P9-DIA-682

CAPITOL MEN

Books by Philip Dray

AT THE HANDS OF
PERSONS UNKNOWN:
THE LYNCHING
OF BLACK AMERICA

STEALING GOD'S THUNDER:
BENJAMIN FRANKLIN'S
LIGHTNING ROD AND
THE INVENTION OF AMERICA

CAPITOL MEN: THE EPIC STORY
OF RECONSTRUCTION
THROUGH THE LIVES OF
THE FIRST BLACK CONGRESSMEN

CAPITOL MEN

THE EPIC STORY OF RECONSTRUCTION
THROUGH THE LIVES OF
THE FIRST BLACK CONGRESSMEN

Philip Dray

HOUGHTON MIFFLIN COMPANY
BOSTON ◆ NEW YORK
2008

www.houghtonmifflinbooks.com

Library of Congress Cataloging-in-Publication Data
Dray, Philip.
Capitol men : the epic story of Reconstruction through the lives of the first
Black congressmen / Philip Dray.
p. cm.
Includes bibliographical references and index.
ISBN 978-0-618-56370-8
1. Reconstruction (U.S. history, 1865–1877) 2. African American legislators — Biography. 3. United States. Congress. House — Biography. 4. Social justice — United States — History — 19th century. 5. United States — Race relations — Political aspects — History — 19th century. 6. Southern States — Race relations — Political aspects — History — 19th century. 7. United States — Politics and government — 1865–1900. 8. Southern States — Politics and government — 1865–1950. I. Title.
E668.D76 2008
973.8'1 — dc22   2008011292

Book design by Melissa Lotfy

Printed in the United States of America

DOC 10 9 8 7 6 5 4 3 2 1

The photographs, lithographs, and Thomas Nast cartoons on pages 9, 20, 38, 54, 60, 62, 69, 83, 95, 105, 120, 126, 152, 164, 183, 194, 244, 256, 296, 301, 308, 328, 335, 360, and 370 appear courtesy of the Library of Congress Prints and Photographs Division Online Catalog. The Nast cartoon on page 27 was provided by the American Social History Project/Center for Media and Learning at the Graduate Center of the City University of New York. The portrait of Blanche K. Bruce on page 206 is from the Blanche K. Bruce Papers, Moorland-Spingarn Research Center, Howard University. The illustrations on pages 41 and 218 are from *Men of Mark: Eminent, Progressive, and Rising,* by William J. Simmons, published by George M. Rewell (Publisher) Cleveland, 1887, and those on pages 4, 7, 21, 50, 156, 187, 250, and 293 are from the Picture Collection of the New York Public Library. Posters reproduced on pages 239 and 290 are in the author's collection.

One of the surprising results of the Reconstruction period was that there should spring from among the members of a race that had been held so long in slavery, so large a number of shrewd, resolute, resourceful, and even brilliant men, who became, during this brief period of storms and stress, the political leaders of the newly enfranchised race.

— BOOKER T. WASHINGTON

Some men are born great, some achieve greatness, and others lived during the Reconstruction period.

— PAUL LAURENCE DUNBAR

CONTENTS

PREFACE

OF ALL THE IMAGES of long-ago America, perhaps few are as poignant as the Currier & Ives lithograph from 1872 depicting the first seven black members of the U.S. Congress. From the midst of Reconstruction, one of the most precarious times in our nation's history, they gaze out confidently in their neatly trimmed beards, vested suits, and ties, indistinguishable, except for their color, from their white counterparts. The portrait, showing Hiram Revels of Mississippi; Benjamin Turner of Alabama; Jefferson Long of Georgia; Robert De Large, Robert Brown Elliott, and Joseph H. Rainey of South Carolina; and Josiah Walls of Florida was a proud symbol of the liberation of America's newest citizens, proof of the tremendous social revolution the Civil War had wrought.

The picture was considered an object of scorn among many Southern whites, however, who refused to countenance the sudden transformation of slaves into holders of public office. Emancipation, and then the appearance of black federal troops in the conquered South, had been offense enough; when, under the terms of congressional Reconstruction, men of color began to vote, win elections, and wield political authority, the patience of Southerners was pushed to its limit. "The North thinks the Southern people are especially angry because of the loss of slave property," wrote the North Carolina Unionist Albion Tourgee. "In truth, they are a thousand times more exasperated by the elevation of the free negro to equal political power." As the Virginian George Mason railed, "The noble Caucasian, in whose very look and gait the God of creation has stamped a blazing superiority, [must] bow down to and be governed by the sable African, upon whom the same God has put the ineffaceable mark of inferiority! A more flagrant desecration of the representative principle . . . is not to be found in the annals of the human race."

Faded prints of the engraving still hung in modest sharecroppers' cabins when researchers from the Works Project Administration visited the Southern Black Belt in the 1930s. The men in the picture were by that time largely forgotten, and the image, and others like it, had become historical curiosities. In the 1870s, the states that had sent the "colored representatives" to Congress were themselves roiled by violent factionalism, undermining what legitimacy these men had in Washington, as the nation backed away from the ideals of Reconstruction. In 1901, resolutions of thanksgiving would be passed in the North Carolina legislature when George H. White, the sole remaining black member of the U.S. House of Representatives, finished his term in office. By then black Southerners had been virtually expunged from politics, even as voters; the greater part of a century would pass before another elected representative of color from a Southern state arrived on Capitol Hill.

Reconstruction was initially a hopeful time. America, emerging from civil war, attempted to reinvent itself. A broadened concept of citizenship was introduced, as were new guarantees of equal treatment under law, commitment to public education and public welfare, efforts to redistribute land, and more equitable methods of taxation. Laws and constitutional amendments were forged to improve upon the vision of the country's founders; new government agencies were formed, such as the Freedmen's Bureau, which assisted the recently freed slaves, and the Justice Department, which helped enforce their new rights. This effort rode on the leadership of resolute national legislators and the actions of countless individuals, organizations, and missionaries, but also on the determination of the freed slaves themselves, four million strong, who grasped the long-awaited chance to steer their own destiny.

But despite this earnest struggle, Reconstruction in the end could overcome neither the resistance of the South, where its innovations had their most meaningful impact, nor the North's mounting apathy and desire for sectional reconciliation. Redemption, or home rule, as it was often called, came to the South, and Reconstruction was denounced as a fatal example of governmental hubris and overreaching. History and popular culture for decades characterized it as an atrocious failure.

The South, it was held, had been punished too cruelly for seccession — its attempted act of self-determination. Its leaders had been humiliated and its people victimized in a grotesque experiment that elevated former slaves to citizenship, placing whites "under the splay foot of the

Negro." Vindictive Northerners had been not only hypocrites, in trying to script how others might coexist with a restive, dangerous black minority, but also fools to think they understood the racial dynamics of Southern life. The myth of the Southland redeemed from Reconstruction's errant policies would become a fixture of American memory, retold in countless memoirs, articles, and works of history, from the 1874 appearance of *The Prostrate State: South Carolina Under Negro Government,* by James Shepherd Pike, to the early-twentieth-century Klan-glorifying novels of Thomas Dixon. It provided the backdrop for two of the most commercially successful films of the twentieth century, *The Birth of a Nation* (1915) and *Gone with the Wind* (1939); it resurfaced in 1956 in John F. Kennedy's award-winning book of political biography, *Profiles in Courage;* and it remained for years a staple of high school and college textbooks.

Yet beyond the distortions and the myths lie Reconstruction's considerable achievements — strides in universal education, the forging of black political know-how and leadership, broad national efforts to solve problems of racial prejudice and injustice, and the creation of laws that, although largely nullified by the Supreme Court, stayed on the books, a valuable heirloom in the nation's attic trunk, available for use at an appropriate future time. They would be crucial to the civil rights revolution of the mid-twentieth century.

Reconstruction's echoes resonate still. When Florida election officials in the year 2000 forced voters in heavily minority districts to wait for hours in line before casting a ballot, and when Ohio Republicans, four years later, stationed poll monitors at voting places to intimidate black voters, they were reviving methods that had proved effective nearly a century and a half before, in the Reconstruction South. The debates heard today over affirmative action, police profiling, school integration, economic parity, and reparations for slavery would be largely familiar to Americans of the 1870s and 1880s, when newspapers carried, almost daily, stories of black citizens denied their rights, when black congressmen pleaded with their white colleagues to treat seriously the terror tactics of Southern vigilantism, and when a justice of the Supreme Court inquired, in an infamous ruling, how long those recently emerged from slavery would continue to be "the special favorite of the laws." Current efforts to safeguard civil rights and the rights of the accused, in an age of terrorism and illegal immigration, have their antecedents in the post–Civil War struggle for national standards of citizenship and personal freedom as well as guarantees of due process.

The black representatives to Congress, the subjects of this book, emerged from diverse backgrounds. Many were of mixed racial ancestry and had the social advantages of white parentage, such as access to education; some were free before the war, whereas others had been slaves; several were professionals — lawyers, teachers, or ministers — while others had worked as skilled artisans or tradesmen; a few had won distinction in the military. As black men who competed successfully to attain elective office in a society dominated by whites, they tended to be exceptional individuals — as resilient as they were resourceful. South Carolina's Robert Smalls had hijacked a Confederate steamer and delivered it to the Union blockade off Charleston. P.B.S. Pinchback of Louisiana started out as an accomplished riverboat gambler. Robert Brown Elliott outdid the former vice president of the Confederacy in a debate on the floor of the House, and his colleague from South Carolina, Richard Cain, when he could not secure government help to make land available to the freedmen, formed his own corporation to do so. The portly, goateed senator Blanche K. Bruce of Mississippi, born a slave, once hid for his life from a Confederate raiding party yet rose to become a prosperous Delta planter who traveled as a dignitary to European courts, where it was said he displayed "the manners of a Chesterfield."

Looking at the congressmen's picture and knowing the expectations it once inspired, it's hard not to wonder how things went so wrong, or how events might have turned out differently. Why did white Southerners find these seemingly decent, conscientious black officeholders, and the newly enfranchised African Americans they represented, so unacceptable? Was it simple race-hatred, a refusal that those low enough to have been slaves should rise to citizenship, let alone positions of authority? Was there truth to the accusations of corruption and incompetence made against them? Were their demands too great for a nation recovering from a devastating war? And how did the black elected officials themselves view their own efforts, those of their white Republican allies, and Reconstruction's prospects for success?

For the sake of narrative I have focused on some of the most prominent black congressional officials of the era, while also attempting to sketch in the background of the challenging world in which they lived and the stories of the men and women of both races whose actions affected their role. These include the presidents Abraham Lincoln, Ulysses S. Grant, Rutherford B. Hayes, and James A. Garfield; Frederick Douglass, the editor, author, and ex-slave who was perhaps the black congressmen's greatest champion and who chronicled their endeavors in his aptly named weekly, the *New National Era;* the abolitionists Wendell Phillips and William Lloyd Garrison; Charles Sumner, the willful Massachusetts senator devoted to civil rights, and his Radical colleague, Thaddeus Stevens; the black nationalist Martin Delany; the women's rights advocates Susan B. Anthony and Elizabeth Cady Stanton; General Benjamin F. Butler, who raised the spirits of slaves crossing Union lines by dubbing them "contrabands," and his daughter Blanche and son-in-law Adelbert Ames, the besieged Reconstruction governor of Mississippi. Other important figures include the carpetbagger governors Daniel Chamberlain of South Carolina and Henry Clay Warmoth of Louisiana; the Union generals William T. Sherman, Rufus Saxton, and Otis Oliver Howard; the Confederate general James Longstreet; and the Supreme Court justice John Marshall Harlan, "the Great Dissenter," who tried valiantly to stem the tide that wiped away Reconstruction's accomplishments and made segregation the law of the land.

The "glorious failure," as Reconstruction is sometimes termed — politically turbulent, riven by corruption, often exceedingly violent — can be a disquieting saga to get to know: a lost opportunity, certainly, and in many ways a shameful time in our nation's history. Yet it is also a powerful story of idealism and moral conflict that belongs only to us and whose arc is as beautiful as it is tragic. At its core is something of undeniable value — the courage of black and white Americans who together aspired to right the country's greatest wrong. That this coalition has always been tentative in our history, or that the grand experiment of Reconstruction failed or was premature, cannot diminish the effort's genius or inherent nobility.

CAPITOL MEN

CHAPTER 1

BOAT THIEF

A PERSON GAZING OUT across Charleston Harbor in the predawn quiet of May 13, 1862, would probably have found it hard to believe that the Civil War had begun at this very spot only a year before, with the thunderous shelling of the federal garrison at Fort Sumter. Certainly the signs of war remained, most noticeably the rebel cannon that guarded the harbor and pointed seaward from numerous shore ramparts, their sights fixed on the ships of the Union blockade positioned three miles offshore. But all was now perfectly still, and the only discernible movement took place aboard the *Planter*, a small Confederate transport that appeared to be preparing to depart.

Hours before, the *Planter*'s white captain, C. J. Relyea, and his officers had gone ashore for the night, leaving the vessel in the hands of its mulatto pilot, Robert Smalls, and creating the very opportunity that Smalls and his fellow slave crewmen had been waiting for. Having discussed in detail their plan to use the boat to make a break for the Union blockade, they stealthily began their chores between 1 and 3 A.M., maneuvering the *Planter* to a nearby pier to pick up Smalls's wife and two children as well as four other black women, a child, and three other men. Because the punishment for what they were about to do would surely be death, Smalls had told the others that if caught, they would not surrender but would destroy the boat, along with themselves and all the Confederate guns and ammunition it carried. Two of the crewmen had heard Smalls's warning and elected to stay behind, disembarking as the new passengers came aboard. At about 3 A.M. final farewells were whispered and the *Planter* eased back from the pier.

Despite the hour and the darkness, the city defenses were on alert against Union raiding or reconnaissance parties. Charleston, known for its cultured antebellum society and its leadership in the Southern secessionist movement, formed the emotional and political heart of the Confederacy; it was also a strategic Atlantic port, and its defenders knew that the federals, having been driven from Fort Sumter in the war's first action, dreamed of recapturing it. To escape the harbor, the *Planter* would have to pass directly under the guns of several formidable batteries, including those of Fort Sumter itself, which was now in Confederate hands. The fort, set strategically in the middle of the harbor's entrance, was a manmade island, a pentagon-shaped fortress with walls sixty feet high and six feet thick and guns protruding from all sides, emanating "an aura of doom and menace."

As the *Planter* moved toward the gauntlet, some on board suggested racing past the rebel installations, but Smalls reminded them that such a panicky move would likely be fatal: their best and only hope was to pretend nothing was out of the ordinary. He was banking on the likelihood that sleepy rebel watchmen would not be suspicious of a work ship nosing its way out of the harbor before dawn, nor would they be inclined to imagine that slaves were stealing it.

With this audacious act, Robert Smalls was exploiting a lifetime of trust and privilege placed in him by his white masters — first as a favored house servant, then as a semi-independent laborer and skilled sailor. Born on the South Carolina Sea Islands in April 1839, he was the son of Lydia, a slave woman, and either the Charleston merchant Moses Goldsmith or John McKee, who was Lydia's master. As a girl, Lydia lived and worked on a McKee plantation on Ladies Island, adjacent to the Sea Island town of Beaufort. Because of the dread fear of malaria, the wealthy planters of Beaufort visited their landholdings on the nearby islands only occasionally. One Christmas, when Mr. and Mrs. McKee toured the plantation, distributing oranges and other small gifts to the slaves, Lydia was precocious enough to compliment her mistress on the dress she was wearing. Mrs. McKee, charmed by the youngster's remark, asked her age. "I was born the year George Washington got president," Lydia replied. When John McKee next returned to the plantation, he asked after "the little girl who knew about George Washington," and took Lydia with him back to Beaufort to serve as a housemaid.

Beaufort was the capital of Port Royal Island, which, with the nearby islands of Ladies and St. Helena's, held a prominent position in the lush coastal region Carolinians call the low country. With its endless bays, rivers, tidal estuaries, and broad wetlands, its vast open distances, swarms of shore birds and marsh cranes, and the ancient live oak trees whose "fingers" almost scraped the ground, it seemed a faraway, other-worldly place. In the seventeenth century it had become a rice-growing mecca after the planters selectively imported West African slaves who had knowledge of rice cultivation; these slaves introduced the complex methods of irrigation, seeding, and flood control that made the Carolina rice plantations profitable. By 1860, the South was exporting 182 million pounds of rice per year, two thirds of it from South Carolina, and the crop's success had helped make both Beaufort and Charleston prosperous towns, with grand white-columned mansions, high-steepled churches, and the Southeast's most cosmopolitan society.

Robert Smalls grew up in the McKee household, childhood playmate to his master, Henry McKee, who was likely his half brother, while his mother, Lydia, served the McKee family. So comfortable was the arrangement that after several years Lydia began to worry that her bright, energetic son might come to difficulty in the town someday by failing to understand his true status. To forestall such a problem, she took the unusual step of forcing Robert to watch the slave auctions and whippings at the arsenal building on Beaufort's Craven Street, reminding him that only good fortune kept him from sharing the fate of the wretched people he saw there. Her strategy was not, however, entirely successful, for at age twelve Robert was caught defying the local slave curfew and soon after told his mother that he had listened with interest as another slave read a passage from a book by the abolitionist Frederick Douglass — the kind of proscribed acts she feared could get him cast out of the McKees' Beaufort house to toil on the family's island plantations, or worse. South Carolina rice plantations by no means presented the worst work conditions. Because the owners relied greatly on African ingenuity, the slaves had managed to negotiate somewhat more favorable work conditions than prevailed elsewhere in the South. Rather than labor from sunup to sundown, they were expected each day to execute assigned tasks; once they had completed them, they were free to hunt, fish, or cultivate their own crops. Still, work in the fields was strenuous; slaves labored long hours in knee-deep water, and there was an ever-present danger of snakes, insects, and malaria — the very risks that kept the white planters on Beaufort's higher ground. Lydia wished to spare Robert from such a fate and finally appealed to the McKees to send her rambunctious son to Charleston, where the family maintained another home and where she believed Robert's insubordinate streak would be less apparent.

In contrast to Beaufort, Charleston was a metropolis, a place of hub-

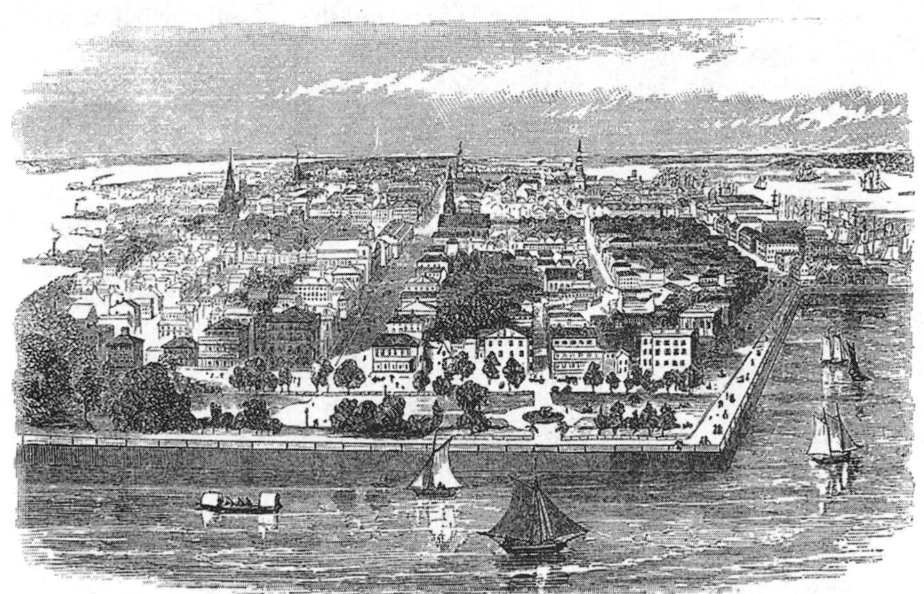

CHARLESTON BATTERY DURING THE MID-NINETEENTH CENTURY

bub, splendor, and riches. Carriages with liveried servants traversed the palm-tree-lined boulevards and waited under the lamplights of impeccable mansions and hotels. Gentlemen strolled the Battery, talking politics and business, as ladies in crinoline window-shopped along fashionable King Street. Beyond the busy central market, with its fish stalls, vegetables, spices, and colorful rows of textiles, hundreds of large-masted ships lined the waterfront, taking on pallets of rice, tobacco, and other foreign-going cargo.

The city ran on the energy of thousands of slaves like Robert Smalls, as well as a substantial community of free blacks, many of whom were small tradesmen or skilled artisans such as roofers or carpenters. Even free blacks, however, were made to wear identity tags and have a white "guardian," for the ongoing political agitation over slavery in the 1840s and 1850s had made local whites jittery. South Carolina, and Charleston in particular, had experienced at least two significant slave rebellions — the Stono Rebellion of 1739, which broke out only twenty miles from the city, and the aborted Denmark Vesey uprising of 1822. In the Stono disturbance, one hundred slaves trying to escape to Florida ravaged plantations and killed two dozen whites before encountering the militia, which slaughtered them and placed their severed heads on posts by the roadside. In response to the affair, the colonial legislature enacted the

Negro Act of 1740, severely restricting slave behavior and mobility. The Vesey rebellion, planned for July 14, Bastille Day, 1822, was the brainchild of a fifty-five-year-old carpenter, Denmark Vesey, a former slave who had purchased his own freedom. Before Vesey could strike, however, two house slaves alerted the authorities, and he, along with several comrades, was arrested and put to death. The threat of slaves' being fired to revolt by conspiracies led by free Negroes remained very real in the minds of white Carolinians, perhaps because after 1820 blacks began to outnumber whites in the state, and free blacks, because of their greater worldliness, were believed to be more likely to stir the embers of discontent.

Although slave-control measures were carefully observed in Charleston as secession and war loomed, Robert Smalls managed to win increased trust and freedom from his white family. He arranged with the McKees to hire himself out as a day laborer and later as a town lamplighter, paying fifteen dollars a month to his owner. In 1856, at age seventeen, he married a thirty-one-year-old slave named Hannah Jones, who worked as a hotel maid. From his modest earnings, Smalls began saving to buy his own and his wife's freedom, as well as that of their daughter, Elizabeth, who was born in 1858. His fortunes brightened considerably when he attained work in the town's maritime trades. From his boyhood in coastal Beaufort he was already familiar with boats and their operation, and he proved a quick study, learning the myriad channels, currents, and shoals of Charleston Harbor. John Simmons, a white rigger and sail maker who took a liking to the young man, mentored him in shipboard work and navigation, and by 1861 Smalls was the wheelman (blacks were not allowed to hold the title of pilot) aboard the *Planter*, a cotton-hauling steamer plying the rivers and inlets between Charleston and the Sea Islands. One hundred fifty feet in length and able to carry fourteen hundred bales, it was, because of its four-foot draft, ideal for maneuvering in the shallow coastal waterways. When war broke out, the boat was quickly commissioned by the Confederacy. Guns were installed on its foredeck and afterdeck, and it was immediately put to use ferrying troops, laying mines, and servicing the work crews building the harbor's fortifications.

Smalls's travels at the helm of the *Planter* frequently brought him into the vicinity of his old home at Beaufort, although after fall 1861 no Confederate vessel could approach the place. On November 7, Union naval forces seeking a Southern anchorage for their blockade had bombarded and then invaded the Sea Islands, one of the first portions of the Confederacy to be conquered by federal troops. The South chose not to defend the outlying region, and local plantation owners fled the arriving Union forces, leaving behind their crops, stately homes, and as many as ten thousand slaves.

The Union toehold on the Sea Islands was of great military value, but the area became another kind of beachhead the following spring, with the arrival of two shiploads of Northern abolitionists. These missionaries, men and women from Boston, Philadelphia, and New York, perceived in the abandonment of the blacks of the coastal islands an unprecedented opportunity to demonstrate that, with the proper guidance, former slaves could exercise the virtues of citizenship and free labor. "The Port Royal Experiment," as it became known, was meant to prove the adaptability of free blacks, their eagerness to be educated, and their viability as wage laborers, so as to ease Northern concerns about emancipation. The endeavor proved more complex than anticipated. Though the departed slaveholders were not missed, their sudden exit was wrenching to the social hierarchy of the islands and raised difficult questions: how to restart the islands' agricultural economy, bring in crops, open schools, and decide whether the former slaves would own land or what civil rights they might enjoy. Indeed, events in the Sea Islands had raced well ahead of the formulation of the federal government's own policy toward slaves liberated from their masters by advancing Union armies: were the slaves to be regarded as other people's property or as free human beings?

If federal authorities continued to wrestle with such matters, there was for Robert Smalls little confusion. It had been no secret to him, or most other slaves, that the victory of Abraham Lincoln in the election of 1860, and the outbreak of war itself, held the definite potential for freedom. Looking out on clear evenings from the pilothouse of the *Planter*, Smalls could see the lights of Beaufort and marvel at the fact that his mother and other relations and friends there were already free.

By spring 1862, with the federal lines so close, Smalls and the other slaves on the *Planter* began talking of crossing over, perhaps using the boat itself as a means of deliverance. Any slave caught plotting such an act, let alone carrying it out, would be killed, and Smalls understood that neither his connections to a good Southern family like the McKees nor his usefulness as a ship's pilot would save him. But he agreed with his mates to discuss the notion further and to watch for an opportunity to escape.

They had several advantages. Smalls knew the placement of the Confederate batteries and the location of all the mines in Charleston Harbor — he had helped put them there — as well as the signals needed to pass by the harbor defenses. He later explained that the scheme for using the boat to escape was partly inspired by a casual remark made by one of his crew that, in height and build, he resembled the ship's white skipper. One afternoon when the whites were elsewhere, the crewman had playfully slapped Captain C. J. Relyea's distinctive straw hat onto Smalls's head and exclaimed, "Boy, you look jes like de captain."

The *Planter* returned to Charleston on May 12 after having spent nearly a week moving guns from Cole's Island to James Island. Smalls suspected that since the boat had not berthed in Charleston for many nights, its white officers would likely choose to spend the night ashore, leaving him in charge. (This violated Confederate naval policy — at least one officer was required to remain with the ship at all times — but the rule was often disregarded.) In the afternoon a wagon carrying two hundred pounds of ammunition and four small pieces of artillery arrived at the wharf for transport to Fort Ripley, a newly built harbor fortification. Realizing this cargo would be a substantial prize for the Union forces, Smalls quietly ordered his men to take their time loading it onto the *Planter,* so that the delivery to Fort Ripley would be put off until the next day.

Once the whites had departed, Smalls and his fellow conspirators made their final arrangements, then laid low until about 2 A.M., when he ordered the boilers fired. As a precaution, Smalls had told the crew that if a sentry came by, they should complain loudly and bitterly about the early morning departure and curse "the cap'n and his orders." A sentry on the wharf did hear the steamer come to life but later recalled he did not "think it necessary to stop her, presuming that she was but pursuing her usual business."

Smalls had timed their departure so that his ability to impersonate Captain Relyea would work to maximum effect. If they tried to pass Fort Sumter in total darkness, he feared the sentry there might demand to speak with him to ascertain his identity; but Smalls surmised that in the half-light just before dawn, Relyea's profile, his naval jacket, trademark straw hat, and even his characteristic way of pacing the deck, which Smalls had learned to mimic, would suffice to allow the boat to pass without inspection. Having positioned himself in the pilothouse as the vessel reached Fort Sumter, he "stood so that the sentinel could not see my color" and nonchalantly gave the correct series of short blasts on the ship's steam whistle. After a pause that must have seemed an eternity, the sentinel replied, "Pass the *Planter*."

Once past Sumter, Smalls at first followed the set route for Confederate vessels departing the harbor, heading southeast in order to hug the coast along Fort Wagner. But he did not complete that final turn. Crying down to the engine room to cram the boilers "with pitch, tar, oil, anything to make a fire seven times heated," Smalls abruptly swung the *Planter* toward the open sea. Confederate signalers atop the shore batteries expressed concern, querying the *Planter* as to why it was heading the wrong way. Had they grasped Smalls's intentions, they might have succeeded in bringing the ship under fire, but with the *Planter*'s furnaces roaring, the boat was in moments safely out of range. As the ocean waves crashed over the speeding bow, Smalls removed Relyea's hat and exulted to his companions, "We're all free niggers now!"

They were in fact hardly out of danger. The Union boat crews manning the blockade had sprung to life as the *Planter* approached, worried that the unknown vessel might be a Confederate ram. Smalls, from his bridge, heard drums being beaten in a call to arms. He quickly ordered the Confederate flag hauled down and a white bed sheet hoisted in its stead.

"Ahoy there," a voice from the Union ship *Onward* called out, "what steamer is that? State your business!"

"The *Planter*, out of Charleston," Smalls replied. "Come to join the Union fleet."

A very surprised Captain F. J. Nichols of the *Onward* was the first aboard the Confederate boat, where he was surrounded by Smalls and his band of exuberant runaways. Nichols later reported that he was told by "the very intelligent contraband who was in charge . . . 'I thought the *Planter* might be of some use to Uncle Abe.'"

The next day's notice in the *Charleston Courier* took a less cheery tone. "Our community was intensely agitated Tuesday morning by the intelligence that the steamer *Planter* . . . had been taken possession by her colored crew, steamed up and boldly run out to the blockaders," the article read. "The news at first was not credited; and it was not until, by the aid of glasses, she was discovered, lying between two Federal frigates, that all doubt on the subject was dispelled." The paper, in its account of "this extraordinary occurrence," noted that one of the Negroes aboard the boat belonged to Mrs. McKee, and reported that it appeared from shore that the Yankees were already stripping the captured ship of its deck guns. This represented a hurtful loss at a time when the Confederacy was desperate for reliable ordnance, but to the federals, the acquisition of the *Planter*'s guns was only a secondary gift. The greater prize was the boat itself, for the Union navy lacked vessels with a shallow draft, able to operate in the channels around the Sea Islands. Equally important, the United States had gained the services of Robert Smalls, whose knowledge of the local waters, as well as his intelligence about the positions of Confederate mines and gun emplacements, would be invaluable.

Harper's Weekly and the *New York Tribune* were among many Northern periodicals to herald the theft of the *Planter; Harper's* ran an illustration of Smalls, terming his feat "one of the most daring and heroic adventures since the war commenced." The blow to the South's pride was commensurate, and its newspapers demanded harsh penalties for the white officers who had allowed slaves to steal a valuable boat. General Robert E. Lee wrote from Richmond that all precautions must be taken to ensure such an avoidable tragedy did not recur. (Captain Relyea and two of his officers were convicted of disobedience in the case but evaded punishment.)

Smalls's daring act not only boosted Northern morale but also represented a decisive victory for his people. At a time when America's leaders could not agree on what to do with blacks freed from bondage by the war, and when even many abolitionists were uncertain about former slaves' potential as independent workers and citizens, the *Planter*'s story made a compelling case for their native pluck and resourcefulness.

ROBERT SMALLS AND THE *PLANTER*

"What a painful instance we have here of the Negro's inability to take care of himself," deadpanned the *Providence Journal.* "If Smalls had a suitable white overseer, he would never have done this foolish and thoughtless thing. Such fellows need a superior who is familiar with the intentions of divine providence and who could tell them where they were meant to stay."

Smalls's action had an immediate effect on a debate then roiling Washington as to whether blacks emerging from slavery could serve as soldiers in the Union armies. Smalls himself was soon given the chance to advocate for their inclusion.

From the war's beginning, a vocal element in the North had argued for emancipating the slaves in order to ground the nation's conflict in a moral cause, demoralize the South, and possibly create a new source of troops. But President Abraham Lincoln hesitated. To cast the fight as a war of emancipation, rather than one that solely aimed to reunite the Union, would, he feared, alienate the border states and push them into the Confederacy. "My paramount object in this struggle," Lincoln proclaimed, "is to save the Union. If I could save the Union without freeing *any* slave I would do it, and if I could save it by freeing *all* the slaves I would do it; and if I could save it by freeing some and leaving others alone I would do that." It was thought by many, including Lincoln, that an emigration program to resettle the slaves would be required if four million blacks were suddenly to become free; until early 1863, the government even entertained the hope that the South, or parts thereof, might return to the Union voluntarily, perhaps with some program of gradual emancipation and compensation to slaveholders for their loss.

Curiously, the militarization of blacks was originally a Southern strategy; Negro regiments were formed in Georgia, Tennessee, and Louisiana in the early months of the war. The Confederacy's battlefield successes in 1861 and 1862, however, convinced its leaders that there was no need to use black troops; the practice was repugnant to most Southerners anyway, and so the men were largely sent home. (Some, like Josiah T. Walls, later a black congressman from Florida, eventually crossed over to the Union forces, becoming one of the few Americans to fight on both sides in the war.) The South did not revisit the idea until early 1865 when, in desperate straits, the Congress of the Confederate States agreed to let General Lee seek the enlistment of black troops; within weeks, however, the rebel cause was lost.

Union policies were ultimately pushed toward resolution by the slaves themselves, for the eagerness of black refugees to flee their masters was evident wherever federal troops advanced. "War has not been waged against slavery," Secretary of State William H. Seward wrote, "yet the army acts . . . as an emancipating crusade." In May 1861 a weak compromise on the issue was reached in Virginia, where the Union general Benjamin F. Butler, commander of Union forces at Fortress Monroe, was confronted with three runaway slaves seeking his protection. One, George Scott, told Butler that the Confederates had put him and other slaves to work building gun emplacements and ramparts. At Butler's behest, Scott guided a Union scouting mission to the enemy's lines to verify this claim. When, soon after, a Confederate officer came to Butler's headquarters under a flag of truce to claim Scott and the other two runaways, Butler refused to release them. In moving his army through Maryland, he had promised state officials he would not act to incite slaves to insurrection. Now, however, he couldn't help but wonder why he should return slaves known to be assisting the Confederate war effort. At the suggestion of one of his aides, Butler resolved the situation by declaring Scott and the others "contraband of war."

The designation was much discussed in Washington. The term "contraband" implied ownership and conveniently did not call into question the legal basis of slavery. It fit nicely within the strictures of the First Confiscation Act, passed in August 1861, which allowed federal troops to take command of any property being used to abet or promote the Southern rebellion, including slaves laboring for the Confederate military effort. Officially the concept of confiscation was to go no further. When the Union general John C. Frémont declared martial law in Missouri in late summer 1861 and pronounced the local slaves free, Lincoln immediately rescinded the order. But even though the president had canceled Frémont's action, and members of his cabinet continued to parse the meaning of Butler's "contraband," the significance for black people still in bondage was clear: they would not be returned to their owners once they reached federal lines.

The pressure on Washington increased in spring 1862 when the Union general David Hunter, relieving General William T. Sherman as commander of the Sea Islands, announced his decision to turn the numerous contrabands in his charge into soldiers. Hunter, upon taking over Sherman's command, had wasted little time in seizing Fort Pulaski, a strategic post at the sea approach to Savannah, and he was eager for additional conquests. He had written to Secretary of War Edwin Stanton of his special desire to retake Fort Sumter for the Union cause. With such ambitions, it was natural that he saw the thousands of ex-slaves gathering at Port Royal as potential troops and hoped that an earlier order from the former secretary of war, Simon Cameron, authorizing Sherman to employ "loyal persons," might effectively cover the action he contemplated. "Please let me have my own way on the subject of slavery," he asked of Stanton as early as January. "The administration will not be responsible. I alone will bear the blame; you can censure me, arrest me, dismiss me, hang me if you will, but permit me to make my mark in such a way as to be remembered by friend and foe."

There were doubts in Washington as to the battle-worthiness of men so recently slaves, but Hunter's bold approach had the support of many who believed black men *would* fight, and fight hard, for freedom. "Nothing would please me more, and bring the race into favor," wrote the abolitionist Frederick Douglass, "than to see Southern chivalry well whipped by an equal number of black men. It would indeed be refreshing." Black Americans, slave and free, had a proud martial heritage extending from Bunker Hill to the Plain of Chalmette — a tradition of loyalty and courage under fire that was often conveniently forgotten by whites. As Douglass later recalled, "I reproached the North that they fought the rebels with only one hand, when they might strike effectively with two — that they fought with their soft white hand, while they kept their black iron hand chained and helpless behind them."

General Hunter acted in stages to bring in blacks as soldiers. On April 4 he wrote to Stanton to request fifty thousand muskets and fifty thousand pairs of scarlet pantaloons, the latter to distinguish contraband troops on the battlefield; on April 13 he declared that some of the contrabands in his district were henceforth to be considered free; and soon after, he announced his intention to organize blacks into military regiments. Recruitment, however, did not go as smoothly as Hunter wished. Many former slaves were eager to join the ranks, but others resisted the idea of returning so soon to any form of white authority. Some fled to the woods at the approach of federal recruiters, fearful because of rumors, spread by Southerners, that the Yankees would ship them to Cuba to be reenslaved or harness them to wagons and use them as horses. To help urge enlistment, Hunter declared all the slaves of Florida, Georgia, and South Carolina free, and on May 9, a few days before Robert Smalls's theft of the *Planter,* which Hunter's actions likely encouraged, he ordered all able-bodied male blacks, ages eighteen to forty-five, to report to Hilton Head for possible induction.

Hunter's decisions confounded official Washington, for the previous fall President Lincoln had ordered General Sherman not to mobilize blacks for regular military service. When Salmon P. Chase, Lincoln's secretary of the treasury, urged the president to allow Hunter's declaration to stand, assuring him that his supporters would rally around the idea, Lincoln testily warned Chase, "No commanding general shall do such a thing, upon *my* responsibility, without consulting me." Lincoln forced Hunter to immediately retract his declarations. Hunter did as he was told but did not relinquish his vision; when the House of Representatives formally inquired by what authority he had sought to arm "fugitive slaves," Hunter assured its members that

> no regiment of "fugitive slaves" has been or is organized in this department. There is, however, a fine regiment of persons whose late masters are "fugitive rebels," men who everywhere fly before the appearance of the national flag, leaving their servants behind them to shift as best they can for themselves . . . It is the masters who have, in every instance, been the "fugitives," running away from loyal slaves as well as loyal soldiers, and whom we have only partially been able to see . . . their heads over ramparts, or, rifle in hand, dodging behind trees in the extreme distance.

Hunter's letter, read aloud in the House, amused the inquiring congressmen and may have helped win a reprieve for his campaign. He followed up by dispatching Robert Smalls as part of a South Carolina delegation to convince President Lincoln of the potential of blacks as loyal fighting men. Smalls was, for the moment, one of the few military heroes the North had; the story of how he turned the tables on his Confederate masters was widely reported, and Smalls himself had quickly developed a knack for self-promotion, cheekily having himself photographed wearing Captain Relyea's uniform.

On August 16, 1862, Smalls and the Reverend Mansfield French, a Methodist minister from Ohio who had helped found Wilberforce University and now worked for the American Missionary Association at Port Royal, arrived in Washington to meet with Lincoln and Secretary of War Stanton. The two also met with other cabinet members, including Treasury Secretary Chase. French and Smalls were well received, their firsthand knowledge of conditions on the ground in coastal South Carolina informing the discussions; but, as Hunter had likely anticipated, what everyone most wanted to hear was Robert Smalls's thrilling story of taking the *Planter*. There simply was no better argument for making contrabands into soldiers.

Powerful support arrived that same week from Horace Greeley, the influential publisher of the *New York Tribune* and a confidant of Chase. In an August 19 editorial titled "The Prayer of Twenty Millions," Greeley called on Lincoln to reconfigure the nation's war policy to acknowledge the root cause of the conflict and alleviate it by freeing the slaves. "On the face of this wide earth, Mr. President," Greeley wrote, "there is not one disinterested, determined, intelligent champion of the Union cause who does not feel that . . . the Rebellion, if crushed out tomorrow, would be renewed within a year if slavery were left in full vigor; that army officers who remain to this day devoted to slavery can at best be but half-way loyal to the Union; and that every hour of deference to slavery is an hour of added and deepened peril to the Union." The article was much-reprinted and quoted, and it bolstered the case for allowing contrabands an active part in the war effort. As James T. Ayers, later a recruiter of black troops in the conquered areas of the South, remarked, "As they waged war on us about the nigger, why, in God's name give them the nigger . . . A wise and good administration, handled by Sambo, at the Britch of a good musket, surely is a plaster good enough for traitors." Through the efforts of men like Ayers, more than half the black soldiers to serve the Union cause would be recruited in the states belonging to the Confederacy.

Lincoln, although advised by many, including Vice President Hannibal Hamlin, of the efficacy of turning slaves into fighting men, still preferred, publicly at least, not to make any sweeping gestures. The president worried that "the organization, equipment, and arming of negroes would be productive of more evil than good," but, according to Chase, "he was not unwilling that commanders should, at their discretion, arm for purely defensive purposes, slaves coming within their lines." Stanton had learned from the Frémont and Hunter episodes that Lincoln did not like bold steps regarding the volatile issue of arming blacks, although he believed Lincoln would accept judicious moves in this direction by responsible officers. The Second Confiscation Act, which Congress passed in July 1862, allowed the president to use confiscated slaves "as he may judge best for the public welfare," implying possible military service. That summer, Lincoln had also begun discussing with his cabinet the idea of using his war powers as president to free all slaves held in Confederate lands. When he shared with them his first draft of the Emancipation Proclamation in late July, he also issued an order that black men, slave or free, could be recruited as noncombat soldiers. In

BLACK TROOPS MUSTERING

late August, when Smalls and French returned to the South, Stanton gave Smalls a letter to take back to General Rufus Saxton, quartermaster at Port Royal, authorizing him to enlist and arm five thousand blacks for guard duty — to keep watch over conquered Sea Island plantations and protect black settlements from possible rebel attacks. The letter further decreed that all black volunteers in this effort, and their immediate families, were to be "forever free."

To take command of the First South Carolina, the first Union force comprised exclusively of freed slaves, General Saxton invited the New England abolitionist minister and writer Thomas Wentworth Higginson to Port Royal. Saxton's choice was largely a public relations move, for Higginson had been a colleague of the abolitionist martyr John Brown. "I had been an abolitionist too long, and had known and loved John Brown too well," Higginson wrote, "not to feel a thrill of joy at last on finding myself in the position where he only wished to be." In the 1840s Higginson had lost his pulpit in Newburyport, Massachusetts, because he advocated the use of violence to overthrow slavery, and he achieved lasting notoriety in Boston in 1854 when he led, and was wounded in, a failed effort to rescue the captured fugitive slave Anthony Burns. He would write a series of influential articles for the *Atlantic Monthly* about his experiences leading black fighting men.

When officials in Massachusetts announced plans to enlist a black regiment, the first one from a free state, Frederick Douglass threw himself into recruitment. "Action! Action!" he enthused. "There is no time for delay. The tide is at its flood that leads on to fortune. From East to West, North to South, the sky is written all over, 'Now, or never.'" He urged black men to join at once. "The iron gate of our prison stands half open. One gallant rush from the North will fling it wide open, while four millions of our brothers and sisters shall march out into Liberty!"

From its unsure beginnings at Port Royal, General Hunter's dream of armed black men in Union blue set to punish the Confederacy became a substantial reality; by war's end almost 180,000 black Americans had worn Union army uniforms, while 24,000 served in the navy; a total of 37,000 sacrificed their lives. The famous assault on Fort Wagner by the Fifty-fourth Massachusetts Volunteers on July 18, 1863, led by Colonel Robert Gould Shaw, is the best-known tale of blacks' Civil War heroism, although Higginson's men skirmished with rebels as early as the winter of 1862–63 along South Carolina's coastal rivers, and ex-slaves showed tremendous valor that spring on the lower Mississippi below Vicksburg, where, on May 23, 1863, black Louisiana regiments advanced against Confederate shellfire at the Battle of Port Hudson.

Two weeks later Confederate forces attacked the federal encampment at Milliken's Bend in an effort to break the supply line supporting General Grant's siege of Vicksburg. The bloody fight became a grudge match between newly minted black soldiers and their former masters. "The planters had boasted," reported the black writer William Wells Brown, "that, should they meet their former slaves, a single look from them would cause the negroes to throw down their weapons, and run." But when the two sides converged, the black troops, although outnumbered, countercharged the advancing enemy. "It was a genuine bayonet charge, a hand-to-hand fight, a contest between enraged men: on the one side, from hatred of a race; and on the other, desire for self-preservation, revenge for past grievances, and the inhuman murder of their comrades." That the fight was fierce and unrelenting was seen clearly in its aftermath. "White and black men were lying side by side, pierced by bayonets, and in some instances transfixed to the earth. In one instance, two men — one white and the other black — were found dead, side by side, each having the other's bayonet through his body."

Of the thousand or so black soldiers engaged in the battle, 652 were reported killed, wounded, or missing, several times the loss of 160 white Union troops. But an enduring statement had been made. A federal captain on the scene, after walking among the dead and dying on the still-smoldering battlefield, told a Northern newspaperman, "I never more wish to hear the expression, '*The nigger won't fight*.'"

For all the freedmen who served under arms, the near-overnight conversion from chattel to soldier, "from the shame of degradation to the glory of military exaltation," had been overwhelming. For Robert Smalls, whose theft of the *Planter* had brought him acclaim and even influence with the authorities in Washington, the effect was hundredfold: national magazines sang his praises, a fort near Pittsburgh was named for him, while back home in the Sea Islands his childhood was recounted by many with special pride and remembered for its early indications of his heroic character.

No one, however, could accuse him of resting on his laurels, as he went on to participate in seventeen deadly encounters with the enemy. The most dramatic came on April 7, 1863, when Smalls piloted the double-turret ironclad *Keokuk* in a fleet of six Union ironclads attempting to retake Charleston. The rebels, having thoroughly mined the waters around Fort Sumter and carefully rehearsed how to concentrate their shore-based artillery in case of assault, pounded the invading federal boats. Two small Confederate ironclads, the *Chicora* and the *Palmetto State,* also engaged the Yankee intruders. The lead Union vessel, the *Weehawken,* got caught in a defensive net while another, the *New Ironsides,* stalled and blocked the ships following in its wake. Smalls's wheelman, standing directly beside him, was killed by a blast to the face, and the *Keokuk,* struck nearly a hundred times by blistering cannon fire from Fort Sumter, was disabled and eventually sank. Smalls was one of the few survivors.

THE BATTLE OF PORT HUDSON

The South thrilled to the victory. A year before at Hampton Roads, in March 1862, the fabled shooting match between the federal ironclad *Monitor* and its Southern counterpart, the *Merrimac*, had ended in a draw, but the repulsion of Union ironclads at Charleston demonstrated that the newfangled boats could be defeated by shore defenses and that the city could withstand an attack from the sea.

Later that year, Smalls was caught in another bloody scrape in the mouth of the Stono River at Folly Island Creek, this time piloting the *Planter*. Whenever Union vessels crept into the watery interior of coastal South Carolina, they risked a loss of maneuverability and the threat of taking close bombardment or sniper fire from shore. The Confederates, trapping Smalls's ship in a narrow part of the river and recognizing it as a stolen prize, resolved to recapture or destroy it, hemming the *Planter* in with an artillery crossfire that shredded the upper part of the wooden boat. When the captain, in the heat of battle, ordered Smalls to ground the vessel and surrender, Smalls emphatically declined. "Not by a damned sight will I beach this boat for you!" he shouted, warning that as far as the rebels were concerned, he and the crewmen were all runaway slaves, and that "No quarter will be shown us!" At that point, according to a later congressional report, "Captain Nickerson became demoralized, and left the pilot-house and secured himself in the coal-bunker." Smalls took control, somehow managing to steer the *Planter* out of range of the Southern guns. Nickerson was dishonorably discharged for his performance, and Smalls, cited for his coolness and bravery under fire, was made the boat's captain.

In the spring of 1864 he was ordered to sail the *Planter* to a shipyard in Philadelphia for repairs; when the work on the boat stretched from weeks into months, Smalls made himself at home in the northern city. Charlotte Forten, a black Philadelphian working as a teacher in the Sea Islands, had written letters of introduction for him to the city's substantial abolitionist community. Smalls busied himself by monitoring work on the *Planter* and raising money to assist the freedmen at Port Royal.

One day in December, Smalls and a black acquaintance were walking back to town from the shipyard when, to escape a sudden downpour, they boarded an empty streetcar. A few minutes later two white men got on, and the conductor told the blacks to leave their seats and go stand on the car's rear platform. Smalls refused. When the conductor insisted, he and his companion got off the car. Smalls was inclined to forget the incident, but the local press learned of it and denounced the fact that "a war hero who had run a rebel vessel out of Charleston and given it to the Union fleet . . . was recently put out of a Thirteenth Street car." Broadsides went up, and a committee of Quakers announced a boycott of the streetcars, vowing to no longer allow a practice by which decent "colored men, women, and children are refused admittance to the cars," while "the worst class of whites may ride." At a spirited mass meeting, concerned Philadelphians were addressed by local luminaries including financier Jay Cooke and locomotive manufacturer Matthias W. Baldwin. In the face of such aroused sentiment, the city's streetcar lines capitulated, the protest helping to inspire the state legislature to ultimately ban discrimination in public transportation throughout Pennsylvania.

That same year Smalls went to Baltimore to join a delegation of black South Carolinians at the Republican National Convention. The group was neither seated nor recognized by the chair, but they made history by formally petitioning the party to include black enfranchisement in its platform. At the time, with emancipation itself a recent development, the request by Smalls and his colleagues for the vote was not likely to get a hearing, even if their presence had been formally acknowledged; however, it was said that the black delegation from the secessionist state of South Carolina was the convention's chief curiosity.

At war's end, Smalls had a place of prominence at the April 14, 1865, celebration in Charleston, marking the anniversary of the firing on Fort Sumter. The ceremonial centerpiece of the day-long event was the hoisting of the Stars and Stripes over the fort by Major General Robert Anderson, the Union officer who had been forced to surrender it in 1861. The Carolina spring day was by all accounts most accommodating, the air "spiced with the aroma of flowers and freighted with the melody of birds, all guiltless of secession, and warbling their welcome." Men, women, and children filled the sidewalks and plazas, waving tiny flags and trying to catch a glimpse of the celebration in the harbor, where hundreds of festooned boats sounded their horns and bells and dispatched fireworks into the sky. On cue, as the American flag rose to its perch above the fort, all the guns in the harbor and those on shore fired a deafening salute.

The abolitionists William Lloyd Garrison, Wendell Phillips, and Henry Ward Beecher were among those who had traveled from Boston and New York to witness the ceremony. Garrison was the editor of the *Liberator,* the nation's most ardent abolitionist publication, and a founder, along with his fellow Bostonian Phillips, of the influential American Anti-Slavery Society. Beecher, the brother of Harriet Beecher Stowe, author of *Uncle Tom's Cabin,* occupied the most famous pulpit in

THE RAISING OF THE FLAG AT FORT SUMTER

the country at Brooklyn's Plymouth Church. This was a day of tremendous vindication for these men and their principled fight against slavery. The abolitionists had been abused for three decades, criticized as hateful agitators, and worse; Garrison had been stripped of his clothes by a Boston mob and almost hanged; Phillips had nearly been killed at a public meeting in Cincinnati by a boulder hurled down from a balcony.

The freed people of Charleston rewarded their travails with a warm welcome. At a mass rally in Citadel Square, the diminutive Garrison was hoisted up into the air to seemingly float on a sea of smiling black faces. In a formal presentation, a speaker assured him that the "pulsations" of the hearts of the black people gathered "are unimaginable. The greeting they would give you, sir, it is almost impossible for me to express; but simply, sir, we welcome and look upon you as our savior." Garrison, equally moved, replied,

> It is not on account of your complexion or race . . . that I espoused your cause, but because you were the children of a common Father,

> created in the same divine image, having the same inalienable rights, and as much entitled to liberty as the proudest slaveholder that ever walked the earth . . . While God gives me reason and strength, I shall demand for you everything I claim for the whitest of the white in this country.

Both Robert Smalls and his now equally famous boat were also objects of interest to the crowd along the waterfront; Smalls posed gallantly atop the *Planter*'s wheelhouse as visitors swarmed over its decks. An American flag was run up the boat's rigging to coincide with the flag raising at Sumter, and as it inched its way to the top, the crowd on the decks below followed its progress with a mounting cheer, until the pennant finally attained the pinnacle, to great applause. "Tears of gladness filled every eye," it was said, "and flowed down cheeks unused to weeping." Even Smalls succumbed to the moment, clumsily backing the *Planter* into another ship loaded with Union dignitaries.

The splendor of the April 14 jubilee in Charleston would glitter all the more in the memory of those who had attended because of the grim event that occurred that very night in Washington: the assassination of President Lincoln at Ford's Theatre. While it was not entirely clear what

THE RUINS OF CHARLESTON

steps Lincoln would have taken to reintegrate the South into the Union, his sudden disappearance at a moment of such profound need could only deepen the country's uncertainty. Immense challenges lay ahead, nowhere more visibly than in South Carolina. Of 146,000 white males residing in South Carolina in 1860, 40,000 had been killed or seriously wounded in the war. Charleston itself, South Carolina's chief commercial port, had endured heavy Union naval shelling; of its five thousand houses, fifteen hundred had been destroyed and many others badly damaged. Much business property had been confiscated or was now worthless. "Of all the states overwhelmed by the rebellion, none lies so terribly mangled and so utterly exhausted as its prime mover, South Carolina," observed the *New York Times,* reminding readers that South Carolina was the birthplace of secession and that "its people have been longer and more virulently alienated from the National Government than those of any other state."

Perhaps of even deeper significance than the physical damage was the sudden shift in the legal status of the bulk of South Carolina's residents: approximately 400,000 slaves, contrasted with a white population of less than 300,000, were now free. Politically, as well as socially, such demographics represented seismic change, auguring a future that few could imagine. Robert Smalls was destined to play a central role in this unprecedented transition, which was already being referred to by the not-yet-familiar term "Reconstruction."

CHAPTER 2

A NEW KIND OF NATION

VICE PRESIDENT ANDREW JOHNSON of Tennessee, who assumed the presidency upon Lincoln's death, was a man of humble origins, a former small-town tailor turned politician and U.S. senator who was added to Lincoln's ticket in 1864 to help the administration reach out to Southerners after the war. He held the South's wealthy planter class responsible for secession and initially viewed the postwar period as a time when *his people* — small farmers, workers, artisans, and merchants — might earn a greater share of the region's leadership. But though he was loyal to the Union and accepted emancipation, the new president differed markedly from men like Senator Charles Sumner of Massachusetts and Congressman Thaddeus Stevens of Pennsylvania, Republicans known as Radicals for their strong views. They saw the South as a conquered foe and called for far-reaching changes in its society and harsh measures for dealing with leading Confederates.

Given that the country was emerging from the trauma of a devastating civil war, the ascent of a man like Johnson after a genial intellect like Lincoln struck the Radicals as tragically unfortunate, for in personal style the new chief executive was a stubborn loner never adept at conciliatory politics. When the need for national healing and inspired leadership could not have been more acute, America was bequeathed not a Washington or a Jefferson, but a man who was *not supposed to be president.*

Even if questions about his character had not arisen, Johnson's reading of the times was to prove errant, and events would soon conspire to make his policies appear inadequate. Trying but failing to grasp the country's mood after four years of strife, he took actions that revealed again and again how hungry the nation was for the kind of leadership he could not deliver — leadership that would project compassion for the freedmen, toughness toward the ex-rebels, and a compelling vision of how the Union might be reestablished. The Radical-led Congress soon became convinced that it, not the president, bore the responsibility for shaping Reconstruction, and its members challenged Johnson at every turn. They overrode his vetoes and passed specific legislation, the Tenure of Office Act, to keep him from forcing from his cabinet those members sympathetic to Congress's views; the act proved a fatal trap for the president; his violation of it in 1868 led to his impeachment.

Johnson had been under a cloud ever since he was sworn in as vice president in March 1864, when he had appeared inebriated at the ceremony. His defenders said that he had been feeling unwell and had swallowed a few glasses of brandy as a pick-me-up. Lincoln, who had heard stories of this intemperance when Johnson served in the Senate, had taken the precaution of sending an aide to Nashville to check up on him before selecting him as his running mate. "I have known Andy Johnson for many years," the president said after the swearing-in. "He made a bad slip the other day, but you need not be scared. Andy ain't a drunkard." Yet despite Lincoln's confidence, Johnson's lack of fitness for high office was a concern in Washington even before he assumed the mantle of the presidency.

Johnson appeared to view the war as a kind of sibling rivalry gone bad, and he acted on the belief that retribution and further animosity between the sections would only impede a return to normalcy. Where the Radicals sought to strengthen federal authority, Johnson opposed them, concerned that the states, if stripped of their autonomy, would atrophy and become "mere satellites of an inferior character, revolving around the great central power." The former slaves he considered basically helpless. Docile, inclined to inertia, they would require guidance and restrictions imposed by whites. Southern society would demand this — having long regarded free black people as dangerous, whites understandably were alarmed by the sudden mobility of the former slaves.

The result was the Black Codes, a system of laws enacted first in Mississippi in November 1865, then in various forms across the South, giving whites what amounted to police powers over the freed people. These new controls enforced labor contracts, kept blacks from accepting better-paying work of their own choosing, and allowed authorities to put "vagrants" — anyone without a fixed abode — to work in the fields or on municipal projects such as road building. Orphans could be compelled into apprenticeships or made to work as house servants. These statutes, "little more than warmed-over slavery," established curfews, prohibited blacks from joining militias, and attempted to govern their private conduct with rules for everything from gun ownership to the use of draft animals.

At first this state of affairs seemed unavoidable. Few people, North or South, imagined that emancipation would entail placing blacks on the same legal plane with whites, and to many observers, the sudden freeing of an unlettered people held so long in bondage looked chaotic, even unsafe. Many Southerners, explained a Northerner living in North Carolina, regarded emancipation as a momentary error, a mistake made in haste, the "temporary triumph of fanaticism over divine truth," which would of necessity be corrected.

Some blacks indeed paid dearly for believing the "delusion" that they were now free. "I met four white men about six miles south of Keachie, De Soto Parish," recalled Henry Adams of Louisiana.

> One of them asked me who I belonged to. I told him no one. So him and two others struck me with a stick and told me they were going to kill me and every other Negro who told them that they did not belong to anyone. One of [the whites] who knew me told the others, "Let Henry alone for he is a hard-working nigger and a good nigger." They left me and I then went on . . . I have seen over twelve colored men and women, beat, shot and hung between there and Shreveport.

The Black Codes, in the end, were likely more offensive than effective; blacks themselves resisted compliance, and federal officers in the conquered South frequently prevented their enforcement. The codes were, however, an accurate gauge of Southern white sentiment and an early sign of the region's will to defy the results of the war.

In Washington, meanwhile, Republicans had grown concerned during the first eight months of Johnson's presidency as he moved to restore the Confederate states to the Union. He pardoned many rebel leaders, appointed Southern men to positions of authority, and ordered that state constitutional conventions be held; often their delegates consisted of former secessionists. When Congress reconvened in December 1865, Republicans called for the dismantling of Johnson's "reconstructed" Southern states and the creation of new state governments in which freedmen would vote and could be elected as representatives of their people. They turned away from Congress's door those Southern Democratic representatives who had been sent to Washington under Johnson's plan.

The bipartisan Congressional Joint Committee of Fifteen was convened to weigh the challenge of Reconstruction — a term that had emerged toward the end of the war and referred to the imperative of restoring the fractured nation, as well as the numerous measures and conditions that would require. The committee was the idea of, and under the control of, Thaddeus Stevens, and despite its alleged bipartisan character it had only three Democratic members. Much of the extensive testimony it heard from 144 witnesses familiar with conditions in the postwar South — including the nurse Clara Barton and the cavalry officer George Armstrong Custer — confirmed the Radicals' suspicion that the rebel spirit had not really been destroyed. Upon deliberating, the group rejected President Johnson's argument that the Southern states were ready to be readmitted to the Union; but the members also spurned a Radical proposal that the states of the Confederacy, having forfeited their rights to sovereignty, should remain under long-term congressional control. The committee, as the historian David Donald explains, came to favor a proposal made by jurist Richard Henry Dana Jr., the so-called "grasp of war" theory, which suggested that Washington use the present, relatively adaptable circumstances of the war's aftermath to "act swiftly to revive state governments in this region and to restore promptly the constitutional balance between state and federal authority."

In early 1866 the committee recommended the passage of two bills — an extension of the Freedmen's Bureau (officially titled the Bureau of Refugees, Freedmen, and Abandoned Lands), which Lincoln had brought into existence in March 1865 to offer physical aid to war refugees and help establish equitable labor agreements between blacks and their former masters; and the Civil Rights Bill, which would undo the nefarious Black Codes and counter the much-lamented 1857 Supreme Court decision in *Scott v. Sandford,* better known as the *Dred Scott* case, which had denied that black people, slave or free, had standing as American citizens. The Civil Rights Bill, referring to the "fundamental rights belonging to every man as a free man," stated that all citizens and their property were entitled to equal protection under the law and that blacks were empowered to make their own labor contracts and initiate lawsuits. The president vetoed both bills, prompting the political cartoonist Thomas Nast, an ardent New York Republican of German descent who drew for *Harper's Weekly,* to depict an ornery Andrew Johnson kicking a chest of drawers containing terrified freed people — the Freedmen's "bureau" — down a flight of stairs.

CARTOON SPOOFING PRESIDENT ANDREW JOHNSON'S TREATMENT OF THE FREEDMEN'S BUREAU, BY THOMAS NAST

That April, the Civil Rights Bill was passed despite Johnson's refusal to sign it, the first time in American history that Congress overrode a presidential veto. Recognizing that Johnson and his states-rights orientation would be more hindrance than help, Congress moved ahead without him and in June proposed the Fourteenth Amendment, which would guarantee the provisions of the Civil Rights Bill and make the federal government the ultimate protector of equal rights and citizenship. The Fourteenth is considered one of the most revolutionary amendments in our Constitution's history, for it redefined notions of individual rights and the balance of states' rights versus federal authority by making personal liberty and equality *federal* guarantees, while empowering the national government to curtail state actions that deprived citizens of these rights.

If Northerners wondered how well the South would comply with these congressional actions, the answer came swiftly. In May, street fighting broke out in Memphis, the culmination of long-simmering tension between white police officers and black soldiers, who had been interfering with arrests of black citizens there. When the troops fired their pistols into the air to keep police from taking a disorderly black man into custody, the police shot back, setting in motion a two-day assault on a black community swollen with war refugees. The so-called Memphis Race Riot, really a massacre of blacks by infuriated white police officers and mobs, killed nearly fifty black men, women, and children, and two whites, and numerous homes, churches, schools, and businesses were looted or set afire.

Even more potent in its effect on Northern opinion was another "riot" in New Orleans, which occurred at the end of July. This city had long seemed a promising one for advances in race relations and the empowerment of black citizens. President Lincoln had begun to view it as "reconstructable" as early as May 1, 1862, when Union army troops, under General Benjamin Butler, took control of the city after Admiral David Farragut completed a successful assault from the sea. Because a substantial Unionist element resided in New Orleans, the president in December 1863 suggested that a form of local reconstruction be started there, based on his Ten Percent Plan. Under this plan, if 10 percent of the men who had voted in the election of 1860 would take an oath of allegiance to the United States, they would be allowed to form a new state government. Subsequently, a state constitutional convention was planned for 1864 to demonstrate Louisiana's willingess to rejoin the Union.

Before the 1864 conclave, more than a thousand New Orleans blacks, and some whites, had petitioned Lincoln to include suffrage for the *gens de couleur*, the free, light-skinned class of Louisiana Negroes, in the new constitution. When Radicals in Congress heard of the petition, they suggested that the franchise be broadened to include all blacks in Louisiana. Formally, Lincoln refused both proposals, but he wrote privately to Michael Hahn, the Unionist governor, to see if certain classes, such as soldiers or intelligent free blacks, might be allowed the vote. Hahn relayed Lincoln's request to the convention, which agreed to grant the state legislature the power to establish limited black voting; but though two such bills were later introduced, neither gained enough support to become law.

Hahn resigned his position in March 1865 and was succeeded by his lieutenant governor, James Madison Wells, a native-born Louisiana Unionist with marked Southern sympathies, who proceeded to evict many leading Radicals from local patronage jobs and appoint ex-Confederates. This encouraged a formidable Democratic power base to grow rapidly, accompanied by the appearance of reactionary political clubs. When in March 1866 President Johnson allowed a city election to take place in New Orleans against the advice of Governor Wells, the forces of Democratic resistance came to power, led by a new mayor, James T. Monroe, who was known as "an unreconstructed rebel."

Governor Wells and the state's Unionists, as well as black leaders agitated by this development, announced in early summer 1866 their intention to reconvene the state constitutional convention of 1864. They sought reconvocation to secure the vote for black Louisianians and, the Monroe faction suspected, disenfranchise ex-Confederates, shifts that threatened to dramatically realign the state's political anatomy and destroy the white-patronage network that Southern veterans were eagerly establishing.

Mayor Monroe informed the local federal commander, Major General Absalom Baird, of his intention to arrest the convention delegates when they gathered on July 30 at the Mechanics Institute, the temporary state capitol on Dryades Street. "The laws and ordinances of the city," Monroe wrote, "declare all assemblies calculated to disturb the public peace and tranquility unlawful." Stronger language about Republican "niggers and half niggers" ran in the Democratic press, along with threats to hang the convention movement leaders Dr. Anthony P. Dostie, a New York–born dentist who had moved to New Orleans before the Civil War, and Michael Hahn, the former governor. It was declared that no man would leave the convention alive. General Baird cautioned Monroe that he had no right to disrupt or defy "the universally conceded right of all loyal citizens of the United States to meet peaceably and discuss freely questions concerning their civil governments, a right which is not restricted by the fact that the movement proposed might terminate in a change of existing institutions." But Monroe, not Baird, had the sympathy of President Johnson, who notified Louisiana's attorney general that federal forces would "sustain the civil authority in suppressing all illegal or unlawful assemblies . . . Usurpation will not be tolerated."

Much as the national policy on Reconstruction remained fluid and unsettled, so officials in New Orleans were left to fend for themselves, with no one — from General Baird to the city police — exactly sure whose rights were to be defended. Baird was "unwilling to assume the attitude of protecting the assembly unless called on by civil authorities" because such activity would only add to local anti-Unionist sentiment, and his superiors likely would not approve of it. Monroe's actions, on the other hand, seemed aimed at making the situation as combustible as possible.

The opening day of the convention was to focus on preliminaries: ascertaining how many vacancies existed in the body, so elections, where needed, could be held. Outside, a cordon of police surrounded the building. Suddenly, a group of approximately two hundred freedmen appeared, marching up Dryades from Canal Street, tooting horns, thumping a big drum, and waving an American flag in support of the convention. Then, according to some reports, a young white bystander insulted one of the parading blacks, who, in anger, drew a gun; when police waded into the column to arrest him, marchers swarmed the officers to free their compatriot. Turning their hatbands around so that they could not be identified, police officers then followed the marchers into the convention. Conventioneers used pieces of furniture to beat back the police, who tried to ram their way through an inner door that had been closed against them. This scenario was enacted four times, as police assaulted the blacks inside with their clubs and were in turn driven back with chairs and sticks. Adding to this scene of disarray, a mob of whites swept into the building behind the police, shooting and clubbing blacks and white Unionists. Policemen were seen on a landing above the meeting hall, firing down indiscriminately.

"Stop firing, we surrender, we make no resistance!" one of the delegates implored.

"God damn you, not one of you will escape from here alive!" was the reply.

Despite claims (never substantiated) that Dostie and other Republicans had incited their followers to riot and were looking for a fight, few if any of those inside the hall had brought weapons — that they had to defend themselves with wooden chairs attests to that fact. The delegates had expected, at worst, to be arrested, and some had even made arrangements to secure bail quickly.

"The crowd in and out of the Mechanics Hall were worked up to a pitch of desperation and madness," recorded the *New Orleans Daily Picayune*, "and firearms were handled as freely as on the battlefield. The reports of pistols were heard in every direction, and balls whizzed by." A former rebel soldier confirmed the combatlike fervor of the confrontation, declaring, "We have fought for four years these god-damned Yankees and sons of bitches in the field, and now we will fight them in the city."

The terrified conventioneers, once they became convinced that submitting to arrest would not save them, took desperate measures. Some jumped from windows, only to be shot as they attempted to flee. "They . . . tried to escape through an alley which runs from Dryades to Baronne, on the Canal Street side," noted the *New York Times* reporter on the scene. "I do not know that any freedmen succeeded in getting away from the building alive . . . I saw several brought in the alley . . . and after they fell I saw crowds of ruffians beating them as they were dying." When convention delegates proved in short supply, the mob began pulling blacks randomly from streetcars and shops, beating them down in the street to cries of "Kill the Yankee nigger!" and "Shoot the nigger son of a bitch!"

More than two hours passed before Baird's federal troops arrived to restore order; the general claimed that he'd been misled about the starting time of the meeting. Baird had obviously been reluctant to insert his men into an emotionally charged local political melee, one in which he did not feel fully empowered to act. In any case, his troops, stationed at the Jackson Barracks three miles southeast of the city, were poorly positioned to respond. All accounts concur that Baird's tardiness had allowed for more carnage, although one official inquiry praised his troops for at least keeping the riot from escalating into the extreme devastation wreaked by the New York Draft Riots of 1863, which had lasted several days.

Forty-six black men were killed and sixty badly injured in the affair; of the attackers, one died of sunstroke, two others were seriously wounded, and a young white student from a nearby medical college was accidentally shot in the neck and killed when he emerged from the school to watch the fighting. The convention's leader, Dostie, was mobbed to death, shot twice in the head and once in the body, then beaten and dragged through the street, while the former governor Hahn was stabbed in the back and suffered a minor head wound. The Congressional Select Committee's inquiry supplied a graphic account:

> Men were shot while waving handkerchiefs in token of surrender and submission; white men and black, with arms uplifted praying for life, were answered by shot and blow from knife and club; the bodies of some were "pounded to a jelly"; a colored man was dragged from under a street-crossing, and killed by a blow; men concealed in outhouses and among piles of lumber were eagerly sought for and slaughtered or maimed without remorse; the dead bodies upon the street were violated by shot, kick, and stab; the face of a man "just breathing his last" was gashed by a knife razor in the hands of a woman . . . one man was wounded by fourteen blows, shots, and stabs; the body of another received seven pistol balls.

"The more information I obtain of the affair the more revolting it becomes," General Philip Sheridan wrote to his superior, General Ulysses S. Grant. "It was no riot; it was an absolute massacre." Congress agreed, concluding, "There has been no occasion during our national history when a riot has occurred so destitute of justifiable cause, resulting in a massacre so inhuman and fiend-like." Sheridan warned President Johnson that "if this matter is permitted to pass over without a thorough and determined prosecution of those engaged in it, we may look out for frequent scenes of the same kind, not only here but in other places."

A government investigation determined that Mayor Monroe and the town's political clubs bore primary responsibility for what had occurred. Carried out largely by policemen and ex–Confederate soldiers — one old colonel showed up "in full uniform and side arms" — the riot was in a sense a supplemental skirmish of the Civil War, its slaughter of unresisting black men a testament to the local disdain for postwar reforms. No one, however, was ever held directly accountable for the butchery. The local grand jury resolved that the whole affair was to be blamed on "political tricksters" who, by staging the meeting, had wrongly attempted to usurp recognized authority.

Legal redress was denied, but the riot's savagery was widely reported, raising concern that President Johnson's version of Reconstruction was insufficiently tough and that stronger federal sanctions were required. Thomas Nast lambasted the president in a cartoon entitled "Amphitheatrum Johnsonianum — Massacre of the Innocents at New Orleans, July 30, 1866." It portrayed Johnson as a Roman emperor seated with other recognizable national leaders in their box at "the Coliseum," watching indifferently as, in the arena below, Mayor Monroe's rebels slaughter the Louisiana Republicans.

The riots in Memphis and New Orleans confirmed for many Americans that "the rebel spirit," though momentarily quashed, was far from dead, and that Southerners, in the absence of slavery, would not hesitate to use extreme violence to maintain supremacy over blacks. Such expressions of fear and resentment would be rekindled easily and often in the Reconstruction South in the coming years. But in the short term "New Orleans!" became the Republican rallying cry, dramatizing the need for severe restraint on former Confederates while creating greater sympathy for Southern freedmen.

In August 1866, with the nation's editorial pages still humming over New Orleans, the president embarked on a circuitous journey through the American heartland, aimed at bolstering his personal image and garnering public support in the run-up to the fall congressional elections. This trip, which became known as the "Swing Around the Circle," included members of Johnson's cabinet, a substantial press corps, and a glittering entourage of heroes meant to set off the president favorably — Generals Ulysses S. Grant and George A. Custer, as well as Admiral David Farragut, the naval hero celebrated for capturing New Orleans in 1862 and Mobile in 1864, where he had famously cried, "Damn the torpedoes! Full speed ahead!" Grant, beloved as "the Man on Horseback" or "the Man with the Black Cigar," was widely credited with winning the Civil War and was hugely popular; many assumed he would soon be president. Custer, with his long yellow curls, thick mustache, and a red bandanna worn as a cravat, was the most dashing military figure of the day. The year before, at a homecoming parade in Washington, he had caught a hurled bouquet on the point of his sword, to thunderous cheers from the crowd.

The framing device for what would become one of the most ill-starred presidential speaking tours in American history was a visit to the gravesite of Senator Stephen A. Douglas of Illinois, who had died in 1861. Making the memorialization of Douglas the excursion's theme was a strange choice. A blustering politico renowned for debating Lincoln over slavery, "the Little Giant" was also the author of the Kansas-Nebraska Act, which in 1854 granted not Congress, but rather the settlers in the new western territories, the right to decide whether a given territory would be slave or free — a bitterly controversial piece of legislation whose passage helped bring on the Civil War. Now the war's outcome had rendered Douglas's views, and his legacy, mostly irrelevant. "Although [he] died five years ago, he seems to have been dead for half a century," wrote one Northern editor. The absurdity of Johnson's homage to Douglas made for some bizarre moments en route, such as when the presidential train slowed near the home of Douglas's elderly mother in upstate New York so that Johnson and Grant could doff their hats from the rear platform as she watched from a chair on her porch.

The tour did not start altogether badly. Johnson's message of national unity and reconciliation carried him through several East Coast appearances — Baltimore, Philadelphia, New York City — but as the train steamed west, the crowded schedule, the almost identical words spoken at every station, and the crush of local well-wishers and dignitaries took their toll. Reporters found Grant stealing a nap in the baggage car. Johnson's stamina seemed about to give out when the tour reached Cleveland, where he came to the balcony of the Kennard Hotel exhausted, maybe a bit tipsy, his voice feeble. After he asked the crowd to tell him when he had ever been false to his own principles, a heckler cried, "New Orleans!"

"Let the negroes vote in Ohio before you talk about negroes voting in Louisiana," Johnson scolded.

"Never!" someone shouted back.

"Hang Jeff Davis!" another voice hollered.

Johnson initially ignored the remark but a few minutes later suggested rhetorically, "Why not hang Thad Stevens or Wendell Phillips?" This prompted the crowd to gasp.

When someone cried "Traitor!" Johnson, in unkind words, chastised his listeners for being cowards who did not volunteer to fight in the war.

"Is this dignified?" a voice asked.

Johnson had never been known for statesmanlike restraint. His political style, honed in the village squares of rural Tennessee, was to give as good as he got, to spar and debate anyone who challenged him. At the moment, such instincts seemed misplaced, and unfortunately the popular Grant, whose appearance always soothed a crowd, had temporarily left the entourage, promising to rejoin it in Detroit.

"President Johnson, in his speech at Cleveland, remarked that he 'did not care much about his dignity,'" observed the *New York Times*. "In our judgment this is greatly to be regretted . . . The President of the United States cannot enter upon an exchange of epithets with the brawlers of a mob, without seriously compromising his official character and hazarding interests too momentous to be thus lightly imperiled."

A few days later in St. Louis, the president was on the defensive again, challenged once more about New Orleans. Apparently stewing about the press coverage of the earlier exchange in Cleveland, Johnson launched into an explanation of how the riot in New Orleans had been caused by Radicals, then lapsed into a self-pitying denunciation of his critics:

> I have been slandered. I have been maligned. I have been called Judas Iscariot . . . If I have played the Judas, who has been my Christ . . . Was it Thad Stevens? Was it Wendell Phillips? Was it Charles Sumner? Are these the men that set up and compare themselves with the Savior of Man, and everybody that differs with them in opinion and that try to stay and arrest their diabolical and nefarious policy, is to be denounced as a Judas?

The *New York Tribune*, like much of the country, was dismayed. "We had thought the President had exhausted his power to offend a national sense of decency," the paper scolded. "This was a mistake. In his speech at St. Louis he passed from vulgarity to blasphemy with a boldness which is almost appalling . . . [and] disgusted every Christian in the land. He has dragged that which is dearest to our hearts into the dirt of his politics and his outrageous defense of the massacre at New Orleans."

Belligerent banter with hecklers, the nation agreed, was not what a president did. Yet the pattern was established; in town after town they descended, interrupting Johnson, demanding that Grant appear, even ordering the president of the United States to "shut up." In the Ohio town of New Market, when Johnson was shouted down, General Custer assumed the role of presidential protector, striding onstage to deal with the harassers. "I was born two miles from here," he fumed, "and I am ashamed of you!" By the time the tour reached Pittsburgh, all was lost; Johnson refused to come to the podium, and after an hour of jeers from the crowd, Grant appeared, only to tell people to go away.

"Never in history had a President gone forth on a greater mission — to appeal for constitutional government and the restoration of union through conciliation and common sense," the historian Claude Bowers would write, "and never had one been so scurvily treated." The newspapers had a field day, depicting Johnson as inept, overly defensive, possibly drunk; rumors also surfaced that Grant's "disappearances" were due to his need to rendezvous with a bottle. The poet James Russell Lowell, writing in the *North American Review*, called the expedition "an indecent orgy" and described Johnson as a performing bear, clownish but excitable, being led about by his handlers. "It was a great blunder of [Secretary of State] Seward to allow [Johnson] to assume the apostolate of the new [Reconstruction] creed in person, for every word he has uttered must have convinced many . . . that a doctrine could hardly be sound which had its origin and derives its power from a source so impure." Lowell judged correctly that a large part of the trouble with Johnson's effort to reach out to America was Johnson himself. He had little aptitude for seeking the middle ground; his character and lack of eloquence ill fitted him for promoting the theme of reconciliation; the public simply did not accept him as the successor to Abraham Lincoln. After all the pain and sacrifice of the recent national conflict, people expected something more.

Concern with the violence in New Orleans and the "unrepentant and still rebellious South," as well as President Johnson's flagging popularity, helped the Republicans sweep the November 1866 congressional elections, giving them the majority they would use to further defy the White House and take over the process of Reconstruction. On March 2, 1867,

Congress once again overrode a presidential veto to pass the first Reconstruction Act (there would be four by midsummer), which mandated that "whereas no legal state governments or adequate protection for life or property now exists in the rebel states," the region should be divided into five military districts, excluding Tennessee, which had already ratified the Fourteenth Amendment. Each of the other former Confederate states was required to ratify the amendment, with its guarantees of citizenship and equal rights, before they could be readmitted to the Union and their representatives welcomed in Congress. State constitutional conventions were called for, to create "a constitution of government in conformity with the Constitution of the United States in all respects, framed by a convention of delegates elected by the male citizens of said state, twenty-one years old and upward, of whatever race, color, or previous condition, who have been resident in the state for one year . . . except such as may be disenfranchised for participation in the rebellion or for felony at common law." Such conventions, the act decreed, were to take place in the former rebel states of Virginia, North Carolina, South Carolina, Georgia, Mississippi, Alabama, Louisiana, Florida, Texas, and Arkansas; all constitutions emerging from these gatherings were to include the right of black suffrage and would be subject to congressional approval.

The Reconstruction Act provided for potentially momentous changes in the lives of African Americans — the opportunity to vote as free men as well as the ability to serve as publicly elected officials. As scholars such as Steven Hahn have stressed, blacks, even as they emerged from slavery, tended to recognize the economic and political issues affecting their situation. But to better know their new rights, the use of the ballot box, and the functioning of a parliamentary democracy, many freedmen turned to the Union League. Begun in New York and Philadelphia during the war, league chapters in the postwar South worked to educate freedmen on the duties of citizenship, provided aid related to labor and land issues, and were strongly allied with Republican sentiments. Naturally, white Southerners distrusted the organization (they derided the chapters as "Loyal Leagues"), based on what the historian Thomas Holt has termed the "new massa" syndrome — the conviction among whites that black people were incapable of independent thought, and that, in the absence of slavery, white Northerners were serving as "thought police" to the ignorant ex-slaves, using the singing of patriotic songs and the teaching of the Declaration of Independence to shape their political attitudes and even direct their actions. It was true that the Union League did not allow those opposed to their work to take part in their meetings, but they were generally open to everyone (many attendees brought their wives and children), and in the final analysis the gatherings probably had significant social and political influence but less than Southerners imagined: the former slaves, after all, needed little convincing that their best interests lay with the Party of Lincoln.

There was probably little that Republicans or Union Leaguers could have done, in any case, to assuage Southern fears of the vast changes taking place. In addition to tens of thousands of new black citizens in every Southern state, legions of Northerners — former soldiers, railroad men, missionaries, teachers, judges, investors, novice cotton planters — had moved south after the war. Whether their business was private enterprise or political work with the Union League or the state conventions, Northerners of either race who entered or remained in the South were categorized uniformly by the derogatory appellation "carpetbagger." While the precise origin of the term is unclear, its negative implication was never in doubt; it referred to persons so scheming, untrustworthy, and "lightweight" that their belongings fit into a cheap piece of luggage, one made of an old carpet remnant with two wooden handles and convenient for sudden departures. The image perfectly captured Southerners' distaste for outside interference in their business. Coupled with other popular mid-nineteenth-century slurs, such as "puppy" (one who is "owned" by others, such as a teacher dispatched by a Northern missionary society), "bummer" (a vagrant who sponges off others, often applied to the members of Sherman's army who decimated Georgia and South Carolina), or the more serious "poltroon" (a duplicitous coward), the effect was utterly and always degrading.

One of the best-known caricatures of Reconstruction is the Thomas Nast cartoon of the 1870s, showing a Southern "black and tan" legislature, a belittling term frequently used for these unprecedented biracial conclaves. Black men in ill-fitting suits gnaw on fried chicken, sip from flasks, and hector one another with all the civility of the barnyard, while at the podium Columbia, Nast's flag-draped female representation of America, gavels in vain for order. Behind her on the wall, ignored by all, is a tattered banner bearing President Grant's famous postwar admonition to his countrymen, LET US HAVE PEACE. As it became known that, by edict of the Reconstruction Acts, black men would sit in elected bodies such as state constitutional conventions, Southern newspapers anticipated Nast's crude depiction. "Can you change a carrot into a melon?" demanded Parson W. G. Brownlow, in a much-reprinted letter.

"Can you grow an oak from a peanut? Will a donkey produce an Arabian horse? . . . Most certainly not! You cannot undo what God has intended shall never be undone. It is, therefore, simply impossible for you to change an African into an Anglo-Saxon."

Most of the state constitutional conventions, however, despite the infamy assigned them by resentful whites "on account of the usurped and

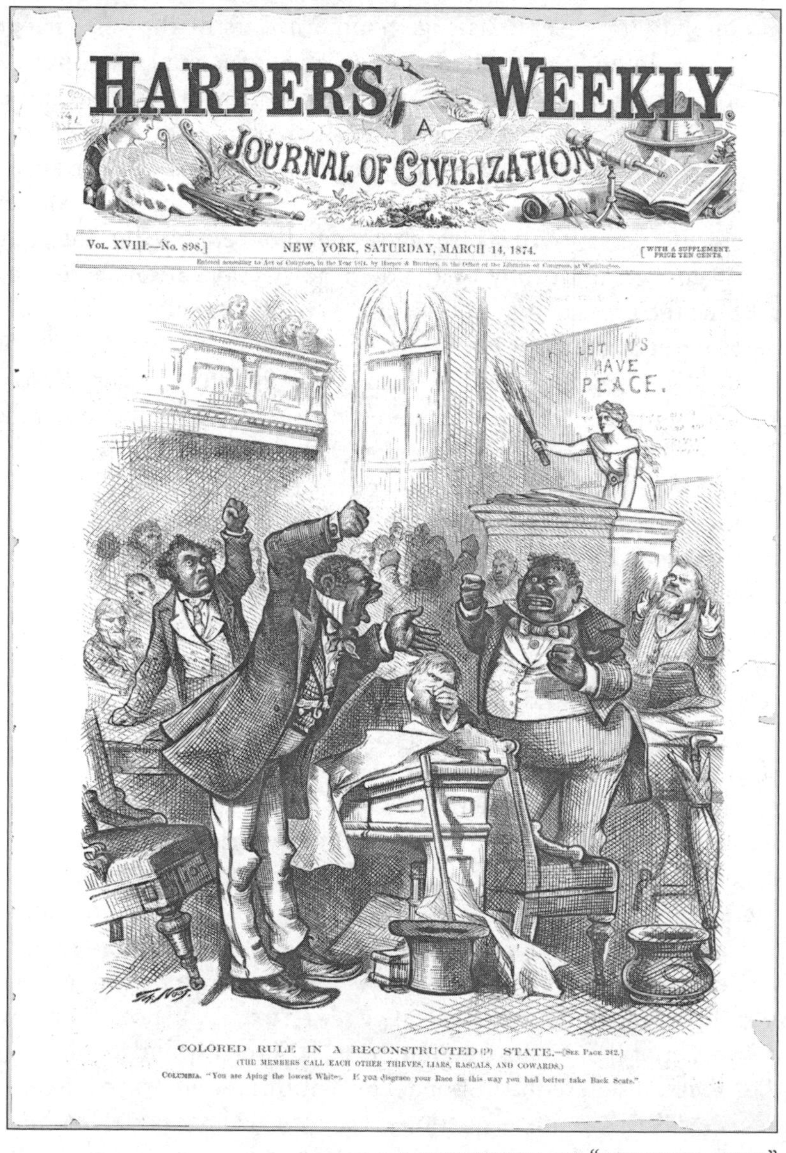

A DEPICTION OF "COLORED RULE"

polluted source from whence it springs" (the Radical Congress) and the appearance of "delegates in every stage of nigritude," would largely demonstrate that such disparagement was unearned. The new constitutions that emerged after weeks of deliberation were often so reasonable that even the white supremacists who, years later, set out to undo them were moved, by practical considerations, to leave many of their tenets intact. "Representing a constituency that previously had been ignored," notes James Underwood of the convention held in South Carolina, the convention's seventy-six black and forty-eight white delegates "crafted a document with a deeper insight into the meaning of freedom, an insight possessed only by the freedmen who had known slavery and the freeborn who knew how precarious freedom could be without constitutional protection."

New England's Gilbert Haven, visiting the South on behalf of the *Atlantic Monthly,* was convinced he was seeing one of the most impressive spectacles of the age: in South Carolina, the very seat of secessionist fervor, the delegates to the convention were black, their aides were black, as were the pages, doormen, and carriage drivers. Haven reminded his readers that in Massachusetts all the considerable effort of the great Senator Charles Sumner had failed to secure a black man a job as chaplain in the state legislature; South Carolina, he concluded, was acting with more ardor than any other part of the country to expand the boundaries of true democracy.

As Haven's observations suggest, the state constitutional conventions held across the South as mandated by Congress were extraordinary events — the nation's first biracial experiment in governance and in most instances the first time blacks had participated in decision-making forums involving whites. Would the freedmen grasp the workings of democratic government? Would they know how to behave, how to listen, how to vote? What attitude would they take toward those who had so recently held them in bondage? There were many Northern men, white and black, involved in these conventions, hoping to see the Southern states adopt "Northern style" or even "New England–like" constitutions. The Northerners were hundreds of miles from their homes, but it was the Southern black participants, many former slaves, who had in fact traveled the most remarkable distance. As convention delegates, they had little time to grow accustomed to this new realm or the responsibilities they'd consented to bear. The gaze of a weary but hopeful nation was upon them.

CHAPTER 3

DADDY CAIN

One of the most notable state constitutional conventions held in response to the Reconstruction Acts took place in South Carolina, the war's birthplace and long a seedbed of antigovernment sentiment. It was one of three former Confederate states — along with Louisiana and Mississippi — in which blacks formed a majority of the population and the state that would ultimately send the most black representatives (six) to Congress during Reconstruction. The convention, which opened in Charleston in January 1868, would also be the setting for an emotional and protracted argument over Reconstruction's most divisive issue — land for the freedmen.

The debate's instigator was Richard Cain, an African Methodist Episcopal minister who would eventually become the first black clergyman to serve in the U.S. House of Representatives. He had been dispatched to Charleston by the leadership of the denomination at war's end to help revive Emmanuel Church, shuttered by the city since 1822 because it was thought Denmark Vesey had used its sanctuary to plot his failed slave insurrection. A freeborn native of Greenbrier County, Virginia, Cain had grown up in Ohio, where he was educated and worked as a steamboat deck hand before attending Wilberforce University and spending the war years behind a pulpit in Brooklyn, New York. Reopened, the Emmanuel slowly gained a substantial congregation, with Cain guiding the membership drive as well as the physical restoration of the building.

Contemporary accounts suggest that Cain was an extremely charismatic man, short in stature but with a compact physique, a booming voice, and a strong, expressive face. His followers bestowed upon him the honorific "Daddy," a term that local whites, who disliked Cain and considered him a Northern interloper, at times used to denigrate him.

RICHARD "DADDY" CAIN

Their own preferred nickname for him was "the Missing Link," an allusion to his thick lips and heavy muttonchop whiskers, which, they claimed, made him resemble an ape. Cain, always willing to give as good as he got, was known to consider most white people "rattlesnakes."

Encouraged by his success at the Emmanuel, he went on to help organize A.M.E. congregations in several outlying South Carolina towns; he was at first disinclined, and probably had little time, to get involved in local politics. The large number of white carpetbaggers flooding into the state troubled him, and he hesitated to affiliate with either political party, leading the *Charleston Mercury* to accuse him of occupying "a position of betwixity." But, devoted to his flock, he came to recognize that their most urgent needs, such as land ownership, were political in nature; and the injustice of South Carolina's Black Codes brought him eventually to side with local Radicals. Along with a partner, the lawyer Robert Brown Elliott, Cain began publishing the *Leader,* later renamed the *Missionary Record,* the first black newspaper in South Carolina during Reconstruction.

"The possession of lands and homesteads is one of the best means by which a people is made industrious, honest and advantageous to the State," Cain believed, contrasting the potential of land ownership to the hardships of the sharecropping, or crop-lien, system. "As long as people are working on shares and contracts, and at the end of every year are in debt, so long will they and the country suffer." He asked that the freedmen receive the chance to "take the hoe and the axe, cut down the forest, and make the whole land blossom as the Garden of Eden."

Despite his initial reluctance, Cain took naturally to the political sphere, first as a city alderman, then as a delegate to the 1868 constitutional convention. His church constituency and his newspaper made him a formidable power broker and spokesman for the dispossessed, and even whites who held him in contempt often had no choice but to respect his authority.

In Cain's Charleston, as elsewhere in the state, blacks experienced a profound upwelling of emotion as they voted, on November 19 and 20, 1867, in the referendum for a new constitutional convention. In the Sea Islands the balloting was held in a building in coastal Beaufort formerly used as a "hall of justice," a place where slaves were sentenced to punishment. This structure was adjacent to the arsenal and the local prison; it had long been the site of slave auctions, whippings, and hangings, the very place where Robert Smalls's mother had taken him to rub his nose in the brutality of chattel slavery. The poignancy of the location was not lost on the former slaves who cast their ballots there that day; it was said some became so overwhelmed, they shed tears.

That the state's freedmen would seize the opportunity to vote should have come as no surprise: black South Carolinians, even before the Civil War had ended, had shown their political fervor. When Union forces marched into Charleston in March 1865, thousands of men, women, and children had swarmed the troops, cheering and hoisting banners that read EQUAL RIGHTS and WE KNOW NO CASTE OR COLOR! while pushing along a float fringed in black — the "hearse" transporting the now quite dead "Body of Slavery." Within two years, they demanded the integration of the city's new streetcar line. At a rally in Citadel Square in March 1867, Daddy Cain was joined by two newly minted black leaders — his publishing partner, the lawyer Robert Brown Elliott, and the former shipping-house clerk Alonzo Ransier — in exhorting the crowd to force the streetcar company to amend its policy. A local white newspaper urged blacks to remember that "the people of Charleston have not, as yet, become accustomed to the presence of colored persons as citizens," but after a black woman was manhandled by white streetcar conductors, officers of the Freedmen's Bureau intervened, convincing the streetcar company to allow equal access on a trial basis. As it turned out, whites seemed to enjoy the novelty and convenience of the new streetcar service too much to care about who sat near them, and, though some feared it, a white boycott of the line did not materialize.

Cain, Elliott, and Ransier were among the seventy-six black and forty-eight white delegates who convened at the Charleston Club House on January 14, 1868, for the opening of the state's constitutional convention, or what the local press enjoyed mocking as "the Crow Congress," "the Menagerie," the "Congo Convention," and even "the Great Unlawful." The town's most reactionary newspaper, the *Charleston Mercury,* offered unflattering caricatures of the individual participants. Robert C. De Large, a mulatto who was a leading Republican operative in Charleston, "might have lived and died without having his name in print, except in an advertisement, if it had not been for the great social revolution which like boiling water has thrown the scum on the surface." Attorney William J. Whipper was "a genuine negro, kinky-headed, who, in the days of slavery, would have been esteemed a likely fellow for a house servant or a coachman." Of Robert Smalls, "the Boat Thief," the *Mercury* noted that although his act of larceny had won "great notoriety for a time, and he was much caressed by his new allies," he "has been gradually subsiding to his proper level, which he has at last attained in the mongrel convention." Cain, in his turn, was described as having "the features of a very ugly white man . . . He came here at the close of the war as a preacher . . . and has, ever since, been engaged in . . . propagating his dusky religion . . . Although black, ugly and shabby, or perhaps because of these exceptional qualities, [he] enjoys considerable influence among the darkies." Nor were the white delegates spared. Daniel Chamberlain, a Yale graduate who came south after the war to settle the affairs of a deceased friend, then stayed to open a successful law practice, was one of the "peripatetic buccaneers from Cape Cod . . . Hell, and Boston."

So annoyed were some of the delegates by the *Mercury*'s barbs that they greeted a resolution to bar the paper's reporters from the convention with loud approval and immediate seconding motions. But Francis J. Cardozo, the college-educated son of a free black woman and a Jewish businessman, spoke against such a rash reaction, as did the lawyer Whipper, who had in preparation for the convention secured copies of the constitutions of numerous Northern states. "To attempt to exclude [the *Mercury*'s] reporter from the bar of the Convention," Whipper declared, "would be only to exhibit a smallness, a pettiness of spite, unworthy of our character. Let us pursue our straightforward course, and the world will judge between us." Whipper commanded respect as a war veteran, but he was countered by Landon Langley, who had served with the legendary Fifty-fourth Massachusetts Volunteers. "I do believe [the *Mercury*] to be utterly incapable of a respectable or gentlemanly course," he said, "and I am not willing for that rebel sheet to burlesque this body. I want it excluded." Alonzo Ransier, however, suggested that the *Mercury* actually benefited "republican liberty" by expressing the "sentiments of those opposed to republican principles" in such undiluted form. Whipper reminded his colleagues that they had gathered "for a great purpose . . . [and] we should not be swerved from it by newspapers, whose chief purpose . . . is simply to make five cent pieces."

Franklin J. Moses Jr., a white native South Carolinian, took the floor.

"I do not stand here to vindicate the *Mercury*. It is no friend of mine," he stated. "I have been abused by it since the Convention assembled more than any other man on the floor, and yet I hope the resolution will be voted down." Moses' opinion carried considerable weight, for he was the convention's most well known scalawag, a Southerner who "traitorously" became aligned with the Republican cause. The son of a prominent Jewish family (his father was the state's chief justice), he had once been a "shouting rebel," or rabid secessionist, and was famous in Charleston as the man who had raised the Confederate flag over Fort Sumter when Union defenders surrendered the fort in 1861. Now Moses had become one of the most-hated men in the South for embracing the tenets of Radical Republicanism. Had his transformation been considered sincere, it would still have won him infamy, but most whites viewed him as gutless and self-glorifying — an immoral "gambler and libertine . . . [who] seized upon the opportunity to share in the plundering of his own people."

The emotions stirred by the demeaning press portraits were hard to set aside. Immediately after the convention adjourned for the day on January 28, the *Mercury* correspondent Roswell T. Logan was gathering his papers at the reporters' table when he was confronted by the white delegate E.W.M. Mackey. "Are you the writer of the article . . . concerning my father?" Mackey demanded. (Mackey's father, Dr. A. G. Mackey, a local customs official, served as the convention's president.) When Logan said that he was, Mackey struck him across the face, exclaiming, "Take that!" Logan attempted to defend himself, and both men were quickly pulled apart by delegates. To protect the journalist, Moses embraced the man in a bear hug and held him against a wall, as blacks watching from a gallery shouted, "Kill the hound! Cut his heart out! Throw him out the window!" Moses refused to relax his grip on Logan, warning that any man who tried to hit the reporter would have to strike him as well. Mackey, in the meantime, hovered about, shouting at Logan for the "mean, contemptible and dirty business" of coming here to "defame the characters of members of the convention."

A police officer arrived, and Logan requested that he escort him back to the *Mercury*'s office. Mackey, in a sudden show of magnanimity, then insisted that *he* would escort Logan back safely, and several other delegates of both races spoke up, saying they would accompany the men. In the end, a group of police and delegates of both races provided an "honor guard" for the reporter as he returned to his newspaper's offices. Thus, having freely maligned the delegates and their character, the *Mer-*

cury provided a test case that proved these judgments erroneous. Even Logan later conceded that the men he had slandered had behaved honorably in seeing that he was not harmed.

As the delegates coolly defused the crisis over the *Mercury,* so did they defy South Carolinians' worst fears about the convention. Some white Charlestonians had joked that the convention participants looked "shabby" and that the clothes they wore were gaudy hand-me-downs distributed to war refugees by the Freedmen's Bureau. But the last laugh, and the sartorial coup of the convention, belonged to the black delegate who showed up one morning in the gray overcoat of a Confederate officer. Even the black observers who filled the gallery were, in deference to their surroundings, generally well behaved; the *New York Times* noted that gentlemen and ladies alike had learned to spit in a civilized manner — that is, into a spittoon.

Most of the whites present, including members of the press, were seeing and hearing for the first time the phenomenon of black men speaking their opinions freely. Two qualities struck them — (1) the ability of blacks to talk compellingly of the hardships they had endured and relate these experiences to the black community as a whole and (2) the African-influenced cadence of speech, influenced by the preaching in black churches. That Daddy Cain could shake the rafters and "call down Heaven" with his forceful eloquence was already well known to his black constituents, but many whites were new to such performances. Robert Brown Elliott was an equally gifted orator just finding his voice; returning to the offices of the *Leader* one evening after addressing a voting rights meeting, he had enthused to his colleagues, "I thundered, and by golly they cheered."

"The colored men in the Convention possess by long odds the largest share of mental caliber," noted the *New York Times.*

> They are the best debaters [and] there is a homely but strong grasp of common sense in what they say, and although the [grammatical] mistakes made are frequent and ludicrous, the South Carolinians are not slow to acknowledge that their destinies really appear to be safer in the hands of these unlettered Ethiopians than they would be if confided to the more unscrupulous care of the white men in the body.

Despite the day's familiar refrain that blacks lacked the education and initiative to be politicians, it began to appear that the reverse might be true; the black participants took readily to their duties, patiently mastering the sessions' procedures and more often than not managing to say their piece. When a visiting correspondent of *The Nation* magazine tried to bait one South Carolina Republican by asking how many of the state's black legislators could read a copy of John Bunyan's *Pilgrim's Progress*, the savvy reply was that they could not only read it but had lived a remarkable "progress" of their own, comparable to Bunyan's, and that they could undoubtedly write better articles about South Carolina than had ever appeared in *The Nation*.

The gathering framed a new constitution that vowed the state's allegiance to the Constitution and the government of the United States, and it promised that South Carolina would remain a member of the Union — a significant point, since the state had led the South into secession. The document also called for direct election of several state officials previously appointed by the legislature, and representation in the state house of representatives based on population. This addressed the power balance in the state, which had long allowed the wealthy coastal section, including Charleston, to dominate state politics at the expense of the backwoods upcountry. A basic bill of rights was established, guaranteeing freedom of speech and assembly. The courts were no longer allowed to take a debtor's last thousand dollars' worth of property or five hundred dollars' worth of personal possessions, meaning that poor whites and blacks alike could not be turned out on the street. Prison sentences for debt were abolished. If a woman owned property outright, her assets could no longer be appropriated to pay her husband's debts; nonetheless, Whipper's resolution that women be given the franchise, despite his passionate urging of the issue (which included his view that women were intellectually superior to men), was rejected without a vote. (Whipper spoke from personal experience: his wife was Frances Rollin, one of several well known, opinionated sisters of a light-skinned, aristocratic Charleston family active in state politics.) The South Carolina constitution also authorized the state to seek loans for sorely needed public works projects — bridges, roads, canals, and other types of infrastructure.

Robert Smalls's most notable accomplishment at the convention was to successfully call for state-sponsored, free, compulsory education for rich and poor, black and white, and the creation of state colleges. In South Carolina at the end of the Civil War, only about 5 percent of the freedmen knew how to read and write, and blacks hurried in a veritable stampede to gain some education after the Freedmen's Bureau opened schools in 1865. The arrival of black suffrage linked education and the all-important ballot, twin priorities among freed people of all ages. Smalls suggested "a system of common schools, of different grades, to be open without charge to all classes of persons" and suggested that it "be required that all parents and guardians send their children between the ages of 7 and 14 to some school, at least 6 months for each year, under penalties for non-compliance." Smalls's keen interest in the subject grew from personal experience. Sensitive about his own lack of education, he had studied diligently since the war to improve his meager reading and writing skills, occasionally working with a tutor.

Some delegates opposed the compulsory aspect of Smalls's plan, deeming it harsh and undemocratic; others thought it placed too great a demand on a people still recovering from the war's devastation or alleged that it was meant to hasten the mixing of the races. But Alonzo Ransier jumped up to defend the point, saying that the success of the republic as a whole relied on the education of its members and that parents should not be allowed to neglect their children's education. Robert Brown Elliott, born in Boston, raised the example of New England, where compulsory education "has made . . . her citizens, poor as well as rich, low as well as high, black as well as white, educated and intelligent." He cast education and understanding as integral to the state's future. "Ignorance is the parent of vice and crime, and was the sustainer of the late gigantic slaveholder's rebellion," he reminded his listeners. "I appeal to gentlemen of the convention to know whether they desire to see a state of anarchy, or a state of confusion in South Carolina . . . I desire to know whether they wish to see an independent people, engaged in industrious pursuits, living happy and contented." Other delegates suggested that parents should willingly pay taxes to keep their children in school rather than maintain them later in penitentiaries; compulsory attendance might keep the state's children from "running around molasses barrels or stealing cotton." One delegate stated that he'd seen, that very morning, "some eighteen colored children standing before the door of the Guard House . . . If those little boys and girls were at school, they would not have been arrested."

The version of Smalls's resolution that ultimately passed provided that all children attend school for a minimum of twenty-four months from age six to sixteen and that each school district keep at least one school open for six months a year. Thus the right to a free education was inserted in the state's constitution for the first time in South Carolina history. Kicking the question of school integration to the state legislature that would enact the relevant laws, the convention resolved that the state's public schools and colleges would be open to all, without regard to race or color. "We only compel parents to send their children to some school," said Cardozo, "not that they shall send them with the colored children; we simply give those colored children who desire to go to white schools the privilege of doing so." Cardozo did suggest that putting children of both races together in schools might serve, in the long run, to diminish racial prejudice, but at this point in time the relative value or harm of mixed schools was a somewhat abstract concern; freed people were primarily interested in education for its own sake.

Education did ultimately prove one of Reconstruction's quiet successes in South Carolina: by 1877 there were nearly three thousand schools in the state, educating 125,000 young people of both races, and Democrats and Republicans continued to allow a statewide property tax to be levied for that purpose. The strong universal desire for learning, and the fact that the issue of integration was never forced by law, probably accounted for this achievement.

The black delegates acted with moderation on two other key issues — the further confiscation of land owned by former rebels and their disenfranchisement; essentially, the freedmen refused to impose additional hardships and kicked the matter to Congress. They knew it would be politically unseemly to appear overly vindictive and no doubt feared that placing restrictions on others' voting rights would undermine the ideal of universal suffrage they themselves so strongly embraced. To some it made no sense that the South, in its greatest hour of need, would not call on the considerable experience of its more prominent white men. Smalls advocated, except in extreme cases, their readmittance to positions of leadership, and, trusting the planters and large landowners more than he did the white yeomanry, looked to a potential coalition between blacks and politically moderate whites; he believed that the state's majority black vote, combined with that of these moderates, would "bury the Democratic party so deep . . . there will not be seen even a bubble coming from the spot where the burial took place." As one member asked the gathering, "Can we afford to lose from the councils of state our best men? No, fellow citizens, no! We want only the best and ablest men. And then with a strong pull, and a long pull, and a pull together, up goes South Carolina."

The prospect of "owning a piece of the land that had once owned them" tantalized the freed people like no other aspect of emancipation, and it was an issue that, in response to Richard Cain's efforts, the delegates explored at great length. South Carolina, because of its head start on Reconstruction in the Sea Islands, already had a substantial history of official efforts to provide land to the former slaves. After July 1862 the federal government had begun taxing abandoned plantations in the Port Royal area, posting notices that landowners would have to make an appearance, swear an oath of allegiance to the United States, and remit the tax. It seemed entirely just that large landholders who had been leading secessionists should help bear the cost of the war they had instigated. "Here, beneath these live oaks," mused the *Harper's Weekly* reporter Charles Nordhoff, "they deliberated, they planned . . . the ruin of their country; here was nurtured that gigantic and inexcusable crime." Where property owners could not or would not pay, lands were seized. The United States also appropriated lands held by ranking Confederate military or civil officials as well as property owned by some rebel soldiers. An 1865 Freedmen's Bureau inventory prepared for General Rufus Saxton of available properties in the Port Royal area suggests both the displacement and devastation wrought by the war:

> Six deserted plantations lie along the "Coosa" river eastward from Port Royal ferry and are perfectly desolate, having neither an inhabitant nor a dwelling . . .
>
> Estate of Rafe Elliott — lies south east of Gardners Corners; has no houses or other improvements; comprises 800 acres of first quality land. Elliott was a surgeon in the C.S.A. and was killed early in the war . . .
>
> Oak Point — belonged to Henry Stewart, a "hard master" who promoted the rebellion in every possible way except to take up arms himself . . .
>
> Estate of Hal Stewart — Lieutenant in the rebel army, the Negroes on his father's place say young "mass Hal" was opposed to the war and only went when "he was scripted"; the place is deserted but several tenements are standing in good order, also cotton and gin houses; there are 600 acres of good land . . .
>
> John Jenkins Place — lying directly on the "Combahee road" all gone to ruin and everything grown up to weeds . . .

In Beaufort, federal commissioners sold almost 17,000 acres subject to sale for nonpayment of taxes at a price of 93.3 cents an acre; blacks bought about 3,500 acres, as well as about 75 homes in Beaufort for as little as $30 to $1,800. Northern missionaries and speculators who had come south with the Union forces obtained additional properties. South Carolina, along with other Southern states, would continue to shift the tax burden onto large property owners or deny them forms of financial relief, with the idea that this would break up once-vast plantations and make small land parcels available to poor whites and freedmen.

The black population of the Sea Islands had grown substantially during the war as refugees by the thousands arrived from combat zones in Georgia and South Carolina. Concerned about this influx, General William T. Sherman and Secretary of War Edwin Stanton on January 12, 1865, convened a meeting at Sherman's headquarters in Savannah with black community leaders, chiefly Methodist and Baptist clergymen. When queried as to how the government might best assist the freedmen, the black spokesmen were unanimous in their reply: *Land!* "The way we can best take care of ourselves," they assured the white men, "is to have land, and turn it and till it by our own labor." In response, Sherman issued Field Order Number 15, establishing the Sea Islands as an area for exclusive black settlement where freedmen and their

THE SAVANNAH HEADQUARTERS OF GENERAL WILLIAM T. SHERMAN

families might be settled on forty-acre parcels. (Sherman mentioned that he had some worn-out army mules he would be willing to give the black settlers to help them get started on their plots of land — the origin of the expression "forty acres and a mule.") Before leaving, the blacks recommended the establishment of separate communities for the two races, for, as one told Sherman and Stanton, "There is a prejudice against us in the South that will take years to get over."

Two months later Congress created the Freedmen's Bureau to deal with the myriad issues now confronting the devastated South and particularly the four million former slaves. In charge were two New Englanders — General O. O. Howard, who had lost an arm in the Battle of Fair Oaks and was known as "the Christian General" for his work with Northern philanthropies that assisted Southern blacks during the war; and assistant commissioner General Rufus Saxton, the wartime governor of the conquered Sea Islands. With about 300,000 acres of confiscated Sea Islands lands in the bureau's possession, Saxton set about leasing forty-acre parcels, with the stipulation that leasers could buy them at any time. He believed the Southerners had forfeited their land with their ill-conceived rebellion and that blacks deserved the soil on which "they and their ancestors passed two hundred years of unrequited toil." A friend and admirer of Robert Smalls, he felt strongly that black war veterans, who "piloted our ships through these shallow waters, have labored on our forts . . . and have enlisted as soldiers in our country's darkest hours," were owed a special debt of gratitude. Smalls had taken advantage of the government's auction of Beaufort properties to purchase the very house where he and his mother had once been slaves.

As General Howard would later note, however, only a tiny fraction of former Confederate lands were ever under federal control; and in any case, the confiscation edicts proved short-lived, for in August 1865 President Andrew Johnson came out against the practice. Johnson allowed all but the most prominent Confederates to seek and obtain presidential pardons and offered to return their seized property. The president's actions did not apply to the Sea Islands, which were covered separately by Sherman's field order, so Johnson directed General Howard to go to South Carolina and work something out between the former property owners and the blacks who had already taken possession of land. Howard suggested to the president that he require Southern men whose property had been returned to "provide a small homestead or something equivalent to each head of family of his former slaves; but," as Howard remembered, "President Johnson was amused and gave no heed to this recommendation. My heart ached for our beneficiaries, but I became comparatively helpless to offer them any permanent possession . . . Why did I not resign? Because I even yet strongly hoped in some way to befriend the freed people."

Reconstruction would be filled with examples of how the federal government backed away from its promises to the freedmen, but none may have been as heart-rending as the scene on Edisto Island in fall 1865 when the "Christian General" had to inform loyal blacks, gathered in a village church, that they would have to forfeit their claim to the land and strike labor contracts with their former owners. In the meeting's "noise and confusion," he recalled, "no progress was had till a sweet-voiced Negro woman began the hymn, 'Nobody knows the trouble I seen, nobody knows but Jesus . . .'"

The singing calmed the meeting, but when Howard began to address the assembled freed people, "their eyes flashed unpleasantly, and with one voice they cried, 'No, no!' . . . One very black man, thick set and strong, cried out from the gallery, 'Why, General Howard, why do you take away our lands? You take them from us who are true, always true to the government! You give them to our all-time enemies! That is not right!'"

After the first of the year, a newly arrived federal officer, General Daniel E. Sickles, ordered all freedmen to move off the property they held "illegitimately" or face immediate eviction. Some freedmen were able to hold on to their land if they had purchased it outright and held titles; others were offered less desirable sites possessed by the government. Robert Smalls was active in making these alternative lands available. But by and large, the dream of the forty-acre land plots had ended. Of the almost forty thousand freedmen who were settled on Sea Islands lands because of Field Order Number 15, only fifteen hundred were ultimately deemed to have valid titles.

Other opportunities did open up. In 1866 Congress passed the Southern Homestead Act, making forty-six million acres owned by the United States in Alabama, Arkansas, Florida, Mississippi, and Louisiana available in eighty-acre sites at a cost of $2.50 an acre. But much of the land was too expensive or too poor in quality, and freedmen lacked the capital to dredge, drain, or otherwise transform it into arable plots. Hopeful blacks who relocated with the idea of acquiring such property often were forced by economic necessity to accept labor contracts from nearby whites.

It was becoming increasingly clear that most of the desirable land in the South would remain in the hands of the landowning class that had held it previously. Many Northern Republicans felt that this repudiated the whole purpose of fighting and winning the Civil War. "Of what avail would be an act of Congress totally abolishing slavery, or an amendment to the Constitution forever prohibiting it, if the old agricultural basis of aristocratic power shall remain?" asked the Indiana congressman George W. Julian. "Real liberty must ever be an outlaw where one man only in three hundred or five hundred is an owner of the soil."

To Julian's colleague from Pennsylvania, Thaddeus Stevens, confiscation still seemed the best way to rectify this imbalance, for Stevens envisioned Reconstruction not as a time simply to patch and mend America but as an opportunity to perform reconstructive surgery. The chief of the House Radicals and perhaps the purest revolutionary of the postwar era, Stevens was an intimidating congressional leader. He moved awkwardly because of a clubfoot, a lifelong disability, and, robbed of his natural hair by a scalp infection, he wore an imposing wig, which accentuated the hatchet-sharp features of his face. The *New York Herald* called him "a strange and unearthly apparition — a reclused remonstrance from the tomb . . . the very embodiment of fanaticism," but his friends claimed that his handicaps were the source of his hatred of all injustice. He had been in the forefront of many key advances of the era — the Confiscation Acts, the arming of black troops, and the enfranchisement of the freedmen. Some historians suggest that President Lincoln valued the prickly Stevens for his willingness to confront difficult issues head-on, in order that the president's own efforts, trailing just behind, might better appear conciliatory. Stevens was most widely known for his role in engineering the 1868 impeachment of Andrew Johnson, nominally for violating the Tenure of Office Act, but really for failing to lead a program of Reconstruction that was acceptable to Congress.

While the franchise was frequently cited as the key to establishing the freedmen in the South, Stevens feared that even with the vote, black Southerners without land would remain vassals; land confiscation would readjust the region's economy and labor practices while providing poetic justice for the slaves. In a speech in his hometown of Lancaster, Pennsylvania, Stevens explained that if the land holdings of seventy thousand of the key rebels in the former Confederacy were confiscated, it would make enough acres available for redistribution to as many as one million freedmen, with plenty of land left over to be sold at $10 per acre both to blacks and also to poor whites. The latter deserved consideration, Stevens felt, because they had been buffaloed by the Southern

THADDEUS STEVENS

aristocrats into fighting an unwinnable war. The income from these sales could pay down the national debt. To those who might question the wisdom of dispossessing the planters, Stevens insisted such a measure made more sense than cockeyed migration schemes to colonize in some foreign land four million black Americans "native to the soil and loyal to the government." Stevens had an ally in the Boston abolitionist Wendell Phillips, who believed "this nation owes the Negro not merely freedom; it owes him land," and that black Americans knew this best of all, for their "instincts are better than our laws." Phillips saw "what few public men in the America of his time appear to have realized," notes his biographer Ralph Korngold, "that economic power was the foundation of political power — that if the land remained in the hands of the planter aristocracy, it would be a question of time before they again ruled the South."

JOSEPH RAINEY

With the antagonisms of the war already fading, however, there was inadequate support in Congress for Stevens's confiscation program. Most Americans, including many Republicans, "believed that a free laborer, once accorded equality of opportunity, would rise or fall in the social scale on the strength of his own diligence, frugality, and hard work," the historian Eric Foner points out. "Confiscation seemed an unwarranted interference with the rights of property and an unacceptable example of special privilege and class legislation." Frederick Douglass could remind America that "when the serfs of Russia were emancipated, Tsar Alexander II saw to it that each received three acres of ground upon which they could live and make a living," but the taking of private property, even that of notorious rebels, somehow did not sit right with most of Douglass's countrymen.

Richard Cain of South Carolina was not ready to give up on the dream of land for former slaves. Even as he saw the efforts of the Freedmen's Bureau and the confiscation policies suggested in Congress fall from favor and eventually from consideration, he continued to hear his own followers' urgent plea — *Land!* — and sought ways to obtain it fairly.

By the time of South Carolina's constitutional convention in 1868, attempts to transfer land to freedmen had already accrued a lengthy and not very pleasant history. Therefore many delegates were inclined to view it as a dead issue. Joseph Rainey of coastal Georgetown won approval of a resolution aimed to prevent the subject from even being discussed:

> That this Convention do hereby declare to the people of South Carolina, and to the world, that they have no land or lands at their disposal, and in order to disabuse the minds of all persons whatever throughout the State who may be expecting a distribution of land by the Government of the United States through the [Freedmen's Bureau], or in any other manner, that no act of confiscation has been passed by the Congress of the United States, and it is the belief of this Convention that there never will be, and that the only manner by which any land can be obtained by the landless will be to purchase it.

Rainey, a native South Carolinian, was a reliable spokesman for local black sentiment. His father had been a successful barber who had purchased his family's freedom, and Rainey, following the family trade, had become a barber at the Mills House, one of Charleston's finest hotels, where he may have himself briefly owned a slave. When war broke out, however, his skilled profession did not save him from being drafted for Confederate service — first helping to build harbor fortifications, later as a steward on a rebel vessel used for running arms and other goods through the offshore Union naval blockade. The blockade runners frequently put in at Bermuda or the Bahamas, where cargoes from big English ships were transferred to the Southern boats for the stealthy journey to the American coast. Rainey managed to bring his wife, Susan, along on one of these voyages, and the two jumped ship in Bermuda. Here Rainey resumed his peacetime vocation to wait out the war, offering "Hair-Cutting . . . Executed in Artistic Style" in a shop near the waterfront, before returning to South Carolina in 1865.

Rainey's resolution was based on humane concern for the frustrations with land acquisition of South Carolina blacks, but Richard Cain's response was to demand a conversation on that very topic. Cain announced that he would offer a resolution to create a state land commission so that freedmen would be able to buy their own land, with the state serving as middleman in the transactions. Many owners of large properties were in disadvantageous financial straits, Cain said, and the planters could make good profits by culling small land parcels from their vast holdings and selling them. Cain believed the commission should be established with the help of the federal government and recommended that the convention petition Congress "to make an appropriation of one million dollars . . . for the purpose of purchasing lands in this state . . . and that said lands when so purchased shall be sold to the freedmen as homes, in parcels of 10, 20, 40, 50, 60, 80 and 100 acres . . . under the supervision of [the] Commissioner of the Freedmen's Bureau." The land would also be available to interested whites. Cain suggested that the $1 million could take the form of a loan from the $7 million said to remain in the Freedmen's Bureau Fund; the loan would be paid back within five years with the income from the land purchases.

Several delegates denounced Cain for raising a proposal bound to give the freedmen false hope. The most animated was Charles P. Leslie, a white New Yorker who had initially come south as an employee of the U.S. Treasury Department and was now trying his hand at operating a plantation. Leslie warned that there was almost no chance Congress would make any such allocation and that after the earlier disappointments in the Sea Islands, it was cruel to dangle such unlikely dreams before the former slaves. "It is the fashion of bogus politicians to get up resolutions," he said, "but gentlemen here are tickling the fancy of the poor people of the state by petitions to Congress that every sensible person from the coast of Maine to the Gulf of Mexico well knows will not get a single dollar. I will not, for that reason, allow my name to be recorded in favor of fooling the people." He mocked Cain's faith in the bottomless largesse of the national Congress. "Suppose I should button up my coat and march up to your house and ask you for money or provisions, when you had none to give," he demanded. "What would you think of me?"

"You would do perfectly right to run the chance of getting something to eat," Cain replied. Leslie frowned, but Cain continued: "The abolition of slavery has thrown these people upon their own resources. How are they to live? I know the philosopher of the *New York Tribune* [Horace Greeley] says root, hog, or die . . . My proposition is simply to give the hog some place to root."

Cain told the convention he regretted that his idea had generated such a caustic reaction.

> When I, in the simplicity of my heart and with a fervent desire for good, snatched a few moments of my time between the hours of twelve at night and two in the morning, to pen the preamble and resolutions of the petition presented, I little thought there would be five persons on this floor who would object to so reasonable, so innocent an operation as simply requesting the Congress of the United States . . . to appropriate . . . money for the benefit of the black men and poor white men in this state, equally involved in a state of starvation.

He recounted the unfairness of the sharecropping system to which many blacks, unable to attain land, had been relegated.

> After fifty men have gone on a plantation, worked the whole year at raising 20,000 bushels of rice, and then go to get their one-third, by the time they get through the division, after being charged by the landlord 25 or 30 cents a pound for bacon, two or three dollars for a pair of brogans that cost 60 cents . . . two dollars a bushel of corn, that can be bought for one dollar . . . after, I say, these people have worked the whole season . . . they find themselves in debt.

He related how on a recent visit to a plantation, "I saw corn cribs piled with corn, and fodder houses filled with fodder. I went into the cabin of the negroes and found but a scanty morsel of corn dodger and a scanty ration of bacon."

In his view, the infusion of $1 million would have multiple effects. It would offer land and homes to the destitute, relieve the Freedmen's Bureau of caring for the needy, and enrich white landowners who were cash poor, thus invigorating the state economy. The bureau was already spending hundreds of thousands of dollars on the indigent, he pointed out; the same investment in homes and land would prove far more meaningful and would help improve the character and work ethic of the Southern Negro.

> I believe if the same amount of money that has been employed by the Bureau in feeding lazy, worthless men and women, had been expended in purchasing lands, we would today have no need of the Bureau . . . There are hundreds of persons in the jail and penitentiary cracking rock today who have all the instincts of honesty, and who, had they an opportunity of making a living, would never have been found in such a place.

Cain's emphatic rhetoric had its effect, and his measure passed the convention with substantial white support, although Robert Smalls, Robert Brown Elliott, and Joseph Rainey concurred with Leslie, opposing Cain on the grounds that it was irresponsible to set up South Carolina's black population for another crushing disappointment.

As Leslie and the others predicted, the land commission idea won no sympathy in Washington; a tersely worded telegram advised the convention that a $1 million loan was out of the question. But it remained popular enough with the delegates that they authored a constitutional provision ordering the state legislature to create such a body. Established in March 1869, the commission was to buy both existing farmland and undeveloped lands, divide the purchases into parcels of twenty-five to one hundred acres, and sell them at reasonable prices to citizens, with the stipulation that the purchase price be repaid within eight years. Settlers would pay only interest and taxes for the first three years and make payments toward the purchase price thereafter. Speculators would be discouraged by the requirement that purchasers begin cultivation within five years.

For reasons that are not entirely clear, Leslie, the harshest critic of Cain's plan, was put in charge of the land commission, perhaps as a means of ensuring the program would be kept under tough scrutiny. Cain was passed over, likely because he was regarded as gifted but eccentric, a man of God whose proclamations at the convention — such as a resolution denying the office of governor to anyone who refused to acknowledge the existence of a supreme being — often appeared softheaded. In any case his real authority lay with his congregation at the Emmanuel, and in his newspaper readership, a base of support that would eventually propel him to national office.

CHAPTER 4

"THE WHIRLIGIG OF TIME"

IN LATE JANUARY 1870 a tall, heavy-set man in his late forties, black but of light complexion, strode purposefully into the corridors of the U.S. Capitol. He wore white gloves, a dignified long black coat, and matching pants and vest, and he carried a dark walking stick. His home state, Mississippi, had recently held a constitutional convention similar to South Carolina's, and was in the process of gaining readmission to the Union. At the time (and until 1913), U.S. senators were not popularly elected but were selected by the state legislature. When Mississippi's had convened, its black members had demanded that one of the state's three open Senate terms go to a black man. Now Hiram Rhodes Revels, a minister and the state's newly appointed senator, had arrived to claim his seat.

Would Congress accept this "Fifteenth Amendment in flesh and blood," as Wendell Phillips called him, an allusion to the amendment passed by Congress in 1869 providing American citizens with the right to vote, regardless "of race, color, or previous condition of servitude"? Throughout the nation's history prior to emancipation there had been only two known elected black officeholders — the lawyer Macon Allen, who in 1848 won a position as a justice of the peace in Massachusetts, and John Mercer Langston, the great-uncle of the poet Langston Hughes, who in 1855 became a township clerk in Ohio. As recently as 1869 J. Willis Menard, a black Louisianian elected to the U.S. House of Representatives, had been sent home by that body, which refused to acknowledge his election as legitimate.

Two factors made Hiram Revels especially interesting to the Washington establishment. The first was that he had come to "replace" none other than Jefferson Davis, who in 1861 had resigned his Senate seat to

HIRAM REVELS

become president of the Confederacy, exclaiming, "The time for compromise has passed, and those who oppose us will smell powder and feel Southern steel." Such a stunning reversal of fortune — black men assuming the places of authority previously held by the leading Confederates — was both meaningful and dramatic; as the black educator and missionary Charlotte Forten noted, "The 'whirligig of time' has brought about its revenges." The other was that Revels was known for speaking his mind; those who knew him said that since he had never been a slave, he lacked the habit of deference to whites. "The Senator-elect . . . has a benevolent expression, a pleasant, impressive voice, and speaks with directness, as one thoroughly convinced of the views entertained," marveled one observer, while the *New York Herald* noted, "The distinguished darky made quite a sensation" huddling with one of his chief white supporters, Senator Sumner of Massachusetts, the two men "thus practically illustrating the idea of political and social equality." "Happy Revels" crowed another account. "He is of popular manners and speaks with great ease, fluency, and generally in good taste. In his intercourse with all classes he conducts himself with decorousness."

Even other men of color considered Revels a curious figure, for Mississippi had never had a large free black population. He was born in 1822 in North Carolina, where, even though his family were not slaves, their freedoms were sharply curtailed after the 1831 slave insurrection led by Nat Turner in neighboring Virginia. Determined to leave the South to receive an education, Revels enrolled at a Quaker seminary in Indiana and briefly attended Knox College in Galesburg, Illinois; he later went as a missionary to Kansas, where he tended to the spiritual needs of itinerant blacks and lectured against intemperance. He was arrested in 1854 "for preaching the gospel to Negroes" in neighboring Missouri, a slave state where abolitionists were making strong inroads. Returning east during the war, he served as chaplain to Maryland's first black regiment and later went south to work for the Freedmen's Bureau, helping to organize schools. Peacetime found him back in Kansas, where an account from the town of Leavenworth commends him for "adding 191 to the church [and] killing off two whiskey shops kept by colored men." Within a few years Revels was living in Adams County, Mississippi, in the river-bluff town of Natchez, where blacks were beginning to take an active role in state politics.

Being something of a political cipher may have helped Revels rise to prominence. According to John Roy Lynch, a young but influential city politician (and future congressman), Revels "had never voted, had never attended a political meeting, and of course, had never made a political speech. But he was a colored man and presumed to be a Republican, and believed to be a man of ability and considerably above the average in point of intelligence." He was also a property owner and a solid family man, married to the former Phoeba Bass of Zanesville, Ohio, with a growing brood that would eventually include six children, all daughters. A dutiful letter-writer when away on his frequent travels, Revels could be counted on to enclose some small amount of money, along with the request that Phoeba "kiss the children for me" and admonitions to his girls to "love God [and] live close to Him."

Revels apparently overcame his initial fears about getting involved in politics, becoming a moderate but loyal member of the party of emancipation. "If ever influenced by the friendship of your Democratic neighbor, you desert the Republican flag, desert the Republican standard, desert the Republican Party that has freed you," he once told his constituents, "you will be voting away your last liberties." Would the Democrats rescind those rights if they were to return to power? "They will do it," Revels declared, "as certainly as the sun shines in the heavens." When in 1868 a Republican nominating convention in Adams County deadlocked while trying to pick a man to run for the state senate, Lynch put the kindly Revels forward as a compromise candidate.

That year saw a divisive presidential campaign between General Ulysses S. Grant and the Democratic governor of New York, Horatio Seymour. Southern Democrats warned that Reconstruction as carried out by the Radical Republicans, who backed Grant, would "Africanize" America, while the Radicals pointed out that the treasonous rebels who refused to accept the consequences of the war needed Grant's stern authority. In February 1869, just after Grant's election, Congress approved the Fifteenth Amendment; in spring 1870 it became part of the Consti-

"THE RESULT OF THE FIFTEENTH AMENDMENT"

tution. Attaining the vote for black men was greeted by many as the crowning glory of the long crusade for abolition and of the war itself, a means for black Americans to, in Frederick Douglass's words, "breathe a new atmosphere, have a new earth beneath, and a new sky above." Wendell Phillips heralded it as the nation's new beginning — the promise of equality enshrined in the Declaration of Independence at last made real.

Of course, the granting of black enfranchisement was not solely altruistic. It was a political necessity. Prior to the war, a black person was counted as 3⁄5 of one person in calculating Southern representation in Congress; now that blacks were citizens and stood to be counted as whole individuals, their aggregate would increase the number of Southern representatives in Congress, allowing Southern states to dominate that body even more than they had by counting 3⁄5 of their slave population. Only by enabling blacks to go to the polls, where they would, at least in the near term, be inclined to support the Party of Lincoln, could the Republicans hope to remain competitive.

This tug-of-war over representation had been a source of political tension throughout the nineteenth century. As western territories were added to the Union, each one's status as slave or free was hotly contested. Southerners pushed for an equal number of new states to be recognized as slave states; they feared that if nonslave states gained a majority in Congress, the South's own slave economy might be marginalized and eventually overwhelmed.

In Mississippi it was said that Revels had clinched his appointment to the U.S. Senate with his eloquence and pastoral mien in the state legislature. His fellow legislators liked what they saw in the sturdy but unassuming clergyman. His reputation would withstand scrutiny, and his cool manner might deflect the harassment he was likely to encounter. Also, because the term he'd be appointed to was fractional, only a year's duration, the experiment, were it to prove unsatisfactory, would not cause serious harm.

Senator Revels, who had once lived in nearby Baltimore, would have noticed upon his arrival in Washington that, among many other dramatic changes, the city's population had grown considerably since the war. Northern entrepreneurs, Union soldiers, merchants, black refugees from the fighting in nearby Virginia — all had been drawn to the capital, and many had stayed. The prewar population of 75,000 had mushroomed by 1877 to 175,000, which included a black population of 55,000. Despite its new residents, the city retained much of its antebellum demeanor, "singularly placid [and] . . . untouched by the intensely competitive spirit of the rest of the country," for, having no industry, it attracted relatively few European immigrants. Freedmen served as its labor force.

This burgeoning metropolis, however, had a dismaying appearance after the war. The few main cobblestone thoroughfares had been destroyed by supply wagons and heavy army guns. Now, on dry days, they formed broad ribbons of caked horse manure and dust; on damp days they turned quickly to mud so thick and deep, it pulled the boots off men's feet. The mall that extended from the Capitol and ran parallel to Pennsylvania Avenue had not seen a blade of grass in years because stables had been built on it for army mules and horses. The lowlands before the Capitol itself remained lined with railroad tracks. Herds of cattle were driven daily through the streets, pigs rooted through the garbage, and the city's waste all went into a canal that was supposed to feed into the Potomac but was often backed up, creating an environment conducive to typhoid fever and dysentery. The dubious symbol of growth amid stagnation was the half-completed Washington Monument. Its construction had ceased during the war, and it resembled, as Mark Twain suggested, "a factory chimney with the top broken off."

Also keeping an eye on the city was another rough-hewn literary character, the poet Walt Whitman, who had come to Washington during the war to help minister to wounded soldiers and then stayed to serve as a clerk in the office of the attorney general. Whitman, "tall . . . portly . . . swinging along like an athlete and looking like Santa Claus," was a regular sight on the town's boulevards, although many who had read *Leaves of Grass,* his magisterial, exotic book of verses, regarded him with a curiosity bordering on disdain. Andrew Johnson's secretary of the interior, the pious James Harlan, got his hands on a copy and promptly dismissed Whitman from a post in his department.

Yet, for all its disarray, Washington was becoming one of the powerful engines of the reunited Union. It was more frequently visited, observed, and commented upon than ever before, though foreign reporters made fun of its provincialism and some of the nation's editorial pages couldn't help but ask whether, since the country's geographic center had shifted westward, the federal capital should migrate as well — perhaps to St. Louis or Cincinnati.

It was President Grant who, in 1869, his first year in office, set out with his customary determination to refurbish the capital district. He found a no-nonsense counterpart in Alexander "Boss" Shepherd, a businessman and faithful Republican whom he appointed to lead the Board of Public Works. Over two busy years Shepherd's laborers planted sixty thousand trees, erected thousands of gas lamps, installed a drainage system, tore up railroad tracks, turned muddy intersections into fountains, and paved 365 miles of sidewalks and streets. Shepherd chose the noted landscape architect Frederick Law Olmsted to design the Capitol grounds, spending three times his $6 million budget along the way. "The old repulsive sheds used in the old times as market-places . . . have been swept away," wrote Frederick Douglass, "and their places taken by imposing and beautiful structures in harmony with the dawn of a higher civilization." Some accused Shepherd and his subordinates of carrying out their mission with too heavy a hand, trampling on bureaucratic niceties, but as Douglass commented, "I may say what all men in Washington are compelled to confess: They have done a great and needed work for the metropolis." Douglass took pride in the fact that although slaves had once toiled on public works projects, including the construction of the Capitol itself, now an army of *freedmen,* receiving pay for their labor, were transforming the city.

While free black men with shovels and picks built a new, glorious capital, others like Hiram Revels, in top hats and custom-tailored suits, took their seats in Congress. Meanwhile, on the site of a 150-acre farm just beyond the city limits, rose Howard University, a black college named for General O. O. Howard, chief of the Freedmen's Bureau. In the city a proud new Freedman's Savings Bank opened its doors, while Frederick Douglass's newspaper, the *New National Era*, began publication. As Congress nailed the Reconstruction amendments into place, the local Washington city council also took giant steps; having ended segregation on the city's streetcars in 1864, it acted in May 1869 to create a civil rights law that prohibited racial discrimination in places of public entertainment, which would improve daily life for thousands of black Washingtonians. In January 1870 a more comprehensive civil rights ordinance was passed to safeguard equal access to hotels, bars, and restaurants. Another law in 1872 extended this policy to bathhouses, barbershops, and ice cream parlors, and it increased the penalties for noncompliance. Some establishments attempted to evade these regulations by ignoring black customers or offering to serve them at exorbitant prices, but an additional law in 1873 stipulated that all public accommodations offered customers be identical, and in several cases brought by black complainants, judges came down hard on uncooperative business owners. As a jurist lectured one offender: "Rights that have cost a revolution will not stand aside for a pretext."

Since early in the century, Washington had been home to some black families, mostly those of partial white ancestry, who had won manumission and certain privileges. During Reconstruction, and for much of the late nineteenth century, it became the capital of America's black aristocracy, a world of black and mulatto arrivistes from the South, such as Senator Blanche K. Bruce and his wife, Josephine; Robert and Mary Church Terrell; Congressman John Roy Lynch; prominent "race men" such as Frederick Douglass; Christian Fleetwood, the black Baltimorean who had won the Congressional Medal of Honor; and members of established local black society such as the Syphax family of Arlington, Virginia. Charles Syphax, a former slave who was related to both Martha Washington and Robert E. Lee, lived long enough to regale Union troops who camped on the family's grounds in Arlington with stories of George Washington, James Monroe, and Thomas Jefferson; his son William, born in 1825, was a longtime employee of the Department of the Interior and a leader in the opening of public colored schools in Washington. Six feet tall and a fine physical specimen, William Syphax submitted his head to be measured by phrenologists, and it was discussed as an example of innate nobility.

Many of Washington's "bon tons," as the local black aristocrats were sometimes called, occupied a singular world, some barely familiar with the inconvenience of prejudice. They acquired property and homes, owned horses and carriages, kept servants, and avoided if possible the company of those of their own color who toted and laundered, scrubbed and hauled, were bawdy and ill-mannered, or worshiped in loud voices at spirited Sunday outdoor "rousers." Some worked for the betterment of the black masses even as they kept the individual representatives of that "unimproved class" at arm's length. The effort of the "betters" to put some distance between themselves and the black hoi polloi was most noticeable on Emancipation Day, the annual freedmen's celebration and the city's biggest outpouring of black pride and celebration, featuring a massive parade, colorful floats, speeches, and daylong parties. Even the egalitarian Frederick Douglass disapproved of the holiday's "tinsel shows [and] straggling processions [that] empty the alleys and dark places of the city into the broad day-light . . . thrusting upon public view . . . the most unfortunate, unimproved and unprogressive class of the colored people," a display, he feared, that could foster negative stereotypes.

The expanded horizons of citizenship made self-improvement a significant mandate among blacks of all classes. Its most fundamental expression was the widespread desire to gain basic literacy, but it extended to matters of social skill, etiquette, and even personal hygiene. The black press was filled with columns of "do's and dont's" and admonitions to stay clean and tidy, avoid shouting in public, refrain from guffawing or laughing like a horse, and keep the mouth closed so as not to show one's teeth. Later, women journalists such as Memphis's Ida B. Wells would blend political commentary with reminders of the special necessity for black women to live a spotless moral life.

A success story that epitomized the rise of the local black establishment was that of James Wormley, who in 1871 opened the five-story Wormley Hotel at 15th and H Street N.W. Like several other black entrepreneurs in Washington, he had made his reputation as a caterer. The term *catering* in Reconstruction Washington didn't refer primarily to the provision of food and drink for weddings and social functions, but rather to the business of delivering warm meals to the many congressmen, senators, and judges who lived in the city's hotels and rooming houses. It was a profession well suited to black advancement, since it was lucrative but whites tended to shun it because they perceived it as servile. Wormley, who in the 1850s went to London as cook and valet for Reverdy Johnson, President Buchanan's minister to the Court of St. James, pulled off an international culinary coup by bringing along, and serving to British aristocrats, a large shipment of diamondback terrapins from Chesapeake Bay. While in England he purchased the fine linen, crystal, and china he would ultimately use in his hotel dining room. His attention to detail and the freshness of his ingredients — he and his son William kept a farm just outside the city — made his establishment, which had an elevator and one of the city's first telephones, a favorite Washington destination. Vice President Schuyler Colfax lived in one of its suites, and Charles Sumner and others were frequent guests.

Reconstruction Washington's most famous social event — celebrated for its extravagance as well as its racial inclusiveness — was the ball held in honor of President Grant's second inaugural in March 1873. Those attending included Louisiana's black governor, P.B.S. Pinchback; South Carolina's congressman Robert Brown Elliott and his wife, Grace; Frederick Douglass; and three thousand other guests, gathered in a specially designed building in Judiciary Square. Grant's first inaugural ball, in 1869, had been something of a bust, poorly managed and plagued by icy cold weather. The 1873 version was similarly troubled by chilly temperatures, which congealed the desserts and forced the guests to waltz in their overcoats, but the mood remained festive. The dining area, about the length of a city block, offered among its various edibles 26,000 oysters, 2,400 quails, 75 roast turkeys, 25 boar's heads, 8,000 sandwiches, 150 cakes, and 24 cases of Prince Albert Crackers, all to be washed down with 300 gallons of punch and an equal quantity of hot coffee. "Praises of the completeness of all the details, and the perfection with which everything moves, are on every tongue," gushed the *New York Times.* General William T. Sherman and other leading military men of the late war, resplendent in their brass and blue, were applauded as they stepped onto the dance floor, but the hit of the evening was a spirited contingent of West Point cadets, some of whom created a delicious stir by dancing with the wives of the black congressmen. Grace Elliott, a visiting Southerner conceded, was "one of the most beautiful and handsomely gowned women at the ball."

Grant's inauguration and the ball were long remembered by those fortunate enough to be in attendance as a unique, glittering moment of black attainment and white broadmindedness. "In the grand procession . . . the advance the nation has made under the genius of liberty was epitomized," cheered the *New National Era.* "Colored cadets . . . marching side by side with white cadets, colored marshals, colored militia, colored Congressmen — all took part in a ceremony in which only a few short years ago none but white persons were allowed to participate. No organization military nor civic withdrew from the line because colored citizens participated, no white person left the inaugural ball . . . There seemed to be a general acquiescence to the new order of things."

Revels was much in demand upon his entry into Washington's political brotherhood. He at first lived with George T. Downing, the black Rhode Island abolitionist and entrepreneur who ran the Capitol Restaurant on the Hill. A dinner hosted by Downing in Revels's honor featured numerous senators and was "of the most recherché character," where "every honor was paid the distinguished successor of Jefferson Davis . . . There were no speeches . . . but the company engaged in lively conversation and remained until a late hour listening to words of wisdom from the lips of the sable Senator from Mississippi." In honor of the occasion, Frederick Douglass's new publication offered a lithograph of Revels for sale, an image "equal to a first rate original oil painting [that] would do no discredit to the walls of any parlor in America." While black people were usually depicted in cartoons or works of art "either as apes or as angels," said the *Era*, it was refreshing to see in the image of Revels "the real man, neither flattered by partiality nor distorted by malice or prejudice."

Although there was much talk of how Revels "replaced" Jefferson Davis, technically Davis's seat had expired in the nine years since his departure. But the prospect of the traitorous Davis being upstaged by a loyal black man was too rich an irony to ignore. In a devastating cartoon by Thomas Nast, Davis — as Shakespeare's Iago — peers in from behind a curtain as Revels takes the secessionist's former place. "For that I do suspect the lusty Moor hath leap'd into my seat," muses Nast's Davis, "the thought whereof doth like a poisonous mineral gnaw my innards." Nast was merciless toward the former Confederate president. Another cartoon, titled "Why He Cannot Sleep," depicts Davis in bed as Columbia reveals to him the ghosts of numerous rebels, one of whom has crawled next to Davis and points to a bullet hole in the center of his skull.

Humiliating Davis had been an irresistible Northern pastime since his capture in May 1865. President Johnson had accused Davis of complicity in Lincoln's assassination, and a $100,000 bounty was placed on his head. Davis was not involved in Lincoln's murder and in fact disapproved of it, but this was not immediately known in the confusing weeks following the war. Davis, his family, and his entourage were at that time in desperate flight through rural Georgia in an effort to reach the Florida coast and secure passage by boat, possibly to Cuba, when on

"TIME WORKS WONDERS."
IAGO. (JEFF DAVIS.) "FOR THAT I DO SUSPECT THE LUSTY MOOR HATH LEAP'D INTO MY SEAT: THE THOUGHT WHEREOF DOTH LIKE A POISONOUS MINERAL GNAW MY INWARDS." — OTHELLO.

JEFFERSON DAVIS AS IAGO

May 10, outside Irwinville, Union troops overtook them. Davis, attempting to escape (or give fight, depending on which account one accepts), either accidentally grabbed his wife's raincoat or slipped her shawl over his head, the origin of the durable tale that the chief rebel tried to flee disguised as a woman.

Davis was kept under lock and key at Fortress Monroe for two years while the government debated what to do with him. Was he a captured enemy leader deserving of official respect or a base traitor ripe for the gallows? (Only one prominent Confederate — Henry Wirz, commandant of the prison camp at Andersonville, Georgia, where 13,000 federal soldiers died — was hanged because of his actions during the war.) The government's indecision and delay favored Davis's cause, thanks in part to the dedicated public relations efforts of his wife, Varina, and their friends. The height of his rehabilitation was the 1866 publication of *The Prison Life of Jefferson Davis* by John J. Craven, Davis's physician, which portrayed Davis as an ill-treated martyr who read the Bible, prayed daily, and saved crumbs of food for a mouse that lived in his cell. His imprisonment ultimately became a political liability for President Johnson, as petitions bearing thousands of signatures demanded Davis's release. (One midwestern businessman offered $30,000 for the right to exhibit the captive, promising to return him in good health.) The predicament worsened when Davis, insisting he was not guilty of anything, refused Johnson's offer of a pardon.

In May 1867, two years after his capture, Davis, looking gaunt and unwell, was released on bail provided by the publisher Horace Greeley, the railroad tycoon Cornelius Vanderbilt, and the reformer Gerrit Smith. There was still talk of putting the ex–Confederate president on trial for treason, a course Davis himself was said to welcome, since it would give him a chance to clear his name and defend the Southern cause, but public sentiment, various legal technicalities, and then the impeachment of Johnson himself kept it from ever taking place.

While Republicans took pride in the arrival of Hiram Revels, the Democrats were not about to allow him a free pass. As soon as President Grant signed Mississippi's readmission into the Union (on February 23, 1870) and Senate Republicans moved to have Revels sworn in, the opposition began to forcefully resist seating him, just as the House had done successfully the year before in the case of Louisiana's J. Willis Menard. The apparent winner of a special election held in Louisiana to fill a seat vacated by the death of a sitting congressman, Menard was certified as the new representative by Louisiana's legislature and its youthful Reconstruction governor, Henry Clay Warmoth. But a white candidate, Caleb S. Hunt, disputed the election results, and in the end neither Menard nor Hunt was seated. Before this rejection, Menard made history by defending his claim on the floor of the House for a quarter of an hour on February 27, 1869 — the first time a black American ever addressed Congress.

The debate over Revels opened when Southerners argued unsuccessfully that the white military governor of Mississippi, the carpetbagger Adelbert Ames, did not possess the authority to certify Revels's election.

But the chief obstacle was constitutional. Democratic critics pointed out that even if Revels (like other blacks) had been made a citizen by the Civil Rights Act of 1866, he had not been a citizen for nine years, a requirement for senators, according to the first article of the Constitution. The Democrats also questioned whether the Founding Fathers had ever intended black people to be citizens, reminding the Senate that in the *Dred Scott* decision of 1857, the Supreme Court had clearly asserted that although free blacks might be citizens of individual states, they (and certainly slaves) were not citizens of the United States. Chief Justice Roger Taney wrote, in his majority opinion, that black people were "so far inferior, that they had no rights which the white man was bound to respect."

Republican senators cried foul at such a tactic; James W. Nye of Nevada insisted that "[*Dred Scott*] has been repealed by the mightiest uprising which the world has ever witnessed." Indeed, much of the Republicans' legislative program since the war had aimed to undo the harm of *Dred Scott;* the Civil Rights Act and the Reconstruction amendments struck at the very themes that Taney had handled so poorly. But the Democrats were relentless. Senator Willard Saulsbury of Delaware characterized the Taney court as "giants! — great, intellectual, mighty giants, in comparison to whom the dwarfed intellects of the present hour are but pygmies perched on the Alps" and declared the Fourteenth Amendment to be "no more part of the Constitution than anything which you . . . might write upon a piece of paper and fling upon the floor." He cleverly asserted that despite the insult rendered by Charles Sumner (who had said "the name of Taney is to be hooted down the page of history") the Republicans obviously *did* accept *Dred Scott,* since they had gone to great lengths to produce the 1866 Civil Rights Bill and pass it over Johnson's veto — an explicit effort to undo Taney's handiwork. Such determination, said Saulsbury, implied the Republicans' recognition of the legitimacy of Taney ruling and provided "evidence that in your own judgment at the time of [the passage of the Civil Rights Act of 1866] . . . negroes and mulattoes were not citizens." Since only four years, not nine, had passed since 1866, Saulsbury concluded, Hiram Revels could not now be considered an American citizen. "Addressing you not as Republicans, but as revolutionists, there is one extent to which your revolutionary movement has not carried you yet, and that is to make a negro or mulatto eligible to a seat in the Senate of the United States."

The Republicans were quick to respond. John Scott of Pennsylvania said that all black persons in the United States had instantly become citizens by the enactment of the Civil Rights Act and the ratification of the Fourteenth Amendment, and he mentioned that most Republicans had never accepted the notion that *Dred Scott* addressed the status of free blacks like Hiram Revels. Missouri's Charles D. Drake suggested that since Revels was technically neither a Negro nor a mulatto but an octoroon, a person who was one-eighth Negro, Saulsbury's anxiety at having to spend time alongside him in the Senate might be somewhat alleviated. Pivoting on Drake's comment, Saulsbury insisted his conscience was troubled only by disobedience to the law and that Reconstruction itself — its hasty amendments and its elevation of blacks like Revels — was little more than a dictatorial coup, a "great and damning outrage."

Saulsbury's opposition to Revels came off as spiteful, but some newspapers also criticized the new senator. A Baltimore periodical dredged up a story that Revels had once stolen money from a church in Kansas and had taken part in a drunken brawl, subdued only when a whiskey bottle was smashed over his head. A former nemesis from Kansas, J. H. Morris, hostile to Revels because the minister had once halted his use of a church for political meetings, distributed among Democratic senators a pamphlet he had written detailing Revels's "offenses," although Revels himself proudly noted that Morris's rantings went directly into most senators' wastebaskets. As for the issue of Revels's eligibility, a writer for *The Nation* pointed out that the residents of Texas had all been granted instant national citizenship when that territory was annexed in 1845 and wondered why residents of Mississippi wouldn't enjoy the same privilege when their state was readmitted. Sumner, the veteran senator, took the floor to remind those who would derail Revels that *Dred Scott* had been "born a putrid corpse" and had become "at once a stench in the nostrils and a scandal to the court itself, which made haste to turn away from its offensive offspring." He asserted that Revels's taking his seat in the Senate would be a milestone in America's realization of the promise of the Declaration of Independence. "'All men are created equal,' says the great Declaration, and now a great act attests this verity."

No sooner had Sumner completed his remarks than a vote was taken and, Saulsbury's fulminations notwithstanding, Mississippi's new senator was approved by a comfortable margin. "Revels, who had been sitting all day on a sofa in the rear of Mr. Sumner's seat, advanced toward the clerk's desk with a modest yet firm step," according to one account.

> He was in no way embarrassed . . . [but] swallowed the iron-clad oath without wincing, and bowed his head quite reverently when the

> words "so help you God" were rendered . . . Judging from the anxiety pictured on their countenances, and the uneasiness manifested to get a good look at the operation of swearing Revels in, the people in the galleries must have expected something terrible to follow.

Comical suggestions had been made about just such a possibility — that the walls and ceiling of the chamber might collapse spontaneously or the chandeliers might fall and shatter in response to the dramatic transition that Revels's confirmation symbolized.

"The colored United States Senator from Mississippi has been awarded his seat," concluded the *Philadelphia Inquirer,* "and we have not had an earthquake, our free institutions have not been shaken to their foundations, nor have the streets of our large cities been converted to blood." It was 4:40 P.M. on Friday, February 25, 1870, and a black American was now a member of the U.S. Congress.

The rebellious spirit of Jefferson Davis may have been exorcised from the Senate chamber, but in the far-off reaches of the former Confederacy it appeared to be enjoying a vibrant second life — in New Orleans, Memphis, and now also Georgia, and the plight of blacks in that state became the subject of Hiram Revels's first speech from the Senate floor on March 16.

Revels challenged the readmission of Georgia to the Union on the grounds that the state had denied blacks the right to serve in its legislature, and had indeed a year and a half earlier expelled those already serving. As in other Southern states, many whites in Georgia deliberately sat out the elections held in 1867 to name delegates to write a new state constitution, a phenomenon known as "masterly inactivity," and they did the same for the state election in April 1868, through which a new biracial legislature was chosen. Then, in September 1868, thirty-two duly elected black members of the Georgia legislature were thrown out (although four of fractional Negro ancestry were readmitted); their white peers claimed that the new state constitution gave blacks the right to vote but not to hold office. Henry M. Turner, a black chaplain in the Union army and a Georgia representative, was the hero of the doomed fight in the legislature. He warned the whites, "You will make us your foes, you will make our constituency your foes. I'll do all I can to poison my race against Democracy . . . This thing means revolution," and then he led the other black legislators out of the hall. That same month political violence erupted at a Republican campaign event in the town of

Camilla, Georgia, at which one of the expelled legislators was to speak, and several blacks lost their lives.

Led by Turner, a delegation of some of the black legislators from Georgia came to Washington in fall 1869 to press the issue and testify before a congressional committee. Calling the state of Georgia "a wayward sister," Frederick Douglass extended support to the visiting representatives. "Every one of them has a moving tale to tell of personal danger and outrage," he wrote, adding, "Upon every side in [Georgia] the indications are clear, that the snake, Rebellion, has been only scotched there, and not killed." The legislator Abram Colby reported that one night in October 1869 thirty disguised men had come to his home. "They broke my door open, took me out of bed, took me to the woods and whipped me three hours or more and left me for dead. They said to me, 'Do you think you will ever vote another damned Radical ticket?' I said, 'I will not tell you a lie.' I supposed they would kill me anyhow. I said, 'If there was an election tomorrow, I would vote the Radical ticket.' They set in and whipped me a thousand licks more, with sticks and straps that had buckles on the ends of them."

A national outcry over these events returned Georgia to federal control; its military governor, General Alfred H. Terry, forcibly reinstated blacks in the legislature while banning an equal number of whites in an action known to aggrieved Georgians as "Terry's Purge," thus setting the stage for the legislature to ratify the Fifteenth Amendment and be readmitted to the Union in 1870. But at the time of Revels's appearance in the Senate, questions remained about how and when new legislative elections would be held in Georgia, and, among national Republicans, how the state could be held in the Republican column with the party's members there so badly disheartened by persistent harassment. (Georgia would rejoin the Union on July 15, 1870; elections there that fall would yield a largely Democratic legislature.)

Just as they did with Revels's swearing-in, the Republicans were eager to show him off as he made his maiden address in the Senate, and a large and quite unprecedented biracial crowd gathered, with hundreds of blacks filling the gallery overhead to gaze down at the white senators. "Never since the birth of the republic has such an audience been assembled under one single roof," recalled a witness. Revels took the floor to a hushed room; he began to speak a bit hesitantly but quickly gained confidence. He attacked the rationale of the Georgia Democrats, who justified the exclusion of blacks from the legislature because of severe antagonism between the races, which would likely cause the blacks to lord their authority over the whites. "As the recognized representative of my downtrodden people, I deny the charge, and hurl it back into the teeth of those who make it, and who, I believe, have not a true and conscientious desire to further the interests of the whole South," he said.

> Certainly no one possessing any personal knowledge of the colored population of my own or other states need be reminded of the noble conduct of that people . . . in the history of the late war . . . While the Confederate army pressed into its ranks every white male capable of bearing arms, the mothers, wives, daughters, and sisters of the Southern soldiers were left defenseless and in the power of the blacks . . . And now, sir, I ask, how did that race act? Did they . . . evince the malignity of which we hear so much? They waited, and they waited patiently. In the absence of their masters they protected the virtue and chastity of defenseless women . . . Mr. President, I maintain that the past record of my race is a true index of the feelings which today animate them.

Revels's speech was loudly applauded, and his measured performance came as a significant relief to his Republican allies. Oliver Morton of Indiana observed that "in receiving him in exchange for Jefferson Davis, the Senate had lost nothing in intelligence."

On May 17 Revels spoke again, this time on an issue far more controversial, the lifting of remaining political disabilities against former Confederates. Amnesty was of particular significance for black politicians, for it was widely believed that the disenfranchisement and political neutering of secessionist leaders had made possible their own political ascendance. Politically, it behooved them to appear conciliatory and to avoid the charge that they meant to "Africanize" the South. "I do not know of one state that is altogether as well reconstructed as Mississippi is," Revels told the Senate. "We have reports from a great many other states of lawlessness and of violence . . . but . . . do you hear one report of any more lawlessness or violence in the State of Mississippi? No; the people now I believe are getting along as quietly, pleasantly, harmoniously, and prosperously as the people are in any of the formerly free states . . . I am in favor of amnesty in Mississippi . . . the state is fit for it." This appeal for harmony reached the Mississippi state legislature then convening in Jackson and brought Revels so much praise that there was talk of naming a county for him.

His celebrity carried him through a summer speaking tour in the Northeast states. In a talk he titled "The Tendency of the Age," Revels located his own success on a vast timeline of human history, positioning himself as a transitional figure in a centuries-old struggle between "aristocracy" and "democracy," which extended from Europe of the Middle Ages to Reconstruction Mississippi. When he was denied a podium at the Academy of Music in Philadelphia, local blacks were outraged; one letter-writer to the *Philadelphia Post* noted that the Academy's "respectable board has the negrophobia so bad it cannot bear the idea of hearing eloquence from anyone who is not lucky enough to be white. It has repeatedly refused Frederick Douglass the privilege of lecturing . . . although he has alone more brains than almost any six members of the board together." Revels was compensated by a triumphant welcome at Boston's Tremont Temple, where, introduced by Wendell Phillips and speaking before an audience of former abolitionists, he received a warm ovation.

Revels's optimism, however, would soon come to seem premature, even to him, and when he left Congress and returned to experience firsthand the tribulations of his rural constituents as they fought to retain the gains of Reconstruction, he would be far from the adoring clutches of sympathetic Boston and the cheers of the Senate gallery. How he handled that challenge would anger many of his own people, and diminish his star.

CHAPTER 5

KUKLUXERY

MEMBERS OF the U.S. Congress in 1870 might have paused to congratulate themselves on the advances made during the half-decade since the war. Their program of Reconstruction had overcome President Andrew Johnson's obstructions, and the Black Codes had been challenged; a new ideal of national citizenship, as well as expanded rights of suffrage, had been set forth; and the former Confederate states had been welcomed to rejoin the Union, but only after holding constitutional conventions and ratifying the Fourteenth and Fifteenth Amendments. With the seating of Hiram Revels in the U.S. Senate and, later that year, South Carolina's Joseph Rainey in the U.S. House of Representatives, black political representation had become a reality at the highest national levels.

These were impressive achievements. But far from the committee rooms of Washington, in the modest African American farm settlements and small courthouse towns of the South, a new, very menacing problem had appeared. Founded by Confederate veterans in Pulaski, Tennessee, in 1866, a white vigilante organization called the Ku Klux Klan had been rapidly emulated in numerous states under names such as the Knights of the White Camellia, the '76 Association, the Pale Faces, and the Council of Safety. Reports of these groups' deadly assaults on freedmen and white Republicans had become increasingly hard to ignore.

Having conquered the rebellious South once before, General Ulysses S. Grant, who had become president in early 1869, seemed the ideal choice to confront this new form of insurrection. The issue of using federal force to smite the Klan, however, quickly became controversial, and the Grant administration, wishing at all costs to avoid reigniting passions related to the war, proved sensitive to criticism that it might be capable of offering only a military solution. As the Klan's activities prompted sharp concern in the North, the president would move cautiously, working with Congress on coordinated legislative and enforcement initiatives.

One of his more dedicated collaborators was Attorney General Amos T. Akerman, a man of Northern birth and education whose résumé uniquely qualified him for the role. A Dartmouth graduate who had relocated in the 1840s to Georgia, where he'd become a successful attorney and started a family, Akerman was faithful to both sections of the country. Having stood with the Confederacy, he now accepted the tenets of Reconstruction and encouraged his fellow Southerners to do likewise. He was thus an inspired choice to head the Grant administration's newly created Justice Department and take on the worst law enforcement crisis in the nation's history. Also important in battling this Southern scourge were the efforts of Joseph Rainey and Robert Brown Elliott, two black congressmen from South Carolina, for it was in upcountry South Carolina that Klan violence was possibly at its worst and where the United States ultimately chose to face down the group.

When in spring 1865 the armies of the Confederacy faced imminent defeat, some of their officers and soldiers suggested resisting the inevitable federal occupation of their homeland by forming guerrilla fighting units, which could disperse into the South's rugged mountains and pine forests and harass the invader from these impenetrable areas. General Robert E. Lee vehemently condemned the idea. But as Southerners became frustrated over equal rights for blacks and other conditions imposed by the national government in the late 1860s, this very strategy had, in a sense, been reborn. "Masterly inactivity," the whites' deliberate nonparticipation in Reconstruction, had not accomplished much. Blacks would not stop voting and engaging in political activity of their own accord. And although white South Carolinians might have enjoyed the racial caricatures and insults that appeared in the pages of the *Charleston Mercury,* those who were honest would admit that the most disturbing element of the 1868 convention and the new biracial state legislature was not black ineptitude, but the very opposite. African Americans, even former slaves, *could* function as aldermen and state legislators, as lieutenant governors and U.S. congressmen, and serve convincingly in parliamentary settings with whites. This performance, together with eager black participation at the polls, exploded the cherished notion that the ex-slaves would be lost without the guiding paternalism of their former masters. As the *Marion Star* conceded, the South's singular dilemma was not how to deal with a chaotic mass of ignorant, unwashed Negroes, but rather with an empowered race. "The enslaved have not been merely emancipated, but invested with every political right of the ruling race. Thus suddenly elevated, [they] outnumber the whites by an overwhelming majority, and have all the power." Statistics supported the *Star*'s fears. In 1870 the black population of South Carolina was 416,000 and that of whites, 290,000; blacks formed a majority in twenty of the state's thirty-one counties.

The new state constitution, completed in spring 1868, seemed to create a kind of tipping point, for by the fall elections of that year, South Carolinian whites were experiencing a political reawakening, staging large, noisy outdoor pageants of racial solidarity in support of the national Democratic ticket headed by Horatio Seymour. Confederate veterans marched to affectionate ovations; the crowds enjoyed fireworks, long tables of barbecued meats, whiskey, lemonade, coffee, banners declaring patriotic themes, and crude depictions of the region's antagonists — General Grant, smoking a filthy cigar butt while squatting on a dead horse or a barefoot freedman looking through a spyglass at the moon under the label FORTY ACRES OF LAND! All of this transpired to the noise of brass bands, the booming of guns, and cheering so fervent, it was said the very "heavens were rent with the sounds of acclamation."

An effort to address the state's political imbalance through more conciliatory means arose two years later, with the founding of the Union Reform Party — Democrats and Republican moderates attracted by the idea of a home state coalition. The Union Reformers reached out to the huge black electorate by acknowledging the legitimacy of the universal franchise but had little success in drawing substantial numbers of freedmen, who remained fiercely loyal to the party of emancipation. The failure of the Union Reformers was particularly hard felt: their candidate for lieutenant governor in 1870, the proud ex–Confederate general Matthew C. Butler, who'd lost a leg in combat, was soundly defeated at the polls by Alonzo Ransier, the black politician who had formerly been a shipping clerk. "This vile, rotten, wicked, corrupt and degrading regime must be reformed or overthrown," the *Winnsboro News* concluded, voicing the anger of many whites toward the entrenched Republicans. "We see no practical method of accomplishing it except by some form of revolution."

A hint of what form that revolution might take had appeared in the deadly night-rider violence that accompanied the election of 1868. Armed vigilantes rode through black settlements at night, shooting into cabins; coffins with Klan markings and other dire warnings were left on doorsteps; and blacks were warned to vote the Seymour ticket or face dire consequences. The Klan's activity was concentrated in the upcountry, most likely because it held a greater number of poor whites, who more readily viewed blacks as political and economic competitors.

Although those who romanticized the movement liked to pretend otherwise, the Klan was not entirely born from a spontaneous urge to redeem the region's honor, nor was it ever a social fraternity. It had roots not only in local regulator movements dating to the Revolutionary era but also in the antebellum Southern patroller system, the "courts on horseback" that policed slaves and free blacks, a method so well established that its organized areas of patrol, sometimes known as "beats," remained as jurisdictional boundaries in some parts of the South well into the twentieth century. Of course, the patroller system represented the privilege every Southern white man took for granted — the right to control black people's movements, judge them when they offended, and mete out penalties. Institutions like the patrollers vanished with emancipation, but not the urge to regulate blacks' behavior. The Klan's "mysteriousness," its system of appellations such as Exalted Cyclops and Imperial Wizard, its disguises and eerie warnings played on the age-old assumption that simple, superstitious slaves could be easily frightened; it also reflected the need for anonymity in the postwar political climate, which, at least officially, disallowed patroller-style vigilantism.

Southerners had long loved gallantry, and a forceful response to insult was part of this tradition. This sense of derring-do was shared across social classes. "The passing of high words and blows, canings, cowhidings, and so on, all terminated by the drawing of knives or pistols, together with hostile correspondences and duels, became everyday occurrences . . . especially in South Carolina and perhaps Mississippi," noted the *Atlantic Monthly* in 1877. Virtually every man (and some women) went about with a gun — on trains, on steamboats, at church; it was not uncommon to see young boys of nine or ten with a bowie knife or a black revolver tucked into the band of their trousers. "Honor is the sentiment by which a high estimate is placed upon individual rights, social repute and personal self-respect," declared "The Code of Honor," a pamphlet written by Robert Barnwell Rhett, a diehard Southern conservative, and published in Charleston in 1878. "These are not always adequately protected by the laws and tribunals of the civil organization.

There are cases of insults grievous and degrading for which there is no action at law." The idea that laws are inadequate and that "determined men" will make and enforce their own is dangerous to any society. In the postwar South this line of thinking served to legitimize all sorts of extra-legal mayhem, from shots fired under cover of night into sharecroppers' cabins to cold-blooded assassinations, race riots, and lynchings.

The spiritual home of the state's opposition to unwanted social and governmental change was upcountry Edgefield County, perhaps the most independent and fiercely "Southern" parts of South Carolina. Edgefield was the abode of no fewer than ten South Carolina governors as well as the Confederate generals Matthew C. Butler and Martin W. Gary, and it wore proudly its reputation as the "region where Liberty finds her constant home." Governor Francis Pickens, an Edgefield native and one of the area's wealthiest landowners, had helped guide the state toward secession in the years leading to the Civil War. So thoroughly identified was he with the cause that an image of his wife, Lucy Holcombe Pickens, a noted beauty, adorned the Confederate one-dollar and hundred-dollar bills.

Edgefield's distinctive character — its farmers' traditional hostility to the gentry of Charleston and the coastal low country, its proud resistance to seated power — was well developed by the late eighteenth century, when the area had been the site of pervasive anti-Tory violence. Its isolation from and suspicion toward the outside world was formalized in the early nineteenth century when a native son, Vice President John C. Calhoun, became the outspoken leader of the nascent states' rights movement by opposing an 1828 federal tariff that he believed was unfair to the agricultural South. Congress responded by revising the conditions of the tariff somewhat, but the rates remained so high that in 1832 South Carolina approved the Ordinance of Nullification, which declared the tariffs of both 1828 and 1832 unconstitutional and forbade the collection of the relevant duties in the state. The Compromise Tariff of 1833 resolved the heated dispute, but the nullification crisis, and Calhoun's ardent defense of South Carolina's rights, remained an important touchstone. His heroism was enhanced when he resigned from President Andrew Jackson's administration over the matter. Settling for a bully pulpit as U.S. senator from South Carolina, he spent the rest of his days eloquently defending slavery and states' rights and inspiring future generations of Southern "fire-eaters." So persistent was Calhoun's influence over the South that when the abolitionists William Lloyd Garrison and Henry Ward Beecher visited Charleston at war's end, they made a special pilgrimage to the great man's tomb in order to satisfy themselves that he was extinct. Placing his hand firmly on the monument, Garrison intoned, "Down in a deeper grave than this slavery has gone, and for it there is no resurrection."

Thus, the secessionist strain in South Carolina as well as white resistance to postwar Reconstruction belonged to a proud tradition, reaching all the way back to the state's greatest Revolutionary War hero, Francis Marion, a lethal guerrilla fighter known as "the Swamp Fox," whose stealth famously confounded the British command; it would be hard to invent a more suitable archetype. It was a natural progression from the Swamp Fox to Calhoun, to Congressman Preston Brooks who in 1856 savagely attacked Charles Sumner with a cane on the Senate floor to defend the honor of an Edgefield relative, to the rebel general Martin W. Gary and to the Red Shirt leader "Pitchfork" Ben Tillman. Rarely did upcountry South Carolina lack some colorful, bellicose character to act out its anti-authoritarian bent.

This template of regional defiance and individual bravado fit the Klan rather easily, and hundreds of incidents of night-rider violence were reported in upcountry counties beginning in the late 1860s. At Newberry Courthouse, Klansmen surrounded the home of a black man named Simeon Young, hurled "turpentine balls" into his house to illuminate the interior, then opened fire, wounding Simeon's wife and child. They visited Charles Johnson, who lived twelve miles north of Edgefield, "for the purpose of inflicting punishment on him for his Republican principles" and "for selling bad whiskey." On a moonlit night, Slap Jeffries, "a colored man of some prominence among his race, was taken from his house and brutally murdered by armed men in disguise, who shot him dead near his own door, and in sight of his family." At Spartanburg, the blacksmith John Good was slain when Klan members learned of his ability to identify local Ku Klux by their horses' hoof prints.

"These vile retches [sic], the white man, are bushwhacking my people," wrote Pastor Hardy D. Edwards of Abbeville. "They are also beating them, whipping them, running them off, in short, they are moving heaven and Earth to subdue my people . . . the retches have killed one man at Cokesbury, one in the Whitehall settlement, one near Lowndesville. They burn the houses of the colored people; they whip them & beat them worse than they did as slaves for then the people had some protection."

From 1868 to 1871, York County, in northwest South Carolina, saw more than a dozen murders, as many as six hundred incidents of whip-

DISGUISED KLANSMEN

ping or beating, and the burning of several churches and homes. A particularly infamous attack involved Elias Hill, a fifty-year-old black Baptist preacher who was a dwarf. The Klan, accusing Hill of agitating the local blacks to demand equal rights, pulled him from his bed in the middle of the night, dragged him into the yard, and enjoyed an hour of sport as they lashed him with a buggy whip, the whole time warning him to quit the Republican Party and cancel his subscription to a Republican newspaper. Hill was so rattled by the incident he and most of his congregation emigrated to Liberia.

"The effect of these numerous threats and outrages upon the negroes is very great," noted a *New York Evening Post* correspondent. "In the most disturbed sections of the state, for months together, hardly a negro man dared to sleep in his home at night. Many of the women and children would leave their homes on the approach of evening. Working in the fields all day, even there frequently harassed by fears of assassination, they sought at night the woods or fields, and there hid until morning."

One of the worst incidents of Klan violence — arguably the largest mass lynching in Reconstruction history — took place in Union County, South Carolina, in early 1871, when black militiamen were arrested for shooting to death Matt Stevens, a local white moonshiner who had donned a Klan costume in an attempt to rob a "contraband whiskey wagon." (His wife, upon learning of his demise, exclaimed, "I told him to stay at home — I knew what he would get when he went Ku-Kluxing!") A posse of white townsmen calling themselves the Black Panther Klan stormed the county jail and lynched two blacks accused of Stevens's murder. Soon after, fifty members of another vigilante group, the Council of Safety, raided the same jail, demanding that several other blacks, who were also being held under suspicion in the case, be turned over to them. These prisoners, however, had surrendered voluntarily on the sheriff's promise of protection; when that officer refused to collaborate with the lynch mob, he was held hostage as the intruders used an ax to break into a cell and abduct five men. Two, including Ellick Walker, the local militia captain, were found dead on the road the next morning; the other three, gravely injured, were promptly re-arrested by the sheriff. When word spread that the three survivors and seven additional suspects were to be moved to Columbia for safekeeping, an army of three hundred Klansmen descended on the jail. After posting guards on the roads leading in and out of town, they roughed up the uncooperative sheriff and his deputy, tied them to a hitching post, and then departed into the night with ten abducted men. The remains of eight were found the next morning; two had been hanged and six shot to death; the other two were never heard of again.

A note left on the body of one victim read, "In silence and secrecy thought has been working, and benignant efficacies of concealment speak for themselves. Once again we have been forced by force to use Force. Justice was lame and she had to lean on us."

Black politicians were frequent targets of the Klan. One of the most notorious assassinations of the period was the shooting, in broad daylight, of the legislator Benjamin Randolph, murdered by whites as he waited on a railroad platform at Hodges Station, in Abbeville County, on October 1, 1868. A minister and Oberlin graduate who had served in the state constitutional convention and advocated the integration of public schools, Randolph had once said of postwar South Carolina, "We are laying the foundation for a new structure here. We must decide whether we shall live together or not." Witnesses to his killing said Randolph's attackers, unconcerned about being seen, nonchalantly mounted their horses afterward and rode away.

While Klan attacks were often related to politics, they could also be prompted by other perceived transgressions, even incidental ones — buying land where poor whites resided; leaving a job or refusing to work; not giving way in a carriage; disrespecting a white woman; operating a moonshine business that competed with whites; or, as one Klansman complained of his victim, for "acting the Big Man and fool generally." Turning to white authorities or courts for help was hardly an option in areas where Klan membership was widespread enough to include almost every white man. Police, retired military men of rank, businessmen, physicians, and even ministers held places in the group's leadership. A teacher at a college in Limestone Springs, unable to obtain a Klan disguise in time for one midnight rendezvous, showed up in his professorial gown. The lower levels of the organization were often filled with teenage boys, most too young to have worn the gray but who identified with the Lost Cause.

Blacks had to be especially careful not to appear to succeed at the expense of individual whites. In 1871 a coachman named Samuel Simmons, representing his widowed employer in a horse trade, apparently got the better of a white neighbor named Beloue. When Simmons and the woman next rode out in their carriage, Beloue intercepted the pair, telling the widow he would "put six balls through your boy" and assuring Simmons he would "bring the Ku Klux on you, and swing you to a limb until you are dead, by God." Beloue was as good as his word: Klansmen with horns on their heads came to Simmons's house in the middle of the night and whipped him, explaining that they were the ghosts of Confederate soldiers slain at Gettysburg. They instructed their terrified victim to observe that one of the Klansman's horns had been bent as he crawled from the grave.

Klan assaults on lonely black settlements, though chiefly meant to intimidate residents and prevent voting and other political activity, often included acts of sexual humiliation and molestation of black women; night riders forced women to lower their dresses, or strip completely, to receive a lashing across the back. Rape was not uncommon. Such acts dehumanized black women, humiliated their male kinfolk, and reinforced the idea that white men controlled the region's sexual dynamics.

The Klan's wrath at times did not even spare ex-Confederates. George W. Garner of Union County, who had fought at Antietam and Fredericksburg, angered local Klansmen by serving as a deputy sheriff for the local Republican government. Irritated by his "damned Radical way of doing," they took Garner from his house one night and administered a painful flogging. "They cut my back all to pieces, and told me if I did not announce myself as a true Democrat, and promise it faithfully, that they would come back and kill me." What the Klan was after — in Garner's case and in many others — were public statements or acts of contrition, meant to shame anyone, white or black, who had been led into wayward alliance with the Republicans. Isaiah Brown of Spartanburg, when threatened, dutifully placed a notice in his local paper, stating, "I did honestly believe that it was in my interest to vote with the Radical party, and that that party was the colored man's friend, but I am now most thoroughly convinced of my error." The black residents of one village became so anxious that they issued a preemptive public proclamation: "We will no longer be used as tools or instruments in placing [Radical] men into office, but will hereafter identify ourselves with the interests of the good people among whom we have been brought up." E. Henry Bates, like Garner a Confederate veteran, was forced to deny publicly any sympathy for the Radicals, stating, "I have an utter abhorrence for their principles and constitutions."

An example of the economic coercion that often accompanied Klan intimidation across the South was Edgefield County's Agricultural and Police Club, founded in 1870. To protect local landholding interests, its members were forced to swear an oath not to sell land to blacks. The club also worked to isolate uncooperative white men, for local backsliding was worrisome: in 1872 a coalition of moderate Democrats and Republicans claimed several municipal positions in an election, and, in an even more glaring affront, a white Republican staged his marriage to a local freedwoman on the steps of the county courthouse. Any man who failed to join, according to George Tillman, a group founder, was to be treated "as a whole nigger should be treated . . . pass him and his whole family with silent contempt . . . let him or any of his household get sick, or even die with none to cheer the lonely hours, or to bury the tainted remains, but his nigger associates." Such ostracism in an insular rural area could be psychologically unbearable: an Edgefield County landowner named Joshua McKie made the mistake of renting property to a black; finding himself shunned by friends, tradesmen, and even his own relatives, he committed suicide. Trapped between their belief in Reconstruction and the mounting hostility of their neighbors, while residing in remote hamlets with little hope of federal protection or even contact with political allies, whites with Republican sympathies increasingly felt endangered. One North Carolina carpetbagger described them as "the worst frightened men you ever saw."

Many Americans, including members of Congress, were reluctant at first to contemplate the scope of the Klan's activities, almost as if the nation, utterly weary of civil war, could not bring itself to acknowledge the evidence of renewed Southern agitation. "The Northern mind, being full of what is called progress, runs away from the past," Attorney General Amos Akerman would observe. Indeed, the ratification of the postwar amendments had created much false hope in the North — the faith that once given the vote, America's newest citizens would soon learn to stand on their own, using their new political power to secure their own safety and confront all manner of social, economic, and educational challenges. This was exasperating to men like Akerman, Frederick Douglass, and Charles Sumner, who were convinced that the willful spirit of secessionist defiance, which had surprised the North in 1861 and had taken four bloody years and all the North's resources to put down, was far from suppressed. "The principle for which we contended," Jefferson Davis had vowed at war's end, "is bound to reassert itself, at another time, and in another form," words that by the early 1870s appeared darkly prescient.

One potential tool to combat the Klan in the South was the militias, which state governments were authorized to use against insurrection or lawlessness; in Tennessee, North Carolina, and Texas, militia units did act to quash Klan activity. But this approach was problematic: militias were expensive to maintain at a time when funds were desperately needed for myriad projects related to Reconstruction; citizens resented having to support a standing military force; and many whites refused to serve as peers of freedmen or subordinates of black officers. Also, because in many places militias were largely made up of blacks, authorities feared that using them against Klan vigilantes would alarm the white populace and possibly excite more general racial violence. In 1871, Governor William Holden of North Carolina paid the ultimate political price for dispatching his state's militia against the Klan; he became the first governor in American history to be impeached and removed from office.

The white public's deep-rooted hostility to black armed men in uniform was occasionally expressed in attempts to banish the playing of drums — the militias' usual means of rousing their members. Also offensive were the militiamen's love of brightly colored outfits, sashes, and hats and the tendency of black men, women, and children to turn out in large numbers to cheer units of black militiamen and military bands, evidently as thrilled with the novel spectacle of armed black pageantry as whites were bothered by it. Reconstruction South Carolina saw several violent incidents related to black militias parading in public. In one example, a streetcar moving along Charleston's King Street on March 27, 1871, came up behind two black militia companies. After the car lurched close to the militia's ranks, the blacks accused the driver of disrespect and began using their bayonets and gunstocks to smash the car's windows. Terrified passengers fled. The next day's *Daily News* blamed "the atrocious policy of allowing excited and vindictive negroes to parade the public streets with arms in their hands. These negroes are not to be trusted with deadly weapons." Disarming militiamen, and blacks in general, thus became a fixation of the Klan, and raids on black households often included an effort to locate and confiscate guns.

In South Carolina the state militia had about twenty thousand members in 1870, but only half were armed; and though they had shown themselves capable of guarding polling places, many militiamen lacked training and were said to suffer an innate reluctance to fight. As the carpetbagger Daniel Chamberlain would inform President Grant,

> The long habit of command and assertion on the part of the whites . . . [and] the fact that at least four fifths of the property of these [Southern] states are in their hands . . . give them an easy physical superiority . . . over the recently emancipated race, who still exhibit the effects of their long slavery in their habit of yielding to the more imperious and resolute will . . . and material resources of the white men.

The Klansmen, many of whom were Confederate veterans, also had the overwhelming advantage of combat experience in battle and a sense of military tactics. As *The Nation* observed: "The fighting men of the South are all on the Ku-Klux side."

In an effort to comprehend the magnitude of the threat the Klan posed, Congress in December 1870 created the Joint Committee to Inquire into the Condition of Affairs in the Late Insurrectionary States, one of the first large-scale congressional investigations in the country's history. Committee members fanned out across the South to hear evidence of Klan outrages. The result was a massive thirteen-volume document — a kind of black book of Southern disturbances, listing abuses ranging from voter intimidation to whippings and murder. The report revealed a clear pattern of white brutality and made novel use of the raw, unfiltered voices of Southern freedmen taken in recorded testimony. Released in February 1872, eight months before the presidential election, its executive summary reminded the country of the need to maintain Reconstruction's authority over the unstable former Confederacy and, as some Southern critics charged, the importance of reelecting President Grant.

Grant took action even before the report was concluded. In May 1870, he encouraged Congress to pass the first of several major Enforcement Acts prohibiting the use of intimidation, bribery, or force to violate voting rights and making it an offense to wear a disguise on public highways or on private property in order to harm or intimidate voters. Another, passed in February 1871, established the means for federal officials to monitor and supervise congressional elections. Despite their name, though, the laws were somewhat vague as to the precise means of safeguarding voters' rights on a reliable basis and punishing abuses. As one congressman lamented, "It is not law that is wanted in the South; it is the execution of the laws."

There was, however, already talk of another major enforcement act that would deal directly with the Klan. It involved extending the judicial reach of the federal government to address criminal acts that had always been a matter for local and state courts. This was extremely controversial, for Southerners already decried the voting-related Enforcement Acts as federal bullying. But was there any alternative? To many Northerners it seemed that the sacrifice of the Civil War would be meaningless unless Ku Kluxism could be stopped. "If the federal government cannot pass laws to protect the rights, liberty, and lives of citizens of the United States in the states, why were guarantees of those fundamental rights put in the Constitution at all, and especially by acts of amendment?" asked Congressman Benjamin Butler, who helped draft the new legislation. If an American citizen was waylaid or assaulted abroad, in a foreign nation, he asserted, it would be expected that "the whole power of the Republic" would be available to "protect him and redress his wrongs." It only made sense that a citizen terrorized as he slept peacefully in his bed, "on our own soil, under his own roof-tree, and covered by our own flag," should enjoy the same security. During the House discussion of the issue, it was said that Butler displayed a bloodied nightshirt worn by a county school superintendent in Mississippi who had been flogged by the Klan — the origin of the expression "waving the bloody shirt," that is, eliciting Northern sympathy for the victims of

Southern vigilantism. There is some question as to whether Butler actually did this, and evidence suggests that the expression was in use earlier, its exact genesis unknown; but whatever its origin, the term, and the concept to which it referred, would recur frequently in debates over Reconstruction.

The South Carolina representative Joseph Rainey reported to his white congressional peers that the Klan situation at home had become so severe not even state authorities were safe and that he himself had been threatened. Rainey had received a message from the Klan, scrawled in red ink, with crude drawings of a skull and crossbones:

> K.K.K.
> Beware! Beware! Beware!
> Your doom is sealed in blood
> Special Order: Headquarters 17th Division, Cyclopian Cyclop Commandery
> At a regular meeting of this post on Saturday it was unanimously resolved that notice be given to J. H. Rainey and H. F. Heriot to prepare to meet their God.
> Take heed, stay not. Here the climate is too hot for you. We warn you to flee. You are watched each hour. We warn you to go.

"When myself and colleagues shall leave these halls and turn our footsteps toward our Southern home," Rainey explained, "we know not but that the assassin may await our coming."

However, many in Congress shunned the idea that the federal government might appropriate local authority to address crimes of murder, assault, and trespass. Indeed, many in Congress, including the Ohio Republican congressman James A. Garfield, worried about the constitutionality of such a step as well as the apparent rush to usurp state authority and thus hand Southern Democrats more cause for protest. Others felt that although bold federal laws had been, of necessity, passed in the war's immediate aftermath, now was the time to rein in such impulses. "We have reconstructed, and reconstructed, and we are asked to reconstruct again," declared Representative John F. Farnsworth of Illinois. "We are governing the South too much."

The Nation expressed an additional fear: that a "Ceasarist" doctrine of federal law enforcement would cause state-level government to atrophy. The magazine called for "restoration of peace and order" in the South "by natural processes" and discouraged the "desperate attempt" to exploit "the humanitarian feelings of the Northern people." Klan outrages, it suggested, were the inevitable result of the ill-conceived disenfranchisement of the South's "natural" leadership and the subjection of Southern whites to "the rule of [the community's] most ignorant members [blacks], aided or managed by knavish adventurers [carpetbaggers]." *The Nation* concluded that empowering the federal government to repress the Klan would simply compound one bad policy decision with another, delaying the moment when the Southern people ultimately made their own peace with the black population in their midst. "We must," it averred, "hand the Government over to the people."

President Grant wrestled with the problem. Certainly, it would be better if local or state law enforcement would put down vigilantism, but it was obvious that the Klan would never be effectively prosecuted that way, for few residents in their areas of operation were bold enough to testify against them, many jurists dared not convict them, and most sheriffs were too frightened or sympathetic to investigate their crimes or hold them in custody. Some Southern courts seemed to act as agencies of the Klan itself. When William Wright, a black citizen of York County, South Carolina, accused Klansman Abraham Sapoch of leading a Klan posse that whipped Wright and set fire to his house, Sapoch slapped Wright with a lawsuit for perjury and false arrest. After a court deliberated, Sapoch was set free to return to his Klan unit, and Wright, the complainant, was dispatched to the state penitentiary.

"Sir, we are in terror from Ku-Klux threats & outrages," a white woman, Mrs. S. E. Lane, the wife of a Presbyterian minister, informed the president in a letter from Laurens County, South Carolina.

> Our nearest neighbor, a prominent Repub'can now lies dead, murdered by a disguised Ruffian Band, which attacked his house at midnight. His wife also was murdered . . . she was buried yesterday, and a daughter is lying dangerously ill from a shot-wound. My husband's life is threatened [and] we are in constant fear and terror. Ought this to be? It seems almost impossible to believe that we are in our own Land.

Another upcountry white, C. F. Jones, confided that

> I am a clergyman, superannuated, dwelling on my plantation, having a number of colored tenants and hired laborers. On Thursday night . . . my farm was invaded by a gang of disguised ruffians, who went from house to house, dragging the inmates out, beating them, firing pistols at them, etc. A bullet has since been extracted from the head of

> one. Another aged, upright, Christian man, was slaughtered, in his own yard, while begging them to spare him.

Such cries for help were impossible to ignore but could not completely outweigh Grant's concern that federal anti-Klan policies might appear overbearing. Attorney General Akerman, however, was less hesitant; his unusual dual background as a Unionist with powerful Southern sympathies, and his intimate knowledge of life in the rural South, allowed him to grasp more readily than others both the evil the Klan represented and the imperative that it be stopped.

Shortly after graduating from Dartmouth in 1842, Akerman, who had respiratory problems related to a childhood swimming incident, was advised by doctors to relocate to a southern climate. He found employment in South Carolina, tutoring the children of the elite, and later moved to Savannah to serve as a private instructor to the children of John M. Berrien, a U.S. senator and a former attorney general under Andrew Jackson. In exchange Berrien provided Akerman with an education in the law. In 1850 Akerman became an attorney in Habersham County, Georgia, and purchased a three-hundred-acre farm, which he worked himself, along with a small "force" of slaves.

Faithful to the principle of the rule of law, he sided with his adopted state when war came, worried that Lincoln's policies toward the South lacked consistency and fearful of the turmoil emancipation might bring. He joined a home guard unit that was activated when Union forces entered Georgia in spring 1864. However, he accepted the war's outcome as inevitable and served as a delegate to Georgia's constitutional convention of 1867–68, believing it his duty "to let Confederate ideas rule us no longer [and] to discard the doctrines of states rights and slavery." Black suffrage had at first seemed to him "an alarming imposition on account of [their] supposed ignorance . . . But on reflection we considered that if ignorance did not disqualify white men it should not disqualify black men. We considered that colored men were deeply interested in the country and had at least sense enough to know whether government worked well or not in its more palpable operations, and therefore would probably be safe voters."

On a visit to Washington he came to the attention of Republican legislators who saw in the transplanted Northerner a potential ally, someone who could help protect freedmen's rights as well as the future of the Republican Party in the South. Congressman Butler helped persuade President Grant of the value of placing a man like Akerman in the cabinet as a show of confidence in and support for all Southern Republicans. Who better than a man with proven loyalty to the South to take the reins of the newly established Justice Department as it faced the politically sensitive dilemma of dealing with the Klan?

Prior to the creation of the Justice Department, the federal government had hired lawyers to argue its cases, a method both expensive and frequently ineffectual. The new department would rely on federal district attorneys as well as the solicitor general — a new position — to see that federal law was observed, a timely adjustment to counter Southern lawlessness and the ineffectiveness of local courts there. Akerman identified thoroughly with his mission but "discovered at Washington, even among Republicans," he told Charles Sumner, "a hesitation to exercise the powers to redress wrongs in the states. This surprised me. For unless the people become used to the exercise of these powers now, while the national spirit is still warm with the glow of the late war, there will be an indisposition to exercise them hereafter, and the 'States Rights' spirit may grow troublesome again."

Akerman was by now impatient with his Southern neighbors' continued rejection of the outcome of the war, and he held the deepest contempt for night riding and political violence, which he called "KuKluxery." What especially worried him, and what he feared most Northerners failed to appreciate, was that Klan intimidation often went well beyond night riding. The midnight visit to a freedman's cabin by a handful of local vigilantes could seem almost quaint compared to what the Klan looked like at full strength — scores of men, some in disguises, some in tattered Confederate gray, raising the dust of a sleepy courthouse town, thoroughly overwhelming its citizens and authorities alike. He also was perhaps the lone high-ranking federal official who knew what it was to live in fear of the Klan, for he had a wife and several children still residing in Georgia.

"One cause of [the] readiness to secede in 1861 was the popular notion that the government at Washington was a distant affair, of very little importance to us," he wrote of his fellow Southerners, emphasizing that the federal response to the Klan must be consistent and thorough. "They have now been taught better. They ought not to be allowed to forget the lesson." He cautioned against any appeasement or "attempt to conciliate by kindness that portion of the Southern people who are still malevolent. They take all kindness on the part of the government as evidence of humility and hence are emboldened to lawlessness by it." Akerman no doubt pleased President Grant with his conviction that Klan activity should be quelled without sending additional federal troops into the South. The trend had been one of gradual withdrawal, as troop levels across the South fell from twelve thousand in 1868 to six thousand a year later; any new buildup would smack of renewed sectional confrontation. Akerman wanted instead to use the federal courts to pursue Klansmen as vicious criminals, isolating them from Southern society. The legal teeth for such an approach would be provided by pending legislation that would become known as the Ku Klux Klan Act.

While Joseph Rainey's plea to Congress about the Klan had been both personal and affecting, it was his colleague, twenty-eight-year-old Robert Brown Elliott, a lawyer and a publishing partner to Richard "Daddy" Cain, who offered the most compelling argument for passage of a special Ku Klux Klan bill.

A square-shouldered man of medium height, "black as a highly polished boot," Elliott appeared to journalist Marie Le Baron a "distinguished and agreeable figure" who evinced "no awkward gesture, no obsequious movement to point back to a life of cringing servitude." He claimed that he was born in Boston in August 1842, that his family had then lived briefly in Jamaica, and that as a young man he had been taken to England, where he attended Eton and studied law before returning in 1861 to America, where he eventually enlisted in the Union army. However, Peggy Lamson, a twentieth-century biographer who diligently examined Elliott's past, found no record of his birth in Boston or his schooling in England, nor any evidence that he ever wore a soldier's uniform. What his contemporaries *did* know was that he was articulate, well educated, capable as a printer, and knowledgeable in the practice of law. He was also multilingual, speaking passable French and Spanish as well as English, and was versed in the classics, to which, like his hero Charles Sumner, he often alluded in his orations. More intriguing was the fact that despite so much time abroad, he was conversant with the "political condition of every nook and corner" of South Carolina, "every important person in every county, village, or town . . . [and] the history of the entire state as it related to politics."

So who was he? A favored slave who had received an education (his African appearance seemed to rule out the likelihood of even partial white parentage), or an opportunistic Englishman who had made his way to the New World? It seems odd that during Elliott's lifetime it was universally accepted that he had lived many years in Jamaica and

ROBERT BROWN ELLIOTT

England, yet there is no mention in accounts of his numerous speeches that he spoke with a British inflection. It's equally remarkable that for a man who had countless political enemies and who was often under assault from the home-state press, the details he gave of his background seem to go unchallenged.

Whatever his origins, Elliott lived well in South Carolina, possessed an extensive library, and married one of the most beautiful quadroons in the state, Grace Lee, who had been a house servant and governess to a prominent white family. Numerous contemporary accounts note her poise and natural elegance as well as Elliott's short temper where his wife's reputation was concerned. Ironically, this most African-looking man had, in addition to his taste for classical scholarship, another trait common to the native-born Southern aristocrat: an easily violated sense of personal honor. In late October 1869 Elliott accused James D. Kavanaugh, a former Union soldier, of writing notes to his wife; confronting the white man outside a government building in Columbia, he shoved him to the ground and repeatedly thrashed him with a whip. Elliott's behavior was not atypical in an age that saw Southern gentlemen routinely cane one another or inflict other "bodily chastisements." What made the assault newsworthy was that, as a black man defending his wife's good name, he was directly challenging the traditional notion that black women were approachable and sexually available to white men, a condition black men had for generations painfully endured. "A Negro from Massachusetts Cowhides a White Carpetbagger" reported the next day's *Charleston Daily News,* slyly inquiring why Yankees kept asserting that blacks were their *equals* when it appeared that Elliott was actually *superior* to Kavanaugh.

In Washington, Congressman Elliott was a tactful spokesperson for his race; several times he led delegations to confer with President Grant. On the House floor, however, he could be combative, as when, in defense of the Ku Klux Klan bill, he tangled with the Democrat Michael C.

Kerr of Indiana. Kerr, arguing states' rights, suggested that the Constitution allowed the federal government to interfere only if a state requested help. "The United States shall guarantee to every State in the Union a republican form of government," Kerr said, citing Article IV, Section 4, of the Constitution, "and shall protect each of them against invasion, and on application of the Legislature or of the Executive (when the Legislature cannot be convened) against domestic violence." There was no basis for federal intervention, he emphasized, when the legislature or the governor did not request assistance. Elliott disagreed with Kerr's interpretation, saying the article meant that the nation *did* have an obligation to defend, in each state, a republican form of government — precisely what was under assault in South Carolina. "In this case the duty imposed upon the Federal Government is to protect the States 'against domestic violence,'" Elliot said. "The clause is not inhibitory, but mandatory. It was evidently not designed to restrict the rights, but to enlarge the duties of the Government."

Elliott pointed out that the clause about the governor's request could not stand as the sole means by which intervention would occur, for the governor himself might be complicit in affiicting the people of a state. "Otherwise," Elliott pointed out, "a faithless and undutiful Executive, assisting the insurgent authors of the 'domestic violence,' might, by withholding his 'application,' render the Government of the United States a torpid and paralyzed spectator of the oppressions of its citizens." Kerr's formula for federal intervention, Elliott quipped, reminded him of the story of the aristocrat who apologized for watching a man drown before his eyes, explaining that they had not been properly introduced. (Elliott's joking at Kerr's expense, a black man openly mocking a white, did not sit well with congressional Democrats, several of whom walked out during his remarks.)

Kerr then argued that the outrages in South Carolina were being carried out by "a very small number of persons," and only in a few localities. "They are merely common criminals," he said, "without politics or higher motives." Elliott countered by reading a long list of known offenses and deadly Ku Klux threats, as well as warnings made to employers not to hire blacks or Republicans. He also called Congress's attention to several local newspaper editorials from South Carolina that called for what had come to be known as the "Straightout" Democratic policy, one that had as its goal not only electoral victory over the Republicans but also their obliteration as an active political entity. Contradicting the frequent charge that "the Republican party is answerable for the existing state of affairs in the South," Elliott stated that "the troubles are usually in those sections in which the Democrats have a predominance in power, and, not content with this, desire to be supreme."

Horace Greeley, the editor of the *New York Tribune,* criticized Elliott for his comments, believing he had unfairly impugned the Southern planter class. Elliott replied in a letter (which Greeley published) that he had not said that planters *were* Klansmen, only that they supported them.

> Possibly, Mr. Editor, your graciousness to recalcitrant Confederates would be somewhat modified if you lived, as I do, within the theatre of their operations. Men often bear the misfortunes of their neighbors with great equanimity, and are ready most graciously to forgive wrongs to which they cannot be personally subjected. Thus the philosopher Seneca, seated in his magnificent villa, surrounded by symbols of opulence, wrote upon tablets of gold his famous "Essay on the Beauties and Advantages of Poverty."

Frederick Douglass joined the debate in the pages of his *New National Era,* arguing that the clarity of the Civil War conflict may have been preferable to the scurrilous mischief of the Klan. "Rebellion, at least, is honest, in so far that it makes war in broad daylight against organized forces, while, on the contrary, those dastardly gangs direct their attacks against single, defenseless individuals, and surprise, torture, and assassinate them in disguise and under the cover of night."

In late March 1871 Grant sided formally with the advocates of the bill, telling Congress, "A condition of affairs exists in some of the states of the Union rendering life and property insecure . . . That the power to correct these evils is beyond the control of the state authorities I do not doubt . . . therefore I urgently recommend such legislation as, in the judgment of Congress, shall effectually secure life, liberty, and property, and the enforcement of the law in all parts of the United States."

The Ku Klux Klan Act, which passed on April 20, expanded on the earlier Enforcement Acts by outlawing conspiracies to obstruct or hinder the equal rights protection of citizens under the law, including the rights of due process, and by asserting that such acts constituted "rebellion against the government of the United States." Its passage meant that cases involving Klan attacks on freedmen and others in South Carolina would receive a hearing in federal court and that the president was authorized to suspend the writ of habeas corpus, which gives imprisoned suspects the right to know why they are being held, so that large-scale roundups of Klansmen could be carried out and the accused held until testimony and witnesses were arranged. It also allowed Grant the option of dispatching federal troops without a state's formal request, and it mandated that both petit and grand jurors sitting on Klan cases would have to swear they had never taken part in the organization's activities.

Visiting South Carolina that summer, Attorney General Akerman went to York County to examine the considerable evidence against the Klan assembled by Major Lewis Merrill, a local commander of federal troops. Merrill, who impressed the attorney general as "very indignant at wrong, and yet master of his indignation," told Akerman he'd gathered evidence of eleven murders and more than six hundred whippings and other crimes, and that numerous victims of the Klan, potential witnesses, were now residing in army encampments under federal protection. Merrill, called "Dog Merrill" by resentful Klansmen, confirmed that prosecutions against alleged Klan suspects in local courts were impossible. Akerman, leaving for the North, concluded that substantial parts of South Carolina were in open rebellion and "under the domination of systematic and organized depravity," and he advised Grant to suspend the writ of habeas corpus in the most troubled parts of the state.

Grant's proclamation ordering martial law and suspending the writ of habeas corpus in nine counties of the South Carolina upcountry came on October 12, but when Akerman returned to York County on October 10, local Klan leaders had already begun to slink away from the scene. In their absence, more junior participants saw the wisdom of cooperating with authorities in order to avoid being locked up indefinitely under the new federal powers. In one instance, an entire Klan den arrived en masse to surrender. They explained that they had formed a Klan unit only out of fear of retribution if they did not conform to the dominant Ku Kluxers in the neighborhood. According to Louis Post, a Northern attorney who assisted with the Klan prosecutions in South Carolina, the locking up of Klan suspects helped get individual members to "puke," or confess, thereby incriminating others. These suspects hoped their cooperation would gain them some leniency. Still, of the 1,500 suspected South Carolina Klansmen arrested by detectives and U.S. marshals under the leadership of Attorney General Akerman, only 168 were convicted of a crime. But this low percentage belies the actual success of the effort. As many as 2,000 Klansmen were rumored to have fled the state rather than risk arrest, and thus the organization was effectively broken in South Carolina. Several of its leaders were convicted and sent to Northern penitentiaries.

By comparison, in Mississippi, another state hard-hit by Ku Kluxism, 585 convictions were obtained out of 1,100 cases; this larger number may be explained by the fact that the penalties for violation of the Enforcement Acts in Mississippi, which was not under martial law, were milder, so it was easier to compel whites to testify about Klan activity, although convincing black witnesses to do so remained difficult. A greater challenge to federal law officers lay in the state's frontier character. Arresting suspects in remote Mississippi villages where the Klan had extensive support was not easy, for the local telegraph office was frequently in Democratic hands, and "spotters" and other busybodies quickly passed the word along when federal marshals approached. Even when arrests were made, marshals often had to transport their prisoners back to the nearest railhead under threats and catcalls from local residents, suggesting that an imminent assault would be staged to free the men in custody. Death threats were common; one U.S. attorney in Mississippi was poisoned (he recovered), one was killed by a sniper firing into his kitchen window, and another was shot to death while he slept in a hotel room; several others were arrested by local law enforcers. In some places federal soldiers could back up the marshals in making arrests, but often infantry troops, rather than cavalry, were available and thus of limited effectiveness because of their lack of mobility. The growing conflict with the Indians in the western territories meant that fewer mounted units were posted in the South.

One quick-thinking U.S. attorney in Mississippi had the presence of mind to photograph several captured Klansmen in their disguises. He passed the images along to Congress and to *Harper's Weekly*, which published them not once but twice in 1872, remarking that "these lawless disturbers of the South . . . are not always so elaborate in their brigand toilet. A white blanket or sheet thrown over the head, with holes for the eyes, is usually sufficient." The photographs were significant because they showed the whole nation, at long last, that the Klan actually existed and was not, as often alleged by Southerners, a "figment of the Northern imagination." In the North, Louis Post lamented, "The general disposition . . . was to assign the Ku Klux Klan to the category of horseplay," and as late as December 1871 one New York newspaper was convinced that most Klan outrages were nothing more than "personal quarrels." *Harper's*, however, assured its readers that "these outlaws will speedily be taught that the government will protect peaceable citizens in the full enjoyment of their rights, life, and property, if it takes the whole military power of the nation to do it."

In spite of the successful prosecutions, President Grant remained ill at ease with this flexing of federal muscle; one of the leading members of his cabinet, Secretary of State Hamilton Fish, had become annoyed by what appeared to be Akerman's obsession with punishing the Klan. Fish believed that the attorney general had the Ku Klux "on the brain," a view soon shared by other advisers close to the president. He had been particularly irritated by Akerman's insistence on relating the particulars of Klan atrocities in cabinet meetings, including one of "a fellow being castrated, with terribly minute and tedious details." Akerman, it so happened, had also made enemies among the nation's powerful railroad interests by introducing stricter rules about the distribution of federal land subsidies to corporations seeking to build rail lines out west. Interior Secretary Columbus Delano, an adviser to some of the rail barons, worked on their behalf to get Akerman dismissed, and at the same time Fish denigrated the attorney general to the president for having become unbearable on the subject of the Ku Klux.

Grant had always been inconsistent in his willingness to enforce Reconstruction policies — in some instances acting convincingly to defend the freedmen's rights, at other times shrinking from that responsibility. Shortly before Christmas 1871 he made what, in retrospect, seems a colossal misjudgment, asking for Amos Akerman's resignation on the basis of "public sentiment." In his eighteen months on the job Akerman had set the new Justice Department in motion, stirred Northern concern about Southern violence, and led a fruitful campaign to vanquish the Ku Klux Klan. Although his successor, Judge George H. Williams of Oregon, would largely continue Akerman's policies, not for another century would the federal government have a leading law enforcement officer similarly willing to vigorously prosecute civil rights violations in the South.

"As a body designed to destroy Reconstruction and all its works, the Ku Klux Klan was a failure," writes historian George Rable. The Klan's terrorism had demonstrated overwhelmingly that black voters and their white allies could be intimidated by violence, but the group's excesses had left Washington no choice but to intervene in the South's affairs; the nation, after considerable doubt and reflection, had done so, breaking the terror organization and honoring Reconstruction's promise to its newest citizens.

This accomplishment, however, was only a momentary triumph. In the prolonged debate leading up to the Ku Klux Klan Act, astute white Southerners had observed that Washington, as well as the Northern press and public, was conflicted about the obligation to protect the freedmen. The Klan's blatant misbehavior had forced the government's hand, and whites in the South recognized that future efforts to restore white rule would likely fare better if pursued with greater subtlety. There was no need to confront Reconstruction directly; better to nibble at its advances, harass its flanks, and wait out its collapse. When such a campaign arose a few years later, Southern tactics would indeed be much more nuanced, and the nation's desire to intercede even more wanting.

CHAPTER 6

PINCH

IT WAS DURING the federal occupation of New Orleans in the early 1860s that Pinckney Benton Stewart Pinchback, the black paladin of Louisiana politics, first appeared. Hated, loved, always dapper, a maker of overly long speeches, a political operator with an ardent concern for black civil rights, Pinchback aroused conflicting passions among Louisianians, such that he could, in the course of a single day, be heckled in the New Orleans press as a "Radical," a "damned nigger," and a "usurper," yet before sundown hear the lusty voices of white men at a political rally, urging, "We are with you! We are with you, Pinchback!" During the war and Reconstruction he served as a Union officer, a delegate to two state constitutional conventions, a Louisiana state senator, the state's lieutenant governor, its acting governor (the first black governor in the nation's history), and — simultaneously — the state's appointee to the U.S. Senate and its elected representative to the House.

Klan night riding had been the defeated Confederacy's most sensational reply to the nation's efforts on behalf of the freedmen, but there was another harmful, more "gentlemanly" response — character assassination, racist demagoguery, and bitter factionalism wielded in the newspapers, legislatures, and political backrooms of the reconstituted Southern states. Reconstruction politics at the state and local levels was often a vicious blood sport, and Louisiana politics, with its endlessly contested election results, dual governments, rumors of poisonings, and murder conspiracies, was easily the most dysfunctional of them all. Just as the term "New Orleans" — meaning the Mechanics Hall riot of summer 1866 — had become a code for the failures of President Johnson's Reconstruction policies, the name "Louisiana" would signify the era's longest-running political soap opera — civic chaos as spectacle, with an ever-changing cast of characters, few of whom would remain unsullied.

"Are you a white man, or what are you?" a policeman once demanded, stopping Pinchback as he strolled along a New Orleans street. Frederick Douglass, who encountered Pinchback during a visit to the city in 1872, thought him "only colored enough to be thus classed by the most skillful discerners of proscribed blood," while a Northern reporter saw "a bronze Mephistopheles . . . his most repellent point a sardonic smile, which, hovering continuously over his lips, gives him an evil look, undeniably handsome as the man is."

He was born in 1837 to a white father, Major William Pinchback of Virginia, and his slave, Eliza Stewart, whom Major Pinchback had married and manumitted. At the time of his birth the family was on its way to Mississippi, then a frontier of vast fertile land tracts, where the major had purchased a plantation in Holmes County, northeast of Yazoo City. For a decade the Pinchbacks flourished in their new life, but when P.B.S. was age ten, his father died. The major had attempted to provide for Eliza and the children in his will, but she had no legal standing in Mississippi, despite having been his lawful wife, and his family back east, who had never approved of the marriage, promptly seized the inheritance, leaving mother and children to fend for themselves. Afraid that her late husband's kin might attempt to reenslave her and her children, Eliza moved the family to Cincinnati, where Pinchback and his older brother, Napoleon, had been attending boarding school at the time of their father's death.

Napoleon eventually suffered psychological problems and left school, and with the family in economic straits Pinchback at age twelve also abandoned his education, finding work on the canal boats operating between Cincinnati and Fort Wayne, Indiana. By 1854 he was a cabin boy on riverboats plying the Ohio River, where he fell in with a gambler named George Devol, who seems to have become a second father. Devol and his companions — "Canada" Bill Jones, Holly Chappell, and Tom Brown — were skilled card sharks. Working as a team on the crowded boats, they fleeced passengers by pretending to be country bumpkins who'd never previously met. They would "foolishly" raise the stakes of a poker game until there was a formidable pot, then swoop in for the kill. From these men, Pinchback, or "Pinch," as he was invariably known, learned numerous games of chance and sleight of hand, including how to throw a wicked game of three-card monte.

A life so colorful was not without risk. Once, aboard the steamboat *Homer,* a group of black deck hands accused Pinchback of cheating at cards. Pinchback drew a pistol to effect a swift exit, then employed a trick he had learned from Devol, hiding under the pilothouse and passing a bribe up to the pilot so he would bring the vessel near shore, allowing Pinchback to leap into shallow water. Spotted by his pursuers as he made his escape, Pinchback managed to scurry to shore as bullets pinged in the water around him.

He eventually worked his way up from cabin boy to steward but bridled at the fact that, although legally free, he was in almost every way a slave "to the unwritten law that the cleverest colored man could rise no higher than steward on a steamboat . . . that the colored man, no matter how intelligent or clever, was lower than the lowest white man." The outbreak of the Civil War, however, heralded great change. In spring 1862 Pinchback was a steward on the *Alonzo Childs* when he jumped ship in Yazoo City and headed for New Orleans, which the Union had just occupied, with the idea of enlisting with the federal forces. That same year he married sixteen-year-old Nina Emily Hethorn of Memphis. A family memoir describes Nina as "a white woman, of English-French stock" and recalls that, physically, the newlyweds dramatically differed: Pinchback at twenty-three looked intense, a man of action, his face "suggesting physical courage and a sort of picturesque recklessness," while Nina, in contrast, seemed delicate, reticent, potentially "a wife and mother, the maker of a home."

Pinchback and Nina struggled at first, since money was tight. "I ate cakes to fill my stomach, and apples to empty it," he recalled." He would later be a partner in both a newspaper and a mercantile business, and dabble, not always scrupulously, in local real estate. But his start in his adopted city was almost brutally cut short on May 16, 1862, when he got into a street brawl with his brother-in-law, his sister's husband, John Keppard. The fight, according to witnesses, was dead serious — Keppard, armed with a knife, appeared intent on taking Pinchback's life — and only through fierce effort (Keppard had jumped Pinchback by surprise) did Pinchback fend off his would-be assassin. Brought before an unsympathetic judge, Pinchback was outraged to hear himself charged with "assault with attempt to kill." On his lawyer's advice, he pled guilty in the hope of leniency; the judge, however, sentenced him to two years in the workhouse. "When it was announced I nearly fainted in court," he later said. "The object of this was blackmail, and before incarceration I was applied to and refused to pay up. I remained there about a month before I effected my release." Pinchback had enough money to ensure that his prison stay was comfortable. "I had my own food, bed, and other comforts which I procured out of my means."

His discharge, in July 1862, came only a week after General Benjamin Butler, the Union commandant of New Orleans, received permission from Washington to begin enlisting blacks for limited duty with the army. Pinchback applied to Butler to recruit a company of black men and by October was a captain in the Louisiana Native Guards. His enchantment with military life was of short duration, however, for despite the uniform that he and his black comrades wore, white Union soldiers regularly abused them; soon, because of complaints from whites, it was decreed that no black man could serve as an officer. Although Pinchback was allowed, nominally at least, to retain his rank, he found "nearly all the officers inimical to me" and wrote to Butler, resigning his appointment, explaining, "I can foresee nothing but dissatisfaction and discontent, which will make my position very disagreeable, indeed."

Pinchback thus abandoned the idea of military service, although he soldiered on in his own way — acting on the belief that emancipation should mean equal treatment for black people in the public sphere. The war years saw the advent of the "star car" system in New Orleans; the streetcars thus marked were set aside for black riders (the term STAR, a precursor to the COLORED ONLY label of the Jim Crow era, was used to designate other segregated facilities as well). As early as 1863 Pinchback refused to board the cars set aside for black people but instead used those meant for whites. On account of his light complexion, his military uniform, or his aristocratic mien, conductors generally did not make him leave, although in some instances they placed objects on the seats around him to create a buffer between him and any objecting white passengers. Other black soldiers and citizens emulated Pinchback's example, and the *New Orleans Tribune* took up the cause of deseg-

P.B.S. PINCHBACK

regating the vehicles. Ultimately the star cars were eliminated and both races were technically free to board any car, although whites' adjustment to the new arrangement was eased by the blacks' tendency to segregate themselves by occupying the seats at the rear.

Pinchback was often frustrated during "Johnsonian" Reconstruction, as he watched the Black Codes imposed and former Confederates assume public office. This was supposed to be the hour of liberation, the moment of black advancement, "the time when every thinking man must come forward and give his best views to the people," as he told a gathering in Alabama during a family hiatus from New Orleans. "No nation ever born has, or ever can, obtain the respect and confidence of the other nations of the earth until it has made some effort in its own behalf."

He warned against a false sense of entitlement created by the Civil War. "There is a sense of security displayed by our people that is really alarming," he said in June 1867, before a Republican meeting in New Orleans that would choose delegates to the upcoming state constitutional convention. "They seem to think that all is done, the Great Battle has been fought and the victory won. Gentlemen, this is a fallacy. The Great Contest has just begun." Having helped determine that the convention's makeup would be half black delegates and half white, Pinchback took the lead in authoring a civil rights article for the new constitution, advocating that all Louisianians should "enjoy equal rights and privileges upon any conveyances of a public character; and all places of business, or of public resort . . . without distinction or discrimination on account of race or color." It was Pinchback's unyielding demand for basic fairness in blacks' daily lives that most endeared him to his followers.

Before the convention ended, the Republicans added Pinchback to the list of men who might be nominated as the party's candidate for governor. He asked that his name be removed, however, saying he didn't think it wise at so volatile a political moment for the state to have a black man in the statehouse. Instead, he backed the white carpetbagger Henry Clay Warmoth, a precocious young attorney from Illinois who had been Louisiana's "territorial delegate" to Congress after the war. So enamored were Louisianians with Warmoth, who was twenty-six years old, that the convention officially lowered the age required to occupy the statehouse from thirty to twenty-five so that he could run for the office. Another key Warmoth backer was Oscar Dunn, a skilled, local black politician who had built a network of support through his work for the Freedmen's Bureau. In April 1868, Warmoth was elected governor and

Oscar Dunn lieutenant governor, making Dunn "the first colored man in America to hold a political position of an executive nature."

Pinchback ran for state senator but lost the election to his white Democratic opponent, E. I. Jewell, by a margin of 899 to 819. Or so it appeared. Pinchback claimed election fraud, and after Warmoth and Dunn came to power, a state committee on elections reviewed the balloting and, finding fraud had been committed on Jewell's behalf, gave the election to Pinchback. But Democrats and even a few Republicans grumbled that Warmoth had made a backroom deal to obtain that result, and some New Orleans newspapers accused Pinchback and his allies of trickery.

No one was more sincere or eloquent than Pinchback in his lifelong crusade for equal rights, but there was substantial basis for the scandalous gossip that shadowed him. He tried to distance himself from his past as a steamboat hustler, particularly as he raised his family; he found it difficult, however, to not see life, and particularly his life in politics, as a game to be cleverly played, and success as a series of "tricks" to be taken, like so many hands of cards. And as he'd done in many a riverboat poker game, he sometimes did not hesitate to improve his chances.

A humiliating incident, which occurred shortly after he had won his election case against E. I. Jewell, did not diminish this characterization. Strolling down Canal Street in the first week of September 1868, Pinchback heard the unmistakable sound of a pistol being cocked. He whirled around in time to see a mulatto named S. C. Morgan, an opponent of Governor Warmoth, take aim at him. Pinchback immediately drew his own gun and returned fire. Both men were shooting through a crowd of pedestrians, who screamed and ducked for cover as bullets ricocheted off a passing streetcar. A policeman, hearing the shots, came running up the block and arrested both men; they offered no resistance. An infuriated Pinchback accused Morgan, who had been grazed by a bullet, of attempted assassination; Morgan claimed his assault was retaliation for a slander that Pinchback had made against him for opposing Warmoth's election. Both were briefly held and released, but the local newspapers were highly critical, chiefly of Pinchback, wondering if black men reckless enough to engage in a gunfight on a crowded street were qualified to fill high positions in the state government. The *Daily Picayune* termed the incident "a shooting affray . . . with intent to kill and murder" and poked fun at the fact that "much sympathy was manifested for 'brudder' Pinchback, [who] endured a season of condolence in the Chief's office before his weeping friends could consent to give him up to the iron shelter of the cell."

Still stewing over the attack, Pinchback demanded the floor of the state senate a few days later to deliver "the most fiery speech ever heard in the history of the Louisiana legislature." Insisting that Morgan had been sent to murder him, he vented his anger at being stigmatized as a desperado for simply defending his life, assailed the unflattering criticisms of him that had appeared in print, and vowed a settling of scores if such harassment recurred. The hall murmured in disapproval; his tone was threatening, his words too caustic. Pinchback later apologized and restated his position a bit more mildly, but the damage was done. The press assaulted him anew, calling his speech "the ravings of a self-deceived man" and citing it as further evidence of "the utter unfitness of this class of which Pinchback is a type to be Senators and rulers in this land."

The abuse saddened Pinchback. Optimistic about the rights and opportunities opening up for the freed people, he had assumed that he could play a role in making these hopes a reality, but the Morgan affair and his contested election were casting him in the role of the black gentleman-outlaw of Louisiana politics, and he resented it. Probably it didn't help much that the other leading black politician in New Orleans, Oscar Dunn, was a native of the city and enjoyed an unassailable reputation, which stood in stark contrast to Pinchback's. Dunn, a fine-looking man of "genuine polish" and "extraordinary dignity and poise," seemed neither a schemer nor a demagogue, or was far more subtle than Pinchback was about getting what he wanted. Even his political opponents regarded Dunn as above corruption.

Once the Morgan affair had died down, Pinchback proved himself a fairly effective legislator in the state senate, helping push through two significant measures. The first one legally sanctioned marriage between a man and a woman who had previously cohabited, regardless of race, a measure that must have held personal resonance for Pinchback, whose parents' marriage had been easily challenged by his father's family upon his father's death. The second, a civil rights bill, imposed a $100 fine on any steamboat master, hotelkeeper, or other owner of a public business who refused equal accommodations because of a person's race. Some legislators complained that the bill's intent was to force whites to mix with blacks socially, which Pinchback vehemently denied. "I consider myself just as far above coming into company that does not want me," he said, "as they are above my coming into an elevation with them."

The civil rights bill passed both houses of the legislature, although Warmoth, in a sop to the state's conservatives, vetoed it — the first indication of a shift in the governor's sympathies that would ultimately alienate him from his black allies. Warmoth's defection — he had hoped the bill would be killed in the legislature, sparing him the trouble of the veto — was emblematic of the growing dissatisfaction that many whites felt about the political ascension of blacks like Dunn and Pinchback. These citizens, set on their heels at first by defeat in the war and then the continuing occupation by federal troops, had begun to chafe under "black Radical rule." Local rivalries intensified during the summer and fall of 1868; street fights and confrontations between politically affiliated gangs, sometimes called "marching clubs," became common; assaults on prominent freedmen and white Republicans increased. Brutal atrocities occurred in the state's outlying parishes, where blacks and even Republican lawmen were attacked and often killed. Warmoth estimated that during one six-week period, 150 people had been slain in the state, a figure that was likely half the actual total; more would come in October, when whites rampaged in the Shreveport area, murdering as many as 200 freedmen. During the final week preceding the election, according to historian Ted Tunnell, "New Orleans resembled a major European city in the throes of violent revolution." White mobs disrupted Republican gatherings while police huddled for safety in their station houses; at least 60 people perished in these assaults. Grant won the national election for president but failed to carry Louisiana; in New Orleans and throughout the state, the Republican turnout stood as evidence that voters had been intimidated; tallies dropped far below those of the April election, which had swept into office Pinchback, Warmoth, and Dunn.

Pinchback took this setback seriously. The violent white backlash was not unanticipated; he knew enough of the racial background of Southern politics to expect that whites, to protect their interests or simply express their frustration, would do everything in their power to diminish black political clout. For this reason he and others were eager to make as much progress as possible while blacks remained a viable political force. Pinchback surely had this in mind when in January 1869 he again urged the passage of his civil rights bill. "We are told, do not legislate on this subject; time will bring it about. Give the people time to get over their prejudices," he warned. "If left to time, the time will never come. Unless this matter is regulated by law, we will not only fail to have these privileges, but we may look to have all our rights, one by one or in a fell swoop, taken away from us. As for me, if I am denied any single right pertaining to American citizenship, I care not how soon I lose them all."

The bill was adopted by his colleagues in the legislature, and although Governor Warmoth signed it, the legislation was, due to a technicality, never enforced. Pinchback and other Republicans were coming to see the governor as an impediment to truly fundamental objectives: the adoption and enforcement of effective civil rights legislation and the appointment of black men to key offices. Warmoth's enthusiasm for these causes had clearly diminished. When, after considerable delay, he vetoed another major civil rights measure in 1870, Republicans who had felt concern about the governor now expressed open resentment, and Lieutenant Governor Dunn initiated an effort to deprive Warmoth of the leadership of the state Republican Party. This move caught Pinchback flat-footed, for he was politically beholden to the governor and hesitated to desert him, despite Warmoth's growing apostasy.

Dunn may have been emboldened because he enjoyed the support of President Grant's brother-in-law, James F. Casey, the collector of customs at the port of New Orleans. Furthermore, Grant was known to dislike Warmoth because of an incident that took place during the war. After returning from a leave of absence taken to convalesce from a wound received during the siege of Vicksburg in May 1863, Warmoth was dishonorably discharged by Grant for malingering and disseminating false accounts of Union casualties. Warmoth pleaded innocent and traveled to Washington to appeal the discharge personally to President Lincoln. The nation's chief executive, taking a liking to his fellow Illinoisan (who somewhat resembled Lincoln in height and build), reinstated the young officer, but Grant never forgave Warmoth for going over his head to win Lincoln's favor.

To resolve his dilemma, Pinchback did not join Dunn in the revolt against the governor but simply shifted his aspirations as a politician. The term of the first Republican senator from Louisiana, John S. Harris, was set to expire in 1871, and Pinchback began to eye the appointment, even cajoling some support from the local press. "Senator Pinchback . . . possesses tact and boldness, and generally succeeds in making himself heard and felt," said the *New Orleans Republican,* favoring his advancement to Washington. Oscar Dunn also aspired to the job. In January 1871, when Louisiana Republicans gathered to select Harris's replacement, Pinchback beat Dunn in the caucus vote but nonetheless lost to Warmoth's choice, a white former Union soldier named Joseph R. West. Warmoth managed to offend multiple factions during this episode. In promoting West he not only turned away the bid by Pinchback, who had remained loyal to him, but once again irritated President Grant, who wished the appointment to go to his relation, James Casey. Warmoth perhaps did himself the most harm by thwarting the ambition of his own increasingly popular lieutenant governor, Oscar Dunn.

In Louisiana politics, Oscar Dunn was a rarity — a popular official, native to New Orleans, whose life story exhibited wholesome elements of integrity and hard work. While he and Pinchback were never far apart politically and shared cordial, if not close, relations, Dunn's untarnished reputation — like that of a more perfect, more adored sibling — was a continual source of aggravation to his colleague; indeed, Pinch was to be haunted by the other's example throughout his political life.

Dunn's trajectory was representative of the black political experience during Reconstruction — the seemingly implausible ascent from obscurity to public authority that only so cataclysmic an event as the Civil War could have made possible. Born in New Orleans in the mid-1820s, Dunn was the son of a free woman of color who managed a boarding house frequented by entertainers. According to one account of his early years, the boarders, in partial exchange for a roof over their heads, tutored Oscar in the dramatic and musical arts. He evidently possessed talent as a singer and guitarist, and in 1841, seeking to better his lot, he fled his job as a painter's and plasterer's apprentice to find work on the Mississippi River steamboats, prompting his employer to run an ad in a local newspaper offering a five-dollar reward for the return of "the negro boy Oscar Dunn," who was described as five feet ten inches in height and "of a *griffe* color."

Griffe, meaning "a person born to a Negro, or pure-blooded African parent, and a mulatto parent," was a familiar term in Louisiana's multilayered caste system. Those of mixed race, sometimes known as *gens de couleur,* in 1860 comprised a full half of the local black population and were known by a variety of designations — griffes, briques, mulattoes, creoles, quadroons, or octoroons, each category specifying a narrowly defined quality of white tincture. Other terms, especially after the war, distinguished *free blacks* — those like Oscar Dunn and P.B.S. Pinchback who had *never* been slaves — from *freedmen,* slaves who had purchased their own freedom, been manumitted by their owners, or been emancipated by the war.

For the youthful Oscar Dunn, as for Pinchback, work aboard the steamboats plying the Mississippi River provided a kind of entrée into the wider world. Steamboats offered one of the more cosmopolitan experiences available in mid-nineteenth-century America; these floating empires gave travelers a chance to mingle in society beyond their usual means, and perhaps even a whiff of risqué adventure. Dunn was a steamboat barber and later a shipboard entertainer, performing on guitar and violin. After the war, working with the Freedmen's Bureau, he managed an employment service that arranged labor contracts between former slaves and their former masters and placed domestic workers in white homes. Holding this position of trust with hundreds of black laborers, he became a skilled organizer and built his first political constituency. He was known for possessing an attribute in short supply in Reconstruction Louisiana: honesty. It was said that he refused a bribe with the remark "Sir, my conscience is not for sale."

Dunn's probity was all the more remarkable because paying for legislative votes, expecting kickbacks from corporations or utilities, padding expense accounts, running up phony printers' bills, cutting insider deals on land sales, and running huge, often nepotistic patronage systems were all common abuses at the time. Dunn also managed to remain fairly insulated from the city's more infamous crises — the Mechanics Institute riot of 1866, the white-on-black terrorism of the 1868 election, and the everyday canings, stabbings, and street brawls that were recounted each morning in the police blotters of the local press.

As lieutenant governor, Dunn kept largely above the fray until 1870, when Governor Warmoth began appointing Democrats to important positions in his administration, including even some former rebels such as Penn Mason, a member of General Robert E. Lee's staff, and General James Longstreet, whom he made head of the Metropolitan Police Force, which served as a kind of private army for the Republican authorities. Dunn and his colleagues worried that Warmoth's penchant for the political center would open the way for Democrats to extinguish Republican power in Louisiana and strip blacks of their newly gained suffrage. "Warmoth," Dunn complained in a published letter to Horace Greeley's *New York Tribune*, "has shown an itching desire to . . . secure the personal support of the Democracy at the expense of his own party, and an equally manifest craving to obtain a cheap and ignoble white respectability by the sacrifice of the support of colored Republicans. We cannot and will not support him."

When Warmoth left New Orleans in early 1871 to recuperate from a foot injury, Dunn in his absence assumed the duties of the governor. The Democrats had a field day; their newspapers boasted that they "preferred a 'nigger' governor to a carpet-bagger." Warmoth, it seemed, was being double-crossed; not only did some Republicans distrust him as an appeaser of Democrats, but also many Democrats showed him disrespect by playing the popularity of Warmoth's own lieutenant governor against him.

Dunn and his Republican faction aimed to take control of the state party at its convention, scheduled for August, and the governor was well aware of this. Warmoth suspected that Dunn would not locate the meeting at the Mechanics Institute, which still served as the statehouse, in order to undermine Warmoth's ability to call upon Longstreet's police; the governor tried to counter Dunn's likely efforts by reserving all the suitable meeting halls in town. In response, Dunn's colleagues enjoined Stephen Packard, the chair of the party's state committee, to withhold, until the last moment, the announcement of the site of the meeting — the federal customhouse. Holding a state political conclave in a federal building was unusual, but it was where Packard, who was a federal marshal, could most effectively wield authority. For good measure Packard arranged for fifty additional marshals to be on hand, as well as a detachment of federal troops. President Grant's brother-in-law, Casey, who had just returned from a visit with the president, fully cooperated in this plan. Moreover, during his visit with Grant, Casey reported on Warmoth's misbehavior in pandering to disaffected Southerners and also broached the idea of elevating Dunn to vice presidential candidate on the national Republican ticket the following year. Grant, confident of a second term, was said to be at least agreeable to considering Dunn.

When the gathering convened, the delegates expressed their resentment of Warmoth by taking the unprecedented step of electing Dunn, not the governor, to preside over the Republican convention. Warmoth, who had showed up on crutches in the company of Pinchback, furiously pulled out his supporters and created a rump convention in a nearby building, Turner Hall, and staged a fake "celebration" down the length of Canal Street with his followers to mark his "revolution." But the Dunn faction, in a rapid exchange of telegrams with Washington, won a guarantee from the president that they were indeed the legitimate leaders of Louisiana's Republican Party.

Grant's willingness to recognize Dunn in preference to Warmoth boxed in the governor. Chastened by being abandoned by the national head of the Republican Party, he found himself denounced anew by Louisiana Democrats, who voiced their contempt at his weakness and lack of discipline in failing to contain the breakaway Dunn element. Exasperated, Warmoth lashed out, accusing Dunn of wanting to "Africanize" Louisiana and railing at the libels printed against Warmoth himself in Democratic newspapers. "I have been called a carpetbagger, a czar, a Caesar . . . a Political Leper, the Pest in the Executive Chair, a traitor to my political party, a robber of the state, and the oppressor of the people," he cried. "I have been accused of having made a fortune out of the office of governor."

Pinchback, siding with Warmoth, agreed to join a committee to travel north and explain the governor's predicament directly to the president. Pinchback and the others found Grant at his summer cottage in Long Branch, New Jersey, where they related the Dunn forces' recent shenanigans; Pinchback at one point dared suggest to the president that Grant's brother-in-law be removed from office (Pinchback would later tell a reporter that Casey "hasn't a handful of brains"). Grant listened to Pinchback but did nothing, refusing to extricate the federal troops who were protecting Dunn and what was now being called the Customhouse faction. This breakaway group had by now elected Dunn as their president, adopted an article expelling Warmoth from the Republican Party, and passed a resolution calling for the governor's impeachment. The charges against him were technical, citing "official misconduct" and "high crimes and misdemeanors in office," but stemmed essentially from his abandonment of the party's aims. The now-flailing governor, agreed the *New Orleans Picayune,* was a "War-moth" who needed to be "exterminated" as soon as possible.

In the midst of the crisis, in November 1871, Oscar Dunn came down with a nagging, debilitating cough, a condition he and his friends assumed had resulted from his strenuous duties. For about a month he had been suffering from what his doctor called "pulmonary catarrh," a respiratory inflammation, and had been taking Cherry Pectoral, a popular cure-all "recommended for weak hearts." The product, however, had been ineffectual in curing his weariness and hoarseness. On Saturday, November 20, Dunn gave a talk at the Third Ward Radical Club and was in good form. Sunday morning he ate a hearty breakfast and spent part of the day with his cohort Marshal Packard. After dinner, however, Dunn had a severe attack of vomiting, and on Monday, E. D. Beach, the family doctor, was called in. Beach diagnosed pneumonia, noting that the lieutenant governor's brain was "evidently much affected," and put him to bed, in the care of a nurse. During the night

Dunn slipped into unconsciousness, and Packard was summoned. Seeing his friend's desperate situation, he called in another physician, Dr. Scott, who declared that Dunn was suffering from congestion of the brain and lungs brought about by excessive vomiting.

Other leading physicians of New Orleans arrived, including Dr. Warren Stone, a local medical pioneer, and Dr. Louis Roudanez, a Paris-educated Creole physician, but they ventured no new diagnosis and expressed puzzlement at Dunn's rapid deterioration. Consulting in hushed tones, they cast pitying looks at the patient's wife, who, along with other family members, had convened a deathwatch by the bed, where Dunn lay emitting "a regular gurgling sob that occasionally changed to a harsh rattle." Mrs. Dunn, alternately clutching a handkerchief and lowering her face into her hands, came and went, unable to remain for long in the presence of a scene so unbearable. Dunn's nurse, "an intelligent quadroon woman," observed that she had "never seen pneumonia like that." Gently wiping the drops of blood and mucus from Dunn's lips, she assured her patient that "Jesus is coming — Jesus will soon be here to take you away." At the sound of her voice, Dunn opened his eyes and appeared to scrutinize the woman's face, "his blank stare mirror[ing] the baffled confusion of his soul." "They've given poison to the Governor," another servant said quietly. "They've poisoned the Governor." Late Tuesday night, November 23, he slipped from consciousness for the last time, and soon one of the physicians signaled that the struggle had ended.

When the local coroner, Dr. Creagh, arrived, he encountered a police physician, Dr. Avila, who was preparing to depart; Avila said that Dunn's family had turned him away. At Creagh's urging, Avila returned with him to the house, where Creagh explained to Dunn's survivors that a rumor of the lieutenant governor's poisoning was already abroad on the streets, and it was Creagh's duty under law to conduct a postmortem to ascertain the true cause of death. The family, supported by Beach and the other attending physicians, refused Creagh as they had Avila, insisting that Dunn had died of natural causes. They also rebuffed Creagh's request to examine a sample of Dunn's bodily waste, which might have helped confirm or dispel the suspicion of poisoning.

Creagh persisted because a week earlier he had handled a similar case involving a black prostitute who had arrived at a New Orleans charity hospital. Complaining of "break bone fever" — aches in her side, back, and head — she soon died. Creagh's autopsy found substantial amounts of arsenic in her stomach. His interest in Dunn's case may have been piqued even more by the fact that two of the white doctors in attendance, Beach and Stone, had disagreed initially about the cause of death.

Was Oscar Dunn poisoned? His overall condition and specific symptoms — vomiting, muscle spasms, shrunken features and whitened face, weak pulse, coma — correspond with classic accounts of arsenic poisoning. Because the symptoms arsenic causes resemble those of natural illness, and because, colorless and flavorless, it can be mixed undetectably with food, this poison was known as a handy means of retribution or a shortcut to an inheritance. Not for nothing was it sometimes called "succession powder." Certain arsenic compounds were used in the nineteenth century to treat syphilis, which might explain Dunn's family's demand for secrecy, although there's no evidence he suffered from the disease. It's also possible that Dunn was poisoned accidentally. The Cherry Pectoral he was taking contained a small amount of arsenic to calm the nerves. Then, too, in an era before refrigeration and government standards for shipping and storing food, tainted provisions were not unheard of; the very week of Dunn's death, the *New Orleans Times* ran an article titled "Beware of Herrings" about reports that containers of arsenic-laden fish had shown up on grocery shelves.

Of course, the theory that had "set tongues upon swivels" on the streets of New Orleans was that Dunn had been murdered for political reasons. Warmoth, in desperate political straits and under threat of impeachment, was a primary suspect. Another was Pinchback; having already replaced Dunn as Warmoth's leading black ally, he stood to succeed Dunn as lieutenant governor and even ascend to the office of governor if Warmoth was impeached. In a bizarre turn, another man in line for the governor's seat, House Speaker George Carter, complained the day after Dunn's death that he *too* was feeling sick, "in a way that he had never before experienced," with abdominal cramps and nausea; he confided to his physician that he feared he had been "dosed" and "foully dealt with." So certain was he that he was about to die, Carter at one point called for a close friend to help him settle his private affairs. He survived his fever and delirium, however, and soon repudiated the rumor that he and Dunn had been the target of a murderous conspiracy.

"Who delivered the fatal cup?" the Louisiana historian A. E. Perkins would ask, several years later. "It ill becomes an historian, or any other chronicler, to dignify rumor with notice. But when rumor swells to established fact, or rests upon evidence all but conclusive, then one may without hesitancy take full notice of it." The *Louisianian*, a newspaper in which Pinchback was an owner and partner, dismissed the rumors as a "hallucination" and a "chimerical notion," and scolded those "classes of people, whose minds suspicion is always haunting, and whose . . . lack of knowledge induce them to attribute every disaster . . . to some second-hand agency." But the idea that something mysterious had attended Dunn's sudden passing would linger for many years. Several informants assured Perkins, whose research took place in the 1930s when many contemporaries of Dunn's remained alive, that the murder by poison had been "an open secret," that the conspirators were known, and that all had been hushed up.

Whether Dunn was poisoned, or his natural, if untimely, removal simply agitated local suspicion, what mattered was that a man who may have had a stabilizing effect on Reconstruction in Louisiana had been cut down in his prime.

While it seems unlikely that Dunn would have been added to Grant's presidential ticket in 1872, and even a politician of Dunn's caliber would have been hard-pressed to survive the local crusade for whites' home rule in the mid-1870s, it is intriguing to consider what impact Dunn might have had. Such questions surely occupied the mourners — numbering more than fifty thousand — who gathered for his funeral, the largest such event held for an African American in the nineteenth century. They lined the curb along a dozen blocks of Canal Street and joined the mile-long procession, which slowly trailed the caisson that conveyed Dunn to his final resting place in St. Louis Cemetery.

Pinchback was cautious in his response to Dunn's sudden death. He did not, like many others, rush to the lieutenant governor's home to sit in the parlor and console the widow, although he was in prominent attendance at the funeral. He discreetly mentioned his regard for Dunn in a speech in the state senate, where, alluding to his own keen interest in civil rights, he observed that Dunn's life, and his ascent to the office of lieutenant governor, "manifested to us the truthfulness of the sublime principle established by the fathers of our country that all men are born free and equal."

Warmoth, meanwhile, was preoccupied with his own troubles. Although no official inquiry investigated whether Warmoth had anything to do with Dunn's death, it was hardly forgotten that the last objective to which the lamented lieutenant governor had devoted himself was Warmoth's impeachment. Dunn's disappearance had, for the moment, left the Customhouse men disoriented, but Warmoth recognized the need to act. Fearful of allowing Carter, the house speaker, who was popular with the Customhouse faction, to remain in line for the governorship, he moved quickly to put the loyal Pinchback in Dunn's seat. His adversaries would be far less inclined to seek impeachment if it meant making Pinchback the governor. At the same time Warmoth had to assuage his white constituency. "Pinchback . . . was a restless, ambitious man and had more than once arrayed himself against me and my policies," Warmoth later recalled. "He was a freelance and dangerous, and had to be reckoned with at all times. He was very distasteful to my conservative friends, and many of them openly condemned me for his election until they became aware of the situation and realized the political necessity for the action we had taken."

After attaining Pinchback's consent, Warmoth shrewdly convened the state senate, not the full legislature, for he knew the house was capable of starting impeachment proceedings against him. On December 6, the senate elected Pinchback as temporary presiding officer, an indication that he was their choice for lieutenant governor. Soon after the New Year, however, a resurgent Customhouse faction attacked Pinchback's elevation as illegal (Warmoth was rumored to have secured Pinchback's victory by paying $15,000 for the vote of a Customhouse-aligned senator) and again made known their aim to impeach Warmoth at the first opportunity.

The governor had executed several clever maneuvers, but the Customhouse clique responded in kind. To approve Pinchback as lieutenant governor, a senate quorum was needed. In order to make such approval impossible, eleven Republican senators and three Democrats were by nightfall sneaked aboard the federal revenue cutter *Wilderness*, which James Casey then ordered to sail offshore and keep the legislators out of sight. Marshal Packard met the vessel by launch every few days to resupply it with food, drink, and cigars, and the ship kept its human cargo secret for a full week. When Warmoth and Pinchback learned of the ruse, they complained directly to President Grant that an official U.S. vessel was being used for questionable political purposes, and Grant ordered the boat back to New Orleans. Officials who met it at the dock, however, discovered no Louisiana state senators aboard, for they had disembarked in Mississippi.

In addition to inserting Pinchback into the line of secession ahead of Speaker Carter, Warmoth sought to undermine Carter by making a show of strength against the Customhouse faction when the full legislature finally convened at the Mechanics Institute. Warmoth called up special police deputies to watch over the meetings; the opposition had federal troops brought in. Cordons of armed men jostled as they surrounded the building. At noon on January 4, 1872, federal marshals entered and arrested Warmoth and Pinchback, Police Chief Algernon S. Badger, and eighteen representatives and four senators. The arrests stemmed from alleged violations of the Ku Klux Klan Act of 1871, involving interference with the Customhouse faction's civil rights, and were dubious in any case since each side was using similar tactics to undermine the other. The apprehended men immediately made bail, but by the time they returned to the institute, Carter had expelled additional senators loyal to Warmoth and put Customhouse men in their place.

Then it was Warmoth's turn. When the legislature finished its business for the day, he told his followers not to venture too far away, and at 4:30 P.M. he used his extant powers as governor to call an extra session. All members of the legislature were immediately notified by messenger, but the Warmoth men who had stayed nearby managed to rush into the hall and, acting as fast as the Carter faction had earlier in the day, voted to wipe clean the record of the earlier arrests and strip Carter of his job as speaker of the house, installing a Warmoth man in his stead. For good measure, the body passed an official vote of confidence in Governor Warmoth.

Carter and his faction were furious, but Warmoth had the organizational advantage and gathered enough men to regain a quorum in the senate, where he and Pinchback set out at once to defeat the opposition's scheme to deny Pinchback the office of lieutenant governor. When it became apparent that only one vote was required to tip the balance, Pinchback, as the senate's presiding officer, resolved matters by simply voting for himself. This went against informal senate tradition, but by this point no element of subterfuge seemed unusual. With Warmoth in charge, Pinchback safely elected, and Carter tumbled from his leadership of the house, the Customhouse group had no choice but to return to their seats in a Warmoth-Pinchback administration. They could only pray that an authority so corruptly installed would be short-lived.

As the election of 1872 approached, friction was also apparent in the leadership of the national Republican Party. This was a matter of special concern to black Americans, whose fate was intertwined with the party's fitness and survival though they yet had little direct influence over its management. The core of the dilemma was the man who sat in the White House and who now sought a second term. President Grant, while still admired personally as a hero of the recent war, had disap-

PRESIDENT ULYSSES S. GRANT

pointed many Americans, even some within his own party. At fault were his persistent cronyism, his seemingly lax attention to important issues, and the corruption that seemed to waft about his office and his closest aides and cohorts.

Perhaps most significant for his black supporters, Grant that year had a bitter public falling-out with the Massachusetts senator Charles Sumner, who, with the death of Thaddeus Stevens in 1868, had become Congress's chief activist for securing equal rights for the freedmen. Sumner and Grant had always made a strange pair of Republican icons — Sumner a man of ideals and searing intellect who expressed himself, at times bombastically, with lofty allusions to classical literature and antiquity; Grant, a bland, silent fellow, seemingly incurious about the world, said to be most at ease when talking about horses in the company of his old army buddies. In the war, Grant had distinguished himself from other Union commanders by his unwavering determination to find and fight the enemy. But this firm steadfastedness often appeared less well suited to managing complex affairs of state. And while Grant personally steered clear of the charges of corruption that dogged the White House, the creeping sense of something rotten in his administration provided fodder for Democrats; among other things, it lent credence to the Democrats' persistent claims that Southern Republicans were guilty of malfeasance and incompetence.

The break with Sumner had begun in 1870, when the president became taken with the idea of annexing the Caribbean nation of Santo Domingo (now the Dominican Republic) for $1.5 million. The appeal of annexation was threefold: access to the island's mineral resources, a place to establish an American outpost that would inhibit European meddling in the Caribbean, and control of a nearby yet isolated locale to which American blacks might be enticed to emigrate.

Sumner, chairman of the Senate Foreign Relations Committee, was harshly critical of the idea, which seemed like unwarranted expansionism. He suspected that the clique that ran Santo Domingo, centered on its autocratic president, Buenaventura Báez, did not truly represent the best interests of its people, for, as Sumner learned, Báez had so little authority over his countrymen that U.S. warships had been dispatched to intimidate his opponents. It also came to Sumner's attention that some of Grant's aides had been busy in Santo Domingo, lining up lucrative real estate deals in anticipation of annexation, and that private speculators were thick in the plot to bring about the purchase. As for the idea of black migration, Sumner believed it wrong to export the nation's racial issues, however intractable they seemed, and feared that a government plan fostering the out-migration of American citizens would be a poor precedent for both the country's domestic initiatives and its foreign policy.

The rift between the two men was exacerbated not so much by Sumner's formal opposition to the plan but by the freighted language he used — comparing the annexation to the South's attempts to expand slavery into the west a generation earlier, alluding to Báez as "a political jockey . . . sustained in power by the government of the United States that he may betray his country." He also made some very personal attacks on Grant, whose "kingly prerogative" toward Santo Domingo he likened to the bullying tactics of the Ku Klux Klan. "Had the President been so inspired as to bestow upon the protection of Southern unionists, white and black, one-half, nay one-quarter the time, money, zeal, will, personal attention, personal effort, personal intercession which he has bestowed upon his attempt to obtain half an island in the Caribbean sea," Sumner told the Senate in March 1871, "our Southern Ku Klux would have existed in name only, while tranquility would have reigned everywhere within our borders." After loud applause, and some hissing and booing from the galleries, Sumner continued. "Now, as I desire the suppression of the Ku Klux, and as I seek the elevation of the African race, I insist that the presidential scheme, which initiates a new form of Ku Klux on the coast of St. Domingo . . . shall be arrested. I speak of that Ku Klux of which the President is the declared head, and I speak also for the African race, whom the President has trampled down." Sumner was known for insensitive and reckless words — his friend Wendell Phillips called him "a cat without smellers" — but even his supporters feared he had overreached in comparing the president of the United States to a leader of the Ku Klux Klan.

Grant felt not only abused but also double-crossed by Sumner, for he had once had reason to believe that he and the Massachusetts senator basically agreed about Santo Domingo. Sumner lived on Lafayette Square, just across from the White House, and on January 2, 1870, Grant had taken the unusual step of paying an unannounced visit to his neighbor. Sumner, at dinner with two reporters, diplomatically invited Grant inside; the ensuing discussion, which the journalists were allowed to witness, included Grant's personal appeal for Sumner to lend his influential support on the annexation question. The president likely hoped that the part of the plan meant to benefit Southern blacks would, if explained carefully, win Sumner over, and apparently he departed that night confident of Sumner's loyalty. "Mr. President," Sumner had told him at the door, "I am an administration man, and whatever you do will always find in me the most careful and candid consideration."

When Sumner began disparaging the idea in the Senate, Grant was livid, and he repaid Sumner's rebellion by launching a successful effort to relieve Sumner of his chairmanship of the Senate Foreign Relations Committee and to recall the current ambassador to Britain, John Lothrop Motley, who was the senator's close friend. Grant could not have calculated a blow to hurt Sumner more, for Sumner was immensely proud of his expertise on American foreign policy; he had traveled extensively in Europe and had dozens of important friends and contacts there.

When Grant enjoyed public favor, his ethical and diplomatic lapses were overlooked. However, when badly handled issues such as the Santo Domingo crisis emerged (the annexation plan was eventually dropped), his opponents could revive them when the moment seemed opportune. A persistent vulnerability was Grant's unashamed nepotism, for he had more than a dozen close relations on the federal payroll; and by the spring of 1872, with the election only a few months away, more questionable incidents had accrued to taint Grant's reputation.

Some said the president's troubles really began with the loss of his good friend and adviser General John A. Rawlins, a trusted military aide who later served as Grant's secretary of war. Rawlins was one of the few people whom Grant allowed to criticize him, even about his drinking. After Rawlins died of consumption in September 1869, the president's administration and policymaking seemed less sure-footed. In that very month the administration became implicated in an attempt to corner the gold market, led by the financiers Jim Fisk and Jay Gould. On September 24, a day that came to be known as Black Friday, the price of gold was driven steeply upward as insiders bought large quantities of it; then, when a satisfactory price was reached, these amounts were suddenly sold, causing the bottom of the market to drop. The Grant administration's complicity lay in suspending the sale of gold, thus further limiting the amount available and driving up the price.

An even greater disgrace was the manipulation of the Crédit Mobilier, a construction company formed to build the roadbed for the Union Pacific railroad, which would bridge America coast to coast. For an estimated $50 million in work and material, Crédit Mobilier received $73 million from the federal coffers, a $23 million windfall for its well-connected stockholders, some of whom also sat on the board of directors of the Union Pacific. When suspicions about the arrangement arose, Oakes Ames, the Massachusetts congressman who had helped create the enterprise, distributed lucrative Crédit Mobilier shares, earning as much as 80 percent interest, to well-placed individuals in Washington, including Vice President Schuyler Colfax and the Ohio congressman James Garfield. One of the lesser beneficiaries of the scandal, Garfield was said to have received $329; this figure, scribbled in the background, became a recurring motif in derisive political cartoons about the future president.

Colfax turned out to be the big fish in the net of Crédit Mobilier. An impeachment effort was launched against him, and although it fell short, it effectively denied him a second term as Grant's number two. As far as Charles Sumner was concerned, however, it wasn't Colfax alone who should be kept from another term in office; he believed President Grant had to go as well. Grant remained popular, however, particularly with blacks, and they recoiled at the attacks made against him, for any diminution of Grant's leadership would only strengthen the Democrats' chances of seizing the nation's highest office. "I may be wrong," wrote Frederick Douglass, "but I do not at present see any good reason for degrading Grant in the eyes of the American people. Personally, he is nothing to me, but as the president, the Republican President of the country, I am conscious if it can be done to hold him in all honor."

If anyone thought Sumner would similarly acknowledge reality and fall in line behind the president, they received a rude shock on the last day of May 1872, weeks before the Republican convention, when the New Englander unloaded another barrage against Grant on the floor of the Senate. For four hours he lambasted the party's standard-bearer as inept, corrupt, and ignorant of the workings of democratic government. Referring to a comparison that someone in the Senate had made between Grant and George Washington, the nation's first president, Sumner listed the current chief executive's distinctions: "first in nepotism, first in present-taking, and first in every species of diplomatic blundering." Accusing Grant of wasting his time on fast horses, expensive carriages, and vacationing at seaside resorts, he declared, "I protest against him as radically unfit for the presidential office!"

Republican loyalists were again deeply troubled by Sumner's antics, for earlier that month a breakaway faction, the Liberal Republicans, had convened in Cincinnati to declare their intention to deny Grant another term. Their pet cause was the overturning of the spoils system — the patronage and nepotism for which Grant was well known. But just as they decried the handing of lucrative offices to those who did not merit them, so did they speak out against the continuing "spoils" of war in the South — the restrictions on once-rebellious Southerners and the "favoritism" shown the freedmen. The movement's leaders — Senators Carl Schurz and Lyman Trumbull, the feminist orator Anna Dickinson, and the influential journalists Murat Halstead of the *Cincinnati Commercial*, Horace White of the *Chicago Tribune*, and E. L. Godkin of *The Nation* — opposed the Ku Klux Klan Bill and the ongoing interference of federal forces in the former Confederacy. In addition to their appeal for sectional reconciliation, they asked that greater attention be given to big business, western expansion, and immigration, as well as the labor strife then gripping the North, such as the demand for an eight-hour day. In short, they wanted the federal government to begin addressing the many ways in which the whole country, not only the South, had been transformed by the war.

The rise of the Liberal Republicans promised to make the election of 1872 the first, since the inception of the party a generation before, characterized by splits and oppositions among party members, which rendered Sumner's assaults on Grant all the more dangerous. As Sydney Howard Gay, a black New Yorker, reminded Sumner, "We believe, as Frederick Douglass has said, that 'The Republican Party is the deck; all the rest is the sea.' We do not propose to go overboard. We have been drifting astern of civilization, hanging on by a rope, for several generations, and have had enough of it." Discussing the president's alleged offenses, Gay offered that they were "infinitely small when weighed against his services to the Republic and to my race," adding, "The *nepotism* which assumes such formidable dimensions in your eyes seems in ours a small blemish when we remember the cruel *despotism* from which this man was the chosen instrument to deliver us."

South Carolina's black congressman Robert Brown Elliott, in an address honoring the tenth anniversary of emancipation in the District of Columbia, seemed to pick up on Gay's theme, warning that the Republicans could not afford the luxury of overconfidence. Speaking on the historical precariousness of social and political progress, he cautioned against faith in the belief that "revolutions never go backward." The Jews, he explained, were led from Egypt after 430 years of slavery, but within a few generations they were enslaved again by the Assyrians and Babylonians. The French staged a noble revolution, but it devoured them, so that they again had an emperor. The Declaration of Independence had vowed all men were created equal, but only eleven years later the Constitution preserved the concept of men as property. Thus, Elliott said, "It will be seen that we hold our rights by no perpetual or irrevocable charter. They are confronted by constant hazards. The enemies of the ancient Israelites, the Egyptian monarch, with his multitude of horsemen and chariots, were buried in the waters of the Red Sea, while our foes have crossed with us. Yet, perhaps by the inscrutable order of Providence, the very dangers that menace our rights are intended to admonish us to be vigilant in guarding them."

Sumner, however, proved impervious to all counsel and advice and broke with the traditional Republican Party to endorse for president the Liberal Republican candidate Horace Greeley, editor of the *New York Tribune*. As many had feared, Greeley's candidacy was also backed by the Democrats, who had not bothered to nominate a candidate of their own. A bookish, awkward-looking man with huge white whiskers and a "big round face of infantile mildness," Greeley was an unlikely choice for high office, and Sumner's endorsement only further rankled and confused the Republican faithful. Greeley had supported emancipation and was friendly to the plight of the freedmen, but his views were eccentric; he had at various times been a booster for socialism, feminism, spiritualism, and vegetarianism, and was hardly a longtime abolitionist, as Sumner now claimed. "I need not tell you, my friends, what Horace Greeley is," Wendell Phillips assured Boston's African American community. "A trimmer by nature and purpose, he has abused even an American politician's privilege of trading principles for success . . . You and I know well when *abolitionist* was a term of reproach how timidly he held up his skirts about him, careful to put a wide distance between himself and us."

WENDELL PHILLIPS

The doubts about Greeley soon were reflected in the difficult fusion of Liberal Republicans and Southern Democrats. There was no real cohesion between the two factions, no plan to win a unified campaign. The Liberals were motivated primarily by their anger with Grant over spoils, corruption, the Ku Klux Klan Act, and Santo Domingo, and the Democrats by the desire to reassert states' rights. Nor did Greeley lose any time in demonstrating his unsuitability as a candidate. In a speaking tour that swept through New England, the eastern seaboard, and the Midwest, he appeared disorganized, wandered off topic, shuffled his papers, became defensive when challenged, and overall cut a poor figure. The demanding schedule of the tour — at one point he made twenty-two speeches in a single day — no doubt also took a toll on the sixty-two-year-old candidate. By the time he limped back to the relative safety of New York, the nation's press was comparing the experience to Andy Johnson's dismal "Swing Around the Circle" of 1866 and praising President Grant as statesmanlike for wisely staying off the campaign trail.

Among the allies Grant had retained, few proved as valuable as the cartoonist for *Harper's Weekly.* After the election of 1868, Grant had credited his victory in part to "the pencil of Thomas Nast," but it was the 1872 contest that saw Nast at the height of his influence on national politics. The artist had deeply admired Abraham Lincoln, but he idolized Grant, whom he saw as a homespun American version of the Italian patriot general Giuseppe Garibaldi, whose insurrectionary campaigns across Italy Nast had covered as a young artist and reporter. The Liberal Republicans, on the other hand, he viewed as betrayers of the war's great sacrifice, and Greeley's exhortation to his Southern Democrat partners that the war's former adversaries "Clasp Hands over the Bloody Chasm" was, in Nast's view, infamous. In a series of cartoons lampooning the slogan, Nast showed Greeley physically propping up a badly wounded freedman and encouraging him to accept the greeting of a white desperado standing on the other side of a pile of black corpses; another depicted the editor extending his hand southward over the graves of the thirteen thousand Union soldiers who had perished at Andersonville.

Nast's other caricatures of the campaign itself were equally devastating: Schurz as a demented pianist-composer writing the same piece over and over; Sumner as a Roman senator breaking his bow as he tries to shoot one last arrow; Columbia using the shield of Truth to protect Grant from Liberal arrows. Nast at one point depicted Greeley as a Ku Klux Klansman, and not having an image handy of Greeley's running mate, the little-known Missouri governor B. Gratz Brown, drew him as a label stuck to Greeley's jacket, reading " . . . and Gratz Brown," perfectly lampooning Brown's insignificance and the general hopelessness of the ticket. Another cartoon presented a comatose Greeley being carried on a hospital litter, with the caption "We are on the Home Stretch." So deadly were Nast's efforts throughout the campaign that *Leslie's Illustrated,* a competitor of *Harper's,* sent abroad for a renowned cartoonist from London to possibly counter him; but the effort was futile. Horace Greeley was a target who only seemed to grow larger, Thomas Nast was at the top of his game, and it appeared certain that Ulysses S. Grant, "the Man on Horseback," would continue to ride in command.

In his new role as the lieutenant governor of Louisiana, Pinchback embarked on a speaking tour of his own that summer of 1872, visiting Maine on behalf of the Republican congressman James Blaine, who was up for reelection. It was a way for Pinchback to shore up his recognition and support among national Republicans and a chance for the party to show off one of its rising Southern stars at a time when confidence in Southern Republicanism was desperately needed. But the journey led to one of the strangest cloak-and-dagger escapades in American political history, and rather than demonstrate Pinchback's readiness for the national political stage, it revealed his provincialism.

At home in Louisiana, where both the national and state campaigns were competitive, Pinchback supported President Grant's reelection, breaking with Warmoth, who aligned himself with the Liberal Republican–Democratic ticket. This brought a sudden thaw in Pinchback's relations with the Grant-oriented Customhouse faction; the state Republican convention even offered to place his name in nomination for governor. Pinchback declined, pointing out that a black gubernatorial candidate on the ballot would only scare more white Republicans into the camp of Horace Greeley. The Republicans ultimately settled on a state ticket of William Pitt Kellogg for governor, C. C. Antoine for lieutenant governor, and Pinchback for congressman at large.

On his way back from New England, Pinchback stopped in New York City, staying at the popular Fifth Avenue Hotel, headquarters of the Republican National Committee and a favorite political gathering place where President Grant was known to keep a suite of rooms. To his surprise, Pinchback learned that one of his fellow guests was none other than Governor Warmoth, who invited his lieutenant to join him in his room that night for a late supper. Pinchback agreed, then went to meet vice presidential candidate Henry Wilson of Massachusetts, who at the Republican national convention in June had been nominated to replace Schuyler Colfax, and William E. Chandler, secretary of the Republican National Committee. When Chandler asked what the party's chances were of carrying Louisiana, Pinchback confessed they were poor. He explained that because of his state's archaic election laws, the voting process could easily be abused, almost certainly resulting in diminished black voter turnout and fewer votes recorded for Grant. So harmful were the regulations, Pinchback said, that the state legislature had recently passed new laws to reform the process and make it more difficult to commit election fraud; Warmoth, however, had refused to sign the reforms into law.

Listening to Pinchback's explanation, Chandler suddenly had an idea: since Warmoth was planning to tarry in New York awhile, and Pinchback was headed home, what if Pinchback were to hurry back to Louisiana and, invoking his status as acting governor while Warmoth was out of the state, sign the election reform bills into law? Wilson and Chandler emphasized that Louisiana's eight electoral votes might be key to a Republican victory for the national ticket and that it would be a "grand thing" if Pinchback were to undertake such a mission. The ambitious Pinchback instantly recognized an opportunity to play hero to both the party leadership and President Grant. "If the success of the Republican party is at stake, I dare do anything that will save it," declared Pinchback, and agreed to start for Louisiana at once. There was a small technicality, however — the promise Pinchback had made earlier to have dinner with Warmoth. To avoid leading the governor to suspect that his lieutenant governor had left town, Pinchback parked his trunk, with his name written on it, outside his hotel room. If Warmoth passed by, he would assume that Pinchback was still in the city and had simply become distracted and forgotten their dinner arrangement.

At first the plan worked. Pinchback failed to appear at Warmoth's room, but Warmoth thought little of it and went to bed, figuring his dinner guest had found something more entertaining to do in the big city. Pinchback had conspired with his friend Henry Corbin, the editor of the *Louisianian,* to seek out Warmoth the next day and make his apologies, explaining that Pinchback had been called away at the last minute to give a speech. But Warmoth, upon going downstairs the next morning, encountered not Corbin but another of Pinchback's friends, A. B. Harris, a state senator from Louisiana. Pinchback had lacked the time to let Harris in on the scheme, and when Warmoth inquired after Pinchback, Harris replied that he had not seen him since the prior afternoon. Warmoth, thinking this information a bit odd, thanked him and walked away.

Pinchback, meanwhile, having left New York by the first train available, had gone to Pittsburgh, then on to Cincinnati, and encountered an exasperating six-hour layover at each stop. The only consolation was that he had not heard from William Chandler back in New York, who had promised to telegraph immediately if Warmoth was seen starting toward Louisiana. Exhausted already from the trip, but fairly confident that Warmoth was not on his trail, Pinchback at last boarded a train for New Orleans, nestled into a comfortable berth, and went to sleep.

Several hours and many miles later he was awakened by someone shining a light in his eyes. "Are you Governor Pinchback?" a voice asked.

"I am that man."

"Then I am directed to inform you that there is a telegram awaiting you in the telegraph office, which the operator is directed to deliver only to you in person."

"Where are we?" Pinchback asked.

"Canton, Mississippi."

Sure that this would be a message from Chandler, Pinchback threw on some clothes and hurried off the train and into the tiny office. Once inside, it seemed to take a very long time for the operator to locate the envelope bearing the telegram. When he finally handed it over, Pinchback opened it, but there was nothing inside except a blank piece of paper. Pinchback, confused and still not fully awake, was struggling to make sense of the situation when he realized that, outside, his train was starting to move. At that moment, as one New Orleans newspaper related, "the consciousness flashed upon the sagacious Pinch that he was sold." He leapt to the office door and found it locked; he rushed to a window and tried to yank it open, but it also was closed tight. Returning to the door, he banged on it loudly enough to attract the attention of someone on the platform, but by the time he was released, the red lanterns on the rear of his train were vanishing around a bend, a quarter-mile away.

Moments after speaking with Harris in New York, Warmoth had suspected what Pinchback was up to and resolved on the spot to return to New Orleans. With the aid of Major E. A. Burke, a Louisiana campaign official and railroad executive, Warmoth arranged the fastest rail connections possible, including a special train consisting of a single car and locomotive for maximum speed, that would wait for him at Humboldt, Tennessee, just north of Memphis, and rush him to New Orleans. At Humboldt, Warmoth learned that Pinchback was twelve hours ahead of him. When the engineer warned Warmoth that the locomotive could do no better than forty-five miles per hour, the governor ordered him to improve on that as best he could, saying his aides were dispatching telegrams to stations down the line to clear the track. Warmoth's men also sent a telegram to the Canton depot, arranging for the deception that would lure Pinchback out of his slumber, and with that, Warmoth's one-car express shot out of Humboldt and headed south. Late the next morning, as it rumbled into the Canton station, Pinchback was waiting on the platform.

"Well, governor," Pinchback greeted Warmoth, "your lucky star is still in the ascendant."

"Hello, Pinch, old fellow." Warmoth smiled. "What are you doing here?"

"I am on my way home," Pinchback replied, "and if you have no objection, I will go on with you the balance of your journey."

Racing, usually involving horses or steamboats, had long been a special passion in Louisiana, and the hometown papers found the contest between the carpetbag governor and his troublesome lieutenant irresistible; by the time the train bearing the two politicians entered New Orleans, hundreds of the curious lined the tracks. The press evaluated this strange "sporting event" in detail, not missing the interesting fact that Warmoth had, in addition to catching Pinchback, set a new record of sixty-two hours for covering the distance between New York City and New Orleans. The *Louisianian* worried that locking Pinchback in a strange office in the middle of the night and forcing him to search in panic for an escape constituted "scandalous and disgraceful measures," but the Democratic *Daily Picayune* was more astute, inquiring, "What have the people of Louisiana done, how have they sunk so low, that they should be subjected to the shame . . . of having a Lieutenant Governor who, by an arrangement with the official partisans of President Grant . . . rushes back from a remote extremity of the Union to seize the state executive office?" As for Pinchback, he seems to have weathered what for any other man might have been a fatal humiliation by considering it from a gambler's perspective. Warmoth, Pinchback conceded, had simply "taken the big trick," and he did not bother chastising himself for having misplayed the hand.

President Grant was reelected by a wide margin that fall, carrying Louisiana, although because of alleged voting irregularities, the state's ballot results in the presidential race were ultimately discarded. In the state gubernatorial election, between the Republican William Pitt Kellogg and the Democrat John McEnery, both Republicans and Democrats claimed victory, with the Warmoth-appointed returning board — a nominally bipartisan panel that threw out fraudulent votes and issued an official statement certifying election results — splitting initially into two rival factions, then three.

Ironically, shortly after the 1872 vote, Warmoth signed into law the very reform bills that had motivated the train race between him and Pinchback; this allowed the governor to abolish the divided returning boards and appoint a single new one. To no one's surprise, the new board announced that the Liberal Republican–Democratic ticket had won the gubernatorial contest, making McEnery the new governor. The Republicans, however, refused to go quietly and remained adamant that Kellogg was the winner. In response, Warmoth, who backed McEnery, called an extra session of the legislature, but before his representatives could certify the election results, Marshal Stephen Packard got federal officers to take possession of the Mechanics Institute where the legislature was to meet. Under this protection, the Republicans gathered and heard Lieutenant Governor Pinchback report that Warmoth, apparently with the backing of certain Democrats as well as Republicans, "had visited him the night before and offered him $50,000 and the appointment of any number of offices if he would organize the legislature according to [Warmoth's] direction." Pinchback said he had replied negatively to the offer, for he was "determined to do my duty to my state, party, and race." Warmoth denied the accusation, contending that the best proof of his innocence was the fact that Pinchback was "not in the habit of resisting such temptations."

Warmoth soon had other problems, however, for with the election still unresolved, the house convened and immediately voted by a wide majority to impeach him. The senate would have to conduct a trial to determine his guilt, but by law the filing of an impeachment brief suspended the governor from office, thus making Pinchback the acting governor of Louisiana — the first African American governor of a state in the country's history.

The ouster of the hated Warmoth was cause for celebration, and Pinchback's supporters were ecstatic. A crowd instantly surrounded him, shouting and offering congratulations, and escorted him to the office of the secretary of state to take the oath of office. Once this formality was complete, the mob swept him along to the governor's office itself, which inconveniently was found to be locked. Someone had to climb in through an unlocked window in order to open the door from the inside. Pinchback, followed by dozens of friends and backers, then marched into the office and, to further cheers, made himself comfortable in Warmoth's chair. In the midst of the revelry, it occurred to Pinchback's aides that they needed at once to send a telegram to inform Washington of what had occurred in Louisiana; several minutes were required to clear the room of well-wishers.

The Democrats immediately denounced Pinchback as a usurper, and an infuriated Warmoth launched various legal and not-so-legal strategies to unseat the "wrong-doer and trespasser" who occupied the executive office. On December 12, however, the telegram that Pinchback had been nervously awaiting arrived. George H. Williams, the attorney general of the United States, informed him

> LET IT BE UNDERSTOOD THAT YOU ARE RECOGNIZED BY THE PRESIDENT AS THE LAWFUL EXECUTIVE OF LOUISIANA, AND THAT THE BODY ASSEMBLED AT MECHANICS' INSTITUTE IS THE LAWFUL LEGISLATURE OF THE STATE . . .

Of course, with Warmoth under the cloud of impeachment and Pinchback able to serve as governor only until the results of the McEnery-Kellogg contest were decided, the two former allies were now simply stalking horses for the actual candidates, each fighting to hold the Louisiana statehouse for their own faction. It was an important struggle, likely to determine the future of Reconstruction in the state, and Washington and the nation watched it closely.

In Pinchback's brief tenure as governor of Louisiana — he served from December 9, 1872, until January 13, 1873 — he took on an increasingly urgent task: the stabilization of law and order in the outlying parishes. As a first step, he sought to neutralize the state's white militia, which was hostile to him, by replacing its leadership with the former Confederate general James Longstreet, whom Warmoth had earlier appointed to head the Metropolitan Police. Unfortunately, though Pinchback hoped the general's credentials would help bring the militia into line, the opposite occurred, for its members widely spurned Longstreet as a scalawag and a traitor. Longstreet was despised because of his political apostasy, but his reputation had also come under assault from fellow ex-Confederates for his wartime action. He had once been friend and confidant to General Robert E. Lee, and he had initially emerged from the Civil War with a reputation for gallantry. Following Lee's death in 1870, however, other members of Lee's staff, most notably Jubal A. Early and William N. Pendleton, began an effort to enshrine Lee as an American hero. This entailed blaming someone else for Lee's worst strategic decision of the war, the deadly headlong rush toward the Union lines at the Battle of Gettysburg known as Pickett's Charge, named after George E. Pickett, the Confederate general who led it. Longstreet, who had differed with Lee over strategy at Gettysburg (and now, as a scalawag, made a likely fall guy), was accused of procrastination in getting his troops ready for battle, thus subverting Lee's plans. Since Gettysburg was seen retrospectively as a pivotal loss for the Confederacy, Longstreet's alleged misdeeds there, and his perceived backstabbing of Lee, had earned him, in the eyes of his critics, excommunication from the Southern cause.

Pinchback encountered another reversal when he sought federal help in disarming hostile whites who opposed Republican authority in rural Louisiana. President Grant informed Pinchback that federal troops could not possibly take part in such a potentially warlike and incendiary campaign. Frustrated that his best efforts were being stymied, Pinchback unleashed a severe denunciation of the McEnery forces' election tactics and their claims to power, accusing them of having "disenfranchised thousands of voters by a denial of registration and thousands more by concealing the places at which the votes were to be cast . . . substituting boxes full of Democratic votes for boxes that were full of Republican votes, [and] . . . through the Governor [Warmoth] attempting to make a purely partisan board of canvassers to count the same and manipulate the final returns." He attacked their efforts to construct a parallel state authority, characterizing them as "foiled and defeated leaders of a minority" who "now propose, through a man pretending to be Governor-elect [McEnery], and a Legislature pretending to be elected, to organize and operate a government in direct conflict with and in violation of the dignity and peace of the existing government of the State of Louisiana and of the United States."

McEnery loyalists were furious to be scolded publicly by a man they respected as little as Pinchback, but the acting governor was not going to be around much longer to deal with the consequences. On January 13, 1873, in dual ceremonies, both John McEnery and William Pitt Kellogg were inaugurated as "governor" of Louisiana. The next day the Kellogg legislature, the one whose existence was sanctioned by President Grant, elected Pinchback to the U.S. Senate.

Somewhere the gods of chance were smiling, for this time Pinch had played his hand expertly. Having eschewed his relationship with Warmoth in the nick of time, he'd managed to ally with and effectively support the ascendant faction in the state, one that was willing to repay his loyalty with an extremely prestigious prize. Seventy-two hours later, his credentials personally signed by Governor Kellogg, U.S. senator-elect P.B.S. Pinchback — in a supremely exultant moment — boarded a train for Washington.

CHAPTER 7

THE COLFAX MASSACRE

HORACE GREELEY MADE an interesting protest candidate in the presidential race of 1872, but he lacked both the requisite stature and vigor to pose a serious challenge to the incumbent. Indeed, his exertions in the campaign proved not only futile but final. Exhausted, haunted by the recent death of his wife, plagued by insomnia, "nervous prostration," and "inflammation of the brain," unable even to resume his editorial duties, he passed away on November 29, only weeks after the election. Greeley's friends claimed it had been Thomas Nast's incessant ridicule that killed him, pointing out that *Harper's* had cruelly published the cartoon depicting the candidate being carted off on a stretcher the very day Greeley's wife had expired.

The Greeley campaign, like many a third-party effort, however, did succeed even as it failed, for it revealed numerous cracks in the edifice of Northern opinion regarding Reconstruction and an eagerness for sectional reconciliation. Greeley's admonishment to his fellow citizens, North and South, to "Clasp Hands over the Bloody Chasm," had, despite Nast's mockery, captured the growing mood, even as the candidate himself had been spurned as the agent for that reunion. The result was that not only Democrats, but also Republicans, now felt freer to openly disapprove of continued federal interference in the South. With the war won, the building-block protections of Reconstruction in place, crowned by the Fifteenth Amendment, it was time, as Greeley had advised, for the former slaves to "Root, hog, or die!"

Impatience with the freedmen's problems found their outlet in one of the era's seminal books, *The Prostrate State: South Carolina Under Negro Government,* by James Shepherd Pike. Although not published until 1874, it was based on a lengthy article by the author, "A State in Ruins," that ran in Greeley's *New York Tribune* in March 1872, and on several subsequent articles Pike filed with the paper after he traveled to the South in January 1873. "Without going into details, it is enough to say that the men who lead and manage the legislature and the state government are thieves and miscreants," Pike announced in the 1872 piece, well before visiting South Carolina. When, ten months later, Pike had a chance to observe the legislature in Columbia at work, his worst fears were confirmed. "Here, then, is the outcome, the ripe, perfected fruit of the boasted civilization of the South, after two hundred years of experience. It lies prostrate in the dust, ruled over by this strange conglomerate, gathered from the ranks of its own servile population. It is the spectacle of a society suddenly turned bottom-side up." That former slaves now held positions of authority over whites struck the author as preposterous. "Seven years ago these men were raising corn and cotton under the whip of the overseer," he complained. "Today they are raising points of order and questions of privilege." He had little trouble explaining the allegations of corruption in South Carolina's government. "Sambo takes naturally to steal, for he is used to it. It was his notorious weakness in slavery . . . The only way he ever had to possess himself of anything, was to steal it from somebody else." One could feel some sympathy for the impulse behind the Ku Klux Klan, insisted Pike; Northerners would no doubt react similarly if forced to share South Carolina's dilemma.

Pike's publishers made much of the fact that the writer had once been aligned with the antislavery cause and had served President Lincoln as minister to the Netherlands. Here was a credentialed Republican whose eyes had at last opened to reality. "Years ago, when abolition was a forlorn hope and its open advocates under the ban, Mr. Pike was one of their leaders," ran a typical comment in the *Savannah Republican*. "He shared in their struggles, he enjoyed their triumphs, and has had no cause, either of interest or ambition, to feel sympathetic toward the Southern people. But he is a man of convictions, and an outspoken one, and the unutterable horror and loathing, surprise and indignation, with which the actual condition of misgovernment and oppression at the South have inspired him, cannot be silenced."

Pike's book, widely lauded as a clear-eyed appraisal, was, however, not all it seemed; both political and personal motives lay behind the author's much-noted change of heart. As a Liberal Republican of the Greeley camp, his criticism of South Carolina was, in a sense, a colorfully written indictment of the Reconstruction policies associated with President Grant; and one of his key sources for information about the state was Senator William Sprague, a Rhode Island millionaire who had been severely disappointed by some financial investments in South Carolina and blamed the state's political culture for his losses. Sprague's financial reversals became, in the author's hands, a larger story of disillusionment about Southern whites trapped in the North's Reconstruction dream-gone-bad, making the "inept" black and white Republicans the easy scapegoats. The book's journalistic credibility was even further compromised by its repetition of many of the points the author had published in the *Tribune* before he had even visited the South, and his sources appear to be almost exclusively people with conservative views of the situation.

That a book so lacking in objectivity could become popular and even well regarded probably had less to do with Pike's gifts as a writer than with the country's shifting mood. The *Literary World* hailed the author's lack of racial prejudice, while *The Nation*, in citing the book's importance, echoed Pike's conclusion that the intelligence of most blacks was "slightly above the level of animals." (When Thomas Wentworth Higginson, the New Englander who had led black South Carolina troops, wrote a letter of protest to *The Nation*, the editor, E. L. Godkin, admitted that his "animals" characterization had been too broad but insisted it still applied to the blacks of the Sea Islands.) Even the judicious *Atlantic Monthly* leapt eagerly into Pike's corner, praising the book and lamenting the fact that its publication had been made necessary by "the ignorant negro rulers" of South Carolina's "sable despotism," who had "carried into their legislation and administration the spirit of the servile raid on the plantation hen-roost and smoke house." Henry Ward Beecher, who knew better, nonetheless accepted at face value Pike's claims that criminals ran South Carolina and that "the ignorant and unprincipled classes," meaning black people, kept them in office. Beecher went so far as to suggest that South Carolina's mulatto population was alarmed because "unmixed Africans" were gaining too much authority — perhaps a dig at Congressman Robert Brown Elliott, but in any case a disappointing loss of perspective by an antislavery man of Beecher's experience.

Pike's success at crystallizing the feelings and fears of so many in the postwar era has led one commentator to term his book "the 'Uncle Tom's Cabin' of the Southern Redemption." Perhaps the real tragedy was that *The Prostrate State* not only was influential during its own time but also became a respected source for many early historians of Reconstruction, helping perpetuate Americans' misunderstanding of the period.

Other writers laboring under Pike's sway would offer similar deprecatory views of Southern state governments, hearing "chuckles, guffaws, [and] the noisy crackling of peanuts" among South Carolina's state representatives while noting that sheer bedlam reigned in the "monkey house" that passed for the Republican-dominated legislature of Louisiana, where "amendments [are] offered that are too obscene to print, followed by shouts of glee." Black legislators were accused of buying expensive cuspidors and chandeliers, abusing their railroad passes, even of stealing office furniture. At restaurants near Southern statehouses, it was alleged, they supped and drank at the people's expense, then departed, their pockets loaded with mints.

Did black politicians really behave this way, or was something else disturbing their white observers? Perhaps it was simple resentment of the changes Reconstruction had imposed, an inchoate rage at the spectacle of Governor Moses of South Carolina, for example, besmirching the glory of his antebellum mansion by opening the doors to "a ring-streaked, striped and speckled" crowd that "rolled up gaily to [the] ancient gateways," wherein the governor deigned to mix with "negroes and low whites puffing cigarettes." Perhaps it was indignation at the fact that Robert Brown Elliott dared reside in a fashionable cottage with "a pretty, rose-tinted light mulatto" (who happened to be his wife) and that black legislators dined in once-exclusive clubs or stood in groups, chatting and bantering on public sidewalks. To many whites such scenes were not just intimidating but also profoundly disturbing; certainly they looked so to the *New York Herald* correspondent who described South Carolina's capital city of Columbia, with its gatherings of black politicians, as "an out-of-door penitentiary . . . where the members browse voluntarily, like the animals in the Zoological Garden."

A particular source of irritation were scenes, no doubt generously enlarged by the imagination, of black women — former "serving-maids" — sitting and taking tea "under the venerable trees" of fine Southern estates, putting on airs, seemingly rubbing their former white mistresses' noses in their new status. In Columbia, the aristocratic sisters of the Rollin family — the eldest, Frances, was married to the politician William Whipper — were so obvious in their enjoyment of the good life that they attracted attention and raised concern. These "colored courtesans swept into furniture emporiums, silk trains rustling in their wake, and gave orders for 'committee rooms.'" They "rode in fine carriages through the streets" and maintained a stylish salon, which its detractors dubbed "Republican Headquarters." There, it was alleged, "mingling white and dusky statesmen wove the destinies of the old Commonwealth."

Gilbert Haven, writing in the *Independent,* was one of the few who took issue with Pike's impressions of South Carolina. He acknowledged that political corruption existed but pointed to several optimistic results of Republican governance — new schools and new road construction (of major significance in a rural state), while noting that whites had worked to suppress the black vote in an effort "to win at the ballot box what was lost with the cannon." Haven advised that Northerners continue to support the South Carolina experiment, warning that "if she is assailed and deserted by her friends, and left to the mercy of her malignant and steadfast foes, she may succumb, and then comes chaos and black night again to all this Southern land." He conceded, however, that "we have only half swallowed this pill of Reconstruction, and we shall spit it up as soon as possible."

According to Oken Edet Uya, a biographer of Robert Smalls, "the charge of corruption and extravagance" in South Carolina was "just a cloak" for whites' real agenda — the restoration of white rule. Smalls himself noted, with irony, that often the very blacks who rose above power's easy temptations were most likely to be targeted by resentful whites. And whatever corruption existed in the Republican leadership, it surely paled in comparison to the far more gross illegalities — voter fraud, intimidation, and violence — practiced by those opposing Reconstruction's reforms.

General Rufus Saxton, recalling the optimism that had attended the announcement of the Emancipation Proclamation in Port Royal, wrote a warm letter to Smalls in December 1871 to say that while he believed that the often-heard charges of Republican corruption in South Carolina were overstated, he knew that "where there is so much smoke there must be some fire." He warned his old friend that "the Republicans of South Carolina must see to it that the state is redeemed by the election of only true and honest men to office in the future." Alluding to Smalls's wartime heroism, Saxton wrote,

> When you brought the *Planter* out from Charleston . . . you knew where lay the torpedo on the right, and the shoals and rocks on the left, you knew where the channel was deep and sailed in it; you did not tarry long before the guns of Fort Moultrie or Sumter, but straight to your purpose, to the beacon of liberty ahead . . .
>
> The ship of state of South Carolina is now in stormy waters. The

> rocks and shoals, torpedoes and hostile guns are ignorance, immorality, dishonesty, and corruption in high places. The beacon lights ahead are honesty, intelligence, the school house and the church.

Keep the helm of the ship of state "steady toward these," Saxton suggested, "and soon the ship shall glide gently by the breakers into the peaceful waters of freedom."

Smalls, much moved by Saxton's words, had the letter published and read it himself before a gathering in Beaufort. He also read to the audience his reply to Saxton, which echoed the general's imagery. "As well as I knew the beacon lights in the time of the *Planter,* I know the beacon lights now, and the channel that leads to honesty, virtue, purity and intelligence, and I trust that I may ever be found working with those who are anxious to guide the ship of state [from] dark and troubled waters." He then asked for and received three cheers for General Saxton, and he vowed before his listeners to safeguard honest government in South Carolina.

In part, Smalls did this by campaigning vigorously in 1874 for the election of Daniel Chamberlain as governor. If one of the early ideals of Reconstruction had ever gained traction — that Northerners would help the postwar South develop a "New England model" of town-meeting democracy — Dan Chamberlain, a native New Englander, Yale man, classics scholar, and onetime follower of Wendell Phillips, would have been the person to implement it. Once in office he impressed even the state's conservatives with his sincerity and dedication to reform. When Smalls challenged the views of James S. Pike and his brethren, he could cite the good example of Chamberlain, mentioning that even the conservative *Charleston News & Courier* consistently praised the governor's performance.

It was perhaps inevitable, however, given his prominence and the lingering contempt for his wartime accomplishments, that Smalls himself would face charges of wrongdoing. Sent to Congress in December 1874 (with his seventeen-year-old daughter Elizabeth, a recent graduate of a New England finishing school, as his secretary), "the Boat Thief" lost no time in becoming an outspoken advocate for his constituency in the Sea Islands, obtaining funds to develop the harbor and waterfront at Port Royal. His celebrity as a war hero, his efforts in the state's constitutional convention, his much-publicized work to enhance life in his beloved Beaufort, and his control of patronage had won him a devoted following in the low country. But the popularity among black Sea Islanders of a man whom many whites still vehemently resented fueled the effort to destroy him. In 1877, after the Democrats seized control of the South Carolina statehouse, he was accused of having received, earlier in the decade, $5,000 as a beneficiary of a bogus printing-expense claim filed with the state legislature. The charges relied on the testimony of Josephus Woodruff, who as public printer of the state had allegedly robbed South Carolina of $250,000, fled to Pennsylvania, then been extradited and offered leniency in exchange for "information" against Smalls and other officials. The question of Woodruff's credibility hardly troubled the Democrats as they savored what one Northern headline termed "The Downfall of Smalls." There was some hand-wringing among Northern papers, which lamented that a man so recently cheered for nobly throwing off the bonds of slavery had fallen into corrupt ways; the *Hartford Times* speculated that the federal government had erred in praising and rewarding Smalls for stealing the *Planter,* since it had clearly given him the idea that crime paid.

The real objective of the prosecution became clear, however, when a man named Cochrane, the head of an investigating committee appointed by the legislature, visited the black congressman. "Smalls, you had better resign," Cochrane warned, according to an account Smalls later provided.

"Resign what?" Smalls demanded.

"Resign your seat in Congress."

"What," Smalls asked, "the seat the people elected me to?"

"Yes, you had better resign, because if you don't they are going to convict you."

"I don't believe that, sir," Smalls insisted. "I am innocent and they cannot do it."

"Well," said Cochrane, "bear in mind that these men have got the Court, they have got the jury, and an indictment is a conviction."

A prominent newspaper editor from Aiken County, a Mr. Drayton, also urged Smalls to comply. "Smalls, we don't want to harm you. We know you were kind to our people just after the surrender . . . We want this government, and we must have it. If you will vacate your office we will pay you $10,000 for your two years' salary."

Smalls, always at his best when pinned down by enemy fire, told Drayton defiantly, "Sir, if you want me to resign my position, you must call meetings all over the Congressional District and get the people who elected me to pass resolutions requiring me to resign, and then you can have the office without a penny. Otherwise I would suffer myself to go to the penitentiary and rot before I resign an office that I was elected to on a trumped-up charge against me for the purpose of making me resign."

As Cochrane had threatened, Smalls was convicted and sentenced to three years in prison, but he spent only three days in jail because, on the advice of some fellow congressmen, he had appealed his case to the U.S. Supreme Court. In the meantime, the Democrats, unable to win Smalls's resignation, found a way to make something of his predicament. A deal was struck between the state of South Carolina and Washington: the case against Smalls would be dropped in return for the federal government's abandonment of several cases pending against whites for election fraud and Ku Kluxing. Smalls was furious when he learned of the arrangement but was pardoned in full.

The positive response to both Horace Greeley's urgings for reconciliation and the writings of James Pike were indicators of a shifting national mood regarding Reconstruction and the South's growing desperation to be free of the policy's constraints. When P.B.S. Pinchback returned to Louisiana from President Grant's second inaugural in March 1873, he was grieved to find his state still paralyzed by dual claims to control of the statehouse, a conflict that had led the Senate in Washington to postpone a ruling on his own status as senator-elect. Although Grant had authorized the administration of William Pitt Kellogg, the Democratic followers of John McEnery had formed a shadow government and had begun commissioning their own public officials.

This impossible predicament soon turned deadly. In April 1873 it triggered the Reconstruction period's most lethal violence, which took place at a remote hamlet in central Louisiana known as Colfax Courthouse. One of the many tragic results of this bloodletting would be a seminal Supreme Court decision to reverse a constitutional guarantee to protect the freedmen.

Colfax lay in Grant Parish on the banks of the Red River, about 350 miles north of New Orleans. The parish, with a racially mixed population of several thousand, had in 1869 been cut out of Rapides and Winn Parishes by the legislature as part of an effort to diminish Democratic authority in the Louisiana countryside; the parish was named for the U.S. president. Similarly, the name of the courthouse village, a former sugar plantation with a handful of buildings and about seventy residents, honored Vice President Colfax. The two-story courthouse itself was a converted stable.

The Democrats C. C. Nash and Alphonse Cazabat had been "certified" as the parish's sheriff and judge by the McEnery forces. However, on March 23, 1873, several Kellogg loyalists, led by William Ward and R. C. Register, who were black, and Daniel Shaw, who was white, took over the courthouse and ejected the McEnery men. Shaw, the new sheriff, instructed local black residents to defend the building from Democratic reprisals. Ward and two other black army veterans — Levi Allen and a Pennsylvanian named E. H. Flowers — began drilling men from the neighborhood in an impromptu militia, although most were armed only with antiquated weapons and some were forced to parade with a hoe or pitchfork in lieu of a rifle. They also busied themselves in constructing earthworks, anticipating that Nash and Cazabat would attempt to retake the courthouse.

Half-hearted efforts were made at some sort of negotiated settlement, but rumor-mongering and fears of a widespread Republican-led black insurrection were rampant. Some freedmen allegedly warned a white settler that "they intended to go into the country, and kill from the cradle up to old age"; another white reported that blacks planned to massacre all the white men in the neighborhood and then "seduce" all the white women, in order to create a "new race" of people. Whites particularly distrusted Ward, a state legislator whose deeply scarred face made him resemble an outlaw; it was widely believed he had been involved in the unsolved murder of a white farmer named Jeff Yawn in 1871. Even the Kellogg legislature had once admonished Ward for "ruffianism," perhaps because he had falsely promised his black constituents that the governor intended to give them their former masters' lands.

One of the worst accusations, however, was made against Ward's friend, E. H. Flowers. The "little sleek black negro," it was told, had broken into the home of the prominent local Democrat Judge William R. Rutland, ransacked the place, then pried the lid off a coffin holding the corpse of one of the judge's children, a little girl who had drowned years earlier and whose remains Rutland was planning to re-inter, and dumped it face-down on the ground. Then, with two jugs of Rutland's wine under his arm, he had departed to spend "the night in riot and debauch."

The story of Flowers's invasion of Rutland's home and his ghoulish act was probably exaggerated. As at lynchings, where lurid descriptions of alleged sexual outrage against virginal Southern maidens stoked mobs to fury, here the rumors of murderous black depravity fed anxiety among white parish residents, helping to drum up the sizable citizens' army that eventually challenged Republican control of the courthouse.

"To get up a body of men for the unwarrantable attack on the peaceable and inoffensive citizens of Colfax and vicinity," the *New York Times* noted, "it was necessary to resort to perfidy, and every conceivable and infamous lie was industriously circulated through the pine woods to accomplish the purpose."

Any hope of a peaceful resolution likely ended when Judge Rutland himself traveled to New Orleans to apply for help from federal troops or state militia but was rebuffed by Governor Kellogg and General Longstreet. Kellogg apparently shared Rutland's request with the federal commander William H. Emory, but like Kellogg and Longstreet, Emory was not convinced the standoff in Grant Parish merited a military response. He knew that because the parish was in a fairly remote part of Louisiana, it would be difficult (as well as politically unpopular) to send and maintain troops there. It's also likely that Kellogg and the others wanted to believe that the contingent of blacks now guarding the courthouse would be up to the job of defending it; black self-sufficiency in such matters was almost always viewed as preferable to outside intervention. In the meantime, troubling news arrived. Jesse McKinney, a black farmer and father of several children, had been murdered by a group of mounted whites near Bayou Darro, three miles east of Colfax, as he was at work building a fence on his property. What provocation, if any, he had committed was unknown. Not long afterward, gunshots were exchanged near a place called Boggy Bayou, and a white man named Jack O'Quinn, "of Kuklux notoriety," was shot out of the saddle and killed.

By Easter Sunday, April 13, the deposed sheriff, C. C. Nash, had gathered from Grant and neighboring parishes about 150 armed whites who assured him that they were "not afraid to die for white supremacy." He then requested and obtained a parley with Levi Allen, the black man left in command of the courthouse by Ward, Register, and Flowers, who had themselves gone to New Orleans to meet with the Kellogg government.

"What do you depend upon doing in there?" Nash asked Allen.

"We are doing nothing more than we were before, standing still as we've been standing," Allen replied.

Insisted Nash, "We want that courthouse."

"We're going to stand where we are until we get United States troops, or some assistance."

"Then go in there and say to your people that I advise them to get out of there."

When Allen again said that his force would hold their ground, Nash extended a thirty-minute truce so that the blacks could send women and children away from the line of fire.

Then Nash brought his men closer to the courthouse, and the two sides began a general exchange of shotgun and rifle fire, which continued with little effect for almost three hours. The blacks had prepared well, building solid defensive breastworks, but their shotguns lacked enough range to hurt the whites. Combat was at first so leisurely that the black defenders had to step up onto their works, showing themselves, in order to draw any white fire; with equal nonchalance, several whites at one point broke off the siege for a meal and a few hands of cards.

During the days leading up to the battle, the blacks had improvised two cannon out of old stovepipes by stopping up the ends, drilling touchholes in each, and mounting them on carriages. These homemade weapons used makeshift ammunition such as pieces of chain, bolts, and nails. The blacks had fired these randomly in the preceding days, frightening nearby residents, although it's not entirely certain whether they were functioning on Easter Sunday. The whites, however, knowing of their existence, countered the opposing "artillery" by appropriating a small cannon from the steamboat *John T. Moore,* which was tied up at a nearby landing.

A breakthrough in the siege came when Ezekiel B. Powell, one of the whites, scouted the blacks' position and suggested to his comrades that they flank the courthouse by having a party quietly maneuver down the river and climb up to an opening in the breastworks. As Powell was new to the area, some were unsure whether to act on his idea, but C. A. Duplissey spoke on his behalf, saying, "This man is an old Confederate soldier, and he has been down examining things, and [he] says if we can take them trenches we can drive them out."

Powell's party carried the small steamboat cannon with them, and seizing a vantage point where the defenders' lines opened, they began pouring steady fire at the enemy and the courthouse itself. As some blacks retreated, the courthouse suddenly burst into flames. Isaiah Atkins, a black survivor of the attack, later said that Nash's men had captured a handful of black defenders and coerced one, a man named Pinckney Chambers, to hold a pine torch to the end of the building; others would claim that the whites ignited the structure; it was also alleged that blacks set the courthouse ablaze to spite those trying to recapture it. Amid the smoke, two white flags of surrender appeared at the windows. "Don't shoot, we are whipped!" cried someone inside. But shots continued to come from the courthouse, and two whites fell. James Hadnot, a Democratic politician, was wounded, shot through the lower abdomen, and another white, Sidney Harris, was also hit. The attackers, infuriated by the false surrender and seeing Hadnot fall (blacks disputed this version, claiming there had been no trick surrender and that Hadnot was shot by his own men), swarmed the black defenders as they fled the burning courthouse and tried to escape toward the river; several blacks were killed. Many "were ridden down in the open fields and shot . . . [and] those lying wounded on the court house square were pinned to the ground by bayonets." Others tried to get away through a cypress pond; while wading through water up to the waist, they were shot from behind. One witness recalled that "by the time the job was finished it looked to me like any one could have walked on dead negroes almost an acre big."

The wound to Jim Hadnot, which proved mortal, evidently at least partly inspired the atrocities committed by the whites. After many blacks were slaughtered in the initial assault, an even less defensible act took place: black prisoners held in a nearby cotton field were led away in pairs under the ruse that they were being to be taken to a nearby town, but then instead they were summarily executed. "I heard Luke Hadnot [the brother of the white man expected to die] say, 'I can take five,' and five men stepped out. Luke lined them up and his old gun went off, and he killed all five of them with two shots. Then it was like popcorn in a skillet. They killed those forty-eight."

"It is our opinion," stated an account by a deputy U.S. marshal who arrived soon afterward, "that when forced by the fire to leave the courthouse [the blacks] were shot down without mercy. The position and condition of many of the bodies go far to prove this." According to the official,

> under the warehouse, between the courthouse and the river, were the dead bodies of six colored men, who had evidently gone under for concealment, and were there shot like dogs. Many were shot in the back of the head and neck. One man still lay with his hands clasped in supplication; the face of another was completely flattened by blows from a broken stock of a double-barreled gun, lying on the ground near him . . . Many of them had their brains literally blown out.

When passengers aboard the steamboat *Southwestern,* happening to pass Colfax the next day, learned that it was possible to tour a "battle ground" with dozens of dead bodies still on it, many disembarked and ascended the bluff to the courthouse area. R. G. Hill, one such passenger, later explained that a young, heavily armed white man had come aboard to ask that the *Southwestern* convey the two wounded whites, Hadnot and Harris, downriver to Alexandria, at the same time telling the passengers

> that if we wanted to see dead niggers, here was a chance . . . Almost as soon as we got to the top of the landing, sure enough, we began to stumble on them, most of them lying on their faces, and, as I could see, by the dim light of the lanterns, riddled with bullets. One poor wretch, a stalwart looking fellow, had been in the burning courthouse, and as he ran out with his clothes on fire, had been shot. His clothes to his waist were all burnt off, and he was literally broiled . . . I counted eighteen of the misguided darkies, and was informed that they were not one-fourth of the number killed.

Walking among the prostrate forms on the ground, the visitors were alarmed to find one that still seemed alive. Revolvers were quickly drawn, and a white man said, "I will shoot that black dog." But when the body was turned over, it was evident the man was already dead. Smoke from the courthouse, which was still on fire, and the stench of burning flesh from the littered corpses, Hill reported, soon drove the tourists back to their boat.

In New Orleans, Kellogg and Emory were staggered by reports of the apparent magnitude of the violence. Now faced with the necessity of moving troops into the area, they met resistance from several steamboat operators, who refused to provide passage on the grounds that visibly aiding federal forces would harm their business. Although the Metropolitan Police from New Orleans and at least one federal officer made it to Colfax within a few days of the battle, the first contingent of a hundred federal troops did not arrive at Colfax until April 21, eight days later. The commanding officer, Captain Jacob H. Smith, listened to various accounts of the affair, including that of C. C. Nash, and concluded that most of the victims had been gunned down after surrendering.

Scholarly and official estimates of how many blacks died at Colfax have always varied widely, from sixty to as many as two hundred. Calculating the death toll was complicated by the fact that many bodies were badly burned, others were lost in the river or in the cypress pond, and some were carried away by friends or relatives. Because many black families were too frightened to claim their dead, dozens of the victims were interred in mass graves — the very trenches they themselves had dug as fortifications to defend the courthouse.

Pinchback traveled upriver to the scene of the massacre and was overwhelmed by the magnitude of the devastation. In his brief tenure as Louisiana's governor a few months earlier, he had tried unsuccessfully to arrange for either General Longstreet or federal forces to establish control of outlying districts like Grant Parish, and it saddened him to see the terrible consequences of that policy's failure. Back in New Orleans he joined concerned black citizens at an emotional meeting, where resolutions of protest were drafted and comparisons made to the wartime slaughter at Fort Pillow, where Confederates under the command of General Nathan Bedford Forrest notoriously massacred surrendering black troops. Pinchback, upon reaching the podium, recited from Shakespeare ("Give me no help in lamentation. / I am not barren to bring forth complaints. / All springs reduce their currents to mine eyes, / That I, being governed by the watery moon, / May send forth plenteous tears to drown the world") and urged the gathering to disregard press accounts that had characterized the events at Colfax as a "race war." It was, he insisted, a confrontation between citizens defending a legitimate Republican state government outpost and bitter Southern men determined to carry Louisiana backward into the past. Refuting the notion that the blacks had been the aggressors, Pinchback noted, "My knowledge of their temperament and disposition teaches me that they would not be guilty of the wrong alleged, for the obvious reason that they know too well what would be the inevitable result, owing to the immense disparity between the numbers of white and colored people in this country."

Pinchback condemned the fact that the massacre would surely intimidate blacks and keep them from voting, and he returned to criticisms he had, as governor, leveled at the McEnery faction — about white Louisianians' unwillingness to accept the changes the war had brought and the weakness of moderate whites who might exercise a controlling influence on the most vicious white element. "A large number of white people feel just as sad as we do," he told his colored listeners, "but unfortunately for them they dare not come out and express their opinion. They are ground down in a slavery worse than ours was. They are slaves to a mistaken public opinion."

Whereas the Memphis and New Orleans riots of 1866 and the Klan violence of 1870–71 had motivated Congress to take action that would safeguard the freedmen, it was the strange fate of the Colfax massacre to spark a federal judicial decision that inhibited that protection. As ever, the Justice Department was faced with the awkward challenge of prosecuting mob violence and murder with statutes designed to protect civil rights. The United States initially indicted ninety-eight whites under the Enforcement Acts, which outlawed conspiracies to deny such rights, but ultimately brought only nine men to trial. Despite graphic testimony from witnesses, one defendant was acquitted; the trials of the remaining eight ended with a hung jury. In a second trial, the defendant William Cruikshank and two others were convicted; these verdicts were appealed to the Supreme Court.

In a landmark decision, *United States v. Cruikshank* (1876), the Supreme Court voted unanimously that the indictments were improper, ruling that the right of citizens to assemble was protected as a federal right only if they did so for the purpose of petitioning Congress or for anything else directly connected with the federal government; any other assembly, such as that of the black defenders at Colfax, was not protected by federal law. Echoing the court's actions three years earlier in the *Slaughterhouse Cases,* the ruling in *Cruikshank* further stipulated that guarantees of due process and equal protection promulgated in the Fourteenth Amendment restricted only the states and offered no protection regarding actions involving individuals. Essentially, this meant that though states could not deprive citizens of life, liberty, property, or equal rights without due process of law, the federal government had no jurisdiction when private citizens, such as a mob or a vigilante army, did so. The part of the indictment that invoked the Enforcement Acts was thrown out on the grounds that there was no allegation that the victims' race had anything to do with the assault on the courthouse.

"This racist and morally opaque decision," argues the historian Ted Tunnell, "reduced the Fourteenth Amendment and the Force Acts to meaningless verbiage as far as the civil rights of Negroes were concerned." After all, notes the scholar Eugene Gressman, "it was private action, not state action, that had caused so much of the postwar bloodshed and atrocities in the South . . . It was private action, not state action, that had been the prime motivation for all the toil and debates that produced the Fourteenth Amendment and the surrounding legislation."

When the case against the perpetrators of the Colfax massacre proved unprosecutable, the highest court in the land concluded that the problem lay in the overreaching nature of the statutes violated; it then proceeded to render those laws meaningless. By gutting the Enforcements Acts and placing private actions beyond the reach of the federal judiciary, the decision left Southern blacks in a position of greatly increased vulnerability.

The only silver lining in the aftermath of the crime was the broadly shared sense of shame and violation; the nation, as had Pinchback and others, reacted strongly to the killings in Louisiana. The blaring *New York Times* headline "A Second Fort Pillow: Surrendered Negroes Butchered in Cold Blood" was typical of the outcry. "The war between the races, so constantly carried on in this distracted state," noted the paper's editorial, "has seldom presented such a horrifying instance as this burning of a courthouse filled with human beings . . . the terrible scenes enacted at Colfax Courthouse . . . appear to be more like the work of fiends than that of civilized men in a Christian country."

America, it seemed, still cared about the inequities Reconstruction aimed to alleviate; the question was how long it would honor that commitment.

CHAPTER 8

CAPSTONE OF THE RECONSTRUCTED REPUBLIC

SENATOR CHARLES SUMNER'S BREAK with President Grant in 1872 was a troubling development in the eyes of most black Americans, and not solely because of its detriment to the electoral fortunes of the Republican Party. Sumner was the primary force behind a controversial piece of legislation then making its way through Congress, a civil rights act (called the Supplementary Civil Rights Act, for it would expand on those rights granted by the Civil Rights Act of 1866) that would for the first time guarantee citizens everywhere equal access to public accommodations. First introduced by Sumner in May 1870, and reintroduced twice in 1871, the bill stipulated that no public inns or places of public amusement for which a license was needed, no railroads or stage lines, charities or cemeteries, no churches or jury boxes, and no schools supported at public expense should make any distinction as to admission on account of race, color, or previous condition of servitude.

This initiative was an effort to finalize the work of Reconstruction by establishing civil rights not simply at the ballot box but in the public sphere where Americans lived their daily lives. As South Carolina congressman Alonzo Ransier said in support of the bill, "We cannot . . . educate our children, defend our lives and property in the courts, receive the comforts provided in our common conveyances . . . and, in short, engage in 'the pursuit of happiness' as rational beings, when we are circumscribed within the narrowest possible limits on every hand, disowned, spit upon, and outraged in a thousand ways."

Sumner found authority for his civil rights law in some inspired

CHARLES SUMNER

places — the Thirteenth Amendment, of course, which had abolished slavery and, by interpretation, all "badges of slavery" (in Sumner's view, discrimination that publicly set blacks apart as an inferior class was surely a "badge of slavery"), but also the Declaration of Independence and the Sermon on the Mount, sources "earlier in time, loftier, more majestic, more sublime in character and principle" than the Constitution itself. Sumner's conviction that the Declaration of Independence's "pledge of universal human equality was as much a part of the public law of the land as the Constitution" was a faith he had in part adopted from former president John Quincy Adams, who, in old age, received Sumner frequently at his home outside Boston. Since the U.S. Constitution was famously evasive on the subjects of race and slavery, Sumner saw the Declaration as a more valuable and useful instrument in relating America's core principles to the problem of racial equality. He considered the Constitution, drafted in Philadelphia in 1787, to be a pragmatic, "earthly body," while the Declaration, penned by Jefferson at the very moment of America's creation in 1776, was "the soul" of the United States.

The federal government could not watch over each and every interaction between white and black Americans, enforcing equality on an individual basis, but Sumner hoped that by authorizing penalties for those who discriminated and offering legal recourse to their victims, the nation would ultimately choose compliance, and race relations would evolve favorably. This formalizing of equal rights under the law was, for Sumner, "the subject of subjects," a matter that would "not admit of postponement or hesitation"; he saw his bill as "the capstone of the Reconstructed Republic" and a fitting culmination to his life's work.

That effort had begun as early as 1849, when he was the attorney in a case seeking change in Boston's segregated schools. Sumner lent his representation pro bono to the plaintiff, a five-year-old child named Sarah Roberts, at the request of her father, Benjamin, who was a local black leader. The complaint in *Sarah Roberts v. the City of Boston* was that the city's policy of segregating pupils by race defied more general Massachusetts standards of equality. The chief primary school used by black children in the city was in disrepair and far inferior to the schools white children attended, yet spokesmen for the schools insisted that the difference was "one which the Almighty has seen fit to establish, and it is founded deep in the physical, mental, and moral natures of the two races. No legislation, no social customs, can efface [it]." Sumner alleged that the school committee had no right to this position, as the Massachusetts Constitution itself had never made such a distinction. To assert the concept of equality before the law, he alluded to the Declaration of Independence, the writings of the eighteenth-century French *philosophes,* and the Bible. The Boston schools, in defying the most fundamental ideals of equality, he said, were "condemned by Christianity."

In arguing the Roberts case, Sumner described both the inferior physical character of the Negro school Sarah Roberts was made to attend and the destructive psychological and sociological effect of segregation on children — both blacks and whites. "The whites themselves are injured by the separation. Nursed in the sentiment of caste, receiving it with the earliest food of knowledge, they are unable to eradicate it from their natures." Later, Sumner would observe that segregation "cannot fail to have a depressing effect on the mind of colored children, fostering the idea in them and others that they are not as good as other children," anticipating by a century the principal rationale used to defeat legalized segregation in America's public schools in 1954 and, by extension, all Jim Crow restrictions. Sumner's brief, however, was rejected by the Massachusetts Supreme Court, which deemed it extravagant and overly reliant on abstract philosophical arguments.

A generation later, the school clause in Sumner's Supplementary Civil Rights legislation helped spark the first national dialogue on the subject, pitting the ideals of equality in education and the eradication of racial prejudice against concerns over states' rights and forced "social equality." Most people declared the nation unprepared for mixed education and were inclined to treat the question of the clause's legitimacy as not only an abstraction but also possibly dangerous, for the certain result of such a mandate would be that whites would desert public schools. Reports had already emerged from the South that Sumner's planned legislation was inhibiting school construction projects. But such warnings emanated not solely from below the Mason-Dixon Line; the *New York Times* also recommended that the matter be tabled until greater national progress in race relations was achieved. Even many black spokesmen, who agreed with Sumner that separation likely had a hurtful effect on black children, were willing for now to surrender the concept of equality in the interest of keeping education itself available.

Sumner remained steadfast, however, his very public leadership on the issue bringing to his desk each day fresh testimony from black Americans relating their inability to enjoy equal access in public life. "How is it possible for one who has never been denied any of these privileges," Sarah Thompson of Memphis asked Sumner in early 1872, "to express so fully and clearly the profound sense of humiliation which we feel?" Thompson explained that she and her four young children had been barred from a railroad waiting room in Louisville:

> To keep ourselves warm, we were obliged to walk to and fro in front of the depot in the sleet and while my dear children were suffering and crying from the severity of the cold. In faltering accents one of them inquired of me, "Why is this, ma? What have we done? Why can't we go in there and warm just like others?" Oh, sir, words are inadequate to express my feelings at that time. How my very soul burned with indignation. We had committed no offense. Our only crime was that of being American negroes.

Charlotte Forten, the black Philadelphia missionary teacher to the Sea Islands, assured Sumner, "I think only those who have suffered deeply from the cruel, cruel prejudice in this country can know how it embitters as well as depresses, how it gradually weakens and undermines one's faith in human nature — and, oh, how that loss of faith darkens the world, as nothing else can."

Even many Southern whites saw the inherent injustice. "For God's sake urge your Civil Rights Bill with all the vehemence of your soul," a man from Tennessee implored Sumner. "Yesterday I bought a R.R. ticket in company with four colored men. They paid the same price for theirs . . . but I . . . because my skin is white, was furnished a nice, soft, quishened [sic] seat in an elegant car; they were forced to occupy 'plank seats' in a filthy box . . . In no sense of the word can this be right." The peripatetic Gilbert Haven was aghast at the conditions the railroads created. "The cars into which [blacks] are thrust are hideous pens," he wrote of a journey by rail in the South, where a fellow clergyman "of the offensive hue" was forced to ride "in a dirty, ill-ventilated, close-packed, unswept car, as mean as mean could be. Yet he was paying first-class fare and two score of seats in my clean car were vacant. But for him to have asked to occupy one would have brought a revolver against his head."

One of the most disturbing testimonials came from Howard University, where it was reported that two black visitors — William White, a student from Fisk University in Nashville, and James Rapier (later a congressman from Alabama) — were treated so poorly by the railroad that White was made seriously ill. Even though he and Rapier held first-class tickets, White reported, "from Nashville to Chattanooga I was compelled to ride in the car next to the baggage car, where smoking, drinking, and obscene conversation were carried on continually by low whites . . . At stations for meals I could get nothing to eat . . . At Chattanooga where I arrived at about 5 o'clock in the morning I was not permitted to enter the sitting room." White and Rapier were forced to stand on the dark station platform in the cold until their connecting train departed at 8 A.M. On that train they were assigned to one half of the baggage car, where the door was left open to the elements because there was a corpse being shipped among the baggage. G. W. Mitchell of Howard remarked, as he passed along White's complaint to Sumner, "This is simply an illustration of what is occurring daily, and to which all are subjected in whose veins flows a perceptible amount of African blood."

In late 1872 the civil rights cause received a boost from an unusual source. John A. Coleman, a white businessman from Providence, Rhode Island, described in an article in the *Atlantic Monthly* how, after attempting to use a New Haven–New York City ticket for travel in the opposite direction, he had been arrested and bodily removed from a train. In "The Fight of a Man with a Railroad," Coleman accused the conductor of pettiness in refusing to honor his ticket, but the larger issue his story highlighted, and with which most readers could identify, was the routine insensitivity of railroad authorities and even the occasional bullying of passengers. This, Coleman wrote, was a particular failing of American railroads, and even an embarrassment, in light of the more civilized treatment accorded European rail travelers. The *New National Era* seized on Coleman's arrest and harsh treatment as valuable testimony; for once, a prominent white person had been victimized by the same "tyranny of railroad corporations" that affiicted black people every day. The *Era* pointed out that unlike Coleman, who had his case heard several times in court and had the satisfaction of venting his anger in the pages of a national magazine, blacks had no choice but to suffer in intimidated silence.

Black congressmen themselves were not immune to prejudice on the rails. "Here am I, a member of your honorable body, representing one

"IF I COME BY WAY OF LOUISVILLE OR CHATTANOOGA, I AM TREATED NOT AS AN AMERICAN CITIZEN, BUT AS A BRUTE."

of the largest and wealthiest districts in the state of Mississippi," John Roy Lynch of Natchez told the House,

> and yet when I leave my home to come to the capital of the nation . . . to participate with you in making laws for the government of this great republic . . . if I come by way of Louisville or Chattanooga, I am treated not as an American citizen, but as a brute. Forced to occupy a filthy smoking-car both night and day, with drunkards, gamblers, and criminals; and for what? Not that I am unable or unwilling to pay my way; not that I am obnoxious in my personal appearance or disrespectful in my conduct; but simply because I happen to be of a darker complexion. If this treatment was confined to persons of our own sex, we could possibly afford to endure it. But such is not the case. Our wives and our daughters, our sisters and our mothers, are subjected to the same insults and to the same uncivilized treatment.

Joseph Rainey told a story of being physically removed from a hotel dining room in Suffolk, Virginia; another black representative asserted that while traveling from Boston to Washington he would need to "carry a basket of bread and wine with him" or go hungry. Robert Brown Elliott, never one to endure a slight, remonstrated with the proprietor when refused a meal at the café in the train station at Wilmington, North Carolina. "[Elliott] was compelled to leave the restaurant or have a fight for it," lawmaker Richard "Daddy" Cain told Congress. "He showed fight . . . and got his dinner." The next time Elliott and Cain passed through Wilmington, they tried to avoid another scene by having food and coffee brought to them on the train, but the train master refused, accusing the congressmen of "putting on airs." Elliott later won some measure of revenge at a restaurant in Washington, where a young white man complained to the management about his presence at a nearby table. Elliott made inquiries, learned the fellow clerked in the Treasury Department, and arranged to have him fired.

Along with railroads, hotels were also an embattled civil rights terrain. Would whites consent to sit in lobbies alongside blacks and take meals with them, or stay in hotel rooms, use bathrooms, and sleep in beds that blacks had occupied? The answer, generally, was a resounding "No!" Hotel managers warned that they would shut down their businesses completely if legislators continued to "push on the dusky column." Even the great Frederick Douglass had been refused dinner at the Planter's House in St. Louis. Staying at the hotel in 1871 while on a lecture tour, he had gone out one afternoon to do some visiting. When he returned for dinner, he was challenged at the door to the dining room and asked if he was a registered guest; he replied that he was, but when the registration book was consulted, it was found that his name had been scratched out. Douglass demanded an explanation, but the hotel offered none. The *New National Era* indignantly cited Douglass's reputation and the fact that he was welcome in some of the world's most dignified salons and lecture halls, and lamented the fact that "Mr. Douglass's experience . . . is the experience of thousands of his race all over the country." To stamp out "the accursed prejudice which deprives colored men of the common courtesies of civilized intercourse," the paper called for "legislation as will teach snobbery everywhere that men who were good enough to fight to save the life of the Republic are also good enough to enjoy the common rights belonging to citizens."

The reports of Douglass's mistreatment prompted P.B.S. Pinchback's *Louisianian* to make a disheartening association, observing that "the roasting of a poor negro lad with kerosene at Port Jervis a few days ago by two or three white brutes, is but the crystallization of a sentiment which in less defined form shut Frederick Douglass from a hotel in St. Louis . . . and turns up its fastidious nose at the negro in street car, the church, or the theatre."

St. Louis also offered harsh treatment to Congressman Lynch, in what would prove an embarrassing gaffe. Beginning in 1869, town fathers there had held occasional "capital removal conventions" as part of a public relations effort to lobby the rest of the country on the idea of relocating the nation's capital from Washington to St. Louis. Lynch, as a member of Congress, was invited to town to be wined and dined and persuaded on the matter by local boosters. But, arriving late at night, he was turned away from the Planter's House, where Mississippi's other congressmen were staying, and he wound up wandering the streets in the middle of the night with his luggage, unable to find a hotel. The incident made the newspapers the next day, much to the chagrin of the host committee. The nation's capital, of course, remained in Washington.

More than that of other public accommodations, the potential integration of hotels and restaurants produced the greatest alarm over "social equality," which whites feared would lead to the eventual amalgamation of America's distinctive racial groups. "Social equality" was one of the most highly charged terms in late-nineteenth-century America, but a misleading "bugbear," as Alonzo Ransier remarked. Attaining equal rights in the public sphere did not imply that blacks and whites would be forced into social intimacy; only whites opposed to civil rights laws insisted on that interpretation. Sumner himself stressed that his proposed law would not regulate social interactions. Any person could freely choose his friends and associates and do so within the walls of his private dwelling, but "he cannot appropriate the sidewalk to his own exclusive use, driving into the gutter all whose skin is less white than his own."

There was of course great hypocrisy to the charge that "social equality" was being forced on the South. As civil rights advocates never failed to point out, whites had for decades permitted close relations with blacks as servants and had indulged them as sexual partners and blood kin. "Why this fear of the negro since he has been a freedman," asked Rainey, "when in the past he was almost a household god, gamboling and playing with the children of his old master? And occasionally it was plain to be seen that there was a strong family resemblance between them." Thomas Cardozo, Mississippi's light-skinned superintendent of education, liked to say he had no trouble understanding what social equality was — he saw "a practical demonstration" of it "whenever I look in the glass."

Charles Sumner envisioned his civil rights act as a final phase in the evolution of national authority that had begun with the Civil War itself, in which the North denied the Confederate states their right to secede. The advance had continued with the Emancipation Proclamation, the Thirteenth Amendment, the Civil Rights Bill of 1866, the Reconstruction Acts, the Fourteenth and Fifteenth Amendments, and the Enforcement Acts — documents that presumed the constitutional duty of the federal government to establish and defend the status of residents of the United States. Sumner's legislation also relied, ironically, on a widely disgraced antebellum law — the Fugitive Slave Act of 1850, which had criminalized the abetting of slave runaways or the failure to return them to their owners. In practice, the Fugitive Slave Act caused few runaway slaves to be returned to their Southern owners, and its implication that all Americans, including Northerners, were now to act as "slave catchers" only served to agitate public opinion in the run-up to civil war. But postwar civil rights advocates like Sumner found a technical advantage to be made of this heinous law, for it had required the involvement of federal officers and judges. By making it incumbent upon the national government to use its branches and agencies to defend a slaveholder's right to his property, the law created a precedent for the idea that an individual's constitutional rights could be not only recognized but actively enforced by Congress.

Sumner was often criticized for bringing too much emotion to the law and ignoring its intricacies, although what really separated him from his congressional brethren was his greater willingness to shape existing laws to meet present social needs, an idea that would not fully engage the American legal establishment for another half-century. One of Sumner's heroes was the eminent New England jurist Joseph Story, who taught that although common law deserved respect for being based on precedent, it was not to be regarded as infallible; wise lawmakers looked not solely backward for guidance, but around them as well. When a fellow senator protested to Sumner, "I have sworn to support the Constitution, which, as I understand, binds me *not* to vote for anything that I believe to be unconstitutional," Sumner replied, "I have *also* sworn to support the Constitution, and it binds me to vote for anything for human rights."

Sumner believed that Congress's duty lay in the enactment of legislation it deemed necessary and that outstanding issues of constitutionality should be left to the courts. Most men in Congress, however, many of whom were lawyers, considered themselves expert on the subject of the Constitution and did not agree that such responsibility should be passed along. They raised numerous objections to his proposed legislation — that enforcing equality in churches was unconstitutional, that the government could not impose rules of conduct on privately owned businesses, and that blacks and whites actually preferred a degree of separation in many of their activities.

The latter point was integral to Southern representatives' perennial argument that race relations were a matter of intimate concern primarily to Southerners, since it was in their section that most black Americans lived. Sumner's crusade for civil rights, in their view, was intrusive. "I am not here to be dictated to by the Senator from Massachusetts," James Lusk Alcorn of Mississippi declaimed on the Senate floor.

> He fights the battles of the colored people from afar off, at a safe distance. I have fought their battles in a hand-to-hand conflict. I hold my place here under their authority . . . I speak for both races; I speak that their friendly relations may not be thus unwisely disturbed. I, sir, whose childhood was nursed in the lap of the negro; who in his boyhood shared every playground with the negro . . . I, sir, have no snobbish prejudice against the colored people.

Rhetoric similar to Alcorn's echoed across the corridor in the House chamber as well, prompting Joseph Rainey to demand,

> If the Democrats are such staunch friends of the negro, why is it that when propositions are offered here and elsewhere looking to the elevation of the colored race . . . the Democrats array themselves in unbroken phalanx, and vote against every such measure? You, gentlemen of that side of the House, have voted against all the recent amendments to the Constitution, and the laws enforcing the same. Why do you do it? I answer, because those measures had a tendency to give to the poor negro his just rights, and because they proposed to knock off his shackles and give him freedom of speech, freedom of action, and the opportunity of education, that he might elevate himself to the dignity of manhood. Now you come to us and say that you are our best friends. We would that we could look upon you as such.

Had Sumner faced only the predictable Southern hostility to his bill, his task might have been easier; but numerous moderate Republicans opposed him as well, most notably the Illinois senator Lyman Trumbull, one of the main architects of the Civil Rights Act of 1866 and the Fourteenth Amendment, as well as Lot Morrill of Maine. Both men thought Sumner's bill overstepped congressional authority — that there was no basis for the federal government to influence the treatment an individual received in a public accommodation; and they challenged specifically its reliance on the Declaration of Independence as a source of legislative powers. Sumner grew impatient with what he saw as Morrill's insistence on the strictest of constitutional interpretations. "He [Morrill] finds no power for anything unless it be distinctly written in positive precise words. He cannot read between the lines; he cannot apply a generous principle which will coordinate everything there in harmony with the Declaration of Independence." Trumbull believed that "in regard to the rights that belong to the individual as man and as a freeman under the Constitution . . . I think we had a right to pass the Civil Rights Bill [of 1866] . . . but I think we went to the verge of constitutional authority." Sumner, in Senate session, accused Trumbull of standing in the way of equal rights.

"Equal rights in what and for what?" Trumbull demanded.

"Equal rights for the colored race."

"Has not a colored man the same right to go anywhere that I have?" Trumbull asked.

"He is exposed to insult wherever he goes," Sumner replied.

"And so is the white man."

Sumner frowned. "My friend ought not to say that. He knows a white man may travel from one end of the country to another, and he is exposed to no insult on account of his color."

"I do not know of any right by law that a white man has to travel that a colored man has not," Trumbull insisted. "And if [Sumner] will show me where any white man has any right to travel that a colored man has not, I will vote with him to correct it. There is perfect equality now."

"Perfect equality!" Sumner snorted. "Will the Senator listen to Mr. Frederick Douglass as he reports his experiences? I wish the Senator would listen to him reporting his experience on his recent visit to New Orleans; how he was insulted on all the railroads, shut out from equal rights." Douglass, describing his journey, had written in the *Independent* of being made to sit in "a second class car, amid filth and smoke," and of being denied refreshments at depots en route.

"I ask the Senator," Alcorn of Mississippi interjected, querying Sumner, "was Mr. Douglass insulted anywhere in the South?"

"He was."

"Whereabouts?"

"At what precise stopping-place, I know not."

"I say that colored men can travel in Mississippi and do travel in Mississippi in first-class cars," Alcorn asserted, "and that there is no insult offered them anywhere."

"Then Mississippi is in a happier condition than I had supposed," Sumner retorted.

"Then," Alcorn proposed, "let your legislation come up to the line and leave Mississippi alone."

"We must legislate generally," Sumner said, exasperated. "There must be one law for every part of the country, the law of equal rights.

Perhaps the bill's chief technical difficulty was that it sought to guarantee equal treatment in public accommodations that, unlike voting, had never been made explicit by previous legislation. And unlike a formal right, such as voting, daily interactions between the races regarding public accommodations were governed by deeply ingrained patterns of prejudice that would be hard to police and perhaps impossible to reform. "Equality," C. Vann Woodward observes, "was a far more revolutionary aim than freedom." Securing equal rights in everyday life "involved many more relationships than those between master and slave . . . It involved such unpredictable and biased people as hotel clerks, railroad conductors, steamboat stewards, theater ushers, real estate agents, and policemen."

To those who questioned whether the government could proscribe private actions, Sumner replied that certain institutions, although in private hands, were nonetheless part of the public weal. Schools, supported by tax dollars and regulated by law, were certainly public, not private, entities; similarly, hotels, railroads, and theaters were licensed and subject to public regulation. "A hotel is a legal institution . . . a railroad corporation is also a legal institution," he insisted. "So is a theater, and all that my bill proposes is that those who enjoy the benefits of law shall treat those who come to them with equality . . . Whoever seeks the benefit of the law, as the owners and lessees of theaters do, as the common carriers do, as hotelkeepers do, must show equality."

Was Lyman Trumbull correct in suggesting that a bill requiring equal rights in the private interactions of citizens went too far? This was the core question, for even if such laws were morally right, even if Congress should be allowed to enact them, how could they be successfully enforced? The uncertainty raised some ancillary questions: Where exactly did the battle for black America's rights end? Did it *ever* end? In 1865 William Lloyd Garrison, believing that with the adoption of the Thirteenth Amendment the longstanding goal of the American Anti-Slavery Society was attained, had tried to disband that organization. Wendell Phillips and Frederick Douglass resisted, however. They believed, as Lincoln had observed of his Emancipation Proclamation, "We are like whalers who have been long on chase. We have at last got the harpoon into the monster, but we must now look how we steer, or, with one 'flop' of his tail, he will send us all into eternity." A significant number of abolitionists were willing to view the Thirteenth Amendment as only the first victory in what would be a long crusade to win true equality for the freedmen, and they remained committed to that struggle, even after the Constitution was amended further to provide citizenship rights and the franchise. The discrimination a black American encountered in his or her daily experience, however difficult to address, could not be swept to the margins; it must be confronted. "While a colored gentleman is . . . unable to obtain admission to the public hotels; while state-rooms are refused in our steamboats, and berths refused in our sleeping-cars, on account of color," Douglass wrote, "the negro is not abolished as a degraded caste."

There was one group of American reformers, once closely tied to the abolition movement, whose active support for new legislation Charles Sumner could no longer take for granted. Many women's rights leaders had become alienated from the civil rights cause, upset that Congress would again immerse itself in the subject of rights for the freedmen, for whom so much had been done already, when their own demands had received scant attention.

Women had organized as supporters of the abolition movement as early as the 1840s, not only because it was the morally right thing to do, but because its aims mirrored their own aspirations for equal rights. They had felt slighted, however, by the Fourteenth and Fifteenth Amendments' transformation of black men (but not black and white women) into citizens and voters. As for the Supplementary Civil Rights Bill, Susan B. Anthony, president of the National Woman Suffrage Association, would offer no more than qualified praise. "I only long for the hour when you shall turn your constitutional law and logic in the direction of women citizens," she wrote to Sumner, encouraging him to speak "as grandly for Equal Rights to *all women* as you have to *all men*," for surely "the majesty of the U.S. Constitution" was meant "to protect *all* of its citizens." She warned him that because "women are absolutely

SUSAN B. ANTHONY

nothing in Republican minds today, as were the Negroes with Democrats twenty years ago . . . I will give no aid or comfort to any pact that fails to recognize the equal rights of women citizens."

This rift between women's rights advocates and civil rights activists — "one of the saddest divorces in American history," the historian William McFeely has termed it — was painful for both sides. Women were understandably angry to be sidelined in the postwar push for freedmen's rights. But civil rights supporters, facing an uphill battle of their own, came to resent the complaints from those they once considered natural allies. It was an embarrassing quandary for which many abolitionists had no good resolution; philosophically they knew the women were right; however, they could not help but take offense when women expressed indignation that "illiterate black men" would be able to vote before educated white women. Garrison and Sumner, Douglass and Phillips, while supporting women's suffrage in principle, denied its alleged urgency. The nation, they believed, had been conditioned by the war's sacrifice to accept the empowerment of the freedmen but was not prepared to endorse women as voters; Phillips insisted that burdening the one good cause with the other would resemble putting too many bundles in a small boat, sinking all of them together.

At the end of the Civil War, Anthony and her colleague Elizabeth Cady Stanton had sought actively to join the two causes. Anthony told audiences that the time was right to remake the government so that it would serve all Americans, white and black, male and female. Her argument went to the heart of the question of what Reconstruction was and should be. Was it to be solely a means of elevating the former slaves to citizenship or a grand retooling of society at large? "We have fairly boosted the Negro over our heads, and now we had better begin to remember that self-preservation is the first law of nature," declared Stanton in May 1866. "Some say, 'Be still, wait, this is the negro's hour.' But I believe this is the hour for everybody to do the best thing for reconstruction. A vote based on intelligence and education for black and white man and woman — this is what we need . . . and [we will] press in through the constitutional door the moment it is open for the admission of Sambo." Douglass, flinching at her use of a racial slur, cautioned the women that while the vote was an important goal for all who did not possess it, for blacks it was absolutely essential, a matter of life and death.

Phillips, in a meeting with Anthony and the editor Theodore Tilton, suggested that the vote for women would likely have to wait another generation. When Tilton concurred with Phillips, Anthony seethed. "I would rather cut off my right hand than ask for the ballot for the black man and not for women!" Stanton displayed similar obstinacy at a larger gathering in New York City in May 1867, explaining that she did not look forward to having black elected officials who were themselves "degraded [and] oppressed" create the laws for her and other women; if women were not to be enfranchised, the qualification for voting should be made an educational one. Otherwise, all the newly created black voters would be men hardly qualified to have authority in public affairs, resembling instead an "incoming tide of ignorance, poverty, and vice." That same year a campaign in Kansas to amend the state constitution to allow both black and women's suffrage drew Anthony and Stanton to the state, but the crusade stalled, newspapers refused to treat it seriously, and a wealthy but wayward male sympathizer, George Francis Train, unleashed nasty words about black people, which the press, and other feminists, denounced. The result was that neither black nor women's suffrage passed the Kansas referendum, confirming fears back east that the two causes could not be combined.

Black elected officials such as Robert Brown Elliott, Hiram Revels, and P.B.S. Pinchback — examples of the "inferior" men Stanton complained of, whom Reconstruction had catapulted to political prominence — were of course unfairly maligned by her words. They were hardly ignorant or illiterate, and in fact they had tended to support women's suffrage and expanded rights for women. In South Carolina, the black attorney William Whipper had been a consistent champion for the cause. According to the historian Benjamin Quarles, some black women had actually managed to vote in some South Carolina districts in the election of 1870; two years later, Republicans there had proposed a female suffrage amendment, provoking a debate so contentious that punches were exchanged in the aisles of the state legislature.

Nationally, Stanton and Anthony had rallied against adoption of the

Fourteenth Amendment, objecting to the fact that, for the first time, it introduced the word *male* into the Constitution; they also opposed ratification of the Fifteenth Amendment. Stanton mocked the Republican Party for "establishing an aristocracy of sex on this continent" and appealed to the nation's most base racial anxieties by suggesting that if "the slaves of yesterday . . . in whose eyes woman is simply the being of man's lust" became legislators, the result would be "fearful outrages" on womanhood, especially in the Southern states.

> Think of "Patrick" and "Sambo" and "Hans" and "Yung Tung," who do not know the difference between a monarchy and a republic, who cannot read the Declaration of Independence or Webster's spelling book, making laws for . . . the daughters of Adams and Jefferson . . . women of wealth and education . . . Shall American statesmen, claiming to be liberal, so amend their constitutions as to make their wives and mothers the political inferiors of unlettered and unwashed ditch-diggers, bootblacks, butchers and barbers, fresh from the slave plantations of the South?

Frederick Douglass, one of the first men in America of either race to support women's suffrage, eventually could stand no more of Stanton's crude allusions. "I must say that I do not see how anyone can pretend that there is the same urgency in giving the ballot to woman as to the negro," he said.

> When women, because they are women, are hunted down through the cities of New York and New Orleans; when they are dragged from their houses and hung upon lampposts; when their children are torn from their arms and their brains dashed out upon the pavement; when they are objects of insult and outrage at every turn; when they are in danger of having their homes burnt down over their heads; when their children are not allowed to enter schools, then they will have an urgency to obtain the ballot equal to our own.

In May 1872 Charles Sumner adopted a new strategy for his civil rights bill, linking it with amnesty legislation intended to benefit those remaining Southern whites still legally stigmatized by their actions in the war, with the exception of former high-ranking Confederate officials. Specifically, it offered to give them back the right to hold elective office — it was thus politically momentous, as it would undoubtedly create more viable Democratic candidates in the South and potentially diminish Republican control of Congress. Representatives such as Robert Brown Elliott, Joseph Rainey, and Robert De Large had been generous in supporting the restoration of rights to former Confederates, although after years of Ku Klux Klan violence and other extreme Southern resistance, they had become more cautious. But they nonetheless concurred with Sumner's approach. "We have open and frank hearts toward those who were our former oppressors and taskmasters," Rainey told Congress. "But . . . we would say to those gentlemen on the other side that there is another class of citizens in the country, who have certain rights and immunities which they would like you, sirs, to remember and respect . . . I implore you, give support to the Civil Rights Bill, which we have been asking at your hand, lo! these many days."

It was becoming evident to all that Sumner's health, never good since the physical assault on him in the Senate in 1856, was beginning to fail. This would likely be his last campaign of spirited advocacy for the bill; to carry Sumner's initiative across the goal line, Southern black Congressmen would have to show leadership, alone and in alliance with other Republicans. This was entirely fitting, of course, for Sumner himself had often used their example in his arguments, pointing to the absurd fact that they sat as equals next to white men in the highest body of the land, yet could not sit with ordinary white citizens in a theater or on a train.

Sumner, staunch in his own beliefs and the righteousness of his cause, apparently neglected to consider what small legislative compromises he might offer to make his bill more acceptable to Congress. He may not have fully appreciated how much the support for Reconstruction's egalitarianism had eroded in recent years, or how much his own standing on Capitol Hill had suffered as a result of his attacks on President Grant. His demand that churches and cemeteries be integrated was particularly troublesome to many, the inclusion of schools was controversial, and without sufficient leeway for adjustment in these areas, his pairing of civil rights for freedmen with amnesty for former rebels seemed to his fellow lawmakers an unattractive bargain.

The bill was voted on and rejected twice that spring, but days after a second defeat on the joined bill, when Sumner was away from the floor, Senate Republicans used parliamentary tricks to break the attached bills apart and, in an all-night session, rushed through passage of the amnesty provision, while the civil rights bill was sidelined and not even addressed.

Learning of the treachery, Sumner hurried to the Senate the next morning. "I sound the cry!" he bellowed. "The rights of the colored race have been sacrificed in this chamber where the Republican Party has a large majority — that party by its history, its traditions, and all its professions bound to their vindication. Sir, I sound the cry! Let it go forth that the sacrifice has been perpetrated." Such heated talk was for the most part wasted on his colleagues. Exhausted from being in session all night, having listened, patiently, numerous times to arguments over civil rights, they informed him they were in no mood to be lectured at, especially in tones of indignation and self-righteousness. Sumner had, for the moment, been outfoxed: the amnesty measure had gone through, while civil rights were left behind.

But civil rights remained for Sumner the ultimate cause — quite literally so. Upon his passing in March 1874 he admonished the faithful gathered at his bedside, "You must take care of the civil rights bill — my bill, the civil rights bill; *don't let it fail!*"

By early 1874, even before Sumner's death, it had fallen to Robert Brown Elliott, who had displayed his skills as an orator in the congressional battle for the Ku Klux Klan Act, to be one of the standard-bearers for the civil rights law. Fate could not have chosen a more provocative advocate for the bill, for as a highly intelligent man of "uninterrupted African descent," Elliott was at once unnerving to white antagonists and fascinating to the press. Until Elliott's arrival in Washington in 1871, whites in Congress had for the most part been exposed to black representatives with marked Caucasian features, such as Hiram Revels and Joseph Rainey. Elliott's countenance made him far less reassuring a presence. "His skin is very black," confirmed the *Chicago Tribune,* "which, with his features, a low, receding forehead, broad, flat nose and thick lips . . . indicate that he has no white blood in his veins." Elliott's debut in Congress, like Revels's, had also contained some neat symbolism: Revels had replaced Jefferson Davis; Elliott had the distinction of representing the same South Carolina district that had once sent to Congress the hotheaded Preston Brooks, who had smashed a cane to pieces over the head of Charles Sumner.

In an age infatuated with pseudoscientific notions about genetic "character," in which subtleties of skin tone were thought to be critical indicators of an individual's worth, the success of men such as Revels or P.B.S. Pinchback was consistently rationalized as stemming from their mixed-blood heritage. Blacks who did possess more thoroughly Negroid features, such as Richard Cain or Robert Elliott, were either mocked outright for their "apelike" appearance (Cain) or suspected of possessing some innate animal-like cunning (Elliott). Broad presumptions about race almost always seemed to come with rather glaring ironies attached — in the case of the congressmen, that they could be deemed simultaneously "ignorant" and "scheming," or that such accomplished individuals might be held up as representing inherent Negro inferiority.

The seats and galleries were packed on January 5, 1874, as it was known that in that day's session Alexander H. Stephens, the former vice president of the Confederacy and now a congressman from Georgia, would speak against Sumner's civil rights bill, and that "Robert Brown Elliott, Negro of South Carolina," would answer his speech. The two sides clashed even before the main event, when Elliott's colleague Alonzo Ransier tangled with the Virginia Democrat John Harris, one of the bill's staunchest opponents. Harris alleged that the civil rights bill was flawed because it "is based upon the purpose, the theory, of the absolute equality of the races. It seeks to enforce by law a doctrine which is not accepted by the minds nor received in the hearts of the people of the United States — that the negro in all things is the equal of the white man. And I say there is not one gentleman upon this floor who can honestly say he really believes that the colored man is created his equal."

"I can," said Ransier.

"Of course you can," Harris barked in reply, "but I am speaking to the white men of the House; and, Mr. Speaker, I do not wish to be interrupted again by him."

Harris continued, "Admit that it is prejudice, yet the fact exists, and you, as members of Congress and legislators, are bound to respect that prejudice. It was born in the children of the South; born in our ancestors . . . that the colored man was inferior to the white."

"I deny that," interjected Ransier.

"I do not allow you to interrupt me!" Harris snapped. "Sit down; I am talking to white men; I am talking to gentlemen!" The gallery hooted at the flustered Harris as the chair used the gavel to restore order.

When Stephens finally gained the floor, the room became hushed in anticipation to hear the words of the legendary rebel orator and statesman. An authority on the U.S. Constitution (he had helped write the Confederate Constitution, which he deemed an improvement over the original), he became a hero to the dawning Confederacy with an address given in Savannah on March 21, 1861, subsequently known as the "Cornerstone Speech." In it, he blamed the nation's founders for failing to deal honestly with the issue of slavery and for enshrining in the early life of the country the questionable theory that "all men are created equal."

"The prevailing ideas entertained by [Jefferson] and most of the leading statesmen at the time," he stated, "were that the enslavement of the African was in violation of the laws of nature; that it was wrong in *principle,* socially, morally, and politically." However, he assured his rapt audience, "our new [secessionist] government is founded upon exactly the opposite idea . . . its cornerstone rests upon the great truth that the negro is not equal to the white man, that slavery — subordination to the superior race — is his natural and normal condition . . . Our new government," he boasted, "is the first in the history of the world based upon this great physical, philosophical, and moral truth."

Never in good health — he suffered from neuralgia and "horrible headaches" — and now at age sixty-three restricted to a wheelchair, Stephens was almost apparitionlike in appearance. Only five feet tall and weighing no more than ninety pounds, he dressed all in black, a purple velvet skullcap on his head, beneath which peeked some strands of silver hair. "With a shrunken, consumptive chest, a sallow, mummified face, in which the bony structure stood forth like a death's head . . . He was," recounts one scholar, "little more than a brain."

Addressing the question of the civil rights bill, Stephens told Congress, "There is a vast difference between civil rights proper and some of those social rights claimed by this bill." A black man who buys a first class railway ticket has the right to a first-class seat, he explained, "but this does not entitle him . . . to a seat in the same car with the white man." And Stephens asserted that in his home state of Georgia, blacks, when presented with the choice, preferred to be with their own race. "They have no desire for anything partaking of the character of social rights; and if the people, colored and white . . . shall be left to themselves to work out their own destiny under the present system . . . without external interference of any sort, it will, in my judgment, be infinitely better for both races."

He also emphasized that any proposed federal civil rights law would defy the sacred ideal of states' rights. "If there is one truth which stands out prominently above all others," he observed, "it is that the germinal and seminal principle of American constitutional liberty is the absolute unrestricted right of state self-government in all purely internal municipal affairs."

Stephens had already touched upon two of the key Southern objections to the general course of Reconstruction — social equality and states' rights. The latter had, of course, been an emotional factor in congressional debates on slavery as far back as the age of Calhoun, and it was still in many ways an unresolved issue. In the early 1870s, advocates for a civil rights law justified it by invoking the Fourteenth Amendment's clause prohibiting states from denying the "privileges and immunities" of citizens and the Thirteenth Amendment's promise to remove the stigma of slavery from those recently freed from bondage. But in *Blyew v. U.S.* (1872) the Supreme Court had severely limited the scope of the concept of "badges of slavery," and the following year, in the *Slaughterhouse Cases*, had dealt the Fourteenth Amendment a wounding blow.

The *Slaughterhouse Cases* arose in 1869 when the state of Louisiana tried to limit all butchering in New Orleans to a central slaughterhouse, where standards of sanitation could be better enforced, rather than in the city's many privately run operations. A group of independent butchers sued on the grounds that such a monopoly violated their rights under the Thirteenth Amendment's ban on "servitudes"; also, they cited the Fourteenth Amendment's edict against a state's enforcing "any law which shall abridge the privileges or immunities of citizens of the United States," arguing that it prohibited the state from interfering with their trade in order to "sustain their lives through labor." The butchers also contended that the slaughterhouse monopoly denied the Fourteenth Amendment's guarantee of due process. This legal strategy, engineered by the butchers' attorney, Joseph A. Campbell, a former Supreme Court justice who had defected to the Confederacy, was cleverly innovative, suggesting that the scope of the Fourteenth Amendment might be broader than its original purpose of safeguarding freedmen's rights.

The Supreme Court, in a 5–4 decision, ruled against the butchers, knocking out the "servitudes" argument and delineating the Fourteenth Amendment's protections as chiefly applicable to the freedmen. It ruled that the organization of slaughterhouses belonged to the police powers of the state. The amendment's "privileges and immunities" was said by the majority to describe a very limited number of rights associated with citizenship and guaranteed by both the state and federal government, such as voting rights. Foes of civil rights legislation pounced joyously on the ruling, for it acknowledged the states' authority to regulate private businesses and their day-to-day interactions with citizens and a limit to the federal government's ability to intervene.

On January 6, the day following Stephens's appearance, Elliott rose to address the House. The mood was expectant, the galleries again packed, and the reporters' tables full to see "the African" challenge "the Brain of the Confederacy." Several dignitaries, including General William Tecumseh Sherman, were present. At that time most congressmen did not have separate offices but carried on their correspondence and other work at their desks on the House floor. "A few extreme Democrats pretended to be busy with letters and documents," noted the *Chicago Tribune,* "but the eloquence of the speaker soon drew them from their preoccupation, and compelled them to listen."

Elliott began by calling attention to the fact that black Americans deserved the civil rights bill and other protections because they had earned their citizenship. "In the events that led to the achievement of American independence," he reminded his listeners, the black American was not "an inactive or unconcerned spectator." To make his point, and in response to James B. Beck, a Kentuckian who earlier had disparaged the courage of black men while boasting of the chivalrous character of his own state, Elliot contrasted the brave actions of black troops at the Battle of New Orleans in 1815 with the less distinguished performance of a unit of Kentuckians. "Under the immortal Jackson, a colored regiment held the extreme right of the American line unflinchingly, and drove back the British column that pressed upon them, at the point of the bayonet," while the Kentucky outfit, in General Jackson's own words, had, at a critical moment, "ingloriously fled" the scene. And in the recent war, Elliott added, while "the negro, true to that patriotism and love of country that have ever characterized and marked his history on this continent, came to the aid of the government," the state of Kentucky "coldly [declared] her neutrality in the impending struggle."

Elliott then turned to the *Slaughterhouse Cases,* dismissing Beck's and Stephens's suggestion that the ruling had determined that the state, not the federal government, had legislative power over its citizens. What the Supreme Court had ruled, he explained, was that a state did have certain police powers, such as offering, for reasons of health and sanitation, exclusive slaughtering rights to a single corporation, but that any effort to conflate the butchers' claims of unfair treatment with those of freedmen was spurious. Elliott reminded Congress that in the *Slaughterhouse Cases,* the Supreme Court had suggested that it was the amendment's equal rights clause, *not* its privileges and immunities clause, that perhaps afforded blacks the most legitimate protection. "No state shall 'deny to any person within its jurisdiction the equal protection of the laws,'" quoted Elliott. "No matter, therefore, whether his rights are held under the United States or under his particular state, he is equally protected by this amendment. He is always and everywhere entitled to equal protection of the laws."

"The [Reconstruction] amendments, one and all," he continued,

> have as their all-pervading design and end the security to the recently enslaved race, not only their nominal freedom, but their complete protection from those who had formerly exercised unlimited dominion over them. It is in this broad light that all these amendments must be read, the purpose to secure the perfect equality before the law of all citizens of the United States . . . If a state denies to me rights which are common to all her other citizens, she violates this amendment, unless she can show, as was shown in the Slaughterhouse Cases, that she does it in the legitimate exercise of her police power.

Elliott clearly relished the opportunity to diminish an ex-Confederate of Stephens's stature. "While the honorable gentleman contended himself with harmless speculations in his study, or in the columns of a newspaper, we might well smile at the impotence of his efforts to turn back the advancing tide of opinion and progress," Elliott mused.

> But, when he comes again upon this national arena, and throws himself with all his power and influence across the path which leads to the full enfranchisement of my race, I meet him only as an adversary; nor shall age or any other consideration restrain me from saying that he now offers this government, which he has done his utmost to destroy, a very poor return for its magnanimous treatment, to come here and seek to continue, by the assertion of doctrines obnoxious to the true principles of our government, the burdens and oppressions which rest upon five millions of his countrymen who never failed to lift their earnest prayers for the success of this government when the gentleman was seeking to break up the Union of these states and to blot the American republic from the galaxy of nations.

"Sir," Elliott continued, addressing the Speaker:

> it is scarcely twelve years since that gentleman shocked the civilized world by announcing the birth of a government which rested on human slavery as its cornerstone. The progress of events has swept away that pseudo-government which rested on greed, pride, and tyranny; and the race whom he then ruthlessly spurned and trampled on are here to meet him in debate, and to demand that the rights which are

> enjoyed by their former oppressors . . . shall be accorded to those who even in the darkness of slavery kept their allegiance true to freedom and the Union. Sir, the gentleman from Georgia has learned much since 1861; but he is still a laggard. Let him put away entirely the false and fatal theories which have so greatly marred an otherwise enviable record.

Murmurs of approval from the gallery had been growing louder as Elliott lashed Stephens, and they crested in loud applause when he declared, "That gentleman would better befit his station if, instead of throwing himself in the way of the progress of the nation that had so magnanimously pardoned him for conspiring to overthrow the Republic, he would lay his shoulder to the wheel and help it on to a better and more glorious future."

The chairman's gavel quieted the room, and Elliott turned to answer Congressman Harris, who had clashed the day before with Ransier.

> To the diatribe of the gentleman from Virginia, who spoke yesterday, and who so far transcended the limits of decency and propriety as to announce upon this floor that his remarks were addressed to white men alone, I shall have no word of reply. Let him feel that a negro was not only too magnanimous to smite him in his weakness, but was even charitable enough to grant him the mercy of his silence. I shall, sir, leave to others less charitable the unenviable and fatiguing task of sifting out of that mass of chaff the few grains of sense that may, perchance, deserve notice.

The audience reacted so enthusiastically to this putdown of the smug Harris, with applause and stamping of feet, that it was several minutes before order could be restored.

"The results of the war, as seen in reconstruction," Elliott said, moving on, "have settled forever the political status of my race. The passage of this bill will determine the civil status, not only of the negro, but of any other class of citizens who may feel themselves discriminated against." Alluding to the popular idea, represented in a well-known allegorical lithograph of the postwar era, that Reconstruction was a process of America rebuilding itself into an impressive new and vast public structure, a pavilion constructed on the firm pillars of justice and fair play, Elliott vowed that the Sumner bill would "form the capstone of that temple of liberty, begun on this continent under discouraging circumstances . . . until at last it stands in all its beautiful symmetry and proportions, a building the grandest which the world has ever seen, realizing the most sanguine expectations and the highest hopes of those who, in the name of equal, impartial, and universal liberty, laid the foundation stones."

Finally, as a parable for the unique dual nature of America, where black and white people lived and worked side by side, Elliott invoked the scriptural story of Ruth. "Our race has 'reaped down your fields,'" he said, and now, having been given their civil rights, he vowed, they would be whites' fellow citizens in the truest sense, sharing with a grateful and faithful heart the nation's endless bounty. "For whither thou goest, I will go," Elliott intoned, "and where thou lodgest, I will lodge; thy people shall be my people, and thy God my God; where thou diest, will I die, and there will I be buried; the Lord do so to me, and more also, if aught but death part thee and me."

That a black man should, on the floor of Congress, deliver so powerful an address on such a theme, a defense of Reconstruction itself, and in so doing skillfully filet three of the South's leading apologists, including the vice president of the Confederacy, was an audacious triumph. To then, in a soaring finale, link America's two races in a bond so enduring that it bore analogy to biblical faith! It was arguably one of the most daring addresses ever proclaimed in Congress. Elliott had replied "by calm, convincing arguments to the conceited assumptions of superiority made by plantation overseers who occupy seats in the House of Representatives," raved the *New National Era,* which gave the story its entire front page. Agreed the *National Republican,* "No more dignified, skillful, exhaustive tearing down of the false theories raised by caste alone has ever been witnessed in legislative halls." The *New York Times* chimed in with fulsome praise: "Mr. Elliott is of the blackest of his race, a fact to which he referred with much feeling, in regretting that it was necessary for him, in an American Congress, to ask for civil rights. His speech was well-written, and it was delivered with the earnestness and eloquence of a natural and experienced orator. The African love of melody was noticeable in the harmony of his delivery." Journalist Marie Le Baron noted that "the blade of sarcasm with which he annihilated his rude Southern opponent was wielded as one would wield a knife, a bone, a stinging snake. 'I am what I am,' was the rude spirit, 'and believe in my own nobility.'" Almost comical was the *Charleston News & Courier*'s churlish reaction to the great address, saying of the debate over the civil rights bill only that "Elliott, of South Carolina, delivered a speech in advocacy of it." This single sentence was the paper's sole mention of the event, although it did devote several columns to Stephens's remarks.

Elliott's speech was instantly immortalized by a popular engraving titled "The Shackle Broken — by the Genius of Freedom." Its several panels reproduced images suggested by Elliott's words — colored troops in combat; Lincoln and Sumner on pedestals; Sumner proclaiming "Equality of rights is the first of rights"; and a representation of a cozy black homestead, captioned "American slave labor is of the past — Free labor is of the present — We toil for our own children and not for those of others." There was, in apparent homage to Robert Smalls, an image of blacks manning a small armed naval vessel, above a quotation of Lincoln's: "So far as tested, it is difficult to say they are not as good soldiers as any." In the center was Elliott himself, holding forth on the House floor to a rapt audience of colleagues and an attentive gallery, and across the bottom ran a line from Elliott's address: "The rights contended for in this bill are among the sacred rights of mankind, which are not to be rummaged for among old parchments or musty records; they are written as with a sunbeam in the whole volume of human nature, by the hand of the Divinity itself, and can never be erased or obscured by mortal power."

At night a large biracial crowd gathered outside Elliott's boarding house on Second Street. A band played, and several speakers hailed the day's hero, who was then introduced, to rapturous applause. No record exists of his remarks, but it's likely he told his hearers much of what he would soon offer a similar group in South Carolina:

> In the recent debate on the civil rights bill, the privilege of replying to the elaborate legal and constitutional argument of Mr. Beck, of Kentucky, and more particularly of Hon. Alexander H. Stephens, of Georgia, was, by general consent, awarded to me . . . No man could have had a more exciting theme, or a more exciting occasion. I must speak under the eyes of crowded galleries, in the presence of a full house, and of many distinguished strangers, attracted by the novel interest of such an occasion. I may confess to you, fellow citizens, that I trembled for the result . . . [However], friends have been delighted, and enemies have been forced to concede that the Vice President of the Southern Confederacy — a man acknowledged to be of the greatest intellectual force, and long public experience — has been met in debate, and that his sophistries have been exposed, and his constitutional arguments overthrown, by one of that race, which, twelve years ago, he described

> as fit only to be "hewers of wood and drawers of water." This triumph I do not chiefly value as a personal one. If it be a triumph, it is a triumph for you as well as for me — a triumph for our whole race.

The national recognition of Elliott as an orator of genius, an heir to Charles Sumner himself, was a particularly meaningful affirmation, granting Elliott the kind of intellectual prominence only Frederick Douglass and a few other black Americans enjoyed. Newspapers began taking an interest in all aspects of his life, even his and Grace's plans to renovate their house in Columbia, and gave significant coverage to his visit to Boston's Faneuil Hall, where he'd been invited to offer the chief eulogy at a memorial gathering for Sumner. In response to the new curiosity about Elliott, an unconfirmed story emerged from a town in upstate New York where, it was said, the teenage Robert Elliott had once bested a local physician in a debate over slavery. The older man was arguing for the gradual emancipation of the slaves when Elliott inquired if, in amputating someone's arm, the good doctor would also do so one finger at a time. "The victory for the colored boy was complete," it was reported, "and the excitement of the audience knew no bounds . . . That boy's name was Robert B. Elliott . . . whose recent speech on the Supplementary Civil Rights Bill has electrified the nation."

Back in the galleries overlooking Congress, Elliott's treatment of Stephens had whetted appetites for more of the sport of black congressmen skewering pompous former Confederates. The next victim was Democrat William Robbins of North Carolina, who, after boasting of his service in the rebel army and his role in several famous battles, argued against the civil rights bill on the grounds that although whites had tried "to bring these barbarians up to civilization," black people were simply not capable of the ascent. The civil rights bill, Robbins declared, would therefore bring the whites of the South down to the level of the ex-slaves. Richard Cain of South Carolina replied that the "civilizing instruments" used by Robbins and his fellow whites "to bring these barbarians up to civilization" had been the lash and the whipping post, but that, despite such abysmal treatment, he and Robbins today stood on the same floor of Congress and that he had come to assert his rights. To Robbins's humiliation, even many white members joined the gallery in chuckling at his efforts and at Cain's wit and eloquence in the exchange. "In the ratio of their numbers," a Republican told a reporter, "it must be conceded that the colored representatives in Congress are better parliamentary speakers than the whites."

The knock-down success of Elliott's address helped gain some momentum, at long last, for Sumner's civil rights bill, which in May 1874 was passed by the Senate. Many saw the vote as a kind of memorial tribute to Sumner, or an homage to the idealism of early Reconstruction, which amounted to basically the same thing. In the House, the bill came up for a vote in early 1875 with the strong backing of Benjamin Butler of Massachusetts and James Garfield of Ohio.

By now, the Republicans had experienced a setback in the November 1874 elections, losing 170 seats in the House of Representatives and control of that body for the first time since 1860. In part this expressed the nation's weariness with Reconstruction but more specifically its unease with the Senate's approving vote, which made passage of Sumner's civil rights law appear imminent. As William Gillette points out, a looming new civil rights law "mandating social equality" was a peril that any Southern voter could understand. Questions such as "Do you wish to be buried in a nigger grave-yard?" or "Do you wish your daughter to marry a nigger?" summed up why many felt that the Republicans could no longer be trusted with the management of Congress, the Southern statehouses, or the nation's racial dynamics. Putting the "nigger into our tea and coffee" was how one Kentucky editor denigrated Sumner's bill. President Grant had spoken supportively of civil rights legislation in his second inaugural address, but even he acknowledged that this issue had turned the tide against the Republicans in the South and border states, a view seconded by the journalist Charles Nordhoff, who saw former white Republican voters desert the party in droves.

Now, with the Democrats set to control the House of Representatives and Butler himself a lame duck, having lost his seat in a close race in Massachusetts, the Republicans were eager to go out on a high note by easing the civil rights legislation through. Not that all were of one mind concerning the bill. Some saw its passage as obligatory — the finishing touch on Reconstruction, or a tribute to Sumner; others feared that by becoming law, it would only further inflame Southern passions, perhaps harming the Republican Party in the upcoming presidential contest in 1876 as it had in the congressional elections of fall 1874.

With the bill before the House, it was Garfield of Ohio who rode to the rescue, reminding his peers that "the measure pending here today is confronted . . . by the first argument that was raised against the anti-slavery movement in its first inception — that it is a sentimental abstraction rather than a measure of practical legislation." The abolitionists, he noted, had once been "denounced as dreamers, abstractionists, who were looking down to the bottom of society and attempting to see something good . . . something that the friend of human rights ought to support in the person of a negro slave. Every step since that first sentimental beginning has been assailed by precisely the same argument." He admitted that the emerging Democratic majority in Congress might "go back and plow up all that has been planted," reversing his and others' efforts to place black Americans safely and securely on the plane of equal rights, yet he urged his own party to act while it still could to usher the civil rights bill into law. He framed his request in a kind of valediction of Reconstruction itself:

> During the last twelve years it has often been rung in our ears that by doing justice to the negro we shall pull down the pillars of our political temple and bury ourselves in the ruins . . . When we were abolishing slavery by adopting the Thirteenth Amendment we were warned that we were bringing measureless calamity upon the Republic. Did it come? When the Fourteenth Amendment was passed the same wail was heard, the wail of the fearful and unbelieving. Again when it was proposed to elevate the negro to citizenship, to give him the ballot as his weapon of self-defense, we were told the cup of our destruction was filled to its brim. But sir, I have lived long enough to learn that in the long run it is safest for a nation, a political party, or an individual man to dare to do right, and let consequences take care of themselves, for he that loseth his life for the truth's sake shall find it.

The bill, minus its provisions for equal rights in schools, churches, and cemeteries, passed the House on February 5 by a vote of 162 to 99; the Senate accepted the House version by a margin of 38 to 26; and on March 1, 1875, with President Grant's signature, "Sumner's Law" at long last went on the books.

CHAPTER 9

DIVIDED TIME

WHILE THE DEBATE over the new civil rights bill was testing Reconstruction's limits in Congress, a parallel struggle was taking shape in far-off Mississippi. This verdant agricultural land had, since war's end, experienced periods of relative political stability, enough so that blacks from more troubled states, such as Georgia, regarded it as something of a mainstay of Republican rule. Yet of the three states with black majority populations — Mississippi, Louisiana, and South Carolina — Mississippi would be the first in which whites achieved redemption, or home rule, and the methods by which this was accomplished, known as the Mississippi Plan, would become a regional model for that transformation.

Perhaps the first sign of the coming political convulsion was a deadly riot at Meridian, an east Mississippi railroad town, in spring 1871. A posse of Ku Klux Klansmen from nearby Alabama had entered Mississippi to track down and discipline some black men for allegedly backing out of work contracts. Meridian's Republican leadership — Mayor William Sturges, a carpetbagger, and his scalawag cohort Robert J. Mosely — challenged the incursion on the grounds that the Klan's leader, an Alabama sheriff named Adam Kennard, had violated his jurisdiction by pursuing the missing workers across the state line. Tensions rose when it was alleged that Kennard had himself been assaulted by Daniel Price, a scalawag who taught in a black school. To help calm the fears of Meridian blacks, who were nervous about possible Klan retribution, Mayor Sturges and local Republican authorities staged a well-attended torchlight rally on the steps of Meridian's Lauderdale County Courthouse. The black spokesmen J. Aaron Moore, William Clopton, and Warren Tyler joined Sturges in urging their supporters to remain calm until the crisis had passed.

A few nights later local Democrats held their own gathering, from which a belligerent resolution emerged: the town's "present [Republican] incumbents must be swept away from the face of the earth." The Democrats also drew up affidavits and swore a formal complaint against Moore, Clopton, and the others, alleging that the town's Unionist leaders had, in their meeting on the courthouse steps, made "incendiary" speeches and used "seditious language." "Damn old Meridian!" Clopton was quoted as having declared. "She has given us a lot of trouble; let's burn her all up tonight."

When a judicial hearing was held to examine the complaint a few days later, numerous Republicans and as many as two hundred Democratic "observers" packed the courtroom. At one point, Warren Tyler interrupted a white witness named James Brantley to demand the right to summon other witnesses who would show that Brantley was not being truthful. "I want to introduce two or three witnesses to impeach your veracity," said Tyler. Enraged at the suggestion that he was a liar, Brantley grabbed a billy club from a court officer's hands and charged Tyler, who, according to witnesses, reached into his coat for a revolver. Instantly, weapons were drawn on all sides, and, after a blaze of gunfire, the presiding white judge fell back dead in his chair. The stunned courtroom froze; then, as furious whites cried murder, the Republicans fled for their lives. Tyler sprinted to a second-floor veranda, swung over the railing, and jumped to the ground; he then ran off, with several whites in pursuit. William Clopton, who'd fallen wounded, was carried to a balcony by two white men and hurled to the brick pavement below. Rioters meanwhile chased down Aaron Moore and "continued their hellish barbarities," beating him severely and later burning his house to the ground. Tyler, the chief target of the mob's rage, was found hiding in a shack, dragged into the street, and killed. As many as thirty other blacks died in the rampage.

Mayor Sturges evaded the mob by hiding in the garret of a boarding house and emerged only when intermediaries worked out an arrangement whereby he would resign his office and leave town. "I wanted to know the whys and wherefore," Sturges explained in a letter to the *New York Tribune* that described the day's events, "but they said they came not to argue any question of right: the verdict had been rendered. They treated me respectfully, but said that their ultimatum was that I must take a northern-bound train. I yielded. At about half past twelve o'clock at night perhaps three hundred came and escorted me to the cars."

Sturges's letter was reprinted widely in the North, feeding the debate then under way about the need for the Ku Klux Klan Act's tougher measures. The duly elected Republican mayor of a large Southern town had been "hunted out like a wolf" by "confederated murderers," lamented the *New National Era.* "It proves the rebel spirit [is] still rampant and murderous." Sturges ended by advising that "martial law be proclaimed through every Southern state. Leniency will not do."

Such a prescription was severe, but the deposed mayor was right that the Meridian riot would not remain an isolated occurrence. Native whites had stumbled upon an almost foolproof tactic for loosening local Republican control: foment some outrage or accusation against black or carpetbagger authorities, then create a physical confrontation. The freedmen, less inclined to engage in a sustained fight, would likely make no effective resistance; the show of massive force would not only paralyze them but also lay bare the tenuousness of the bond between them and their white Republican allies. The *Era,* which headlined its piece about Sturges "The Peril of the Hour," saw the danger vividly: isolated acts of Klan violence, while troubling, involved solitary victims and terrorists who could potentially be prosecuted; a riot, on the other hand, carried out by an anonymous mob, inflicted more wholesale damage and could demoralize an entire community.

The Mississippi senator and former military governor Adelbert Ames also understood instantly that something ominous had taken place at Meridian. He had monitored the rise of a home-rule mentality in his state and had come to suspect that native whites, despite their at times conciliatory rhetoric, were at heart driven by a deep-seated contempt for the idea of blacks as citizens or equals. "The South cares for no other question," Ames later noted. "Everything gives way to it. They support or oppose men, advocate or denounce policies, flatter or murder, just as such action will help them as far as possible to recover their old power over the negro."

Ames knew that the rights and security of the freed people, and civil society itself, could not be sustained unless white violence was quelled; the future of Reconstruction itself in Mississippi likely hung in the balance. But what were the appropriate remedies, and how could such policies be enforced in this remote place?

One glance at Adelbert Ames showed that fate had made a curious choice. With his receding hairline, pleasant smile, and neatly trimmed mustache, he resembled a small-town bank manager far more than a

ADELBERT AMES

professional soldier. Yet the Maine native and West Point graduate had emerged from the war with a distinguished reputation for gallantry, winning the Congressional Medal of Honor for his heroism at First Bull Run, where, though badly wounded, he had remained with his two-gun battery even after being ordered to the rear, directing fire at the enemy until he collapsed from loss of blood. "Every one who rode with him . . . soon discovered that Ames never hesitated to take desperate chances under fire," an aide recalled. "He seemed to have a life that was under some mystic protection. Under the heaviest fire . . . he would sit on his horse, apparently unmoved by singing rifle-ball, shrieking shot, or bursting shell, and quietly give his orders." Ames went on to serve at Gettysburg and in numerous other engagements; not yet thirty years old at war's end, he was made a brigadier general and appointed Southern district commander of the Union occupying forces based in Jackson, the capital of Mississippi.

In 1867 he received his first lesson in the peculiarities of Southern justice when not a single witness could be coaxed to testify before a military court that he convened to prosecute a lynch mob, forcing the case to be abandoned. Then, in 1869, after Ames was appointed military governor of Mississippi, the native spirit struck closer to home. To the position of provisional mayor of Jackson he had appointed Lieutenant Colonel Joseph G. Crane, the tall, likable son of a longtime Ohio congressman. Crane, in the course of his duties in recovering overdue taxes, ordered seized and sold at public auction a piano belonging to Edward M. Yerger, the eccentric scion of a once-prominent Mississippi family. Yerger was away in Memphis when notice of the piano's sale was posted; upon his return he was livid and sent several notes to Crane, demanding satisfaction. A go-between who delivered one of the missives warned Crane that Yerger's "passions were greatly intensified by liquor."

When Yerger finally caught up with the mayor, Crane was at the corner of State and Capitol Streets, one of the town's main intersections, inspecting a sidewalk said to be in need of repair. "Angry words" were heard by several witnesses as Yerger confronted the young Northerner over the "theft" of the piano. When Crane tried to calm his antagonist, Yerger proclaimed him a "God damned cowardly puppy," to which Crane replied, "I do not want to have anything to do with you, except officially," and, making a gesture with his hand, turned to walk away. Yerger, infuriated by the dismissal, struck at Crane's hand; the mayor replied by bringing his cane down on his attacker's neck; Yerger then drew a knife and plunged it into Crane's side, killing him.

The mayor's wife, learning of a commotion involving her husband, rushed to the scene, where a crowd had formed. Pushing others aside, she threw herself on the lifeless body and, hysterical, demanded that he speak, clinging to him for several minutes until her own clothes were soaked with blood. She "was borne from the spot almost a maniac," the next day's paper reported, "amidst the sympathy of the entire gathered population."

At court-martial Yerger's relatives conceded that the killer, whose family nickname was "Prince Edward," was an unbalanced personality, a rabid secessionist who "went into ecstasies" over Lincoln's assassination. They nonetheless challenged the right of a military court to try their kinsman. Ultimately the U.S. Supreme Court ordered him released to the civil authorities — the first time in Reconstruction that the high court had curbed the powers of the federal government in the South. His lawyer then managed to convince a civilian court that a second trial would constitute double jeopardy, so Edward Yerger, to the dismay of Crane's family, Governor Ames, and many others, went free, eventually leaving the state.

Incidents such as Crane's murder, and reports of abuses of the freedmen, had a radicalizing effect upon Ames, transforming him gradually from a bureaucrat of the federal occupation into an indignant advocate committed to upholding the law and defending black people's rights. In 1869 he oversaw the first free election for governor, in which former-Confederate-turned-Republican James Lusk Alcorn was elected. Alcorn, one of Mississippi's leading men of property, promised his constituents a "harnessed revolution" that would offer blacks opportunity even as it retained white authority. To be safe, however, Ames disqualified other officeholders he thought insufficiently repentant and put solid Republicans in their places. "The contest [here] is not between two established parties . . . but between loyal men and a class of men who are disloyal," Ames explained, when some in Washington questioned the move. "The war still exists in a very important phase here." The following year, as Republicans, including many black representatives, moved into the state legislature, they repaid Ames's devotion by electing him U.S. senator.

As a Northern white official who had seen the mounting Southern resistance firsthand, Ames in Washington became an influential advocate for the freedmen's security. But by 1871 Alcorn had joined him in the Senate, where the two broke over the Ku Klux Klan Act. Ames challenged Alcorn's claims that Mississippi by itself could tamp down the Klan, citing the Meridian riot and the fact that more than two dozen black schools and churches had been torched recently and more than sixty freedmen killed, with no significant action taken by the state to prosecute such crimes. Eventually, in 1873, both Alcorn and Ames resigned their Senate seats to vie for the Republican nomination for governor of Mississippi, a job they knew would be far more central to the state's future than representing it in the far-off capital.

Back in Mississippi, Alcorn immediately stepped into political quicksand, angering his white constituents by appealing to black voters with promises of equal treatment and seating on the railroads, a vow that, to whites, reeked of "social equality," though for most blacks the promise had little credibility. Because of Alcorn's miscues and a large black voter turnout, Ames won the election easily. Also of help was his developing skill as a political stump speaker. In the nineteenth century perhaps no accomplishment, outside of military valor, was more respected than public oratory, and the buttoned-down officer from Maine took immense pleasure in his newfound ability to hold crowds of Mississippi blacks and whites with his words. As he laid out his appeal for unity and progress, a real depth of feeling for the people of his adopted state seemed to inspire him and to grant his thoughts eloquence.

Blanche Butler was one of Washington's most sought-after belles when Adelbert Ames courted and married her in the early 1870s. Known for her striking appearance as well as her artistic flair and independent nature, she had been the subject of a series of photographs taken by the famous Matthew Brady and exhibited in his Washington gallery. When in 1873 Adelbert Ames decided to abandon the capital to return to Mississippi, she accompanied him, if a bit reluctantly, for she was the daughter of one of the most despised men in the South, the Massachusetts congressman Benjamin F. Butler, known as "Beast Butler" for his infamous stint as the wartime military governor of New Orleans.

The short, walleyed General Butler, who had introduced the term *contraband* to describe fleeing slaves, was dispatched by President Lincoln to oversee New Orleans after the city was taken by Union forces in spring 1862. Finding the place conquered but its people defiant, Butler responded by seizing control of the local press, arresting those openly disloyal to the Union, and using the recently legislated Confiscation Acts to attach the holdings of New Orleans households owned by absent Confederates. He also ordered the public hanging of a youth named Billy Mumford, who had climbed onto the roof of the U.S. mint to remove the American flag as federal troops arrived in the city. For allegedly pilfering silverware and fine china from elite residences, or allowing his officers to do so, Butler earned the nicknames "Silver Spoon" and "Spoon-Thief." But his action that most infuriated Southern whites was General Orders Number 28, the so-called Woman Order, which labeled as a prostitute any female who disrespected occupying Union troops. Local women were said to have insulted federal officers and even spit at their feet; one had been caught mocking the funeral cortege of a fallen Union soldier. Though Butler understood that his occupying forces would be resented, he was outraged that women would act so abominably toward his men. He later claimed that the controversial order had its desired effect, that "these she-adders of New Orleans were at once tamed into propriety of conduct," but so gross an insult to Southern womanhood was not soon forgotten, nor was the martyrdom of young Billy Mumford, who in death became a Confederate hero.

The depth of Southern loathing for Butler only seemed to increase with time. One Democratic paper late in the war accused him of seeking to disembowel dead soldiers in order to send their corpses north filled with silverware — "this representative of Hell in garb of man, this cock-eyed insulter of woman, this sensuous incarnation of all that is damnable — this beast, Benjamin Butler."

Blanche Butler Ames, although devoted to her husband, didn't fully share his commitment to navigating Mississippi safely through the shoals of Reconstruction; and after the whirlwind of Washington society, a posting in tiny Jackson must have seemed bleak. Despite its handsome state capitol and governor's mansion set on a central hill, the place was still more or less a crossroads town; the state's sparsely populated frontier began almost at the city limits. With greater prescience than

Adelbert, she viewed the surroundings as not merely tedious but immensely hostile, and thus feared for her own, and later her children's, safety. Because of this, she rarely left the "great barn of a house," as she called the mansion. As if to compound her sense of vulnerability, the residence was situated on a prominent site just behind the capitol, not far from where Edward Yerger had killed Colonel Crane, and it was under the almost constant "surveillance" of the walking and carriage-borne public.

Blanche recognized Mississippi's "multitudinous disadvantages . . . the malarious atmosphere, with its baleful influence upon mind and body, the red, clayey, turfless soil, filled with watercourses and gullies, the slothful indolence of all its people," which she registered as "insurmountable reasons why I could never regard it with favor." But she made an effort to welcome to the mansion Jackson's gentry and her husband's political acquaintances, occasionally asking them onto the lawn to play croquet, although she thought the local women nosy and "lynx-eyed" and was disheartened to find that the town had no qualified engraver of invitations and that the servants were inadequately trained, by eastern standards. Gatherings that mixed her husband's black and white

STATE CAPITOL, JACKSON, MISSISSIPPI

political followers were less frequent and called for greater circumspection, as they could potentially inflame local opinion.

Despite the presence in Mississippi of conciliatory former rebels such as James Lusk Alcorn and the capable executive Adelbert Ames, efforts to achieve a governing alliance of whites and blacks in the state eroded steadily through the early 1870s. They foundered on the elemental fact that most whites remained unwilling to recognize blacks as their political equals, a resistance that had evolved from the "masterly inactivity" of the constitutional convention phase of Reconstruction, to the bloodshed of the Meridian riot, and finally to ever more strident calls for home rule. By late 1874, agitated by the national debate over a civil rights bill and encouraged by the Democratic Party's reclamation of the House of Representatives, even midstream papers like the *Jackson Clarion* and the *Hinds County Gazette* joined the call from the small-town Mississippi press for "a white man's government, by white men, for the benefit of white men." The *Forest Register* inserted in its masthead the soon-popular motto "A white man in a white man's place, a black man in a black man's place, each according to the eternal fitness of things"; the paper also urged its readers to "carry the election peaceably if we can, forcibly if we must." The *Westville News* offered the headline "Vote the Negro Down or Knock Him Down" as it editorialized, "Let us have a white man's party to rule a white man's country, and do it like white men."

The usual allegations were made that blacks wielded too much authority in the state, although even with 226 black officials serving Mississippi during all twelve years of Reconstruction in every position from U.S. senator to county tax collector, their influence was never truly dominant. There was one black secretary of state, James D. Lynch, and one black lieutenant governor, Alexander K. Davis; the state's nine positions in Congress saw only three black representatives — Hiram Revels and Blanche Bruce in the Senate, and John Roy Lynch (unrelated to James) in the House — and never was there more than one black Mississippian in either body of Congress at the same time. Of Mississippi's seventy-two counties, only a dozen ever had black sheriffs, and these men did not all serve at the same time. Similarly, blacks never held anything near a majority in either chamber of the state legislature. And while Mississippi whites inevitably complained of excessive taxation and black and carpetbagger corruption, Governor Ames would point out in congressional hearings held in 1876 that Mississippi taxpayers paid only an average of seventy cents a person in 1875, as compared with sixteen dollars in New York State and thirty-six dollars per inhabitant of New York City. Republican counties in the state tended to be on better financial footing and freer from "plundering" than Democratic ones, Ames cited, and there were few examples anywhere of wholesale corruption.

The most notorious "black desperado" in Mississippi was probably Thomas Cardozo, the state superintendent of education, a confidant of Governor Ames, and the younger brother of South Carolina's Francis Cardozo. "Part of the drift-wood that floated into the state after the war," as one Mississippi newspaper described him, he arrived in 1871, hoping to ply his trade as a teacher to the state's ex-slaves and possibly dabble in politics, since Mississippi, unlike some other reconstructed states, had no significant native class of free, educated blacks ready to assume the duties of public office. Cardozo operated a school in Vicksburg and, a skilled writer, authored a column on Mississippi politics for the *New National Era* under the pen name CIVIS. By the mid-1870s he had won elective office in Vicksburg as clerk of the circuit court for Warren County, but it was there that his career began to unravel, for he was accused of creating false witness affidavits in order to steal the witness expense money, and was also said to have embezzled state education funds. To compound matters, a scandal from his past surfaced in the press. In late 1865 he had been dismissed from the American Missionary Association for having an affair with a female student (and funneling some of the organization's funds to her), and despite his apologies and his vow to reform, the AMA had shut its doors to him permanently. Subsequently, the press he received in Mississippi was almost uniformly hostile, characterizing him, among other things, as "a fugitive from justice" and "an ex-convict from a N.Y. prison-house." When his case involving the affidavit fraud came to trial, a jury — despite the defendant's being "shingled all over with indictments" — was unable to reach a verdict. Cardozo, faced with impeachment, would eventually resign his post and leave the state.

The ruin of Cardozo's reputation was unfortunate since he did have an impact on the evolving politics of Reconstruction Mississippi, writing a civil rights resolution that was adopted by local Republicans and eventually emerged in legislation, much as P.B.S. Pinchback had done in neighboring Louisiana. But black Mississippians had little interest in testing the progress of civil rights in their state by provoking challenges under the 1873 law. Even elected officials were known to abide by segregated traditions on railroad trains and on the Jackson horse cars, leading Cardozo to express frustration with men who roared defiance in political gatherings, but then went meekly to take their seat in the most squalid "colored" railroad coach.

In the summer and fall of 1874, only months after Adelbert Ames had returned from Washington to become governor of Mississippi, the pressure for change in the state, for "a white man's party to rule a white man's country," began to increase noticeably. One provoking factor was what one state Democratic leader called "The Black Cloud," the influx of blacks from other parts of the South, particularly from Georgia and Alabama. As those states experienced powerful Democratic movements in the early 1870s, black residents headed west to Mississippi because it had a stable Republican government and a black majority in many counties. It was estimated that between ten and fifteen thousand new black residents were entering the state each year, alarming Democrats with the prospect that Mississippi would become "a receptacle of the colored men generally in the South, and that they would resort to that state as a home," irretrievably "Republican-izing" the political landscape.

The flashpoint for this brooding concern proved to be the western river town of Vicksburg, where Democrats broke Republican control of the city by sweeping the municipal elections in fall 1874. Republicans still held the Warren County government, but the newly energized Democrats formed citizens' organizations to drive black and white county officials from power as well, rallying around alleged claims of tax abuse and misuse of government funds. A half-dozen of these "people's clubs" were assembled, each containing from sixty to one hundred men. The main target of their wrath was the black sheriff Peter Crosby, a native Mississippian and Union war veteran whom they charged with not being adequately bonded to serve his office. In Mississippi the sheriff wasn't solely a law enforcer but was also responsible for collecting taxes, making Crosby the very personification of the tax burden most whites thought unjust. After the town's newspapers published incendiary articles about Crosby and other black officials, a "people's club" visited him on December 2, which happened to be a tax collection day, and demanded his resignation. When he refused, a white mob marched on the courthouse, occupied the sheriff's office, and forced him to leave. Crosby fled to Jackson to consult with Governor Ames.

Isolated in the capital, Ames had less than adequate control over events in the state's outlying communities. In his earlier role as military governor, he had federal troops available to quash insurrections or intercede in local disputes. As the civilian governor, however, he was required to ask Washington for such aid, and federal troop levels in the state had by now declined significantly to a total of only about five hundred, stationed mostly at Jackson, Vicksburg, and the northern Mississippi town of Holly Springs. And although scattered local militia units existed, no state militia could be readily mobilized.

Ames's instructions to Peter Crosby have always been the subject of historical debate. He apparently advised him to arm a contingent of black men and return and take back the Warren County courthouse by force. Given the governor's own reputation for unflinching courage under arms, it's possible he did endorse this line of action, believing as he did that Mississippi blacks would eventually need to demonstrate their ability to stand up to white aggression. But it seems unlikely Ames ever uttered any of a number of more inflammatory statements later attributed to him by his political enemies, such as "I and other white men have faced the bullets to free the colored people, and now if they are not willing to fight to maintain that freedom, they are unworthy of it."

Over the weekend of December 5 and 6, Crosby printed and distributed in Warren County an appeal for support in reclaiming the courthouse. "Let us, with united strength," read the appeal, "oppose this common enemy, who, by all the base subterfuges of political tricksters, and the audacious mendacity of heartless barbarians, are trying to ruin the prospects and tarnish the reputation of every Republican, colored or white . . ." Black ministers reputedly read the proclamation from the pulpit on December 6, inspiring many congregants to join the ragtag army that, the next morning, Sheriff Crosby led back toward Vicksburg. Some of Crosby's "troops" had rifles and shotguns, but many clutched only hoes, axes, and pitchforks, and a fair number had no weapons whatsoever. Additional volunteers fell in as they advanced, although Crosby himself was said to have sudden misgivings about the enterprise and at one point tried to send some of his forces away. His instinct proved correct, for as his followers emerged from the woods near town they met a superior mass of armed whites, including even some former Union soldiers now settled in Vicksburg, as well as a party of Louisianians who had crossed the Mississippi River that morning to help put down the "black rebellion." Word of Crosby's threat to retake Vicksburg, it seemed, had passed through white vigilante channels as far away as Texas, from which a telegram had arrived: "Can raise good crowd within 24 hours to kill out your negroes."

One curiosity of the confrontation was that the former enemies Charles

E. Furlong, an ex–Union cavalry officer, and a Confederate, Horace Miller, were united against Crosby's invaders. Furlong had been the head of the Republican Party in Warren County but had undergone a political change of heart after being toppled from his post by party blacks. Miller, acting to stop the confrontation before it could begin, managed to capture Crosby himself and demanded that he order his followers to disperse before a bloodbath ensued. Outmanned and seriously outgunned, the blacks were no match for the whites, Miller cautioned. Crosby was willing to try, and a number of blacks did turn in retreat. But despite his efforts, it was now too late to head off a conflict, as the two "armies" were already in close proximity. According to a later congressional investigation, the whites rushed upon "unresisting and retreating men, who in good faith were carrying out the agreement [to depart] . . . It was no battle; it was a simple massacre, unutterably disgraceful to all engaged in it."

"The whites who came in from the plantations were particularly desperate and bloodthirsty," reported the *New York Times.* "They must have known that the ignorant negroes were misguided and misled, but, blinded by passion, they had no mercy for them." The blacks "were met at the city limits and slaughtered — simply slaughtered and butchered. They were chased through the woods and the fields and were shot down like dogs. Many were shot after they gave up, and some were shot on their knees, while begging for mercy."

Much of the struggle took place in the vicinity of the Pemberton Monument, also known as the Surrender Monument, the site where General Grant had accepted the capitulation of Vicksburg from the Confederate general John C. Pemberton on July 4, 1863. The symbolism of the locale could not have been more fitting. The drawn-out wartime siege of Vicksburg by General Grant and the city's ultimate defeat had long weighed on the minds of local whites — an indignity to erase, if possible. Such was the whites' zeal at this opportunity for retribution that when there remained no more of Crosby's "militia" to fight, they turned on residents of Vicksburg's black neighborhoods.

Casualty estimates in the so-called Second Battle for Vicksburg varied dramatically, from as few as fifteen to as many as three hundred; the *New York Times* reporter on the scene quoted a Republican officeholder as saying "not less than 200 were shot [but] . . . where these men were buried is a mystery, and how they were conveyed from the battlefield no one seems to know." Congress's report estimated that twenty-nine blacks and two whites had died, and cited an investigator who learned from a local man the trick of locating bodies lying in dense growth by watching where buzzards gathered overhead. The investigator, despite this newly gained skill, concluded that the total number of men missing and unaccounted for was "impossible to ascertain."

Notwithstanding the broad condemnation heaped upon them, the whites of Warren County had achieved an important emotional victory, demonstrating that they could defy the state's Republican authority and defeat what passed for an armed Republican force. After Crosby's men had been routed, one white suggested that the Pemberton Monument's inscription be changed to read "Here surrendered the Confederate chieftain in 1863, and here fell 100 Dupes to the unhallowed ambition of Adelbert Ames in 1874."

Vicksburg was the future that the Meridian riot had augured back in 1871, and Ames perceived in the calamity a severe reversal that could not be ignored. Upon reading the terrible dispatches from the scene, he convened an emergency session of the legislature and shared with the state's lawmakers his fear that if whites in one community could oust legitimate black officeholders by brute force, the entire state would follow suit. He urged them to vote on an immediate appeal to request President Grant's help. On December 21 Grant responded, issuing an order for Vicksburg's white vigilante groups to disperse; at the same time, a local board of supervisors in Vicksburg rescinded Crosby's resignation since it had been made under duress. On January 18, 1875, U.S. forces, without bloodshed, reinstalled Peter Crosby as sheriff of Warren County.

Although order was momentarily restored in Mississippi, a troubling series of events in Louisiana boded poorly for Governor Ames and his Reconstruction government. The first took place in the remote north central Louisiana town of Coushatta, where the Vermont carpetbagger Marshall Harvey Twitchell had used his influence as a state senator to carve out a new parish known as Red River, with a population of eleven hundred blacks and three hundred whites. To the White League, founded in spring 1874 to protest continuing Republican authority and operating openly as the paramilitary wing of the Democratic Party, Red River was a hated "Yankee Colony." When, in the last week of July, Twitchell traveled to New Orleans to attend the state Republican convention and seek help in dealing with White League activity in Red River, the league took advantage of his absence to abduct six prominent white Republicans, including Twitchell's brother Homer and Sheriff

THE WHITE LEAGUE AS A COUNTERPART TO THE KU KLUX KLAN, IN A CARTOON BY THOMAS NAST

Frank Edgerton, as well as several black men, accusing them of fomenting a black insurrection. After forcing the white captives to resign their official offices, the league offered them safe passage as far as Shreveport, on the condition they would there board trains for the North and never return. The Republicans had little choice but to agree although, concerned by the number of armed white belligerents in Coushatta, they insisted their captors escort them to Shreveport early on a Sunday morning, in the hope that their departure would be little noticed.

All went well for a few hours as the party rode northward on the morning of August 31; then, suddenly, a cloud of dust raised by horses' hooves was seen approaching rapidly from behind. Near a place called McFarlane's Plantation, about forty miles north of Coushatta, a fast-riding band of White League pursuers came into view. "Mount and ride for your lives!" one prisoner shouted to his friends, but too late: in moments, the ambushing party was upon them. Three of the Republicans were shot down in cold blood; the others were executed later that day.

Readers of newspapers north and south were by now accustomed to reports of vigilante violence in which black people were put to death;

the Coushatta attack was startling because this time it was six whites, Republican men of standing, who had been wantonly slaughtered. So bold an atrocity sent a tremor of fear through the entire state. In New Orleans, rumors abounded that the White League would attempt to topple the Republican government of William Pitt Kellogg and possibly kidnap or even assassinate the governor (just such an attempt had occurred on a New Orleans street once before).

In response, in early September police loyal to Kellogg seized a number of arms shipments entering the city and destined for the league, infuriating the intended recipients. On September 12, Kellogg authorized General James Longstreet and the state militia to intercept the steamer *Mississippi,* which had arrived, loaded with a large cargo of guns, at a dock in New Orleans. That night inflammatory White League broadsides were posted along the riverfront, and when the next day's papers reported that federal troops were en route to the city, the conservative press screeched angry defiance. "If the soldiers choose to get mixed up in broils with which they have no concern," warned the *New Orleans Bulletin,* "they must expect to come out with punched heads and torn uniforms. The time has passed when a blue coat stuck up on a pole can make us bow in abject submission."

On September 14, 1874, an estimated five thousand whites rallied on Canal Street, denounced the "usurper" Kellogg government, and threw up barricades of old furniture, bales of cotton, pieces of iron fences, and whatever else came to hand. When the police and Longstreet's mostly black militia, numbering about thirty-five hundred men, marched into lower Canal Street from the French Quarter, the whites opened fire from behind their rude defenses and from sniper perches in high windows. Longstreet's forces fought valiantly but were eventually pushed back with eleven dead and numerous injuries, including a wound to Longstreet himself. Witnesses said the former Confederate general had visibly blanched at hearing the rebel yell from the throats of his "enemies." As the police and militia retreated, the White League, also having lost about a dozen fighters, declared victory, seizing the state arsenals and all the city police stations — every official building but the customhouse and the federal mint — while the remnants of the Republican government, including Kellogg, retreated to the customhouse, guarded by a handful of federal troops. By the evening of September 15, the league had confiscated numerous weapons, including four cannon, and had even invaded the statehouse; there, a mob violated the sanctity of the governor's office and hurled from its windows all manner of books, documents, journals, envelopes, and sheaves of paper, which fell to the street, to the cheers of riotous citizens below. The *New Orleans Times* reported that dozens of police and militiamen had deserted, retired to their homes, or surrendered to the White League forces.

The league and the Democratic newspapers exulted in their success — one termed New Orleans "the happiest city in the universe" — and went to work at once to impress and reassure federal authorities that their sure-footed victory at "the Battle of Liberty Place," as a lower section of Canal Street was known, meant that the Democratic government of John D. McEnery deserved to be deemed legitimate. Some of the foremost citizens of New Orleans dispatched messages of friendship and loyalty to Washington; local bankers sent wires assuring federal authorities that they were able to provide enough cash for the new government; a consortium of bishops issued a proclamation blessing the league's actions, then rang the city's church bells in a chorus of deliverance and thanksgiving.

The revolutionists had surprised even themselves with the extent of their achievement. But as they awaited Washington's formal acknowledgment of their victory, Kellogg and his Republican cohorts were also busy working the telegraph lines, imploring the Grant administration to restore their authority. The White Leaguers had demonstrated convincingly the weakness of the present state regime, but it was Governor Kellogg, captive and isolated in the town's single fortified federal building, who over the next few days managed to win the country's sympathy. The national press scorned the seizing of a state government by armed revolt. Citing his constitutional obligation to defend Kellogg's government, Grant issued a proclamation commanding "turbulent and disorderly persons to disperse and retire peaceably to their respective abodes . . . and hereafter to submit themselves to the laws and constituted authorities of the state." He backed his words with additional troops and three federal gunboats bound for New Orleans.

The White League was momentarily caught off balance. Convinced, in the thrall of victory, that their triumph in the streets of New Orleans had earned them the right to govern, the group's leaders were chastened by the nation's disapproval and by Washington's rejection of their rebellion. However, they wisely took heart from all they had accomplished, decided to look ahead with greater confidence to the November elections, and agreed to surrender New Orleans to the Republicans.

The fall elections were relatively peaceful, although the Democrats contended that the Kellogg forces had used election trickery and fraud to gain a slight majority in the legislature. The Republican returning board had rewarded their own party with the votes of blacks who had not actually voted, claiming these citizens *would* have voted Republican if they had not been intimidated — a tactic of questionable legality. It was doubtful the Democrats would quietly accede to its outcome, and when the newly elected state legislature convened in January 1875, President Grant dispatched General Philip Sheridan to New Orleans to oversee the situation.

Sheridan, known as "Little Phil," had been for the past decade a ubiquitous figure in American military and civil affairs — helping to cut off Lee's army and force the surrender at Appomattox, distinguishing himself in the Indian Wars, and directing recovery efforts after the Great Chicago Fire of 1871. A stern administrator, he was familiar to New Orleans residents from his tenure there earlier in Reconstruction, and local memories of him were far from pleasant. When, on January 4, Democratic legislators who insisted they had won their elections tried to physically occupy five contested seats, armed federal troops led by Colonel P. Regis de Trobriand entered the hall and removed them. In protest, all the Democrats walked out of the building. At the same time, Sheridan sent two telegrams to Secretary of War William Belknap, which were made public, offering to arrest the local leaders of the White League. The most inflammatory read:

> I think that the terrorism now existing . . . could be entirely removed and confidence and fair-dealing established by the arrest and trial of the ringleaders of the armed White Leagues. If Congress would pass a bill declaring them *banditti* they could be tried by a military commission. The ringleaders of this *banditti* . . . should, in justice to law and order and the peace and prosperity of this southern part of the country, be punished. It is possible that if the President would issue a proclamation declaring them *banditti,* no further action need be taken, except that which would devolve upon me.

Sheridan's suggestion that Congress or the president declare citizens outlaws, to be hunted down by soldiers, and also the armed federal entry into the Louisiana legislature itself were poorly received. "It is surprising that a very able graduate of West Point, and a soldier who has so faithfully fought for the supremacy of the Constitution," the *New York Times* said of Sheridan, "should know so little of its requirements." The reported images of U.S. troops routing legislators "by bayonet," coupled with Sheridan's ill-chosen words — by using the term *banditti* he was not only calling white Southerners criminals, but also employing a racist term suggestive of foreign brigands — brought howls of disapproval from almost every segment of American society, in sharp contrast to the generally favorable Northern response to Grant's policy after the recent Liberty Place coup. The offense common to both instances seemed to be the unconscionable application of force to achieve political ends.

The Sheridan-Belknap *banditti* telegrams were reprinted in newspapers across the country, much to the administration's embarrassment, solidifying public anger and resentment toward Reconstruction's heavy hand, even as "Little Phil" himself, ever defiant, accused his critics of "manufacturing sensational protests for northern political consumption." Ironically, after the Mechanics Institute violence of 1866 in New Orleans, a comment that Sheridan made — "It was no riot; it was an absolute massacre" — had helped galvanize Northern concern about the irreconcilable rebel spirit; now his colorful language from the same troubled city had bent public opinion the opposite way. Disapproving editorials appeared in many big city newspapers, as state legislatures across the country sent resolutions of solidarity to the Louisiana Democrats, demanding an end to federal interference. More surprising were the sympathetic public meetings held in New York's Cooper Union and Boston's Faneuil Hall, long considered reliable Republican forums, decrying both this new federal aggression and the president's failure to immediately censure Sheridan.

The vehemence of the national reaction seemed out of proportion to the specific incidents and hasty words that inspired it; the insult of federal intrusion into the Louisiana legislature resonated with a significance that quickly dwarfed the event itself. What the points of Colonel de Trobriand's bayonets had really done, it appeared, was to deflate the country's reservoir of patience.

In summer 1875, Mississippi's white Republican postmaster, Henry Roberts Pease, appointed Milton Coates, a black man, to a job at the Vicksburg post office. A local newspaper warned that "the men of Vicksburg would not submit to have a negro assigned to the duty of waiting on their wives and daughters." But what most rankled local sentiment was a widely reported encounter between Pease and "a respectable citizen." "I hear, sir, by God, that you are going to appoint a damned nigger to be a clerk in your post office," the man told Pease. When Pease acknowledged the fact, his interlocutor declared, "Then, sir, I tell you it's a damned outrage, and this community won't stand it, sir," to which Pease infamously replied, "You will have to stand it." The exchange, and the Republican's menacing words — *You will have to stand it* — were soon the talk of the town.

Post offices, and the federal patronage jobs that went with them, were frequently a source of contention in the Reconstruction South, as they were relatively secure from local interference. But although it was useless for native whites to rail against the arrogance of Postmaster Pease, they found numerous other outlets for their fury. Increasingly, a Republican's ability to earn a living anywhere in the state was becoming endangered, as conservatives, with the cooperation of local newspapers, initiated a form of economic and social ostracism called "the preference policy." These papers published the names of known Republicans and advised readers to avoid hiring them, patronizing their businesses, or selling or renting property to them. One paper in Canton went so far as to intrude upon their love lives, warning that the amorous attentions of "Radicals" must be shunned by "every true woman." These pressure tactics threatened social isolation and often succeeded; white Republicans were usually the first to succumb. They "returned to the fold of the Democracy in sackcloth and ashes and upon bended knees, pleading for mercy [and] forgiveness," according to John Roy Lynch, the black congressman from Natchez. "They had seen a new light; and they were ready to confess that they had made a grave mistake, [and] . . . hoped that they would not be rashly treated nor harshly judged."

Economic intimidation was not always as effective with black Republicans; they had less to risk in a material sense and were more loyal to their political goals. It would take deadly riots, like those at Meridian and Vicksburg, to undermine most black people's sense of security; repeated outbreaks reinforced just how vulnerable black communities were and took a cumulative toll on residents' morale. Many such disturbances occurred at political rallies where Democrats demanded what was known as "divided time," an equal exchange of Republican and Democratic views to be heard by adherents of both parties. Some divided-time events were conducted with notable fair play. At their best, they provided an irresistible source of entertainment for people of both races living in rural areas, an opportunity that might come only once in an election season to see and hear one's political favorites up close and measure them against the opposition. With a fortitude unique to the age before radio and television, audiences sat through day-long programs of speeches, each of which might last as long as two hours as orators lectured, read from official reports, and laid out searing indictments of political opponents, keeping their voices supple with drafts of whiskey and branch water.

In the turbulent Mississippi of 1875, however, these events frequently turned volatile. It became common for Democratic speakers, railing at the heavy hand of Republican rule, to use the divided-time meetings to denigrate Republican standard-bearers to their faces; their supporters often joined in with boos and catcalls. Such provocations were particularly distracting at Republican rallies with a large black turnout, for the Democrats' insults and hissing inhibited the playful call-and-response of the political "sermon" that black speakers thrived on and their listeners enjoyed. Tempers flared when men saw their leaders disrespected publicly; shoves and punches would be exchanged, a weapon shown or perhaps fired, and violence would engulf the meeting and possibly the surrounding community.

On the evening of September 1, 1875, in Yazoo City, fifty miles north of Jackson on the edge of the Mississippi Delta, Sheriff Albert Morgan, a white carpetbagger from Wisconsin and an influential state senator, was heckled by Democrats while addressing a Republican rally. Yazoo was a Republican town with a majority black population, and Sheriff Morgan was roundly disliked by the area's whites. Not only had he effectively held together a biracial Republican government and promoted racial equality, but he had also acted personally on the latter ideal by marrying a black teacher and temperance reformer, Carrie Highgate. Moreover, Morgan's résumé was stained with what many whites considered a political "murder." When he had won the election and became sheriff, the losing Democratic incumbent, Francis P. Hilliard, had refused to vacate the sheriff's office, prompting Morgan and his supporters to storm the premises in a predawn raid. Hilliard and his own men then attempted to retake the office, and in the ensuing fight Hilliard had been shot dead.

The rally, which gathered on the second floor of Wilson Hall, had drawn perhaps one hundred blacks and a small number of whites. It began peacefully, but soon a well-known Democratic antagonist, Henry M. Dixon, whose vigilantism had won him the ominous nickname "The Rope Bearer," arrived in the company of several other White Liners, Mississippi's less regimented version of Louisiana's White League. Dixon soon left the hall and, as an act of provocation, returned with a black man named Robinson, a local barber known for his eccentric outbursts.

As expected, Robinson took to haranguing the meeting and would not be silenced. Some of Morgan's friends suggested adjournment, but the sheriff replied that "if we should adjourn the meeting under such pressure, we could not attempt to hold Republican meetings in the county afterward." He had been warned that Dixon was out to cause trouble and had heard that he and some other whites had earlier that day terrorized blacks by knocking dry goods boxes and other objects into their path as they walked down the street. Still, as Morgan later recalled, "I did not believe that they intended to break up the meeting by force, but to intimidate us, if possible, and I did not propose to be intimidated."

Once Robinson finished ranting and sat down, Morgan resumed the meeting by praising some recent efforts by the local Republican board of supervisors as honest and conscientious. Dixon loudly protested. In a response aimed at defusing the tension in the room, Morgan pointed out a member of the board, a Captain Bedwell, who happened to be in the audience and whose reputation was unsullied. "You can have no objection to him," Morgan offered, attempting to placate Dixon.

"Bedwell is a thief!" Dixon exclaimed. "They are all thieves!"

A voice nearby declared, "That's a lie!"

"Show me the man who said that," Dixon demanded, rising to his feet.

A chair was overturned and shots were fired as the lights in the hall were doused. Morgan, swarmed by Democrats, fought his way to a window, climbed out, and dropped to the ground. Other men spilled from the building, through the windows and out the front door. On the street, the town fire bell began to clang, bringing more armed whites from their homes. As Republicans fled, White Liners calling themselves "the Dixon Scouts" roamed the city in pursuit, spreading word of a Negro insurrection. At morning's light it was found that a white deputy who worked for Morgan had been killed, along with several black men; few blacks remained in Yazoo, and the followers of "the Rope Bearer" occupied the town.

From a hiding place, Morgan smuggled a letter to Governor Ames:

> My friend, I fought four years, was wounded several times, suffered in hospitals, and as a prisoner, was in 27 different engagements to free the slaves and save our glorious Union . . . I know how you are situated. I do not blame you. I would not give you more pain than you already feel at your inability to help; but can't you get an officer to come

> here? Is there no protection for me? I am ready to die, if it is necessary . . . but to be butchered here by this mob after all I have done is too cruel.

Ames, who was receiving a steady flow of bad news from Yazoo, wrote to his wife on September 2. "These white liners will do anything to carry the state . . . So far has this intimidation gone that I cannot organize a single company of militia . . . The old rebel armies are too much for our party, and the colored men dare not organize even though they know their liberty is at stake . . . Our only hope is through the U.S. enforcement laws." Ames had met recently with President Grant and was under the impression that federal troops were available if needed, although he knew the administration had little desire to intervene.

Blanche Butler Ames frequently left Jackson, preferring to spend time with her family in the North. Her husband, although glad his wife and children were not exposed to the difficulties of living in a place hostile to them, suffered in their absence, and the two corresponded almost daily. Having come to share some of her misgivings about Mississippi, he admitted, "This house does not seem a natural place for you and the children . . . It seems more like a hotel where we stayed, but for a day. This is not home and never can be. Slavery blighted [the white] people," he wrote, "then the war — then reconstruction — all piled upon such a basis destroyed [their] minds — at least impaired their judgment and consciousness to that extent that we cannot live among them."

The conclusion that Ames shared with his wife would be reinforced two days later, on September 4, at a Republican rally and barbecue in Clinton, west of Jackson. Nearly two thousand exuberant blacks entered the town, along with about one hundred white Republicans, their numbers swollen by a rumor that Governor Ames would speak. The party faithful paraded in celebration, their mules and horses "trimmed fantastically and patriotically in red, white and blue ribbon," a witness recorded, "in some instances there being more ribbon than horse." From the town square they marched triumphantly a quarter-mile to the site of a former plantation known as Moss Hill, where a rousing band welcomed the audience. As at Yazoo, however, a group of white men had come as agents provocateurs. "There is no doubt [the riot] had its origin with some young white men carrying whiskey, who, as all accounts agree, seemed likely to raise a row from the start, if they were not there for that express purpose," recorded the *Cincinnati Commercial.*

The program included divided-time speeches. The second speaker of the day, a Republican named Captain Fisher, had just taken the podium and was congratulating the first speaker, a Democrat, Judge Johnston, for the orderly and peaceful nature of his remarks. Then one of the white troublemakers shouted, "Well, we would have peace if you would stop telling your damn lies!" The band momentarily began to play, in order to calm the disturbance, while a few blacks tried to hush the whites. "Efforts, it appears, were made several times to quiet them, until at last they were approached by one of the negro policemen." When the police officer asked the whites why they could not show the same courtesy to Captain Fisher as had been shown Judge Johnston, the whites mobbed him, grabbing the collar of his uniform and dragging him along the ground. The local black leaders Charles Caldwell, who was a state senator, and Green Tapley swiftly intervened, freeing the policeman and urging onlookers to return to the rally, but suddenly a shot was heard. Lewis Hargraves, a black man, fell to the earth dead, shot through the forehead.

"The thing opened just like lightning, and the shot rained in there just like rain from heaven," said one witness of the sudden violence. Amid shouts and gunshots, hundreds of blacks fled, most on foot, leaving behind their horses and buggies. "[Whites] . . . chased [the blacks] for miles and miles, killing them as a sportsman would kill the scattered birds of a covey," reported the *Commercial.* One black later testified that he ran in horror from the gathering, pursued by men with "long guns," took to the woods, and barely stopped running until he'd reached the streets of Jackson, ten miles distant. "What can we do?" he implored of an acquaintance there. "It looks like Judgment."

At the scene of the riot, abandoned mules, horses, and carriages stood unclaimed for days afterward; some of the latter were set afire by marauding whites. The death toll included three white men and four blacks, including a woman, her child, and an aged man nearly a hundred years old; many others were wounded. Two of the whites killed were among those who had initiated the disturbance; there were reports that their corpses had been hacked at and otherwise mutilated. A diamond ring was taken from the finger of one of them.

When word of the melee spread, especially the ghoulish details about the dead white men, vigilantes quickly organized. White Liner units similar to the Dixon Scouts and bearing names such as the Southerns, the Flanagan Guards, and the Jackson Road Modocs, took the train from Vicksburg to Clinton, there to embark on a second and more deadly phase of violence: they roamed the countryside, seeking prominent Republicans. "One fellow, bearing a gun . . . said the train got there late and the darkies were hard to find," stated a news account, "that they killed only four or five last night, but that this morning they popped over eight." It was later estimated that as many as thirty blacks — including clergy, political leaders, and teachers — were murdered in vengeance killings in the wake of the Clinton affair.

"Oh, we didn't do much," one of the shooters from Vicksburg confided to a Northern reporter. "A few negroes committed suicide, damn 'em, that's all."

As Margaret Ann Caldwell, wife of the state senator Charles Caldwell, remembered, "They went to a house where there was an old black man named Bob Beasly, and they shot him all to pieces. And they went to Mr. Willis's and took out a man named Gamahel Brown, and shot him all to pieces. It was early in the morning; and they goes out to Sam Jackson's . . . and they shot him all to pieces. He hadn't even time to put on his clothes. And they went out to Alfred Hastings; Alfred saw them coming . . . and they shot Alfred Hastings all to pieces."

When Mrs. Caldwell asked a white acquaintance why whites had disrupted a peaceful event at Moss Hill and were hunting down black people, he replied indignantly, "You all had a big dinner yesterday, and paraded around with your drums and flags. That was impudence to the white people. You have no right to do it. You have got to leave these damned negroes; leave them and come on our side. You have got to join the democratic party. We are going to kill all the negroes. The negro men shall not live."

It had been a dreadful week for Mississippi and for the Ames administration. Within shouting distance of the state capital, a Republican meeting at Yazoo and an outdoor pageant at Clinton had become murderous riots, and once again the governor had been unable to protect the state's most vulnerable citizens from devastation and deadly reprisals. The state economy was at a standstill, harvests were in jeopardy, and many blacks were afraid to go into the fields to pick cotton. Wrote a citizen of Yazoo City to the governor, "I beg you most fulley [sic] to send the United soldiers here . . . they have hung six more men since the hanging of Mr. Fawn; they won't let the Republicans have no ticket . . . send help, help, troops. . . ." A pitiable plea arrived from Warren County: "The rebles turbulent; are arming themselves here now today to go to Sartaria to murder more poor negroes. Gov[ernor], aint [there] no pertiction?"

Ames was running out of options. He feared that black militias would only incite a greater reaction from the disaffected whites, as borne out by the Vicksburg debacle of late 1874, and he suspected that militias made up of whites would hesitate to confront White Liner forces. A proposal he made to the legislature to create special police units was defeated, while his public appeal to the vigilantes to stop harassing black people and return peacefully to their homes was greeted with derision.

After informing President Grant by telegram that "domestic violence prevails in various parts of this State, beyond the power of the State authorities to suppress," Ames on September 10 received a response from Attorney General Edwards Pierrepont, who asked for more details about the troubles in Mississippi and inquired as to why Ames could not handle them. Ames replied that he understood the official reluctance to intervene but assured Pierrepont that the crisis was all too real and offered to assume responsibility for calling in federal troops. "As the Governor of a State, I made a demand which cannot well be refused," he reminded the attorney general, an allusion to Article IV of the U.S. Constitution, which allows a state's chief executive to request federal support when a state's republican form of government is threatened by either foreign invasion or domestic unrest. "Let the odium, in all its magnitude, descend upon me," Ames declared. "I cannot escape the conscientious discharge of my duty toward a class of American citizens whose only offense consists in their color, and whom I am powerless to protect."

To help plead his case in Washington, Ames turned for support to Blanche K. Bruce, a U.S. senator from Mississippi. A Republican landowner in the Delta region's Bolivar County, Bruce was a large man whose girth made him one of the state's more recognizable black politicians. As sheriff, tax collector, and school superintendent in Bolivar, as well as a newspaper publisher, his low-key style had earned him the esteem of both races in western Mississippi. Ames so admired Bruce he had originally wanted him for his lieutenant governor, but Bruce, with the help of the state's leading black Republicans, had in early 1875 won appointment to national office.

Born in 1841 in Farmville, Virginia, to a slave mother and her white master, Bruce, like South Carolina's Robert Smalls, enjoyed a relatively favorable upbringing for a child who was by birth a slave. He became the servant to one of his owner's "legitimate" sons and was educated alongside him. However, "the white boy gave little heed to lessons, while the colored boy seized and held every scrap of knowledge that came his way," according to one account. The family had relocated to Missouri by

BLANCHE K. BRUCE

the time war came in 1861, and Bruce's young master hastened to enlist in the Confederate army. Bruce, having different aspirations, headed to neighboring Kansas, a non-slave state. He took up residence in Lawrence, a hub of abolitionist sentiment, where he found work as a teacher. But the great conflict that had seized the nation found him even there. It was his misfortune to be present on the morning of August 21, 1863, when the notorious anti-Unionist bushwhacker William Clarke Quantrill, furious over the previous month's Confederate reversals at Gettysburg and Vicksburg, sacked the town. The populace, roused from sleep by the dawn raid, fled for their lives as Quantrill led his desperadoes on horseback through the streets, shouting, "Kill! Kill, and you will make no mistake!" The mounted raiders, needing little encouragement, smashed windows and storefronts, set fires, and shot or bludgeoned anyone in their path. As many as two hundred people were killed or maimed, and numerous buildings left in ruins.

"Quantrill's band certainly would not have spared a colored man," Bruce later recalled.

> The night before the raid I had been watching and nursing a sick friend, and when the day broke I heard firing . . . Looking out of the window I saw armed men riding by firing pistols, and immediately realized that the enemy was upon us. To remain with my sick friend would have been to invite certain death, so I bade him *adieu* and with no clothing on my person but shirt and drawers, watched for my opportunity, got out of the house and hid in the brushes behind a fence.

After watching from his hiding place for some time, Bruce, still in his underclothes, perceived a lull in the action and made a break toward the Kaw River. He was seen, however, by some of Quantrill's men, who charged him on horseback as he dove into the water. "Fortunately, keeping my head under water, I managed to hide beneath a hedge of vines and roots close to the shore. The troopers rode to the river and searched everywhere without discovering my retreat, although they came within a few feet of me a dozen times. Finally they rode away, and I remained concealed in the river all day and did not venture to emerge . . . until after nightfall."

After the war Bruce briefly attended Oberlin, the abolitionist-founded school in Ohio, although he soon left for lack of tuition money. He was working as a porter on a Mississippi River steamboat when he began to hear of the public role blacks were starting to play in the postwar South. He was especially curious about Oscar Dunn, Louisiana's black lieutenant governor, and the urbane state senator P.B.S. Pinchback, both of whom he'd read about and who had, like him, worked the riverboats. "In the midst of their vassalage," Bruce was convinced, "my race had still preserved in full force and vigor, their original love of liberty."

The man who had narrowly escaped Quantrill's raiders was savvy enough to know Reconstruction's idealism might not last long, and he was eager to make something of it, and of himself, while good prospects remained. Visiting Mississippi in 1868, Bruce heard a speech given by James Lusk Alcorn and was impressed by the extent to which the former Confederate general was reconciled to the dawning of a new era in the South. Alcorn termed the citizenship rights granted by the Civil Rights Bill of 1866 and the Fourteenth Amendment "the logical sequence to the freedom of the negro," and he characterized resistance to Reconstruction as "a childish display of spite," which would only weaken the "influence of our friends and of the moderate men in the Republican party." Bruce liked what he heard, was introduced to Alcorn, and on the spot decided to remain in the state. He settled in solidly Republican Bolivar County in the fertile plantation-rich Delta, with its 2,084 black and 590 white voters, and immediately befriended H. T. Florey, the white carpetbagger who held sway there. "[Florey] had a big drum at his office which could be heard for miles around," a memoirist of the period writes, "and when this drum beat, like the great war drum of the Aztecs, it summoned the faithful, and they came from far and near."

Bruce quickly won the attention of state Republicans. Even though his weight hovered somewhat below three hundred pounds, he was always neatly groomed and carried himself with a certain regal deportment. He had a large man's knack for taking the world in stride and was known for his sense of humor, even when the subject was his own physique. "He stands very straight and is very dignified," the *Washington Bee* noted, when Bruce later lived in the nation's capital. "His face is round and very full about the jaws, which are clean shaven. His eyes are black, with a sparkle of fun in them . . . A small dark mustache curls in at the corners of his full-lipped mouth . . . He dresses quiet, always wears a high hat, and raises it French fashion to everyone when he bows."

Bruce's talent, honed perhaps by the dual nature of his upbringing, was an ability to interact confidently with both whites and blacks; thus began his political ascent in Boliva. In a debate during the election for sheriff, Bruce's white opponent allowed that Bruce was "a decent man" but unqualified as a leader of men because he had once been a slave and done menial labor. Bruce replied coolly that he had indeed once been a slave, but whereas he "had outgrown the degradation and ignorance of slavery and was a free man and a good citizen . . . the difference between my adversary and myself [is that] had *he* been a slave . . . [he] would be performing menial offices even now."

The Delta's white planters grew satisfied with Bruce's basic decency and, more important, with the evidence that he was not a wild-eyed Radical. His success as superintendent of education bore that out. Many whites had rebelled against the idea of supporting black schools with their tax dollars, but Bruce assured them the schools were to be segregated and would not be forums for political resentment; furthermore, Northern white missionary teachers (often derided as potential agitators) would be phased out as qualified black instructors became available. Bruce also emphasized that educating blacks in basic reading and arithmetic would make them more adaptable laborers and perhaps less inclined to malingering or drunkenness. So effectively did he sell the need for education that some planters contributed to build schools in places where none had ever existed. By late 1872 Bruce had twenty-one schools up and running in Bolivar County, teaching a thousand pupils.

When exactly Bruce learned of Governor Ames's plan to make him lieutenant governor is unclear, but he had reason to regard the offer with caution. He had closely watched affairs in neighboring Louisiana and had corresponded with P.B.S. Pinchback, who had become Louisiana's lieutenant governor upon the death of Oscar Dunn. The incessant political infighting there was a very poor advertisement for engaging in politics at the state level in the postwar South. To Bruce, the U.S. Senate, with its Republican majority and its prestige as a federal legislature, seemed a far friendlier destination.

As Governor Ames had requested, Senator Bruce visited Attorney General Edwards Pierrepont in summer 1875 to encourage him to heed Mississippi's plea for federal intervention. Pierrepont held distinctly negative views on Reconstruction, once characterizing it as a "false doctrine of despotic sovereignty," and had joined the administration in the wake of the public relations disaster caused by the federal intrusion into the Louisiana legislature. His skepticism was by now hardly unique. Bruce told Pierrepont that Ames's warnings about the present political turmoil in Mississippi were accurate and that without federal help, the growing crisis would mean the end of the Republican Party in the state, as well as the final snuffing out of the freedmen's voting and political rights. A show of commitment from President Grant, the black senator explained, in the form of federal troops and other technical assistance, might possibly stem the rise of White Liner outrages, which threatened to destabilize the outlying Mississippi counties.

Pierrepont received Bruce politely, heard him out, yet promised nothing, in part because at that very moment a number of Mississippi conservatives were paying him visits and writing him letters, offering exactly the opposite advice. They included Bruce's own senatorial colleague, James Lusk Alcorn. They criticized Governor Ames, suggesting he had not explored all possible options for controlling the situation, including the arming of white militias to be led by "the most responsible citizens in Mississippi." Even Hiram Revels, Mississippi's original black senator, whom Ames had removed from the presidency of Alcorn College after Revels defected to the Democratic Party, wrote Grant a public letter predicting that white Mississippians, if Washington would only leave them alone, would ultimately do right by the state's black citizens.

It did not help that considerable bad blood existed between Alcorn and Bruce. After inspiring Bruce's move to Mississippi, Alcorn had felt hurt when Bruce abandoned him in the gubernatorial race of 1873 to shift his allegiance to Adelbert Ames. So poor were their relations that on March 4, 1875, when Bruce was sworn in as U.S. senator, Alcorn showed him the ultimate disrespect by refusing to honor the Senate tradition of escorting his state's new member to the podium.

Of course, by late summer of 1875, convincing the Grant administration to authorize new military endeavors in the former Confederacy would have been a tall order for even the most persuasive legislator, black or white. Indicative of how greatly attitudes had changed, even in the North, the influential New York press largely concurred with Hiram Revels's apostate missive to the president; the *New York Tribune* suggested that Governor Ames suffered from an "excited imagination," and the *New York Times* proposed that if the Republicans indeed controlled Mississippi, now was the time to prove it, without anyone's help.

Pierrepont duly forwarded Governor Ames's telegrams, notes from his meeting with Senator Bruce and the other men he'd received, as well as some press clippings and his own recommendations to President Grant, who was vacationing at Long Branch. Relaxing at the edge of the serene Atlantic, the president began the chore of sifting through the information, weighing the hardship in the ever-troubled South against the duty of the national government, and pondering what, if anything, was to be made of the once-grand experiment of Reconstruction.

CHAPTER 10

THE ETERNAL FITNESS OF THINGS

After President Grant had considered the plight of Mississippi and its stricken Republican government, and weighed the various testimonies and advice received from Mississippians of both races and political parties, it was Attorney General Pierrepont who informed Governor Ames that there would be no troops sent to Jackson. "The whole public are tired of these annual autumnal outbreaks in the South," read Pierrepont's telegram, "and the great majority are ready now to condemn any interference on the part of the Government."

"This flippant utterance," Ames would later remark, "was the way the executive branch of the National government announced that it had decided that the reconstruction acts of Congress were a failure." Pierrepont went on to gently scold Ames for his decision not to arm loyal men in his state. "I suggest that you take all lawful means and all needed measures to preserve the peace by the forces in your own state, and let the country see that the citizens of Mississippi, who are largely favorable to good order, and are largely Republican, have the courage and manhood to fight for their rights and to destroy the bloody ruffians who murder the innocent and unoffending freedmen."

The historian William Gillette has shown recently that Pierrepont had in fact edited Grant's thoughts on the Mississippi predicament. The president, while expressing frustration about "autumnal outbreaks," had conceded that federal assistance would likely be needed in the state because Ames's request, "if made strictly under the Constitution and Acts of Congress there under," could not be refused; but he also told Pierrepont that, in the short term, Ames would do well "to strengthen his position by exhausting his own resources in restoring order before he receives govt. aid."

"Taking advantage of Grant's fatal ambiguity," observes Gillette, "Pierrepont proceeded to impose his own will and to block federal intervention. Quoting from Grant's letter, but out of context, he eliminated the president's appraisal of the situation, narrowed his interpretation of the reach of federal authority, and related nothing but the idea of pressing the Ames government to take defensive action on its own." Still, it's difficult to blame the attorney general for the abandonment of Mississippi . The president knew that the fight there could not likely be won, certainly not on terms favorable to his administration or to the national Republican Party. Pierrepont certainly colored Grant's thoughts with his own bias, but he was delivering a message that the president fundamentally approved.

The governor in Jackson had few, if any, alternatives to pursue if Washington would not act. Black self-defense was a chimera; no one wanted to provoke another Vicksburg, and even black leaders warned Ames to avoid at all costs anything resembling a race war. Ames nonetheless felt he had no choice. He could not relinquish Mississippi to the enemy without a struggle. He arranged for two militia units to be pulled together in Jackson, and one at Edwards Station, a small junction near Clinton, informing Blanche, "I have taken steps to put all the arms I have or can possess into the hands of colored people and shall demand that they fight." No doubt with the humiliating rout at Vicksburg in mind, he ordered one hundred copies of a manual entitled *Upton's Infantry Tactics* from a publisher in New York for distribution to black militia leaders.

Ames was foundering on what the historian Richard Zuczek has described as "the paradox of law enforcement during Reconstruction . . . In using the militia, Republicans incurred charges of military oppression; in not using the militia, Republicans betrayed a weakness that ex-Confederates were all too ready to exploit." Given local whites' deep-rooted dread of black rebellion, Ames's action could not have been more provocative — a carpetbag governor arming black men and encouraging the use of deadly force. The governor was denounced as "a hyena in human form, unfit to live and wholly unfit to die." As things turned out, Ames's bravado and the militia crisis both quickly fizzled: there was a shortage of qualified recruits and insufficient time to create, train, and mobilize a functioning citizen military from scratch. Only two black militia units became active in response to Ames's alert, and the leader of one, the state legislator Charles Caldwell, would pay a high price for his loyalty.

Caldwell, a blacksmith and former slave, had been a delegate to the state's constitutional convention of 1868. Shortly after it, he was assaulted in Jackson and, in a gunfight, had slain his white attacker. When an all-white jury concluded he had fired in self-defense, Caldwell became probably the first free black man in Mississippi ever to be tried and acquitted for taking the life of a white person. A resident of Clinton, he had been present at the rally-turned-riot of September 4 and had tried to head off the violence, but he had fled, along with many other Republicans, to Jackson when whites began their campaign of terror. Upon Ames's call for militia, Caldwell agreed to lead Company A, Second Regiment of Mississippi Infantry, the thirty miles from the capital to Edwards Station to deliver a shipment of arms and ammunition to other militia commanders from a reserve that Ames had kept under federal guard at the capital. The governor and other officials watched nervously as Caldwell's outfit marched and were greatly relieved when the blacks were not harassed while going to or returning from the railhead. Later it was learned that White Liner forces suspected Ames of using Caldwell's force to draw them into a fight, a spectacle that might bring federal troops, so they had shrewdly refused to take the bait. Having allowed Caldwell to march unmolested, the whites simply went back to the kind of terror tactics they knew best, targeting individual blacks.

Ames regretted that he had not earlier demanded that the militia be organized. "Election day may find our voters fleeing before rebel bullets rather than balloting for their rights," he wrote to Blanche.

> They are to be returned to a condition of serfdom — an era of second slavery. It is their fault (not mine, personally) that this fate is before them. They refused to prepare for war when in time of peace, when they could have done so. Now it is too late. The nation should have acted but it was "tired of the annual autumnal outbreaks in the South" . . . The political death of the negro will forever release the nation from the weariness from such "political outbreaks." You may think I exaggerate. Time will show you how accurate my statements are.

In desperation he made one last request for assistance to President Grant, noting that "domestic violence prevails in various parts of this State, beyond the power of the State authorities to suppress . . . The Legislature cannot be convened in time to meet the emergency." The administration reiterated its refusal of troops, but this time Pierrepont responded to Ames's plea by sending a Justice Department envoy, the New

York attorney George K. Chase, to console the governor and assess the situation on the ground.

Chase, arriving in Mississippi in the first week of October, met the state's leading Democratic representatives, the party executive committee chairman and former Confederate general James Z. George and Ethelbert Barksdale, a prominent newspaper editor. He helped schedule a conference with Ames at the governor's mansion. The Democrats sensed that Ames by now knew the cause of Reconstruction in Mississippi was lost and that he would be glad to accept a dignified compromise that would avoid more riots and killing. But still they worried about a federal insertion of troops as well as a rumor that Charles Caldwell and the deposed sheriff Albert Morgan intended to lead black militiamen back into Yazoo City. Ames continued to back Morgan's reinstatement as sheriff. Chase, however, was assured by Democrats that a large, dangerous white contingent at Yazoo awaited any such black "invasion" and that a massacre would be the certain result. Having noticed that many of the so-called black militiamen in Jackson lacked shoes, the New Yorker had a difficult time imagining them as an effective fighting force. On October 12, to everyone's great relief, Sheriff Morgan announced that he would not attempt to retake Yazoo.

In the meeting at the mansion, held the next day, the two sides agreed that the militia units Ames had activated would stand down, and no new units would be mobilized; in return, the Democrats would allow a fair, safe election to be held in November. Chase later recalled that

> the [Democratic] citizens expressed themselves well-satisfied with the Governor, and regretted very much that they had not known him personally before. General [Thomas J.] Wharton . . . said he was never more surprised in his life, and that it was hard to tell whether they had captured the Governor or the Governor had captured them. They said they were delighted with the turn affairs had taken, and that there would be no more killing, but there would be peace and quiet, and everybody would have a chance to vote.

The compromise in Mississippi was endorsed by many in the Northern press even as it was understood what Democratic guarantees about voting would likely mean. "Notwithstanding the apparent injustice of driving the negroes away from the polls, it might be better in the end for them, and it might be better for the white people, if that action were suffered, so as to be done with present troubles, at least," said the

Cincinnati Commercial. "The state needs peace . . . and it needs it badly . . . even at the sacrifice of a large share of justice and principle." One of the immediate benefits of the new understanding was General George's willingness to alleviate the problem caused by black farm workers who had fled to the state capital, seeking shelter from White Liner violence; the seasonal cotton harvest was not being brought in. "The city of Jackson was almost literally filled with negroes who had abandoned their work on the plantations and fled there for safety," Ames later told Congress. George personally wrote "passes" to black field hands who had become refugees in Jackson, to enable them to return home without being harassed.

Of course, the Democrats could afford to be lenient that fall in "allowing a fair election," for they had already succeeded at intimidating the black electorate. Not willing to take anything for granted, however, they spent the final weeks of the campaign working to seduce any remaining black voters by hosting several barbecues expressly for blacks, with bands, the firing of cannon, and stem-winder speeches from the candidates. At other Democratic gatherings the imagery was darker, including parades of wagons bearing empty coffins with the names of known carpetbaggers and scalawags inscribed on them. Isolated reports of violent attacks on leading Republicans also continued; the White Liners targeted influential men such as ministers in order to frighten their followers. "One smart nigger in some localities would control the votes of two or three hundred niggers," Chase later said, "and the Democrats wanted to get those recognized leaders out of the way; if they could not scare him out, then they would kill him." When, in the days just before the election, Chase complained of such abuses to George and Barksdale, they explained them away as misunderstandings or incidents of a personal nature. As Chase had feared, the Democrats were reneging on their agreement, but the election was now too close for federal troops to be sent to safeguard the balloting, even if Grant was to approve such a measure.

The tactics of harassment seen in the campaign proved mild compared to those of election day itself. Chase, in later testimony before a congressional committee, described the situation in Yazoo County. "Sublit had a band of . . . about 100 armed men . . . that went about the country scaring the niggers . . . they would start out on a raid with a rope hitched to each saddle, and would ride over the country firing their guns and scaring the niggers, and . . . when the niggers would see the ropes tied to their saddles, that was enough for them." Chase also witnessed an attempt to terrorize Governor Ames following a large Democratic barbecue in Jackson:

> They went to the United States camp and borrowed a cannon, a Government gun and caisson, hitched up four mules to it . . . The mob, as they passed the executive mansion . . . would stick their fingers up to their noses and make all sorts of grimaces at the windows . . . and hoot and holler at the governor, and several pulled out their pistols and fired at the mansion; while I was standing there a ball went up over my head in the window-casing. The marks are in the mansion and can be seen there.

These efforts at intimidation proved effective, erasing black voting majorities. Thus the Democrats gained control of both houses of the state legislature, while winning back four of the state's six congressional districts. There was no clearer example of the fraud that attended the election than the results from the bitterly contested turf of Republican Yazoo County. There, in the election of 1873, Republican votes had tallied almost 2,500, as opposed to 411 Democratic votes; by contrast, in 1875 the Democrats gathered more than 4,000 votes, against 7 for the Republicans. Not only had black voters stayed away (it was said the seven Republican votes were cast by Democrats in an attempt to suggest a balanced election), but more people had voted than actually resided in the county.

With the election over, the time had come for whites' final reckoning with Charles Caldwell. They had allowed him to play the hero as he led his loyal band of freedmen to Edwards Station, but his kind of courage could not long be endured. Shortly before Christmas 1875, whites in Clinton badgered Caldwell's nephew, David Washington, about his role in the Moss Hill riot; when Caldwell ventured into town to inquire about his relative's mistreatment, a white acquaintance named Buck Cabell invited him into a store basement to share a drink of holiday cheer. Caldwell at first demurred, but eventually acceded to Cabell's request. The invitation, however, was a setup for Caldwell's assassination. "They jingled the glasses, and at the tap of the glasses . . . someone shot him right through the back, from the outside of the gate window, and he fell to the ground," his wife explained. Caldwell, badly wounded, begged to be taken out of the store. "He wanted to die in the open air, and did not want to die like a dog closed up." He was dragged out into the street, where he told the armed assailants standing over him, "Remember, when you kill me, you kill a gentleman and a brave man. Never say you killed a coward. I want you to remember it when I am gone." His body was then filled with bullets.

Caldwell's wife came on the run when told about her husband, but it was too late, and she was driven off by the whites. "I went over to the house," she said, "and went upstairs and back to my room, and laid down — a widow." Tragically, Caldwell's brother Sam was also hunted down and killed that same day. When the bodies of the men were laid out in the parlor the next day, mourners witnessed a bizarre ceremony. "At one o'clock the train came from Vicksburg" carrying a group of White Liners, Mrs. Caldwell remembered. "They all marched up to my house, and went in to where the two dead bodies laid, and they cursed them, those dead bodies . . . and they danced and threw open the melodeon, and sung all their songs, and challenged the dead body to get up and meet them, and they carried on there like a parcel of wild Indians."

Ames, stunned by the death of a man he'd so recently lauded as a hero, confided to Blanche, "I have never read of such depravity among enlightened people . . . and what seems the saddest is that no class of Democrats, it matters not what may be their intelligence or position, frown upon these crimes." He shared his concern that "some of our party are indignant at me because of my action [in reaching a compromise with the Democrats]. By and by they will thank me for it. It was the only way they could be secure . . . My dread is that I fear somebody will think I have 'sold out' — but I have not, in any sense."

This concern, and his sense of honor, was all that kept Ames from resigning on the spot. Now that Republicanism in Mississippi had ended, he could never again hope to be an effective public officer, only the object of scorn and repugnance. Chase, who had remained in Mississippi at Ames's request, tried to cheer him. Describing his own successful professional and social life in New York City, he encouraged the governor to look ahead to new opportunities, to consider resettling in the North, perhaps in a big city where he could pursue a business career. Ames didn't know it, but he was fortunate to be able to contemplate his future at all. According to the Mississippi Democrat W. Calvin Wells, a conspiracy had been put in place to assassinate the governor just before the election. A "committee," Wells reported, "was . . . importuned to allow a squad of men to enter Jackson, surround the mansion at night, and take Ames and hang him to a post. We protested, not because we loved Ames, but we knew if this were done, troops would be sent by the President and we would fail to carry the election, and military despotism would be the result."

Shortly after the Mississippi election of November 1875, the black Mississippi congressman John Roy Lynch, who still controlled a substantial amount of black patronage in the state, visited President Grant at the White House to discuss a postmaster appointment in Mississippi. What Lynch most wanted to ask Grant, however, was why he had withheld federal support from Governor Ames.

Lynch, born in 1847 at Vidalia, Louisiana, was the son of a slave mother and an Irish American plantation manager who, before his death, promised both mother and son their manumission. The white friend who was supposed to carry out the dying man's wishes, however, went back on his word, keeping Lynch and his mother in bondage and eventually selling them across the river to Mississippi. Freed by Union forces in 1864, Lynch studied in missionary schools, worked as a photographer's assistant in Natchez, and eventually ran his own photography business and acquired local real estate.

Distinguished in appearance, possessing an innate gentlemanly reserve, Lynch had the advantage of speaking a very clear English, with no trace of "negroisms" or regional accent. In the late 1860s he volunteered on behalf of Natchez's black community to travel to Jackson to meet with Adelbert Ames, then military governor, to discuss the political situation in the Natchez area. Lynch hit it off with the governor, impressing Ames as the kind of person most needed in the state's postwar transition; the twenty-one-year-old Lynch returned home with an appointment as a justice of the peace. He soon rose to prominence in the state legislature, in 1872 becoming speaker of the house at age twenty-five; the next year the state sent him to Washington as the first black Mississippian in the House of Representatives.

JOHN ROY LYNCH

Once President Grant and Lynch had dealt with the issue of the postmaster's job, Lynch broached the subject he most wished to discuss; Grant, according to Lynch, appeared eager to unburden himself on the matter. The president explained that upon receiving Ames's request for aid, he had alerted both the War Department and Attorney General Pierrepont to review the possibility of sending troops. But a short time later, a delegation of Republican Party leaders from Ohio visited him, pleading with him not to intervene in Mississippi. Ohio at the time was "an October state," meaning its election was held a month earlier than Mississippi's. His guests pressed upon him the point that the Democrats would most likely win the election in Mississippi. Why put the Ohio Republican ticket in jeopardy by granting Ames his request? If the federal government intervened there with troops or through the courts, voters in Ohio would be angered and might throw their support to the Democratic ticket, endangering the gubernatorial campaign of Republican Rutherford B. Hayes. Grant was reminded that in recent elections in Maine, Republicans had fared poorly. Ohio could and must be saved, even though Mississippi would surely be lost. Grant told Lynch that this kind of sacrifice went against his own views as well as his sense of duty — indeed, he had acknowledged as much in his instructions to Pierrepont — but he also recognized the merit of the Ohioans' argument.

Lynch was bothered by what he heard; the president was saying that he had knowingly voided the Constitution in order to better his party's chances in a state election. It is unlikely Lynch expressed himself so forcefully in his interview with the president, but years later he recalled saying,

> What surprises me . . . Mr. President, is that you yielded and granted this remarkable request. That is not like you. It is the first time I have ever known you to show the white feather. Instead of granting the request of that committee, you should have rebuked them and told them that it is your duty as chief magistrate of the country to enforce the Constitution and laws of the land and to protect the American citizens in the exercise and enjoyment of their rights, let the consequences be what they may, and that if in doing this Ohio would be lost to the Republicans, it ought to be lost — in other words, no victory is worth having if it is to be brought about upon such conditions as those — if it is to be purchased at such a fearful cost as was paid in this case.

Grant recognized that his decision may have been technically wrong but said that he felt a powerful obligation to safeguard the party's future and that it was important to keep Ohio in the Republican column. "If a mistake was made, it was one of the head and not one of the heart," Grant acknowledged. "If I had believed that any effort on my part would have saved Mississippi I would have made it, even if I had been convinced that it would have resulted in the loss of Ohio to the Republicans. But . . . Mississippi could not have been saved to the party in any event, and I wanted to avoid the responsibility of the loss of Ohio in addition. This was the turning point in that case."

In the difficult fall 1875 election in Mississippi, Lynch had himself only narrowly managed to retain his House seat. The congressional district that he represented in the Delta had been gerrymandered to include the large but slender Republican districts that hugged the east side of the Mississippi River for the entire length of the state; for this reason it was known as "the Shoestring District." Democrats had traditionally conceded it to the Republicans, but in the run-up to the 1875 election, Democratic appetites were so large that party members set their sights on taking "the Shoestring" away from Lynch. To oppose him, the Democrats nominated the former Confederate general James R. Chalmers, who had been present at the infamous Fort Pillow massacre of 1864. Lynch's diplomatic nature and his generally good standing among the state's political commentators spared him some of the worst baiting and harassment of the campaign, although he had to dodge a last-minute effort by the Chalmers forces to rig the election. Seeking to artificially increase the Democratic votes in Adams County, Chalmers's men asked a Natchez newspaper editor what the expected vote total for Lynch was there; the editor in turn asked Lynch himself, who said he anticipated 1,200 votes in the county. The Democrats then arranged to fix the county's returns by having their candidate receive 1,550, seemingly a safe margin of victory. But Lynch, to his own surprise, actually polled 1,800; and because the Democrats had already fixed the results at 1,550 votes for Chalmers, they could not then contest the election.

The Democrats would make no such amateurish missteps when the new Mississippi legislature convened in early 1876. They promptly impeached Alexander K. Davis, the black lieutenant governor, so that he could not succeed Ames, and then won the governor's resignation by threatening him with the same punishment. (The infamous Thomas Cardozo, Ames's superintendent of education, was impeached at the same time.) Among the trumped-up articles of impeachment against Ames was the accusation that he had intended to incite a riot by sending colored citizens, "whose Captain was one Charles Caldwell . . . a notoriously dangerous and turbulent and obnoxious man of that race, to march, with guns and accoutrements of war," from Jackson to the town of Edwards Depot in 1875. They also cited him as the prime mover behind Sheriff Peter Crosby's attempt to "cause bloodshed" in Vicksburg in December 1874. Among the dubious statements attributed to Ames was the claim that he had callously informed Crosby that even if some blacks were killed in retaking Warren County, it would benefit the Republican Party: "What if it does cost blood. The blood of the martyr is the seed of the church."

Reporting to his wife on the legislature's actions, Ames explained that "their object is to restore the Confederacy and reduce the colored people to a state of serfdom . . . I am in their way, consequently they impeach me." Yet remaining in office until the next scheduled gubernatorial election in 1878 was out of the question. It was Blanche Ames who came up with a workable solution: if the legislature would withdraw the impeachment charges, Ames would resign. On March 29, 1876, the day his trial was to begin, Adelbert Ames stepped down as governor. With this act, the curtain fell on Reconstruction in Mississippi.

"He had given the state an excellent administration," Congressman Lynch said of Ames. "But these facts made no difference with those who were flushed and elated over a victory they had so easily won. They wanted the offices and were determined to have them."

Along with Lynch, Senator Blanche Bruce was active in demanding a U.S. Senate inquiry into the election and numerous instances of voter fraud, intimidation, and ballot fixing. Bruce was angered when the senators dragged their feet on the matter, and he warned that the events in Mississippi did not result from one political party's besting the other in a fair fight, but constituted a grossly undemocratic assault on the rights of black and white citizens. He cautioned (prophetically, as it turned out) that the tactics used in his home state would soon be emulated across the South.

Ames himself came to Washington to offer testimony. When asked his impression of the "true sentiments" of Mississippi whites toward the federal authority and the freedmen, he answered, "In one phrase, hostility to the negro as a citizen. Justice is what the Democratic leaders do not want. They want supremacy — absolute despotic control of the negro — to make him powerless in politics and in the courts of law, so that they can re-establish their old-time control of his labor as far as it is possible after the abolishment of property in man." The Senate committee heard plenty to raise their suspicions, but as the House of Representatives was now Democratic and officials in both chambers were fed up with the seemingly endless inquiries into Southern elections, the Democratic victory in Mississippi was allowed to stand.

There remained, however, a very high profile election case for Congress to resolve, that of the popular black Louisianian P.B.S. Pinchback. Appointed to a seat in the U.S. Senate in January 1873 by the Republican administration of Louisiana's governor, William Pitt Kellogg, Pinchback had run into a competing claim for the seat from the Democratic rump government of John McEnery, and the Senate had long debated the matter and deferred it.

Pinchback spent part of the summer of 1873 traveling in Europe with his wife, Nina, and returned from the Continent "invigorated by the free air . . . breathed even under monarchial governments" and "determined to devote his remaining years toward an effort to acquire for the colored people of America free and equal rights of citizenship." His optimism, however, failed to impress the Senate's owlish gatekeepers. On December 4, 1873, they passed along Pinchback's claim for his seat to the Committee on Privileges and Elections, which considered the case for eleven days before its members reported themselves hopelessly deadlocked. Pinchback was upset to learn that the reason the committee had stalled was because Charles Sumner had been absent from its deliberations. He had backed Sumner as a presidential candidate against Greeley at the Liberal Republican convention of 1872 (before ultimately switching to Grant), and even though Sumner was in fragile health, he was known to push himself physically when an important matter was at stake; his absence from the committee, where his eloquence might have swayed the opposition, was for Pinchback an inconvenient loss.

With Sumner unavailable, Oliver Morton of Indiana became Pinchback's advocate. The wartime governor of Indiana, credited with helping to keep the neighboring border state of Kentucky out of the Confederacy, Morton counseled his Senate peers that Pinchback should be seated at once because the Louisiana Supreme Court as well as the Grant administration had recognized the Kellogg state government, and Kellogg's legislature had chosen Pinchback. But Democrats on the committee continued to question that legislature's legitimacy, and Morton grew exasperated, accusing them of simply using Pinchback's case as a chisel to grind away at the president and his policies in the South. Of course, Pinchback was in fact being used by both sides. His insistence on claiming his seat was, by extension, the Kellogg administration's way of demanding Congress's respect and recognition; and, as Morton had cited, Congress's unwillingness to approve him reflected its own dissatisfaction with the endless political machinations in Louisiana and Grant's sometimes awkward way of handling them.

It also didn't help that Pinchback's personal history was well known. His past as a gambler and street fighter, his years as a protégé of the unpopular Henry Clay Warmoth, stories of his political maneuverings in Louisiana, and even his good looks and rumors about his romantic life — one linked him to the spiritualist and free-love advocate Victoria Woodhull — contributed to the image of Pinchback as a skilled operator and undermined his integrity. Like most state legislators of his era, he had indulged in the practice of buying and selling votes, although his most lucrative ploy was his participation in a scheme, as head of a committee on public parks, to purchase land chosen for a city park and then resell it at a profit to the city of New Orleans. Pinchback's cut of the booty was so generous, even his co-conspirators believed they'd been swindled. His name was also blemished by a congressional inquiry into Louisiana's 1872 election. Among the worrisome points were Pinchback's overnight elevation to lieutenant governor in the wake of Oscar Dunn's sudden (and to some minds, still suspicious) demise and the likelihood that a deciding vote in Pinchback's favor had been bought by Warmoth.

Pinchback never hid the fact that there were steamboat saloons and card games in his past — many of his contemporaries, after all, had worked the riverboats; the charge that stung him most was that he was selfish, a man on the make, not really dedicated to the interests of black Louisianians. He was justly proud of his advocacy for civil rights and his rapport with his constituents, and he bristled at the suggestion that the martyred Oscar Dunn had been the true people's champion and he, Pinchback, a mere pretender. "I desire to inform the members of the Senate and the members of the congressional committee in what my infamy consists," Pinchback said. "I am infamous because I cannot be frightened or coaxed into supporting the Democracy; I am infamous because from the very day the constitutional convention met in [New Orleans] I have championed the cause of the down-trodden colored people. From that day to this I have not failed . . . to cast my vote and raise my voice in behalf of the class I represent."

In Washington he had his share of defenders. The *New National Era* disparaged those senators who might hold Pinchback's early life or character against him. "The period of slavery was itself so monstrous," noted the paper, "that the blackest charges and the most obstreperous rumor grow clean under its awful enormities. Some become great rowers in Harvard or Cambridge who would have been boatmen without the opportunities of an education, others gamble with cards because they are reduced by the laws to the level of a position where they cannot contend for the management of men." Senator Blanche Bruce, who had made a personal crusade of helping to place qualified black men in government, also spoke for Pinchback. The two were friends with somewhat similar backgrounds — successful businessmen, Tidewater roots, mixed parentage, a riverboat apprenticeship. "As a father, I know him to be affectionate; as a husband, the idol of a pleasant home and cheerful fireside; as a citizen, loyal, brave, and true," asserted Bruce.

When the Senate resumed its work after the Christmas holiday, Pinchback returned to Washington with news that the Kellogg administration had reaffirmed him as its choice for senator. He went personally to lobby the president, although he was disappointed to find Grant hesitant to take a strong position on the matter. The *Era* admonished the president and other leading Republicans, noting that their candidates would need the black vote in the upcoming elections and that blacks would not view favorably a well-liked party loyalist like Pinchback being kept "knocking at the door."

In late January 1874 a new complication arose. A man named George Sheridan, a Democrat who claimed election to a House seat from Louisiana, was staying in the capital with Henry Clay Warmoth, who was serving as Sheridan's adviser. On January 19 they received a visit from E. E. Norton, a Louisiana Republican, who told them a strange story. He claimed that he was Kellogg's original choice for U.S. senator, but when Kellogg informed Pinchback of this, Pinchback objected in strenuous terms that he had already spread $10,000 among Kellogg's legislators in order to secure the job. Kellogg then promised Pinchback that Norton would reimburse him for his outlay. Pinchback took Norton's $10,000 but then double-crossed both Norton and Kellogg by successfully winning the post for himself. Only with great difficulty had Norton retrieved his money from Pinchback. How much of this story was true is hard to fathom — it's unclear why Kellogg would certify Pinchback for the Senate if he was not his preferred choice — but its outline, even in vague form, was highly damaging because it seemed to confirm, as many already suspected, that Pinchback was an unscrupulous opportunist.

Warmoth sent Sheridan to relate the story to Senator Morton, who listened with interest but questioned its veracity. Sheridan, on a tip from

Warmoth, then suggested that Morton simply ask Pinchback about it, predicting that Pinchback was so vain, he would likely admit to cleverly outmaneuvering Norton. Morton did so, and apparently heard enough to be upset, for he abruptly asked the Senate to remove Pinchback's resolution for admission until the Committee on Privileges and Elections could again review his credentials. "I will state to the Senate that since the adjournment of the Senate on last Friday evening I have received information which I think makes it important . . . that an investigation touching the circumstances of this election be made." Morton specified that his concern was not with the Kellogg government's legitimacy, but with Pinchback's personal conduct. According to Warmoth, "That was really, and in fact the end of Pinchback's ever being a Senator of the United States."

Pinchback was furious when he realized that someone within the Kellogg government had revealed the Norton story, and he lashed out, threatening to share some secrets of his own. "Let the investigation proceed," he declared. "Of one thing I am certain and that is that the result of a fair investigation will be to make me a minor figure in the grand cavalcade of damned scoundrels who will have to march in my van." Pinchback's outburst and his threat to tell all about his political confreres caused nervous Republicans in Washington to remonstrate with Morton; back in Louisiana, meanwhile, Pinchback's supporters cautioned the senator-elect to tread lightly; anyone familiar with the melodrama of Louisiana politics knew that an inquiry into members of the Kellogg government would lead nowhere good.

Pinchback did have another option: in the campaign of November 1872 he had been elected congressman at large; due to conflicting ballot results, both he and his rival, George Sheridan, claimed victory, although neither had been seated by Congress. With his Senate appointment now blocked, Pinchback renewed his interest in the congressional seat, again citing the fact that since the Republican faction had won the Louisiana statehouse and had been recognized by President Grant, his own election must be valid. If Kellogg had won in November 1872, so had Pinchback. As a result, Congress asked Sheridan and Pinchback to defend their claims before the House. Both addressed that body on June 8, 1874. Sheridan suggested that Republican fraud had brought about the appearance of two Louisianians claiming the same House seat and mocked Pinchback's interest in both Senate and House seats as unseemly, asserting that the ex-governor would be all too glad to pocket both salaries, if possible.

Pinchback in turn defended his loyalty to the Republican Party, even citing his willingness to attempt, at the suggestion of the party's chairman, the ill-fated "railroad race" from New York to New Orleans. "I demand simple justice, I am not here as a beggar" he told the House. "I do not care so far as I am personally concerned whether you give me my seat or not. I will go back to my people and come here again; but I tell you to preserve your own consistency. Do not make fish of me while you have made flesh of everybody else."

There was, however, a technical problem: if Pinchback was accepted by the House, he would have to drop his bid to be a senator, the latter obviously the more prestigious position. Characteristically, he decided to go for broke, renewing his efforts to gain the Senate seat. On January 12, 1875, though the House still had not resolved the claims of Sheridan and Pinchback, the Kellogg legislature reelected Pinchback as U.S. senator, and on February 8 the Senate's Committee on Privileges and Elections at last advised the full body that Louisiana had given him a right to his seat. Morton told his colleagues that with this new certification, Pinchback had a "prima facie title to admission."

The full Senate, however, continued to stall, citing the fact that the Committee on Privileges and Elections was not functioning at full strength. Pinchback, understandably exasperated, petitioned the Senate to act speedily on his claim. Prompting his demand was the fact that Nina had tired of Washington. No doubt in part because her husband's political status was ambiguous, she had never found her legs socially in the city, and despite support from some of the local black elite, she informed her husband that she preferred to wait out his ongoing Senate challenge at home in New Orleans.

On February 15, 1875, Morton once again called on the Senate to resolve the issue. It was a month after the national outrage concerning the federal bayonet entry into the Louisiana legislature, and the fall 1874 congressional election results had brought a Democratic majority to the U.S. House; therefore, for the Republicans, Pinchback's admission to the Senate had higher stakes than before. With a newfound party fervor arising from defeat, they were more eager than ever to seat him and help legitimize the Kellogg government, thus also granting legitimacy to the president's handling of the recent crisis in Louisiana. But the Democrats, recognizing this game, were uncooperative. The matter remained unresolved by mid-March, when the Senate agreed to table the issue until December. In the meantime, since Pinchback had largely abandoned his quest for seating in the House, that position was awarded to Sheridan, who was sworn in on March 3, 1875.

In December 1875, nearly two years since Pinchback had first arrived triumphantly in Washington to claim the Senate seat, W. L. McMillen, who had long been his competitor for it, abruptly removed his application and acknowledged the Kellogg government in Louisiana. But so determined were some Southern senators to halt Pinchback that they first tried to block McMillen's withdrawal; then, when that failed, they dug up minor procedural obstructions to slow Pinchback's appeal. The following month, January 1876, brought another surprise: the Louisiana Republican Party, frustrated with Pinchback's inability to win confirmation, had gone ahead and elected another man, J. B. Eustis, to the seat. The Senate reacted unkindly to Eustis's claim; the body was already consumed with resolving Pinchback's.

This latest delay proved too much for the usually subdued Senator Bruce. Pinchback's appointment, Bruce stated, was the only action taken by the Kellogg legislature that had been challenged by Washington, and to disregard Pinchback was to disavow all federal support for Republicanism in Louisiana. He pointed out that since Louisiana had a majority of almost fifty thousand black people, the charge that Pinchback did not represent the state's population was meritless. "Under these circumstances," Bruce concluded, "holding the question in abeyance is, in my judgment, an unconstitutional deprivation of the right of a state, and a provocation to popular disquietude; and in the interest of good-will and good government, the most judicious and consistent course is to admit the claimant to his seat."

In an executive session of the Senate, Bruce used more forceful language. Louisiana's white Republican senator, Joseph R. West, had just told the Senate that the confirmation of a U.S. judge, E. C. Billings, was a matter of urgent importance to the Republican Party in his state. Bruce blew up, indignant that Louisiana's white senator could demand urgent attention to a judicial appointment when Pinchback's case had lingered for so long. Citing the unconscionable delay, Bruce accused the Senate Republicans of abusing the trust of black Americans, waving the bloody shirt when convenient to help keep themselves in power, but behaving disingenuously when it came time to allow a deserving Southern black man the Senate seat to which he'd been elected. Blacks might no longer be slaves, Bruce complained, but politically they were still in bondage to the Northern wing of the Republican Party — good enough to help elect white men to office, but not hold office with them. He vowed to depart the Senate and return to the Mississippi Delta. "I can make $15,000 a year on my plantations, and the $5,000 I receive here is of no importance . . . Nor am I particularly anxious to remain here with a lot of old-time abolitionists."

Bruce then stunned his fellow Republicans by turning on the president. "General Grant has deceived us long enough. He is untruthful, treacherous, and insincere. My people will make terms with the whites who owned the country. They are honest and truthful and will protect the negroes in their rights." When a colleague tried to remind Bruce that Grant had been a loyal friend to the freedmen, Bruce would have none of it, insisting that he and other Southern blacks understood the dynamic of Republican hypocrisy; and he vowed to repeat his criticism of Grant in the open Senate. "You have upheld the Kellogg government in one breath," he scolded, "yet have refused a seat in this body to the Senator elected by the legislature, which you have solemnly declared to be lawful. I do not want to belong to a body which stultifies itself in this manner, and if when the Louisiana case is again called, it be not settled, I will resign my seat in a body which presents this spectacle of asinine conduct."

On March 8, 1876, Bruce got what he demanded: a final vote on Pinchback's appointment. By a close tally of 32–29, Pinchback was rejected. His own and his allies' lobbying efforts had failed to overcome partisan resistance, the persistent doubts about his character, and the simple fatigue many senators felt by now with his presence and the byzantine details of his struggle. In recognition of the three years he had spent in Washington lobbying for his own cause, the Senate awarded him $16,000 in compensation, about what he would have earned, had he held the job.

Thus the remarkable ascent of one of the country's most enigmatic black politicians ended. "[I]n the country the tides were changing," his biographer James Haskins writes, "and now Pinchback had been swept back just as he had been swept forward over a decade earlier. Then, the changing of the tides had heralded a warm season of political power for the black man and of political equality . . . But it had been for America an artificial season."

His last hand played, Pinchback did not dally in Washington but went home straightaway to Nina and New Orleans.

CHAPTER 11

BLACK THURSDAY

OF THE EX-CONFEDERATE STATES that the Reconstruction Acts of 1867 sought to reform, South Carolina, Mississippi, Louisiana, and Florida held on to their Reconstruction governments the longest. The others had, by the mid-1870s, already been restored to "home rule" or were in the process of caving in to the forces of redemption. Strenuous efforts to undo Reconstruction were nothing new; the difference now was that the resistance had grown ever more savvy, patient, and sophisticated in its ability to humiliate the occupying foe. In South Carolina, the state's black political leaders, including Robert Brown Elliott, recognized that purposeful measures were needed if the state's Republicans were to ride out the wave of white reaction.

Elliott returned home in February 1874, fresh from his triumphant civil rights speech in Washington, during which he'd gotten the better of former Confederate vice president Alexander Stephens and blazed a name for himself as a Republican orator of note. But when he took the podium at a homecoming gathering in Columbia on February 16, he did not, as some expected, commence a recitation of his now-famous address to Congress. In Washington he had eloquently defended black Americans' claims to Reconstruction's advances; now, at home in South Carolina, he wanted to speak about their responsibility. Deserved or not, the state's politics had become a national subject of ridicule, its Republican leadership deemed incompetent and corrupt. Though the characterizations were obviously exaggerated and inflamed by racial enmity, leaving them unaddressed entailed great risk.

As Elliott knew, whites in South Carolina felt that the Republican state government was excessive and wasteful, and this belief was linked to outrage at how the state had shifted the local tax burden. A central tenet of the constitutional convention of 1868, where the Republicans had laid out their blueprint for reform, was the idea that raising land taxes would drive the state's planters to break off small parcels to sell to blacks and poor whites. But this meant higher taxes for one segment of the population, with the potential rewards reaped by those who paid little or no tax. The higher rate of taxation, coupled with their loss of their slave "property" and other economic reversals associated with the war, had hit many landowners hard. Newspapers were filled with listings of properties that had gone up for sale as a result of unpaid taxes. Since many whites also felt excluded from politics generally, they described this imbalanced situation as taxation without representation.

Elliott was willing to concede that the taxpayers' anger had some justification. "Fellow citizens, rights impose duties," he told his supporters. "The question is . . . can the colored people of this state maintain and administer the government of this state upon the basis of self-government and unrestricted suffrage? The power we have will be our condemnation, unless we arouse ourselves to our responsibilities."

Realigning the state's tax burden might be one means of quelling the citizens' outrage, but in Elliott's view, reforming the culture of corruption and "easy takings" was at least as essential. Then, as now, this was a high-minded ambition. So pervasive was official thievery among both black and white officials during the 1870s that even once-decent men became, in the novelist William DeForest's description, "blinded by long confinement in the dark labyrinths of political intrigue as the fishes of the Mammoth Cave are eyeless through the lack of light." In New York City, William Marcy "Boss" Tweed and his ring bilked the public out of millions; Wall Street financiers rigged the markets and tweaked railroad stocks; in Louisiana, elected representatives gave themselves a stipend for "stationery" that was used mainly to buy hams and cases of champagne; in South Carolina the "Robber Governor," Franklin Moses Jr., arranged for the legislature to cover his losses at the horse track while running up an unpaid tab of a thousand dollars at a local cigar stand. Many officials, north and south, would have readily earned the droll estimation Lincoln once offered of Simon Cameron, his own first secretary of war: "The only thing he *wouldn't* steal is a red-hot stove."

But the question of who was corrupt was perhaps the wrong question; more to the point was who was most vulnerable to being exposed as corrupt, and who had the authority to make such accusations stick. A charge of corruption was "somewhat like the charge of communism in more recent times," notes Thomas Holt. "The key issue remained one not of corruption, but of power." In South Carolina and other locales where blacks, carpetbaggers, and scalawags commanded what struck natives as an inordinate and undeserved rein on state government, and where resentful Democrats were represented by a vocal press, the charges of theft, perfidy, and abuse all seemed to flow in one direction. Because many whites believed that blacks held elected office by special dispensation, they seemed to consider them less entitled to the usual illicit, opportunistic sweepings that came with political power. Elliott saw that black politicians were being held to a higher standard than whites, and resented it, but he warned nonetheless that inattention to even the appearance of the proper functioning of government could doom the Reconstruction experiment — in part by causing it to lose support in the North. "Misgovernment works its own suicide," he said. "We may shout our party shibboleths, we may repeat our party watchwords, we may discourse ever so eloquently upon the glorious principles of the Republican Party, but all this will not save us from overthrow and defeat, unless we maintain good government in South Carolina."

The home-state press was surprised by Elliott's "remarkable harangue" of his fellow black South Carolinians, and certainly far more pleased by it than by his civil rights oration. "With the courage and good sense which have marked his entire public career, Mr. Elliott condemned the state administration, and declared that the salvation of the Republican Party depended upon its instantly putting an end to the existing abuses," the *Charleston News & Courier* stated with approval. The *New York Times* noted that "Mr. Elliott has rendered a public service of the very highest importance" and encouraged the black men of South Carolina to take heart from New York City's own recent example of political housecleaning: its exposure of Boss Tweed.

Elliott, perhaps in part because he had been passed over by the state legislature for a recent appointment to the U.S. Senate, had decided to leave Congress in order to return to South Carolina. As had Adelbert Ames in Mississippi, he had become convinced that he could do more good at home than away in the distant capital. And in Columbia dramatic political change appeared to be afoot. The various scandals surrounding Governor Moses meant that Moses would almost certainly not win the party's nomination for reelection in 1874, leaving the way open for Daniel Chamberlain, the attorney general, to become governor. Elliott's biographer Peggy Lamson entertains the possibility that Chamberlain, who shared many of Elliott's ideas about reform, had encouraged Elliott to leave Congress and enter the state legislature, with a promise to appoint him speaker of the state's house of representatives, a perch of considerable influence. "Together, then," Lamson speculates, "the two men would work miracles in cleaning up the state's administrative and legislative stables." She hypothesizes further that Chamberlain, who may have had his long-range sights on one day being chosen by the South Carolina legislature as a U.S. senator, a job that was slated to open in 1876, eyed Elliott as Adelbert Ames of Mississippi did Blanche Bruce — a respected black Republican to whom stewardship of the state party could eventually be handed off.

Chamberlain applied himself with considerably more dexterity than his fellow carpetbagger, Louisiana's Henry Clay Warmoth, to righting his ship of state by appeasing Democrats and creating a solid center; and Elliott at first accepted Chamberlain's inclusive policies, confident in the sheer numerical superiority that Republicans enjoyed. Neither man recognized fully the growing depth of feeling among whites that South Carolina had to be redeemed from Republican rule at any cost, or the possibility that the state's black vote could be reduced to near-invisibility by determined Democrats.

It was Elliott who inadvertently helped push South Carolina in that direction when, in December 1875, in reaction to Chamberlain's handing out of patronage to Democrats, he participated in a black Republican campaign to pack an upcoming round of judicial appointments with men of their choosing, including William J. Whipper and the disgraced former governor, Franklin J. Moses Jr. Both were by now associated in the minds of South Carolinians with the worst kind of Radical arrogance, Whipper more unfairly so. Chamberlain was slow to get wind of Elliott's scheme. He was scheduled to travel to the town of Greenville to deliver a lecture on Thursday, December 16, and award scholarships to students of classical studies. A devotee of Greek and Roman literature and oratory since his youth, he had looked forward to the outing. Aware that the election of the judges in the state senate was slated for that same day, Chamberlain asked Elliott, as speaker of the house, to reschedule the vote. Chamberlain later said he had written Elliott a personal note making this request and that Elliott had visited the governor's office on the morning of December 15 and agreed to do what he could to postpone the election; the next day, however, with Chamberlain away in Greenville, the legislature went ahead and voted. In what came to be known in the annals of South Carolina politics as "Black Thursday," Republicans swept all eight judicial posts, including placements for Whipper and Moses.

The *News & Courier* termed this maneuver "the triumph . . . of the worst elements of negro radicalism." Whipper was described as "a full-blood negro . . . known to be ignorant and malignant . . . believed to be utterly corrupt," while "Moses is known throughout the length and breadth of the land as the Robber Governor, as a man whose rascality is equaled only by his audacity." The election of such purportedly nefarious men to sensitive judgeships could lead the paper to only one conclusion: "*War is declared upon the honest people of South Carolina.*" Across the border in North Carolina, the *Charlotte Observer* worked itself into a purplish lamentation: "South Carolina, noble old mother of learned jurists and pure statesmen, where has thy manhood and chivalry fled? Radicalism found her a garden, they have left her a wilderness. They found her a paradise, they have made her a pandemonium — a hell!" The paper, alluding to rumors of sexual impropriety that had long affixed themselves to the former governor, dismissed Moses as a "moral ulcer and despoiler of female virtue," while Whipper was simply "a stupid negro . . . What more can we say?" Even the Republican *Daily Union-Herald* feared the party in which it placed its faith had signed its own "death-warrant" and scolded Elliott and his allies for being oblivious to public opinion. Meanwhile, whites residing in the circuit over which "Judge Moses" would preside vowed to bar him from the courtroom by any means necessary, even "with muskets on our shoulders . . . [to] defend that temple of justice from desecration."

Black Thursday's chief victim, however, was Governor Chamberlain. The surprise election of eight Republicans, including the despised Moses, had so shaken South Carolina that Chamberlain's cautious efforts to build a partnership of conservatives and independent Republicans stood out suddenly as tepid half-measures. It was widely agreed that the affair had been the doing of roguish blacks seeking to demonstrate their independence from the governor and to gain greater judicial control of Charleston and the low country — a plan, according to the *News & Courier,* "to Africanize the state and to put the white man under the splay foot of the negro and hold him there" — and if Chamberlain's administration could permit such a thing, whether by design or ineptitude, it must be rejected, along with the black rascals.

Chamberlain knew that terrible damage had been done. In a letter to President Grant, he compared the absurdity of Moses's election to the improbability that New Yorkers would accept the elevation of Boss Tweed to a judgeship. "One immediate effect," Chamberlain acknowledged to the *News & Courier,* "will obviously be the reorganization of the Democratic Party within the state, as the only means left, in the judgment of its members, for opposing . . . this terrible crevasse of misgovernment and public debauchery."

Considerable sympathy accrued to Chamberlain, who clearly had been ambushed and who in desperation tried to issue an emergency order nullifying the ascent of Moses and Whipper (in the end he blocked them from assuming their judgeships by refusing to sign their commissions). In a bizarre, self-glorifying appraisal of what he perceived to be his own historic role in facing down the abuse of the Elliott forces, whom one paper had dubbed "The Black Band," Chamberlain informed the New England Society of Charleston that

> I cannot attend your annual supper tonight; but if there ever was an hour when the spirit of the Puritans, the spirit of undying, unconquerable enmity and defiance to wrong ought to animate their sons, it is the hour, here, in South Carolina. The civilization of the Puritan and the Cavalier, of the Roundhead and the Huguenot, is in peril. Courage, Determination, Union, Victory, must be our watchwords. The grim Puritans never qualified under threat or blow. Let their sons now imitate their example.

The *News & Courier* seemed willing to credit him for the effort, but most of the state's conservatives were having none of it. Black Thursday told whites that a carpetbagger governor could not, would not, keep the lid on black political mischief, and as Chamberlain himself had predicted, it emboldened them to pursue a Straightout approach that sought to drive every vestige of Republicanism from their midst. "A rumpus has begun in South Carolina which will end in the white people getting control of the state," noted the *Cincinnati Commercial*. "For a long time the whites have wanted a sufficient excuse to rise up and overthrow the African government under which they live, and now they have it."

The Fourth of July, 1876, was a momentous day, the century-mark of a nation conceived in liberty and dedicated to the proposition that all men are created equal. As elsewhere across the United States, the residents of Hamburg, a black South Carolina village located across the Savannah River from Augusta, Georgia, were in an exuberant mood. Hamburg had in antebellum days been an important cotton shipping port and link between train and ferry, but after a bridge was built spanning the Savannah, trains no longer stopped there, and the once-thriving town waned in significance. By the end of the Civil War it was, according to one history, a "ghost city" of about five hundred residents, "inhabited almost exclusively by Negroes and governed completely by Negro officers." The latter included Prince Rivers, a Union army veteran and former state legislator who was now the town's magistrate, and Dock Adams, who captained the Hamburg militia. Rivers, like Robert Smalls, enjoyed a local reputation for a colorful act of "self-emancipation" during the war, stealing his master's horse and fleeing across Confederate lines to join a Union regiment. His commander, the New England abolitionist Thomas Wentworth Higginson, had once described Rivers as "a man of distinguished appearance . . . six feet high, perfectly proportioned, and of apparently inexhaustible strength," adding, "If there should ever be a black monarchy in South Carolina, he will be its king."

Early on that Independence Day in Hamburg, Dock Adams was parading his militiamen on a city street when two white men, Henry Getzen and Thomas Butler, rode up in a carriage and insisted that the militia break ranks and make way for them. Suspecting that the whites were simply trying to provoke a scene, Adams informed them that the militia had a right to parade and that the carriage should go around; but ultimately he relented and ordered his men to open their ranks and let the buggy through.

Adams had good reason to think the two whites were looking to start trouble. July Fourth, an embodiment of the nation's creed of human equality, had always been a source of discomfort to Southern whites and a focal point for their fears of black rebellion. Since the war, the holiday had grown substantially in meaning for the freedmen, as had the festivities, which often included day-long barbecues, the firing of cannon, and public readings of both the Declaration of Independence and the Emancipation Proclamation. But even such humble demonstrations of patriotism could cause friction. On a July Fourth only two years earlier, in Edgefield's Meriwether Township, not far from Hamburg, a flamboyant black militia leader named Edward Tennant (known for the ostrich plume he wore in his hat) had disturbed whites with the "excessive" noise of his fife-and-drum band. When angered white citizens shot into his home that night, Tennent called out his militia; by daybreak on July 5, two hundred armed blacks had gathered. A local white vigilante group, the Sweetwater Sabre Club, roused by fear of a general assault, quickly assembled their own force of seventy men. A deadly clash was averted only when a U.S. army officer intervened.

Once Getzen and Thomas had whipped their buggy through his men's ranks, Dock Adams assumed he'd seen the end of the matter. He was surprised to learn, a day or two later, that the white men had accused him of having blocked a public highway; Prince Rivers ordered him to appear in court. On July 8, the day of the hearing, several vigilante "rifle clubs" showed up in Hamburg, along with Edgefield's Matthew C. Butler, a former Confederate general who had come as the attorney for Getzen and Thomas. Butler, whom some called "the handsomest man in the Confederacy," was Francis Pickens's son-in-law and had managed Pickens's successful 1860 gubernatorial campaign. But neither the war nor Reconstruction had been kind to him. At the Battle of Brandy Station, Virginia, in June 1863, a Union shell landed under his horse, blowing the animal to smithereens and damaging Butler's leg below the knee, forcing its amputation. He came home, it was written, "twenty-nine years old, with one leg gone, a wife and three children to support, seventy slaves emancipated, a debt of $15,000, and, in his pocket, $1.75 in cash." In 1870 he experienced the further humiliation of losing the election for lieutenant governor to the black candidate, Alonzo Ransier. Edgefield blacks viewed Butler as "one of the most malignant of the unreconstructed rebels" who, easily angered, was wont to address them with "a most highly sulphurated vocabulary." Even his white neighbors knew that "with all of his beautiful manners, when he wanted to he could be the most cold-blooded, insolent human being that mortal eyes ever beheld."

Butler, conferring with Rivers, insisted that Dock Adams's militia, which had turned out to support its leader, disarm before any hearing was held. Rivers advised Adams of Butler's demand, recommending that under the circumstances it would be best if the militia complied. But when Butler refused as a matter of principle to assure the black militia leader that his men would not be molested if they stacked their guns, Adams in turn declined to disarm, a response Butler perceived as insolent. With the situation about to turn "squally," the blacks withdrew to a brick structure that served as the local armory. "During this time, while the militia were taking refuge," noted an eyewitness who later sent an account of the affair to Robert Smalls, "the white desperadoes were coming into the town in very large numbers, many armed with guns, others with hatchets and clubs, not only from the adjacent county of Edgefield, but also from the city of Augusta, Georgia, until they numbered over 1,500 well-armed and ruffianly men." This figure seems unlikely, but certainly the blacks were outnumbered by the whites who surrounded the armory where they waited.

The rifle clubs loyal to Butler immediately laid siege, sending a group of skirmishers close to the building. Adams and his men returned fire, and one of their shots struck in the forehead a twenty-three-year-old white Georgian named McKie Meriwether, killing him instantly. Meriwether's father, who was present, screamed in anguish and rushed forward to pull his son's body from the firing line. "[McKie's] death exasperated his friends to the highest degree," noted the *News & Courier*, "and, their fire making no impression upon the house, they sent to Augusta for an old cannon, a six-pounder, playing it in an exposed position within fifty yards of the house." The cannon, a local antique used on ceremonial occasions, was loaded with rocks, nails, and whatever else came to hand, and discharged several times at the militiamen's stronghold. Although it caused little damage, it made enough noise to panic those inside, who, in the gathering darkness, attempted to escape out the back windows and disappear into a cornfield. Dock Adams managed to elude capture, but within half an hour most of his men had been hunted down, including some who had crawled under a neighboring house.

A kangaroo court was promptly held to adjudge the blacks' "guilt." Some of the captives recognized whites in the group and pleaded for mercy, to little avail. Henry Getzen, one of the men who had sworn out the complaint against the militia, fingered Allan T. Attaway, the commissioner of Aitkin County and a black militia member, as one of "those of the meanest character and most deserving of death." Attaway's mother had rushed to the scene to help her son, and according to a report made by the state attorney general William Stone and sent to Governor Chamberlain, "begged for his life, but in vain." Reported Smalls's informant, "[Attaway's own] pleadings were met with curses and blows, and he was taken from the sight of his comrades and a file of twelve men fired upon him. He was penetrated by four balls, one entering his brain . . . [and] after he was dead the brutes in human shape struck him over the head with their guns and stabbed him in the face with their bayonets." Four other men — David Phillips, Albert Minyard, Moses Parks, and Hampton Stevens — were led off a short distance and shot to death. Another chosen for execution, Pompey Curry, was shot as he attempted to escape, but he survived by feigning death.

The rifle clubs then joined with local Augusta whites — who were, it was reported, "inflamed with liquor" — to riot through the town, destroying storefronts, stealing furniture, tearing down fences, and even cutting the ropes of the public wells. Prince Rivers's home was looted. James Cook, the black chief of police, was slain, his head bashed in with muskets. The bodies of Cook, Attaway, and the other black dead were mutilated, an act witnesses ascribed to the whites' rage at the death of young McKie. A few of the marauding whites terrified black children with an offer to feed them pieces of the men they had killed.

The incident at Hamburg galvanized South Carolina politics. At first moderate whites denounced it; the *News & Courier* wrote sympathetically that the only offense committed by the black militiamen was "in being negroes and bearing arms." It condemned the cowardly killing of "negro prisoners who were shot down like rabbits long after they had surrendered," while reminding readers that the whites' natural intelligence and superiority over blacks made the use of the "shot gun and bludgeon" unnecessary. But Governor Chamberlain saw immediately that the massacre had created a trap: if he did not express disapproval of what had occurred, he would be false to his own values and to his constituents, but to denounce Butler and the rifle clubs and demand their prosecution risked further alienating the state's conservatives. It was readily apparent that Butler had provoked the trouble; however, Southern whites still tended to view any black resistance to white authority as unacceptable, no matter what the circumstances, and black militias were widely seen as disreputable. As the *Charleston Journal of Commerce* observed, no one could expect unruly black men "to be treated as prisoners of honorable warfare according to the laws of nations." In addition, for anyone to suggest that Butler, a gentleman and veteran soldier, as well as other whites, had lied about what had taken place would be construed as a monstrous insult. When a Republican newspaper did call for Butler's arrest, even many moderate whites leapt in, passionately defending a native son who had forfeited a limb for the Confederacy.

Still, Chamberlain had no choice but to speak out. "Shame and disgust must fill the breast of every man who respects his race or human nature, as he reads this tale," he wrote in a letter that was made public. "What hope can we have when such a cruel and blood-thirsty spirit avails in our midst for its hour of gratification? Is our civilization so shallow? Is our race so wantonly cruel?" But his initial fears were confirmed: instead of statewide revulsion at the Hamburg massacre, the incident only hardened existing attitudes while vanquishing any hope of collaboration; some Democrats were already warning that Chamberlain would use Hamburg as a pretext to increase the number of federal troops in the state before the November elections. "We have supported Governor Chamberlain's reform measures, and we have frankly expressed our opinions of the Hamburg riot," said the *News & Courier,* "but we must protest against any move that wears the appearance of taking advantage of a local disturbance to prop up the waning fortunes of South Carolina Republicanism."

Robert Brown Elliott was hampered by no such concern. He had moved swiftly to organize public sentiment over the massacre, appearing along with Daddy Cain and William Whipper at a rally in Charleston's Citadel Square on July 17 "to express our indignation, and to adopt resolutions setting forth the enormity of General M. C. Butler's outrage in Hamburg So'Ca." The rally protested "the late unwarrantable slaughter of our brethren at Hamburg . . . an unmitigated and foul murder" by Butler and the "lawless men . . . ex-Confederate soldiers . . . outlaws and semi-barbarians who, ever since the war, have practiced wrong and outrage upon the helpless, unoffending colored people because of their emancipation by the war." The rifle clubs were accused of having deliberately provoked the clash. From the podium Cain demanded to know if whites would stand for blacks insisting they give up their arms, as Butler had demanded of blacks at Hamburg. "No!" shouted the crowd. "No!" Cain answered back. The whites know their rights, he declared, but the blacks are learning from them rapidly.

"Remember," Cain told his followers, "there are 80,000 black men in this state who can bear Winchester rifles and know how to use them, and there are 200,000 black women who can light a torch and use the knife, and that there are 100,000 boys

ATTENTION!

Colored Citizens Attention!!

There will be a mass meeting of the Colored Citizens on Monday night, July 17th, in front of Market Hall, to express our indignation, and to adopt resolutions setting forth the enormity of General M, C, Butler's outrage in Hamburg So'Ca'. The following gentlemen will address the Meeting.

Rev. R. H. Cain.
Genl. R. B. Elliott.
Rev. E. Adams.
Hon. W. J. Whipper.

POSTER FOR A RALLY IN PROTEST OF THE HAMBURG MASSACRE

and girls who have not known the lash of a white master, who have tasted freedom once and forever, and that there is a deep determination never, so help their God, to submit to be shot down by lawless regulators." Cain had so fired up the crowd that ecstatic cheers burst out when a number of men from the rally blocked a horse car trying to pass along King Street. Police swooped down to arrest one of the instigators, but other protestors quickly intervened, chanting, "This is not Hamburg! This is not Hamburg! This is not Hamburg!" and hurried the man away into the safe anonymity of the throng.

Elliott called for a convention to be held three days later in Columbia to protest the murders. From this gathering came "An Address to the People of the United States," written by Elliott, which recounted the details of the affair. Signed by three score black citizens, the address dismissed the idea of Hamburg as a local misunderstanding, characterizing it instead as the fruit of the rifle clubs' long-running efforts to terrorize the African American settlements in the upcountry. The document implored the state's leading whites to reject rifle club vigilantism, invited all Americans to look on black South Carolinians' plight with concern, and sought President Grant's assistance in suppressing further violence.

Chamberlain enclosed a copy of "An Address to the People of the United States" with a letter he sent to Grant inquiring whether additional federal troops might be available for posting in South Carolina. The governor knew that Washington had begun to spurn such requests, but he was duty-bound to try. As it happened, Congress at that moment was discussing the redeployment of federal soldiers from the South to the West, an issue made more poignant by a military disaster in Montana only two weeks earlier — the annihilation of General George Armstrong Custer's Seventh Calvary at the Battle of the Little Bighorn. To Chamberlain, the Indian fighters' fate offered a tempting parallel to Hamburg, the latter "a darker picture of human cruelty than the slaughter of Custer and his soldiers." Custer's men "were shot in open battle," Chamberlain pointed out. "The victims at Hamburg were murdered in cold blood after they had surrendered, and were utterly defenseless."

The debate in Congress about troop deployment reflected the nation's evolving priorities and did not bode well for African Americans. As William Gillette explains, there had been twelve thousand federal troops in the South in 1868, but that number had been halved by the next year. More were siphoned off for western duty in the early 1870s, leaving about thirty-four hundred; by the time of the Hamburg crisis in summer 1876, there were likely fewer than three thousand soldiers in a region stretching from the Carolina Piedmont to the Mississippi Delta; although the number of garrisons was increased, no new troops were introduced, meaning that those available were spread out over an even greater area. And the soldiers left in the South tended to belong to "slow-moving infantry outfits rather than the fast-moving cavalry, which was reserved for the Indian wars."

Representative Joseph Rainey, in urging his congressional colleagues to increase troop levels in the South, could bear personal witness to the soldiers' importance. Traveling by horseback to a Republican rally one day in the town of Bennettsville, South Carolina, he and about sixty fellow Republicans were confronted suddenly by an armed contingent of more than a hundred whites who had gathered from the surrounding counties; a few had crossed the border from North Carolina. They brandished shotguns, ax handles, and other weapons. Not a moment too soon, a company of federal troops rode into view. They had been tipped off about the confrontation and quietly defused what could have been a very bloody scene. "The presence of the troops was most providential," Rainey told the House. "I am confident that members of both parties who are alive at this time, if it had been otherwise, would have been numbered among the dead."

When white congressmen seemed unable to grasp the full import of what had occurred at Hamburg, Rainey used an analogy to issue a powerful demand:

> What would be thought if here in Washington City, when a military company was parading on the Fourth of July, two men should come up in a buggy and demand of the officers that the company should get out of the way, and, if they did not, should at once set to work and murder the men of that military company? I ask you, citizens of the United States, would you stand for it? I ask you, proud Southern men who boast of your gallantry and your intelligence and your superiority to my race, would you stand it? I ask you, men of the North, who sacrificed your blood and treasure, who sacrificed the lives of your sons and your relatives, would you stand it?
>
> Do you, then, expect Negroes to stand all this? Do you expect my race to submit meekly to continual persecution and massacre by these people in the South? In the name of my race and my people, in the name of humanity, in the name of God, I ask you whether we are to

> be American citizens . . . or whether we are to be vassals and slaves again? I ask you to tell us whether these things are to go on, so that we may understand now and henceforth what we are to expect.

Robert Smalls also worked to ensure that Hamburg would not be swept under the carpet, producing in Congress the graphic letter he had received from an eyewitness to the Hamburg affair. When he was pestered by Democratic representatives to name the writer of the letter, he replied, "I will say to the gentleman, if he is desirous that the name shall be given in order to have another negro killed, he will not get it from me," and insisted that he himself could vouch for the letter's authenticity. The Ohio Democrat Samuel Cox, known for his sarcasm, then asked Smalls who would vouch for *him.* "A majority of 13,000," Smalls shot back, referring to his Sea Islands constituents and cutting off the titters Cox's query had prompted. Cox then began reading from *The Prostrate State* by James S. Pike, but had not gone far when Smalls, unwilling to hear South Carolina demeaned, inquired, "Have you the book there of the city of New York?"

The entire House burst into laughter. A New York Republican then chimed in, reminding Cox that "nothing in South Carolina could match his own state's record of extravagance and dishonesty under the Democrats." Cox, fuming, insisted that "South Carolina is today a Republican state and the worst governed state in the Union; it is bad all around, bad at its borders, bad at its heart; bad on the sea-coast . . . everywhere rotten to the core. Give South Carolina a democratic government," Cox vowed, "and you will see that every man, black and white, will be cared for under the law."

Deadpanned Ohio's James Garfield, "As they were at Hamburg?"

Smalls managed to tack on an amendment to the troop redeployment bill ensuring that adequate troop levels would be maintained in South Carolina.

In their correspondence, Chamberlain pointed out to President Grant that what had occurred at Hamburg did not auger well for the coming elections, in that it had terrorized the black population and brought "a feeling of triumph and political elation" to "the minds of many of the white people and Democrats. The fears of the one side correspond with the hopes of the other side." Grant responded that he too feared for the upcoming fall election, when the country's greatest civil right, "an untrammeled ballot," might well be put in jeopardy, and agreed that South Carolina was on the brink of the same violence that had so recently restored Mississippi to the hands of the former slave-owning class. "Mississippi is governed today by officials chosen through fraud and violence, such as would scarcely be accredited to savages, much less to a civilized and Christian people," Grant conceded. "How long these things are to continue, or what is to be the final remedy, the Great Ruler of the universe only knows."

When in early September a court convened in Aiken County, South Carolina, to consider charges of murder and conspiracy against Mathew Butler and other whites involved at Hamburg, every lawyer in the county offered to work pro bono to defend the accused. For good measure, a local vigilante leader Benjamin Tillman led a large contingent of men "armed to the teeth," many from his Sweetwater Rifle and Sabre Club, to surround the courthouse and await the court's deliberations. Because in the wake of Hamburg, Republicans like Elliott and Chamberlain had so vehemently "waved the bloody shirt," Tillman had the sympathetic womenfolk of Aiken daub forty shirts with red ink and turpentine, which some of his men wore to mock the traditional Republican complaint, a vivid form of protest that had originated the year before in Mississippi. He also had a huge mask created of a "Negro" with kinky hair, covered it with threatening slogans, and filled it with bullet holes. On one side read the motto AWAKE, ARISE, OR BE FOREVER FALLEN, and on the other, NONE BUT THE GUILTY NEED FEAR.

Dressed in their "bloody" clothes, carrying the grotesque mask, Tillman's mounted men began galloping back and forth through the streets of Aiken, with the horses' hooves raising an immense cloud of dust. It frightened away any would-be black spectators yet won cheers and applause from some of the federal troops on hand. When the judge hearing the cases announced he was considering waiting until the next morning to begin, the sheriff whispered, "You had better let these men get out of town tonight else they may burn it, and hang you before morning." The court wisely wrapped up its proceedings, saying it would bring no indictments, and the "red shirt" that day became the popular uniform of the Edgefield movement in South Carolina. The state, and the nation, would soon hear much more of Captain Tillman and his men.

With no legal action pursued against Butler's men, whatever moderate sympathy that had existed in South Carolina for the Hamburg victims quickly melted away, especially as the hotly contested 1876 elections approached. When, during a campaign appearance in rural Abbeville that fall Governor Chamberlain began to speak of the tragedy that had befallen Hamburg, he recognized the unmistakable sound of numerous pistols being cocked — a reliable indication in Reconstruction South Carolina that an audience had wearied of a subject.

Eighteen seventy-six was a year of well-deserved celebration, as Americans gathered at the Centennial Exposition in Philadelphia to mark the hundredth birthday of the United States. It was a moment to anticipate the future and to survey with pride the tremendous distance the nation had come from its colonial origins a century before.

The country was now several times the size of the original thirteen colonies (that year adding Colorado as the thirty-eighth state), with a population that had grown ten times over and now approached forty million. American industry, no longer located at the village forge or clockmaker's, was to be found in sprawling mills and factories. Manufacturing had been transformed by automated lathes and the sewing machine, agriculture by mechanized plows and threshers. Railroads spanned the country coast to coast, and San Francisco to New York was now a six-day run; harbors and rivers teemed with vessels carry-

PROMOTIONAL ARTWORK FOR THE CENTENNIAL EXPOSITION OF 1876

ing passengers and freight; and from port cities steamships embarked on transoceanic voyages. Chicago, still rebuilding from the great fire of 1871, had taken over from Cincinnati as the nation's meat-packing center, helping to launch a new system of nationalized food production and distribution. The first professional intercity baseball organization, the National League, was recently formed; Alexander Graham Bell had patented a newfangled device he called "the telephone"; and Mark Twain, one of America's leading humorists, had just published a semi-autobiographical novel of simpler times titled *The Adventures of Tom Sawyer.*

The reach of the nation's press had expanded. News of catastrophes such as train wrecks and the massacre of Custer and his troops were sped to readers, and the first sensational kidnapping for ransom riveted the public when four-year-old Charley Ross was abducted from the front yard of his family's home in Germantown, Pennsylvania, held for $20,000, and never seen again. The press coverage of "Little Charley's" vanishing was obsessive enough to compete with that surrounding the Beecher-Tilton scandal, which involved a sexual dalliance between the sanctimonious Henry Ward Beecher and Elizabeth "Lib" Tilton, wife of the New York editor Theodore Tilton. The Beecher-Tilton saga, the decade's longest-running newspaper soap opera, featured free-love advocates, spiritualists, and eastern intellectuals, and it made for irresistible copy while offering proof of the moral turpitude of even America's "best people." Less salacious but equally steadfast were the reports of official wrongdoing, thievery, and crooked financial dealings emanating from Washington and Wall Street, as well as accounts of abusive labor practices in the steel mills and on the railroads. "There has been so much corruption," one observer could only conclude, "the man in the moon has to hold his nose as he passes over the earth."

Also darkening the centennial mood were lingering economic woes from the Panic of 1873, which had begun in September of that year, with the failure of Jay Cooke and Company, America's leading investment house. Depositors rushed their banks and investors besieged brokerage houses, and for ten days the New York Stock Exchange remained shuttered. Ripples from the collapse in the East coursed across America to the plains and to the cotton plantations of the Mississippi Delta. Falling agricultural prices exacerbated tensions related to land and labor in the South; farmers cried out against railroads' price gouging; in Northern cities, hard-pressed workers and the unemployed marched for relief.

The widely shared anguish caused by the downturn served as another breaking point in the North's interest in the freedmen. CIVIL RIGHTS HAVE PASSED, NOW FOR THE RIGHTS OF WORK, a banner read at a rally in New York's Cooper Union, a blunt expression of a shift in mood as the dilemma of black field hands in the plantation South gave way to the growing concern for industrial labor relations and the plight of the immigrant working classes. The ex-slaves, many Americans felt, had already enjoyed a very long day as the nation's darlings.

Moreover, public faith in the president had fallen off even more precipitously. By now, the country was nearly a full decade removed from the days of Andrew Johnson's "Swing Around the Circle," when audiences stood in the rain and begged for a glimpse of Grant, the Union's military savior. To the glory of his battlefield successes, unfortunately, were now added years of bruising politics and widespread concern about his probity and competence. In the Whiskey Ring affair that came to public attention in 1875, it was revealed that midwestern businessmen had bribed members of Grant's inner circle to issue an illegal tax abatement on whiskey, causing the United States to forfeit almost $3 million in tax revenues. Later it was discovered that some of the money wound up funding Grant's reelection campaign of 1872 and paying for gifts for him and some of his associates; these included a team of horses given to the president and a $2,400 diamond shirt stud presented to Orville E. Babcock, the president's secretary.

A more embarrassing scandal involved Secretary of War William Worth Belknap, who was found to have engaged in a number of profitable schemes, including the "sale" of a U.S. military trading post in the West. Belknap was married to one of Washington's most fashionable society women, Amanda "Puss" Tomlinson, the sister of his late wife, Carrie. Before her death from consumption in 1870, Carrie Belknap had made arrangements so that a friend, Caleb P. Marsh, would receive the post tradership at Fort Sill, Oklahoma. The sale of these lucrative positions was common, but Marsh's case was complicated in that the present owner of the Fort Sill tradership, John Evans, did not wish to relinquish it. Marsh arranged for Evans to keep the post but pay him $15,000 annually (later reduced to $12,000), half of which — Marsh agreed with Carrie Belknap — would go to maintain a trust for her infant son. When Amanda Tomlinson assumed her deceased sister's place as the new Mrs. Belknap in 1873, she continued with the scheme, even though the child had died in 1871. Puss apparently used money from the "trust" to enhance her wardrobe and to fund her and her husband's active social life. That the secretary of war himself knew of the arrangement was made evident by Marsh's testimony that he had on occasion paid the money to Belknap directly.

When word of the scandal broke in March 1876, Belknap rushed to the White House and in tears gave the whole story to Grant, who on the spot accepted his resignation, thus allowing him to escape impeachment. Grant did this no doubt out of personal regard for Belknap (they had served together at Shiloh), but perhaps as well because Grant knew that his own brother Orvil and his brother-in-law, John Dent, profited handsomely from similar arrangements with post traders. Belknap also had much to fear from any further scrutiny of his affairs; he was rumored to have pocketed a kickback for awarding a contract to erect headstones in a soldiers' cemetery.

The Democrat-controlled House of Representatives smelled blood over the quick acceptance of Belknap's resignation. Not willing to miss a political opportunity to rub the nation's face in the affair, the House went ahead and impeached Belknap, although he was acquitted by the Senate amid questions as to whether an impeachment of a man no longer in office was legitimate. Meanwhile, the case packed no end of melodrama. Press accounts feasted on the recurring evidence of the Belknaps' personal collapse — a cabinet officer weeping before his president; the ruin of the once-celebrated Puss, now unable to face her peers; Caleb Marsh's ill-conceived escape attempt to Canada, during which he "showed symptoms of mental agony bordering on insanity." If war heroes and glamorous Washington figures close to the president could be seduced by such petty and cynical greed, what did it say about others entrusted with authority? What did it say about America? "Considering the official rank of Mr. Belknap, and Mrs. Belknap's position in what is called 'Administration society,'" concluded *The Nation*, "the whole story is revolting."

The scandal led the periodical to stigmatize Grant as a man lacking in character and inept at statecraft and civic affairs. "Pierce and Buchanan, and Lincoln and Johnson all had their faults as administrators," *The Nation* said, "but they were men who had grown up in office or in the forum, and who had sat at the feet of teachers in whom the original ideal of the Government was still strong . . . The crisis came when an ignorant soldier, coarse in his tastes and blunt in his perceptions, fond of money and material enjoyment, and of low company, was put in the Presidential Chair."

One effect, among many, of Grant's diminished reputation was to stain his party's image further and deny him and his administration some of the moral authority required to make hard decisions to defend his policies in the South. In the months ahead Southern Democrats would continue to exploit these weaknesses, denigrating Republicanism everywhere and portraying themselves as the necessary redeemers of what the *Vicksburg Monitor* termed "the albatross of Reconstruction."

If anyone might have managed to stem the tide of Straightout-ism in South Carolina it was Daniel Chamberlain, a successful moderate Republican governor with a comparatively honest record, whose efforts at meeting conservatives halfway had been lauded by the state's leading newspapers. He had even impressed many residents recently with his solicitous attention to state pride, seeing to it that South Carolina was well represented at the Centennial Exposition in Philadelphia and arranging for a hallowed local Revolutionary War unit, the Washington Light Infantry, to be honored at centennial events in Boston and at South Carolina's own Fort Moultrie.

However, the mood for redemption was strong, and Chamberlain's style had never sat well with natives. His precise, elegant manners and well-turned phrases tended to sail over the heads of his listeners; his speeches were "models of style and diction . . . suited to cultivated audiences," one contemporary said, but were "delivered to people who . . . enjoyed and understood only rant, shrieks, arm waving, foot stomps and funny stories about hogs . . . and hound dogs." On a personal level, the sick headaches from which he suffered were just one indicator that Chamberlain was beginning to flag at the strenuous effort he'd been forced to make — a New Englander with a degree from Yale and a penchant for classical verse, attempting to govern the deepest secessionist state of the Confederacy. It was said that his wife, Alice, "a perfect type of high-born, high-bred, Anglo-Saxon loveliness, noble in bearing," was increasingly unhappy in the South. She cared little for her husband's white political allies and had even less interest in receiving socially his black Republican colleagues. Visiting the legislature one day, Mrs. Chamberlain was spotted by Robert Brown Elliott, who strode down from the speaker's chair in hopes of being introduced. At Elliott's approach, however, she shivered noticeably and stepped back, simply saying the word, "No!" Elliott, understandably offended, never forgave the insult.

Chamberlain's discomfort stemmed from the mood of the South, which had shifted underneath his feet as he held office. In 1874 a Democratic majority had returned to the U.S. House of Representatives and included several ex-Confederate generals, and by the end of 1875, with

Mississippi's redemption and (in early 1876) the forced resignation of its Republican governor, Adelbert Ames, only South Carolina, Florida, and Louisiana, of all the Southern states, remained in Republican hands. Whites in the region saw clearly that there was no reason to come to terms with the Republicans and Reconstruction governments in their midst; they could chase them out or wait them out; either way, home rule would be restored, and in the new order of things there was no need to make room for even reasonable, conciliatory carpetbaggers like Daniel Chamberlain.

As recently as June 28, 1876, the governor had been welcomed by the state's rifle clubs at a dinner for Palmetto Day, a holiday honoring South Carolina's triumph over British troops in the Revolutionary War; speeches were given, elaborate toasts exchanged, but this last momentary light of reconciliation soon flickered and died. When the Democrats convened six weeks later to choose candidates for the upcoming election, they imported a campaign "expert" from Mississippi to describe some of the techniques whites had used there the previous fall to restore home rule. This character likely was either James Z. George or Ethelbert Barksdale, the fathers of what had become known as the Mississippi Plan, a skillfully managed campaign of intimidation just strong enough to keep blacks from the polls but subtle enough to avert any real protest from the North. Among other steps, the expert suggested that South Carolinians impress black voters with "a spectacular uniform, and . . . the parade of long processions of armed white men through the country."

Encouraged by the advice, South Carolina's Martin W. Gary, a former Confederate general, prepared a thirty-three-point Democratic agenda for achieving victory at the polls in November; it featured guidelines for physically intimidating the opposition. It included specific instructions on how to maintain discipline in the rifle clubs, many of which were organized like regular military units, with orders, drills, and a system of rank that reprised positions of authority once held under arms in the Confederacy. The campaign would be sweeping in scope, aimed not to achieve parity with the Republicans but to wipe them out, ultimately placing a Democrat in every elective or appointed office in South Carolina. Point 12 advised that "every Democrat must feel honor bound to control the vote of at least one negro, by intimidation, purchase, keeping him away or as each individual may determine, how he may best accomplish it." Point 16 cautioned Democrats to "never threaten a man individually if he deserves to be threatened, the necessities of the

CONFEDERATE TROOPS IN RETREAT

times require that he should die. A dead Radical is very harmless — a threatened Radical or one driven off by threats from the scene of his operations is often very troublesome, sometimes dangerous, always vindictive."

Gary was the descendant of old Edgefield aristocracy, an attorney and cotton planter "devoted to his fine horses . . . game chickens, and the . . . merry music of the hunter's horn." He had a violent temper and was considered too unpredictable — some thought genuinely crazy — to be part of the Democratic brain trust. Nonetheless he was highly visible at events during the campaign of 1876, his head "as bald as a billiard ball" (he was known as "the Bald Eagle of the Confederacy"), an impulsive man who seemed in a perpetual state of agitation and who spoke in a rush of words. "He goes off in conversation like a skyrocket," explained a sympathetic biographer. "Five feet eleven in height, with an elegant, well-proportioned form, he bore himself with an air of distinction. His classic features, mobile and full of expression, were lighted by the searching grayish-blue eyes of the natural fighter, and more than one man was to quail before his fiery glance."

He was most renowned for a valorous utterance on the field of battle at Second Bull Run, where, during pitched fighting, a Yankee colonel had demanded the surrender of Gary's troops. "What, sir?" Gary famously exclaimed. "These are South Carolinians, and will never surrender!" The next day he led an attack that destroyed an entire federal unit. Placed in charge of the defense of Richmond in spring 1865, he was said to be the last officer to flee the Confederate capital before the Union advance into that city. It was characteristic of Gary that while Grant and

Lee were discussing surrender at Appomattox, he was dodging federal patrols and boasting of his will to fight on; it was a point of great pride that he had never actually surrendered to the Yankees, never formally conceded the cause — a resolve that informed his belligerence toward Reconstruction and his will to overthrow it.

The special talent of Gary and his Red Shirts, whose distinctive "uniform" had been christened at Hamburg, was their ability to intimidate black and white Republicans, frequently by unlawful means, while posing as the orderly legions of the righteous. Earlier Klan violence in South Carolina in 1870–71 had been instructive: Klan actions were too random and indiscriminate, merely punishing individuals without being linked to an orderly call for change. Without an overarching political agenda, night riding could frighten and alienate even would-be sympathizers and possibly trigger federal intervention. The Red Shirts improved on this model by amassing huge legions of "troops," charging them with the idea that they were the vanguard of a new dawn in the South and keeping a modicum of control over who rode in their ranks; young boys and known hoodlums were discouraged from taking part.

By August of 1876 somewhere between two hundred and three hundred rifle clubs had formed in South Carolina, with a total of nearly fifteen thousand members. They were most active in Edgefield, Laurens, Aiken, Barnwell, and Abbeville Counties, upcountry areas in the southwest part of the state. Armed to the teeth and riding in groups that ranged from fifteen to two hundred, they broke up or interfered with Republican rallies, sent deadly warnings to Republican leaders, published proclamations in newspapers, and placed the names of black Republicans in so-called "dead books" — individuals who would be reckoned with in good time. "They do not claim to be Americans," a *New York Times* correspondent wrote of the Red Shirts, "[but] proudly boast that they are South Carolinians, and they are fully prepared to follow Gen. Gary's terrible instructions. I do not exaggerate . . . when I say that they are again animated by the same spirit of disorder and rebellion which brought on the civil war sixteen years ago. They are better organized than they were then, and they are better armed."

They also had brought forward an ideal candidate to lead the state's redemption, the former Confederate general Wade Hampton. A major landowner in both South Carolina and Mississippi, Hampton was the grandson and namesake of a renowned Revolutionary War figure who had also served in Congress. His father had been with Andrew Jackson at the Battle of New Orleans. Fiercely loyal to South Carolina, he had never been an ardent secessionist, yet responded to the tocsin of battle by using his personal fortune to finance his own Confederate regiment, "Hampton's Legion," at whose head he won acclaim as a battlefield tactician, despite his lack of formal military training.

But Hampton's most winning trait was a cool demeanor borne of entitlement, a gentlemanly restraint that separated him from the more combustible Martin Gary or Mathew Butler. For all his wealth and aristocratic Southern ways, he was markedly democratic in his openness to people of all rank. At war's end, he had been gracious in accepting the fundamental results of the conflict, saying of the freedman, "As a slave, he was faithful to us; as a free man, let us treat him as a friend. Deal with him frankly, justly, kindly."

There was, however, nothing soft or effete about Hampton. In combat he was said to have been fearless, wading into the thick of battle and dispatching Union cavalrymen with a broadsword, apparently some sort of family heirloom. On the campaign trail he took delight in mocking the aides and reporters who tried to keep pace with him, since much of the travel was done on horseback. "He was a big, powerful, athletic man," remarked a contemporary, "carrying just enough extra flesh to become his 58 years. When in the saddle he looked as if he and the horse were one."

One of the more significant effects of Hampton's candidacy was that it converted F. W. Dawson, the influential British-born editor of the *Charleston News & Courier,* to the Democratic cause. Dawson had enlisted in the Confederate navy during the war, then joined the Army of Northern Virginia, rising to an officer's rank, and saw action in numerous battles before being made a prisoner of war. Managing Charleston's leading paper after the peace, he became a barometer of moderate white opinion. In 1868 he organized biracial political meetings in Charleston for the local city council elections, gatherings Dawson proudly claimed were the first of their kind in the state. By the mid-1870s, he and his paper supported Daniel Chamberlain's reforms and voiced skepticism of hotheaded Democrats like Gary and Butler. "Straightout-ism, with its threat and bluster, with its possible disturbances and certain turmoil, is the foe of mercantile security and commercial prosperity," he wrote in May 1876. The threats of federal intervention or disruptions to commerce were the editor's chief apprehensions.

When Hamburg occurred, however, and the Straightout movement burst forth, the *News & Courier* found itself editorially stranded.

Readers canceled subscriptions. Several whites, including Gary, challenged Dawson to duel, as if to ascertain how Southern a man Dawson really was (a threat the editor took seriously, as he regarded Gary as unbalanced). So long as the Straightout policy was represented by the likes of Butler and Gary, Dawson remained convinced it was suicidal; the harsh mistreatment of blacks in denying them the ballot would only bring more federal troops into the state. But when the Democrats chose the rocklike Wade Hampton as their standard-bearer, Dawson had a change of heart, and the *News & Courier* restyled itself as a Straightout paper, dropping its fealty to Chamberlain. Dawson's turnabout was "an audacious, masterly somersault at which everybody laughed," but it was a move that most people approved of and one that ended a long-simmering tension.

The newspaper immediately demonstrated its new mien by lampooning the black politician Joseph Rainey, who in his reelection bid for Congress had warned his constituents against the Straightouts, citing their ultimate intention to disenfranchise blacks. Calling Rainey "a very light mulatto, of limited ability," the *News & Courier* endorsed his Democratic competitor, a white man named Richardson who, it vowed, "will guard the interests of the colored people far more vigilantly than Rainey has done. Colored Congressmen have no earthly influence in Washington," the paper alleged, "even among Republicans. Intelligent, highly educated and influential whites are what the Southern people, irrespective of color, need in Congress, and such are the Democratic candidates."

The conversion of Dawson was but one indicator that the choice of Wade Hampton had been an inspired one. Even some blacks were susceptible to his charms, awakening the longstanding Republican fear that the planter class would manage to reunite emotionally with its former slaves. One of the more notable blacks to espouse support for Democratic positions was Martin Delany, an abolitionist and Harvard-educated physician who attained the rank of major in the war and served in the Freedmen's Bureau. His speeches and writings stated that the experiment of Reconstruction had failed to convince the nation that blacks could be taken seriously as custodians of government. They must now strike the best bargain possible with Southern whites, whatever compromise they could salvage, before the final curtain of Reconstruction was rung down. "Rest assured of this," said Delany, "that there are no white people North or South who will submit to see blacks rule over the whites in America. We may as well be plain and candid on this point, look each other in the face, and let the truth be known." Francis Dawson thought Delany "a black prophet" and called his advice to his fellow black citizens "a solemn warning . . . They cannot hereafter complain that there was not one of their race who possessed the boldness and ability to expose their faults, and point out to them the edge of the precipice on which, in blind security, they stand."

By assuring the freedmen that he would respect their rights to free labor, to the ballot, and to education ("I pledge my faith," he wrote in a campaign pamphlet, "that if we are elected . . . we will observe, protect, and defend the rights of the colored man as quickly as [of] any man in South Carolina"), Hampton held out the vision of a government run by the South's native leadership class, one that would reconstitute the caring paternalism of antebellum times while respecting the blacks' new status as citizens.

Certainly most blacks remained skeptical, and even some whites murmured that Hampton's vaunted heroism and wealth were mostly illusions — that he was more shabby genteel than true aristocrat, a man who banked on the glory of his ancestors. ("Like a beet," quipped the *New York Times,* "the better part of him is underground.") But the program was seductive, appearing to offer the best of all worlds, or at the least an alternative to the tumult of Reconstruction. The Hampton forces went out of their way to coddle those blacks curious about joining the Democracy, staging free barbecues "for colored brethren, and engaging speakers [who] tried to amuse, instruct, and interest them." At every rally Hampton's aides made sure a section of chairs with quality views of the stage were set aside for black attendees. "The only way to bring about prosperity in this state is to bring the two races in friendly relations together," the candidate assured an audience at Abbeville in mid-September. "If there is a white man in this assembly [who] believes that when I am elected Governor, I will stand between him and the law, or grant to him any privileges or immunities that shall not be granted to the colored man, he is mistaken."

The Democratic campaign was thus from its inception double-edged. While Hampton offered chairs with good views and free dinners to black people and gentlemanly composure and reassurances to Northern onlookers, Butler, Gary, and the Red Shirts provided the intimidation. Hampton occasionally hurled red meat to the faithful by invoking his Confederate service, railing about federal "bayonets," and vowing that he would unflinchingly take up his famous broadsword again if South Carolina were to call upon her sons.

As early as 1868, the *New York Times* had warned that the results of the Civil War would be rendered meaningless if the South should "again become impregnated . . . with a fixed spirit of disloyalty which will need but the favoring moment to precipitate itself into a sweeping revolution." Now, in 1876, the signs of impending upheaval were unmistakable: the Fort Moultrie centennial observance that year turned into a giant Confederate reunion, with armed veterans reconstituting their former regiments, marching in ranks to martial music, and cheering an afternoon of "hot Southern speeches." During the event word came that, at St. Louis, Samuel Tilden had just been nominated as the Democratic candidate for president, and there were hoorahs for his victory. When war veterans who had ridden in from Georgia for the occasion expressed disgust "at the unwonted spectacle of negroes in office" in the Palmetto State, locals assured them the offending situation would not long persist.

"Hampton's Triumphant Progress," "The Fires of Patriotism Everywhere Aglow," and "The Spirit of Seventy-Six!" were a few of the exuberant headlines that greeted Wade Hampton's campaign of redemption, which marched across South Carolina from seacoast to upcountry hamlet. "Never has there been so general an uprising of the people of the upcountry as there is at present," recorded the *News & Courier.* "At Anderson, Greenville, Spartanburg, Union, Laurens, Walhalla, Pickens and Newberry . . . Hampton . . . has received grand ovations . . . The people have said, and they mean it, that they will either redeem South Carolina or die in the attempt."

There was no denying that with these events, known as "Hampton Days," white South Carolina had experienced a genuine rebirth; here were the pride and self-respect so sorely missing since 1865; here were Southern men, valorous and once again full of purpose. The impact of strutting brass bands and booming cannon on sleepy towns that had not heard such fanfare since the days of secession can well be imagined. It was redemption in the fullest sense of the word — redemption from unwanted Republican political domination and federal policies, but more important, redemption of the South from inglorious defeat. The campaign even took on the sense of a religious crusade, with a prayer day, fasting, church services, and its own "Joan of Arc" — Francis and Lucy Pickens's teenage daughter Douschka, a skilled horsewoman, who rode through Edgefield Village at the head of a column of whooping Red Shirts.

Hampton himself observed that South Carolinians seemed more de-

WADE HAMPTON

termined to secure his election than they had been to win the Civil War. At one rally in Manning, country people arrived "three on a mule" to witness a promised display of pageantry. Thirty-seven young women appeared on stage draped in white costumes identifying them as the individual "United States"; but face-down on the floor laid one dressed in a black robe — South Carolina, "the Prostrate State." The moment the candidate strode onstage to deafening cheers, "the Prostrate State" arose and, "throwing off her somber draperies, appeared a fair white robed figure like the others. Her deliverer, Wade Hampton, had come."

Spectacle on such a scale proved hard for the state's Republicans to match. An infamous debacle in August 1876 in Edgefield made this plainly evident. The incumbent Republican gubernatorial candidate, Daniel Chamberlain, accompanied by Robert Smalls and the white Republican E.W.M. Mackey, arrived for a party rally, only to be greeted by six hundred mounted Red Shirts under the command of Gary and Butler. The Democrats demanded "divided time." The Republicans at first refused, saying they had called the gathering expressly to meet with their own faithful and to ratify the national ticket of Rutherford B. Hayes and William A. Wheeler. But the Democratic presence was overwhelming, with a crowd of townspeople swelling the Red Shirt ranks. Smalls, directly facing Butler and his rifle clubs, must have felt he had stepped into the very Hamburg massacre he had so eloquently criticized to Congress. Having little choice, the Republicans agreed to share the platform, with speeches of one half-hour allocated to each presenter.

This ostensibly fair format quickly broke down. Governor Chamberlain was heckled as he vowed to continue his reform efforts, and whites even nudged loose the posts holding up the speaking platform, nearly causing it to collapse as Chamberlain completed his remarks. Butler then came to the podium to denounce Smalls and Chamberlain for having accused him of membership in the Ku Klux Klan. Mackey bounded up to defend Chamberlain, urging listeners to help secure the governor's return to office as the best way to maintain peace in the state. When Gary's turn came, Chamberlain was moving to one side of the stage in order to speak with an aide; Gary loudly, and to the glee of his followers, commanded the governor to return to his seat at once, or the Red Shirts would force him to remain there. "I spoke to him in rude and rough language in order that the rude and rough negro might understand it," Gary later said. "This is what killed the spirit of the negro, to see the governor of the state and the chosen leader of their party abused in such unmeasured terms." Gary went on to castigate the governor as "a damn bald-headed renegade and bummer of Sherman's army," then turned his wrath on Smalls, "who has used my name in the Halls of Congress as being the leader of the Ku Klux." He defied Smalls to "open his lips on this stand today." The audience roared its approval, shouting, "No, that God damn nigger shall *not* speak here today!" Butler then returned to the stage to take a turn at haranguing Chamberlain, standing over him and shaking his finger in his face, but the crowd's enmity seemed to shift to Smalls. When Butler mockingly asked for the crowd's "opinion" of "the Boat Thief," the cries were loud and unanimous: "Kill the damn son of a bitch! Kill the nigger!" Many of the black Republicans in the audience, understandably cowed by what they'd seen and heard, began quietly leaving the rally.

As if things could become any more chaotic, at this moment the stage finally did collapse, sending Governor Chamberlain and his two fellow Republicans to the ground, with Butler left standing erect on the only section to remain upright. "This mishap was received by the Democrats with cheer after cheer," observed a reporter, "as significant that Radicals would go down and the Democrats stay up." Shaken but unhurt, Chamberlain and his party left the area as quickly as possible, with several Red Shirts trailing at their heels, shouting threats at Smalls. Even after the Republicans had managed to board their train, whites on horseback began riding up and down alongside the cars, searching for "the nigger congressman." There was talk he should be hanged. Cooler heads among the Democrats talked down the idea of a lynching, but some of the whites persisted, stating that Smalls should not be allowed to escape without some form of physical humiliation; they demanded that a lock of his hair be cut off. To the passengers' great relief, the train soon lurched into motion and gathered speed, leaving behind the Red Shirt horsemen, the day's humiliation, and proud Edgefield — the "county that has never been reconstructed."

CHAPTER 12

A DUAL HOUSE

FREDERICK DOUGLASS FOUND it impossible to walk by the Freedman's Savings and Trust Company on Washington's Pennsylvania Avenue without pausing to admire it. "I often peeped into its spacious windows," he said of the institution founded during Reconstruction to aid the nation's freedmen, "and looked down the row of its gentlemanly and elegantly dressed colored clerks, with their pens behind their ears and button-hole bouquets in their coat-fronts, and felt my eyes very enriched. It was a sight I had never expected to see."

The concept for the bank had originated during the Civil War in the form of ad hoc military "savings banks," which the Union army established for black soldiers and their families to assist the ex-slaves in their first experience with handling money. General Nathaniel Banks in New Orleans and General Rufus Saxton in Beaufort had seen that the freedmen often frittered away their enlistment bonuses and salaries or were easily cheated by army sutlers. To address this problem, the savings program allowed for part of a soldier's salary to be put aside, paid directly to a close relative, or held by the government for payment at the time of the man's discharge.

John W. Alvord, an abolitionist minister and army chaplain, sponsored the idea of making these "Negro savings banks" permanent. Surely, Alvord believed, the need for such an organization would only grow at war's end as freedmen, for the first time, began drawing wages as laborers. Alvord's notion moved successfully up the chain of command, and on March 3, 1865, the same day he signed the bill establishing the Freedmen's Bureau, President Lincoln created the Freedman's Savings and Trust Company. "This bank is just what the freedmen need,"

Lincoln famously said, a remark that would be quoted extensively in promoting it. The board of trustees included the philanthropist Peter Cooper, the editor and abolitionist William Cullen Bryant, and General O. O. Howard, who headed the Freedmen's Bureau. These "patriotic and philanthropic citizens," noted Senator Blanche Bruce, who later investigated the bank's operations, commended the institution "to the confidence of the many thousand simple-hearted and trustful people who subsequently became its depositors." Passbooks from the bank bore patriotic images of Lincoln, Generals Grant and Howard, the American flag, and written testimonials that helped foster the idea that the bank was run (and its deposits guaranteed) by the government.

Alvord was a missionary at heart and believed ardently in his creation. Beginning in 1865 he traveled throughout the South, supervising the opening of new bank branches; ultimately there would be thirty-three in the Southern states, New York, and Baltimore, with headquarters in Washington. The bank offices in the South were often attached to Freedmen's Bureau offices — Alvord was simultaneously president of the bank and superintendent of education in the bureau — and bureau agents frequently acted as cashiers.

The bank was instantly popular among black soldiers and other freedmen. It soon became a show of status to have a savings account, and the bank encouraged participation by allowing accounts to be opened with as little as five cents; between 1865 and 1874 the bank took in more than $50 million from as many as 100,000 depositors. As Senator Bruce noted, "The need for such an institution was real . . . it not only supplied a great convenience to those for whose benefit it was ostensibly established, but it stimulated in them a spirit of thrift, frugality, and foresight."

The misleading statements about the bank's governance, and the true nature of its problems, might never have become an issue, had the bank stayed afloat, and until about 1870 all went well. A report made that year by Alvord for the bank's trustees and excerpted by the *New National Era* gave satisfactory marks to eleven Freedman's Banks across the South. Alvord related that he had visited many black schools where children held accounts in the bank and mentioned that even "old time slave owners" who now hired their labor appreciated the fact that the bank offered blacks a sense of money's worth and a means of saving it. He noted that the only parties opposed to it were "whiskey dealers, lottery gamblers, circus men, and a certain class of bounty and claim agents" —

in other words, those accustomed to benefiting from Negro profligacy. He wrote,

> At Charleston, S.C., we have a choice property, well-purchased, commodious, and everything properly secured . . . at Beaufort we own the office and over 20,000 feet of land . . . at Macon, [where] a branch recently opened . . . $1,000,000 was . . . paid to freedmen for their share of last year's cotton; a goodly portion of this sum has been deposited . . . A branch is strongly urged at Lexington, Ky. In that city I found 12,000 colored people, the most prosperous of any freedmen I have yet seen at the South . . . Kentucky is full of Ku Klux, [but] a bank in Lexington will be safe.

"Permit me to say," Alvord concluded, "that no one can visit our branch institutions — note their progress, freedom hitherto from losses, increasing patronage and popularity — without astonishment. This institution has been the child of a protecting Providence . . . the system we have adopted seems as safe as anything of the kind in human affairs can be."

The bank's charter stipulated that two thirds of the available funds be invested in government securities and the other third held with the bank. In June 1870, however, around the time Alvord was circulating his upbeat report, the bank fell into the hands of a Washington-based clique whose duties related to the Freeman's Bank overlapped with their participation in various local real estate and investment schemes. The charter was amended to enable the new trustees to invest in a more aggressive and speculative way, allowing for one half of the money held for government securities to be used for investment in real estate. Such a drastic redirection had never been intented by the bank's cautious founders; and because the original basis for the bank had been largely philanthropic, its charter lacked the kind of penalties designed by most financial businesses to keep those in charge from disregarding the depositors' best interests. Most of the men who had helped put the bank in business had by now departed, and neither the aging Alvord nor the bank's actuary, D. L. Eaton, possessed enough expertise to fully understand the danger.

Despite warnings from a handful of onlookers, the bank began making speculative loans to a risky class of borrowers. Jay Cooke and Company (Jay's brother Henry sat on the bank's financial board), Howard University, the YMCA, and the Seneca Sandstone Company were among the entities that, along with certain well-connected individuals, secured extremely advantageous loans from the Freedman's Bank. Henry Cooke, the president of the First National Bank of Washington, shifted poor securities from First National to the Freedman's Bank and took advantage of his role as territorial governor of the District of Columbia to borrow heavily in the district's name. In the Panic of 1873, which started with the crash of Jay Cooke and Company and soon devastated many other national financial institutions, these loans quickly went bad. The bank's trustees did what powerful men in such circumstances have often done — feathered their own nest, protected their friends as best they could, and scurried away.

Suddenly, instead of a beacon of thrift and promise, the bank became a worrisome disaster, an example of the era's worst tendencies, heaping woe upon the freedmen. Frederick Douglass, as ever their outspoken guardian, was sickened by the institution's distress, and in March 1874 he took charge of the bank in an effort to correct its course and restore its good name in the eyes of "the sable millions," as he announced in printed circulars. But Douglass, one of the bank's early boosters, was to become a convenient scapegoat for a debacle that was without remedy. The bank's assets, he found, were mostly tied up in uncollectible real estate loans; also, knowledge that the institution was in trouble had led depositors to make three devastating runs on the bank, withdrawing $1,800,000 over an eighteen-month period. In desperation, Douglass loaned $10,000 of his own money to keep it afloat, dollars that were never recouped. "The false building, with its marble counters and black walnut finishings, was there, as were the affable and agile clerks," Douglass grieved, "but the Life, which was the money, was gone, and I found that I had been placed there with the hope that by 'some drugs, some charms, some conjuration, or some mighty magic,' I would bring it back." He would later compare the experience to being "married to a corpse." To make matters worse, Douglass soon discovered that a bank examiner's report describing the institution's true predicament had been withheld from him. On June 28, 1874, the day Douglass informed Congress that the bank should be shut down, it owed 61,114 depositors a sum of $2,993,790, but had just a little over $31,000 on hand. (At about the same time, in depressing counterpoint to the bank's collapse, Douglass's own *New National Era* went out of business.)

In spring 1879 Senator Bruce pushed through two resolutions asking for an inquiry into the bank and was put in charge of the Senate investigating committee. In the House, Joseph Rainey of South Carolina, who since the inception of the crisis had insisted that the government make good on the deposits, joined a similar conclave. It was a curious congressional alliance urging the issue forward — Southern black representatives like Bruce and Rainey seeking resolution (and reimbursement) for their constituents and Democrats eager to heap political embarrassment on the Republicans who had created the bank and on whose watch the mismanagement had occurred.

The nearly yearlong Senate inquiry found that several sections of the bank's charter had been "disregarded, violated, or misinterpreted." The findings included reckless loans, embezzlement at the branch banks, and recordkeeping so shoddy that deposits had sometimes been entered as withdrawals, and withdrawals as deposits. Other transactions were so confusing as to defy categorization. Many reports of corruption and sleight-of-hand surfaced concerning cashiers; the worst transgressors were Washington branch tellers "Daddy" Wilson and his son-in-law, Boston, who "lived in style beyond their means" and whose petty schemes took cruel advantage of the freedmen. Boston, it was found, had for years fleeced an illiterate depositor named Watkins who was unable to read his own passbook. Believing that he had $900 on deposit with the bank, Watkins arrived one day to learn from another cashier that his account had been emptied of all but forty cents. In other testimony, General Howard, who had supervised the bank's affairs early on, recollected that in some instances federal soldiers had solicited deposits or served as tellers while wearing their army uniforms. He stopped short of suggesting a deliberate effort to deceive but agreed that depositors had every reason to believe the bank was operating under government auspices.

Investigators found that wayward investment policy alone had not done all the damage. No group of "sane and honest men could so trifle with a serious trust and so recklessly administer the funds of others," it was concluded; the "dishonesty of men holding official positions in the institution" was cited as the immediate cause of the bank's collapse. But by the time Bruce's committee issued its report, few culpable persons were left to blame. Alvord and the actuary D. L. Eaton had died, while the surviving ex-trustees either "pleaded forgetfulness or ignorance of the violated law" or simply blamed Alvord, who, it was now revealed, had suffered from mental lapses and had been briefly committed to a sanitarium. Only one person was convicted in relation to the collapse of the bank, an Atlanta branch cashier and minister named Philip Cory, who had embezzled $10,000. Sentenced to four years in prison, Cory was pardoned after he agreed to move west and become an Indian agent. To try to recoup some of the loss, those who made the inquiry advocated that the federal government purchase the Freedman's Bank building in Washington and appoint a single person to oversee the process of dissolving the bank.

As the historian James M. McPherson points out, the Freedman's Bank, over the nine years of its operation, was technically less of a failure than is commonly believed. But the symbolism of its collapse was powerful, for the bank, rightly or wrongly, was perceived as yet another example of how the nation tried to confer new status on black Americans, only to default on that commitment and eventually shun accountability.

In the wake of the bank's collapse, many people, most notably General Howard and Frederick Douglass, called on Congress to make good on all remaining deposits. These demands were revived sporadically over several years, by Senator Bruce in 1880 and by the Mississippi congressman John Roy Lynch in 1883, among others. (Bruce, for his efforts, wound up with the consolation prize of a load of discarded Senate office furniture to donate to a home for colored women and children.) Despite many editorials and petitions in support of this equitable and humane idea, the motion was ignored, even as hand-scrawled notes from former depositors or their relatives seeking information about lost savings continued to arrive on Capitol Hill. These appeals were still showing up as late as the 1920s, a half-century after the doors of the bank had closed.

In 1876, a year of national self-reflection, Americans at last had a presidential election with the potential to resolve the issues left over from the Civil War. The Republicans, grouping behind Rutherford B. Hayes, the kindly but unexciting governor of Ohio, were intent on blocking the further ascent of the opposition symbolized by the Democratic sweep of the House in 1874; the Democrats, in turn, led by the New York reformer Samuel Tilden, saw the Republican Party, which had held power since 1861, as a bloated political machine long overdue for dismantling, along with its wayward Southern policy.

The results of this close election were elaborately disputed, amid extensive partisan maneuvering and delay, and the end came only with a backroom compromise struck in Washington. The deal itself soon became infamous, accusations of fraud and manipulation lingered, and neither candidate emerged whole from the experience. Hayes, the nominal winner, was a one-term president who never truly earned his countrymen's respect (he became known as "His Fraudulency"), while

Tilden wound up conceding the election despite strong evidence he'd been cheated out of victory.

Both camps initially believed that Tilden, having amassed a larger share of the popular vote, was the victor. But Tilden's electoral vote total stopped at 184, one vote shy of the 185 needed, leaving the election's result in question. Nineteen yet unclaimed electoral votes belonging to Florida, Louisiana, and South Carolina were in dispute. If Hayes, with his 166 electoral votes, could win those 19, his total would become 185, sufficient to make him, not Tilden, president. (The architect of the Republican scheme to seize these votes was none other than William E. Chandler, the party operative who had instigated the Pinchback-Warmoth railroad race of summer 1872.) By the end of November 1876 all three states were reporting Hayes as the winner, "results" that the Democrats immediately challenged. If Reconstruction had taught America anything, it was that inquiries into contested elections could drag on indefinitely and were rarely conclusive or satisfactory, so on January 25, 1877, President Grant and Congress created a bipartisan electoral commission made up of five senators, five representatives, and five justices of the Supreme Court to determine who had won the Hayes-Tilden election.

In South Carolina, the election that pitted Daniel Chamberlain against Wade Hampton was also being contested. The Republican-controlled returning board had thrown out the votes from Laurens and Edgefield Counties, where it appeared that more whites had voted than actually resided there. On election day in Edgefield, Martin Gary and his Red Shirts had seized both local voting locations, the courthouse and the Masonic hall. Black leaders appealed to General Thomas H. Ruger, who led a nearby detachment of federal troops, to intervene, but Gary's men far outnumbered Ruger's, and with the words "By God, sir, I'll not do it," Gary brushed off Ruger's entreaties to move his followers. Ruger had no choice but to direct black voters to a small schoolhouse nearby — a place that proved inadequate to the great number of freedmen who had turned out to vote. "Gary's doctrine of voting early and often changed the Republican majority of 2,300 in Edgefield to a Democratic majority of 3,900," the Red Shirt captain Benjamin Tillman later said, "thus giving Wade Hampton a claim to the office of governor. It was Edgefield's majority alone which gave to Hampton a chance to claim to have been elected." President Grant, however, citing rampant Democratic voting fraud in the state, recognized Chamberlain as the victor. Within days, however, Chamberlain notified Grant that the state capital of Columbia was under siege, with hundreds of armed rifle-club members milling about the streets. The president immediately ordered federal troops in South Carolina to guard the statehouse and protect the incumbent governor.

On November 28, Wade Hampton led Democrats in an orderly march on the statehouse. Blocked by U.S. soldiers, they retreated to Carolina Hall, a public lecture space, and declared themselves the legal house of representatives of the state of South Carolina. The state constitution, the Democrats pointed out, stipulated only that the legislature convene in the city of Columbia, not necessarily in the statehouse; therefore, said the Hampton forces, their representatives could legitimately claim to be in charge. The Republicans, of course, issued similar declarations of sovereignty.

On November 30, the Democrats again besieged the statehouse. Because the press, both north and south, had strongly criticized the use of federal troops to safeguard Chamberlain's government — some had dubbed the Republicans' Columbia bastion "the Bayonet House" — this time the Democrats were allowed to enter and fill in the available seats on one side of the chamber across from the Republicans. Democratic Speaker W. H. Wallace immediately went to the podium and gaveled for order; the Republican speaker, E.W.M. Mackey, "trembling with excitement and gasping for breath," challenged the interloper.

"You will please vacate this seat."

"I have been elected by a majority of the House of Representatives of the State of South Carolina," Wallace replied. "We are here in pursuance of our rights . . . we desire to oppress no one . . . we desire to claim only the rights that belong to us, and those rights we intend to have."

Mackey insisted that he had been elected speaker "by a legal quorum" and that "these men who are visiting this hall without our consent must keep order. I must again demand that you, General Wallace, leave this chair."

"I have already declared that I am the legally elected Speaker of this House," Wallace insisted, "and I must request you to retire."

Mackey announced that he had sent a message to Governor Chamberlain that the "house was disturbed by men not members" and had asked him to order soldiers to enter and eject the intruders; but no uniformed protectors appeared. "Mackey gazed with longing eyes toward the door of the House for the troops that should enable him to usurp the control of the House," noted the *Charleston News & Courier*, "but none came, and Dennis [John B. Dennis, a partisan of Governor Chamberlain] came in, after a long absence, looking sad. He had a conference with Mackey, and he looked sad also."

Seeing that Wallace would not budge, Mackey directed the sergeant at arms to "please step forward and enforce my order." Wallace then called upon the Democrats' sergeant at arms to eject Mackey. The sergeants at arms for both sides approached, each followed by a crowd of supporters. A confrontation appeared imminent as each group glared at the other; then someone pushed forward a chair for Mackey to sit on alongside Wallace, and suddenly the solution had presented itself: a "dual house," operating with two speakers.

After federal troops failed to materialize, another omen of the shifting political mood appeared. Thomas Hamilton, a black Republican from Beaufort, stood to announce his acquiescence to a Democratic victory. While acknowledging his loyalty to his own party, he said, "In my opinion the verdict of the people at the ballot-box has been in favor of home rule, and against a stranger [Chamberlain] holding the reins of government in South Carolina any longer. I do not say that strangers cannot come among us and live amongst us as friends, but I do say that it has been the popular verdict that they must keep their hands off of politics." Hamilton became so moved during his remarks that he began crying — tears he attributed to his remorse "in describing the pass to which his own race had brought South Carolina."

As Republicans scoffed and rolled their eyes over Hamilton's histrionics, a Democrat, Robert Aldrich, rose to praise him. "We have just seen a brave, honest, patriotic man weeping in the halls of the South Carolina legislature over a spectacle which is calculated to bring tears from any depths." Invoking the by now well known image of the "prostrate state," Aldrich stated, "If [Hamilton's] wife or children were lying dead before him, he could not feel more keenly than he does today." Other Democrats seconded Aldrich's words, demanding that the supporters of Chamberlain walk away in shame for persisting with "a defeated administration that has to be upheld by United States bayonets."

With neither side daring to leave the room even for a recess, the "dual house" remained in session for four days and nights without pause; friends and supporters supplied the legislators with food and other necessities. "The scene in the House . . . is picturesque in the extreme," it was reported. "The members, wrapped in blankets, are lying asleep on the desks or sofas. The aisles are strewn with coffee pots and trays of provisions. Those of the members who are awake are smoking and discussing the situation, while the negroes are singing 'Hold the Fort for

Hayes and Wheeler.'" When either side attempted to conduct business, the two speakers talked simultaneously, as did everyone else, so that nothing could be accomplished. At one point a former black representative named Abraham Smith, identified by the local press as "a Charleston coon," became intoxicated and started yelling to drown out the Democrats' speeches and had to be restrained. Otherwise, the tense standoff eventually gave way to a sense of camaraderie, even laughter and singing. "The Mackey house members, mostly negroes, who are born songsters, enlivened us with loud songs," the Democrat John G. Guignard recalled. Mackey himself quipped, "I perceive that the state of South Carolina has brought forth twins, but the chastity of the good mother is under suspicion because they are of different colors." The *Charleston News & Courier* depicted the blacks of the Mackey House as more good natured about the situation than the Democrats, although some blacks became upset at the newspaper's caricatures. One representative had been described as a "ringtail roarer," while another read with displeasure that "he would be more in his place if he were in his native jungles munching the shin bone of a Wesleyan missionary."

The threat of physical confrontation lingered just beneath the surface. On December 4 rumors reached the hall that the Republicans had called for a gang of black toughs from Charleston, known as the Hunkidories, to come and remove the Democrats. Wade Hampton warned General Ruger, the federal officer in charge, "If such a thing is carried out, I cannot insure the safety of your command, nor the life of a Negro in the state." The Hunkidories and another black Charleston gang, the Live Oaks, were thought to be responsible for street disturbances there in early September, when blacks rioted after a Democratic turncoat of their own race stated publicly that the wives of Republican men took jobs as domestics in order to steal food for their husbands. Whether the gang members ever truly embarked for Columbia to brawl anew with the Democrats is unclear, but certainly the anticipation was real, and Hampton's warning to Ruger was backed up by fresh legions of Red Shirts arriving in Columbia. Confident they had made their point by occupying one side of the house for several days, the Democrats eventually retreated to Carolina Hall.

With the federal troops on hand outnumbered and, in any case, largely indifferent to the outcome, Hampton's forces could have easily chased the members of Chamberlain's government all the way to the hills, if Hampton had so ordered. The Republicans knew this, and knew also that the stalemate was playing poorly in the North. Most people there had heard enough about the state's fractious situation to allow that it probably deserved an attempt at "self-government," whether or not it was obtained by proper means. Public feelings about the crisis were probably best glimpsed in reports of a New York pageant where the shabbily costumed, ever-prostrate "State of South Carolina" was "made" to crawl down Broadway in chains.

While the situation in South Carolina remained at a standstill — in December both Chamberlain and Hampton had themselves inaugurated — the presidential election was being decided in favor of Hayes, who received all 19 of the contested electoral votes, allowing him to inch past Tilden by a tally of 185 to 184. Although the nation's Democratic editorial pages were incensed, the party's spokesmen had agreed, during the bipartisan electoral commission's drawn-out negotiations, which included a pivotal gathering at Wormley's Hotel in Washington, to strike a deal and drop their challenges to the three contested elections in the South. The Democrats offered not to filibuster or otherwise block Hayes's election under the condition that the federal government cease intruding in Southern politics and appoint Southerners to more federal offices; also, they stipulated that more federal funds and private Northern money be allotted to the region's infrastructure, especially the building of a Southern transcontinental railroad. While vowing to honor the laws protecting the right to vote and other rights for blacks, the Democrats secured a promise that the Southern states would henceforth be allowed primacy in dealing with race relations. At 4:10 in the morning of March 2, 1877, Hayes was declared the winner of the presidential election and was sworn in, a few hours later, at the White House.

This then was the price of a Republican victory in the presidential election — an arrangement that formally suspended what remained of the vast egalitarian experiment known as Reconstruction. The far-reaching efforts of the Freedmen's Bureau, Northern missionaries, black congressmen, the Union League, the rebuilt Southern state governments, the hard-won constitutional amendments and Enforcement Acts, were to be set aside or wiped away entirely. Had all the "reconstructing" been a monstrous error, a crime (as most Southerners believed), or an accomplishment? History would have to judge. For the moment, the Republican Party was set free from its political obligations to the former slaves and their children while, for the Democrats, the compromise was made easier by the fact that the Southern wing of the party had never been particularly loyal to Tilden. Like Horace Greeley before him, the candidate had agreeable political ideas, but Southern whites professed little affection for the man; sacrificing him to attain broader goals was not difficult, and caused no remorse.

It was assumed that Tilden, if elected, would act on the long-simmering dissatisfaction with Reconstruction by drastically reducing federal forces in South Carolina, thus dooming the Chamberlain government, but it was not widely expected that Hayes would act similarly. Immediately after the election in early November, when it appeared that he had lost, Hayes confided to his aides and reporters, "I don't care for myself . . . but I do care for the poor colored men of the South. The result [of a Tilden win] will be that the Southern people will practically treat the constitutional amendments as nullities, and then the colored man's fate will be worse than when he was in slavery, with a humane master to look after his interests." But he also allowed that the South deserved "the blessings of honest and capable local self-government." Blacks deserved "absolute justice and fair play," he insisted, although that might best be achieved by empowering "the honorable and influential Southern whites."

Only two days after Hayes was sworn in, Judge Stanley Matthews, a close ally of the new president, wrote to Chamberlain to ask if "an arrangement could not be arrived at which would obviate the necessity for the use of federal arms to support either government [in South Carolina], and leave that to stand which is able to stand of itself. Such a course," Matthews explained, "would relieve the [Hayes] administration . . . of making any decision between the conflicting governments, and would place you in a position of making the sacrifice of what you deemed your abstract rights for the sake of the peace of the community, which would entitle you to the gratitude not only of your own party, but the respect and esteem of the entire country." With the letter came a friendly note from William M. Evarts, who was in line to be Hayes's secretary of state, so Chamberlain could only conclude that the request that he step aside originated with the president himself. Hayes was a careful, deliberate man. ("His tongue, unlike his mind, is not active," the *New York Times* had observed, "and is under the most perfect government.") The White House was asking Chamberlain to vacate his office on the grounds that his administration would not be able to sustain itself without federal troops, and thus could no longer make a legitimate claim to represent the people of South Carolina. This was a far different standard than that previously applied, but it suited Washington's outlook at this precarious moment.

"I desire to aid and relieve President Hayes," Chamberlain wrote in reply to Matthews, as he reminded him of the moral responsibility the Republican Party had to the people of South Carolina.

> This is a life or death struggle, and I know that I should consign myself to infamy in the eyes of all Republicans here, who know the situation by fearful experience, if I were to accept any terms or do any act which could result in the success of the monstrous conspiracy against law and humanity which the Democracy of this state embody and represent . . . Of one thing I am sure, neither you nor any man moved by a sense of justice can understand the situation here and be willing, for any political advantage or freedom from embarrassment, to abandon the Republicans to the fate that awaits them whenever Hampton becomes the undisputed governor of this state.

Since Matthews's attempt to gently nudge Chamberlain aside did not succeed, the South Carolina governor was summoned to Washington by W. K. Rogers, Hayes's personal secretary, who assured Chamberlain of the president's strong desire "to be able to put an end as speedily as possible to all appearances of intervention of the military authority . . . In this desire the president cannot doubt he truly represents the patriotic feeling of the great body of the people of the United States." Wade Hampton had received a copy of the same letter and had likewise been asked to come immediately to Washington.

In the capital, Chamberlain argued with Hayes, noting that the president's predecessor, Ulysses S. Grant, had personally authorized federal protection for the duly elected government of South Carolina, and that he as governor and the people of the state were entitled under the Constitution to be safeguarded from violence. If troops were withdrawn from Columbia before the issue of the "dual house" governments was formally resolved, Chamberlain said, Democrats would seize the statehouse by force. To demonstrate that the Republicans of the state were willing to move expeditiously to settle the matter, Chamberlain, along with Senator John Patterson and Senator-elect David L. Corbin, presented Hayes with a plan by which the South Carolina election results would be submitted to a bipartisan commission, including the Chief Justice of the United States, to be appointed by Hayes. But after this offer was discussed at a cabinet meeting on April 2, Chamberlain received word that since an actual civil disturbance was not then occurring in South Carolina, the federal government was not bound by the Constitution to supply troops, and they would be withdrawn from the statehouse on April 10. Wade Hampton stated that after the exit of federal soldiers, he would attempt to oversee a fair adjudication of the electoral dispute, but Chamberlain waved the offer away, anticipating that any such inquiry would be a sham.

Chamberlain, who had now run out of options, immediately began drafting a letter "to the Republicans of South Carolina." He applauded them for winning the state for Hayes but regretted that in the process "you became the victims of every form of persecution and injury . . . You were denied employment, driven from your homes, robbed of the earnings of years of honest industry, hunted for your lives like wild beasts, your families outraged and scattered, for no offense except your peaceful and firm determination to exercise your political rights." Ultimately, he explained,

> by the recent decision and action of the President of the United States, I find myself unable longer to maintain my official rights, and I hereby announce to you that I am unwilling to prolong a struggle which can only bring further suffering upon those who engage in it . . . I have hitherto been willing to ask you, Republicans, to risk all dangers and endure all hardships until relief should come from the government of the United States. That relief will never come. I cannot ask you to follow me further. In my best judgment I can no longer serve you by further resistance to the impending calamity.

The governor's words, though well meant, could hardly soothe those black South Carolina voters who had risked their lives to cast ballots in the recent election. "To think that Hayes could go back on us now," complained a man from Edgefield, "when we had to wade through blood to help place him where he is." Robert Brown Elliott and other leading South Carolina Republicans, however, wrote to Chamberlain to encourage his decision. They described themselves as "unanimous in the belief that to prolong the contest . . . will be to incur the responsibility of keeping alive partisan prejudices which are . . . detrimental to the best interests of the people of the state, and perhaps of precipitating a physical conflict that could have but one result to our defenseless constituency. We cannot afford to contribute, however indirectly, to such a catastrophe, even in the advocacy of what we know to be our rights."

April 10 was the day chosen for the formal transfer of power from Chamberlain to Hampton. At Columbia, the federal officer in charge at the statehouse, having calibrated his watch with that of the city hall clock, which was in turn calibrated with a telegraph office in Washington, marked the final minutes of Reconstruction in South Carolina. A reporter, who headlined his account "The Day of Deliverance," saw "a score of the colored special constables . . . hanging about the entrance watching our movements with sullen, unfriendly glances," and "a confused crowd of perhaps 150 persons, mostly negroes . . . moving about aimlessly, or . . . engaged in low and dispirited conversation. Here and there were to be seen one or two smaller groups of white Republicans of the better sort similarly occupied, and all looking badly demoralized." As a nearby church tower began to toll the hour of twelve o'clock, the soldiers barked out the commands — "Attention, guard! Carry arms! Right shoulder arms! Two's right, march!" Before the bell had reached its fifth stroke the troops' heavy boots had tramped all the way down the statehouse corridor and reached the door. "Twelve strokes sounded, and the twelve long, weary wretched years of carpetbag misrule were tolled off one by one." When the last of the troops had gone, a huge bar was dropped into the brackets of the door.

The meticulous protocol with which so epochal a transition had come to pass may have helped render it anticlimatic; the rest of the day was reportedly quiet in the South Carolina capital. When in the afternoon the deposed governor Daniel Chamberlain left his office for the last time, his carriage was surrounded by a throng of citizens — but neither to cheer nor harass him: they were on their way to attend a circus recently arrived in town, and most, in their excitement, barely noticed the passing coach with its solitary occupant sitting behind curtains half-drawn.

CHAPTER 13

EXODUSTING

THE FREEDOM TO PICK UP and seek better prospects elsewhere is in many ways the story of America, and for its citizens something of a national birthright. It was, however, a privilege largely denied African Americans. Thus, when Reconstruction ended in the late 1870s, the nation could only look on with surprise and no small amount of concern as substantial numbers of Southern blacks began acting on the impulse to emigrate. Reports came from the Carolinas, Louisiana, and Texas of families hoarding their pennies, even canceling long-held plans to purchase small plots of land, in order to travel and begin life anew in distant Liberia or the American West.

This development and the collapse of the Freedman's Bank had a common origin — the loss of economic stability that had helped make Reconstruction viable. In the bank's case, poor management and a lack of oversight had exacerbated the effects of the crisis related to the Panic of 1873; in the rural South, regional financial strains related to the economic depression had lowered the price of cotton, placing greater pressure on the always precarious crop-lien, or sharecropping, system, in which the black sharecropper's profits were marginal even in the best of circumstances. Hard times weren't the only impetus, of course; the advent of home rule and the corresponding decline of civil and political rights, most notably the vote, accompanied by diabolical new forms of white-on-black violence, such as lynching, also led many to the point of despair.

The prospect of large numbers of blacks, particularly laborers, exiting their usual locales naturally created apprehension among whites. From the standpoint of history, the exodus movements of the late 1870s have a fairly distinct beginning and end, but at the time, the contours of the situation were unknowable. No one — not Congress, nor black leaders such as P.B.S. Pinchback and Blanche K. Bruce, nor the white planters who watched with mounting alarm as their work force decamped — could predict with certainty how vast the movement would prove to be, or where it would end: at times, it appeared the entire black population of the former Confederacy might empty out.

What was most startling about the exodus was the determination of ordinary black citizens to take their fate into their own hands. No longer willing to be supplicants who demanded that things be done for them, they decided, with what meager means were available, to do for themselves. "The Negro," wrote Frederick Douglass, "long deemed to be too indolent and stupid to discover and adopt any rational measure to secure and defend his rights as a man, may now be congratulated . . . [on] the quiet withdrawal of his valuable bones and muscles from a condition of things which he considers no longer tolerable." By acting on their own initiative, the emigrants defied the myth that they possessed none; and with their newfound confidence they ultimately challenged even those very black spokesmen, including the wise Douglass, who had long presumed to know their interests.

Although the exodus fever of 1878–80 caught the nation largely unawares, the idea of an out-migration of blacks from the South was in fact almost as old as the United States. Robert Finley, the Presbyterian minister from New Jersey who in 1816 founded the American Colonization Society (ACS), envisioned it as a benevolent means of returning free American blacks to their native Africa, and in the process helping to Christianize "the Dark Continent." His associates included Francis Scott Key, the composer of "The Star-Spangled Banner"; the Kentucky senator Henry Clay; and the former president James Monroe of Virginia, an ardent supporter of repatriation who was instrumental in urging Congress to donate $100,000 to the cause. The ACS, in collaboration with the federal government, established in 1822 the Republic of Liberia on the western coast of Africa; the capital of the new nation was named Monrovia in honor of its leading benefactor.

Finley's original objectives for the organization unfortunately became diluted when slaveholders embraced the society as a means of ridding the country of free blacks, who were deemed a threat to slavery after the insurrections led by Nat Turner and Denmark Vesey and the advent of the abolition movement in the 1830s. "Of all classes of our population, the most vicious is that of the free colored," declared Clay at an ACS meeting in 1827. "Contaminated themselves, they extend their vices to all around them, to the slaves and to the whites."

Not surprisingly, abolitionists and blacks themselves came to distrust the ACS as a front for slaveholders' interests. "The fostering agency of Liberian colonization was rotten in moral sentiment and hypocritical in its professions," Frederick Douglass later wrote. "With more than Jesuitical deceit and unscrupulousness, it enlisted on its side negro-haters and negro aspirations for freedom." Douglass, like William Lloyd Garrison and others, had faith that slavery would ultimately be abolished in America and that racial prejudice could be conquered over time; slaves, after all, were Americans, not Africans, and they too would someday become citizens. "We live here — have lived here — have a right to live here, and mean to live here," Douglass vowed. This faith, as well as the logistical and financial difficulty of transporting large numbers of people across the sea and situating them in a foreign land, hindered massive relocation. In its first half-century of existence, the ACS was estimated to have dispatched no more than 12,000 Americans to their new Liberian home, an average of 240 per year. Black interest in emigration increased after 1847, when Liberia became an independent nation, but waned when America began edging toward a decisive civil war that blacks, no less than whites, understood would likely determine the future of slavery.

The shifting and sometimes contradictory beliefs on this subject can be charted in the career of the abolitionist and physician Martin Delany, who after initially opposing emigration was converted by his travels in Africa in the 1850s; he later attempted to found a colony in Niger for black Americans. At a meeting of the National Negro Convention in 1854, he spoke favorably of "establishing the rights and power of the colored race" where such things were attainable (in Africa), rather than continuing to struggle against impossible odds in the United States. The Civil War, however, revived his confidence that blacks might yet attain equality in a reconstructed South, and as one of the few men of color to attain an officer's rank he served the Union cause with distinction. By the mid-1870s, however, he had become a critic of Reconstruction and a black nationalist, so disgusted with the Republican program that he backed the Democrats in the election of 1876 and returned to his earlier emigrationist views.

It seems astonishing, in retrospect, that anyone ever seriously considered the likelihood that America's enormous black population — four million at war's end — could actually be put aboard a steamship and sent away. On the other hand, few, if any, models of bi- or multiracial democratic societies existed anywhere in the world, and in the early nineteenth century hardly any Americans, with the possible exception of abolitionists, genuinely envisioned a republic in which citizens would accept coexistence as equals with nonwhites. "Deep rooted prejudices entertained by the whites," Thomas Jefferson had warned, "ten thousand recollections, by the blacks, of the injuries they have sustained; new provocations; the real distinctions which nature has made; and many other circumstances, will divide us into parties, and produce convulsions which will probably never end but in the extermination of the one or the other race." This imagined tableau of racial apocalypse brewed in the national imagination. "Do you intend to turn the three millions of slaves you may emancipate . . . loose among the free whites of the Southern states where they are now held in bondage?" the Democratic congressman Robert Mallory of Kentucky demanded of his colleagues in 1862. "Do you intend, by a course like this, to inaugurate scenes like those which occurred in Haiti some years ago, a war of extermination between the white and black races? I hope not, for the sake of humanity."

President Lincoln, like many of his contemporaries, assumed that America would function best as a racially homogeneous nation. In 1852 he concurred with Henry Clay that there was "a moral fitness in the idea of returning to Africa her children, whose ancestors have been torn from her by the ruthless hand of fraud and violence." During a debate with Stephen Douglas in 1854 he conceded that while his "first impulse would be to free all the slaves and send them to Liberia . . . a moment's reflection would convince me that, whatever high hope there may be in this, in the long run its sudden execution is impossible." Three years later, however, in a speech in Springfield, he suggested that although "the enterprise is a difficult one . . . where there is a will there is a way, and what colonization needs most is a hearty will."

Once in office, Lincoln continued to examine various emigration schemes, pondering which foreign countries might be the recipients of American blacks and whether emigration would be voluntary or compulsory. Treaties would have to be struck, and perhaps generous aid provided, in order to convince other nations to accept America's outcasts. One area considered was the so-called Chiriqui Tract, a swath of land on the Central American isthmus in present-day Panama and Costa Rica. In spring 1862, when Congress passed an act abolishing slavery in the District of Columbia, the law also offered funds to colonize former slaves outside the United States; additional legislation enacted that July allowed the president to "make provision for the transportation, colonization, and settlement in some tropical country . . . of such persons of the African race, made free by the provisions of this Act, and [who] may be willing to emigrate." In August, Lincoln followed up by asking five leaders of Washington's "colored community" to the White House to discuss emigration, the first time in American history that a president met formally with a delegation of black Americans. Lincoln carefully outlined the advantages he perceived in emigration, saying, "There is an unwillingness on the part of our people . . . for you colored people to remain among us . . . It is better for us both to be separated." Looking hopefully around the room at his visitors, he mentioned that he would need able spokesmen to help stimulate wider interest in his proposal. His guests, however, were largely unsympathetic to the idea and offered no assistance, while Frederick Douglass and other abolitionists lost no time in denouncing it outright. Garrison's *Liberator* compared the notion of a massive out-migration to an "attempt to roll back Niagara to its source, or to cast the Allegheny Mountains into the sea." Black Americans, the magazine insisted, "are as much the natives of the country as any of their oppressors. Here they were born; here, by every consideration of justice and humanity, they are entitled to live."

Such opposition, however robust, could not in itself quiet the talk of settling the freedmen elsewhere; it took an actual emigration experiment ending in disaster to still the impulse. On December 31, 1862, the federal government contracted with a man named Bernard Kock to colonize 5,000 black Americans on Cow Island off the coast of Haiti at a cost of fifty dollars apiece. Kock agreed to transport the emigrants and furnish them with homes, schools, churches, and acreage, and assured the Lincoln government of Haiti's cooperation. When the administration learned that Kock was also soliciting support for the plan from private investors, its officials grew concerned and tried to withdraw, but Kock moved forward, sending an initial "shipment" of 435 blacks to the island. Sickness broke out among the arrivals, few of the promised facilities were ready, and Kock soon declared himself "governor" of the black colony, a hint of tin-pot despotism that further unnerved the White House. Lincoln dispatched an investigator, who promptly reported that sanitary conditions in Kock's kingdom were dismal and that the émigrés wanted badly to come home. The president ordered a vessel sent at once for that purpose, and the federal government never again ventured down the path of emigration planning.

When the impulse reasserted itself in the late 1870s, it came chiefly from the freedmen themselves. With Reconstruction on the wane, tens of thousands of letters seeking information about Liberia were received by the ACS and other colonization groups. "Fifty families in Granville County desire to obtain tickets for passage to Liberia next autumn, numbering from two to ten in my family," wrote A. G. Rogers of North Carolina. "Ages from six months to fifty years; occupation: mechanics of different kinds, farmers, school teachers, tobacconists, two ex-members of the N.C. Legislature. They are willing to pay $25 on a family . . . We wish to know of you if the ship could be sent to Norfolk, Va. to meet us provided we can get passage . . . We would be pleased to have a package of circulars, hundreds are demanded of us." Emigration organizations like the ACS, however, were capable of sending at most two sailings per year to Africa, each carrying no more than one hundred passengers. And though the interested parties were mostly indigent residents of the rural South, the colonization societies were based in the Northeast and sailed generally from New York; therefore the plans of many applicants died when they were confronted with the cost of getting themselves and their families to the East Coast.

South Carolina saw a powerful surge of black interest in a Liberian exodus following the "dual house" confrontation of spring 1877. On July 4 an emigration rally was held at Charleston's Morris Brown A.M.E. Church; a few weeks later, on July 26, at a mass meeting convened to honor the thirtieth year of Liberian nationhood, four thousand blacks heard a stirring reading of the Liberian Declaration of Independence. The Liberian Exodus Joint Stock Steamship Company was founded, and a local black news-sheet bannered the words "Ho for Africa! One million men wanted for Africa!" across its front page. The promotional pitch to would-be emigrants was uncomplicated and required no elaboration: with the advent of a Straightout Democracy in the state, conditions would become increasingly unbearable for blacks and would not improve any time soon.

The state's Republicans were in a poor position to be of much help, since their powers had declined precipitously in the wake of Governor Chamberlain's abdication. Those who had been part of Chamberlain's clique managed to hang on to their offices for weeks at most. The Democrats, not content merely to chase their enemies from authority, established its massive fraud investigation to pore over the alleged misdeeds of the previous dozen years and to tar individual Republicans for good as thieves and manipulators of the public trust. After wide-ranging indictments of numerous persons including Francis Cardozo, Richard Gleaves, Franklin Moses Jr., Robert Smalls, and Daniel Chamberlain, exhaustive show hearings were held. Prosecutors alluded to patterns of "monstrous corruption" and labored to show the existence of an intricate web of deceit and wrongdoing, but in the end only three men were convicted of fraud — Cardozo, Smalls, and a white man, L. Cass Carpenter. All were pardoned in a deal whereby Wade Hampton got federal and state charges dropped against whites accused of election fraud and Ku Kluxing.

Governor Hampton, true to his campaign vows, went through the motions of proffering paternalistic concern for the state's blacks, even appointing some black Democrats to minor posts, but this magnanimity was soon quashed by the Negrophobe wing of his own party, led by Martin Gary, Matthew Butler, and Ben Tillman, and by the renewed effort to permanently disenfranchise black voters.

Butler, whose brutality at Hamburg had helped inspire the determined Straightouts, took advantage of the changing political tides to ascend to the U.S. Senate, where in a contested election he edged aside the Republican David L. Corbin. Known to Democrats as "Ku Klux Korbin" for his zealous prosecution of upcountry Klansmen in the Amos Akerman era, Corbin had been a Union major in the Civil War and then stayed on in South Carolina, where he served the Freedmen's Bureau and became a state senator and district attorney. Since the U.S. Senate was Republican and Corbin's credentials were impeccable, it was assumed the infamous Butler could not emerge the victor in this contested election. But in an unmistakable sign that the carpetbagger era had closed, South Carolina's other sitting senator, the Republican "Honest John" Patterson, dramatically announced that he would cast his vote for Butler. Witnesses long remembered Patterson's speech on November 26, 1877, as one of the most pathetic spectacles in Senate history. "Honest John" tried to explain his abrupt change of heart, mopping his brow ineffectually with a large handkerchief and offering feeble justifications for abandoning his own party; derisive laughter from the floor and from the gallery nearly drowned his remarks.

One of Butler's initial efforts in the Senate was to request federal funds to carry any of his willing black neighbors back to Africa. He saw the prospect of large numbers of blacks departing South Carolina as a pleasing one, for it would diminish the state's colored electorate. But more clear-headed whites saw the risk of allowing the state's cheap labor to disappear. As an editor in Laurens noted, "It will not do to shut our eyes to the fact that if the present emigration fever . . . is not abated . . . the agricultural interests of the country must suffer. It will not do to treat the matter lightly, and say, 'Let the "nigger" slide.' We need his services and it is too late now to look elsewhere for a substitute." State officials had indeed tried to "look elsewhere," but their efforts to attract white immigrant laborers to South Carolina had been unsuccessful. In contrast to Northern states, with their large urban populations, South Carolina did not have established settlements of European immigrants to lure newly arrived kin; the chief nonagricultural industry was limited to low-paying work in textile mills; and the state's history of intolerance and racial violence was no secret, even to those just setting foot on America's shores.

Some whites, determined to frighten black workers into staying put, revived the hoary myths of the 1862 Yankee invasion of the Sea Islands, suggesting to blacks that emigration was in reality a secret plan to carry blacks to Cuba and reenslavement. The *Columbia Daily Register* denounced "the Liberian Fraud" as a scheme "gotten up by a few sharpers of your own race and a lot of white rascals, who would delude you by first robbing you of your little hard earnings and then leave you to die in the jungles." The Liberian relocation project did have a millenarian aspect: its boosters described a "promised land" of deliverance where potatoes grew so large that one sufficed to feed a family, syrup flowed from trees as if from a spigot, and the sunlight shone so intensely that there was never a need to build a fire.

As black South Carolinians waited throughout the autumn of 1877 for the Liberian Exodus Joint Stock Steamship Company to produce a ship, Senator Blanche K. Bruce submitted in Washington a petition from more than four hundred black Mississippians asking for $100,000 to move to Liberia. Bruce explained that he had begun to see "mischievous consequences not only to my race, but to the section generally in which they live," from the prospect of an exodus, but he felt that he could not in fairness disregard a request from so large a number of his constituents. In a letter to the *Cincinnati Commercial* he worried that the back-to-Africa movement was dangerously out of date, for "the motives that inspired and prompted the creation of [the American Colonization Society] were derived from a historic period of the Negro utterly unlike the present." The ACS, Bruce reminded readers, had indeed acted to put the free blacks somewhere where they could enjoy freedom, but the organization also "looked to the protection and perpetuity of the institution of domestic slavery, as it then existed in the Southern states, by removing from all contact with the subordinated Negro communities of the South the freemen of color, whose example was supposed to breed discontent among his subject brethren."

Recent history had dislodged these presumptions, Bruce asserted. Now black Americans had participated in a "great revolution" that had made them citizens; they had earned a stake in the agricultural South, a region whose economy would collapse, were the blacks to disappear. Furthermore, Bruce suggested, the black American of the late 1870s would surely find Liberia an alien experience — "a land without roads and without vehicles of transportation; a community without a system of public schools, and a Republic without a press." With native Africans "he would find no common bond of union except simply in the color of the skin." After all, "the Negro of America is not African, but American — in his physical qualities and aptitudes, in his mental development and biases, in his religious beliefs and hopes, and in his political conception and convictions . . . He is not a parasite, but a branch, drawing its life from the great American vine, taking on the type of American civilization and adapting himself to the genius of her institutions, as readily and unreservedly as his Caucasian brother."

In Congress, Bruce was consistently humane; he fought against efforts to restrict Chinese immigration and suggested civilizing the Plains Indians rather than exterminating them; he was also pragmatic, one of the first national figures to call for badly needed federal coordination of navigation and flood control improvements along the lower Mississippi River. But his vision of a coming racial enlightenment in the South — that blacks would someday "entertain independent political opinions without prejudice, and . . . assert and exercise all rights without hindrance and without danger" — no doubt felt very remote and unreal to those who remained there, dwelling in fear of white violence, mourning their loss of the vote, and harnessed in the traces of the crop-lien system. With recent "reforms" in that institution increasing the size of the lien and hence the economic power of landowner over tenant, black farmers had to fight even harder for their family's sustenance and scrap of land, and more than a few, understandably, had come to see the struggle as futile.

At Charleston, meanwhile, the Liberian Exodus Joint Stock Steamship Company, with inexperienced management and only $6,000 in hand, was under siege from those who had put down money for their trip to Africa. Hundreds of emigrants had arrived in Charleston in anticipation of a spring sailing. Finally, a battered but sturdy old seawagon, the *Azor,* was purchased and lashed to a Charleston wharf; the boat, despite its dilapidated condition, became an object of fascination to all who rushed to gaze upon her. The ship was so overbooked when it finally departed for Liberia in late April 1878 that some 175 would-be pioneers were left standing with their luggage on the dock, watching their dream of emigration sail away over the horizon.

The *Azor* tacked out of Charleston Harbor with its passengers shouting joyful hallelujahs and declaring, "The Gospel ship is sailin'! We're boun' for the promis' land!," according to Alfred B. Williams, a *Charleston News & Courier* reporter who was aboard for the journey. Williams noted that most of the men and women had never seen the ocean before, let alone sailed on it, but that none expressed remorse as the coastline of America faded from view with the first sunset. Their chief complaint was that the sea was a more monotonous place than they had anticipated, as they did not find the "whales, leviathans, sharks, mermaids, sea cows, and all the real and mythical monsters of the deep" they had heard about. But more substantive difficulties lay ahead. Many suffered for days with seasickness, supplies of food and water were soon badly diminished, and in violation of a law requiring that a physician be aboard any transatlantic vessel, the *Azor*'s passengers had to rely on the ministrations of a volunteer named George Curtis, "a blundering ignoramus," according to Williams, with as much knowledge of proper healing methods "as a street car mule." Shipboard burials of children and the elderly became common. Of the 206 emigrants aboard the outgoing vessel, 23 died before reaching their ancestral homeland.

Forty-two days out from Charleston, the *Azor* arrived in Monrovia, where the emigrants found a stark, brutal country with few amenities and little infrastructure. Some who later made their way back to South Carolina reported that they had survived only by relying on handouts from native Africans. Although the tales of hardship brought home were probably exaggerated and were told by those who had not succeeded in resettling (many others did remain in their new home), the apparent failure of the *Azor* experiment broke the enthusiasm for African migration in South Carolina. The Liberian Exodus Joint Stock

Steamship Company soon floundered and went bankrupt, its single ship sold quickly to the highest bidder; never again would the *Azor* or any other vessel carry black emigrants over the Charleston bar.

The fascination with Liberian emigration was soon eclipsed by a domestic resettlement of far greater significance — the mass departure of thousands of disaffected black Southerners for the Kansas frontier, the so-called Exoduster Movement. Like the interest in Liberia, the western exodus was fueled by the perception that Reconstruction's demise had rendered life untenable in the South. "The government of every Southern state is now in the hands of the old slave oligarchy, and . . . both departments of the national government soon will be," Frederick Douglass observed, "and [blacks] believe that when the government, state and national, shall be in the hands of the old masters of the South, they will find means of reducing the freedmen to a condition analogous to slavery." As one migrant told a reporter, who rendered his statement in Black Belt patois, "The Democrat party was de party dat kep' us in slavery, an' de Republican party was de party dat sot us free. When de party dat sot us free goes out, an' de party dat kep' us in slavery comes in, it's time for de nigger to look out for himself."

Because the western exodus was seen as a far more threatening crisis than its Liberian counterpart, the movement's root causes were weighed closely by the national press. The *Atlantic Monthly* explained to its readers that the theft of the vote could only have a staggering impact on the freedmen who, only a dozen years before, had been handed this precious right and whose self-image was now bound up with it. "Voting is widely regarded at the North as a disagreeable duty, but the negro looks upon it as the highest privilege in life. To be frightened out of the exercise of this privilege or compelled to exercise it in conflict with his convictions and preferences, is to suffer from a cruel injustice."

In addition to a loss of political standing, the migrants most often cited dissatisfaction with sharecropping. A reporter from the *New York Tribune* who toured rural South Carolina in 1878, the year before the exodus began in earnest, found that black families who managed to farm their own property "live as happy as a big sunflower," raising cotton, corn, peas, sweet potatoes, and rice, and keeping livestock such as pigs and chickens. Those who worked a piece of someone else's farm, however, were often given the poorer land; were expected to supply their own seed, manure, mules and labor; and were at the mercy of the landowner in terms of rent charged and the ultimate sale of their crop, from which proceeds the owner deducted for various equipment or provisions. Many, after an entire year of work, received — less the expenses the landlord took — as little as five or ten dollars from the sale of their crop. The hardest lot was that of the day laborers, who picked cotton or corn for forty or fifty cents a day, much of which was paid in provisions whose value was adjudged by the landowner.

Sharecroppers of course had more than the landlord to reckon with. "The Negro's necessities have developed an offensive race, called merchants by courtesy, who keep supply stores at the crossroads and steamboat landings, and live upon extortion," a Northern magazine wrote. "These people would be called sharks, harpies, and vampires in any Northwestern agricultural community." ("The male [Negro] is an enormous consumer of tobacco and whiskey," the writer added, and "the female has an inordinate love of flummery; both are fond of sardines, potted meats, and canned goods generally.")

Piled onto the inequities of sharecropping and farm labor was the fear of white harassment or problems with the law. With slave labor no longer available, many Southern states had turned to convict labor programs to construct state roads, monuments, and public buildings; they also profited by selling prisoners' labor to municipal or, at times, private enterprises, such as farms or railroads, in what was known as the convict lease system. To busted state economies, convict lease arrangements were irresistible; they were self-supporting and in many cases profitable. But for those trapped inside it, the system was a kind of living purgatory. Arrested for even a minor violation of the law, a black man could find himself stuck for weeks or months on a convict work gang, working off his "debt to society" under a blazing sun.

Abject violence, night riding, lynching, and other forms of terror were of course also a powerful inducement to exit the region. An elderly man arriving in the exodus at its main transfer point in St. Louis related that "I know, within the last three years, of seventy-five men who left their houses at night, and were never found until the buzzards found them in the fields or in the valleys." Such accounts were often belittled by Southerners as shopworn rumors being repeated by impressionable blacks. But President Grant, on December 6, 1876, sent to Congress a catalog of outrages carried out against Louisiana freedmen — ninety-eight pages of atrocities, including murders and whippings from 1868 through 1876 that had left about 4,000 blacks dead or maimed. General

Philip Sheridan quoted official records indicating that in 1868 alone, 1,884 people had been killed or wounded in Louisiana.

In the white South, debate about the exodus focused on possible political chicanery. Some suspected it was a Republican plot to take over neighboring states or to diminish the South's political representation by reducing the number of its black citizens. It was whispered that the Yankees had sent agents provocateurs into the South to effect these developments. "The Southern white man is inconvertibly fixed in the belief that the negro is incapable of any such thing as an independent, self-assertive movement," observed a Northern paper. "He looks upon every migrative or aspiring tendency as the result of some outside . . . malignant influence." The idea that anyone other than the black emigrants themselves was responsible for the exodus struck Frederick Douglass as amusing. "Political tricksters, land speculators, defeated office seekers, Northern malignants, speeches and resolutions in the Senate," he advised, "could not have, of themselves, set such a multitudinous exodus in motion." In an allusion to the 1875 redemption in Mississippi, Douglass joked that the state's departing black residents had simply gotten around at last to presenting whites with their own "Mississippi Plan." The magazine *Puck* neatly captured the reversal in a cover illustration: an immaculately dressed, smiling black family, luggage and tickets in hand, ask of a haggard white planter who is laboring miserably with a shovel in a ditch, "Now, boss, how you like it you' self?" In any case, the possibility that Republicans would foment a black migration to "take over" Kansas was dubious since the state was already largely Republican. It was, in fact, the state's well-known rejection of slavery that helped attract migrants. Given its history, a congressional committee noted, "It is not surprising that the Negro looks with longing eyes to that great and noble state . . ." The *Missouri Republican* extolled Kansas as the place "where John Brown's soul is doing perpetual guard duty."

But recriminations in the South swelled as whites began to appreciate "the humiliating fact," as Douglass put it, "that the prosperity and civilization of the South are at the mercy of the despised and hated Negro." The *New Orleans Times* in April 1879 urged planters to lose no time in assuring laborers and sharecroppers that their rights would be protected, that they would be safe, and that it would ultimately be possible for them to purchase land. P.B.S. Pinchback suggested that the exodus might be quelled if planters would quickly enact policies that offered blacks a route to land ownership, although, as historian Nell Painter observes, such promises and inducements "smacked too much of the Freedmen's Bureau and Radical Reconstruction" and would have been a very hard sell to the freedmen at this late date.

In mid-March 1879 Pinchback decided to have a firsthand look at the exodus, and traveled by steamboat from New Orleans to what had become a staging area, the river town of Delta, Louisiana, just south of Vicksburg. "You may . . . judge of my surprise, on nearing the Delta ferry landing," he wrote in a dispatch, "to find the banks of the river literally covered with colored people and their little store of worldly goods." Mingling with the travelers, who were waiting to pay four dollars for passage to St. Louis, Pinchback noted that while "numerous reasons are alleged for this remarkable exodus . . . so far as I have been able to learn, the *real* cause is an apprehension of undefined danger in the near future." He was assured by those fleeing Louisiana that an upcoming state constitutional convention, under the sponsorship of "home rule" Democrats who had reclaimed their state in April 1877, aimed to reinstitute slavery. "They religiously believe that the constitutional convention bodes them no good; that it has been called for the express purpose of abridging their rights and liberties . . . They are absolutely panic stricken." He also heard a number of completely groundless reports, including one that Jefferson Davis himself "was on the loose again, this time in command of ten thousand troops, supported by a flotilla of four gunboats, and he [has] threatened to send back into slavery every black who tried to go up the river."

One can imagine the gentlemanly Pinch, walking among the roughhewn, desperate emigrants, listening to their stories and patiently trying to quell their fears. He came away fully convinced that the travelers' dread fear of the new Democratic governments in the former Confederate states, of worsening conditions or even reenslavement, were genuine and unfeigned. "There is no doubt in my mind," he concluded, "that this movement has assumed formidable shape and, unless some means are devised to arrest it, this portion of the state will soon be entirely depopulated of its laboring classes."

While there were, as Pinchback witnessed, elements of anguish and uncertainty in the western exodus, the migration was not the panicked stampede that some correspondents had implied. The idea of departure from the Southland had germinated among the freedmen for several years, through word of mouth and through the educational and promotional efforts made by homegrown black advocates of emigration.

Henry Adams of Louisiana, a former slave and Union soldier, had as early as 1870 become concerned about anti-black violence and the assault on political freedoms, and with some other war veterans he helped form a committee, the Colonization Council, to "look into affairs and see the true condition of our race, to see whether it was possible we could stay under a people who had held us under bondage." Adams, described later by a Congressional report as "an uneducated colored laborer, but a man of very unusual natural abilities," helped orchestrate one of the most impressive grassroots information-gathering campaigns in American history, dispatching "investigators" across the former Confederacy to examine the conditions under which blacks lived and forwarding the group's findings to the Justice Department in Washington.

Worried that his agents would learn very little if they simply asked questions and moved on, Adams insisted they work and live in the communities they were studying. "You can't find out anything till you get amongst them," Adams later reported. "You can talk as much as you please, but you got to go right into the field and work with them and sleep with them to know all about them." Monitoring the trend in violence and intimidation closely, Adams and his cohorts were among the first to sound the alarm that retrenchment in the area of voting rights and civil rights might soon make life unsustainable for blacks in parts of the Deep South. One of the more consistent, and depressing, findings reported to the council was that white bulldozing, as the routine harassment of black voters was termed, usually worked. Counties with solid Republican majorities, once its black residents were visited by political terrorism, tended to be reborn as Democratic strongholds; in some elections, not a single Republican vote was cast.

Adams and his council wrote letters of appeal to President Grant, asked Congress to set aside a territory for black settlement, inquired about transportation to Liberia, and even considered approaching "governments outside of the United States to help us get away from the United States and go and live there under their flag." By 1877 he and his team had given up hope of remaining in the South and resolved "to go anywhere on God's earth, we didn't care where; we said we was going if we had to run away and go into the woods."

In addition to studying and collating information about conditions in the South, representatives of emigration societies such as the Colonization Council as early as 1871 sent emissaries to the West to examine the prospects there for black settlement. A report on agricultural conditions in Kansas, submitted by Alabama's George F. Marlow to an 1872 convention of blacks, noted that

> The weather and roads here enable you to do more work here than elsewhere.
> The climate is mild and pleasant.
> The country is well watered.
> Fine grazing country; stock can be grazed in winter.
> Climate dry, and land free from swamps.
> Railroads are being built in every direction.

Marlow concluded,

> It is within the reach of every man, no matter how poor, to have a home in Kansas. The best lands are to be had at from $2 to $10 an acre, *on time.* The different railroads own large tracts of land, and offer liberal inducements to emigrants. You can get good land in some places for $1.25 an acre. The country is mostly open prairie, and level, with deep, rich soil, producing from forty to one hundred bushels of corn and wheat to the acre. The corn grows about eight or nine feet high, and I never saw better fruit anywhere.

More than any other individual, it was Benjamin "Pap" Singleton of Nashville who came to personify the spirit of the exodus. A former slave who supported himself as a carpenter, Singleton wore his own humble provenance on his sleeve. Educated blacks he derided as "tonguey men" and believed that "the colored race . . . invests too much confidence in Professor Tom Cat, or some of the imported slippery chaps from Washington, Oberlin, Chicago." He held that the success of prominent "race men" such as Frederick Douglass, Robert Brown Elliott, and Blanche Bruce, and their acceptance as spokesmen by white society, was exceptional and, in any case, left them incapable of relating to the quandary of Southern blacks. "They had good luck, and now are listening to false prophets," he stated. "They have boosted up and got their heads a whirlin', and now they think they must judge things from where they stand, when the fact is the possum is lower down on the tree — down nigh to the roots." The Louisiana minister and editor William Murrell concurred with Singleton when he said of the exodus, "Those who had been leading the colored people in political matters could not lead them any more when it came to this matter."

Born in 1809 — the year of Lincoln's birth, as Singleton himself liked to point out — Pap had been a most troublesome slave. His owner sold him a dozen times, often to planters far from Nashville, but he managed to escape each time and return home. When he did depart for good, it was by his own volition; he made his way to Canada along the Underground Railroad. Back in Nashville after the war, Singleton worked as a carpenter, and one of his tasks was building coffins for black victims of local political violence and occasionally for young black women who had been sexually outraged and murdered by whites. He also dabbled in real estate, and his Tennessee Real Estate and Homestead Association helped blacks buy small tracts of land, although success was limited because the only land they could afford consisted of worn-out plots "where peas would not sprout." Deciding that the local whites lacked even the small amount of noblesse oblige the planter class had exhibited before the war, Pap became convinced of the need to separate the races. "I had studied it all out," he recalled later, "and it was clear as day to me. I don't know how it come to me; but I suspect it was God's doing. Anyhow I knowed my people couldn't live there." In 1873, after a number of Nashville blacks went to Kansas to work on railroad construction crews and returned speaking favorably of the locale, Singleton organized the first group of three hundred emigrants. "Place and time have met and kissed each other," he told his followers, before leading them to Kansas to found the "Singleton Colony." They sang,

We have Mr. Singleton for our President,
He will go on before us, and lead us through;
Marching along, yes we are marching along,
To Kansas City we are bound . . .

Pap knew the value of printed promotional materials, and his colorful broadsides and circulars were distributed widely; he made a special effort to get them into the hands of train porters, steamboat employees, and ministers. Thanks to his own formidable marketing skills and the help of two other dedicated Tennessee emigrationists, Columbus M. Johnson and A. D. DeFrantz, Singleton quickly became the movement's best-known advocate, proclaiming himself "the Moses of the Colored Exodus" and boasting ultimately of having brought more than seven thousand blacks to settle in Cherokee and Lyons Counties, Kansas.

Singleton's promotions, and those of other agents, exhorted potential travelers with posters exclaiming "Ho for Kansas!, Brethren, Friends, and Fellow Citizens," "All Colored People That Want to Go to Kansas . . . Can do so for $5.00," and "See What Colored Citizens Are Doing for Their Elevation." Representatives of the Kansas Pacific Railroad also encouraged the move, circulating pamphlets that showed "illustrations of high colored life in Kansas" accompanied by enticing captions. A black landowner was seen "lassoing a buffalo going through a rich corn field" and relaxing beneath a tree on his property, "surrounded by squirrel, coon, rabbit, and chicken, so dear to his heart." The *Vicksburg Commercial Daily Advertiser* complained that "gloriously illuminated chromolithographs of Kansas scenes have been distributed among the blacks," showing "Old Auntie . . . on the veranda knitting stockings while she gazes on herds of buffalo and antelope, which are feeding on the prairies beyond the wheat fields." Complicating efforts to separate fact from myth was the traditional tendency of western communities to exaggerate their attractiveness to prospective residents; some emigrants arrived

Ho for Kansas!

Brethren, Friends, & Fellow Citizens:
I feel thankful to inform you that the
REAL ESTATE
AND
Homestead Association,
Will Leave Here the
15th of April, 1878,
In pursuit of Homes in the Southwestern Lands of America, at Transportation Rates, cheaper than ever was known before.
For full information inquire of
Benj. Singleton, better known as old Pap,
NO. 5 NORTH FRONT STREET.
Beware of Speculators and Adventurers, as it is a dangerous thing to fall in their hands.
Nashville, Tenn., March 18, 1878.

AN ADVERTISEMENT FOR SINGLETON'S SETTLEMENT PLAN

in St. Louis clutching a brochure that had been prepared by the state of Kansas for the nation's centennial gathering at Philadelphia, listing its scenic and civic virtues.

Unlike many other blacks who endorsed or joined the exodus, Singleton gave no credence to the idea that the move might improve blacks' political status. He had little patience for men and women foolish enough to think the whites would ever give them their equal rights; rather, he saw himself as a divinely inspired actor in a much grander struggle akin to the biblical story of Exodus, in which an eternally suffering people kept in bondage are at last set free. Like the pharaohs of Egypt, Singleton preached, Southern whites would be punished for slavery: when crops ripened on the stalk and fruit withered on the vine, with no labor to bring in the harvest, perhaps then they would recognize the error of their ways.

Senator William Windom of Minnesota didn't share Pap's millennial vision, but he likewise wondered if the exodus might have a reforming effect on the South. "If such a policy [of federally aided black migration] could be inaugurated," he stated, "it would do more to keep the peace and put the 'bulldozers' on their good behavior than would 20,000 soldiers marching through that country." A Minnesotan of Quaker background who had first learned of the exodus from Blanche Bruce, Windom was a longtime advocate of homesteading. On January 16, 1879, he introduced a resolution that Congress study the westward exodus with an eye toward assisting it. Predictable voices decried the resolution as unwarranted meddling, although Windom believed that blacks had the right to depart "those states and congressional districts where they are not allowed to freely and peacefully exercise and enjoy their constitutional rights," and enter "such states as may desire to receive them."

Several days later Windom met with the South Carolina congressmen Robert Smalls, Richard Cain, and Joseph Rainey, as well as Richard Greener, Harvard's first black graduate, who had served as professor of metaphysics and logic at the University of South Carolina but departed after Wade Hampton's election and was now a law professor at Howard University. Greener was blunt about the choices facing black Southerners in light of the collapse of Reconstruction. Black people had become accustomed to liberty and suffrage, he told Windom, and would no longer submit meekly to injustice, adding, "If the advice of leading colored men had been listened to ten years ago, many of the mistakes of Reconstruction might have been prevented, and the black man would not have been left, as now, naked and helpless in the hands of his enemies." Smalls, Cain, and Rainey suggested that a western territory might be formally set aside for black Southerners, one headed by recognized black leaders whose presence would in turn help attract and reassure black farmers and workers considering relocation. They pointed to the example of the South Carolina Sea Islands, where blacks were in a comfortable majority and lived in relative peace and prosperity. The capital of the islands, the town of Beaufort, had itself become a kind of black "promised land," they explained; as many as fifteen hundred black emigrants from elsewhere in South Carolina had arrived there during 1878 and 1879. Smalls had always disapproved of emigration to Liberia or other foreign lands (as did Windom), but he continued to welcome to his beloved Beaufort any blacks whose lives were made unbearable in other parts of the cotton South.

Gatherings of prominent black leaders supported Windom's idea of government sponsorship. In May 1879 Congressman John Roy Lynch of Mississippi presided at a Nashville meeting that voted to request half a million dollars from Congress to enable "the colored people [to] emigrate to those states and territories where they can enjoy all the rights which are guaranteed by the laws and Constitution of the United States." This request, like many others, was turned down. Indeed, no legislation to aid the Exodusters ever emerged from Congress, despite a significant number of proposals. Southerners on Capitol Hill opposed vehemently any federal aid that would, by appearances, grant legitimacy to the exodus and encourage more departures from the fields, while the Democratic *Washington Post* labeled the Minnesotan's efforts misguided, referring to those blacks decamping from the South as "the wretched dupes of Mr. Windom's windy rhetoric." The paper blamed the exodus on "rascally demagogues" who had already robbed the freedmen "through the agency of the Freedmen's [sic] Bank." Flabbergasted at being accused of having instigated the exodus, Windom fired back that it was Southern Democrats who were truly responsible, having subjected blacks to "outrages never before practiced upon any free people on the face of the earth," including shooting at them as they waited to board northbound steamboats.

The sole exception to Congress's passivity was an agreement to allow a Kansas aid society to avoid paying import duty on a 1879 shipment of used clothing sent by a reform group in England. Blanche Bruce won that bill's passage by reminding his Senate colleagues that money was often raised in America to aid the Irish poor overseas, and he asked that

EXODUSTERS LEAVING VICKSBURG

the English organization's charity be honored similarly. Most of the $40,000 in relief funds and gifts of food, clothing, and bedding that did reach exodus-assistance groups such as St. Louis's Refugee Relief Board and the Kansas Freedmen's Relief Association, based in Topeka, came from Quakers back east, Christian women's groups in the Midwest and Northeast, and communities in Kansas.

President Hayes, who held a benign view of the migration, managed to steer clear of direct involvement until a black cleric named Thomas W. Conway, incensed at stories that steamboats had stopped picking up black passengers en route to St. Louis, made public his idea that the government should dispatch boats armed with troops to ferry emigrants north. Hayes had met with Conway and apparently given him some mild encouragement, but Democrats pounced on the rumor that Conway's armed federal "invasion" of the South might enjoy the president's approval. At his aides' urging, Hayes quickly disavowed any "endorsement" of Conway, not only to placate Democrats but to discourage emigrants from the belief that the government would guarantee their transportation.

Of course, the world of presidential disclaimers and senators' resolutions was far removed from the disorder and uncertainty of the exodus itself, where black families of three and four generations, "fluttering in rags and wretchedness," their bundles and boxes stacked upon wagons, sat waiting for a steamboat to carry them north to St. Louis. "It is computed that up to date about 5,000 colored persons have left this region," a Northern reporter based in New Orleans wrote in early April 1879, "and the Anchor Line of steamboats, which plies between Vicksburg and St. Louis, takes them to the latter place at half price, where they are met by the Kansas Immigration Committee. They sell out their little stock, such as mules, etc., at great sacrifices." One emigrant from Mississippi said he had sold his home, valued at $400, for $6. A Missouri resident who aided a boatload of emigrants determined to reach Kansas recalled, "There was an offer of $80 a month for 500 of them to work on a railroad in Iowa, but they didn't know where Iowa was. They were afraid it was down South somewhere."

Most observers who saw the hundreds of souls camped for days on the shores of the river, or huddled in tents or makeshift charity housing in Missouri or Kansas, would doubtless have considered them refugees rather than emigrants. But despite the hardships, few considered turning around.

Elected black officials and other prominent men were made uncomfortable by a mass movement that negated their significance and whose homespun leaders publicly mocked them as superfluous. Senator Blanche Bruce was among the first national figures to discern and sympathize with the westward exodus, yet the impulsiveness of so vast a relocation ran counter to his own sense of what constituted progress for black Americans. "It is a matter of sincere regret," he said of the Kansas fever in the pseudonymous column he wrote under the name VINDEX for Pinchback's *Louisianian,* "that hundreds of our people, listening to the wild quixotic stories of railroad and steamboat agents, have been induced to abandon their homes at the South, and, without preparation or a definite idea of the geography, climate or productions of the new Eldorado to which their hopes point, have started on what may be called 'a wild goose chase.'"

What troubled Bruce about the exodus was both the chaotic scenes of mass flight along the Mississippi shore and the celebrity of men like Pap Singleton, who insisted on seeing the movement in biblical terms.

> I feel that I do not overstate the case if I say that this criminal mismanagement . . . is due largely to the influence of an illiterate and unguided clergy . . . The truth is . . . that the negro has too much religion, rather than not enough, of the kind now in vogue. If less

> attention was paid to sensational prayer meetings, class meetings, festivals, bazaars, lotteries, societies of all sort . . . and a thousand and one other fooleries, upon which the clergy of today live and luxuriate . . . the colored people would be in far better condition than we now find them.

A stampede of frightened people led by strange black men claiming divine appointment represented everything that Blanche Bruce was not. He suggested that a halt be called "until this matter is at least better understood and better organized."

Bruce was concerned that the exodus would "jeopardize the industrial interests of at least eleven states," endangering the livelihoods of the sharecroppers, laborers, and their families who remained, and that the abrupt departure from the South would for many blacks prove unsuitable, even unnatural. "The colored people are the most unmigratory class of people in the world," he wrote. "Their love of home, the places rendered sacred by old associations, the buried places of their dead, and numerous other charms which fill their imagination, render them the most immovable of any of the races." Bruce's Mississippi congressional colleague James R. Chalmers believed that blacks possessed a "climatic fitness" for the South that worked to their advantage, since the intense sun and heat inhibited the ability of other races to work there. "The sun is the colored man's friend," Chalmers told his constituents. "Stay where your friend, the sun, aids you in the contest."

The black congressman Joseph Rainey of South Carolina differed sharply from Bruce; he saw not chaos in the exodus but the refreshing sign of the freedmen's determination to enjoy the citizenship rights won by the war. Theirs was a positive act of free will. As he told the *New York Herald*, "The freedman may lack education, but I'll assure you he is not quite the fool imagined . . . Humanity forbids that this patient people should longer remain in the midst of their persecutors."

It was Frederick Douglass who voiced perhaps the most significant disapproval of the exodus. Despite his basic admiration for the emigrants' initiative, he felt their movement constituted a retreat from the principle that all citizens deserved fair and equal treatment anywhere in the United States. Fleeing the South, he said, only postponed the inevitable struggle that must occur to ensure civil rights. He viewed that battle as one the blacks could ultimately win, given their concentrated political power in the region, but he feared that very power would be dissipated by the exodus. "Bad as it is," he wrote of the conditions in

FREDERICK DOUGLASS

the South, "it is temporary. It will soon be seen that the South cannot suppress a half million of voters without great damage to itself . . . The resentments and passions of the war must wear away." He also thought it prudent that blacks learn to stand their ground. "It is sometimes better to bear the ills we have than fly to others we know not of . . . When you part with your pig, your pony and your little lot to go a thousand miles to look for a pig and a pony, your money will be gone, and your pig and your pony will not easily be replaced. Life is too short, time is too precious to be wasted in such experiments."

Douglass's views on the subject were so unpopular, his name was booed at Southern Exoduster gatherings. "Some say 'stay and fight it out, contend for your rights, don't let the old rebels drive you away, the country is as much yours as theirs,'" remarked the novelist William Wells Brown, referring to the great abolitionist. "That kind of talk will do very well for men who have comfortable homes out of the South, and law to protect them [Douglass resided in Washington]. But for the negro, with no home, no food, no work, the land-owner offering him conditions whereby he can do little better than starve, such talk is nonsense." At a meeting in New Orleans, someone raised the question as to how Douglass, who had himself escaped from the South to the North as a runaway slave, could now object to those who also sought to depart. Douglass replied in the pages of the *New York Herald*, "I doubt very much if I had found in the Constitution a Thirteenth, Fourteenth, and Fifteenth Amendment, if I had seen a powerful political party pledged to the maintenance of my liberty, I would have run away. I think I would have stayed there . . . I have full faith in the ultimate establishment of justice and liberty in the Southern states, and would have the colored man stand in his place and bide his time."

Senator Windom's request for congressional involvement in, or at least scrutiny of, the westward migration, received backing from an unexpected source in December 1879, when the Democrat Daniel W.

Voorhees of Indiana, concerned about a stream of black immigrants from North Carolina entering his state, joined the call for an inquiry. This was a step Windom had requested eleven months earlier, and he welcomed it even as he questioned Voorhees's motives, for he knew the Indianan viewed the exodus negatively and suspected him of setting up a Democratic whitewash. Windom demanded that any investigation not look at the movement solely as a problem but also search for possible remedies, a suggestion Voorhees accepted so long as the inquiry would examine closely whether malignant forces were involved.

The "Exodus Committee," as it was dubbed by the press, made up of five senators including Voorhees and Windom, interviewed 159 witnesses between January and April 1880. Democrats held the majority on the committee, and it proceeded to do as Windom feared, denying that blacks had any reason to be upset with conditions in the South and ascribing the migration to baleful Northern influences. So-called relief societies, stated the committee's official conclusions, were in fact operatives for the Republican Party, seeking to tip the balance of political might in the North and the West. The committee used the pejorative term "outside agitators" to describe those fanning the flames of discontent from afar (likely one of the first times this infamous phrase appeared in discourse on Southern race relations) and overall painted a rosy picture of life for blacks in the Southern states. Reports of racial violence, claimed the study, tended to be retold years after their occurrence "by zealous witnesses," and most were "all hearsay, and nothing but hearsay, with rare exceptions." The committee noted that "many of the witnesses before us were colored politicians, men who make their living by politics, and whose business it was to stir up feeling between whites and blacks, [to] keep alive the embers of political hatred." These leaders' "inflammatory appeals," combined with the "misdirected philanthropy" of some fawning whites, had led Southern blacks to abandon their homes.

Windom protested the findings. It was apparent that Voorhees and the other Democrats had reached their "conclusions" long before any actual testimony had been heard; indeed, most of the testimony made it clear that the exodus was no act of conspiracy but the more or less spontaneous result of pent-up frustrations among blacks. Windom dismissed as "an utter absurdity" the notion that the movement was an effort "on the part of Northern leaders of the Republican Party to colonize [Kansas] with Negroes for political purposes" and scolded Voorhees and his brethren for wasting the taxpayers' money. Congress had refused to aid the migrants themselves but had spent $30,000 to fund Democratic propaganda, or, as it struck the black educator Booker T. Washington, "thousands of dollars to find out what was already known to every intelligent person, and almost every schoolboy in the country . . . thousands of dollars to ascertain the cause of the poor Negroes' distress, but not one cent to relieve it."

It was, however, in the end Voorhees who had most accurately gauged the public mood. The lack of interest in Washington and elsewhere for black political rights generally defeated the possibility of federal involvement in the exodus. Windom's efforts were made to appear quixotic at best, and, as the committee report had implied, evidence of unworthy political manipulations at worst. In any case, the westward flow of emigrants soon slowed; the frenzied activity of 1879 and early 1880 seemed to substantially exhaust the number of Southern blacks willing to act on the migration urge. Reports that steamboats plying the Mississippi had ceased picking up black migrants under threats from planters and intimidation from white vigilantes no doubt also helped curtail the movement.

Probably somewhere between 30,000 and 50,000 blacks departed the South altogether for western lands during the late 1870s. For 25,000 or so who made the journey to Kansas(during 1870–80 the black population of Kansas more than doubled, from 17,108 to 43,107) their new life was hardly without difficulty. Black farmers experienced at working the rich alluvial lands of the Deep South were challenged by clearing and cultivating less cooperative ground, and white immigrants to the state brought unanticipated competition and sometimes outright hostility.

But although Kansas was not the agricultural paradise its boosters had claimed, the exodus was in numerous ways a success. Many blacks did thrive there, often by throwing themselves with superhuman effort into their labors, mindful that they had come too far to countenance failure. The Tennessean Henry Carter and his wife walked the sixty-five miles from Topeka to the town of Dunlap, Kansas; within a year they had cleared forty acres, built a small stone cottage, and purchased a horse and two cows. In Graham County, a determined black farmer was said to have turned five acres of "raw prairie" with a hand spade. One emigrant wrote to his family in Louisiana, "They do not kill negroes here for voting. I am living here as a lark. You can buy land at from a dollar and a half to two dollars an acre." Fortunately for the new arrivals, many of whom lacked necessary supplies, the winter of 1879–80 was one of the mildest in the state's history. "God seed dat de darkies had thin clo's," according to one grateful witness, "an' he done kep'd de cole off."

In retrospect, the western migration of black Americans from the South at Reconstruction's end appears more a deliberative — and decidedly prescient — act of collective survival than an impulse borne of momentary uncertainty. The Exodusters had, in fact, read accurately the drift of history and of recent events: a long night of national disregard for their rights and humanity was indeed at hand, and the Deep South was to prove an ever more unfortunate habitat. "The exodus presented proof that Afro-Americans did not quietly resign themselves to the political or economic order of the Redeemed South," concludes Nell Painter. "Exodusters on their way to Free Kansas said no, we do not acquiesce in Redemption; we do not believe that this is the way of American democracy."

In contrast, established black spokesmen such as Blanche Bruce and Frederick Douglass had a harder time accepting that "the Reconstruction dream of black assimilation into white American society had died." They had believed fervently in that dream and had fought ably for civil rights, Enforcement Acts, and Constitutional reforms. But when those attainments were reneged upon, it was the ordinary black citizen who knew what to do.

CHAPTER 14

A ROPE OF SAND

SOME MEN ARE BORN GREAT, some achieve greatness, and others lived during the Reconstruction period," wrote the African American poet Paul Laurence Dunbar. Even by the standards of that unforgiving era, however, the decline of South Carolina's "savior," Wade Hampton, came with astonishing swiftness. The candidate who had served as the moderate face of redemption soon found himself undermined and made to appear superfluous by the potent conservative wing of the Democratic Party.

The Straightouts had overthrown the reform governor Daniel Chamberlain by talking a great deal about "reforms" of their own, although it became increasingly apparent that they were obsessed chiefly with one — the eradication of black Americans from elected office and from the balloting place. As Martin Gary proclaimed within two years of the election that had brought Hampton to power, "We regard the issues between the white and colored people of this state, and of the entire South, as an antagonism of race, not a difference of political parties . . . white supremacy is essential to our continued existence as a people."

Despite the triumph of home rule, the will to violence that had characterized the 1876 campaign had in no way abated; if anything, it intensified as a younger generation of Edgefield men emerged, who, in the words of their one-eyed leader, Benjamin Tillman, "rode hard and delivered strong licks." Tillman, a founding member of the Sweetwater Sabre Club, which had been involved in the massacre at Hamburg, was at heart "a dairy farmer and cotton planter," reported the *New York World,* but also "a rough, fierce, masterful leader . . . powerfully built, with a square head, heavy jaws and powerful mouth — the sort of man who

BENJAMIN TILLMAN

can lead mobs. His one gleaming eye gives an expression of fierceness to his countenance . . . [it] burns in his head, a menace to his enemies and an inspiration to his friends."

His larger-than-life personality and embrace of popular reactionary sentiments — his distrust of cities, Yankees, big business, and wealthy planters; his advocacy for farmers (he had been instrumental in founding Clemson University, an agricultural school for the state's native sons); and his personal heroic connection to the hallowed days of Red Shirt activism — made him an irresistible figure to many white South Carolinians. Supremely confident, Tillman's style was to ride into and over potential hindrances. One night, while delivering a talk from the steps of Charleston's city hall, his words were suddenly drowned out by the tolling bells of a nearby cathedral; another speaker might have been thrown off, but Tillman shrewdly met the distraction. Pointing to the tower he cried, "They ring out the false and ring in the true!"

It might be argued that the powerful white-supremacist attitudes, which opened into full flower across the South in the 1890s and the early twentieth century, first took shape with the Tillman movement in South Carolina. Certainly they were nowhere better articulated or successfully promoted, with Tillman himself a prototype for the familiar modern demagogues of the American South, who combined adherence to "the Southern way of life" with open defiance of the federal government. But unlike some of his successors, the public Tillman was not particularly lovable or even lampoonable. He appeared to savor his role as the supreme bad man of redemption, even goading audiences and the press:

> You of the north shoved the Negro into our mouths, but you couldn't make us swallow him, and by the holy God you never will.

> We have ten million Negroes and only one Booker Washington, and even he's half white.

> All we of the South want is for you to . . . keep your long Yankee noses out of the Negro question.

> We have done our level best [to disenfranchise blacks]. We have scratched our heads to find out how we could eliminate the last one of them. We stuffed ballot boxes. We shot them. We are not ashamed of it.

"Pitchfork Ben," as he would come to be known (for offering to stick the said implement in the "fat old ribs" of President Grover Cleveland), was to have an outsized impact on not only state but national politics, holding several high offices, including governor and U.S. senator, as the Edgefield spirit morphed into a creed known as "Tillmanism." Its guiding principle was simple: the "control" of white people's lives by black men like Robert Smalls, Richard Cain, and Robert Brown Elliott was the nemesis of civilization, and such a state of affairs, once all too real during Reconstruction, could never, ever recur; the only logical response was to choke the possibility at its source — the ballot box. And because South Carolina contained more blacks than whites, the fear of black domination could be manipulated to make it seem that the biological survival of the white population was at stake, licensing all manner of outlandish interventions. The emotional touchstone of this crusade was always and forever 1876, the year of redemption. "That we have good government now," boasted Tillman, "is due entirely to the fact that the Red Shirt men of 1876 did all and dared all that was necessary to rescue South Carolina from the rule of the alien, the traitor, and the semi-barbarous negroes."

In the interim between the rise of the rifle clubs of 1876 and the legislated disenfranchisement that would arrive under Tillman's guidance in the 1890s, a number of devious means were employed to thwart black and Republican South Carolina voters and still their voices. One well-known deception instituted in the early 1880s was the "eight box law." It turned the ballot box into a maze of interchangeable slots labeled with the names of various offices, such as governor, lieutenant governor, and congressional representatives, making it impossible for illiterate voters to know which box should receive a particular ballot. To defeat those who tried to memorize the location of the appropriate slots, the signs denoting them were frequently rearranged. Illiterate people whose votes *were* desired could be directed by poll workers to vote properly; others would be disqualified for having been placed in "the wrong box." When the Republican state convention met in 1882, delegates agreed that the trickery of the eight box likely disenfranchised as many as 80 percent of the state's Republican voters.

Poll managers, registrars, and vote tabulators appointed by the sitting governor had many other discretionary means available to tamper with voting and the vote count. For one, the registrars could, in reviewing the credentials and identification of blacks aspiring to vote, object to any minor irregularity, even in so minute a question as the applicant's middle initial; at times poll workers might simply hide out, or close the polling place, forcing black voters to wait or return home in frustration. In another act of deceit, poll managers stuffed the ballot box with more ballots than there were voters registered; the law then allowed them to shake the box and "randomly" withdraw ballots until the number inside matched that of the number registered; in the process, of course, large numbers of Republican ballots could be discarded. Or the manager might create an opening in the ballot box that was too small; in this way, many of the ballots placed inside could be declared to be "mutilated" and thrown out.

Congressman Joseph Rainey, who provided a journalist with other examples of Democratic ballot box "rascality," explained how at one precinct, Democratic poll managers were hired who were not properly qualified for the job. When Republicans demanded to know if this state of affairs would invalidate the ballot count, they were assured it would not, but after Republican candidates carried the district, the total vote was vacated on the grounds that one of the poll managers had not been qualified, in direct violation of state law. Rainey pointed out that few if any such irregularities occurred in districts where the black vote, even honestly tallied, did not threaten a Democratic victory.

With time, the Democrats refined their methods so that disenfranchisement needn't wait until official balloting. Joel W. Bowman, an examiner with the Justice Department who visited South Carolina in fall 1882, was told by Democrats "that it is much easier and looks better to adopt means to prevent the registration of negroes . . . than to be compelled to intimidate and sometimes kill them on election day." When registrars went into a predominantly black precinct to register voters, they would form two lines of applicants, one black, one white, and take the whites first. As much time as possible would be consumed registering the whites, and when black registration started, Bowman reported, the process would slow even further, as the supervisors challenged blacks with all sorts of "nonsensical and frivolous questions, with evidently no other object in view than to . . . register as few colored voters as possible, till the time expired for registration in that precinct."

Blacks who did not manage to register would be told to try doing so at the county seat, but there, similar delaying tactics would be used, including the demand that the black aspirant present a white person who could vouch for his identity (although such was not required by law). "Thereby the time would be frittered away to the disgust and despair of the large mass of applicants, who would finally be forced to return to their homes without their certificates of registration, and were therefore disenfranchised." When, however, Democrats failed to obtain the required certificate, registrars found ways to add them to the list of eligible voters on election day, a courtesy rarely extended to blacks. These kinds of election law violations became so standard after 1876, with few if any prosecutions of the abuses ever sought, that black people understandably became demoralized about voting.

Such developments did not sit altogether well with Governor Hampton, who gradually came to resent the extremists' efforts to nullify moderate aspects of his agenda, particularly the idea that the black electorate, though humbled under Democratic authority, would nonetheless retain its power of the franchise and would have a voice in state affairs. By 1878 he had come to distrust Martin Gary's wing of the party, though he had joined Gary in achieving redemption and feared his own efforts were being set aside at the peril of the state's future. "If you are to go back upon all pledges that I have made to the people," stated Hampton, "if you are to say that the colored men that have sustained us are no longer to be citizens of South Carolina — if you require me to go up and give my allegiance to a platform of that sort, then, my friends, much as I would do for you and South Carolina, much as I desire to spend or be spent in her service, willing as I am to give even my life for my state, I should have to decline. I would give my life for South Carolina, but I cannot sacrifice my honor, not even for her." That summer he warned explicitly against ballot-box fraud in the upcoming election, pointing out that it would demean all that had been struggled for. "If you once countenance fraud, before many years pass over your heads you will not be worth saving, and will not be worthy of the state you live in. Fraud cannot be successful, because the chosen sons of South Carolina form the returning board now. The men placed there as representing the truth and honor of South Carolina would die before they would perjure themselves by placing men wrongfully in office." Perhaps Hampton wished for too much; the program of voter bulldozing and Red Shirt intimidation that had helped boost him to high office was not easily abandoned by those who'd mastered it.

Governor Hampton learned for himself what it was like to be targeted by the Edgefield forces after he and his state superintendent of education were invited to dine with the president of Claflin College in Orangeburg. To their surprise, they found that two eminent local black men — a judge and a professor — were joining them at the table. There is no evidence that the dinner was anything but cordial, but rumors spread that the old, once-proud Confederate general, the "Giant in Gray," had weakened, had taken to "dining or dancing with the colored brothers and sisters," as Gary disparaged it, a sign of political foolishness if not moral depravity. (For white politicians, sharing a meal with a black man, no matter how distinguished, could be a serious misstep, as President Theodore Roosevelt would discover in 1901 when he received the educator Booker T. Washington for dinner at the White House.)

Then a bizarre accident caused Hampton even more embarrassment and pain. Having announced his intention to challenge vote fraud in the 1878 state elections, the governor left the capital to enjoy some autumn deer hunting. Hampton was a renowned hunter; his specialty as a younger man was the taking of black bears, with his hunting knife, in the swamps of Mississippi. But somehow, during this particular outing in South Carolina, he wandered off from his party, and then the mule upon which he was riding tripped and fell against a tree, crushing the governor's leg. Unable to pull himself to his feet, Hampton lay for several hours alone in the deep woods, signaling with his gun in the gathering darkness until a search party located him and a cart was brought from Columbia to the difficult-to-access spot. The wounded man was carefully hoisted aboard and endured a bumpy, painful ride along a rutted path before reaching a hospital back in town. The incident seemed suspicious — why was the governor of South Carolina, under any circumstances, off by himself in the woods? The *New York Times,* under the headline "Mule Fraud," accused South Carolina Democrats of concocting the entire story so that the governor would not be held to his promise to explode fraudulent election results. Such speculation halted abruptly when physicians were forced to amputate Hampton's injured right leg.

Although he won reelection as governor in fall 1878, soon after, the state legislature chose him to represent South Carolina in the U.S. Senate. To attain national office was a great honor, although in leaving the governor's chair Hampton knew he was abandoning his state to elements far less conciliatory than he was. The image of restraint and temperance Hampton had paraded in 1876, which had won him sympathy beyond the state's borders, had always been based on his own reputation as a gentleman-patriot; there was thin support for such moderation now. In 1879, at a rally in Abbeville, the site of a triumphant "Hampton Day" appearance only three years earlier, he was actually booed and shouted down. He warned that he would return to the state and run again for governor, in order to confront the likes of Gary and Tillman, but instead he remained in Washington, serving two terms in the Senate.

When the Democrats looked out over the political landscape of South Carolina, they saw a state largely swept clean of Republicanism by the restoration of home rule. Marring the view, however, was one stubborn corner of Republican control, Robert Smalls's Sea Island sanctuary of Beaufort County. Long known as "the Negro's Paradise," it was to Pitchfork Ben Tillman a "niggerdom," one requiring immediate redemption. The state's transformation would not be complete, he declared, so long as such an enclave remained. The Democrats in control of the state legislature proceeded to gerrymander the Sea Islands into improbable districts that reduced black voting power and made it physically difficult for blacks to reach polling places.

This effort complemented a campaign to discredit Smalls personally. In October 1878 Wade Hampton himself had been dispatched to Beaufort to humiliate Smalls before his own people, bringing with him a portfolio of "evidence" from the recently published "Report on Public Frauds," the Democratic effort to permanently tarnish those Republican "miscreants" who had once held authority in the state. Hampton told a gathering there that their beloved congressman had taken a $5,000 bribe, and he offered to show the audience the very checks Smalls had cashed. A number of black men came forward to have a look and "shook their heads significantly," as Smalls, who had been in the crowd, was seen making a convenient exit. The *New York Times* wrote disapprovingly of the incident, admonishing Hampton to cease "the vengeful political persecutions of South Carolina" and to "call off the bloodhounds of the law from the ex-slave, Robert Smalls, charged with bribery, but really suffering for the old crime of grand larceny in running off with the steamer *Planter,* taking her over Charleston bar, and delivering her to the commander of the United States blockading squadron."

Hampton, or whoever had sent him to embarrass Smalls, was in a sense being ungrateful, for Smalls had played a key role in quelling a potentially violent race conflict that had come close to spiraling out of control during Hampton's winning campaign in 1876. Rice planters in the Carolina lowlands that summer, moved by the economic imperatives of a drought year, had begun reducing the amount they would pay for tasks performed by black laborers and introduced the unpopular system of paying workers in scrip, in lieu of cash. Local merchants would redeem the scrip, but because the planters themselves controlled these plantation stores, the overall effect was less pay for the workers; ten dollars was no longer worth ten dollars when, as scrip, it purchased only six or seven dollars' worth of goods. Laborers went on strike at a plantation along the Combahee River, and soon neighboring ones also fell quiet. The planters sought to negotiate, but the angry workers insisted on immediate concessions and began blocking rice shipments and threatening other blacks who refused to join the shutdown. When local white vigilantes invaded the plantations to arrest strike leaders said to have violated the law, the strikers counterattacked, driving off most of the whites.

With the situation deadlocked, the state appealed to Smalls for help. Warned by militant strikers that if they caught him double-dealing, they would "tie him up and give him 150 lashes on his big fat ass," Smalls managed to wave off a threatened intervention by the state militia; after placating the workers, who feared retribution, he obtained an agreement from the planters to resume weekly cash payments. He won safe passage for some white vigilantes out of the neighborhood and convinced the strike's ringleaders, who refused to surrender to white authorities, to walk the fourteen miles to Beaufort with him in order to turn themselves in to a black judge. Smalls and his "prisoners" were cheered by onlookers as they entered Beaufort, and the next morning a judge dismissed all the charges against them.

Smalls's history as a useful liaison between the races, however, was little valued by the Red Shirts. In fall 1878, around the time of Hampton's visit to Beaufort, they arrived en masse to harass Smalls and his followers at a Republican rally in the hamlet of Gillisonville. The white Sea Islands missionary teacher Laura Towne recounted that "eight hundred red-shirt men, led by colonels, generals, and many leading men of the state, came dashing into the town, giving 'the real rebel yell' and," as Smalls himself recalled, "whooping like Indians." The Red Shirts, according to Towne, "drew up and as a body stood still, but every few

ROBERT SMALLS

minutes a squad of three or four would scour down [the] street on their horses, and reaching out would 'lick off the hats' of the colored men or slap the faces of the colored women coming to the meeting, whooping and yelling and scattering the people on all sides. This made the colored men so mad that they wanted to pitch right into a fight with the eight hundred, but Robert Smalls restrained them, telling them what folly it was." One of the Red Shirt leaders then proposed a divided-time meeting, but Smalls, a veteran of more than one disastrous divided-time affair, refused. As the invaders fingered their weapons, Smalls and several other black men retreated into a general store, where Smalls directed those who had guns to aim at the door, but not to fire unless the Red Shirts actually broke in. With Smalls and his band effectively held prisoner, a body of Democrats moved off a short distance and began giving political speeches.

Witnessing Smalls's predicament, residents quickly spread the alarm throughout the community. According to Towne, "Every colored man and woman seized whatever was at hand — guns, axes, hoes, etc., and ran to the rescue. By six o'clock [in the] afternoon a thousand negroes were approaching the town, and the Red Shirts thought best to gallop away." Still, the invaders left a posse behind to ambush Smalls when he tried to board the train that would carry him back to Beaufort, and as a precaution he hid in some dense brush a safe distance from the station and waited until he could leap aboard the train as it departed. If Smalls was exhausted and disappointed by the day's brush with violence, he was buoyed to find at almost every station large numbers of armed black men waiting to travel in the opposite direction, toward Gillisonville, because they had learned that their "King of Beaufort" was in trouble.

Smalls was again in his element during a rare visit by former president Grant and his wife in 1880. A boisterous crowd of five thousand turned out to greet the general, with Smalls, resplendent in his uniform and ceremonial sword as captain of the Beaufort Light Infantry, an all-black honor guard, leading the welcoming committee. When President and Mrs. Grant appeared, the crowd erupted in boisterous shouts of "Hallelujah!" Many fell on their knees, weeping and laughing, crying, "'Fore God, that's the man; he's come, 'fore God, sir." The throng at one point pressed so hard around the former first couple that soldiers and police had to push back the people. Under Smalls's command the troops made a sharp demonstration of maneuvers in the street, and artillery pieces were fired to salute the ex-president. Grant then embarked on a scenic drive around the little city, followed by numerous other vehicles, horse carts, and dozens of young barefoot admirers who "hurrah'd" him up and down the picturesque streets.

The honored visitor, a man of few words, appeared genuinely moved by the enthusiastic turnout. Noting that Beaufort "has occupied a conspicuous place in the history of our country for the past twenty years," he declared it "a place where the best qualities of the newly emancipated race are to be developed. I hope that they will become worthy and capable citizens." Smalls had the privilege of presenting Mrs. Grant with the light infantry's gift of a "handsomely-ornamented cake." When the president signaled to his aides to offer some token present in return, Smalls gallantly reassured him that seeing Mrs. Grant up close was all the reward his men required, a remark that brought laughter and applause. Waxing hopeful about Grant's chances of reclaiming the presidency that fall, Smalls announced, to wild cheering, "I am going to Washington with my company to see General Grant inaugurated on the 4th of March, 1881."

Despite Smalls's personal popularity, the Democratic redistricting and bulldozing tactics, such as parading Red Shirt units near polling places, ultimately contributed to his first electoral defeat, which came in 1878. To his credit, he refused to be cowed by such maneuvers. He had given considerable thought to the nature of the South's desire for white rule and the many ploys used to turn aside the black vote. In a speech delivered to Congress the year before, "An Honest Ballot Is the Safeguard of the Republic," he had offered the view that, though Southern whites were not without their good qualities, slavery had worked a corrupting influence on them. Decades of absolute power over a servile race had made them cruel, lazy, arrogant, and incurious. Now that the federal government had set both races on an equal plane, "the late slave holding class will not submit peacefully to a government they cannot control, believing they are a superior race." It was this profound resentment of black equality, he said, that drove otherwise decent people, in their weakness and fear, to commit horrible crimes — to threaten, to defraud, to kill. Such actions taken by whites "against a harmless race" became "the blacker with their boasted chivalry, their claim of superior gentleness" and threatened to "make the history of the new South one of blood and . . . the subject for one of the darkest pages in American history."

Understanding the grudge that whites refused to relinquish, Smalls reacted to his first defeat at the polls without dejection; rather, he took heart from the knowledge that the Democrats had been forced to use extraordinary measures to defeat him. He dug in to better prepare for the next election two years hence.

Unfortunately, Democratic gerrymandering and ballot-box manipulations in the Sea Islands were only part of the Republicans' problem. Loyalty among blacks to the Party of Lincoln had waned over the years in the face of voter intimidation, incessant attacks on the party as corrupt and wasteful, and diminished anxiety about possible reenslavement. So pervasive was the Democrats' dominance over South Carolina politics that when a white Republican named T. B. Johnson managed to be elected to the state house of representatives, the Democrats insisted that before he could take his seat, he had to publicly apologize for supporting Daniel Chamberlain in the "dual house" showdown of 1877; when Johnson refused to honor so absurd a demand, he was denied entry to the legislature. The outlook appeared so dire at the state Republican convention in September 1880 that Robert Brown Elliott warned Smalls and others to not bother mounting political campaigns, since they would surely fail and only further dishearten black constituents. The spirit of change and possibility that had attended the 1868 South Carolina constitutional convention was now such a remote memory, Elliott said, it was hard to believe such things had ever been. Virtually all the postwar aspirations of the ex-slaves, the means by which they were to pull themselves upward to freedom and equality, had dissolved in their grasp "like a rope of sand." Smalls dismissed Elliott's defeatism and plunged ahead anyway, although, as in his 1878 campaign, plagued by the same Democratic harassment, he came up short, losing by a substantial margin to George Tillman, Pitchfork Ben's brother.

This time, however, Smalls was ready, and he officially contested the results. He pointed out to a special committee appointed by the U.S. House of Representatives that at numerous polling places across the state, Democrats had stuffed ballot boxes and cast out Republican votes;

in Edgefield, Democrats wearing red shirts had seized the voting stations the night before the election, while others on horseback "rode through the town discharging guns and pistols." In Aiken County a loaded cannon had been wheeled ominously close to the polling place. In Hampton County, Republican ballots were taken from the poll manager, so that Republican voters could not vote; and elsewhere "polls were opened at unusual places and at improper hours, of which Republican voters had no knowledge." When the committee found Democratic fraud in four South Carolina counties where blacks formed the majority, Smalls insisted that the vote totals from these counties be thrown out, leaving him with a majority of 14,393 to George Tillman's 12,904.

Tillman offered a unique defense. Rather than attempt to explain away alleged polling station abuses or uphold the vote's legitimacy, he simply argued that it was essential that whites govern South Carolina — that their restored authority was important to the national reconciliation then taking place between North and South. He added, in a twisted allusion to then-prevailing notions of social Darwinism, that the whites' willingness and ability to "win" the election by whatever means necessary, in this case intimidation and trickery, only proved their natural racial superiority. Democratic supremacy in South Carolina politics, in his view, merely evinced "the great universal law of nature — the inevitable law of the survival of the fittest." Despite Tillman's candor, or more likely because of it, the House committee gave the election to Smalls.

But by 1882, it was apparent that only fate or luck could spare Smalls from the Democratic efforts to eliminate him from Congress in the upcoming election. Sensing that he would not be able to muster enough delegates to win the nomination of the Republican Party that year, Smalls threw his weight behind the white candidate, E.W.M. Mackey, who had played an active role in the constitutional convention of 1868 and in the "dual house." Mackey won the election but died soon after, and Smalls was selected to replace him and finish out his term. He was then reelected in his own right in 1884.

In 1886 Smalls mounted his last congressional campaign. Time and again he had plucked victory from seemingly impossible odds, but by now the move to oust him and collapse the black enclave he ruled in Beaufort had become something like a national Democratic crusade. So phalanx-like were the forces opposing him that even a modest bill he managed to pass in the House to provide a pension to Maria Hunter, the widow of the former Union general David Hunter, was blocked. Hunter's memory was sacred to the black Sea Islanders because of his

1862 declaration that slaves in South Carolina were "forever free," helping pave the way for the eventual enlistment of black soldiers in support of the Union. Smalls told Congress, "Less than a quarter of a century ago that class of which I am a representative were 'hewers of wood and drawers of water. Our lives were one long eternal night . . . [thus] we can never forget the Moses who led us out of the land of bondage." But the eloquence of Smalls's appeal failed to impress President Cleveland, who vetoed the appropriation.

One affront led to another. In Boston in 1882 Smalls was denied a hotel room on account of his race. Blacks across the nation were outraged by this mistreatment, which was reported in the press, although Smalls himself insisted the matter be dropped. More painful for him was the Democrats' success, in the 1886 campaign year, at turning even some of his long-faithful neighbors against him over issues of color. As a one-man bastion of power in the low country, he relied heavily on the spoils system — distributing patronage to maintain his base of support. Smalls himself was a mulatto and his patronage tended to favor other light-skinned blacks. Challenged by the pure black, or "African," members of his constituency, Smalls argued that it had simply made sense for him to appoint to office men who could read and write, had seen something of the world, or had had dealings with whites; this, he insisted, did not imply these individuals were better than others, only that they were better equipped to work for the interests of the Sea Islands. But many had come to view this practice as exclusionary and did not countenance Smalls's argument. Due in part to the death from malaria of W. J. Bowen, his chief Republican opponent, Smalls secured his party's 1886 nomination, but he lost the general election. As in 1880 he made a formal protest on the grounds that Democratic fraud had tilted the results. Unlike 1880, however, this time Congress refused to come to the rescue.

As Robert Smalls fought to defend his Sea Islands from the encircling forces of redemption, elsewhere in America "Sumner's Law," the hard-won Supplementary Civil Rights Act of 1875, faced increasing hostility as the idea of equal rights lost favor.

No one had expected the new law to erase prejudice overnight; the hope had been that by assuring "citizens of every race and color, regardless of any previous condition of servitude," the right "to the full and equal enjoyment of the accommodations, advantages, facilities, and privileges of inns, public conveyances on land or water, theaters, and other places of public amusement," a process of assimilation and mutual acceptance would be encouraged: black and white Americans might learn to exist as equals in their daily lives.

But any sense of triumph accompanying the law's enactment had proved fleeting. At its birth it was widely denounced as impractical, unenforceable, and perhaps unconstitutional; it was nearly friendless from the start. Neither President Grant nor any member of Congress spoke out with enthusiasm to support it, and even some of the law's original backers were alienated when Congress cut the provision for school desegregation. While Northern newspapers expressed skepticism as to the law's chances for success, the South declared open defiance. "A thousand federal lawsuits and fines cannot establish . . . negro equality" was the opinion heard from Georgia. "We would ride in wagons or walk, live in boarding-houses or starve, live without a laugh or public entertainment, rather than be dictated to, and forced to mingle with an element inferior, ill-bred, ignorant, and forced by law upon us."

Early attempts to apply the law in real-world situations encountered immediate resistance from local courts, including the stirrings of a philosophy that would, within a generation, come to dominate race relations in America — "separate but equal" — the belief that equal standing in the eyes of the law was sufficient to assume equal treatment.

Unquestionably, the courts were put off by the ambiguity in this legislation. Federal judges both north and south made numerous requests to the office of the attorney general in Washington, asking questions that needed clarification: Did the civil rights law cover all kinds of steamboats and water conveyances? Did the term *inns* refer to hotels only or also saloons and restaurants? Could a defendant evade punishment by demonstrating that although a complainant might not be allowed access to "white" accommodations, the accommodation offered was equivalent?

The *New York Times* worried that sensation seekers would exploit the law. Blacks living in the North were "quiet, inoffensive people who . . . have no desire to intrude where they are not welcome," one editorial assured its readers, but the South held "colored men and women who delight in 'scenes' and cheap notoriety . . . Such men as Pinchback of Louisiana . . . [who] would take no small delight in breakfasting at the Café Brunswick, in attending a fashionable ball, or occupying seats in the dress circle at the opera."

The paper's confidence in the moderation of Northern blacks was, however, misplaced, and some of the first tests of the new law occurred there. William E. Davis Jr., the business manager of a black newspaper, "a respectable-appearing colored man . . . intelligent and well-educated . . . [who] converses and dresses well," went to the box office at the Booth Theatre on West 23rd Street in New York City and was refused when he attempted to purchase seats for either the orchestra or the parquet. The theater's treasurer, William Tillotson, told Davis that he would have to be content with seats in the "upper circle," an area of the balcony set aside for colored patrons. The next morning Davis filed a complaint with the U.S. attorney, who ordered Tillotson arrested, but a grand jury failed to return an indictment.

In another incident in New York, a black man complained that a confectioner on Sixth Avenue had refused to sell him ice cream. Authorities declined to order the confectioner's arrest on the grounds that an ice cream peddler's business was not covered by Sumner's legislation. "What good is the civil rights law, "the frustrated complainant asked, "if a colored man cannot get a plate of ice cream the same as a white man?"

Mrs. Henry Jones of Philadelphia also found the law unhelpful. As she and her family marched in procession with her husband's remains to the Mount Moriah Cemetery, where she had purchased a double plot, the funeral was stopped by a group of men claiming to represent a "cemetery association." They informed her that no black person could be buried there, for, like schools, cemeteries had been excised legislatively from the civil rights act's guarantee of equal access.

There were, however, a few positive signs. In early June, Henry Greenwall, manager of the Tremont Opera House in Galveston, was convicted under the law for refusing to sell tickets to two black women who wished to sit on the main floor. The judge fined Greenwall $500 but didn't stop there; in addition, he hurled a "contempt" ruling at a local newspaper that had criticized his judgment. In Virginia a hotel clerk named Newcomer refused lodging to a black minister, Fields Cook, telling him there were no rooms available but suggested to the clergyman that, if he wished, he could sit in a room off the lobby all night. While sitting, Cook kept count as Newcomer admitted eighteen white arrivals to the hotel. At one point a white guest, learning of Cook's plight, offered to allow the clergyman to sleep on a spare bed in his room, but the hotel clerk would not allow it. A jury, instructed by a judge about the new law and offended by Newcomer's special cruelty to Cook, found the clerk guilty.

The case of a black woman named Green, who was put off a steamboat, exemplified how courts would use the emerging doctrine of "separate but equal." Green was on board the *City of Bridgeton,* traveling between Savannah, Georgia, and various points in Florida, and by her own account, she

> demanded to ride in the same cabin with the white people and on the same deck, and demanded [the] same and equal accommodations which the white people enjoyed . . . [but] the purser insisted that if I did he would put me ashore at Doboy. He used no abusive language to me, with the exception of the tone of his voice, just as if I was a brute or something. He came to the passengers and collected the fare politely and turned to me and said, "Say, have you a ticket?" and I said "No, but here is the money." And he said, "Go downstairs, or I will put you off at Doboy." . . . I went ashore because I was afraid, from the way he spoke to me, that he would put me off, and having my nephew I was afraid one or the other of us would fall overboard.

The master of the steamboat later insisted that Green had been unruly and that when she went ashore at Doboy, she continued to holler at and threaten the purser, "daring him to come out on the wharf, saying what she would do with him." The woman and her nephew ended up waiting six hours for another boat so they could continue their trip.

When Green's case came before the federal district court judge John Erskine, he criticized any interpretation of the new law that would "put passengers in the same cabin or stateroom, who would be repulsive or disagreeable to each other." Better, he said, to prevent "contacts and collisions arising from natural and well known repugnancies," which might "breed disturbances where white and colored persons are huddled together without their consent." He pointed out that the Civil Rights Act did not forbid steamboat owners from regulating the business of their vessels "in such manner that the accommodations for colored passengers . . . may be distinct and separate from those assigned to white passengers" and concluded that "the cabin and state rooms reserved for colored passengers on the *City of Bridgeton* were substantially equal" to those from which Green and her nephew were excluded.

The policy of providing "separate but equal" services and accommodations for blacks thus became a handy means of sidestepping the law without directly challenging its constitutionality. Still, the hypocrisy of the policy was evident even in its earliest applications. The "separate" facilities offered to blacks were almost always inferior and rarely "equal"; and although blacks were separated on the grounds that their presence was offensive to whites, loutish, drunken whites were never forcibly separated from well-behaved blacks.

In Baltimore, Judge William F. Giles articulated an objection to a civil rights case that foreshadowed the law's ultimate fate. On June 9, 1876, a group of twenty men and women of color were traveling from Rockville, Maryland, to Washington on their way home from a large black political meeting. After the conductor informed them they would have to ride in the smoking car, they brought suit against the Baltimore & Ohio Railroad. Judge Giles, citing both the *Slaughterhouse Cases* and *United States v. Cruikshank,* ruled that under the Fourteenth Amendment the federal government could punish only state actions that deprived citizens of certain rights, not the actions of individuals or businesses such as railroads. Congress, he declared, had no right to enforce penalties for violations of rights that belong to a citizen *as a citizen of a state,* and therefore the Civil Rights Act of 1875 was unconstitutional.

This was, in the eyes of many supporters of the new law, a willful misreading of the Fourteenth Amendment, an opinion more expressive of contemporary views than sympathetic to the goal of the amendment's authors, who had intended that it *would* reach individual, not state, acts of discrimination. As one advocate of the act inquired, "If the states are to be allowed through the corporation . . . to trod upon the privileges of the negro, then where is the good from the amendment contemplated by its framers?" The hearings of the Congressional Joint Committee on Reconstruction, which informed the framing process, had showed clearly that most discrimination against blacks originated with individuals or businesses, not state governments or state agencies.

By 1877, only two years after the law's passage, its judicial history of complaints was already hopelessly scrambled, and the law's application limited. Several representative legal actions that had deadlocked in lower courts, ultimately known as *Civil Rights Cases,* were bundled and presented to the Supreme Court, where, it had been long believed, the law's many inconsistencies would find resolution.

Senator Blanche K. Bruce of Mississippi seemed to flourish as a living example of the doctrine of equal rights, despite how embattled this concept was in the legal sphere. With his "manners of a Chesterfield" and the remarkable trajectory of his life, from slavery to Capitol Hill, Bruce demonstrated beyond a doubt the potential of allowing equal access and opportunity to all Americans. Little remembered today, in part because his political agenda was modest and his methods conciliatory, Bruce was widely viewed in the late nineteenth century as both a consummate representative of his race and a symbol of the social mobility made possible by Reconstruction.

Bruce's rotund yet distinguished appearance and his political fame — he was the first black American to be elected to and serve a full six-year term in the Senate — ensured that the public would follow his private life with no little interest. Long one of Washington's most eligible bachelors, he became half of the capital's most elegant couple when, on June 24, 1878, he married Josephine B. Willson, a schoolteacher and the daughter of a prominent family from the crème de la crème of black Cleveland society. Josephine, gifted at languages and music, was almost Caucasian in appearance; as a Washington society page noted, she was "a slender, shapely woman [with] delicate, high-bred features, singularly full of repose."

The nuptials, held in the Willsons' home as a crowd of the curious assembled outside, represented for Bruce the reversal of a personal misfortune: only four years earlier he had been engaged to another Cleveland woman, Namee Vosburg, who died of an illness only weeks before their wedding date. This tragedy occurred just as Bruce was assuming his job in the Senate, and it encouraged gossip and curiosity. To fend off speculation about his private life, Bruce made a habit of attending social functions with John Roy Lynch, the black congressman from Mississippi, and a Washington schoolteacher named Emma Brown, with whom he appears to have enjoyed a brotherly friendship. Miss Brown later described Bruce as "a great big good natured lump of fat" who was "gentlemanly and very jolly . . . just the kind of fellow to go around with."

After a respectable period of mourning, he courted Miss Willson, whom he had met in 1876. Her family in Cleveland belonged to the Social Circle, an organization founded in 1869 "to promote social intercourse and cultural activities among the better educated people of color." The Willsons were so integrated into the city's elite class that many of Dr. Willson's patients were white, and Josephine's brother, an attorney, practiced at a white law firm. Of course, for Bruce, the marriage signified an enormous leap across social boundaries. For a self-educated man who had been born a slave, who had narrowly survived Quantrill's Raiders, and who had come to political maturity in the rough-and-tumble of the postwar Mississippi Delta, winning a U.S. Senate seat as well as the hand of one of America's leading black society belles was a remarkable attainment.

Upon their marriage, Bruce and his bride sailed to Europe for a four-month honeymoon. The first black elected American official to ever visit abroad, Bruce was received as something of a phenomenon and made an immensely favorable impression on the Continent, abetted no doubt by his attractive new wife. While in Paris in December 1878, he encountered ex-president Grant and his family, who were also making the grand tour. "General Grant was less reserved in conversation than when he had been President of the United States," Bruce told a reporter. "In Paris he spoke freely and instructively, and seemed in a happier mood than I have ever known him to be at Washington." The normally taciturn Grant, perhaps a tad homesick and glad to see a familiar face, opened up to Bruce on a number of topics, including the future of black America. He informed Bruce that based on his military experience with black soldiers and his observation of the effective work of black elected representatives in Congress, he held high hopes for the race's eventual success. He also let Bruce know he was considering another run for the presidency, and Bruce, although he'd resented Grant for not aiding Pinchback during his fight in the Senate, came away from the European encounter an ardent fan of the general, predicting, a few months later in the *Louisianian,* that even moderate Republicans "will again march to battle under the banner of 'the Man on Horseback.' There is no denying that Grant is the coming man and [will] receive the Republican nomination."

Bruce's popularity within his own party led to his serving as temporary chair at the Republican National Convention in 1880. After the first ballot, Grant had the largest number of delegates' votes but not enough to clinch the prize. Over the course of twenty-seven more ballots, the former president deadlocked with the popular James Blaine, once the Speaker of the House but now a U.S. senator. Frustrated by the stalemate, Blaine's supporters rallied around the dark horse candidacy of the respected House Republican James A. Garfield, who became the nominee on the thirty-sixth ballot. Bruce backed Grant's candidacy as he had promised, but he wound up being a lucky catalyst for the convention's ultimate choice by recognizing Garfield from the podium during a chaotic moment when many delegates were simultaneously demanding the floor. Garfield, who went on to secure not only the nomination but the presidency, would not forget Bruce's helpful act.

Settling back home in Washington, the fashionable Bruces were much talked about and in demand; an invitation to one of Josephine's soirees denoted insider status, at least among Republicans, and the newspapers made this clear. "The most *unreasonable disturbance* in Washington society at present is Mrs. Senator Bruce, who presides over her capital residence with true womanly grace, making it a fit rendezvous for the distinguished circle of friends with which she and her husband have been so closely identified." Such accounts left no doubt that "Mrs. Bruce is a lady of great personal beauty . . . [She] wore a magnificent black velvet dress, made for her by [the English couturier Charles] Worth during her recent visit to Paris, and handsome diamonds. As to her toilets, they are simply elegant, and can not be outshone by any in the wardrobes of the white ladies whose husbands are in the Senate."

When Josephine began receiving callers — Thursday was her "at home" day — the first person to visit was Lucy Hayes, wife of the president. Mrs. Hayes, known as "Lemonade Lucy" for her strict ban on alcohol in the White House, was so charmed by Mrs. Bruce that she soon came a second time. Upon hearing that Lucy Hayes had already called on Mrs. Bruce twice, the wives of cabinet members, Supreme Court justices, and various senators also beat a path to her door.

Conspicuous by their absence from Josephine's parlor were the wives of Democratic senators. When gossip circulated that Mrs. Allen G. Thurman, wife of the powerful Ohio Democrat and presidential aspirant, had also visited Mrs. Bruce, Thurman's office immediately issued a formal statement to set to rest so damaging a rumor. "I know it would be the political ruin of any Southern Democrat to recognize us socially or have his family do so," Senator Bruce told a reporter. "And I want it understood that while Mrs. Bruce and I are glad to see all our friends at any time at our house, we would feel very badly if any persons compromised themselves by paying us attention." He emphasized that when he had first arrived in Washington, "I made up my mind to let the society question adjust itself without any of my intervention. I have never attempted to force my way into society, and in letting things take their natural course I have never had a particle of trouble. I believe that it is only the one who seeks trouble from the 'color line' that finds it."

The backlash against the kind of nouveau black aristocracy that the Bruces represented came not only from Democratic politicians but also at times from other blacks. Bruce's counterpart from Mississippi, John Roy Lynch, was snickered at for his high-profile Washington wedding to Ella Somerville, a light-skinned woman from an affluent family in Mobile, Alabama. The bride was lampooned in the local black press for her delicate ways and her flawless French; it was even hinted that her snobbery would harm the political career of her husband, who was well regarded as a champion of civil rights. The *Washington Bee,* a black newspaper edited by V. Calvin Chase, created a stir by protesting that Ella's own sister was upset with Ella "because she married a nigger" and that the wedding had been segregated, with whites attending a fancy early supper and black friends invited to a more plebeian celebration later on, just before the newlyweds boarded a train for Niagara Falls. "Mr. Lynch has, we don't believe, elevated himself in the estimation of the colored people by his marriage to a young lady who is so prejudiced against color," the *Bee* complained.

Chase's candor in print piqued readers who felt insulted to attack him in the street on several occasions. He was most critical of those who, in his view, suffered from "white fever." He resented how their light skin gave them greater access to jobs and other opportunities, and he accused them of exhibiting "color phobia" toward darker blacks. Intraracial hostility was not an entirely new phenomenon in postwar America; it was as old as the antagonism between the house servant who interacted regularly with whites, and perhaps had kinship bonds with them, and the black field hand, who rarely encountered or spoke with white people. (In some instances, as in prewar Louisiana, affluent free blacks had themselves owned slaves.)

The worst criticism was reserved for the so-called bon tons, those who appeared to distance themselves most assertively from the black masses. In addition to Calvin Chase, another well-known critic of "blue veinism" was John E. Bruce (no relation to Blanche), a prolific writer whose column "Bruce Grit" ran in black newspapers for decades. Born of slave parents, John E. Bruce could be merciless in his editorial savaging of blacks who cultivated their "whiteness" and aristocratic backgrounds, such as black New Yorkers who chose to keep the Dutch prefix *Van* in their names. He complained bitterly of the black community's tendency to give its leadership roles to the light-skinned, those who, he reminded his readers, actually bore the blood of the slave masters. A man of similarly strong views on the "whitening" of black America was William Monroe Trotter, editor of the *Boston Guardian,* who refused to publish advertisements for any products, such as skin creams and "hair straighteners," designed to erase Negro features.

The real misfortune of the bon tons, of course, was not that they were subjected to the occasional maulings of Calvin Chase or "Bruce Grit," but that the powerful changes affecting race relations in the decades following the collapse of Reconstruction would soon render distinctions between black aristocrats and their less-benighted brethren largely meaningless. By the turn of the century, the comprehensive assault on black rights in America would cripple the notion that fair-skinned blacks or those who achieved economic independence could escape the stigma of race.

This change was accompanied by a series of downward realignments reflecting blacks' diminished status as voters and citizens. In antebellum literature, the "tragic octoroon" had been a beautiful, accomplished young lady, raised by a caring white father, who comes to grief as an adult because, despite her near-white appearance, she cannot escape the insidious effects of slavery. By the late nineteenth century the tragic octoroon was a Louisiana man named Homer Plessy, who was prohibited from entering the whites-only car on a local railroad train. The Supreme Court's 1896 decision in *Plessy v. Ferguson* ruled that Plessy, despite being of fractional black ancestry, could be made to ride in a separate railroad car from whites, establishing once and for all the doctrine of "separate but equal" as the law of the land.

It was perhaps foreseeable that the U.S. Military Academy at West Point would become, in the late 1870s and early 1880s, a kind of proving ground for questions of equal treatment of the races, since it had been as soldiers that many ex-slaves initially sought inclusion in American society. As Frederick Douglass had predicted during the Civil War, "Once let a black man get upon his person the brass letters, *U.S.*, let him get an eagle on his button, and a musket on his shoulder and bullets in his pocket, and there is no power on earth which can deny that he has earned the right to citizenship in the United States."

While most Americans were probably only vaguely aware that the Civil Rights Act was being tested in court rulings around the country, the stories of efforts to integrate West Point often appeared as front-page news, serving up identifiable heroes and villains whose actions reflected the national conundrum. Surely it didn't hurt that the school was located on the Hudson River not far from New York City, making it accessible to big-city reporters.

Senator Bruce was among several leading officials drawn into one of the most racially charged West Point cases, an alleged assault on Cadet Johnson Whittaker by a gang of his fellow cadets in spring 1880. Appointed to the academy from South Carolina at age seventeen, Whittaker had been one of the most promising students at the University of South Carolina, which during Reconstruction served as a training school for freedmen. There, the young man's talents had been recognized and nurtured by Richard Greener, who worked closely with Whittaker to prepare him for the academic rigors of the military school.

When he arrived in 1876, another black cadet, Henry Ossian Flipper, was in attendance and became a companion and help to Whittaker. Flipper successfully graduated from West Point in 1877, the first black man to do so. But without Flipper for company, the ostracism and "silent treatment" that Whittaker suffered grew more unbearable. After he filed a complaint about a cadet who had harassed and attacked him, Whittaker's classmates accused him of being a snitch, and even his officers let it be known that he should have shown more manliness by defending himself physically, rather than reporting the offender. Ultimately, Whittaker was given his own dorm room since no one else wished to share one with him.

On the morning of April 7, 1880, Whittaker failed to appear at roll call. When a cadet was sent to check his lodgings, he came upon a gruesome sight: Whittaker lay unconscious, trussed to his bed, with wounds to his ears and to his left hand. Someone had chopped off hunks of his hair, and there were streaks of blood on the floor. Whittaker, when brought around, gave a bizarre account of what happened: in the middle of the night, three disguised men had entered his room and attacked him with a knife, then bound him to the bed and smashed him in the face with a mirror. "Let's mark him as we mark hogs down South," he recalled one of his assailants saying. The trio, as they left, warned Whittaker not to report the incident. Two days earlier, he explained to his superiors, he had received a note: "Mr. Whittaker, You will be fixed. Better keep awake . . ." [Signed] A friend." But since he had received similar threats before, he had not mentioned this one to anyone.

"This thing has passed beyond the dignified charge of 'hazing,'" one faculty member admitted to reporters, who had hastened upriver to cover the story. "It was an offense equaled only by acts of masked burglars and robbers from the slums of New York City." But the next day, April 8, an investigating officer announced his startling conclusion: what had happened to Whittaker was not the work of "masked burglars," but rather a tall tale fabricated by Whittaker to avoid an upcoming exam.

Senator Bruce, who headed a congressional inquiry into the affair, knew too much of the recent history of West Point's ignoble treatment of black cadets to accept the notion that Whittaker had faked the incident. He told his Senate colleagues that such an outrageous event was unacceptable even if, as some suggested, it could be shown to be an act of hazing with no taint of race hostility. Whittaker himself had by now demanded an official investigation, and President Hayes responded to the hubbub in the press by appointing Martin Townsend, the U.S. district attorney for the northern district of New York, to look into the matter.

Townsend, from his own preliminary inquiries, concluded that Whittaker had been the victim of a real attack and proposed that the boy's long isolation at West Point had inhibited him from defending himself. Townsend's suggestion offended General John M. Schofield, the school's supervisor. "If you think the rule is taught at West Point that a cadet is to tamely submit to a blow without returning it or defending himself you are greatly mistaken," Schofield insisted. "That rule may perhaps be taught in the Bible, but it is not taught here." The general seemed less concerned about a racial assault on campus than the suggestion that his cadets did not know how to stand up for themselves. He also had little patience for the intervention of Townsend, Bruce, or even President Hayes; he viewed their meddling as chiefly a political charade to impress blacks and sentimental Republicans.

Townsend's inquiry came to focus on the warning note Whittaker said he had received. According to handwriting experts, the black cadet had himself penned the note, and one authority even claimed to have matched the piece of paper it was written on with another that Whittaker had used. On May 29, 1880, Townsend's panel concluded that Whittaker had staged the entire incident, writing the warning note and then mutilating himself. The white cadets under suspicion were exonerated, but the controversy lingered, encouraged by extensive second-guessing in the nation's press.

In August, President Hayes summoned General Schofield to Washington and, expressing concern that a spirit of intolerance permeated West Point, informed him he was to be replaced as the school's head. Schofield was stunned. A war hero who, over the years, had handled a number of sensitive diplomatic chores for Presidents Johnson and Grant (including the arrangements for a naval base to be established in the Hawaiian Islands at Pearl Harbor), he vehemently defended the school by placing the recent trouble in a societal context: if racial equality was not yet accepted in American society at large, why should the U.S. Military Academy have to be the exception? Why should black and white cadets, who were, after all, made to live, study, and work in very close quarters, be expected to practice mutual acceptance and tolerance when such courtesies were not observed by other Americans?

Hayes heard Schofield out but was determined to set a new tone at West Point, so he went ahead and replaced Schofield with a man whose very name had come to imply fair-mindedness and a balanced approach to racial justice: the former Freedmen's Bureau chief General O. O. Howard. In explaining his new job to Howard, the army commander, William T. Sherman, said, "I am willing to go as far as the furthest in this question, but I do not believe West Point is the place to try the experiment of social equality . . . [it] must be admitted in civil life, in Congress, the Cabinet, and the Supreme Court before it is enforced at West Point."

Whittaker, meanwhile, insisting that the academy's inquiry had been biased, asked for a full court-martial in order to clear himself. This trial began in New York City in February 1881. The prosecutor, Asa Bird Gardiner, a veteran military attorney, accused Whittaker of faking the attack "with the design and intention to excite public sympathy, to bring discredit upon [West Point], to obtain notoriety, and further to avoid and escape an approaching public examination." He also charged the cadet with having lied during the original inquiry. Whittaker's counsel was none other than Daniel H. Chamberlain, the former governor of South Carolina, who was now in private practice in New York. Chamberlain went to work raising questions about the methods used in the official inquiry. He cast doubt on the handwriting experts, the initial medical analysis of Whittaker's injuries, and the general atmosphere of prejudice at West Point, which had made it impossible for Whittaker to get a fair hearing. The ever-meticulous Chamberlain, in a three-hundred-page summation, carefully impeached almost all of the evidence used by the prosecution and concluded that the institution lacked the proof to convict Whittaker of any wrongdoing.

The nation followed the trial closely, cognizant of its implications for the larger debate over civil rights. Had Whittaker been treated as a pariah because he was black or because he lacked admirable qualities? Could whites, in their personal lives or in their business, be made to associate with blacks? And, as it was human nature to discriminate among those one wished to befriend, wouldn't blacks, who were, after all, a stigmatized minority, always complain of exclusion?

Gardiner, in response to Chamberlain, acknowledged that the black cadet had been made unwelcome, "but whether this occurred because he made himself unpopular . . . or because of certain disagreeable personal peculiarities . . . or whether it was on account of his colored skin merely, or all combined, is something difficult to determine." Whittaker conceded he was not well liked, and some of the cadets who knew him explained to the court that they found certain of his grooming habits, such as putting grease in his hair, offensive; they also testified that Whittaker possessed an evasive quality that made them uneasy. Gardiner charged that this ostracism, which Whittaker likely deserved, led him to seek revenge on the institution and his fellow cadets by shamming an attack. Invoking some of the pseudo-scientific hokum on race then prevalent in the nation's magazines, the prosecutor explained, "Negroes are noted for their ability to sham and feign. 'Playing Possum' is an Africanism that has come to be generally adopted, and the colored person is — according to all anthropologists — endowed with cunning and the power of mimicry."

Leaving no stone unturned, Gardiner then adopted a version of Schofield's view: Whittaker was a liar who had made up the tale of the assault; but even worse, he was a coward — and clearly unsuited for the academy — because he did not have the presence of mind to punish his attackers with his fists. Whittaker was, the prosecutor concluded, "a person born to obey far more than to command" — a pointed attempt to defame Whittaker, since it was well known that the purpose of the cadets' training was to make them leaders of men. The charge was hardly fair to Whittaker: in standing alone to defend his honor, insisting on his innocence, and enduring endless accusations and inquiries, he was, if nothing else, showing considerable strength of character.

On June 10, 1881, Whittaker was judged guilty, and the court recommended that he be spared harsh punishment and simply thrown out of the academy. Chamberlain and Richard Greener quickly raised technical issues concerning the conviction to D. G. Swaim, the judge advocate general of the army, who in December dismissed the court-martial's findings on the grounds that the introduction of Whittaker's private letters as evidence had been inappropriate and that the prosecution had not proved satisfactorily that Whittaker's own version of the event was untrue. On March 22, 1882, President Chester Arthur, who thirty years before, as a brash twenty-one-year-old attorney, had successfully defended the civil rights of Elizabeth Jennings, a black woman beaten by a conductor and ejected from a New York City streetcar, formally vacated Whittaker's sentence. Theoretically, Whittaker should then have been allowed to return to West Point, but the school that same day discharged him permanently for his poor performance on examinations held in June 1880, at the height of the affair.

When in late 1883 the Supreme Court at last took up *Civil Rights Cases,* the five claims that had piled up under the Civil Rights Act of 1875, the court acted as many observers had anticipated and applied a narrow focus to the wording of the Thirteenth and Fourteenth Amendments, setting aside their possible link to related legislation as well as the intent of the amendments' framers. Justice Joseph P. Bradley, in the majority 8–1 opinion, attacked the Thirteenth Amendment as insufficient to support the law, finding that there was no "badge of slavery" in the denial of a public accommodation. The Illinois senator Lyman Trumbull had used the term "badge of servitude" in proposing the Civil Rights Act of 1866, suggesting that the Thirteenth Amendment could be interpreted to address not only slavery but related discrimination. The Supreme Court appeared to agree in several cases in the late 1860s, but it changed course in *Blyew v. U.S.* (1872), when it ruled that denying black witnesses the right to testify against a white person in court did not constitute a "badge of slavery" under the Thirteenth Amendment. The following year, in the *Slaughterhouse Cases,* the high court specifically limited the amendment's relevance to the condition of chattel slavery.

Bradley, curiously, had argued for a broader definition of "badges of slavery" in *Blyew,* but now he came down firmly against such an expanded interpretation. "It would be running the slavery argument into the ground," said he, "to make it apply to every act of discrimination which a person may see fit to make as to the guests he will entertain, or as to the people he will take into his coach or cab or car, or admit to his concert or theatre, or deal with in other matters of intercourse or business." Bradley went so far as to propose, as an example, that the antebellum practice whereby inns and conveyances turned away blacks for fear they could be runaway slaves was not a "badge of slavery," since the act "was merely a means of preventing such escapes, and was no part of the servitude itself." With the court willing to slice the interpretation of "badges of slavery" that thin, the concept's application to the broader issues at stake in *Civil Rights Cases* had little chance.

As for the Fourteenth Amendment, Bradley declared that

> [the Civil Rights Law of 1875] proceeds *ex directo* to declare that certain acts committed by individuals shall be deemed offences, and

> shall be prosecuted and punished by proceedings in the courts of the United States . . . In other words, it steps into the domain of local jurisprudence, and lays down rules for the conduct of individuals in society towards each other, and imposes sanctions for the enforcement of those rules, without referring in any manner to any supposed action of the state or its authorities.

The section of the Fourteenth Amendment securing Congress's right to "adopt appropriate legislation" to adjust state laws, said Bradley, did not allow Congress to "legislate upon subjects which are within the domain of state legislation." So long as proprietors of trains and steamboats and other businesses stayed within state regulations, they could discriminate among their passengers as they saw fit. Bradley concluded, "When a man has emerged from slavery, and by the aid of beneficent legislation has shaken off the inseparable concomitants of that state, there must be some stage in the progress of his elevation when he takes the rank of a mere citizen, and ceases to be the special favorite of the laws, and when his rights as a citizen, or a man, are to be protected in the ordinary modes by which other men's rights are protected."

The gist of the court's ruling, handed down on October 15, 1883, was that Congress possessed no constitutional authority to enforce equal rights in public accommodations. "Sumner's Law," so nobly intended, so ardently fought for, was after less than a decade of existence about to be lowered ignominiously into its grave.

It would, however, receive an eloquent send-off. The lone dissent in the case came from the pen of Justice John Harlan, "the Great Dissenter," as he would later be known, and it was his brief — far more than Bradley's — that would achieve immortality. Coupled with Harlan's eloquent objection to the majority in *Plessy v. Ferguson,* the Louisiana railroad case that in 1896 established the doctrine of "separate but equal," the writings sound a powerful intellectual protest to the Supreme Court's wayward drift in the post-Reconstruction era.

A son of Kentucky, John Harlan had grown up in a family that opposed secession but also looked disapprovingly on abolition, fearing that an instantaneous freeing of the slaves would rupture Southern society. The Harlans voiced support for African colonization schemes, quietly manumitted some of their own slaves, and held fast to the notion that the states should be left to deal with the issue. But in the war John Harlan served with a Union regiment and by the late 1860s had joined the Republican Party, for he accepted the Reconstruction amend-

JUSTICE JOHN HARLAN

ments and was offended by the belligerence of "the irreconcilables," the Kentucky Democrats who refused to acknowledge the changes the war had brought. President Hayes appointed Harlan to the Supreme Court in 1877.

Deeply devout, the justice came to view slavery as "the most perfect despotism that ever existed on this earth," and the ascent of black people from bondage to citizenship as divinely informed, a special destiny the United States had been particularly suited to fulfill. "In Harlan's imagination, the Revolutionary War became a prototype for the Civil War," according to one biographer. "With the help of God, Americans had first overthrown the hierarchy of monarchy and nobility, then they overthrew the hierarchy of race."

Harlan's wife, Malvina, who was known to host "race elevation" classes for blacks in their home, played a role in the writing of his dissent in *Civil Rights Cases.* Mallie, as she was known, saw that her husband was having a difficult time collecting his thoughts. As his would be the only dissent in the case, he was under extreme pressure and was at first unable to commit any ideas to paper. "Many times he would get up in the middle of the night, in order to jot down some thought or paragraph which he feared might elude him in the morning," she later explained. Watching him struggle, she remembered Justice Taney's inkstand.

Her husband had long had a keen interest in antiquities, especially ones with historical significance. When he first joined the Supreme Court, he expressed curiosity to a court officer about an old inkstand that had once belonged to Justice Roger B. Taney, which, it was said, he had used while writing the infamous *Dred Scott* decision. The officer insisted that Harlan help himself to the inkstand. Harlan gratefully brought home this piece of American history, one he thought "a great treasure." A short time later, however, the Harlans met the wife of the Ohio senator George H. Pendleton, who happened to be Taney's niece.

When she learned of the memento Harlan possessed, she declared she would like to have it as a souvenir of her uncle's career — Justice Taney had died in 1864 — and Harlan, ever the Southern gentleman, graciously agreed, saying he would send her the inkstand the next day. Mallie, however, knowing that her husband was being polite and that the inkstand actually meant a lot to him, hid it. Harlan looked high and low, but, unable to find the item, ultimately wrote to Mrs. Pendelton and apologized, saying that it had apparently gone missing.

Over several years, Harlan forgot about the antique, but Mallie did not, and when her husband became stalled on his dissent in *Civil Rights Cases,* she polished the old inkstand, filled it, and took away all the others from his study. One Sunday noontime after he returned from church, she mentioned that a surprise awaited him upstairs by his writing desk. He went up to the room and, after a minute's silence, Mallie heard the scratch of his pen. "The memory of the historic part that Taney's inkstand had played in the *Dred Scott* decision, in temporarily tightening the shackles of slavery upon the negro race in the antebellum days, seemed, that morning, to act like magic in clarifying my husband's thoughts in regard to the law that had been intended . . . to protect the recently emancipated slaves in the enjoyment of equal 'civil rights.' His pen fairly flew on that day and, with the running start he then got, he soon finished the dissent."

Whether it was the inkstand that inspired Harlan or not, his prose in the dissent was fired with indignation at what he believed was the majority's misreading of Reconstruction. "Constitutional provisions adopted in the interests of liberty, and for the purpose of securing, through national legislation . . . rights inhering in a state of freedom, and belonging to American citizenship," Harlan alleged, "have been so construed as to defeat the ends the people desired to accomplish." He could not "resist the conclusion that the substance and spirit of the recent amendments of the Constitution have been sacrificed by a subtle and ingenious verbal criticism" and that the court had willfully ignored the framers' intentions. "It is not the words of the law but the internal sense of it that makes the law," he cautioned. "The letter of the law is the body; the sense and reason of the law is the soul."

As had Charles Sumner, Robert Brown Elliott, and others before him, Harlan pointed out that certain pre–Civil War statutes had demonstrated unequivocally Congress's ability to make laws affecting individuals. Under the Fugitive Slave Law of 1850, Harlan reminded the court, "the Constitution recognized the master's right of property in his fugitive slave and . . . the right of seizing and recovering him, regardless of any state law, or regulation, or local custom whatsoever." Not only did Congress pass such a law, but "the fair implication was that the national government was clothed with appropriate authority . . . to enforce it." To deny Congress the right to guard and protect the privileges and immunities gained by the Reconstruction amendments, Harlan emphasized,

> would lead to this anomalous result: that whereas, prior to the amendments, Congress, with the sanction of this court, passed the most stringent laws — operating directly and primarily upon states and their officers and agents, as well as upon individuals — in vindication of slavery and the right of the master, it may not now, by legislation of a like primary and direct character, guard, protect, and secure the freedom established, and the most essential right of the citizenship granted, by the constitutional amendments . . . I insist that the national legislature may, without transcending the limits of the Constitution, do for human liberty and the fundamental rights of American citizenship, what it did, with the sanction of this court, for the protection of slavery and the rights of the masters of fugitive slaves.

While he agreed that the Civil Rights Act did not reach the social choices individual citizens made, he believed strongly that because businesses such as hotels, railroads, and theaters were either licensed or authorized to function by the state, they could be subject to federal laws. Only six years earlier, in *Munn v. Illinois*, the court had found that when one devotes "property to a use in which the public has an interest, he, in effect, grants to the public an interest in that use, and must submit to be controlled by the public for the common good, to the extent of the interest he has created." Thus, railroads and steamboats that used public thoroughfares, and hotels and theaters whose operations were publicly licensed, Harlan insisted, could be expected to treat all citizens equally under the law.

He was also troubled by the majority's position that race discrimination could not be considered a badge of slavery. One of Harlan's chief fears, which he would amplify in *Plessy*, was that black citizens, stigmatized by having been slaves, would become a peasant class condemned to occupy permanently a lower tier of American society. Recalling that the Civil Rights Act of 1866, building on the Thirteenth Amendment, had expressly countered the infamous Southern Black Codes, he observed that since slavery as an institution "rested wholly upon the inferiority, as a race, of those held in bondage, their freedom necessarily involved immunity from, and protection against, all discrimination against them, because of their race."

As for the issue of "social equality" so often raised, Harlan was clear that

> the rights which Congress, by the act of 1875, endeavored to secure and protect are legal, not social rights. The right . . . of a colored citizen to use the accommodations of a public highway, upon the same terms as are permitted to white citizens, is no more a social right than his right, under the law, to use the public streets of a city or a town, or a turnpike road, or a public market, or a post office, or his right to sit in a public building with others, of whatever race, for the purpose of hearing the political questions of the day discussed. Scarcely a day passes without our seeing in this court-room citizens of the white and black races sitting side by side, watching the progress of our business. It would never occur to anyone that the presence of a colored citizen in a courthouse, or courtroom, was an invasion of the social rights of white persons.

Addressing the core of Bradley's opinion, he concluded, "My brethren say that when a man has emerged from slavery . . . there must be some stage in the progress of his elevation when he takes the rank of a mere citizen, and ceases to be the special favorite of the laws . . . It is, I submit, scarcely just to say that the colored race has been the special favorite of the laws . . . The one underlying purpose of congressional legislation has been to enable the black race to take the rank of citizens, and to secure the enjoyment of privileges belonging, under the law, to them as a component part of the people for whose welfare and happiness government is ordained."

The majority opinion in *Civil Rights Cases* was a regrettable one, as flawed in its reasoning as the Taney court's decision in *Dred Scott.* It was, however, a fair indicator of the nation's prevailing mood, so utterly in sync with public opinion that it failed to produce even a sliver of the reaction that had greeted Judge Taney's ruling a generation before. Harlan's dissent, of course, was widely published and commented upon. Frederick Douglass assured the author that it "should be scattered like the leaves of Autumn over the whole country, and be seen, read and pondered upon by every citizen of this country." Douglass consoled Harlan that the majority's ruling was simply "one more shocking development of that moral weakness in high places which has attended the conflict between the spirit of liberty and the spirit of slavery from the beginning" and predicted "that it will be so regarded by after-coming generations."

If "Sumner's Law" had been "the capstone of the reconstructed republic," the fullest expression of "the nation's equalitarian aspirations," its rejection was equally symbolic, a final, painful reversal that, along with other judicial setbacks, revealed the nation's inability to ensure civil or voting rights. This was partly due to choices made by the Supreme Court, in several instances, to creatively challenge the new constitutional amendments or read them not for their inherent meaning but for those technicalities that might be exploited as weaknesses. Perhaps the amendments could have been better worded, made more specific and assertive, although Justice Harlan was probably right in thinking that the fault was not technical, but lay in the majority's intellectual reluctance to see in the amendments and in civil rights legislation the main purpose of the Civil War — the end to chattel slavery and the reunion of the nation based on the concepts of national citizenship and equal rights.

The nation did achieve reconciliation in the postwar years but partly by agreeing to sacrifice once-important demands for equality and racial justice. It showed itself unwilling to follow through on the promise that black citizens would be integrated into American society. Worse, it acted increasingly, and with uncommon determination, to ensure that such a transformation did not occur.

CHAPTER 15

"THE NEGROES' FAREWELL"

DEMOCRACY HAS WON a great victory unparalleled," Benjamin Tillman, the newly elected governor of South Carolina, declared in his inaugural address on December 4, 1890. "The triumph of Democracy and white supremacy over mongrelism and anarchy is most complete." A white man's government in South Carolina was now secure, but Tillman and his followers had begun to eye another objective: a new state constitutional convention that would give redemption a permanent constitutional grounding, in large part by obliterating the black franchise.

Doctoring the constitution had long been a pet ambition of the state's conservatives. They had bridled under the "Radical Rag" — the "Black and Tan" constitution that had emerged from "the Crow Congress" at the Charleston Club House in 1868, and they still felt humiliated and resentful that the Reconstruction Acts had forced it upon them. And while the "eight box law" and other measures had diminished black voting in the years since 1878, there remained moderate Democrats in the state government, heirs to the views of Wade Hampton, and more than ten thousand blacks still on the voting rolls.

Rectifying this situation was a priority. The retooled constitution would ensure that black politicians like Robert Smalls, Robert Brown Elliott, and Joseph Rainey would never again exploit their numerical superiority, alone or in coalition with moderate whites. Tillman had given considerable thought to how this might be accomplished without defying the U.S. Constitution, although concern for appearances and possible intervention from Washington kept him from doing anything about it immediately; by 1894, however, Tillman's loyalists far outnumbered the state's more mainstream Democrats, and he had enough influence in the legislature to win a referendum for a constitutional convention.

The 1894 election was among the nastiest in state history, with Tillman and "his white supremacy howlers" using voting fraud freely, against whites as well as blacks. The offenses were blatant and widespread, but because Tillman's forces controlled the courts and the legislature, there was little purpose in contesting what had occurred. When the convention met the following year, Robert Smalls and the few other black delegates who attended were so much in the minority, they were described by one observer as "inert and perspiring at every pore." Smalls and his colleagues, fearing the permanent disenfranchisement that the Tillman forces had in mind but painfully aware of their own isolation, attempted to reach over the heads of their fellow delegates and raise a national alarm by writing an appeal that was published in the *New York World*. They pointed out that Tillman's rationale for preventing "black rule" was exceedingly paranoid and not historically accurate; even at the height of Reconstruction in 1868, Smalls and the others noted, South Carolina blacks had shared power with whites — indeed, whites had always held the highest positions of authority in the state. But the plea for help from South Carolina received no significant national response.

Not that there was much surprise in that. Even the state's onetime Republican white knight, Daniel Chamberlain, had long since given up on the cause of the black ballot. Resentful of his own mistreatment at the hands of the Republican Party, which had brought Reconstruction into being and then abandoned it, and bothered by poor health, Chamberlain had succumbed to a deepening cynicism on race relations and the South. "The only course for reasonable and patriotic men is to recognize the facts as they exist, and to deal with the situation according to its nature and causes," he wrote in the *Yale Review*, counseling that a patient process of education was necessary to draw black Americans fully into society's current. "The foremost fact is the ignorance and inexperience of the colored race. From that single, indisputable fact has come the determination of the white race at the South to suppress the vote of the colored race . . . To change this situation . . . requires the removal of its causes." He asked, rhetorically, who deserved blame for the South's rejection of equal rights and its embrace of the Ku Klux Klan. "The answer must be, to those who devised and put in operation the Congressional scheme of reconstruction, to their unspeakable folly, their blind party greed, their insensate attempt to reverse the laws which control human society."

BOOKER T. WASHINGTON

By calling for "understanding" of the Southern situation and an end to the demand that Congress intervene there, Chamberlain anticipated the ideas soon expressed by Booker T. Washington, the ex-slave who had become the head of Tuskegee Institute and a leading spokesman for his race. In a famous address at the Cotton States and International Exposition in Atlanta in 1895, Washington emphasized that black Americans should focus on practical goals, suspending their agitation for new laws and protections. Blacks should accept their role as laborers and resolve to make their way up society's ladder slowly, winning the respect of whites through hard work and the attainment of useful skills. He also advocated that they remain in their Southern homeland. "Cast down your bucket where you are," Washington exhorted; the South was hospitable to black people if they would only relinquish their constant grievances for rights for which they were unprepared. "No race," he said, "can prosper till it learns that there is as much dignity in tilling a field as in writing a poem . . . The opportunity to earn a dollar in a factory just now, is worth infinitely more than the opportunity to spend a dollar in an opera house." He expressed to whites the wish that they in turn would rely on the labor of those they knew so well, who had long been loyal to the region, and eschew that of foreigners, who could potentially be disruptive. As for the coexistence of the two races side by side, Washington offered a compelling analogy: "In all things that are purely social we can be as separate as the fingers, yet one as the hand in all things essential to mutual progress." His speech, known as "The Atlanta Compromise," was hugely popular and immediately enhanced the educator's national status. With its seamless solution to the nation's vexing racial issues, it became, in its time, the best-known public address given by an African American.

Washington's suggestion that blacks abandon their agitation for reform likely found a receptive hearer in Ben Tillman, but Tillman meant to meet the educator's idea more than halfway; he intended to fix the "problem" of Negro voting once and for all. The Tillmanites perhaps sensed some new urgency in this project, for with the election of Benjamin Harrison in 1888, the Republicans controlled the White House and both houses of Congress again for the first time since the end of Reconstruction. Such a majority could mean a revived threat of federal intervention, and indeed, beginning in early 1890, the Republicans came close to passing two pieces of legislation that were anathema to the South.

The first, introduced by Senator Henry W. Blair of New Hampshire, was an education bill that would provide money to upgrade the region's schools. Many Southerners recognized the need for such help, but the bill also provoked anxieties of federal meddling in school curricula, teacher qualifications, and, far worse, the desegregation of its schools and pupils. It suffered a narrow defeat when Senate Republicans, confronting a bloc of Democratic opposition, failed to hold their own majority. An even sharper concern for Southerners was the legislation crafted by Congressman Henry Cabot Lodge of Massachusetts, which would establish federal supervision of elections. The merit of Lodge's proposal was obvious: dire statistics clearly showed how blacks were being disenfranchised. But the bill resembled the infamous Enforcement Acts and other intrusive laws and thus ran into a shatterproof wall of Southern resistance, with the assistance of some feckless Republicans.

Although the bills that Blair and Lodge proposed were turned back, the extended debates they generated in Congress and in the press hardened Southerners' determination to further marginalize the black electorate. In 1865 Mississippi had been the first state to write and enforce a series of Black Codes, which other states then emulated; in 1875 it had again shown the way, bringing about home rule with its Mississippi Plan; now it achieved another first, convening a state constitutional convention in late summer 1890 that aimed, among other reforms, to devise more permanent means of disenfranchising the state's black majority.

For white Mississippians, as later for Ben Tillman, key legal and constitutional issues stood at stake. Any steps to relegate the black voter to the sidelines could not directly violate the Fifteenth Amendment, which stated, "The right of citizens of the United States to vote shall not be denied or abridged by the United States or by any state on account of race, color, or previous condition of servitude." In addition, each state of the former Confederacy readmitted to the Union during Reconstruction did so under the condition that its constitution would never "be amended or changed as to deprive any citizen, or class of citizens of the United States, of the right to vote." The renovation of the state constitution in Mississippi had to cleverly void or nullify these federal restrictions without openly defying them. If federal law could prohibit states from denying blacks access to the ballot, state law might establish criteria for the exercise of suffrage that would erect insurmountable hurdles and permit wide discretion on the part of official registrars, effectively accomplishing the same result.

The most ingenious of these was put forward in 1890: the "understanding clause" was the brainchild of James Z. George, one of the architects of the Mississippi Plan. By requiring that every voter "be able to read any section of the Constitution of this State; or he shall be able to understand the same when read to him, or give a reasonable interpretation thereof," the clause provided registrars not only with a rigorous means of challenging would-be voters but also with enormous latitude in judging who had failed or succeeded in qualifying.

At first, the state's press and public were taken aback by the prospect of enshrining so ignoble and blatant a fraud in a section of the new constitution. One delegate termed it diabolical, noting that "the mephitic vapor that arises from the section actually stinks in the nostrils of an honest man." As a small-town editor cautioned, if the legendary minds of Daniel Webster and John C. Calhoun could not agree about what the U.S. Constitution meant, then surely in Mississippi there would be "honest differences of opinion between a corn-field nigger and inspectors of election."

The outcry gradually subsided though, because even the critics of the proposed clause came to agree that it was a kind of silver bullet — an indestructible means of attaining the objective of black disenfranchisement while maintaining the voting privileges of ignorant, even illiterate whites. Its cleverness and potential efficacy simply could not be denied. Leading newspapers from Jackson and Vicksburg began to tout the clause, and at the convention even the sole black delegate, Isaiah T. Montgomery of the all-black town of Mound Bayou in the Mississippi Delta, acquiesced to it, apparently recognizing that resistance was futile. On November 1, 1890, the new Mississippi constitution, including the "understanding clause," was successfully adopted.

Thus with rather dismal expectations the South Carolina blacks saw their own state constitution opened for adjustment and repair. "The convention which met [in Columbia] in 1895 was very different both in intent and personnel from that of 1868," notes the historian Okon Edet Uya. "The latter had been called for the special purpose of giving the blacks political rights consonant with their status as citizens; that of 1895 met for the expressed purpose of taking those rights away." John Gary Evans, the new governor and convention president (Ben Tillman had become a U.S. senator but essentially controlled the convention), opened the proceedings by urging delegates to "do our duty in this matter boldly and fearlessly, without regard to the censure of foreigners and aliens. We have experienced the cost and hardship of the rule of the ignorant, and know what it means."

The six African American delegates, sent by districts so overwhelmingly black that even Tillman had not managed to expunge these men, would be allowed their say, for the Tillmanites were keen on dressing the convention in as much propriety as possible. Held in a building with the marks of General Sherman's cannonballs still visible outside and the original ordinance of secession hanging inside, the gathering had from the start a self-willed sense of historic importance and inevitability, a "momentous" event, averred the *Charleston News & Courier,* "for millions of people now living and for millions more yet unborn."

For Robert Smalls, the gathering seemed more likely a "momentous" nightmare, a topsy-turvy world in which everything he had accomplished was to be mocked or destroyed. Listening to Pitchfork Ben, a man Smalls considered a degenerate and a criminal, arraign Reconstruction and the state's black leadership, would have been especially painful. Equally disturbing were the idiotic remarks offered by delegates in defense of white supremacy, such as Robert Aldrich's characterization of the federal mandate for the 1868 convention as "the greatest crime of the nineteenth century," or worse, Henry C. Burns's view that "slavery to the negro was a blessing in disguise," for "when [they] landed at Jamestown they were . . . barbarians, idolaters, they ran about like turkeys, catching grasshoppers and lizards and eating them with the highest relish."

If there was anything encouraging about the situation, it was the extent to which men like Smalls, and the other black delegates including William J. Whipper, had evolved as politicians. (Whipper, the former state legislator who had figured unfavorably in the Black Thursday fiasco under Chamberlain, had become a judge in the Sea Islands.) Long mistreated as upstarts or "aliens," it was they who possessed the status of political veterans and carried the institutional memory of the state's government, they who spoke most knowledgably about the past three decades of its political history. Yet if their battle with the Tillmanites was one of wisdom versus cleverness, cleverness unfortunately had the greater numbers, as well as the podium and the gavel.

Tillman's own speech to the convention coarsely summed up the evolution of state politics since the war. He began by linking the arrival of the carpetbaggers to the national agitation over the Black Codes. "[The Codes] gave the black Republicans, Thad Stevens and his gang, excuse for their Reconstruction deviltry," Tillman said, "and caused these hellhounds, actuated by hate for the Southern people, to determine upon degrading us to the lowest level possible, and they had at hand an instrument which the most fertile imagination, if it had been given a thousand years to concoct a scheme of villainy, could not have surpassed. It was the presence among us of our slaves set free by the results of the war.

"How did it come about and who must bear the blame [for Reconstruction]?" he asked.

> We are told the negroes didn't do it. "Oh, we didn't do it," they say [mimicking the blacks seated in the hall]. You blindly followed and obeyed the orders of the Freedmen's Bureau and the Union League and ignored the appeals of your former masters, who treated you with kindness and furnished you with your daily bread. I myself can testify that appeal after appeal was made by me, and by almost every white man in the state . . . But every one of you, almost up to 1876, blindly followed wherever these white thieves ordered.
>
> The negroes furnished the ballots . . . The negroes put the little pieces of paper in the box that gave the commission to these white scoundrels . . . and this must be our justification, our vindication and our excuse to the world that we are met in convention openly, boldly, without any pretense or secrecy, to announce that it is our purpose, as far as we may, without coming in conflict with the United States Constitution, to put such safeguards around this ballot in future, to so restrict the suffrage and circumscribe it, that this infamy can never come about again.

Tillman read aloud some of the evidence from that hallmark of innuendo, the 1877 "Report on Public Frauds," which alleged that the black members of the Reconstruction state legislature had indulged in expensive and needless articles, such as 40¢ spittoons, 25¢ hat pegs, $4 looking glasses, $200 crimson plush sofas, Havana cigars, champagne, and $600 mirrors, in addition to defrauding the people with extravagant printing costs. Tillman assailed the name of the former state senator Charles P. Leslie, disgraced as the inept head of Richard Cain's state land commission in the early 1870s, who had once said, according to Tillman, "The state had no right to be a state unless she could pay and take care of her statesmen." But Leslie was an easy target. Corrupt, slipshod in his administrative methods at the land commission, he had provided conservatives for many years with a ready illustration of Republican and carpetbag excess. When a black delegate, James E. Wigg, interrupted Tillman to remind him that Leslie was a white man, Tillman shushed him, warning, "I will find you a plenty of nigs after a while."

This rant about Reconstruction-era expense accounts was deeply hypocritical, of course, for even the worst allegations in the "Report on Public Frauds" could hardly be measured against the momentous fraud Tillman and his friends wished to perpetrate in disenfranchising thousands of South Carolina citizens; and one point seldom conceded — or ever mentioned — was that prior to the Civil War, state politicians tended to be wealthy landowners who had little need of government-provided supplies, travel costs, or even a salary.

Looking now to the future, Tillman demanded, "Can we not rise to the necessities of the occasion, and put into this Constitution such an Article in reference to suffrage as will guarantee, as far as the law can guarantee, to future generations that they shall have the blessings of Anglo-Saxon civilization and liberty in this State? How pitiable, how puerile, how ineffably, unutterably contemptible appear the personal ambitions and petty spites of men alongside of this grand and glorious purpose!"

In addition to Mississippi's example, the Tillmanites had for inspiration a pamphlet by a former state legislator named Edward McCrady Jr., bearing the innocuous title "The Necessity of Raising the Standard of Citizenship," which explained how certain simple proofs of citizenship could be legalized that would effectively deny the vote. McCrady, the father of the "eight box law," had outlined the danger of allowing even a significant black voting minority to exist, for fear it would at some point be exploited by whites in an unscrupulous coalition. An old-fashioned conservative in the mode of Wade Hampton, McCrady was known to disapprove of Tillman, but Tillman's convention seized upon many of McCrady's ideas for placing severe "citizenship" restrictions on the state's voters, such as rules concerning place of residency, literacy, and past criminal records. The crimes enumerated were those that blacks were more often accused of, such as burglary, arson, forgery, adultery, bigamy, wife beating, fencing stolen goods, and sodomy. Curiously, murder, rioting, and lynching — more typically white crimes — were not listed. (The black delegates proposed that lynching be added to the list, but the resolution was not carried.)

The most controversial proposed rule was Mississippi's "understanding clause," the loophole that empowered local registrars to quiz voting applicants to see whether they "understood," and could explain to the registrar's satisfaction, a paragraph chosen from the state's constitution. Smalls, seeing the clause for what it was — a means of barring blacks from the polls while admitting any white — spoke out against it, calling instead for a straight-up literacy test. There were, as of the census of 1890, he said, a total of 102,657 white males over the age of twenty-one in South Carolina, and 132,949 black males. Of the whites, 13,242 were estimated to be illiterate; of the blacks, 58,086. Thus, if a fairly applied test kept all illiterate men from the ballot, the whites would reverse the blacks' voting majority in the state by about 15,000. What many delegates knew, however, was that since virtually all the white illiterates in the state belonged to the Tillmanite faction, the blacks of the state might still attain a majority if they managed to forge an alliance with moderate whites — the very coalition that had worried McCrady and that existed briefly in the decade's Southern Populist movement. As the black delegate James Wigg noted, "The doctrine so persistently taught that the interests of the negro and Anglo-Saxon are so opposed as to be irreconcilable is a political subterfuge; a fallacy so glaring in its inception, so insulting to Providence, so contrary to reason and logic of history, that one can scarcely refrain from calling in question either the sanity or honesty of its advocates." It was the truth of Wigg's statement, and the fear of just such a partnership, that made an across-the-board literacy test unacceptable to the Tillmanites.

Smalls warned that Tillmanite abuses of voting rights would be ultimately destructive: they would further alienate black South Carolinians, perhaps driving them away and creating labor shortages as did the Exodus of 1879, and they would reinforce the state's, and the region's, already glaring reputation for racial injustice. He added that since 1865 as many as fifty-three thousand blacks had been killed in the South, but no more than two or three whites had ever been held accountable for these deaths. In response, Tillman accused Smalls and other blacks of corruption and high-handedness during Reconstruction's "era of good stealing." Smalls vehemently denied the characterization, citing evidence that the charges against him, as enumerated in the "Report on Public

Frauds," had been trumped up. "I stand here the equal of any man," Smalls declared. "I started out in the war with the Confederates; they threatened to punish me and I left them. I went to the Union army. I fought in seventeen battles to make glorious and perpetuate the flag that some of you trampled under your feet. Innocent of every charge attempted to be made here today against me, no act of yours can in any way blur the record that I have made at home and abroad."

It was heartening that a resounding national reaction greeted Smalls's stand in the South Carolina convention. Letters and telegrams of approbation poured in from across the country, many daring to suggest that Smalls's eloquence had demolished the basis of the Tillmanites' assault on black rights. As one editorial noted of Smalls's "brilliant moral victory," white anxiety about blacks in politics "is not born so much of regard for their numbers as their intellectual ability. It is not Negro ignorance but Negro intelligence that is being feared."

This theory was conveniently demonstrated when "the Boat Thief" managed to turn the tables on the dominant party one more time. The Democrats had sought to establish codes of punishment in the new constitution for committing the social taboo of racial intermarriage. In response, Smalls counterproposed an amendment stating that any white person caught in cohabitation with a black person should be barred from holding public office and that any offspring from such a union should bear the father's name. And since it was common knowledge that a black man who dared even a romantic pass at a white woman was asking to be lynched, he suggested that a similar, but legal standard be made to apply to white men who sexually exploited black women. "The coons had the dogs up the tree for a change," laughed the *Columbia State*, for Smalls had successfully indicted a long tradition of misbehavior and hypocrisy among white males, and in doing so he had probably made every Democrat in the chamber squirm. His amendment was refused, but not before Tillman's convention was made to discuss and consider its ramifications.

The voting measures adopted by the convention gave the franchise to males over the age of twenty-one who had resided in the state for two years, their county one year, and their precinct four months. (These requirements were meant to set limits on black voters, who tended to be more transient.) A poll tax would be paid in May, six months before November elections. (This deadline preyed on farmers, for the late spring was a time when they were traditionally cash poor.) In addition, the convention approved both the literacy test and the "understanding clause," to be applied at the registrar's discretion, although anyone who had paid taxes on $300 worth of property would be exempt. (The U.S. Supreme Court would uphold the "understanding clause" in an 1898 decision, *Williams v. Mississippi,* refusing to rule that it and other suffrage provisions were discriminatory. Similar clauses were duly enacted by Louisiana in 1898, North Carolina in 1900, Alabama and Virginia in 1901, Georgia in 1908, and Oklahoma in 1910.) The idea of a grandfather clause, requiring black registrants to prove they'd had an ancestor who was a registered voter, was dropped as unnecessary, and Tillman dismissed Robert Aldrich's suggestion that no black person ever be allowed to hold public office as inflammatory and likely to excite Northern opinion. Given the new restrictions on black voting, it was in any case now superfluous.

The Tillmanites got pretty much all they wanted from their convention, which approved the new constitution by a vote of 116 to 7. Ironically, for all their fulminations against the Reconstruction constitution of 1868, the Tillman convention had little choice but to retain many of its structural reforms. There was a moral in this. As Smalls had attempted to assert, establishing a new state constitution based on essentially undemocratic ideas flew in the face of basic good government. The fixation on race above all else, "the subject of subjects," unified regional law and politics but also rendered them perverse, hypocritical, and self-defeating. An example was the South's rejection of potentially beneficial federal assistance in education, for fear that it would arouse national concern about segregated schools. As the white politician Ellery Brayton, a witness to the Tillman revolution, observed with considerable foresight, strict discipline on the issue that mattered most tended to create closed societies in which debate and the airing of differences on other matters became inhibited; this corrupted the region intellectually, and probably morally as well.

When Smalls refused to sign the finished constitution, another delegate informed him that his travel expenses would not be paid if he did not affix his signature. "Then I'll walk home," he said. "I'd rather walk than put my name to a constitution with such an article on suffrage." Ever the Lincolnesque optimist, Robert Smalls walked out of the convention and did not stop. Almost immediately he embarked on a speaking tour in support of William McKinley, who would become the successful Republican candidate for president in 1896; Smalls used every stop on a tour that took him as far west as Kansas to describe the horrors of Tillmanism in South Carolina and to castigate the entire South for efforts to nullify black participation in politics and the democracy at large.

Senator Shelby M. Collom of Illinois made a proposal that appealed to Robert Smalls. Completely legal, its goal was to reduce the South's proportional representation in Congress because so many of its citizens had been disenfranchised. This idea had been floated before, unsuccessfully, but Smalls loved its simple logic and thought it an ideal way of bringing the Southern states to task. In 1898, the Republican congressman Edgar D. Crumpacker of Indiana suggested that a 40 percent reduction in the Southern representation in Congress would adequately reflect the extensive disenfranchisement of Southern black citizens. During the South Carolina convention, the Tillman forces had actually agreed that they would willingly reduce the state's representation in the electoral college and in Congress, if necessary, because from their perspective, the ability to dominate state politics along racial lines meant far more than having a slightly larger voice in Washington.

So sweeping an initiative, however, so utterly sectional and punitive in character, was likely to go nowhere, given the prevailing mood of regional reconciliation. Americans were by now paying far more attention to foreign troublemakers than to homegrown ones like Pitchfork Ben Tillman, and the crises of the nation's cities, its powerful corporate trusts, and its restive masses of ethnic laborers had largely supplanted concern for the most vulnerable residents of the Southern Black Belt.

Even in the face of the post-Reconstruction hostility to black suffrage, Southern black voters continued to send black men to Congress, often from formidable black redoubts such as the Sea Islands and North Carolina's Second Congressional District, known as "the Black Second." Although North Carolina had been redeemed in 1870, the state sent four blacks to Congress from 1875 to 1900. Still, the overall trend was disheartening. The Forty-fourth Congress (1875–77) included eight black members, the maximum for the nineteenth century. After that, black participation fell off precipitously; no more than two at a time served in Congress during the 1880s, three were present for the Fifty-first Congress (1889–91), and from 1891 to 1901, no more than one participated.

The liveliest black North Carolinian to make it to Washington was probably James O'Hara, the son of a black mother and an Irish sea captain, who came to the Tarheel State in 1868 and ascended rapidly through state Republican ranks, serving two terms in Congress in the 1880s. His quick wit and sound legal mind won him the admiration of his constituents but disparagement from many whites, who considered him "a mulatto with cheek a plenty." O'Hara lived up to his reputation in 1875, celebrating the passage of the Civil Rights Act by personally integrating the saloon of a famous steamboat, the *Cotton Planter.* Another strong-willed presence in Congress was the minister Jeremiah Haralson, elected from Alabama in 1874. An unlettered, straight-talking man who had once been auctioned as a slave, Haralson was described by the *Mobile Register* as "a burly Negro . . . black as the ace of spades and with the brogue of the cornfield." He fell out of favor with voters in 1879–80 over his opposition to the Exoduster movement, although Haralson himself ultimately migrated west to Colorado, where he tried his hand at mining, among other schemes, and in 1916 met a grisly death, devoured by wild animals.

Probably the most distinguished black member of Congress in the latter half of the century was John Mercer Langston, great-uncle of the poet Langston Hughes. An Oberlin graduate, Langston became in 1854 the first black person to practice law in Ohio, and soon after, one of the first black Americans ever elected to public office, serving as the town clerk of Brownhelm, Ohio. He went on to have a superlative career, helping to raise black fighting units during the war and working for the Freedmen's Bureau, then serving as dean of the law school at Howard University, as minister to Haiti, and, in the 1880s, as president of the Virginia Normal and Collegiate Institute. Since high elective office was the one prize Langston had not attained, in 1888 he sought a congressional seat from Virginia's Fourth District. The campaign splintered black and white Republicans in the state; Langston's candidacy was opposed not only by Virginia's white Republican leader, Senator William Mahone, but by the influential spokesman Frederick Douglass. Langston and Douglass shared an enduring animosity. Douglass may have resented the life of relative privilege that Langston had enjoyed, while Langston was known to have sniped at Douglass over his handling of the Freedman's Bank debacle. In any case, this ill will motivated Douglass to write an open letter to voters in Langston's district, suggesting that the candidate sought status and influence without being truly devoted to the cause of racial progress. Langston was livid, although Douglass's missive, widely perceived as mean-spirited, galvanized support for Langston. He managed, however, to hold his seat in Congress for only one term.

George H. White of North Carolina was to have the honor of being the last black Southerner of his century to serve in Congress (another,

Andrew Young of Georgia, along with Barbara Jordan of Texas, would not return until 1973). From 1897 to 1901 White was the body's sole black representative, and this isolation, as well as his own obstinacy, made his a most contentious posting. His performance in Congress was noteworthy also because, with the passing of Frederick Douglass in 1895, John Mercer Langston in 1897, and Blanche K. Bruce in 1898, White became by default one of the nation's leading African Americans. Booker T. Washington and his message of quiet assimilation were far better known and respected, but unlike the Wizard of Tuskegee, White had remained true to the emancipationist vision of Douglass and the postwar black Republicans, and in Congress he did not hesitate to assail racial injustice and inequality head-on. Among other initiatives, he revived the idea that Southern states deserved a diminished representation in Congress because of their broad disenfranchisement of blacks, he urged that the federal government reimburse depositors who had lost money in the Freedman's Bank, and he demanded that his white colleagues stop telling "darkey stories" and using "dialect and old plantation language" when trying to represent blacks' views and beliefs (a habit to which even Booker T. Washington often succumbed).

White was also the first member of Congress to propose federal legislation to quell the epidemic of lynching then ravaging the nation. Violence had always been, to some extent, the real story of Reconstruction, and possibly of American race relations in general. The riots at Memphis and New Orleans had convinced the North of the South's intransigence; Ku Kluxing had worn down the resolve of the Northern public even as it brought forth tough federal laws to punish the practice; then came the Red Shirts, the White Liners, and the White League, more sophisticated than their Klan forbears but still using armed might and intimidation to control the black vote and determine political outcomes. In the postbellum South, violence, or the threat of it, had replaced slavery as the key mechanism by which whites controlled African Americans; it wasn't the sole means of oppression, of course, but the most immediately effective at terrorizing the black populace, breeding apathy and disillusionment in the North, and ultimately enabling the Southern redemption.

Lynching, the punishment of a person accused of a crime or other transgression without due process of law, had long been viewed as a necessary means of "people's justice" in places beyond the reach of ordinary courts. Before the Civil War the term could still denote nonlethal retribution, such as tarring and feathering; later it came to refer exclusively to extralegal execution, usually by rope or gun. By the 1880s, fewer lynchings were occurring on the western frontier as settlement there increased; at the same time their frequency grew sharply in the South, with black men the primary victims. South Carolina's Daniel Chamberlain had been one of the first to criticize the trend when, in 1876, six black men were arrested in Edgefield for killing John L. Harmon and his wife, Catherine, and were taken from the sheriff and shot to death without benefit of trial. As Chamberlain pointed out, Edgefield was not a

> new or imperfectly organized community in which concerted violence must sometimes supplement or supersede the laws . . . The courts are everywhere accessible and frequent . . . Nor were there special circumstances attending this affair which could give occasion or excuse for this defiance and overthrow of the law and its officers. The persons charged with the crime were in the custody of the officers of the law. Escape was impossible . . . No ground whatever existed for fearing executive clemency after due conviction. And yet . . . six citizens covered by the aegis of our laws . . . have been summarily, deliberately, openly, and ruthlessly slain, without legal trial, without proper legal scrutiny of the evidences of their guilt, and without the smallest chance of legal defense.

After rising steadily through the 1880s, such race-related lynchings by 1892 were occurring at a rate of almost two hundred per year — *more than one every other day.*

Like other historical examples of community-sanctioned terror, the upsurge of lynching in the 1890s resists easy explanation. Perhaps it was, to a degree, a result of the collision between whites' dread fear of black people and their perceived loss of control over the South itself. A generation of black people who had never known slavery had now come of age. Compared to their forbears, their independence of thought and action as, increasingly mobile, they left farms and headed for work in the cities, inevitably struck whites as troublesome, if not "insolent." Such freedom triggered many anxieties, the most surprising of which was sexual in nature. The exploitation of black women by white men had long been custom; to rationalize such behavior, white men had elevated their own women to a kind of sexless, virginal sainthood; but now that black men were potentially free to mingle with white women, the only recourse was to reimagine the black man as a sexual monster. As economics drove white women off their pedestal — out of the old family homestead and into the wider world of textile mills and cities — protecting their sanctity became conflated with defending white dominion in the South. At stake was a crusade far too sacred to brook interference from courts or ordinary laws. As Ben Tillman infamously declared, "Whenever the Constitution comes between me and the virtue of the white women of the South, I say to hell with the Constitution!"

Also, the region's traditional impatience with legal remedies and due process, the "mistrials and acquittals" won "through the instrumentality of ingenious lawyers or ignorant juries," according to the *Charleston News & Courier,* played a role. When a black was the alleged perpetrator of a crime, the heritage of slavery made it seem logical to disregard legal formalities; after all, in that context all blacks were suspected to be criminals and all white men were entitled to act as police. Blacks were, for ample reasons of their own, alienated from the justice system because Southern courts were traditionally used by whites to deny blacks their earnings, their property, and sometimes their freedom. Lynchings often could be attributed to misunderstandings that, in other settings, mutual trust in local justice might have resolved — the sharecropper or farm worker disputing wages or work conditions with an employer; a black man's panicked flight when confronted by the law; and of course, alleged crimes or transgressions involving interracial sex.

Lynching in the 1890s became so accepted a brake on black "criminality," and the activities of lynch mobs were viewed so commonly as heroic, that some killings took the form of macabre, picnic-like spectacles. These events — egged on by the press, at times serviced by special excursion trains from nearby towns — attracted thousands of men, women, and children, and ended usually in the torture and immolation of the accused before a frenzied crowd. In such well-publicized "entertainments," the victim's demise seemed both an expiation of white people's shame at their loss of status and an affirmation of racial solidarity. It was, perhaps needless to say, also an effective means of keeping the black populace for miles around terrorized and utterly cowed.

Two disquieting events in North Carolina in 1898 drew Congressman White's attention to the issue of lynching and mob violence. In one, local Red Shirts, emulating the South Carolina Red Shirts of a generation before and seeking to expunge blacks from elected and appointed office, rioted in coastal Wilmington. Vigilantes rampaged through the streets, killing and wounding dozens of blacks, setting fires, and driving most local black leaders from town and hundreds of ordinary citizens into the woods. In the other incident, the black postmaster of Lake City, North Carolina, Frazier B. Baker, was mobbed and killed, along with his infant daughter; his house was set afire and his wife and three other children were wounded by gunfire as they escaped the flames.

White brought the Lake City attack to Congress's attention and submitted a resolution asking for funds so the surviving members of Baker's family could attain medical care, since Baker had been a federal employee. In remarks to Congress he then tackled the Southern rationale for lynching — that it was necessary to curb blacks from committing sex crimes against white women. "I have examined the question and I am prepared to state that not more than fifteen percent of the lynchings are traceable to that crime," he reported, adding, "there are many more outrages against colored women by white men than there are by colored men against white women."

For such candor White was widely denounced; he had lifted the veil on a form of licentiousness that had underlaid Southern society for many decades. The seeking of relationships in the slave quarters both dishonored white men's wives and families and created a mulatto race, while inhibiting the maintenance of familial relations among the slaves. Emancipation had thwarted this pattern but hardly obliterated it. Of course, the shrouded truth about many accusations made against blacks was that liaisons between black men and white women were often consensual. Such relations were so taboo, most Southern courts refused to acknowledge their existence until well into the twentieth century.

White was not the first black person to challenge the lynching ethos. For printing almost identical thoughts, the journalist Ida B. Wells had been run out of Memphis in 1892; a similar fate befell Alex Manly, editor of the *Daily Record*, a black newspaper in Wilmington, in 1898; his remarks had helped inflame the deadly riot there.

"It is bad enough that North Carolina should have the only nigger Congressman," the *Raleigh News and Observer* complained of White — let alone one who would foster such foolish ideas for federal legislation. It was particularly annoying that an official representative of the state of North Carolina had dared utter, in Congress, secret truths about the white South's sexual peccadilloes and, furthermore, that black people in the gallery had applauded his words. "As the blatant mouthing of a mere negro, White's utterances are not worth notice," said the *News and Observer*.

> As a fresh manifestation of negroism, of what the negro's attitude is toward the white man . . . its significance should not be allowed to escape us. If there were no other reason, this utterance of White's is

> sufficient to show the absolute necessity of permanent white rule in this state . . . The "inoffensive negro official" is largely a myth. The negro may be inoffensive as a private citizen, but with his induction into office he becomes a new individual. White is typical . . . venomous, forward, slanderous of the whites, appealing to the worst passions of his own race, he emphasizes anew the need of making an end of him and his kind.

Undaunted, White reiterated his statement in Congress and this time defied anyone to disprove it. He backed up his claim that sexual outrage was exaggerated by producing statistics that showed the diverse "reasons" for lynchings. Of sixty-three people lynched between April 24, 1899, and October 20, 1899, he explained, only sixteen were accused of sexual assault; nine had been accused of murder; three of sheltering a murderer; one of trespass; one of barn burning; one had "put hand on white woman"; two had "talked too much"; two "spoke against lynching"; and one had "entered a lady's room drunk." White did not fail to condemn actual cases of rape and sexual assault, but he insisted that conviction and punishment for such heinous crimes were the business of a court, not a mob.

White's anti-lynching measure was based on the "equal protection" and "due process" clauses of the Fourteenth Amendment but was unusual in that it also cited lynching as a form of treason. This strategy was aimed at circumventing the Southern claim that local police matters (that is, combatting lynching) were the business of states, not the federal government. Of course, in reality, the states had been slow or unwilling to deal with the problem, and state or county officials such as judges and sheriffs were themselves frequently complicit in lynchings, often enabling mobs to extract prisoners from jail. In invoking treason, White was a generation ahead of his time, for the mob mindset that lynching represented *would* ultimately come to offend Americans as dangerous and *un*-American, once they'd been exposed, through news accounts, to the horrors of the World War I and the "anarchy" associated with the Russian Revolution and other European civic disorders. White was also prescient in pointing out the psychological damage inflicted on young people of both races in the South who were made to witness or learn about atrocious incidents of mob violence. His bill, however, held up in the House Judiciary Committee, never made it to the floor.

In North Carolina, meanwhile, the state constitution had in 1900 been retooled as in Mississippi and South Carolina to include an "understanding clause" for would-be black voters, and White, recognizing that under this and other new restrictions neither he nor any other black could win election, on January 29, 1901, offered a "Negroes' valedictory message" to Congress. He lamented the fact that his lynching bill "still sweetly sleeps in the room of the Committee to which it was referred," and again he condemned white congressmen who regularly slandered blacks. He then offered "a brief recipe for the solution of the so-called American negro problem" — that the black American "be given the same chance for existence, for earning a livelihood, for raising himself in the scales of manhood and womanhood that are accorded to kindred nationalities."

"This, Mr. Chairman, is perhaps the Negroes' temporary farewell to the American Congress," said White of his own imminent departure, "but let me say Phoenix-like he will rise up some day and come again. These parting words are in behalf of an outraged, heart-broken, bruised and bleeding, but God-fearing people, faithful, industrial, loyal people, rising people, full of potential force . . . The only apology I have for the earnestness with which I have spoken is that I am pleading for the life, the liberty, the future happiness, and manhood suffrage for one-eighth of the entire population of the United States."

On March 4, 1901, at noon, both houses of the North Carolina legislature passed resolutions of thanksgiving that, with the conclusion of White's term, the thirty-one years during which black men had been allowed to occupy seats in Congress, the era of Hiram Revels and Blanche K. Bruce, Robert Brown Elliott, Joseph Rainey, Robert Smalls, and the tenacious George H. White, was finally over. With black Americans segregated in public life to the point of invisibility, denied the ballot, and now banished at long last from the halls of Congress, it was safe to welcome the bright promise of a new century.

EPILOGUE

Although no epoch in history can be condensed into the simple, straightforward narrative we might wish for, it is difficult to imagine another period in America's past as complex as Reconstruction, or one that has been as controversial in the telling. The years 1865–77 were an unprecedented test for a nation barely a century old, bringing rapid corporate and territorial expansion, novel modes of transport and technology, and the flexing of vast new federal authority, as well as the sudden citizenship of four million freed slaves, factional struggles for control of the "late insurrectionary states," and finally, the reuniting of those states with the national government. In the end, the country brought about the latter, reconciliation, by agreeing to set aside the former, the civil rights of black Americans, even to the extent of undoing laws enacted on their behalf — an expediency many view as perhaps the most significant moral failure in our history. Until the fight to rectify that collapse became a national crusade in the mid-twentieth century, historical commentary about the Reconstruction era was frequently clouded by intense sectional feeling, distortion, and myth.

As long as forces largely inimical to Reconstruction dominated Reconstruction scholarship, Robert Brown Elliott and P.B.S. Pinchback, Joseph Rainey and Blanche K. Bruce, and other black officials were often depicted as incompetents and thieves, or worse, simply airbrushed from the historical record. Later, when greater objectivity was brought to the subject, the black representatives nonetheless often remained marginal figures, their role in Congress and on the national political stage considered largely symbolic. Either view tends to invalidate black political initiative and, in any case, flies in the face of the evidence, which indicates that when the reconstructed states of the South began holding elections that included their enfranchised black populations, men of color were elected to Congress and to state and local positions, or were appointed by their state legislatures to seats in the U.S. Senate, in relatively fair proportion to their constituencies and even with the support of whites.

Given the nature of that era, black officeholders tended to be — *had* to be — exceptional individuals, survivors who had emerged from a world of slavery and war to stand as spokesmen for their race, "men of mark," as they were called by a contemporary biographer. In general they brought an impressive degree of competence and dedication to their jobs, dispelling critics' claims that they possessed no aptitude for politics or statesmanship. Facing major issues related to the integration of black citizens into American life — the desire for land and education, the establishment of new state constitutions, the necessity of confronting the Ku Klux Klan and its successors, the passage of laws safeguarding the vote and expanding civil rights — they were often more humane, perceptive, and prescient than their white colleagues. When they spoke as the first official representatives of a long-despised and mistreated class, their words were at times a revelation to white ears, offering a perspective few whites had known, in vocal cadences most had never heard. Ultimately they gave America a great gift, a demonstration of the loyalty and intelligence of its newest citizens.

Their example not only defied the expectations of many whites but also inspired millions of black Americans. The walls of black homes and even modest sharecroppers' cabins were often graced with a print of the image that adorns the cover of this book, or any of the many similar lithographs of the era, such as the portrait of Senator Hiram Revels, the first black senator, which was sold with pride by the *New National Era*, or the multipaneled color lithograph depicting Robert Elliott's famous civil rights speech before Congress on January 6, 1874, which bore the stirring caption "The Shackle Broken — by the Genius of Freedom."

There is, I believe, something eminently decent about their brief transit across history's pages.

Of course, they were public figures in an era infamous for a lack of probity and the casual disregard of ethical standards in business and politics, and some were compromised by easy temptation. Neither did they always judge correctly the shape of coming events or the right path to take. In Congress, the forces of resistance were aligned almost perpetually against them. Without seniority, they could neither head nor wield influence within prominent committees and had to struggle to leverage power as best they could. One handicap was their want of entrenched political support. With the exception of Robert Smalls and John Roy Lynch, most were not natives of the districts they represented, and their constituencies, while substantial, tended to be comprised of voters of modest means. Thus they lacked the capability enjoyed by other members of Congress to call upon established political networks in their home districts or states, and in Washington were often forced to rely on white allies whose own influence might rise or wane unexpectedly.

They were not so naive as to assume the permanence of the authority they had gained, but few imagined the extent to which redemption would strip away Reconstruction's many achievements. Placing considerable faith in the power of the franchise, they did not fully gauge the determination of the Southern states to annihilate it, nor necessarily foresee a time when their access to the ballot could no longer be protected by the federal government. The ratification of the Fifteenth Amendment in 1870, coinciding with the arrival of the first black representatives in Congress, brought a sense of accomplishment and relief, a hope that the black vote might serve as a cure-all, and that with it the work of the postwar transition would be completed. This proved an utterly misplaced confidence. Radical optimists "living too frequently in a paper world of ideal proposals and proclamations of principle," notes one scholar, proved better at making new laws than enforcing them. "When the flimsiness of all the statutory words was confronted with political opposition, deep-seated prejudice, and physical force, the designated programs made little headway and their minor accomplishments did not endure."

The situation in the South likely would have evolved more satisfactorily had larger numbers of blacks attained property, although it may be wishful thinking to assume that land would have automatically brought the freedmen economic stability. "The trouble was . . . not that the grant of political liberty lacked an economic basis — land for black people," suggests Herman Belz, "but that it did not rest on a firm emotional and ideological commitment" to political and racial equality in the South as well as in the North. That commitment, W.E.B. Du Bois once imagined, would of necessity have been deeper and more broadly shared, and included not only a means of land distribution but a system of equal education, civil rights legislation whose tenets could be made acceptable and enforceable, impartiality in the courts, and a permanent cabinet department based on the concept of the Freedmen's Bureau to monitor, evaluate, and guide the way forward.

In the eradication of slavery a noble principle had been achieved, a ruinous war waged, and a president martyred. By the mid-1870s, however, the country had suffered a harsh financial crisis and, facing new social and economic demands, sought to leave the past and particularly the discord of the war behind; eager for sectional reconciliation, it tired of the seemingly endless difficulties in the South, and began to turn a blind eye to the freed people's still-precarious plight. No doubt if Southerners themselves had requested more of the nation's help and stamina, the outcome would have been different, but they had made it clear that further efforts to transform their society were unwanted and would be vehemently resisted, at least for the foreseeable future. Reconstruction, then, a once-great democratizing impulse, collapsed in on itself — missing by now much of its initial leadership, worn down by the South's intransigence, and devoid of public willingness to any longer sustain the antagonisms of the late war. The "moral debt" to black Americans created by that conflict was simply "found to be beyond the country's capacity to pay, given the undeveloped state of its moral resources at the time."

Of the various personalities who rose to shimmer on the surface of public life in Reconstruction, few were so fully invested in the era's possibilities as the black congressmen who arrived in Washington. They, more than anyone, had taken the country at its word, aligning themselves closely with a program of national refurbishment and expanded citizenship, giving their all to the representation of a previously ignored class. They did so with a minimum of vindictiveness and a good deal of patience and creativity, in the faith that the civil and political well-being of their constituents mattered, and was integral to America's future.

As contentious a subject as the history of Reconstruction has been, there's little disagreement about one aspect of its legacy — that it served as a basis for the modern civil rights movement of the 1950s and 1960s, which has been called America's Second Reconstruction.

In the intervening years the struggle for racial justice was by no means idle. The National Association for the Advancement of Colored People (NAACP), founded in 1909, undertook vigorous campaigns for improvements in housing, employment, and education, and a quest for a federal anti-lynching law; the International Labor Defense's numerous courtroom endeavors included a crusade to save the Scottsboro Boys, nine young black men wrongly accused of rape in Alabama in 1931; A. Phillip Randolph and the March on Washington Movement in July 1941 forced Franklin D. Roosevelt's executive order desegregating the defense industries; and later, the Congress of Racial Equality (CORE) emerged as pioneers of modern protest regarding blacks' restricted access to public accommodations. These were only some of the many groups and individuals that tended the flame of civil rights advocacy.

Not until midcentury, however, did the country appear ready to support another broad frontal assault on segregation and white supremacy. What had changed was that a substantial African American population shift to the North had gained blacks a degree of national political influence, while in urban areas such as Atlanta, Nashville, and New Orleans they had achieved economic clout sufficient to force retail businesses and municipal services to take seriously their growing demands for fair and equal treatment. Perhaps most crucial, America, having emerged from a victorious global crusade against fascism, was newly sensitive to the blatant intolerance it found in its own backyard. Conditioned by the successful programs of the New Deal and the winning of the war, the country seemed newly sympathetic to the idea of civil rights reform and to the possibility that the federal government and judiciary would play a supportive role.

At the 1948 Democratic National Convention, progressive forces within the party, especially the liberal Americans for Democratic Action (ADA), led the gathering and its candidate, President Harry Truman, in adopting a strong civil rights platform. The ADA spokesman Hubert Humphrey, who was the mayor of Minneapolis, challenged the delegates, "There are those who say to you — we are rushing this issue of civil rights. I say we are a hundred and seventy-two years too late . . . The time has arrived for the Democratic Party to get out of the shadow of states' rights and walk forthrightly into the bright sunshine of human rights." So bold a declaration provoked many Southerners to abandon the national Democratic Party in disgust, splintering off as Dixiecrats who vowed to defend white supremacy and the separation of the races at all costs.

Battle lines were now drawn for a showdown over civil rights, and the South reacted with predictable outrage to the Supreme Court's landmark 1954 ruling in *Brown v. Board of Education,* which ended school segregation. Southerners decried it as unwanted meddling, much as their forbears had attacked the Blair education bill of 1890. When fourteen-year-old Emmett Till was lynched in August 1955, brutally murdered in Mississippi for allegedly "wolf-whistling" at a white woman, Southern race hatred was revealed at its ugliest, filling Americans from all walks of life with shame and inspiring protest. Soon after, the contours of the coming struggle were refined by the successful Montgomery (Alabama) bus boycott and the emergence of its charismatic leader, Martin Luther King Jr., as well as by President Dwight Eisenhower's decision to send troops to safeguard the integration of Central High School in Little Rock, Arkansas, in 1957, the first show of armed federal force in the South since Reconstruction.

King's appeal to America's core beliefs of equality and fairness, combined with his creative use of Mohandas K. Gandhi's principles of nonviolent protest, fostered the methods for social change that thousands of young civil rights activists adopted in the early 1960s. They fought bravely across the South for integration and the recognition of voting rights. In his "I Have a Dream" speech of August 1963, King alluded unambiguously to the "promissory note" America had signed with the Emancipation Proclamation and the Reconstruction amendments, the debt to African Americans that the Civil War had incurred and which had never fully been paid. The link to Reconstruction King spoke of could not have been more clear: the civil rights movement wasn't a revolution seeking to radically remake society (although it felt that way to Southern whites), but a crusade to remind America of constitutional guarantees already in place, laws that the nation had once had the courage to enact but had ignored or nullified over the past century.

Civil rights workers soon discovered that Reconstruction had left behind not only a constitutional blueprint of sorts but also some very useful tools. Its commitment to black education and equal rights was echoed in the NAACP Legal Defense Fund's breakthrough in *Brown.* The founding in the 1860s of black colleges such as Alcorn, the Hampton Institute, and Fisk, as well as the political empowerment of the black church, largely provided the modern movement's initial intellectual and spiritual energy as well as its legions of youthful foot soldiers. The language and even some of the tactics of the struggle surrounding the Civil Rights Act of 1875 returned to life in the Montgomery boycott and in the lunch counter sit-in movement that flowered in North Carolina in the early spring of 1960; that movement became, overnight, a national phenomenon as masses of young protesters integrated restaurants, department stores, and even public swimming pools. The next year CORE activists known as Freedom Riders broke down segregation on interstate bus lines. Resistance was strong and often bloody, and the jailing and beating of civil rights "agitators" frequent. The steadfastedness of the activists, however, abetted by public support, a largely sympathetic national media, and eventual congressional and Justice Department action, combined ultimately to break the Southern opposition.

Voting rights guaranteed by the Fifteenth Amendment and the Enforcement Acts provided a basis for the voter registration campaigns that swept Mississippi and Alabama in the 1960s, as young workers from the Student Nonviolent Coordinating Committee (SNCC) fanned out across rural hamlets where the nefarious "understanding clause" of late-nineteenth-century origin, and various other impediments, still kept would-be voters from the polls. In many areas black voting had become so depressed over the years that it existed only in historical memory; civil rights volunteers met longtime residents of the Black Belt who were unsure what the term even meant.

SNCC workers encouraged and helped educate black residents to appear before the registrars who had long intimidated them. At one point an SNCC researcher discovered an obscure Mississippi law dating from Reconstruction, originally meant to protect disenfranchised Confederates, that allowed for "unacceptable" votes to be tallied as a protest in the hope of being considered at a later time. The inspired result was the Mississippi Freedom Vote of 1963, in which civil rights workers held a mock election of disenfranchised blacks, calling the nation's attention to the injustice of Southern suffrage laws and laying the groundwork for the Freedom Summer of 1964. A federal reaffirmation of Americans' unhindered right to the franchise arrived with the Voting Rights Act of 1965, which did away with the "understanding clause," poll taxes, and other longstanding schemes of disenfranchisement.

Perhaps the most striking example of Reconstruction measures being revived for modern purposes involved the Enforcement Acts. When concerted NAACP efforts at securing a federal anti-lynching law died in Congress in the two decades after World War I, the Justice Department's newly created Civil Rights Division began considering other means of challenging racial violence, including the use of long-dormant anti-Klan conspiracy laws. By prohibiting mob violence carried out in concert with the police, or "under color of law," the laws once aimed at the Reconstruction Klan, government attorneys believed, could be adapted to prosecute contemporary lynchings and murders. Unfortunately, getting Southern federal judges and grand juries to cooperate proved difficult, and the Justice Department brought several such cases before finally, in the 1960s, working closely with the FBI, it won its first convictions against Southern terrorists. The most notable courtroom victories were related to the 1964 Klan-and-police conspiracy killings of the civil rights workers Andrew Goodman, Michael Schwerner, and James Chaney in Mississippi and the shooting death of Viola Liuzzo, a white Northern woman murdered while assisting in the March on Selma in 1965.

Reconstruction, after slumbering for decades in the attic of American history, was thus able to play a key, if belated, role in dragging the old Confederacy into the twentieth century. The fortresslike mindset the region had developed in response to emancipation and Reconstruction, and the warped antics of segregation's modern defenders, crude figures such as the Birmingham police commissioner Eugene "Bull" Connor and the Mississippi governor Ross Barnett, appeared particularly base and anachronistic when exposed in the glare of network news cameras or in the pages of *Life* magazine. Their white-supremacist ranting and demagoguery, and tactics such as siccing police dogs and playing fire hoses on black citizens, contrasted starkly with the moral decency of the civil rights cause itself.

Of course, as in the first Reconstruction, not all was smooth sailing. Some changes — desegregation in restaurants, in hotels, and on buses — came fairly readily; some, such as voting rights, required years of determined effort; others proved more or less intractable. Despite the victory over segregation and the passage of new laws such as the Civil Rights Act of 1964, there remained a painful gap between white and black Americans in income, employment, education, and housing — problems not easily remedied. And in another echo of Reconstruction, the ensuing frustration among reformers undercut the movement's idealism, and by 1966 dissent rankled among civil rights workers; some threw their support behind Black Nationalism. Martin Luther King Jr. and other leaders were led to rethink their strategies and begin addressing poverty and labor issues at the grassroots level.

While no one can question the overwhelming success of the civil rights movement or doubt the ways in which it irrevocably transformed America, its legacy, like that of Reconstruction, has also involved a conservative backlash. Politically, since the late 1960s, conservative forces have played skillfully upon Southern whites' traditional views on racial matters to solidify electoral support across the region. Nationwide, forced school desegregation (busing), preferences in employment and education (affirmative action), and welfare have all undergone judicial and legislative retrenchment, while fundamental challenges such as economic disparity between the races, inequality of opportunity, and bias in America's systems of justice and law enforcement continue unresolved.

One of the most dramatic allegorical images of Reconstruction America is captured in the 1867 Horatio Bateman lithograph of the republic as a giant pavilion being renovated. Against a background of men and women mingling in peaceful village squares and along city streets, the pavilion's timbers of SLAVERY are carted away, to be replaced by new ones representing JUSTICE, DEMOCRACY, and GOOD GOVERNMENT; overhead a cloud of spirits includes Lincoln, Washington, Webster, and Calhoun, all of them gazing down with approval.

When the actual edifice of Reconstruction fell, however, the hovering angels of the country's destiny hurriedly disappeared, leaving the mortals below to make good their own escape. Franklin Moses Jr., the "Robber Governor" who had raised the Confederate flag over Fort Sumter but then disgracefully used the South Carolina treasury to pay off his horseracing debts, became a drug addict and later went north to peddle sordid "inside" tales of Southern Reconstruction to big-city newspa-

HORATIO BATEMAN'S RECONSTRUCTION LITHOGRAPH

pers; his actions so mortified his family that they changed their name. Three of Daniel Chamberlain's children had perished by 1887 when his wife, Alice, died, leaving him the sole parent to his young son Waldo, who succumbed to illness in 1902 at the age of sixteen. Vanquished and alone, Chamberlain, who suffered from ailments he linked to his stressful years as governor of South Carolina, spent his remaining years traveling in an elusive search for health, and died in Charlottesville, Virginia, in 1907. Henry Clay Warmoth, the carpetbagger governor of Louisiana who, despite having been born in Illinois, always claimed that he was at heart a Southerner, remained in his adopted state to operate a successful sugar plantation.

Adelbert Ames enjoyed careers as a flour mill owner in Minnesota and a textile mill operator in Massachusetts, while dabbling in numerous inventions, such as pencil sharpeners and extension ladders for fire engines. He returned to military service in the Spanish-American War and retired, a wealthy man, to Florida, where he golfed with John D. Rockefeller and became known, thanks to his longevity, as "the Last General of the Civil War." He died in 1933 at age ninety-seven. Although Ames made many friends among ex-Confederates over the years, his memory was not entirely dear to Mississippians; in 1958 Henry M. "Doc" Fraser, a Dixiecrat who had led the state's walkout from the 1948 national Democratic convention, launched a movement to have Ames's official portrait removed from the capitol in Jackson. "Are the portraits of Hitler, Mussolini, Joe Stalin and others of their ilk hanging in the capitol building in Washington?" Fraser demanded. Governor J. P. Coleman insisted that Ames's portrait remain on display, although he stressed to newsmen that the place where it and other governors' images could be viewed was not a "hall of fame."

Most of the black national political figures of the generation of 1868 had disappeared with far less recognition. Hiram Revels collapsed and died during a church meeting in Aberdeen, Mississippi, in 1901. Joseph Rainey worked as a federal tax agent in Charleston until 1881, failed in business, then fell into poor health and died in 1887. Today his name graces a waterside park in his native Georgetown, South Carolina. The former congressman Alonzo Ransier, who had spoken so eloquently of education's role in sustaining a republican form of government, and who once famously got the better of a white antagonist on the floor of the House of Representatives, worked as a street cleaner in Charleston until his death in 1882. A story was told that Ransier one day found in the gutter an old newspaper that contained an article about him from the long-ago heyday of his political career. "Hardly can it be supposed that he was without emotion as he crumpled the vagrant sheet, and tossing it into the dust cart went on humbly with his street-cleaning task."

Ransier's journey to obscurity was not unique. The diners at the Jefferson Club, an elite Washington restaurant in the late 1890s, would have been surprised to learn that the courtly black waiter who filled their water glasses, Richard H. Gleaves, had once been the lieutenant governor of South Carolina. He worked as a server at the restaurant, within sight of the U.S. Capitol, until his death in 1907.

Others survived by securing patronage jobs from the Republican Party. In the case of Blanche K. Bruce, the expectation of reward was particularly high; his favor to Garfield at the 1880 Republican National Convention had not been forgotten, and his term in the Senate ended just as Garfield became president in early 1881. Bruce was offered a post as minister to Brazil or a high-ranking position in the post office, both of which he rejected, asking instead to be appointed register of the treasury. Garfield hesitated, telling Bruce that he feared white women in the Treasury Department might resent working under him. Irritated by Garfield's prevarication, Bruce, according to one account, told other Republicans he would "give the story to the country" if so shabby an excuse for denying him the job was sustained. On May 23, 1881, Garfield appointed Bruce register of the treasury, which meant that Bruce's signature would appear on some of the nation's currency, an accomplishment that seemed to impress Bruce as much as his having served in the U.S. Senate. "Who would have thought of this spectacle a score of years ago!" he exclaimed. "This is an incident of interest worthy of a place upon the bright pages of the history of a public man's life."

Although Bruce was satisfied with the appointment, the editor T. Thomas Fortune criticized Garfield for not elevating Bruce to the cabinet. Bruce's great prestige, Fortune complained, "was hid away . . . with his hands tied to his sides and his voice effectually stifled. The dignity of the Senatorial office and the faithful adherence, through thick and thin, of a million black voters, were stowed away in the oblivion of one of the bureaus of the Treasury Department."

Fortune's confidence in Bruce was not off the mark. The senator from Mississippi may well have been the most fully formed black politician of Reconstruction, a steady but quiet reformer who pushed hard on occasion, but who learned early how to maneuver and survive among influential whites. Known sometimes as "the Silent Senator," he usually waited until near the end of a debate so as to have a better "lay of the land" before he went on the record. Perhaps because he spoke up so rarely, his words were that much more effective. No great intellectual like Frederick Douglass nor a firebrand like Ida B. Wells, he nonetheless made a popular tour of the lecture circuit after his Senate term ended (his seat was taken by James Z. George), speaking about the problems and promise of the black race in America and also about the need for equitable treatment for two of America's other minorities, the Indians and the Chinese. It was said that in 1886 he gave one hundred speeches for one hundred dollars apiece.

Bruce spent the rest of his public life in the government's employ and, due to his easy comportment and level-headedness, became a key distributor of jobs and favors; powerful whites often consulted him about the advancement of other blacks to various positions, a deference also given to Booker T. Washington. Bruce took patronage very seriously, convinced that he helped his race each time he boosted a talented black man into a government job. "It is of supreme importance to us as a class that our best and not our worst men be put forward for official recognition, for by them will the public judge as to our worthiness and capacity," he once said. While still a senator, Bruce had managed to work out an arrangement with the Mississippi congressman L.Q.C. Lamar whereby Bruce agreed to no longer defend white Republicans who held patronage jobs in the state in exchange for being allowed to appoint respectable blacks. But he remained loyal to Mississippians of both races, once procuring a government clerkship for a white woman from his state who had washed up in the nation's capital, bereft of funds or friends, after her husband was sent to prison on a murder conviction. She initially demurred at the idea of asking any favor of Bruce, a man who might well once have been her slave, but thankfully took the position he offered. Characteristically, Bruce spent the last morning of his working life, in spring 1898, shoring up another black man's promotion in a government agency. After lunch he took ill and died a few weeks later of complications from Bright's disease and diabetes.

In the claustrophobic racial atmosphere of the late 1890s Bruce's restrained character, his courtly and undemanding ways, rendered him an appealing figure, a man from an earlier and better time, and his loss was sharply felt. "He was one of the apostles of kindness," noted the *Washington Post,* "one of the prophets of love and mutual forgiveness who stemmed the tide of rancor and misunderstanding . . . [and] taught by the example of his own daily life the gospel of a rational evolution."

Robert Brown Elliott's views of the potential of Southern race relations were somewhat less sanguine than those of some of his colleagues, but even he did not anticipate how completely the advances they had won would stall in the years following Reconstruction. It was especially disconcerting to him that the Democrats of South Carolina wanted more than to simply consolidate their gains after the election of 1876, but, with the "Report on Public Frauds," were intent on rewriting and distorting the story of one of the state's most productive eras. On a personal level, the atmosphere in redeemed South Carolina became so unwelcoming that Elliott could no longer earn a living as an attorney, partly because even blacks had come to understand that having black representation could diminish one's chances before a judge or jury.

Facing financial hardship, he was rescued by John Sherman, secretary of the treasury in the Hayes administration, who found the former congressman a patronage job as a customs inspector in the port of Charleston. It was a significant step down for a man whose ringing words on the House floor had once commanded the nation's headlines and inspired a popular lithograph, but Elliott took his new duties seriously and even appeared to enjoy the work. He returned the favor by campaigning ardently to secure Sherman's nomination for president at the 1880 Republican convention in Chicago. Elliott was allowed to address the convention, probably his last time on the national political stage, and although Sherman didn't get near the nomination, Elliott was gratified to see James Garfield, an admired colleague from the House, become the party's choice.

In May 1881 Elliott was forced to leave South Carolina when the customs service ordered him to New Orleans. Although disguised as a promotion, the transfer was not something Elliott wanted; he owed money, however; his wife Grace was in poor health, and he had little choice but to go where he was sent. His own strength had also become precarious. The previous summer, just after his appearance at the Chicago convention, Elliott had contracted malaria while on a customs inspection tour of the coastal areas of the Florida Panhandle, and the illness lingered. With the debilitation, his mood seemed to darken as well, and his enthusiasm for the job rapidly ebbed. After complaining to Washington about the conditions and personnel in the New Orleans Customs Office, he was released from the service and returned to work as a lawyer in private practice. For two years he and Grace struggled to stay afloat, living in apartments and boarding houses in New Orleans as he fought both his creditors and recurring bouts of tropical disease. He died at age forty-two, on August 9, 1884, virtually unknown in the city, a black gentleman-pauper. Word of his passing reached Charleston, where the *News & Courier* headlined its obituary "Another of the South Carolina Thieves Gone to his Account."

P.B.S. Pinchback was known to keep a photograph of Elliott, among other black congressmen, on display in his home, although the two men apparently had a falling out once Elliott came to New Orleans, probably over patronage issues. Pinchback himself, after being dismissed by Congress in spring 1876, had remained the loyal Republican soldier, marching off to Indiana to campaign on behalf of his Senate sponsor, Oliver Morton. Partly this was to repay Morton's kindness, possibly to obligate future acts of patronage, or perhaps to simply avoid local election-year politics in Louisiana during the summer of 1876. Those elections devolved into their by-now-familiar chaos: Stephen Packard and C. C. Antoine were "elected" on the Republican ticket, while Francis T. Nicholls and Louis A. Wiltz "won" for the Democrats; as in South Carolina, dual inaugurations took place, with the state government, and the last local vestiges of Reconstruction, falling to the Democrats in spring 1877.

Pinchback, however, remained a political figure with considerable clout, describing himself in an 1879 letter to Blanche Bruce as "the liveliest corpse in the dead South." That year he attended the new Louisiana Constitutional Convention, which, dominated by the Democrats and the spirit of redemption, set out to undo much of the progress of the late 1860s. Although the convention was inimical to blacks, Pinchback retained enough influence to win a provision authorizing the legislature to create a state college for black Louisianians. Ex-president Grant visited New Orleans in 1880 to curry support for his quest for the Republican presidential nomination and a third term, and he made a point of seeking out Pinchback for an extended chat.

Like many others of his generation, Pinchback understood that the end of Reconstruction represented an end, also, to the old biracial abolitionist coalition that had guided racial progress in America since the 1830s, and he became active in efforts to create national civil rights organizations that would shift the responsibility for leadership onto blacks themselves. The Exoduster movement of 1878–80 had not pleased everyone in the national community of black leadership, but it had surely proved that black Americans were capable of shaping their own destiny. Led by T. Thomas Fortune and others, blacks organized themselves to tackle vital issues by founding the American Citizens Equal Rights Association in February 1890; the organization was dedicated to securing civil rights for all citizens and improving their moral, intellectual, and material interests. Pinchback was a high-ranking spokesman and took charge of organizing Louisiana. The association ultimately foundered, chiefly because the sensibility it embraced — defending and building on the rights gained in Reconstruction — had widely given way to the more gradualist doctrines of Booker T. Washington. At about the same time, black suffrage in the South virtually became a dead letter, as the number of black voters registered in Louisiana fell within the decade of the 1890s from 130,000 to 5,000. For Pinchback, one last tenet of a cherished era collapsed in 1902, when the New Orleans streetcars he had helped make available for all citizens were forcibly resegregated.

Increasingly finding himself an artifact of a time few knew or understood, his influence and health waning and his brand of political activism eclipsed, Pinchback left New Orleans and settled in Washington, where he and Nina lived out the rest of their days. Their son Bismarck, who had attended Yale to study medicine, and their daughter Nina died, and the two remaining children, Walter and Pinckney, were by now long gone from the house, Pinckney a pharmacist in Philadelphia, Walter an attorney. Nina's son, the Harlem Renaissance writer Jean Toomer, reflected later that Pinchback, conscious of his own unpolished background, may have too forcefully demanded that his children attain conventional academic distinction; all four Pinchback children spent time at Northern universities or finishing schools. "In doing all this, my grandfather had the very best intentions, without doubt. But . . . though part of his nature was affectionate and sincerely good-wishing, another part was egotistical, domineering, and headstrong. With too little wisdom he cut his children's patterns, particularly the boys', and then tried to force them to fit in." Toomer recalled that Pinchback never relinquished his love of entertaining and fine things, of attending banquets and stag parties, and that even in Washington, many years and miles removed from the heady days of Reconstruction New Orleans, friends and family unfailingly addressed him as "Governor."

There was the occasional monument unveiling or testimonial dinner to attend, and he still corresponded and advised where he could, but for the most part he was the historically interesting black gentleman in coat and top hat who, it was said, had once been the governor of Louisiana. With his dignified bearing and handsomely trimmed Vandyke beard, he bore a strong resemblance in old age to the philanthropist Andrew Carnegie, for whom, much to his amusement, he was occasionally mistaken in his perambulations around the capital. After Pinchback's death in 1921, when Toomer brought his grandfather's body back by train from Washington, barely a quorum of his gray-haired former associates gathered at the New Orleans depot. The local press took scant notice; the *Daily Picayune* headlined its short obituary "Negro Who Held State Office Dies" and inexcusably referred to Henry Clay Warmoth as "Womack."

While surviving black Reconstruction figures grew accustomed to such slights, John Roy Lynch of Mississippi chose to make a corrective response. Never relinquishing his egalitarian vision of American race relations, he became an active memoirist of the Reconstruction period because he was concerned that most historians and other commentators were distorting it. He would produce two informative books, *The Facts of Reconstruction* (1913) and an autobiography, *Reminiscences of an Active Life* (not published until 1970), but his most daring literary exploit was to challenge two of America's most prominent early historians of Reconstruction, James Ford Rhodes and Claude G. Bowers. Rhodes's multivolume history dealing with the war and Reconstruction, *History of the United States from the Compromise of 1850 to the Final Restoration of Home Rule at the South in 1877*, appeared in 1906, although a decade passed before Lynch saw it. He then informed his friend George A. Myers, a black Ohioan who managed the barbershop in the lobby of Cleveland's Hollenden Hotel and who knew Rhodes, of his displeasure with the work's inaccuracy. Rhodes replied through Myers that Lynch's objections did not surprise him since he (Lynch) "was a severely partisan actor at the time while I, an earnest seeker after truth, am trying to hold a judicial balance and to tell the story without fear, favor, or prejudice." Myers offered to introduce the two men, but Rhodes declined, instead saying, "Why does not Mr. Lynch write a magazine article and show up my mistakes and inaccuracies and injustice?"

Taking Rhodes's suggestion, Lynch produced a lengthy two-part article titled "Some Historical Errors of James Ford Rhodes," which appeared in the *Journal of Negro History* in October 1917 and April 1918 (both sections were published together in book form in 1922). Lynch began with a shot directly across the bow, writing of Rhodes's work, "I regret to say that, so far as the Reconstruction period is concerned, it is not only inaccurate and unreliable but it is the most biased, partisan, and prejudiced historical work I have ever read." He took issue with the very title of Rhodes's book, pointing out that in terms of the region's demographics, the South had actually enjoyed home rule, if that phrase meant democratic rule by the broadest number of residents, only under the Reconstruction governments of the late 1860s and early 1870s. Lynch parodied Rhodes's contentions that it had been wrong to enfranchise blacks after the war, that those who entered politics were incompetent, or that they ever dominated Southern politics. He argued that blacks in elected offices were no more incompetent or corrupt than whites and that the Reconstruction governments achieved many significant breakthroughs; indeed, Lynch ventured that "the Southern reconstructed governments were the best governments those states ever had before or have ever had since." Myers sent Lynch's lawyerly article on to Rhodes with his own scribbled admonishment: "I think one of your mistakes was made in not seeing and talking with the prominent Negro participants that I could have put you in touch with."

Years later Lynch also laid siege to one of the most popular books ever written about Reconstruction, Claude G. Bowers's *The Tragic Era: The Revolution After Lincoln,* published in 1929. Bowers's entertaining work drew ruthless caricatures of Republicans, blacks, and carpetbaggers and offered a vivid purplish-prose account of the era's drama, while suggesting that the nation had erred in not accepting President Andrew Johnson's version of Reconstruction. To Bowers, a veteran author of popular nonfiction in the 1920s, the complete marginalization of blacks in American society was so much the entrenched status quo that congressional Reconstruction could perhaps only appear as a sad, painful burlesque; but Lynch was merciless in taking the white author to task for numerous inaccuracies.

His high-society marriage to Ella Somerville having ended in a bitter divorce, Lynch ultimately married a woman much younger than him and lived out the rest of his ninety-two years in Chicago, dying there in 1939.

While Lynch had the satisfaction of knowing he had tried to set the historical record straight, Richard Cain of South Carolina lived to see the partial realization of his own long-held dream, that of enabling people of color to own their own land. Having watched his plans for congressional underwriting of land distribution and the state's own land commission flame out ingloriously, Cain in 1871 founded his own land development company. It was a project launched perhaps less on sound business principles than on Cain's charisma and the support of his religious followers, but it would see tangible results.

The scheme began, legend has it, with an epiphany beside a railroad track. Daddy Cain was leaving Charleston one day in the company of six other A.M.E. church trustees when their train stopped for wood and water about twenty miles west of the city at a depot known as Pump Pond. Glancing out the window, he became intrigued by a land-for-sale sign, and to his colleagues' surprise, insisted they immediately get off the train.

Cain ultimately purchased about two thousand acres of land around Pump Pond. Renaming the location Lincolnville, he subdivided it into lots of two to ten acres and offered them for sale at reasonable prices to settlers who agreed to clear their own property and erect homes. Over the next decade Cain sold about sixty of these lots, including one for the construction of an A.M.E. church. Unfortunately, he had begun selling off land parcels in Lincolnville before he could make the first payments on the land, which were due six months after the purchase agreement. Therefore a grand jury indicted him for taking money under false pretenses, that is, selling land that he did not himself own. He was arrested, but his legal counsel and friend, Robert Brown Elliott, arranged for Cain's case to be dropped under the condition the money be refunded.

When the *New York Times*, reporting on Cain's troubles on June 15, 1874, noted that, "It can very safely be said that South Carolina has more criminals in office than any other state in the Union," Cain fired back a lengthy letter, which the newspaper published. "I have settled more colored people in comfortable houses than any other man in the state," he asserted, "and not one family have lost a dollar by any sale which I ever made to them. Anyone may go to South Carolina today and find the people who know me, and they will testify to the facts. The village of Lincoln[ville], twenty miles from Charleston, is a settlement of colored people. If your correspondent will take the trouble to go there he will find 40 odd families comfortably situated — a church, a school, and a most happy and prosperous community, and not one of them will charge me with defrauding them."

Despite the long-ago retraction of General Sherman's Field Order Number 15, the mismanagement that plagued the state land commission, and the quixotic nature of real estate ventures like Lincolnville, South Carolina fared surprisingly better than most other states in promoting black ownership of land during Reconstruction. The land commission had bought 168 plantations, for a total of almost ninety-three thousand acres, and about two thousand black families were able to take advantage of the land offered for sale on reasonable terms. Between these efforts and the land forfeitures of the immediate postbellum period, it is estimated that four thousand black South Carolina families obtained land in the decade or so following the war, as compared with the thirty thousand who had done so across the South by 1870. By the 1890 census, the number of landholding black South Carolinians had more than tripled, as families subdivided lands under their control and whites continued to sell off small parcels of once-vast plantations.

Lincolnville, notwithstanding its rocky start, was by the mid-1880s a nearly all-black town of one hundred homes, and the community Cain had brought into being maintained its growth even after he died in Washington in 1887. Today, it remains a biracial working-class enclave of suburban Charleston, where residents chiefly own their own property; many continue to honor the locale's history, which is ennobled by an "official town poem":

Seven men of color had a dream, where men could live and toil
Among the stately pines that stand, enriched in fertile soil,
Soil that had been nurtured by those who fought and died,
Oh Lincolnville, Oh Lincolnville, what heritage and pride.

Cain's insistence on land for South Carolina's freedmen and even the validity of the land commission he'd done so much to instigate were to

THE PROSPECT OF "OWNING A PIECE OF THE LAND THAT HAD OWNED THEM" TANTALIZED THE FREE PEOPLE.

an extent later vindicated by Carol Bleser, a researcher who in the 1960s met with descendants of some of the original land commission settlers. They resided in an upcountry hamlet known as Promised Land, created in 1870 and consisting of seven hundred acres sold by the commission; by 1872 fifty black families had settled there, paying ten dollars down for farms of fifty to one hundred acres. Unlike the Sea Islands, with their overwhelming black majority, Promised Land was situated in an area where blacks were in the minority and tended to reside in isolated settlements. "Those we talked to were devoid of the embarrassment often felt by Negroes who have had the color line constantly emphasized in meeting white people," Bleser reported. "The possession of land gave them a sense of self-assurance and a certain feeling of equality, both attitudes usually lacking in black tenants and urban workers in the South."

According to Bleser, Promised Land settlers thrived in part by having little to do economically with the surrounding whites. Instead of raising a potentially profitable cash crop like cotton, they diversified their agriculture and concentrated on subsistence farming, growing vegetables and corn and keeping livestock. Crop diversity protected them from the vagaries of the cotton market and allowed them to steer clear of the ruinous debt that haunted many black sharecroppers; they also were able to avoid buying seed, fertilizer, and other goods at overpriced plantation stores. "The genius of this kind of farming," another researcher would conclude, "was that it kept them from getting trapped in the 'crop lien' system that destroyed so many other families, both black and white. They did not get rich, but they endured."

Like P.B.S. Pinchback and John Roy Lynch, many black figures prominent in Reconstruction ultimately drifted away from the South, relocating to Washington, New York, or Chicago. A notable exception was Robert Smalls. His political career at an end following the Tillman-dominated constitutional convention of 1895 in South Carolina, he returned to live out the remainder of his life in Beaufort, in the same house on Prince Street where he and his mother had once served as slaves and which Smalls had purchased at government auction in 1864. Smalls's wife, Hannah, died in 1883, and in 1890 he married Annie Wigg, a teacher from Savannah, whom the *News & Courier* considered "an exceedingly handsome woman of respectable connections"; they had a son, William. Of the three children from his first marriage, Robert Jr. had died as a child, Sara became a music teacher, and Elizabeth, who had served as her father's secretary in Washington, married the editor of the *Beaufort Free South;* when her husband died she became the Beaufort postmistress.

President William McKinley, for whom Smalls had campaigned, appointed him collector of customs for the port of Beaufort, a position of authority and extensive patronage that suited Smalls well. Whatever local observers thought of his politics, there was no question that Smalls was devoted to his Sea Islands community and its people; from long habit, it seems, he never stopped thinking of them as his constituents. When a hurricane swept over the islands in late August 1893, drowning four hundred men, women, and children and causing an estimated $2 million in damage, Smalls assumed a leading role in the rescue and recovery. "These sea islands are the homes chiefly of negroes who by thrift and industry have made themselves homes, with no one to molest or make them afraid," Smalls wrote of his friends and neighbors. "In one night all has been swept away."

With the turn of the century Smalls remained a familiar figure in the scenic coastal town, a genial old war hero whose most visible public role arrived each May 30, Decoration Day, when he led a procession to the national cemetery just beyond the city limits. The cemetery was the largest enduring testament to the substantial federal presence in Beaufort during the Civil War, as it contained the remains of Union dead from Pennsylvania, Indiana, New York, and numerous other Northern states, as well as African Americans who had served with the federal forces. For the occasion, blacks from the vicinity would pour into Beaufort, and Smalls, now a portly, stooped, but still exceedingly proud man, strapped on his sword and other ceremonial effects and marched at the head of the Beaufort Light Infantry, up Carteret Street to the graveyard. Later there would be a reception at his house, perhaps with distinguished out-of-town visitors. One year he arranged for Booker T. Washington to attend. Surely Washington had Smalls in mind when he observed that "one of the surprising results of the Reconstruction Period was that there should spring from among the members of a race that had been held so long in slavery, so large a number of shrewd, resolute, resourceful, and even brilliant men, who became, during this brief period of storms and stress, the political leaders of the newly enfranchised race."

Lionized as he was in Beaufort, however, Smalls was made to ride Jim Crow when he traveled to Columbia or Charleston by train, seated in a dirty coach with cigar stubs on the floor and broken windows; in 1904 he was told to move to the back of a Charleston streetcar. As he had in Philadelphia forty years earlier, he chose to get off rather than be humiliated, but this time no citywide protest gathered to defend his rights.

Smalls's long connection with federal patronage finally ran out in 1913, when, with the advent of the Democratic administration of Woodrow Wilson, he lost his post as a customs official; at the same time his health began to deteriorate. It was said that as long as he could muster the strength, prior to his death in February 1915, he liked to visit the local schoolhouse set aside for use by black students, where he urged the youngsters to take seriously the opportunity for education he had never had. Invariably, the children reported to their parents that "the General" had come by again, telling the story of the great war and the night he had run the Confederate ship *Planter* out of Charleston Harbor.

Beaufort still talks of how, in the days immediately after the end of that conflict, Jane McKee, the wife of Smalls's former master, showed up at the house on Prince Street late one evening, disoriented and without means. Smalls took her in. Mrs. McKee, apparently unable to countenance a world so utterly changed, continued to believe that she was living in earlier times, and Smalls allowed her to stay with him in her old house until her death, never confronting her with the fact that a terrible war had been fought, that slavery had ended, and that her former slave had gone off to the nation's capital to serve in Congress, make laws, and confer with presidents.

The story may well be apocryphal, but Smalls did assist Jane McKee and other members of the McKee family during Reconstruction, and there would have been a kind of elegant symmetry to the fact that Smalls, who in a sense kept Reconstruction alive in Beaufort longer than anywhere else in the South, was at the same time maintaining a private fantasy of antebellum life for his former owner's widow. It was a deception only the "Boat Thief" could have managed, or would have been gracious enough to perform.

ACKNOWLEDGMENTS

NOTES

BIBLIOGRAPHY

INDEX

ACKNOWLEDGMENTS

THE LIBRARIANS AND ARCHIVISTS at dozens of Southern research centers have been enormously generous in responding to my requests for help and information. In particular I wish to thank Ms. Grace Cordial of the Beaufort, South Carolina, Township Library and the archivists at the South Carolina Room of the Charleston Public Library. I was also welcomed at the Charleston Historical Society; the South Caroliniana Library at the University of South Carolina in Columbia; the Clemson University Library; the Mississippi Department of Archives and History in Jackson; the Southern Historical Collection at the University of North Carolina, Chapel Hill; and the Louisiana Room at the New Orleans Public Library.

In Washington, I made extensive use of the Manuscripts and Periodical Reading Rooms at the Library of Congress; the Moorland-Spingarn Collection at Howard University; the National Archives (Freedmen's Bureau Records Group 105); and the National Archives branch in Beltsville, Maryland (Department of Justice Records Group 60). I also was able to perform valuable research at the Houghton Library, Harvard University; the Schomburg Center for Research in Black Culture, New York Public Library; and the New York Public Library's Main Research Branch as well as its Prints and Pictures Collection.

Several books were instrumental in guiding my approach to the subject of Reconstruction, including *Exodusters: Black Migration to Kansas After Reconstruction* by Nell Irvin Painter; Ted Tunnell's *Crucible of Reconstruction: War, Radicalism, and Race in Louisiana*, and *Rehearsal for Reconstruction: The Port Royal Experiment* by Willie Lee Rose, a deservedly respected source on the wartime missionary effort in the Sea Islands. Thomas Holt's *Black over White: Negro Political Leadership in*

South Carolina During Reconstruction, and *After Slavery: The Negro in South Carolina During Reconstruction*, by Joel Williamson, were excellent on the era in South Carolina. Similarly, Vernon Lane Wharton's classic *The Negro in Mississippi*, and *Redemption: The Last Battle of the Civil War*, by Nicholas Lemman, were indispensable regarding Adelbert Ames and the Mississippi of 1875. I also relied on *Retreat from Reconstruction* by William Gillette; Steven Hahn's *A Nation Under Our Feet: Black Political Struggles in the Rural South from Slavery to the Great Migration;*, and James M. PcPherson's *The Abolitionist Legacy: From Reconstruction to the NAACP.* The administration of Ulysses S. Grant is vividly resurrected in *Grant: A Biography* by William McFeely.

Eric Foner, a professor of American history at Columbia University, has written eloquently on virtually every aspect of Reconstruction. His *Freedom's Lawmakers: A Directory of Black Officeholders During Reconstruction; A Short History of Reconstruction; Forever Free: The Story of Emancipation and Reconstruction;* and *America's Reconstruction: People and Politics After the Civil War*, written with Olivia Mahoney, were all essential sources.

When it came to writing about the black congressmen of Reconstruction, I was fortunate to have a number of talented predecessors, most notably Peggy Lamson and her book *The Glorious Failure: Black Congressman Robert Brown Elliott and the Reconstruction in South Carolina;* Sadie D. St. Clair, author of *The National Career of Blanche Kelso Bruce;* Okon Edet Uya's *From Slavery to Public Service: Robert Smalls 1839–1915*, and James Haskins's colorful *Pinckney Benton Stewart Pinchback.* A valuable overview of the subject is found in William J. Simmons's *Men of Mark: Eminent, Progressive, and Rising*, published in 1887. Some of my initial thoughts for embarking on this project were stimulated by Dorothy Sterling's excellent *The Trouble They Seen: The Story of Reconstruction in the Words of African Americans.*

The manuscript was improved by technical comments from Professor Ted Tunnell of Virginia Commonwealth University.

For their encouragement, support, and advice I wish to thank Alison Dray-Novey, Gary Gerstle, Annette Gordon-Reed, Jan Gross, David Levering Lewis, Jerry Mitchell, Stacy Schiff, Robert Sietsema, Lianne Smith, Stephanie Steiker, and Matt Weiland. I benefited from the sound professional guidance of Geri Thoma of the Elaine Markson Literary Agency and Scott Moyers of the Wylie Agency.

At Houghton Mifflin, I am grateful for the efforts of associate editor

Will Vincent, senior manuscript editor Susanna Brougham, and book designer Melissa Lotfy. Senior editor Amanda Cook's enthusiasm for the project never flagged over several drafts; she proved a gifted collaborator and was a pleasure to work with; her numerous contributions were welcome and invaluable.

NOTES

PAGE *Preface*

ix *Of all the images . . .* My discussion of this iconic portrait, titled "The First Colored Senators and Representatives," is indebted to Dorothy Sterling's description in *The Trouble They Seen: The Story of Reconstruction in the Words of African Americans*, pp. 174–75. Sixteen black men would serve in Congress during Reconstruction (1865–77); a total of twenty-two would occupy seats before the end of the nineteenth century. Nationwide there were about two thousand black elected and appointed officeholders, including a governor, several lieutenant governors, state legislators and treasurers, attorneys general, members of state supreme courts, federal customs officials, and foreign ambassadors. The most comprehensive account is in Eric Foner's *Freedom's Lawmakers: A Directory of Black Officeholders During Reconstruction.*

"The North thinks the Southern people are especially angry": Tourgee, p. 383.

As the Virginian George Mason railed: Norfolk Journal, quoted in *Fredericksburg News*, June 22, 1868; see Russ, "The Negro and White Disenfranchisement During Radical Reconstruction," *Journal of Negro History.*

1. Boat Thief

2 *"An aura of doom and menace": Ebony Magazine*, Nov. 2001.

"I was born the year George Washington got president": Information from family correspondence in possession of Dolly Nash, great-granddaughter of Robert Smalls, transcribed by Jeff Berg, Robert Smalls Vertical file, Beaufort Public Library. Some accounts render Lydia's remark as "I was born the year after George Washington got president," which would be more accurate. She was born in 1790, a year after Washington took office.

4 *In the Stono disturbance:* Brown, *Strain of Violence*, pp. 191–92. This act, known as the Barbardian Code for its origins in Barbados, centered on controlling and subduing the slave population through a number of harsh measures, with only scant attention paid to safeguarding slaves from unjust abuse.

5 *In 1856, at age seventeen:* Smalls and his wife and daughter escaped to freedom before this amount ($800) was paid.

7 *"Boy, you look jes like de captain": Charleston Evening Post* and *Charleston News & Courier,* June 15–16, 1962.
Once the whites had departed: New National Era, May 30, 1872.

8 *"We're all free niggers now!":* Lamson, Roswell H., p. 62.
"Ahoy there," a voice from the Union ship Onward *called out:* Sterling, *Captain of the Planter,* p. 70.
"I thought the Planter *might be of some use to Uncle Abe":* E. G. Parrott to Flag Officer S. F. DuPont, May 13, 1862, in Simmons, *Men of Mark,* p. 171.
"Our community was intensely agitated": Charleston Courier, May 14, 1862.

9 *"One of the most daring and heroic adventures":* Quoted in Uya, p. 15.

10 *"What a painful instance we have here": Providence Journal,* quoted in the *National Anti-Slavery Standard,* May 31, 1862; see Uya, pp. 17–18.
"My paramount object in this struggle": Carroll and Noble, p. 217.
Curiously, the militarization of blacks: For discussion of Confederate recruitment of blacks, see McPherson, *Battle Cry of Freedom,* pp. 831–38.

11 *"War has not been waged against slavery":* Quoted in Woodward, *The Burden of Southern History,* p. 60.
"The significance for black people still in bondage was clear": Blacks entering Union lines often brought timely intelligence on Confederate gun emplacements and troop movements. Several ex-slaves, including Harriet Tubman, who went behind Confederate lines in South Carolina dressed as a field hand, were later honored for their service delivering these "Black Dispatches," as the reports became known.
The pressure on Washington increased: Similar steps were taken by General John W. Phelps in Louisiana and, in Kansas, by Senator James H. Lane, although Hunter's efforts are better known.

12 *"Please let me have my own way on the subject of slavery":* Korngold, *Two Friends of Man,* p. 294.
"Nothing would please me more, and bring the race into favor": Quoted in *Frederick Douglass: Selected Speeches and Writings,* ed. Philip Foner, p. 447.
General Hunter acted in stages: Westwood, "Generals David Hunter and Rufus Saxton and Black Soldiers," *South Carolina Historical Magazine.*

13 *"No commanding general shall do such a thing":* Quoted in Goodwin, p. 435.
"No regiment of 'fugitive slaves' has been or is organized": David Hunter to Edwin M. Stanton, June 23, 1862, quoted in Fleetwood, pp. 7–8.

14 *"On the face of this wide earth, Mr. President": New York Tribune,* Aug. 19, 1862.
"As they waged war on us about the nigger": Diary of James T. Ayers, quoted in Franklin, pp. 234–35.
The president worried that "the organization, equipment, and arming of negroes": Thomas and Hyman, pp. 238–39.
In late August, when Smalls and French returned to the South: Edwin Stanton to Rufus Saxton, Aug. 22, 1862, War Department Records, National Archives; cited in Uya, p. 19.

15 *"I had been an abolitionist too long":* Higginson, p. 3.
"Action! Action!" he enthused. "There is no time for delay": Douglass, "Men of Color, to Arms!" in *Frederick Douglass: Selected Speeches and Writings,* ed. Philip S. Foner, p. 525.

16 *"The planters had boasted":* Brown, *The Negro in the American Rebellion,* pp. 137–41.

17 *"From the shame of degradation to the glory of military exaltation":* Williams, *History of the Negro Troops,* pp. xiii–xiv, 67.
For Robert Smalls, whose theft of the Planter: The historian Carter Woodson reports the following conversation between two residents of Beaufort (paraphrased here): "I tell you, Smalls is the greatest man in the world," one man stated. "Yes, he is great," his friend admitted, "but not the greatest." "Pshaw man, who's greater than Smalls?" "Why, Jesus Christ," was the reply. "Oh," said the first speaker with confidence, "Smalls is young yet." See Woodson, "Robert Smalls and His Descendants," *Negro History Bulletin.*

18 *The South thrilled to the victory: New York Times,* July 9, 1883. Ironclads, despite their impregnable look, were greatly weakened when subjected to a direct hit and could take on little water before sinking. An additional problem in the Union assault in which Smalls took part was that the warm Southern saltwater had fouled the ironclads' bottoms with barnacles, rendering the ships incapable of speeds greater than four knots. Heavy and cumbersome even under ideal conditions, they made easy targets for the rebel shore gunners.
"Not by a damned sight will I beach this boat for you!": Report to the Committee on Naval Affairs, accompanying H.R. Bill 7059, House of Representatives, Jan. 23, 1883, quotedin Simmons, pp. 166–69. This report was made to secure Smalls a modest payment of $1,500 for his taking of the *Planter.*
Smalls took control, somehow managing to steer: Rosbow, "The Abduction of the *Planter,*" *Crisis,* Apr. 1949; see also Uya, p. 22.
One day in December, Smalls and a black acquaintance: Philadelphia Press, Dec. 12, 1864, and Jan. 13, 1865; see also Uya, pp. 26–27.

19 *The Carolina spring day was by all accounts:* Ibid., p. 28.

20 *"It is not on account of your complexion or race":* Korngold, *Two Friends of Man,* p. 334.

21 *Tears of gladness filled every eye:* Uya, p. 29.

22 *"Of all the states overwhelmed by the rebellion": New York Times,* Sept. 13, 1865.

2. A New Kind of Nation

24 *"I have known Andy Johnson for many years":* Quoted in Bowers, p. 37.
"Mere satellites of an inferior character": Ibid., p. 30.

25 *"Little more than warmed-over slavery":* Painter, *Exodusters,* p. x.
"Temporary triumph of fanaticism over divine truth": Tourgee, pp. 86–87.
"I met four white men about six miles south of Keachie": Sterling, *The Trouble They Seen,* p. 7.

26 *"Grasp of war":* Donald, *Liberty and Union,* pp. 194–95.

27 *The so-called Memphis Race Riot:* Ryan, "The Memphis Riots of 1866," *Journal of Negro History.*

28 *Formally, Lincoln refused:* Tunnell, *Crucible,* pp. 40–41, 60–65.

29 *Mayor Monroe informed the local federal commander:* James Monroe to Absalom Baird, July 25, 1866, and Baird to Monroe, July 26, 1866; both cited in full in *New York Times,* Aug. 7, 1866; also see "New Orleans Riots 1866," *House Executive Documents,* 39th Cong., 2nd sess., no. 68, serial 1292.
President Johnson, who notified Louisiana's attorney general: Andrew Johnson to Francis J. Herron, July 30, 1866, quoted in Hollandsworth, p. 143.

29 *Baird was "unwilling to assume the attitude":* "New Orleans Riots 1866."
The opening day of the convention: For a description of events, see "Report of the Select Committee on the New Orleans Riots," Washington GPO, 1867.

30 *"The crowd in and out of the Mechanics Hall": New Orleans Daily Picayune,* July 31, 1866.
"We have fought for four years these god-damned Yankees": Quoted in Hollandsworth, p. 115.
"They . . . tried to escape through an alley": New York Times, Aug. 1, 1866.

31 *More than two hours passed:* "Report of the Select Committee on the New Orleans Riots."
Although one official inquiry praised his troops' belated presence: "New Orleans Riots 1866."
"Men were shot while waving handkerchiefs": "Report of the Select Committee on the New Orleans Riots."
"It was no riot; it was an absolute massacre": Philip Sheridan to Ulysses S. Grant, Aug. 2, 1866; see Hollandsworth, frontispiece.
"There has been no occasion during our national history": "New Orleans Riots," *House Report No. 16,* 39th Cong., 2nd sess., serial 1304.

32 *"If this matter is permitted to pass over":* Philip Sheridan to Andrew Johnson, Aug. 6, 1866; quoted in Hollandsworth, p. 145.
A government investigation determined: "New Orleans Riots 1866."

33 *"Although [he] died five years ago": North American Review,* Oct. 1866.
The absurdity of Johnson's homage: New York Times, Sept. 2, 1866.
After he asked the crowd to tell him: New York Times, Sept. 5, 1866.

34 *"President Johnson, in his speech at Cleveland": New York Times,* Sept. 7, 1866.
"I have been slandered": New York Tribune, Sept. 10, 1866.
"We had thought the President had exhausted his power": New York Tribune, Sept. 10, 1866.

35 *"Never in history had a President":* Bowers, p. 138.
"It was a great blunder": North American Review, Oct. 1866; also see coverage of Johnson's tour in *New York Tribune* and *New York World,* Aug. 28–Sept. 4, 1866; Bowers, pp. 135–39; Foner, *A Short History of Reconstruction,* pp. 118–19.
"The unrepentant and still rebellious South": Vandal, "The Origins of the New Orleans Riot of 1866, Revisited," in *Black Freedom/White Violence, 1865–1900,* Donald G. Nieman, ed.

36 *Begun in New York and Philadelphia during the war:* Holt, pp. 29–31.

37 *"Can you change a carrot into a melon?":* W. G. Bronlow to "Payne," Oct. 26, 1860, reprinted in *Charleston Daily Courier,* Oct. 1, 1868.

38 *"On account of the usurped and polluted source": Anderson Intelligencer,* Apr. 22, 1868, quoted in Bleser, p. 26; see also *New York Times,* Jan. 23, 1868.

39 *"Representing a constituency that previously had been ignored":* Underwood and Baker, p. 26.

3. Daddy Cain

40 *It was one of three former Confederate states:* Blacks constituted 60 percent of the population of South Carolina in 1870, and over 50 percent in Mississippi and Louisiana. In Alabama, Florida, Georgia, and Virginia, blacks made up 40–50 percent

of the population; just over 33 percent in North Carolina; and between 25 percent and 33 percent in Arkansas, Tennessee, and Texas. See U.S. Bureau of the Census, Negro Population, 1790–1915, p. 51, cited in Foner, *Freedom's Lawmakers,* p. xiii.
Contemporary accounts suggest: For Cain's background, see Mann, "Richard Harvey Cain," *Negro History Bulletin.*

41 *"A position of betwixity": Charleston Mercury,* Jan. 28, 1868.
The possession of lands and homesteads: Proceedings of the Constitutional Convention of South Carolina, pp. 379, 382.

42 *The poignancy of the location was not lost: Beaufort Gazette,* Sept. 8, 1998.
At a rally in Citadel Square: Charleston Daily News, Apr. 2, 1867.
A local white newspaper urged blacks to remember: Charleston Advocate, Apr. 6, 1867.
Officers of the Freedmen's Bureau intervened: Charleston Daily News, May 6, 1867.
"Might have lived and died without having his name in print": Charleston Mercury, Jan. 28, 1868.

43 *"A genuine negro, kinky-headed": Charleston Mercury,* Feb. 20, 1868.
He "has been gradually subsiding to his proper level": Ibid.
"The features of a very ugly white man": Charleston Mercury, Jan. 28, 1868.
One of the "peripatetic buccaneers from Cape Cod": Proceedings of the Constitutional Convention of South Carolina, Introduction.
So annoyed were some of the delegates: Ibid., pp. 27–31.

44 *Most whites viewed him as gutless and self-glorifying:* Bowers, p. 350.
The emotions stirred by the demeaning press portraits: Charleston Mercury, Jan. 29, 1868.

45 *As the delegates coolly defused the crisis: New York Times,* Jan. 20, 1868.
"I thundered": New York Globe, Aug. 16, 1884; see also Lamson, Peggy, p. 23.
"The colored men in the Convention possess by long odds": New York Times, Jan. 21, 1868.

46 *When a visiting correspondent of* The Nation *magazine: The Nation,* Mar. 30, 1871.

47 *Smalls suggested "a system of common schools": Proceedings of the Constitutional Convention of South Carolina,* p. 100.
"Ignorance is the parent of vice and crime": Ibid., pp. 691–92.
Other delegates suggested that parents: Ibid., pp. 701–2; see also Knight, p. 67.

48 *"We only compel parents to send their children to some school": Proceedings of the Constitutional Convention of South Carolina,* p. 703; see also Knight, p. 66.
Education did ultimately prove: Botsch, p. 73.
"Bury the Democratic party so deep": Robert Smalls to Whitfield McKinlay, Sept. 12, 1912; in Carter Woodson Papers, Library of Congress.
"Can we afford to lose from the councils of state": Quoted in Uya, p. 50.

49 *"Six deserted plantations":* Inventory prepared by Freedmen's Bureau agent H. G. Judd for General Rufus Saxton, Aug. 1, 1865; *Records for the Assistant Commissioner for the State of South Carolina,* Bureau of Refugees, Freedmen, and Abandoned Lands, 1865–1870, National Archives Microfilm Publication M869 Roll 34.
In Beaufort, federal commissioners sold: Beaufort Gazette, undated clipping in Reconstruction vertical file, Beaufort Township Library.

50 *"The way we can best take care of ourselves": New York Daily Tribune,* Feb. 13, 1865, quoted in Cox, "The Promise of Land for the Freedmen," *Mississippi Valley Historical Review.*

51 *"Piloted our ships through these shallow waters":* Rufus Saxton to O. O. Howard, Aug. 22, 1865, Freedom Bureau Records for South Carolina, vol. 9, quoted in Abbott, p. 55.
As General Howard would later note: Howard, p. 229.
"Provide a small homestead or something equivalent": Ibid., pp. 236, 238.
52 *"Their eyes flashed unpleasantly":* Ibid., pp. 238–39.
Of the almost forty thousand freedmen: See Abbott, p. 63. In the 1870s Smalls won a legal case to retain the McKee house at 511 Prince Street, one of several properties that he had purchased at government auction immediately after the war. His was a test case for other blacks who owned confiscated property in the Sea Islands (*De Treville v. Smalls;* see *Beaufort Tribune,* Jan. 6 and Nov. 3, 1875; also *Beaufort Republican,* June 27, 1872).
53 *"Of what avail would be an act of Congress": Congressional Globe,* 38th Cong., 1st sess., p. 2251.
"A strange and unearthly apparition": New York Herald, Mar. 14, 1868.
54 *"Native to the soil and loyal to the government":* Korngold, *Two Friends of Man,* p. 320.
"This nation owes the Negro not merely freedom": Ibid., pp. 321–22.
"Believed that a free laborer, once accorded equality": Foner, "Thaddeus Stevens, Confiscation, and Reconstruction," *Hofstadter Aegis.*
55 *"When the serfs of Russia were emancipated":* Korngold, *Two Friends of Man,* p. 335. See also Williamson, p. 144.
"That this Convention do hereby declare": Proceedings of the Constitutional Convention of South Carolina, p. 213.
Rainey, a native South Carolinian: Bermuda, as a sanctuary for blockade runners, was a crossroads for news and intelligence about the war, and Rainey, cutting the community's hair each day, managed to hear a lot. Before the war's end, he was called upon to testify in the case of Confederate sympathizer Dr. Luke Blackburn, who was caught scheming to spark a yellow fever epidemic in New York and Philadelphia by shipping contaminated clothing, in the guise of charity, to the cities' poor. See Packwood.
56 *"To make an appropriation of one million dollars":* Proceedings of the Constitutional Convention of South Carolina, p. 196.
"It is the fashion of bogus politicians": Ibid., p. 376.
57 *"You would do perfectly right":* Ibid., p. 379; "Root, hog, or die!" was an old folk saying, referring to the practice of turning domestic hogs loose so they could forage for their own food. In Reconstruction it was applied to the ex-slaves, who were expected to make their own way in the postwar economy.
"When I, in the simplicity of my heart": Ibid., p. 423.
In his view, the infusion of $1 million: Ibid., pp. 381, 418–19.

4. *"The Whirligig of Time"*

60 *"The time for compromise has passed":* Korngold, *Two Friends of Man,* p. 276.
"The 'whirligig of time' has brought about its revenges": Forten, "Life in the Sea Islands," *Atlantic Monthly.*
"The Senator-elect . . . has a benevolent expression": National Republican, Jan. 31, 1870.

"The distinguished darky made quite a sensation": New York Herald, Feb. 3, 1870.
"Happy Revels": Memphis Daily Avalanche, Jan. 22, 1870.
Even other men of color considered Revels a curious figure: In 1860, out of a statewide black population of 437,303, there were only 775 free blacks residing in Mississippi. See Wharton, pp. 12–13.
"For preaching the gospel to Negroes": Borome, "The Autobiography of Hiram Rhoades Revels," *Midwest Journal.*

61 *"Adding 191 to the church [and] killing off two whiskey shops":* "Letter to the Editor" in unnamed news clipping, Hiram Revels Scrapbook, Hiram Revels Collection, Schomburg Center for Research in Black Culture, New York Public Library.
Revels "had never voted, had never attended a political meeting": Lynch, *Facts of Reconstruction,* p. 41.
A dutiful letter-writer when away on his frequent travels: Hiram Revels Scrapbook, undated clipping, Hiram Revels Collection.

62 *"Breathe a new atmosphere":* Frederick Douglass's speech at Rochester, New York, Apr. 5, 1870, in the Collection on the American Negro, Columbia University Library, New York; Wendell Phillips's sentiments recorded in *National Anti-Slavery Standard,* Mar. 20, 1869; both quoted or described in Gillette, pp. 22–23.

63 *"Singularly placid [and] . . . untouched":* Green, *The Secret City,* p. 120.

64 *"Tall . . . portly . . . swinging along like an athlete":* Bowers, p. 247.
"The old repulsive sheds": Frederick Douglass, "A Lecture on Our National Capitol," 1876, Frederick Douglass Papers, Library of Congress.

65 *"Rights that have cost a revolution":* Green, *The Secret City,* p. 109.

66 *"Unimproved class": Washington Bee,* Feb. 1, 1890, quoted in Gatewood, p. 50.
"Tinsel shows [and] straggling processions": Ibid., p. 51.

67 *"Praises of the completeness of all the details": New York Times,* Mar. 5, 1873.
"One of the most beautiful and handsomely gowned women": Lamson, Peggy, p. 173.
"In the grand procession": New National Era, Mar. 6, 1873.

68 *"Of the most recherché character": New York Herald,* Feb. 2, 1870.
"Equal to a first rate original oil painting": New National Era, Feb. 28, 1870.

70 *In May 1867, two years after his capture:* In 1878 the state of Mississippi offered to appoint Davis to the U.S. Senate, an honor he could not accept because his citizenship had been removed (it would not be formally restored until 1977).

71 *"So far inferior, that they had no rights": Dred Scott v. Sandford,* 19 How. 60 US, 393 (1857).
"[Dred Scott] *has been repealed by the mightiest uprising":* Swisher, "Dred Scott One Hundred Years After," *The Journal of Politics.*
"Giants! — great, intellectual, mighty giants": Congressional Globe, 41st Cong., 2nd sess., 2-24-70, appendix, p. 127.
"The name of Taney is to be hooted down": Swisher, p. 582.
"Evidence that in your own judgment": Congressional Globe, 41st Cong., 2nd sess., 2-24-70, appendix, p. 127.
"Addressing you not as Republicans": Ibid.

72 *A former nemesis from Kansas, J. H. Morris:* Hiram Revels Scrapbook, Hiram Revels Collection.
As for the issue of Revels's eligibility: The Nation, Feb. 3, 1870; see also Smith, *The Negro in Congress.*
"Born a putrid corpse": Congressional Globe, 41st Cong., 2nd sess., pp. 1566–67.

72 *"Revels, who had been sitting all day"*: Undated news clipping from *Philadelphia Inquirer* in Hiram Revels Scrapbook, Hiram Revels Collection; see also *National Republican*, Feb. 26, 1870.

73 *"You will make us your foes"*: Turner's speech was printed as a pamphlet and is often quoted. See Coulter, "Negro Legislators in Georgia During the Reconstruction Period," *Georgia Historical Quarterly.*

74 *"A wayward sister"*: *New National Era*, Mar. 17, 1870.
"They broke my door open, took me out of bed": Colby's testimony appears in the Georgia section of *House Report 22*, 42nd Cong., 2nd sess.; see also Sterling, *Trouble They Seen*, p. 374.
A national outcry: See Les Benedict, p. 55.
"Never since the birth of the republic": *Philadelphia Inquirer*, Mar. 17, 1870.

75 *"As the recognized representative"*: *Congressional Globe*, 41st Cong., 2nd sess., Mar. 16, 1870, pp. 1986–88.
"In receiving him in exchange for Jefferson Davis": *New York Tribune*, Mar. 17, 1870. An unsubstantiated rumor circulated among Democrats, stating that Charles Sumner had ghost-written Revels's speech. Revels was apparently in the habit of receiving some coaching from Sumner. Later that spring, before giving a speech in Philadelphia, he wrote to the veteran senator, "I will call at your office on next Wednesday night, for the purpose of reading in your hearing." Hiram Revels to Charles Sumner, Apr. 9, 1870, Charles Sumner Papers, Houghton Library, Harvard University.
"I do not know of one state that is altogether": *Congressional Globe*, 41st Cong., 2nd sess., p. 3520.

76 *When he was denied a podium:* Undated letter to the editor in the *Philadelphia Post*, Hiram Revels Scrapbook, Hiram Revels Collection.

5. *KuKluxery*

79 *"The enslaved have not been merely emancipated"*: *Marion Star* (undated), quoted in *Charleston News & Courier*, Nov. 10, 1870.
"Heavens were rent with the sounds": *Charleston Daily News*, Aug. 17, 1868; also *Charleston Daily Courier*, Sept. 12, 1868.
"This vile, rotten, wicked, corrupt and degrading regime": *Winnsboro News* (undated), quoted in *Charleston News & Courier*, Apr. 1, 1871.

80 *"The passing of high words and blows"*: Anonymous, "South Carolina Morals," *Atlantic Monthly.*
"Honor is the sentiment": Tindall, p. 235.

81 *"Region where Liberty finds her constant home"*: *Charleston News & Courier*, Sept. 19, 1876.

82 *"Down in a deeper grave than this"*: Korngold, *Two Friends of Man*, pp. 333–34; Walt Whitman, tending to the Union wounded in the nation's capital, overheard two young soldiers who had visited Charleston, one of whom boasted of having seen Calhoun's monument. "That you saw is not the real monument," replied the other, "but I have seen it. It is the desolated, ruined South; nearly the whole generation of young men between seventeen and thirty destroyed or maimed; all the old families used up; the rich impoverished; the plantations covered with weeds; the slaves unloosed and become the masters; and the name of *Southerner* blackened with every shame — all that is Calhoun's real monument." See Whitman, p. 242.

"These vile retches": Hardy D. Edwards to N. E. Edwards, Sept. 10, 1868, quoted in *Charleston Daily News,* Oct. 2, 1868; see also *New National Era,* May 25, 1871.

83 *Hill was so rattled by the incident:* With the help of the American Colonization Society, Hill arranged to immigrate to Liberia along with 136 men, women, and children.

"The effect of these numerous threats": Quoted in *New National Era,* Sept. 21, 1871.

84 *"I told him to stay at home":* South Carolina congressmen Warren Wilkes and Samuel Nuckles to President Grant, Mar. 2, 1871; Grant, p. 260.

"In silence and secrecy": Post, "A 'Carpetbagger' in South Carolina," *Journal of Negro History;* Nelson, p. 128; also see *New National Era,* Apr. 20, 1871.

"We are laying the foundation": Benjamin Randolph, quoted in Botsch, p. 81.

85 *"Acting the Big Man":* R. N. Hemphill to W. R. Hemphill, Apr. 20, 1871, Hemphill Papers, Duke University Library; quoted in Williamson, p. 264.

"Put six balls through your boy": Nelson, pp. 132–33.

86 *"They cut my back all to pieces":* Thomas, "Spartanburg's Civil War," *Carologue.*

"As a whole nigger should be treated": Burton, "Race and Reconstruction," *Journal of Social History.*

87 *"The worst frightened men":* Albion Tourgee to Thomas Settle, June 24, 1869, Thomas Settle Papers, University of North Carolina Library, quoted in Gillette, p. 182.

"The Northern mind, being full": Amos Akerman to Benjamin Conley, Dec. 28, 1871, Akerman Letterbooks, University of Virginia Library; quoted in McFeely, "Amos T. Akerman: The Lawyer and Racial Justice," in *Region, Race, and Reconstruction.*

"The principle for which we contended": Jefferson Davis, quoted in Washburne, p. 32.

Also offensive were the militiamen's: Charleston Daily News, Mar. 28 and 29, 1871. For more background on militias, see Zuczek, *Encyclopedia of the Reconstruction Era,* vol. 1, pp. 410–14.

88 *"The long habit of command":* Daniel Chamberlain to President Grant, July 22, 1876, quoted in Allen, p. 322; Louisiana's P.B.S. Pinchback concurred with Chamberlain's view: "The whites . . . [are] possessed of every avenue of communication and transportation, the telegraph wires, railroads and steamboats all being at their disposal, [so that] in a few hours they can concentrate a large armed force. On the other hand, the colored as a class are poor, without experience, unarmed, no channels of communication or transportation open to them, naturally docile and peaceable, utterly without organization, they scatter at the first appearance of danger." Draft of speech on upcoming Hayes-Tilden election, summer 1877, P.B.S. Pinchback Papers, Moorland-Spingarn Collection, Howard University Library.

"The fighting men of the South": The Nation, Mar. 23, 1871. This professional élan no doubt helped the Klan build and maintain its hierarchical structure of klaverns and dens. "A county was divided into a certain number of districts, and each district composed a camp, which was under the command of a captain," a North Carolina Klansman reported. Recounted another, "The meetings were to be held in secret places — in the woods, or some other place distant from any habitation, in order to avoid detection. The disguise prescribed was a long white gown, and a mask for the face . . . The sign of recognition of the [Klansmen] was by sliding the

right hand down along the opposite lapel of the coat. If the party to whom the sign was made was a member of the organization, he returned it by sliding the left hand in the same manner down along the opposite lapel of the coat. The word of distress was 'Shiloh.'" *Congressional Globe,* 42nd Cong., 1st sess., Mar. 28, 1871.

89 *"It is not law that is wanted in the South": Congressional Globe,* 42nd Cong., 1st sess., appendix, p. 71.

"If the federal government cannot pass laws": Butler, "Ku Klux Klan Outrages in the South," speech to House of Representatives, Apr. 4, 1871, pamphlet in Benjamin Butler Papers, Library of Congress.

"Waving the bloody shirt": Trelease, p. 294; see also Zuczek, *Encyclopedia of the Reconstruction Era,* vol. 1.

90 *"K.K.K. Beware! Beware! Beware!": New National Era,* May 25, 1871.

"When myself and colleagues shall leave": Congressional Globe, 42nd Cong., 1st sess., quoted in Sterling, *Trouble They Seen,* p. 371.

"We have reconstructed, and reconstructed": Congressional Globe, 42nd Cong., 1st sess., appendix, pp. 116–17; for discussion of resistance to the Klan bill, see also Gillette, p. 52–53.

"Restoration of peace and order": The Nation, Apr. 6, 1871.

91 *"The rule of [the community's] most ignorant members": The Nation,* Mar. 9, 1871.

"We must . . . hand the Government over to the people": The Nation, Mar. 30, 1871.

"Sir, we are in terror from Ku-Klux threats": S. E. Lane to President Grant, Apr. 19, 1871; Grant, pp. 263–64.

"I am a clergyman, superannuated": C. F. Jones to President Grant, May 12 1871; Grant, p. 264.

92 *"To let Confederate ideas rule us no longer":* Amos Akerman to George W. Heidy, Aug. 22, 1876, Akerman Letterbooks, University of Virginia Library; quoted in McFeely, "Amos T. Akerman: The Lawyer and Racial Justice."

"An alarming imposition": Amos Akerman to George W. Heidy, Aug. 22, 1876, Akerman Letterbooks; ibid.

Congressman Butler helped persuade: Ibid.

93 *Akerman identified thoroughly with his mission:* Amos Akerman to Charles Sumner, Apr. 6, 1869, Charles Sumner Papers, Houghton Library, Harvard University.

"One cause of [the] readiness to secede": Amos Akerman to E. P. Jackson, Aug. 18, 1871, Akerman Papers, University of Virginia Library; see McFeely, *Grant,* p. 371.

94 *"Black as a highly polished boot":* Morgan, James M., p. 331.

"Distinguished and agreeable figure": The Louisianian, May 2, 1874.

More intriguing was the fact: Lamson, Peggy, pp. 22–33, offers an in-depth discussion of Elliott's mysterious past.

95 *"A Negro from Massachusetts Cowhides a White Carpetbagger":* The story is covered in *Charleston Daily News,* Oct. 23–26, 1869.

In defense of the Ku Klux Klan bill, he tangled: Congressional Globe, 42nd Cong., 1st sess., Apr. 1, 1871.

97 *"Possibly, Mr. Editor":* Greeley-Elliott exchange in *New National Era,* Mar. 16, 1871.

"A condition of affairs exists in some of the states": Grant's message to Congress, Mar. 23, 1871, quoted in *Charleston Daily News,* Mar. 24, 1871.

98 *"Very indignant at wrong, and yet master of his indignation":* Amos Akerman to General Alfred H. Terry, Nov. 18, 1871, Akerman Letterbooks; quoted in Trelease, pp. 402–3.

"Under the domination of systematic and organized depravity": Quoted in Williams, Lou Falkner, p. 44.
When Akerman returned to York County on October 10: New York Times, Oct. 31, 1871.

99 *"These lawless disturbers of the South":* Cresswell, "Enforcing the Enforcement Acts," *Journal of Southern History;* see also *Harper's Weekly,* Jan. 27, 1872, and Oct. 19, 1872.
"The general disposition . . . was to assign": Post, "A Carpetbagger in South Carolina," *Journal of Negro History.*
One New York newspaper was convinced: New York Herald, Dec. 1, 1871.
"These outlaws will speedily be taught": Cresswell, "Enforcing the Enforcement Acts"; see also *Harper's Weekly,* Jan. 27 and Oct. 19, 1872.

100 *In spite of the successful prosecutions:* Foner, *A Short History of Reconstruction,* p. 197.
He had been particularly irritated by: Hamilton Fish Diary entry, Nov. 24, 1871, quoted in McFeely, "Amos T. Akerman: The Lawyer and Racial Justice."
Shortly before Christmas 1871: See McFeely, *Grant,* pp. 373–74, for a discussion of Akerman's forced departure.
"As a body designed to destroy Reconstruction": Rable, p. 189.

6. Pinch

103 *"Only colored enough": Louisianian,* May 11, 1872.
"A bronze Mephistopheles": New York Commercial Advertiser, Feb. 25, 1875; Haskins, p. 216.

104 *"To the unwritten law that the cleverest colored man":* Ibid., p. 18.
"A white woman, of English-French stock": Toomer, p. 23.
"I ate cakes to fill my stomach": Ibid.
"When it was announced I nearly fainted": New Orleans Times, Mar. 11, 1872.
"Nearly all the officers inimical to me": P.B.S. Pinchback to Benjamin Butler, Sept. 10, 1863; in Grosz, "The Political Career of P.B.S. Pinchback," *Louisiana Historical Quarterly.* He tried joining the Union's fight again the following year, using $1,000 of his own money to recruit a company of black cavalry. General Nathaniel Banks, however, who had replaced Butler, denied Pinchback's request for a commission.

106 *Ultimately the star cars were eliminated:* Fischer, "A Pioneer Protest," *Journal of Negro History.*
"The time when every thinking man must come forward": Draft of Pinchback speech, Montgomery, Alabama, 1865–1866, P.B.S. Pinchback Papers, Moorland-Spingarn Collection, Howard University Library.
"There is a sense of security displayed by our people": Draft of Pinchback speech to Louisiana Republican state convention, June 19, 1867, P.B.S. Pinchback Papers.
Pinchback took the lead in authoring: Constitution of the State of Louisiana with Amendments, New Orleans, 1875; see Article 13.

107 *"The first colored man in America":* Perkins, "Oscar James Dunn," *Phylon.*
A humiliating incident: New Orleans Crescent, Sept. 2, 1868; see also Haskins, p. 63.
"A shooting affray . . . with intent to kill and murder": New Orleans Daily Picayune, Sept. 2, 1868.

108 *"The most fiery speech ever heard": New Orleans Daily Picayune,* Sept. 4 and 8, 1868; see also Haskins, p. 64.
Dunn, a fine-looking man: Perkins, "Oscar James Dunn."
"I consider myself just as far above": Quoted in Haskins, p. 66.
109 *Brutal atrocities occurred:* Tunnell, *Crucible of Reconstruction,* pp. 154–57.
"We are told, do not legislate on this subject": Draft of Pinchback ppeech, Jan. 4, 1869, P.B.S. Pinchback Papers.
110 *"Senator Pinchback . . . possesses tact and boldness": New Orleans Republican,* Nov. 27, 1870.
111 Griffe, *meaning a person:* Reuter, p. 115. The *gens de couleur* figured prominently in state history, having fought heroically at the Battle of New Orleans on the nearby Plain of Chalmette in the War of 1812 and been famously commended for their gallantry by none other than General Andrew Jackson. Reportedly it was a slave who suggested to the American commanders the idea of using cotton bales as breastworks against the British, a strategy credited with playing a key role in the American victory. Jordan B. Noble, a black drummer boy in the battle, was an elderly man in Reconstruction New Orleans, telling the story of the great confrontation between American and British forces to anyone who cared to listen and sometimes delighting children by playing on his old drum. Many *gens de couleur* families were socially prominent, assimilated, and well-to-do; President Lincoln had counted on them to enable Reconstruction to take root in Louisiana.
112 *"Sir, my conscience is not for sale":* Kletzing, p. 185; see also Christian, "The Theory of the Poisoning of Oscar J. Dunn," *Phylon.*
"Warmoth," Dunn complained: Warmoth, p. 145.
The Democrats had a field day: Ibid., p. 112.
113 *Elevating Dunn to vice presidential candidate: Louisville Courier-Journal,* Nov. 23, 1871, quoted in Perkins, "Oscar James Dunn."
114 *"I have been called a carpetbagger, a czar, a Caesar":* Warmoth, p. 191.
"Hasn't a handful of brains": New Orleans Republican, Sept. 2, 1871.
115 *"A regular gurgling sob": Louisianian,* Nov. 23, 1871.
"Never seen pneumonia like that": Christian, "The Theory of the Poisoning of Oscar J. Dunn."
"They've given poison to the Governor": New Orleans Times, Nov. 22, 1871.
116 *"Beware of Herrings":* See "Beware of Herrings" in *New Orleans Times,* Nov. 24, 1871. Prominent in New Orleans voodoo lore was the dreaded "gris-gris," a satchel filled with spices, fingernail parings, or pieces of reptile that, left on the doorstep, brought harm and illness to a house's occupant. Dunn himself was said to have once attended a voodoo exorcism at which priestess Malvina Latour "rescued" a man from a curse by conjuring from his throat a small black mouse. See also Asbury, pp. 202–3.
"Set tongues upon swivels": Christian, "The Theory of the Poisoning of Oscar J. Dunn."
"In a way that he had never before experienced": New Orleans Times, Nov. 23–25, 1871; *New Orleans Republican,* Nov. 23, 1871.
"'Who delivered the fatal cup?'": Perkins, "James Henri Burch and Oscar James Dunn in Louisiana," *Journal of Negro History.*
Dismissed the rumors as a "hallucination": Louisianian, Nov. 23, 1871.

117 *"Manifested to us the truthfulness":* *New Orleans Republican,* Dec. 7, 1871.

118 *"Pinchback . . . was a restless, ambitious man":* Warmoth, p. 20.

120 *In the war, Grant had distinguished himself:* See discussion in Gillette, p. 179.

121 *"A political jockey":* "Naboth's Vineyard," speech by Charles Sumner in Congress, Dec. 21, 1870, in Sumner, *Works,* vol. 14, p. 94; see also *New York Times,* Dec. 21, 1870.

"Had the President been so inspired": Sumner's Senate address of Mar. 24–25, 1871, quoted in *New York Times,* Mar. 28, 1871, and *Charleston Daily News,* Mar. 28, 1871.

122 *"A cat without smellers":* Donald, *Charles Sumner and the Coming of the Civil War,* p. 117.

But even his supporters feared he had overreached: Sumner was not alone in his opposition to the Santo Domingo plan, which split Republican allies; for instance, Frederick Douglass and Congressman Joseph Rainey supported annexation, but William Lloyd Garrison did not. Douglass paid for his loyalty to Grant by being made to endure a tawdry racial snub. Invited to join a presidential fact-finding commission that traveled to Santo Domingo, he was excluded from both the dinner table aboard the ship as it returned to Washington and a dinner that Grant hosted at the White House for the commissioners, who, as expected, presented him with a favorable opinion of the annexation scheme. Grant, it appeared, had appointed Douglass to the commission as a way of countering Sumner's influence with the old black-abolitionist alliance, but after the commission's and the president's discourtesy toward the revered Douglass, there was little likelihood anyone from the anti-annexation camp would be swayed by Douglass.

"Mr. President . . . I am an administration man": Bowers, p. 297; see also Donald, *Charles Sumner and the Rights of Man,* pp. 434–37.

Some said the president's troubles really began: Bowers, p. 263.

123 *The Grant administration's complicity:* Finally, but too late to save several Wall Street brokerage houses, the president authorized the treasury to release $1 million in gold in an attempt to right the market. His personal collusion in the scheme was never proved, although Assistant Treasurer Daniel Butterfield, accused of aiding the conspiracy, was forced to resign.

Garfield was said to have received $329: Garfield's reputation may have withstood assault in part because of an enduring tale of his wartime heroism. At the Battle of Chickamauga in June 1863, Garfield, possibly by coincidence, was seen riding *toward* the advancing Confederates while most of his Union comrades, including his superior officer, General William Rosecrans, were heading in the opposite direction. "Garfield's Ride," as the incident became known, proved a serviceable rejoinder to those who doubted his integrity. See Morris, *Ambrose Bierce,* pp. 59–60.

"I may be wrong": Frederick Douglass to Charles Sumner, Jan. 6, 1871, Charles Sumner Papers, Houghton Library, Harvard University.

124 *"First in nepotism":* "Republicanism vs. Grantism," speech by Charles Sumner in the Senate on May 31, 1872, in Sumner, *Works,* vol. 15, pp. 85–171; also in Donald, *Charles Sumner and the Rights of Man,* pp. 547–48.

Their pet cause was the overturning: See Foner, *Forever Free* p. 179, for discussion of the Liberal Republican cause.

As Sydney Howard Gay, a black New Yorker, reminded Sumner: Sydney Howard Gay to Charles Sumner, Aug. 8, 1872, Charles Sumner Papers.

125 *"Revolutions never go backward":* Elliott, "Oration Delivered by the Hon. R. B. Elliot, Apr. 16, 1872, at the Celebration of the Tenth Anniversary of Emancipation in the District of Columbia."

"Big round face of infantile mildness": Bowers, p. 380.

Sumner's endorsement only further rankled: So irritated were the Republicans with Sumner that he found himself in disrepute even when, in fall 1872, he proposed that the names of Union victories in the Civil War not be noted in army records or used in ceremonial connections, as these had been battles not with alien foes but other Americans. Sumner had raised this idea twice before, once during the Civil War and once in 1865, and his political allies had warmly received it. Now, however, the notion was attacked; the Massachusetts legislature went so far as to formally censure him, terming his resolution "an insult to the loyal soldiery of the nation . . . depreciating their grand achievements in the late rebellion." An editorial accused him of "seeking the overturn of soldiers' gravestones" (quoted in Pierce, pp. 551–52). Sumner was surprised by the severe reaction, but the legislature's rash action ultimately served his purpose. The issue was thrust even more emphatically before the public, which, upon reflection, agreed with him. Phillips to J. B. Smith, Massachusetts House, Mar. 10, 1873, Manuscript Dept., Moorland-Spingarn Research Center, Howard University; see also *Congressional Globe,* 42nd Cong., 3rd sess., p. 2, and Pierce, p. 550.

"I need not tell you, my friends": New York Herald, Aug. 17, 1872.

126 *The doubts about Greeley soon were reflected:* See discussion in Gillette, pp. 66–69.

"The pencil of Thomas Nast": Bowers, p. 231.

128 *"If the success of the Republican party is at stake":* Simmons, pp. 777–79; Haskins, pp. 151–52.

129 *"Are you Governor Pinchback?": Louisianian,* Sept. 21, 1872; see also Haskins, pp. 153–55, and Simmons, pp. 775–81.

130 *Racing . . . had long been a special passion: New Orleans Republican,* Sept. 20, 1872. Horseracing, and racing and gambling in general, constituted a huge passion in Louisiana. Detailed newspaper columns headlined "TURF ACTION" were prominent on front pages even during moments of intense local political upheaval. In 1870, the region thrilled to a series of celebrated races between two legendary steamboats, the *Natchez* and the *Robert E. Lee.* The contests had political overtones, as the captain of the *Natchez,* Tom Leathers, was an unreconstructed rebel who wore Confederate gray and occasionally flew the stars and bars on his vessel; the *Robert E. Lee* was captained by John W. Cannon, who idolized the boat's namesake and, like Lee, was a political moderate. The races upriver, from New Orleans to St. Louis, were watched by thousands of fans and bettors who lined the shores at Memphis, Cairo, and elsewhere. The *Lee* ultimately emerged the winner, achieving a time of three days, eighteen hours, and fourteen minutes, a record that stood for decades. Governor Warmoth rode aboard the *Robert E. Lee* during one of the heats. See Way, pp. 71–89.

The Louisianian *worried that locking Pinchback: Louisianian,* Sept. 21, 1872.

"What have the people of Louisiana done": New Orleans Daily Picayune, Sept. 20, 1872.

131 *"Had visited him the night before"*: Lonn, p. 207; Haskins, p. 159.
Warmoth denied the accusation: Grosz, "The Political Career of P.B.S. Pinchback," *Louisiana Historical Quarterly*; Haskins, p. 159.
133 *Pinchback hoped the general's credentials:* See Piston.
Pinchback unleashed a severe denunciation: Louisianian, Jan. 5, 1873.

7. The Colfax Massacre

135 *Exhausted, haunted by the recent death:* Riddleberger, "The Break in the Radical Ranks," *Journal of Negro History.*
136 *"Without going into details": New York Tribune,* Mar. 5, 1872.
"Here, then, is the outcome": Pike, pp. 11–12.
"Seven years ago these men": Ibid., pp. 21, 29–30.
"Years ago, when abolition": New York Tribune, Apr. 19, 1873.
Pike's book, widely lauded: Durden, "The Prostrate State Revisited," *Journal of Negro History.*
137 *"Slightly above the level of animals": The Nation,* Apr. 16 and 30, 1874.
"The ignorant negro rulers": Atlantic Monthly, Feb. 1874.
"The ignorant and unprincipled classes": Charleston News & Courier, Jan. 6, 1874.
"The 'Uncle Tom's Cabin' of the Southern Redemption": Bowers, p. 418.
138 *"Chuckles, guffaws":* Ibid., p. 353.
"Monkey house": Ibid., p. 364.
Did black politicians really behave this way: Ibid., p. 424; see also *New York Herald,* Oct. 17, 1874.
"Serving-maids" — sitting and taking tea: Avary, pp. 353–57.
139 *"To win at the ballot box what was lost with the cannon": Independent,* Mar. 12 and Aug. 6 and 13, 1874; see also McPherson, *The Abolitionist Legacy,* p. 42.
"We have only half swallowed this pill": Haven, *Independent,* Aug. 13, 1874.
"The charge of corruption and extravagance": Uya, pp. 105–8; see also Smalls, "An Honest Ballot Is the Safeguard of the Republic — Speech of Hon. Robert Smalls in the House of Representatives, Feb. 24, 1877," *Congressional Record,* 44th Cong., 2nd sess., appendix, pp. 123–36.
"Where there is so much smoke": Rufus Saxton to Robert Smalls, Dec. 25, 1871, published in *Beaufort Republican,* Jan. 4, 1872.
140 *"As well as I knew the beacon lights":* Robert Smalls to Rufus Saxton, Jan. 1, 1872, published in *Beaufort Republican,* Jan. 4, 1872.
141 *In 1877, after the Democrats seized control: Charleston News & Courier,* Nov. 12, 1877; Uya, pp. 82–83.
"'Smalls, you had better resign'": Ibid., pp. 85–86.
143 *"'They intended to go into the country'":* "History of the Riot at Colfax, Grant Parish, Louisiana, April 13, 1873," prepared by the "Committee of 70," New Orleans, Apr. 13, 1874.
In order to create a "new race" of people: Rable, p. 127.
"The little sleek black negro": "History of the Riot at Colfax."
144 *"To get up a body of men for the unwarrantable attack": New York Times,* Apr. 16, 1873.
"Not afraid to die for white supremacy": Johnson, "The Colfax Riot of April 1873," *Louisiana Historical Quarterly*; see also *New Orleans Republican,* Apr. 25, 1873.

145 *"This man is an old Confederate soldier":* Johnson, "The Colfax Riot of April 1873."
Powell's party carried the small steamboat cannon: Ibid.; see also *New Orleans Republican,* Apr. 18, 1873.
146 *"It is our opinion": New Orleans Republican,* Apr. 25, 1873.
147 *R. G. Hill, one such passenger: New Orleans Republican,* Apr. 16, 1873; see also *Boston Daily Globe,* Apr. 17, 1873.
In New Orleans, Kellogg and Emory were staggered: Dawson, pp. 145–46.
148 *Pinchback traveled upriver:* Haskins, pp. 184–86.
Pinchback, upon reaching the podium: "Horrible Massacre in Grant Parish, Louisiana: Meeting of Colored Men in New Orleans, Address and Speeches," pamphlet printed at the Republican Office, New Orleans, 1873.
"A large number of white people feel just as sad as we do": Ibid.
149 *"This racist and morally opaque decision":* Tunnell, *Crucible of Reconstruction,* p. 193.
"It was private action, not state action": Gressman, "The Unhappy History of Civil Rights Legislation," *Michigan Law Review.*
150 *"A Second Fort Pillow": New York Times,* Apr. 16, 17, and 19, 1873.

8. Capstone of the Reconstructed Republic

151 *"We cannot . . . educate our children": Congressional Record,* 43rd Cong., 1st sess., Jan. 5, 1874.
152 *"Earlier in time, loftier, more majestic":* Pierce, vol. 4, p. 501.
"Pledge of universal human equality": Donald, *Charles Sumner and the Coming of the Civil War,* p. 153.
A pragmatic, "earthly body": Congressional Record, 42nd Cong., 2nd sess., p. 825.
"The subject of subjects": Sumner, quoted by William Lloyd Garrison, William Lloyd Garrison to Sumner, Aug. 3, 1872, Charles Sumner Papers, Houghton Library, Harvard University.
153 *"One which the Almighty has seen fit to establish":* "Extracts from the Majority Report of the Caste School," in the *Liberator,* Aug. 21, 1846; quoted in Levy and Phillips, "The Roberts Case," *American Historical Review.*
"Condemned by Christianity": Pierce, vol. 3, pp. 40–41; quoted in Murphy, "The Civil Rights Law of 1875," *Journal of Negro History.*
"The whites themselves are injured": "Argument of Charles Sumner . . . in the case of Sarah Roberts v. the City of Boston, Boston, 1849," quoted in Levy and Phillips, "The Roberts Case."
"Cannot fail to have a depressing effect": New National Era, May 5, 1870.
Sumner's brief, however, was rejected: Donald, *Charles Sumner and the Coming of the Civil War,* pp. 180–81.
154 *"How is it possible for one who has never been denied":* Sarah H. Thompson to Charles Sumner, Feb. 5, 1872, printed in *New National Era,* Feb. 15, 1872.
"I think only those who have suffered deeply": Charlotte Forten to Charles Sumner, Jan. 28, 1872, Charles Sumner Papers.
"For God's sake urge your Civil Rights Bill": George W. Richardson to Charles Sumner, Jan. 27, 1872, Charles Sumner Papers.
The peripatetic Gilbert Haven was aghast: Independent, Aug. 13, 1874.

155 *One of the most disturbing testimonials:* G. W. Mitchell to Charles Sumner, Jan. 27, 1872, with attached statement by J. William White, Charles Sumner Papers.
"In late 1872 the civil rights cause received a boost": Coleman, "The Fight of a Man with a Railroad," *Atlantic Monthly,* Dec. 1872; for comment, see *New National Era,* Nov. 28, 1872.

156 *"Here am I, a member of your honorable body":* "Civil Rights Speech of Hon. John R Lynch, of Mississippi, in the House of Representatives, Feb. 3, 1875," GPO, Washington, 1875.
Joseph Rainey told a story: New National Era, Dec. 7, 1871; Lamson, Peggy, pp. 120–21.

157 *"The roasting of a poor negro lad with kerosene": Louisianian,* Mar. 21, 1872.

158 *"He cannot appropriate the sidewalk": Congressional Globe,* 42nd Cong., 1st sess., p. 382.
"Why this fear of the negro": Joseph Rainey, speaking in the House of Representatives, Feb. 3, 1872, quoted in *Louisianian,* Feb. 29, 1872.
"A practical demonstration": New National Era, May 29, 1872.

159 *In practice, the Fugitive Slave Act:* Korngold, *Two Friends,* p. 210.
The law created a precedent for the idea: Kaczorowski, "To Begin the Nation Anew," *American Historical Review.*
"I have sworn to support the Constitution": Congressional Globe, 42nd Cong., 2nd sess., p. 3263 (italics added by author).

160 *"I am not here to be dictated to":* Ibid., pp. 3262–63.
"If the Democrats are such staunch friends": New National Era, Mar. 14, 1872.

161 *"He [Morrill] finds no power for anything": Congressional Globe,* 42nd Cong., 2nd sess., pp. 728–30.
"If the Democrats are such staunch friends": New National Era, Mar. 14, 1872.

161 *"In regard to the rights that belong to the individual":* Ibid., p. 901.
"'Equal rights in what and for what?'": Independent, May 2, 1872.
"'I ask the Senator'": Congressional Globe, 42nd Cong., 2nd sess., p. 3264.

162 *"Equality . . . was a far more revolutionary aim than freedom":* Woodward, *Burden of Southern History,* p. 64.
"A hotel is a legal institution": Congressional Globe, 42nd Cong., 1st sess., p. 280.

163 *"We are like whalers who have been long on chase":* Korngold, *Two Friends,* p. 338. Lincoln recognized the critical contribution the abolitionists had made, as suggested by a reminiscence of Daniel Chamberlain's: "It was my privilege once, and only once, to talk with Abraham Lincoln [in] Virginia, Apr. 6, 1865. I spoke to him of the country's gratitude for his great deliverance of the slaves. His sad face beamed for a moment with happiness as he answered . . . 'I have been only an instrument. The logic and moral power of Garrison, and the anti-slavery people of the country and the army, have done all.'" *New York Tribune,* Nov. 4, 1883.
"While a colored gentleman is . . . unable to obtain admission": National Standard, May 1870. Like Charles Sumner, Douglass and others were convinced the battle for civil rights must be national in scope. That principle was underscored by the efforts of veteran Quaker abolitionist Aaron M. Powell, who in 1870 established the National Reform League to crusade for equal rights. While Powell's campaign had some success in New York, where the desegregation of restaurants and places of lodging led to a state public accommodations law in 1873, it soon became evi-

dent that localized efforts to end certain forms of segregation would be scattershot and ineffective.

"I only long for the hour": Susan B. Anthony to Charles Sumner, Feb. 19, 1872, Charles Sumner Papers.

"As grandly for Equal Rights to all women *as you have to* all men": Susan B. Anthony to Charles Sumner, Dec. 9, 1872, Charles Sumner Papers.

"Women are absolutely nothing in Republican minds": Susan B. Anthony to Charles Sumner, Apr. 23, 1872, Charles Sumner Papers.

164 *"One of the saddest divorces in American history":* McFeely, *Frederick Douglass,* p. 266. Women had been active in the movement to end slavery as early as the 1830s, when the sisters Angelina and Sarah Grimké, Charleston-born daughters of an elite slaveholding family, rebelled against their surroundings and came north, publishing antislavery tracts and holding parlor meetings to abet the cause. As white women of a slaveholding family, their condemnation of "the peculiar institution" was imbued with unique legitimacy, and they did not stop at criticizing slavery's cruelty but described it as a system destructive to the South as a whole.

"Garrison and Sumner, Douglass and Phillips": In 1848, Frederick Douglass attended the founding meeting of American feminism in Seneca Falls, New York, where a broad agenda of women's rights were discussed. At the time, women's claim to suffrage was considered a bold demand even among many of the women present — "Why, Lizzie, thee will make us ridiculous," the Quaker Lucretia Mott famously told Elizabeth Cady Stanton, who put forward the idea — but Douglass concurred with Stanton's resolution.

"We have fairly boosted the Negro": Elizabeth Cady Stanton to Martha Coffin Wright, Dec. 20, 1865, quoted in Goldsmith, p. 102.

165 *Douglass, flinching at her use of a racial slur: New York Tribune,* Nov. 21, 1866.

"I would rather cut off my right hand": Stanton et al., p. 193.

"Incoming tide of ignorance": Painter, p. 228.

"According to the historian Benjamin Quarles": Quarles, "Frederick Douglass and the Women's Rights Movement," *Journal of Negro History.*

Two years later, Republicans there: William Whipper's was perhaps South Carolina's most passionate black voice for the female vote. His wife, Frances Rollin, and her sisters — known collectively as "the Misses Rollin" — were noted characters in Reconstruction South Carolina. In 1867 Frances had been one of the first people of color to file a civil rights complaint in the state. Her case was handled by the Freedmen's Bureau agent Martin Delany, who encouraged her literary aspirations and eventually arranged for her to write his biography. The book was published in 1868 under the name Frank A. Rollin, as the publisher feared the public would not deem a female author credible. Returning to South Carolina, she began work as a secretary in Whipper's office in Columbia; Whipper's wife had died recently, and she and Whipper were married in 1868 over the objections of her father, who considered Whipper a rough-and-tumble "Negro politician" and not suitable for his aristocratic daughter. In Columbia "the Whippers" — husband and wife — were an acknowledged political team, he the legislator, she the knowing insider. See Gatewood, "The Remarkable Misses Rollin," *South Carolina Historical Magazine*; see also *New York Sun,* Mar. 29, 1871.

166 *"Establishing an aristocracy of sex":* Stanton et al., pp. 348–56, 382–83; quoted in Goldsmith, pp. 180–82; also in Lutz, pp. 162–65.

In May 1872 Charles Sumner adopted: Not until 1896 would restrictions on all former Confederates be abolished.

167 *"We have open and frank hearts":* Quoted in Russ, "The Negro and White Disenfranchisement During Radical Reconstruction," *Journal of Negro History.*

168 *"'I sound the cry!'": Congressional Globe,* 42nd Cong., 2nd sess., pp. 3739–40.

"You must take care of the civil rights bill": Pierce, vol. 4, p. 598; also see McPherson, "Abolitionists and the Civil Rights Act of 1875," *Journal of American History.* To his old Senate colleague, who was now Vice President Henry Wilson, Sumner vowed, "If my Works were completed and my Civil Rights bill passed, no visitor could enter that door that would be more welcome than death." See Henry Wilson's letter read at Faneuil Hall, Boston, Mar. 13, 1874.

"His skin is very black": Chicago Tribune, quoted in *New National Era,* Jan. 22, 1874.

169 *Broad presumptions about race:* Some of the most half-baked theories of racial determinism emanated not from the lips of the coarse and uneducated, but from the lecture halls of Ivy League colleges (the Harvard professor Nathaniel Southgate Shaler was a leading offender) and the pens of prominent editorialists, such as *The Nation*'s E. L. Godkin. See Gossett.

Elliott's colleague Alonzo Ransier tangled: Congressional Record, 43rd Cong., 1st sess, Jan. 5, 1874.

170 *"The prevailing ideas entertained":* For Stephens's "The Cornerstone Speech," see Cleveland, pp. 717–29.

"With a shrunken, consumptive chest": Hendrick, p. 59.

"There is a vast difference": Congressional Record, 43rd Cong., 1st sess., Jan. 5, 1874.

171 *The Slaughterhouse Cases arose:* Ross, "Justice Miller's Reconstruction," *Journal of Southern History.* Campbell, assistant secretary of war in the Confederate cabinet, was said to have been the first person to use the term *reconstruction* in reference to the war's aftermath during a peace conference with President Lincoln in winter 1865.

172 *"A few extreme Democrats pretended": Chicago Tribune,* quoted in *New National Era,* Jan. 22, 1874.

Elliott began by calling attention: Congressional Record, 43rd Cong, 1st sess, Jan. 6, 1874.

175 *Elliott had replied "by calm, convincing arguments": New National Era,* Jan. 8, 1874; Lamson, Peggy, p. 182.

"No more dignified, skillful": National Republican, quoted in *New National Era,* Jan. 8, 1874; Lamson, Peggy, p. 182.

"Mr. Elliott is of the blackest of his race": New York Times, Jan. 7, 1874.

"The blade of sarcasm with which he annihilated": Louisianian, May 2, 1874.

Elliott, of South Carolina, delivered a speech: Charleston News & Courier, Jan. 7, 1874.

176 *"In the recent debate on the civil rights bill": New National Era,* Mar. 19, 1874.

177 *The national recognition of Elliott:* Among other things, Robert Brown Elliott's bravura performance on January 6 hushed once and for all the rumors that Charles Sumner, Daniel Chamberlain, or some other white man wrote Elliott's speeches. The rumor had proven intractable, even though Elliott himself cited to his critics

the many times he had spoken effectively in impromptu, unscripted circumstances.

"The victory for the colored boy was complete": *New York Times,* Feb. 5, 1874.

177 *"In the ratio of their numbers":* Ibid., Jan. 25, 1874.

178 *As William Gillette points out:* The editor Henry Watterson, quoted in *National Republican,* Sept. 2, 1874; see also Gillette, p. 217, and *New York Herald Tribune,* Aug. 10, 1874.

A view seconded by journalist Charles Nordhoff: Vaughn, p. 133.

"The measure pending here today is confronted": *Congressional Record,* 43rd Cong., 2nd sess., 1875, pp. 1004–5.

9. Divided Time

181 *"I wanted to know the whys and wherefore":* William Sturges, letter to *New York Tribune,* Mar. 15, 1871, reproduced in *Congressional Globe,* 42nd Cong., 1st sess., Mar. 28, 1871; for Meridian events, see also Harris, pp. 396–99, and Horn, pp. 156–62.

182 *"The South cares for no other question":* *New York Times,* May 2, 1876.

183 *"Every one who rode with him":* Colonel Henry C. Lockwood, quoted in frontispiece of Ames, *Adelbert Ames..*

184 *"Angry words":* *Jackson Tri-Weekly Clarion,* June 10, 1869.

At court-martial Yerger's relatives: Current, *Those Terrible Carpetbaggers,* p. 173; Harris, pp. 59–61. Yerger moved to Maryland, edited a newspaper, and ran unsuccessfully for Congress.

Transforming him gradually from a bureaucrat: Lemman, p. 37.

"Harnessed revolution": Foner, *Forever Free,* p. 139.

185 *"The contest [here] is not between two established parties":* Adelbert Ames to John Sherman, Aug. 17, 1869, John Sherman Papers, Library of Congress; Adelbert Ames to William T. Sherman, Aug. 17, 1869, William T. Sherman Papers, Library of Congress; quoted in Current, *Those Terrible Carpetbaggers,* pp. 174–75.

Photographs taken by the famous Matthew Brady: Lemman, p. 41.

186 *"These she-adders of New Orleans":* Capers, p. 68.

"This representative of Hell in garb of man": *La Crosse Weekly,* Jan. 1865, undated news clipping in Clippings Scrapbook, Benjamin Butler Papers, Library of Congress.

187 *"Multitudinous disadvantages":* Ames, *Chronicles from the Nineteenth Century,* vol. 1, p. 202; vol 2, p. 667. See also Current, *Those Terrible Carpetbaggers,* p. 195.

188 *By late 1874, agitated by the national debate:* Wharton, "The Race Issue in the Overthrow of Reconstruction in Mississippi," *Phylon.*

"'Vote the Negro Down or Knock Him Down'": *Westville News,* undated clipping appears in Appendix to "Mississippi in 1875: Report of the Select Committee to Inquire into the Mississippi Election of 1875," GPO, Washington, 1876.

Governor Ames would point out in congressional hearings: Testimony of Adelbert Ames, "Mississippi in 1875."

189 *"A fugitive from justice":* *Jackson Weekly Clarion,* Sept. 4, 1873, and Oct. 9 and 16, 1873; see also Brock, "Thomas W. Cardozo," *Journal of Negro History.*

"Shingled all over with indictments": Nordhoff, p. 74; see also Foner, *Freedom's Lawmakers,* p. 40.

"Leading Cardozo to express frustration": Wharton, "The Race Issue in the Overthrow of Reconstruction in Mississippi"; see also Lynch, *Reminiscences of an Active Life,* pp. 131–36, and Brock, "Thomas W. Cardozo."

190 *"A receptacle of the colored men":* Testimony of Adelbert Ames, "Mississippi in 1875."

191 *"I and other white men have faced the bullets":* Ames, *Chronicles,* p. 336.

"Let us, with united strength": New York Times, Dec. 17, 1874.

"Can raise good crowd": "Vicksburg Troubles," *U.S. House Report No. 265,* p. xi.

192 *"Unresisting and retreating men":* Ibid., p. viii.

"The whites who came in from the plantations": New York Times, Dec. 18, 1874.

The blacks "were met at the city limits": New York Times, Dec. 14, 1874.

"Not less than 200 were shot": New York Times, Dec. 23, 1874.

193 *"Impossible to ascertain":* "Vicksburg Troubles," p. xi.

"Here surrendered the Confederate chieftain": Rable, pp. 149–50.

"Reinstalled Peter Crosby as sheriff": Harris, pp. 646–48; Garner, pp. 335–36; Rable, pp. 147–49. Peter Crosby, having survived the Democrats' rebellion and the "second battle of Vicksburg," was wounded in early 1875 when a disgruntled employee shot him in the head. Unable to fully recover, Crosby resigned his post in October 1875. See Rable, p. 149. Vicksburg itself remained a hotbed of anti-Republican sentiment. As the town had fallen to General Grant on July 3–4, 1863, Independence Day had not been observed there since the war. When, on July 4, 1875, a black Republican rally was called to commemorate the holiday, whites were duly provoked. One of the scheduled speakers, the much-disliked Thomas Cardozo, was struck on the head with a revolver as he arrived at the train depot. Hours later a fight broke out when he and Secretary of State James Hill tried to address the gathering; shots were fired and a black deputy fell dead. White men and boys then invaded the rally, howling the rebel yell and scattering terrified black celebrants. Cardozo and Hill took refuge in the courthouse cupola. *Vicksburg Herald,* July 7, 1875.

194 *"Mount and ride for your lives":* Twitchell, *Carpetbagger from Vermont,* pp. 146–47.

195 *"If the soldiers choose to get mixed up in broils": New Orleans Bulletin,* Aug. 28, 1874, quoted in Dawson, pp. 162–63.

By the evening of September 15: New Orleans Times, Sept. 16, 1874; see also Gillette, pp. 117–19.

196 *"The happiest city in the universe": New Orleans Bulletin,* Sept. 16, 1874.

"Turbulent and disorderly persons to disperse": New Orleans Times, Sept. 16, 1874.

197 *"I think that the terrorism now existing":* Sheridan's telegrams and Belknap's replies appear in "Affairs in Louisiana," *U.S. Senate Executive Documents,* 43rd Cong., 2nd sess., Mar. 1875, serial 1629.

"It is surprising that a very able graduate": New York Times, Jan. 6, 1875.

198 *The Sheridan-Belknap* 'banditti' *telegrams were reprinted:* Gillette, p. 124.

"Manufacturing sensational protests": Philip Sheridan to William Belknap, Jan. 7, 1875, quoted in Gillette, p. 124.

"It was no riot; it was an absolute massacre": Philip Sheridan to Ulysses S. Grant, Aug. 2, 1866; see also Hollandsworth, frontispiece.

More surprising were the sympathetic public meetings: At Faneuil Hall, where abolitionist oratory had shaken the rafters, where the Fugitive Slave Act and *Dred Scott* had been denounced, now resolutions of censure condemning Grant, Sheridan, and the government's actions in Louisiana were drawn up. On January 15, Wendell Phillips, the "Golden Trumpet" of the abolitionist movement, defended the legality of the federal government's acts in the South, warning that Southern blacks were the true victims of any Northern resolution against Grant and Sheridan. His words were greeted by *boos* and remarks such as "Sit down!" and "That's played out!" The meeting's resolutions were passed over Phillips's objections. See *New York Times,* Jan. 16, 1875; see also Korngold, *Two Friends,* pp. 328–29.

The vehemence of the national reaction: See Tunnell, *Edge of the Sword,* pp. 184–231.

"The men of Vicksburg would not submit": Nordhoff, pp. 74–75.

199 *"Every true woman":* Wharton, p. 183.

"Returned to the fold of the Democracy in sackcloth and ashes": Lynch, *Reminiscences of an Active Life,* p. 148.

200 *Moreover, Morgan's résumé:* Lemman, p. 101.

201 *"I did not believe that they intended":* Testimony of A. T. Morgan, "Mississippi in 1875."

"You can have no objection": An account of the Yazoo riot appears in the *Yazoo City Democrat,* Sept. 7, 1875.

"My friend, I fought four years": Albert Morgan to Adelbert Ames, Sept. 9, 1875, quoted in Ames, *Adelbert Ames,* pp. 420–21.

202 *"These white liners will do anything":* Adelbert Ames to Blanche Butler Ames, Sept. 2, 1876, quoted in Ames, *Chronicles,* pp. 156–57.

"This house does not seem a natural place": Adelbert Ames to Blanche Butler Ames, Aug. 7, 1874; Adelbert Ames to Blanche Butler Ames, Aug. 2, 1874; Adelbert Ames to Blanche Butler Ames, Aug. 12, 1874; quoted in Ames, *Adelbert Ames,* pp. 399, 396–97, 401.

"Trimmed fantastically and patriotically": Brough, "The Clinton Riot," *Publications of the Mississippi Historical Society.*

"There is no doubt [the riot] had its origin": Undated clippings from *Cincinnati Commercial,* early to mid Sept. 1875, Blanche Kelso Bruce Papers, Library of Congress.

203 *"The thing opened just like lightning":* Testimony of E. B. Welbourne, "Mississippi in 1875."

"[Whites] . . . chased [the blacks] for miles and miles": Undated clippings from *Cincinnati Commercial,* early to mid Sept. 1875, Blanche Kelso Bruce Papers.

"What can we do? . . . It looks like Judgment": Testimony of D. C. Crawford, "Mississippi in 1875."

The death toll included: Undated clippings from *Cincinnati Commercial,* early to mid Sept. 1875, Blanche Kelso Bruce Papers; see also Testimony of D. C. Crawford, "Mississippi in 1875."

Two of the whites killed: Rable, pp. 155–56.

204 *"Oh, we didn't do much":* Undated clippings from *Cincinnati Commercial,* early to mid Sept. 1875, Blanche Kelso Bruce Papers.

"They went to a house where there was an old black man": Margaret Ann Caldwell, quoted in *New York Times,* Aug. 7, 1876.

"You all had a big dinner yesterday": Testimony of Margaret Ann Caldwell, "Mississippi in 1875."

"I beg you most fulley [sic] to send": *Senate Reports,* 44th Cong., 1st sess., "Docu-

mentary Evidence," quoted in Wharton, "The Race Issue in the Overthrow of Reconstruction in Mississippi," *Phylon.*

205 *"Domestic violence prevails in various parts of this State":* Adelbert Ames to President Grant, Sept. 8, 1875, quoted in Harris, pp. 663–64.

"As the Governor of a State, I made a demand": Quoted in St. Clair, p. 84.

"Ames so admired Bruce": Ames wanted Bruce to serve as his lieutenant governor because he imagined that he himself might eventually return to the U.S. Senate. He sought a man with a reputation so solid that the legislature, when the time came, would be willing to accept him as successor, freeing Ames for duty in Washington. When Bruce informed Ames he was not interested, Ames chose Alexander K. Davis, a state legislator from Noxubee County. Installing Davis as lieutenant governor would satisfy the black contingent in the state legislature, but it meant that, in all likelihood, Ames would never get to return to the Senate in Washington. As Ames's wife wrote to her mother back north, "In Mississippi the Lieut. Gov. becomes Governor as soon as the Governor leaves the state and if he is inclined to be troublesome this gives a fine opportunity to do many objectionable things." Such a crisis did occur in spring 1874 when Davis, taking advantage of Ames's absence on business in New Orleans, began making appointments and issuing pardons that lacked the governor's approval. State officials had to telegraph Ames and beg his immediate return. See Blanche Butler Ames to Sarah Butler, May 9, 1874, quoted in Ames, *Adelbert Ames,* p. 395.

"The white boy gave little heed to lessons": New York Times, Mar. 18, 1898.

206 *It was his misfortune to be present:* Stiles, p. 95.

"Quantrill's band certainly would not have spared": Kansas City Times, Oct. 17, 1886; St. Clair, pp. 263–64.

207 *"In the midst of their vassalage": Congressional Record,* 45th Cong., 2nd sess., pp. 382–83.

"The logical sequence to the freedom of the negro": Montgomery, pp. 267–68.

"[Florey] had a big drum at his office": Ibid., p. 272.

"He stands very straight and is very dignified": Washington Bee, July 21, 1883, quoting *Boston Herald;* quoted in St. Clair, pp. 253–54.

208 *He "had outgrown the degradation and ignorance of slavery":* Bruce to the *Kansas City Times,* Oct. 17, 1886; quoted in Urofsky, "Blanche K. Bruce," *Journal of Mississippi History.*

By late 1872 Bruce had twenty-one schools: Harris, "Blanche K. Bruce of Mississippi," in Rabinowitz, pp. 8–9. In the 1880s Bruce became interested in Booker T. Washington's ideas about industrial education, and after a visit to Washington's school at Tuskegee, he joined a group of Mississippians trying to establish a similar institute to serve young blacks from Arkansas and Mississippi.

209 *"False doctrine of despotic sovereignty": New York Times,* June 25, 1874.

"The most responsible citizens in Mississippi": St. Clair, p. 85.

Alcorn showed him the ultimate disrespect: Simmons, p. 703. Bruce was rescued by Senator Roscoe Conkling of New York. "When the names of the new Senators were called out for them to go up and take the oath, all the others except myself were escorted by their colleagues," Bruce later said. "Mr. Alcorn made no motion to escort me, but was buried behind a newspaper, and I concluded I would go it alone. I had got about half way up the aisle when a tall gentleman stepped up to me and said: 'Excuse me, Mr. Bruce, I did not until this moment see that you were without an escort. Permit me. My name is Conkling,' and he linked his arm in mine and we marched up to the desk together." Bruce so esteemed Conkling's gesture he named his only son, born in 1879, Roscoe Conkling Bruce. See Bruce's letter to Conkling, Sept. 21, 1879, in St. Clair, pp. 280–81. Senator Conkling would perform a similar service a year later for Frederick Douglass at the Centennial Exposition in Philadelphia, when an attempt was made to keep Douglass from taking his seat on a reviewing stand.

An "excited imagination": New York Tribune, Sept. 21, 1875.

The New York Times *proposed that if the Republicans:* New York Times, Sept. 16, 1875.

10. The Eternal Fitness of Things

211 *"The whole public are tired":* Grant, vol. 26, p. 314n.

"This flippant utterance": Adelbert Ames to E. Benjamin Andrews, May 24, 1895, J. W. Garner Papers, Mississippi State Archives; see also Wharton, p. 194.

"I suggest that you take all lawful means": Grant, vol. 26, p. 314n; Lemman, p. 123.

212 *"Taking advantage of Grant's":* Grant, vol. 26, pp. 312–13; Gillette, p. 157; Lemman, pp. 122–23.

"I have taken steps to put all the arms": Adelbert Ames to Blanche Butler Ames, Sept. 22, 1875, in Ames, *Chronicles,* vol. 2, p. 191; see also Lemman, pp. 125–26.

"The paradox of law enforcement": Zuczek, *Encyclopedia of Reconstruction,* vol. 1, p. 414.

"A hyena in human form": Hinds County Gazette, Oct. 13, 1875.

213 *"Election day may find our voters":* Adelbert Ames to Blanche Butler Ames, Oct. 8 and 12, 1875, Ames, *Adelbert Ames,* pp. 431–32, 433–34.

"Domestic violence prevails": Adelbert Ames to President Grant, Sept. 8, 1875, ibid., p. 424.

214 *Having noticed that many of the so-called:* Testimony of George K. Chase, "Mississippi in 1875: Report of the Select Committee to Inquire into the Mississippi Election of 1875," GPO, Washington, 1876.

"The [Democratic] citizens expressed": Ibid.

"Notwithstanding the apparent injustice": Undated clippings from *Cincinnati Commercial,* early to mid Sept. 1875, Blanche Kelso Bruce Papers, Library of Congress.

215 *"The city of Jackson was almost literally filled":* Testimony of Adelbert Ames, "Mississippi in 1875."

"One smart nigger in some localities": Testimony of George K. Chase, ibid.

"Sublit had a band of . . . about 100 armed men": Ibid.

These efforts at intimidation: Rable, p. 161; also see Testimony of Adelbert Ames, "Mississippi in 1875."

With the election over, the time had come: Testimony of Margaret Ann Caldwell, ibid.; also see *New York Times,* Aug. 7, 1876.

217 *"I have never read of such depravity":* Adelbert Ames to Blanche Butler Ames, Aug. 31, 1875, in Ames, *Adelbert Ames,* p. 419.

"Some of our party are indignant": Adelbert Ames to Blanche Butler Ames, Oct. 15, 1875, ibid., pp. 439–40.

Ames didn't know it but he was fortunate: Wells, "Reconstruction and Its Destruction in Hinds County," *Mississippi Historical Publications,*; quoted in Ames, *Adelbert Ames,* p. 436.

219 *"What surprises me . . . Mr. President":* Lynch, *Reminiscences of an Active Life,* pp. 173–75.

220 *In the difficult fall 1875 election:* Ibid., pp. 181–86.

"Whose Captain was one Charles Caldwell": Ames, *Chronicles,* pp. 335–37. These allegations were also shared with the congressional select committee investigating the 1875 election in Mississippi by Hiram Revels; see Testimony of Hiram Revels, "Mississippi in 1875."

221 *"Their object is to restore the Confederacy":* Garner, p. 402.

"He had given the state an excellent administration": Lynch, *Reminiscences of an Active Life,* p. 187.

"In one phrase, hostility to the negro": Testimony of Adelbert Ames, "Mississippi in 1875"; see also *New York Times,* May 2, 1876.

222 *"Invigorated by the free air": New York Times,* Aug. 26, 1873.

223 *"I desire to inform the members of the Senate": New Orleans Republican,* Feb. 11, 1872.

"The period of slavery was itself so monstrous": New National Era, Jan. 2, 1873.

224 *"As a father, I know him to be affectionate": Congressional Record,* 44th Cong., 1st sess., pp. 1444–45.

"Knocking at the door": New National Era, Jan. 15, 1874.

225 *"I will state to the Senate that since the adjournment": Congressional Record,* 43rd Cong., 1st sess., p. 775.

"That was really, and in fact the end": Warmoth, p. 236. Warmoth found himself the subject of a public scandal later that year when, on December 26, he stabbed the New Orleans journalist Daniel C. Byerly in a street altercation over published insults regarding Warmoth's political career in Louisiana. The killing was ruled justifiable homicide — Byerly had assaulted Warmoth with a cane — and the ex-governor was freed after being briefly held in jail. See *New York Times,* Dec. 27 and 28, 1874.

"Let the investigation proceed": New Orleans Republican, Feb. 7, 1873.

Both addressed that body on June 8, 1874: Congressional Record, 43rd Cong., 1st sess., appendix, pp. 426–38.

226 *"Prima facie title to admission": New York Times,* Feb. 9, 1875.

227 *"Under these circumstances": Congressional Record,* 44th Cong., 1st sess., pp. 1444–45.

In an executive session of the Senate: New Orleans Times, Feb. 17, 1876. Bruce was so angry, he initially refused to meet with Grant but was coaxed into it by colleagues. Bruce later became a leading supporter of Grant's bid for a possible third term at the 1880 Republican convention.

"In the country the tides were changing": Haskins, p. 222.

11. Black Thursday

230 *"Fellow citizens, rights impose duties":* Elliott's remarks in *New National Era,* Mar. 19, 1874.

"Blinded by long confinement": DeForest, *Miss Ravenel's Conversion,* p. 348.

"The only thing he wouldn't *steal"*: Bowers, p. 76.
"Somewhat like the charge of communism": Holt, p. 196.

231 *"Misgovernment works its own suicide"*: Elliott's remarks in *New National Era,* Mar. 19, 1874.
"With the courage and good sense": *Charleston Courier,* quoted and remarked upon in *New York Times,* Feb. 21, 1874.

232 *"Together, then," Lamson speculates:* Lamson, Peggy, p. 199.
She hypothesizes further: Ibid., p. 200.

233 *The* News & Courier *termed this maneuver: Charleston News & Courier,* Dec. 17, 1875.
"South Carolina, noble old mother": *Charlotte Observer,* quoted in *Charleston News & Courier,* Dec. 21, 1875.
Even the Republican Daily Union-Herald *feared: Columbia Union-Herald,* quoted in *Charleston News & Courier,* Dec. 20, 1875.
"With muskets on our shoulders": Woody, "Franklin J. Moses Jr., Scalawag Governor of South Carolina," *North Carolina Historical Review.*
"To Africanize the state": *News & Courier,* Dec. 18, 1875; Lamson, Peggy, pp. 223–24.
"One immediate effect": Quoted in Allen, p. 195.

234 *"I cannot attend your annual supper"*: *Charleston News & Courier,* Dec. 23, 1875.
"A rumpus has begun in South Carolina": Allen, p. 221.

235 *By the end of the Civil War it was:* MacDowell, "Hamburg: A Village of Dreams," *South Carolina Magazine*; see also Williamson, p. 267.
"If there should ever be a black monarchy": Higginson, pp. 43–44. Rivers was such a fine physical specimen that, like Smalls, he had been sent north during the war to promote the idea of making slaves into soldiers. In New York City, however, the sight of the tall, coal-black sergeant in a federal uniform disturbed passersby, and a riot nearly ensued. Rivers himself held off the mob until police arrived.

236 *He came home, it was written:* Avary, p. 161.
"One of the most malignant of the unreconstructed rebels": Morgan, James M., pp. 362, 373.

237 *"[McKie's death] exasperated his friends"*: *Charleston News & Courier,* July 11, 1876.
"Those of the meanest character": Martin, p. 210.
"Begged for his life, but in vain": Attorney General William Stone's report, July 12, 1876, quoted in Allen, pp. 313–18.
The rifle clubs then joined: Charleston News & Courier, July 11, 1876, and *New York Times,* July 24, 1876.

238 *It condemned the cowardly killing of "negro prisoners"*: See coverage of *Charleston News & Courier,* July 10, 11, and 12, 1876.
As the Charleston Journal of Commerce *observed:* Quoted in Allen, p. 320.
"Shame and disgust must fill the breast of every man": Daniel Chamberlain to U.S. senator T. J. Robertson, July 13, 1876; quoted in Allen, p. 319.

239 *"We have supported Governor Chamberlain's reform measures"*: *Charleston News & Courier,* Aug. 10, 1876; quoted in Holt, p. 200.
"The late unwarrantable slaughter": *New York Times,* July 24, 1876.
"Remember," Cain told his followers: New York Times, July 21, 1876.

240 *To Chamberlain, the Indian fighters' fate:* Daniel Chamberlain to U.S. senator T. J. Roberston, July 13, 1876, quoted in Allen, p. 319.
The debate in Congress about troop deployment: Gillette, p. 35.

241 *"The presence of the troops was most providential": Congressional Record,* 44th Cong., 2nd sess., appendix, p. 218; quoted in Packwood, p. 19.
When white congressmen seemed unable to grasp: Congressional Record, 44th Cong., 1st sess., p. 4645.
242 *Robert Smalls also worked to ensure that Hamburg:* Uya, p. 95; see also *Congressional Record,* 44th Cong., 1st sess., pp. 4605–4607, 4641–44.
In their correspondence, Chamberlain pointed out: Daniel Chamberlain to President Grant, July 22, 1876, quoted in Allen, p. 322.
Grant responded that he too feared: President Grant to Daniel Chamberlain, July 26, 1876, quoted in Allen, p. 325.
243 *"Waved the bloody shirt":* Tillman, "The Struggles of '76,"Charleston Historical Society. The exact origin of the red shirt uniform used by Democrats during Reconstruction is unclear. Some scholars suspect it was inspired by the costume of the revolutionaries who rode with the famous Italian military leader of the 1860s, Giuseppe Garibaldi. See Zuczek, *Encyclopedia of Reconstruction,* vol. 2.
245 *"There has been so much corruption":* Bowers, p. 498.
247 *Belknap also had much to fear from any further scrutiny: Nation,* Mar. 9, 1876.
"Showed symptoms of mental agony": New York Tribune, Mar. 6, 1876.
"Considering the official rank of Mr. Belknap": The Nation, Mar. 9, 1876.
248 *"The albatross of Reconstruction": Vicksburg Monitor,* undated clipping in "Mississippi in 1875: Report of the Select Committee to Inquire into the Mississippi Election of 1875," Washington GPO, 1876.
His precise, elegant manners and well-turned phrases: Martin, p. 202.
Visiting the legislature one day: Avary, p. 357.
249 *Among other steps, the expert suggested:* Tillman, "The Struggles of '76."
"Every Democrat must feel honor bound": Martin, p. 211.
250 *Gary was the descendant:* Sophie M. Fair, "Distinguished Confederate War Record of Ge. M. W. Gary," imprint of article from the *Southern Herald* and *Working Man of New York and Columbia, South Carolina,* Feb. 13, 1878, in "Martin Gary," vertical file, South Carolina Room, Charleston Public Library.
"He goes off in conversation like a skyrocket": Bowers, pp. 502–3.
251 *"They do not claim to be Americans": New York Times,* Oct. 13, 1876.
252 *"As a slave, he was faithful to us":* "Wade Hampton" entry in *Appleton's Cyclopedia,* compiled 1887–89; see edited *Appleton's Cyclopedia* (2001) at Virtualology.com.
"He was a big, powerful, athletic man": Williams, Alfred B., *Hampton and His Red Shirts,* p. 89.
"Straightout-ism, with its threat and bluster": Charleston News & Courier, May 9, 1876.
253 *Several whites, including Gary, challenged Dawson to duel:* Clark, pp. 64–66. Francis Dawson engaged in a war of insults in print with both Gary and *Journal of Commerce* editor Robert Barnwell Rhett Jr., while he steadfastly refused to duel, on religious grounds. He was known to editorialize against the practice. However, for all his principled opposition to mindless bloodshed, Dawson met a violent and somewhat tawdry end in 1889. Helene Marie Burdayron, a young governess who lived in his home, had aroused his protective or perhaps amorous feelings, and when rumors reached him that she was being pursued by a neighbor, Dr. Thomas McDow, Dawson became incensed. He confronted McDow, who denied seeking the girl's favors; Dawson then allegedly rushed at McDow, who drew a gun. In a

sensational murder trial, McDow was acquitted; the court ruled that he had killed Dawson in self-defense. See Clark, pp. 215–24.

"An audacious, masterly somersault": Sass, pp. 42–43.

Calling Rainey "a very light mulatto, of limited ability": Charleston News & Courier, Sept. 14, 1876.

"Rest assured of this": Ullman, p. 444.

254 *"I pledge my faith":* Jarrell, p. 73.

"Like a beet": New York Times, Dec. 27, 1876.

The Hampton forces went out of their way: Avary, pp. 360–61.

"The only way to bring about prosperity": Quoted in Bowers, p. 515.

As early as 1868, the New York Times *had warned: New York Times,* Aug. 15, 1868.

255 *"Never has there been so general an uprising": Charleston News & Courier,* Sept. 18, 1876.

256 *At one rally in Manning:* "Recollections of a Red Shirter." Undated clipping from *The State Magazine,* Reconstruction vertical file, South Carolina Room, Charleston Public Library.

This ostensibly fair: Uya, pp. 100–1; *New York Times,* Oct. 20, 1876; Select Committee on Recent Elections in South Carolina, House of Representatives, 44th Cong., 2nd sess., misc. document 31, part 3, pp. 197–99; also Allen, pp. 374–77. Political violence also flared that fall at Cainhoy and around Ellenville, South Carolina.

12. A Dual House

258 *"I often peeped into its spacious windows":* Douglass, *Life and Times,* pp. 487–93, quoted in Fleming, p. 89.

259 *"Patriotic and philanthropic citizens":* "Report from the Select Committee on the Freedman's Savings and Trust Co.," *Report No. 440,* printed Apr. 2, 1880, 46th Cong., 2nd sess.

"The need for such an institution": Resolution in the Senate of the United States, Apr. 2, 1880, Mr. Bruce, Chair, Select Committee on the Freedman's Savings and Trust Company, quoted in St. Clair, p. 147.

260 *"At Charleston, S.C., we have a choice property": New National Era,* Mar. 10, 1870.

261 *"Married to a corpse":* Douglass, *Life and Times,* p. 493, quoted in Fleming, p. 93.

On June 28, 1874, the day Douglass: Foner, *Forever Free,* p. 194.

262 *The nearly yearlong Senate inquiry:* Du Bois, p. 600.

Many reports of corruption: Fleming, pp. 62–63.

In other testimony, General Howard: Gilbert, "The Comptroller of the Currency and the Freedman's Savings Bank," *Journal of Negro History.*

"Sane and honest men could so trifle": Resolution in the Senate of the United States, Apr. 2, 1880, Mr. Bruce, Chair, Select Committee on the Freedman's Savings and Trust Company, quoted in St. Clair, pp. 291, 293.

"Pleaded forgetfulness or ignorance": Ibid., p. 293.

263 *As the historian James M. McPherson:* McPherson, *The Abolitionist Legacy,* p. 75.

In the wake of the bank's collapse: Smith, p. 37.

The deal itself soon became infamous: Morris, *Fraud of the Century,* pp. 1–5.

264 *"By God, sir, I'll not do it":* Burton, "Race and Reconstruction," *Journal of Social History.*

265 *On November 30, the Democrats: Charleston News & Courier,* Dec. 4, 1876.

266 *"We have just seen a brave, honest, patriotic man": Charleston News & Courier,* Dec. 2, 1876.
"A defeated administration that has to be upheld": Charleston News & Courier, Dec. 1, 1876.
"The scene in the House . . . is picturesque": Charleston News & Courier, Dec. 2, 1876. William A. Wheeler, an upstate New York congressman, was Hayes's running mate.
267 *"The Mackey house members":* Guignard, "How the Wallace House Met in Carolina Hall," Charleston Public Library.
One representative had been described as a "ringtail roarer": Charleston News & Courier, Dec. 4, 1876.
The threat of physical confrontation: Avary, p. 368.
269 *"I don't care for myself . . . but I do care for the poor colored men":* Williams, Charles Richard, *Life of Rutherford B. Hayes,* vol. 1, pp. 488–89, 496; Woodward, *Reunion and Reaction,* p. 26, and Logan, *Betrayal of the Negro,* p. 15.
"An arrangement could not be arrived at": Stanley Matthews to Daniel Chamberlain, Mar. 4, 1877, quoted in Allen, pp. 469–70; *New York Times,* Dec. 10, 1876.
270 *"I desire to aid and relieve President Hayes":* Daniel Chamberlain to Stanley Matthews, Mar. 7, 1877, quoted in Allen, pp. 470–71.
"To be able to put an end as speedily as possible": W. K. Rogers to Daniel Chamberlain, Mar. 23, 1877, quoted in Allen, pp. 472–73.
271 *"You became the victims of every form of persecution":* Daniel Chamberlain, "To the Republicans of South Carolina," Apr. 1877; quoted in Allen, pp. 480–82.
"To think that Hayes could go back on us now": W. F. Rodenbach to Daniel Chamberlain, Apr, 4 1877, cited in Burton, "Race and Reconstruction: Edgefield County, South Carolina."
"Unanimous in the belief that to prolong the contest": Robert B. Elliot et al. to Daniel Chamberlain, Apr. 10, 1877; quoted in Allen, pp. 482–83.
April 10 was the day chosen: Charleston News & Courier, Apr. 11, 1877.

13. Exodusting

274 *"The Negro . . . long deemed to be too indolent and stupid":* Douglass, "Negro Exodus from the Gulf States," Sept. 12, 1879, Frederick Douglass Papers, Library of Congress.
Robert Finley, the Presbyterian minister: Finley was inspired by the example of Paul Cuffee, a black New England shipowner who a few years earlier had sailed successfully to Sierra Leone with thirty-eight black American emigrationists.
The ACS, in collaboration: Moses, p. 42. American interests directly controlled Liberia until 1847 when, in order to keep it from becoming a British colony, it was made a free and independent republic.
"Of all classes of our population": The ACS Tenth Annual Report, published in 1827, is quoted in Streifford, "The American Colonization Society," *Journal of Southern History.*
275 *"The fostering agency of Liberian colonization": New National Era,* Feb. 17, 1870.
"We live here — have lived here": Douglass, "Colonization," *North Star,* Jan. 26, 1849; see Douglass, *Selected Speeches and Writings,* pp. 125–26.
In its first half-century of existence, the ACS: New National Era, Dec. 19, 1872.

The shifting and sometimes contradictory beliefs: Delany, "Political Destiny of the Colored Race," quoted in Rollin, p. 337; see also Hahn, p. 122.

276 *"Deep rooted prejudices":* Jefferson, pp. 189–90.

"Do you intend to turn the three millions of slaves": Congressional Globe, 37th Cong., 2nd sess.

"A moral fitness in the idea": Eulogy on Henry Clay, July 16, 1852, quoted in Wesley, "Lincoln's Plan for Colonizing the Emancipated Negroes," *Journal of Negro History.*

During a debate with Stephen Douglas in 1854: Lincoln-Douglas Debates, Oct. 16, 1854; ibid.

"The enterprise is a difficult one": Lincoln speech, June 26, 1857; ibid.

277 *"There is an unwillingness on the part of our people":* Lincoln, quoted in Foner, *Forever Free,* p. 48.

An "attempt to roll back Niagara to its source": Goodwin, p. 469.

On December 31, 1862, the federal government contracted: Wesley, "Lincoln's Plan for Colonizing the Emancipated Negroes," *Journal of Negro History.*

278 *"Fifty families in Granville County":* G. Rogers to American Colonization Society, Mar. 9, 1879, ACS Papers, Library of Congress.

And though the interested parties: Painter, *Exodusters,* p. 140.

279 *Patterson's speech on November 26, 1877: New York Times,* Nov. 27, 1877.

One of Butler's initial efforts: Congressional Record, 51st Cong., 1st sess., p. 972.

280 *It will not do to shut our eyes:* Quoted in *Charleston News & Courier,* Jan. 9, 1882; see Tindall, pp. 177–78.

The Columbia Daily Register *denounced: Columbia Daily Register,* August 19, 1877; quoted in Tindall, p. 159.

The Liberian relocation project did have a millenarian aspect: Charleston News & Courier, Aug. 21, 1877, quoted in Tindall, p. 157.

Bruce explained that he had begun to see: Blanche K. Bruce to *Cincinnati Commercial,* Feb. 19, 1878; quoted in St. Clair, pp. 273–80.

281 *In Congress, Bruce was consistently humane:* Bruce's 1879 bill to create a permanent Mississippi River Improvement Commission was one of the first attempts to bring federal oversight to the issue of flood control on the lower Mississippi. Several damaging floods had occurred between the end of the Civil War and 1874, and during that period more than one hundred miles of levees had collapsed. Bruce proposed a commission to coordinate efforts to protect the alluvial lands adjoining the river as well as a plan for the "correction and deepening" of channels for navigation. He, like many others, believed federal involvement was necessary because the river was an interstate waterway, and local fixes had always been piecemeal. As the Ohio congressman James A. Garfield had said, "The statesmanship of America must grapple with the problem of this mighty stream; it is too vast for any state to handle; too much for any authority less than that of the nation itself to manage" (Garfield, quoted in Humphreys, p. 40). Congress failed to support Bruce's proposal. Federal coordination of flood control along the Mississippi would not begin in earnest until after the devastating flood of 1927. See "An Act to Provide for the Organization of the Mississippi River Improvement Commission," H.R. Bill 4318, U.S. Senate, 45th Cong., 3rd sess., Feb. 6, 1879.

But his vision of a coming racial enlightenment: Blanche K. Bruce to *Cincinnati Commercial,* Feb. 19, 1878, quoted in St. Clair, pp. 273–80.

282 *The* Azor *tacked out of Charleston Harbor:* Williams, Alfred, *The Liberian Exodus,* pp. 1–6.

Forty-two days out from Charleston: Tindall, pp. 162–65.

283 *The so-called Exoduster Movement:* The idea of black westward migration had been in the air since the 1860s, when debates over land distribution to the freedmen in the South dovetailed with enthusiasm for western lands made available under the Homestead Act of 1862. The reformer Sojourner Truth, working among freed people in the Washington area immediately after the war, envisioned a system of land distribution in the West similar to that of Indian reservations, where blacks could become educated, work for a living, and be safe from hostile whites.

"The government of every Southern state": Douglass, "Negro Exodus from the Gulf States."

As one migrant told a reporter: New York Daily Herald, Apr. 17, 1879.

"Voting is widely regarded at the North": Atlantic Monthly, Aug. 1879.

"Live as happy as a big sunflower": New York Tribune, Dec. 19, 1878.

284 *"The Negro's necessities have developed an offensive race": Atlantic Monthly,* Aug. 1879.

"I know, within the last three years": St. Louis Globe Democrat, Mar. 12, 1879, quoted in Athearn, p. 10.

But President Grant, on December 6, 1876, sent to Congress: Executive Documents, 44th Cong., 2nd sess., no. 30; *Senate Reports,* 46th Cong., 2nd sess., part 1; quoted in Van Deusen, "The Exodus of 1879," *Journal of Negro History.*

285 *"The Southern white man is inconvertibly fixed in the belief": New York Times,* Apr. 7, 1879.

"Political tricksters, land speculators": Douglass, "Negro Exodus from the Gulf States."

The magazine Puck *neatly captured:* Cartoon by Joseph Keppler, *Puck,* Apr. 16, 1879, Prints and Photographs Division, Library of Congress; Foner, *Forever Free,* p. 184.

"It is not surprising that the Negro looks": Windom and Blair, "The Proceedings of a Migration Convention and Congressional Action Respecting the Exodus of 1879," *Journal of Negro History.*

"Where John Brown's soul": Missouri Republican, Apr. 17, 1879; Athearn, p. 32.

"The humiliating fact": Douglass, "Negro Exodus from the Gulf States."

The New Orleans Times *in April 1879 urged planters: New Orleans Times,* Apr. 22, 1879; Painter, *Exodusters,* p. 241.

286 *"You may . . . judge of my surprise": Louisianian,* Mar. 15, 1879; Painter, *Exodusters,* p. 181.

He also heard a number of completely groundless reports: Athearn, p. 245.

"There is no doubt in my mind": Louisianian, Mar. 15, 1879.

287 *"Look into affairs and see the true condition of our race":* Hahn, p. 319.

"You can't find out anything till you get amongst them": Windom and Blair, "The Proceedings of a Migration Convention and Congressional Action Respecting the Exodus of 1879," *Journal of Negro History.*

Adams and his council wrote letters of appeal: Ibid.

288 *"The weather and roads here enable you":* Ibid.

Educated blacks he derided as "tonguey men": St. Louis Post Dispatch, undated clipping from 1879, in Singleton Scrapbook, Kansas State Historical Society; quoted in

Fleming, "'Pap' Singleton, the Moses of the Colored Exodus," *American Journal of Sociology.*

"Those who had been leading the colored people": Foner, *Freedom's Lawmakers,* pp. 156–57.

289 *"Where peas would not sprout":* Fleming, "'Pap' Singleton, the Moses of the Colored Exodus," *American Journal of Sociology.*

"I had studied it all out": Senate Report No. 693, Part 3, 46th Cong., 2nd sess., p. 379; quoted in Fleming, "'Pap' Singleton, the Moses of the Colored Exodus," *American Journal of Sociology.*

289 *"We have Mr. Singleton":* Singleton Scrapbook, Kansas State Historical Society; quoted in Painter, *Exodusters,* p. 129.

290 *The* Vicksburg Commercial Daily Advertiser *complained: Vicksburg Commercial Advertiser,* May 6, 1879.

291 *If such a policy [of federally aided black migration]: New York Times,* Feb. 17, 1879.

Windom believed that blacks had the right to depart: Congressional Record, 45th Cong., 3rd sess., p. 483.

"If the advice of leading colored men": St. Clair, p. 137.

292 *They pointed to the example:* Salisbury, p. 191; *New York Times,* Jan. 23, 1879.

To request half a million dollars from Congress: St. Clair, pp. 143–44; also see Tindall, pp. 169–70.

"The wretched dupes of Mr. Windom's windy rhetoric": Washington Post, Dec. 18, 1879.

"Outrages never before practiced upon any free people": Salisbury, p. 192.

293 *Hayes quickly disavowed any "endorsement":* Athearn, pp. 145–46.

"Fluttering in rags and wretchedness": Douglass, "Negro Exodus from the Gulf States."

294 *"It is computed that up to date about 5,000 colored persons": New York Times,* Apr. 3, 1879.

One emigrant from Mississippi: Athearn, p. 26.

"There was an offer of $80 a month": St. Louis Republican, quoted in the *New York Herald,* Apr. 3, 1879.

"It is a matter of sincere regret": Louisianian, Mar. 29, 1879.

295 *"Until this matter is at least better understood": Louisianian,* Mar. 29, 1879.

Bruce was concerned that the exodus: Louisianian, Apr. 26, 1879.

"The sun is the colored man's friend": Missouri Republican, July 18, 1879, quoted in Athearn, p. 149.

"The freedman may lack education": New York Herald, Apr. 11, 1879.

"Bad as it is": Douglass, "The Negro as a Man" (speech), Frederick Douglass Papers.

296 *"Some say 'stay and fight it out'":* Brown, William Wells, *My Southern Home,* pp. 247–48.

"I doubt very much if I had found in the Constitution": New York Herald, May 13, 1879; see also Painter, *Exodusters,* p. 213.

297 *The "Exodus Committee," as it was dubbed:* Windom and Blair, "The Proceedings of a Migration Convention and Congressional Action Respecting the Exodus of 1879," *Journal of Negro History.* The Voorhees committee concluded that "on the whole, [we] express the positive opinion that the condition of the colored people

of the South is not only as good as could have been reasonably expected, but is better than if large communities were transferred to a colder and more inhospitable climate . . . When we come to consider the method in which the people were freed . . . and that for purposes of party politics these incompetent, ignorant, landless, homeless people, without any qualifications of citizenship . . . were suddenly thrown into political power, and the effort was made not only to place them upon an equality with their late masters, but to absolutely place them in front and hold them there by legislation, by military violence . . . when we consider these things no philosophical mind can behold their present condition . . . without wonder that their condition is as good as it is."

Windom protested the findings: Salisbury, pp. 193–95.

298 *"Thousands of dollars to find out":* Washington, *A New Negro,* p. 290; Wood, p. 267; Athearn, p. 225.

During 1870–80 the black population of Kansas: Reports of the U.S. Census, 1860, 1870, 1880.

Their new life was hardly without difficulty: By the mid-1880s Pap Singleton had soured on Kansas. He founded a new organization, the United Transatlantic Society (UTS), to promote an exodus to Liberia or Ethiopia. The reputation of "Old Pap" attracted numerous members, but the UTS never sailed anywhere. See Fleming, "'Pap' Singleton, the Moses of the Colored Exodus."

"They do not kill negroes here for voting": Windom and Blair, "The Proceedings of a Migration Convention and Congressional Action Respecting the Exodus of 1879"; see also Athearn, p. 205.

Fortunately for the new arrivals: Wood, pp. 274–76.

299 *"The exodus presented proof":* Painter, *Exodusters,* pp. 260–61.

"The Reconstruction dream of black assimilation": Harris, "Blanche K. Bruce of Mississippi," in *Southern Black Leaders of the Reconstruction Era,* Howard Rabinowitz, ed.

14. A Rope of Sand

300 *"Some men are born great":* Reuter, p. 249.

As Martin Gary proclaimed: Charleston News & Courier, June 4, 1878; Tindall, p. 26.

Tillman . . . was at heart: New York World, Sept. 30, 1895.

301 *He had been instrumental in founding Clemson:* Thomas G. Clemson was a wealthy widower (he'd married a daughter of John C. Calhoun) and owned a vast estate, formerly owned by Calhoun, named Fort Hill, in western South Carolina. Clemson ceded the site to the state for a public college at his death in 1888, stipulating in a codicil that it would be privately managed, a means of restricting enrollment to whites.

"They ring out the false": W. W. Ball, "An Episode in South Carolina Politics," Reconstruction pamphlet collection, Charleston Historical Society.

"You of the north": Congressional Record, 56th Cong., 1st sess., pp. 2242–45, quoted in Logan, p. 91; see also Press Clippings File, Benjamin Tillman Papers, Clemson University Library.

302 *"That we have good government now":* Tillman, "The Struggles of '76": An Address Delivered at the Red Shirt Reunion, Anderson, South Carolina, Aug. 25, 1909, Reconstruction pamphlet collection, Charleston Historical Society.

303 *Rainey pointed out: New York Tribune,* Dec. 19, 1878.

304 *"Thereby the time would be frittered away":* Joel W. Bowman to Benjamin H. Brewster, Nov. 2, 1882, South Carolina files, National Archives RG 60 (Justice Department).

"If you are to go back upon all pledges": Columbia Daily Register, July 7, 1878; Tindall, p. 29.

"If you once countenance fraud": Wade Hampton, quoted in Testimony of E.W.M. Mackay, "South Carolina in 1878," *Senate Report Serial 1840,* GPO, Washington, 1879.

306 *Long known as "the Negro's Paradise":* Simkins, p. 153.

"Shook their heads significantly": The Nation, Nov. 7, 1878.

The New York Times *wrote disapprovingly: New York Times,* Jan. 14, 1878.

307 *With the situation deadlocked:* Hahn, pp. 347–49.

"Eight hundred red-shirt men": Towne, pp. 289–91.

308 *Smalls was again in his element: Louisianian,* Jan. 10, 1880; *New York Times,* Jan. 10, 1880.

309 *In a speech delivered to Congress:* "An Honest Ballot Is the Safeguard of the Republic," speech of Hon. Robert Smalls, House of Representatives, Feb. 24, 1877, *Congressional Record,* 44th Cong., 2nd sess., appendix, pp. 123–36.

310 *Loyalty among blacks to the Party of Lincoln:* Uya, pp. 111–12.

So pervasive was the Democrats' dominance: New York Times, Jan. 13, 1878.

"Like a rope of sand": Charleston News & Courier, Sept. 3, 1880.

311 *"Polls were opened at unusual places": New York Times,* Dec. 15, 1880.

When the committee found Democratic fraud: Smalls v. Tillman, Congressional Record, 47th Cong., appendix, in Uya, pp. 113–15. This reversal involving Tillman fed the determination of the state's Democrats to move beyond polling-place fraud to more permanent methods of choking off black suffrage.

312 *"Less than a quarter of a century ago": Congressional Record,* 49th Cong., 1st sess., appendix, pp. 319–20, in Uya, pp. 123–25.

As a one-man bastion of power: Ibid., pp. 127–30.

No one had expected the new law: Persons violating the law would have to pay the aggrieved party $500 and could also be fined by the court or imprisoned for up to a year. Another clause ensured that "no citizen possessing all other qualifications . . . shall be disqualified for service as grand or petit juror" in any federal or state court "on account of race, color, or previous condition of servitude."

313 *"A thousand federal lawsuits and fines":* Quoted in *New York Times,* Mar. 6, 1875.

The New York Times *worried: New York Times,* Mar. 6, 1875.

314 *"A respectable-appearing colored man": New York Times,* Apr. 22 and 27, 1875; also Nov. 25, 1879.

"What good is the civil rights law": New York Times, June 12, 1875.

Mrs. Henry Jones of Philadelphia also found: New York Times, Sept. 29, 1875.

The judge fined Greenwall: New York Times, June 8 and 9, 1875.

In Virginia a hotel clerk named Newcomer: U.S. v. Newcomer, Feb. 29, 1876, Federal Cases, vol. 27, pp. 127–28.

315 *"Demanded to ride in the same cabin":* Ibid., vol. 10, pp. 1090–93.

The "separate" facilities offered to blacks: Franklin, p. 127.

316 *On June 9, 1876, a group: New York Times,* Mar. 23, 1877.

"If the states are to be allowed": John M. Harlan to John Harlan (son), Oct. 21, 1883, quoted in Yarbrough, p. 144.

317 *Little remembered today:* Bruce's ascent from obscurity was perhaps nowhere better illustrated than in a story he loved to tell that had its origin in the streets of prewar St. Louis. One day, when he was twelve or thirteen years old, he was commanded by a well-dressed white man to carry a heavy suitcase to the docks, where the man said he was hurrying to catch a steamboat. Bruce obediently hefted the suitcase onto his shoulder and carried it to the wharf, but once there, the white man grabbed his luggage and raced aboard his boat, rudely neglecting to pay the boy. Years later in the Senate, when Senator Lewis Vital Bogy from Missouri approached Bruce to ask for his vote on a measure important to his home state, Bruce studied Bogy carefully and then introduced himself as the young man he had long ago failed to compensate on the St. Louis waterfront. After recovering from his shock, the embarrassed Bogy offered at once to compound the original amount owed. The two men were said to have become friends. See Smith, pp. 25–26.

"A slender, shapely woman": Boston Journal, Jan. 29, 1879; *New York Tribune,* Dec. 1878; both in Clippings File, Blanche Kelso Bruce Papers, Library of Congress.

"A great big good natured lump of fat": Emma V. Brown to Emily Holland, Mar. 31, 1875, quoted in Sterling, *We Are Your Sisters,* p. 293; see also Gatewood, pp. 4–5.

"To promote social intercourse": Ibid., p. 4.

318 *"General Grant was less reserved in conversation": New York Times,* Dec. 7, 1878.

"Will again march to battle under the banner": Louisianian, Feb. 15, 1879.

319 *"The most* unreasonable disturbance *in Washington:* Simmons, p. 702.

"Mrs. Bruce is a lady of great personal beauty": Boston Journal, Jan. 29, 1879; *New York Tribune,* Dec. 1878; both in Clippings File, Blanche Kelso Bruce Papers.

"I know it would be the political ruin": Undated, untitled news clipping in Clippings File, Blanche Kelso Bruce Papers.

"I made up my mind to let the society question": Baltimore American, Jan, 25, 1880, in Clippings File, Blanche Kelso Bruce Papers.

320 *"Mr. Lynch has, we don't believe, elevated himself": Washington Bee,* Dec. 20, 1884.

321 *"Once let a black man get upon his person": Douglass's Monthly,* May 1861, pp. 452–53, and Aug. 1863, p. 852, quoted in Moses, p. 52.

322 *"Let's mark him as we mark hogs": New York Times,* Apr. 7, 1880.

323 *"If you think the rule is taught at West Point":* Marszalek, "A Black Cadet at West Point," *American Heritage.*

324 *"I am willing to go as far as the furthest":* Ambrose, p. 236. Thirteen black cadets were admitted to West Point in the half-century following the Civil War; only three graduated.

Gardiner, in response to Chamberlain: Marszalek, "A Black Cadet at West Point."

326 *Bradley, curiously, had argued:* See Vorenberg, pp. 239–40.

"It would be running the slavery argument": Civil Rights Cases, 109 U.S. 3, 3 S Ct 18 (1883); also see Vorenberg, p. 241.

As for the Fourteenth Amendment: Civil Rights Cases, 109 U.S. 3, 3 S Ct 18 (1883).

327 *"Sumner's Law," so nobly intended:* The part of the Civil Rights Act of 1875 making it illegal to deny black representation on juries was upheld by the Supreme Court in 1880 in *Ex parte Virginia* and *Strauder v. West Virginia.*

The Harlans voiced support: One Harlan family slave, Robert James Harlan, likely the justice's own half-brother, was allowed to go west in the gold rush of 1848, returned a wealthy man, and purchased his freedom for $500. He became a businessman and community leader in Cincinnati.

328 *"The most perfect despotism":* Quoted in Westin, "John Marshall Harlan and the Constitutional Rights of Negroes," *Yale Law Journal.*

"With the help of God": Przybyszewski, p. 47.

329 *"The memory of the historic part":* Harlan, pp. 108–14. A more private source may have also helped inspire the sanctity Harlan granted the cause of equal rights. His eldest daughter, Edith, had served as a teacher in an impoverished black elementary school in Washington and was the family member most personally committed to the eradication of racial injustice. As a representative of a younger generation, she espoused views that seemed progressive to her father. When she died prematurely in 1882 — only a year before Harlan would write his dissent in *Civil Rights Cases* — he was profoundly stricken. "Wherever I go, and whatever I may be doing," Harlan wrote to one of his sons, "her presence will be recognized in its influence upon me. She was to me not simply child, but companion. I am quite sure no character more noble and elevated ever appeared on this earth." John Harlan to James Harlan (son), Nov. 25, 1882, quoted in Yarbrough, p. 145.

"Constitutional provisions adopted in the interests": Civil Rights Cases, 109 U.S. 3, 3 S Ct 18 (1883).

330 *Only six years earlier: Munn v. Illinois,* 94 U.S. 113 (1877).

He was also troubled: Civil Rights Cases, 109 U.S. 3, 3 S Ct 18 (1883).

331 *It "should be scattered like the leaves of Autumn":* Frederick Douglass to John Harlan, Nov. 27, 1883, quoted in Yarbrough, p. 152.

"One more shocking development of that moral weakness": Civil rights advocates met at Lincoln Hall in Washington on October 22, 1883, a week after the unhappy court ruling. Resolutions were introduced demanding renewed legislative and political action on equal rights from both political parties and calling on black citizens everywhere to form civil rights associations through which "proper agitation" could be pursued. The failure of the white man's Congress and the white man's courts, it was agreed, had crystallized the need for intensified black organization and militancy. "Fellow citizens!" Frederick Douglass declared, "while slavery was the base line of American society . . . it admitted no quibbling, no narrow rules of legal or scriptural interpretations of Bible or Constitution . . . It was enough for it to be able to show the *intention* to get all it asked in the Courts or out of the Courts . . . O for a Supreme Court of the United States which shall be as true to the claims of humanity as the Supreme Court formerly was to the demands of slavery!" See Proceedings of the Civil Rights Meeting, held at Lincoln Hall, Washington, Oct. 22, 1883, Frederick Douglass Papers, Library of Congress; see also Douglass, *Selected Speeches and Writings,* pp. 685–93; *Chicago Tribune,* Feb. 6, 1875; *National Republican,* Mar. 1, 1875; *The Nation,* Mar. 4, 1875. Douglass quotations also appear in Douglass, *Life and Writings,* vol. 4, p. 393.

332 *"The nation's equalitarian aspirations":* McPherson, "Abolitionists and the Civil Rights Act of 1875," *Journal of American History.*

15. "The Negroes' Farewell"

333 *"Democracy has won a great victory":* Simkins, pp. 171–75; Logan, Rayford W., p. 74.

334 *"His white supremacy howlers": Beaufort New South,* Mar. 7, 1895.

They pointed out that Tillman's rationale: New York World, Sept. 30, Oct. 1, Nov. 7, 1895; quoted in Uya, pp. 138–39.

"The only course for reasonable and patriotic men": Chamberlain, "The Race Problem at the South," *Yale Review.*

"The answer must be, to those who devised": Chamberlain, "Reconstruction in South Carolina," *Atlantic Monthly.*

335 *"Cast down your bucket where you are":* Washington's remarks appear in Woodson, pp. 580–83.

337 *"The mephitic vapor that arises":* Wharton, pp. 213–14.

The outcry gradually subsided: The idea of other blacks taking part in the convention had been scotched early in the delegate-selection process when F.M.B. "Marsh" Cook, a black activist, was killed in a hail of bullets while canvassing in Jasper County. "The people of Jasper are to be congratulated that they will not be further annoyed by Marsh Cook," concluded the *Jackson Clarion-Ledger* in summarizing the crime. *Jackson Clarion-Ledger,* July 31, 1890; Wharton, pp. 210–11.

"The convention which met [in Columbia] in 1895": See Uya, pp. 139–51; see also *Journal of Proceedings,* South Carolina Constitutional Convention, Charles A. Calvo, State Printer, Columbia South Carolina, 1895, p. 12.

338 *"For millions of people now living": Charleston News & Courier,* Oct. 29, 1895.

"The greatest crime of the nineteenth century": New York World, Sept. 30, 1895.

"Slavery to the negro was a blessing in disguise": Charleston News & Courier, Oct. 25, 1895.

If there was anything encouraging: One of the other black delegates was the former congressman Thomas E. Miller, who, on account of his very light complexion, was known as "Canary Bird." Born into a free black family in Hilton Head and the grandson of Judge Thomas Heyward, a signatory of the Declaration of Independence, Miller had been educated at Lincoln University in Pennsylvania and then returned to South Carolina to serve as a lawyer and state legislator. He was in Congress from 1889 to 1891. Known for his candor, he once told Congress of his Southern white neighbors, "There is no people in the world more self-opinionated without cause, more bigoted without achievements, more boastful without a status, no people in the world so quick to misjudge their countrymen and to misstate historical facts of political economy and to impugn the motives of others. History does not record a civilized people who have been so contented with so little and who can feed so long on a worthless, buried past." See *Congressional Record,* 51st Cong., 2nd sess., pp. 2691–96; in Smith, p. 104.

339 *Tillman's own speech to the convention: Journal of Proceedings,* South Carolina Constitutional Convention, 1895, pp. 462–64.

340 *But Leslie was an easy target:* Mismanagement had plagued the land effort from the start. Purchase agents were impeded by a lack of solid information about what they were buying, as numerous plots of land had not been surveyed since the Revolutionary War, and the agents, many of whom hailed from the North, often did not know their way around the more isolated parts of the state. Many parcels were either overvalued or completely unsuited for cultivation; some turned out to be literally under water — swamplands that would require expensive drainage before they could be used. After Leslie was maneuvered out of his job, the black party operative Robert DeLarge stepped in, although he too proved incapable. By the time

more responsible leadership took the reins, the commission, its work never accepted by whites, was in desperate financial straits. It had spent nearly $750,000 on slightly more than 90,000 acres, twice what it had been directed to spend; and many of the lands were of substandard value. In February 1872 the legislation that had created the commission was repealed, ending the experiment.

"Can we not rise to the necessities": *Journal of Proceedings*, South Carolina Constitutional Convention, 1895, pp. 462–64.

341 *There were, as of the census of 1890: Columbia Daily Register*, Oct. 4, 1895, quotes the *New York World* article; statistics cited in Kindall, "The Question of Race in the South Carolina Constitutional Convention of 1895," *Journal of Negro History.*

"The doctrine so persistently taught": Miller, Mary J., pp. 16–21.

Smalls warned that Tillmanite abuses: Columbia State, Oct. 27, 1895.

342 *"I stand here the equal of any man"*: *Journal of Proceedings*, South Carolina Constitutional Convention, 1895, p. 476; see pp. 473–75 for Smalls's explanation of the case brought against him.

Smalls's "brilliant moral victory": New York press, Oct. 5, 1895, cited by Smalls in Miller, Mary J., pp. 24–25; in Uya, p. 145.

"The coons had the dogs up the tree": *Columbia State*, Oct. 4, 1895; in Uya, pp. 146–47.

343 *The U.S. Supreme Court would uphold:* See *Williams v. Mississippi*, 170 U.S. 213 (1898).

Strict discipline on the issue that mattered most: Brayton, p. 11.

"Then I'll walk home": Sterling, *Captain of the* Planter, p. 223.

James O'Hara, the son of a black mother and an Irish sea captain: Anderson, "James O'Hara of North Carolina: Black Leadership and Local Government," in Rabinowitz, p. 103.

345 *An unlettered, straight-talking man: Mobile Register*, June 18, 1874; in Smith, p. 83.

George H. White of North Carolina was to have the honor: Other nineteenth-century black Southern congressmen included John A. Hyman and Henry P. Cheatham of North Carolina; Charles E. Nash of Louisiana; and George W. Murray of South Carolina. Black representation from northern states began with the arrival in 1929 of Oscar DePriest of Illinois.

346 *White was also the first member of Congress:* In 1891, President Benjamin Harrison had proposed a federal law to stop lynching, but he did so in response to pressure from the Italian government after eleven Italian Americans were lynched in New Orleans on suspicion of having conspired in the assassination of Police Commissioner David C. Hennessey on October 15, 1890. Harrison's proposal received some discussion in Congress but was not presented in the form of a bill. See Dray, pp. 130–32.

347 *Edgefield was not a "new or imperfectly organized community"*: Proclamation of Daniel Chamberlain, June 1876; Allen, pp. 307–308.

348 *"Whenever the Constitution comes between"*: Simkins, p. 396.

Mistrials and acquittals" won "through the instrumentality": Allen, pp. 309–10.

349 *"I have examined the question and I am prepared"*: *Congressional Record*, 56th Cong., 1st sess., p. 1365.

"It is bad enough that North Carolina": *Raleigh News and Observer*, undated clipping, quoted in ibid., p. 1507.

351 *"Still sweetly sleeps in the room of the Committee"*: Ibid., 2nd sess., p. 1638.

"This, Mr. Chairman, is perhaps": Ibid., p. 1638; White tried to remain active in Republican politics in North Carolina, but threats of violence soon drove him from the state. In an act reminiscent of Richard "Daddy" Cain's, the founder of Lincolnville, White eventually bought two thousand acres in Cape May County, New Jersey, and as head of the George H. White Land Improvement Company founded the all-black community of Whitesboro, offering lots for $50 and up. White laid out the streets and supplied "portable" houses that could be easily erected. The impetus for White's purchase may have been the Wilmington, North Carolina, riot of 1898, which had forced a mass exodus of blacks from the city; some of Whitesboro's first inhabitants were from there. By 1906 the town had eight hundred inhabitants, a school, two churches, a railway station, a hotel owned by White, a post office, and a phone. Poet Paul Laurence Dunbar was an early partner in the Whitesboro plan.

Epilogue

354 *Radical optimists "living too frequently":* Gillette, p. 365.

"The trouble was . . . not that the grant of political liberty": Belz, "The New Orthodoxy in Reconstruction Historiography," *Reviews in American History.*

That commitment, W.E.B. Du Bois once imagined: Lynd, "Rethinking Slavery and Reconstruction," *Journal of Negro History.*

355 *The "moral debt" to black Americans:* Woodward, *Burden of Southern History,* p. 67.

356 *"There are those who say to you":* McCullough, p. 639; see also Foner, *Forever Free,* pp. 225–38.

361 *"Are the portraits of Hitler, Mussolini, Joe Stalin": Jackson Daily News,* Jan. 20, 1958.

Governor J. P. Coleman insisted: New York Times, Jan. 22, 1958.

362 *"Hardly can it be supposed":* Post, "A 'Carpetbagger' in South Carolina," *Journal of Negro History.*

"Who would have thought of this spectacle": St. Clair, pp. 174–75.

Bruce's great prestige, Fortune complained: T. Thomas Fortune to the *New York Times,* Aug. 14, 1883.

363 *"It is of supreme importance to us as a class": Louisianian,* Mar. 4, 1879.

She initially demurred: National Republican, July 6, 1878.

"He was one of the apostles of kindness": Washington Post, May 19, 1898.

364 *Elliott was allowed to address the convention:* One final honorific awaited Elliott when, in January 1881, he led a delegation of Southern black leaders to meet with president-elect Garfield at his home in Ohio. Elliott made the group's formal presentation, stressing the abuse to which Southern blacks were now increasingly subjected at the polls and in their daily work, factors that were leading many "to seek relief in strange and uncongenial parts of the country." A rumor emerged, however, that the president-elect had received the Elliott-led delegation with something less than full respect. According to T. Thomas Fortune, Garfield demanded to review a copy of the address Elliott intended to give during the visit and excised parts of which he did not approve, and "otherwise tampered with the document, so emasculating it as to destroy all its saliency." After Elliott had spoken, said Fortune, Garfield "advised the delegation to go home and study, and encourage others to study 'Webster's blue-back speller.'" See *New York Times,* Feb. 15, 1881, and also T. Thomas Fortune to the *New York Times,* Aug. 14, 1883.

365 *"Another of the South Carolina Thieves": Charleston News & Courier,* Aug. 13, 1884; a far more appropriate eulogy came from Frederick Douglass, who said of Elliott: "Living as I have in an atmosphere of doubt and disparagement of the abilities of the colored race, Robert B. Elliott was to me a most grateful surprise, and in fact a marvel. Upon sight and hearing of this man I was chained to the spot with admiration and a feeling akin to wonder . . . To all outward seeming he might have been an ordinary Negro, one who might have delved, as I have done, with spade and pickax or crowbar. Yet from under that dark brow there blazed an intellect and a soul that made him for high places among the ablest white men of the age . . . We are not over rich in such men and we may well mourn when one such is fallen in the midst of his years." Lamson, Peggy, p. 289.

The two men apparently had a falling out: Simmons, pp. 471–72; Smith, p. 60.

Pinchback, however, remained a political figure: P.B.S. Pinchback to Blanche K. Bruce, Mar. 22, 1879; Blanche K. Bruce Papers, Moorland-Spingarn Research Center, Howard University.

Ex-president Grant visited New Orleans in 1880: Pinchback mellowed over the years but was never a pushover. When in early 1880 the black newspaper editor George T. Ruby ran an item in his paper, the *Observer,* suggesting that Pinchback did not deserve a patronage post because of alleged links to organized gambling, Pinchback was livid. Calling Ruby "a cowardly cur," "a vile wretch," "a slanderer," and "a sychophantic fraud," Pinchback accused him of blemishing the reputation of an innocent family (his own) and trying to increase, by cheap tactics, the circulation of the *Observer.* Two weeks later he announced in the *Louisianian* that he had upbraided the "cowardly malingerer . . . in a public thoroughfare" and would not hesitate "to rid this community of his worthless presence" but that Ruby was so low a character to do so "would render it extremely disgraceful for me to take any further notice of him." *Louisianian,* Feb. 21, 1880, and Mar. 6, 1880.

Like many others of his generation: P.B.S. Pinchback to Blanche K. Bruce, Mar. 22, 1879; Blanche K. Bruce Papers.

366 *For Pinchback, one last tenet of a cherished era collapsed:* Fischer, "A Pioneer Protest: The New Orleans Street Car Controversy of 1867," *Journal of Negro History.*

"In doing all this, my grandfather": Toomer, p. 26.

367 *"Negro Who Held State Office": New Orleans Daily Picayune,* Dec. 22, 1921.

"Why does not Mr. Lynch write a magazine article": James Ford Rhodes to George A. Myers, Apr. 5, 1917, in Myers, pp. 42–43.

"I regret to say that, so far as the Reconstruction period": Lynch, "Some Historical Errors of James Ford Rhodes," *Journal of Negro History.*

368 *"I think one of your mistakes was made":* George A. Myers to James Ford Rhodes, Nov. 21, 1917, in Myers, pp. 73–74.

To Bowers, a veteran author: Bowers's far more nefarious literary predecessor was Thomas Dixon, the author of novels that vilified Reconstruction while glorifying the role of the Klan. Dixon's novels served as the basis for D. W. Griffith's landmark film *Birth of a Nation,* released in 1915 to thunderous acclaim but also to complaints and protests from civil rights organizations that it grossly misrepresented the era's history. For a discussion of that controversy, see Dray, pp. 190–207. For John Roy Lynch's post-Reconstruction writings and career, see John Hope Franklin's introduction to *Reminiscences of an Active Life: The Autobiography of John Roy Lynch.*

While Lynch had the satisfaction: Lynch's efforts to challenge the prevailing myths surrounding Reconstruction were joined in 1935 with the publication of W.E.B. Du Bois's *Black Reconstruction in America, 1860–1880,* a major study that offered the first comprehensive account of black Americans' enormous role in the social, political, economic, and philosophical life of the period. Du Bois's book did not reverse single-handedly the trend of Reconstruction historiography, although historians have long considered it seminal. Because the changes in how Reconstruction is viewed have been so dramatic, there has been extensive writing on the historiography itself. See "Reconstruction Revisited" by Eric Foner in *Reviews in American History,* vol. 10, Dec. 1982.

369 *"It can very safely be said that South Carolina": New York Times,* June 22, 1874.

The land commission had bought: Williamson, p. 155; Foner, *Forever Free,* p. 81.

370 *"Seven men of color had a dream":* "Oh Town of Lincolnville" by Frank Dunn, in Lincolnville subject file, South Carolina Room, Charleston Public Library.

371 *"Those we talked to were devoid":* Bleser, pp. 153–54.

"The genius of this kind of farming": Botsch, p. 79.

372 *"These sea islands are the homes": New York Times,* Sept. 2, 1893.

"One of the surprising results of the Reconstruction Period": Washington, *The Story of the Negro,* vol. 2, pp. 22–23; in Uya, p. 164.

373 *Invariably, the children reported to their parents: Savannah Tribune,* Mar. 6, 1915; Uya, p. 162. Smalls died on February 22, 1915, and was buried next to the A.M.E. church on Craven Street. His funeral, enlivened by the music of Allen's Brass Band, which had often accompanied him on his political campaigns, was said to be the largest ever held in Beaufort.

BIBLIOGRAPHY

Books

Abbott, Martin. *The Freedmen's Bureau in South Carolina, 1865–1872.* University of North Carolina Press, Chapel Hill, 1967

Allen, Walter. *Governor Chamberlain's Administration in South Carolina.* Negro Universities Press, New York, 1969; originally published 1888

Ambrose, Stephen. *Duty, Honor, Country: A History of West Point.* Johns Hopkins Press, Baltimore, 1966

Ames, Blanche Butler. *Adelbert Ames, 1835–1933.* MacDonald, London, 1964

———. *Chronicles from the Nineteenth Century: Family Letters of Blanche Butler and Adelbert Ames.* Clinton, Massachusetts, 1957

Aptheker, Herbert. *To Be Free: Studies in American Negro History.* International Publishers, New York, 1948

Asbury, Herbert. *The French Quarter: An Informal History of the New Orleans Underworld.* Pocket Books edition, New York, 1949; originally published 1936

Athearn, Robert G. *In Search of Canaan: Black Migration to Kansas 1879–80.* Regents Press of Kansas, Lawrence, 1978

Avary, Myrta Lockett. *Dixie After the War.* Doubleday, Page, New York, 1906

Ball, William W. *The State That Forgot: South Carolina's Surrender to Democracy.* Bobbs-Merrill, Indianapolis 1932

Barry, David S. *Forty Years in Washington.* Little, Brown, Boston, 1924

Bleser, Carol K. *The Promised Land: The History of the South Carolina Land Commission: 1869–1890.* University of South Carolina Press, Columbia, 1965

Blight, David W. *Race and Reunion: The Civil War in American Memory.* Harvard University Press, Cambridge, 2001

Botsch, Carol S. *African-Americans and the Palmetto State.* South Carolina State Department of Education publication, Columbia, 1994

Bowers, Claude G. *The Tragic Era: The Revolution After Lincoln.* Blue Ribbon Books, New York, 1929

Brodie, Fawn M. *Thaddeus Stevens: Scourge of the South.* W. W. Norton & Co., New York, 1966; originally published 1959

Brown, Richard. *Strain of Violence: Historical Studies of Violence and Vigilantism.* Oxford University Press, New York, 1975

Brown, Thomas J., editor. *Reconstructions: New Perspectives on the Postbellum United States.* Oxford University Press, New York, 2006

Brown, William Wells. *My Southern Home.* A. G. Brown, Boston, 1880

———. *The Negro in the American Rebellion.* Lee & Shepard, Boston, 1867

Bruce, Henry C. *The New Man: 29 Years a Slave, 29 Years a Free Man.* P. Anstadt and Sons, York, Pennsylvania, 1895

Buck, Paul H. *The Road to Reunion: 1865–1900.* Alfred A. Knopf, New York, 1937

Canfield, Cass. *The Iron Will of Jefferson Davis.* Harcourt, Brace, Javonovich, New York, 1978

Capers, Gerald M. *Occupied City: New Orleans Under the Federals, 1862–1865.* University of Kentucky Press, Lexington, 1965

Carney, Judith A. *Black Rice: The African Origins of Rice Cultivation in America.* Harvard University Press, Cambridge, 2001

Carroll, Peter, and David Noble. *The Free and the Unfree.* Penguin Books, New York, 1977

Christopher, Maurine. *America's Black Congressmen.* Crowell & Co., New York, 1971

Clark, E. Culpepper. *Francis W. Dawson and the Politics of Restoration: South Carolina, 1874–1889.* University of Alabama Press, Tuscaloosa, 1980

Clay, William L. *Just Permanent Interests: Black Americans in Congress, 1870–1991.* Amistad, New York, 1992

Cleveland, Henry. *Alexander H. Stephens, in Public and Private.* National Publishing Co., Philadelphia, 1866

Collins, Gail. *America's Women.* HarperCollins, New York, 2003

Current, Richard Nelson. *Those Terrible Carpetbaggers: A Reinterpretation.* Oxford University Press, New York, 1988

———. *Three Carpetbag Governors.* Louisiana State University Press, Baton Rouge, 1967

Dawson, Joseph G. III. *Army Generals and Reconstruction: Louisiana, 1862–1877.* Louisiana State University Press, Baton Rouge, 1982

De Forest, John William. *Miss Ravenel's Conversion from Secession to Loyalty.* Penguin Books, New York, 2000; originally published 1867

———. *A Union Officer in the Reconstruction.* Yale University Press, New Haven, 1948

Devol, George. *Forty Years a Gambler on the Mississippi.* Johnson Reprint Corp., New York, 1968; originally published 1926

Dodd, Dorothy. *Henry J. Raymond and the New York Times During Reconstruction.* Ph.D. Dissertation, University of Chicago, 1933

Donald, David Herbert. *Charles Sumner and the Coming of the Civil War.* Chicago University Press, Chicago, 1960

———. *Charles Sumner and the Rights of Man.* Alfred A. Knopf, New York, 1970

———. *Liberty and Union.* Little, Brown, Boston, 1978

Douglass, Frederick. *Frederick Douglass: Selected Speeches and Writings.* Philip S. Foner, editor; Lawrence Hill Books, Chicago, 1999; originally published 1950

——. *The Life and Times of Frederick Douglass.* Gramercy Books, New York, 1993

——. *The Life and Writings of Frederick Douglass.* Philip S. Foner, editor; International Publishers, New York, 1950–75

Dray, Philip. *At the Hands of Persons Unknown: The Lynching of Black America.* Random House, New York, 2002

Du Bois, W.E.B. *Black Reconstruction in America, 1860–1880.* The Free Press, New York, 1992; originally published 1935

Durden, Robert F. *James Shepherd Pike: Republicanism and the American Negro, 1850–1882.* Duke University Press, Durham, 1957

Eaton, John. *Grant, Lincoln, and the Freedmen: Reminiscences of the Civil War.* Negro University Press, New York, 1969; originally published 1907

Elkins, Stanley, and Erick McKitrick, editors. *The Hofstadter Aegis: A Memorial.* Knopf, New York, 1974

Ellis, John B. *Sights and Secrets of the National Capitol.* U.S. Publishing Co., New York, 1871

Fleetwood, Christian A. *The Negro as a Soldier.* Howard University Printing, Washington, D.C., 1895

Fleming, Walter L. *The Freedmen's Savings Bank.* Negro University Press, Westport, Connecticut, 1970; originally published 1927

Flipper, Henry O. *The Colored Cadet at West Point: The Autobiography of Lt. Henry O. Flipper.* Homer & Lee, New York, 1878

Foner, Eric. *A Short History of Reconstruction, 1863–1877.* Harper & Row, New York, 1990

——. *Forever Free: The Story of Emancipation and Reconstruction.* Alfred A. Knopf, New York, 2005

——. *Freedom's Lawmakers: A Directory of Black Officeholders During Reconstruction.* Louisiana State University Press, Baton Rouge, 1996

Foner, Eric, and Olivia Mahoney. *America's Reconstruction: People and Politics After the Civil War.* HarperCollins, New York, 1995

Forten, Charlotte L. *The Journal of Charlotte L. Forten: A Free Negro in the Slave Era.* W. W. Norton, New York, 1981; originally published 1953

Franklin, John Hope. *Race and History: Selected Essays 1938–1988.* Louisiana State University Press, Baton Rouge, 1989

Fry, Gladys-Marie. *Night Riders in Black Folk History.* University of Georgia Press, Athens, 1991; originally published 1975

Garner, James. *Reconstruction in Mississippi.* Peter Smith, Gloucester, Massachusetts, 1964

Gatewood, Willard B. *Aristocrats of Color: The Black Elite, 1880–1920.* Indiana University Press, Bloomington, 1993; originally published 1990

Gillette, William. *Retreat from Reconstruction 1869–1879.* Louisiana State University Press, Baton Rouge, 1979

Goldsmith, Barbara. *Other Powers: The Age of Suffrage, Spiritualism, and the Scandalous Victoria Woodhull.* Alfred A. Knopf, New York, 1998

Goodwin, Doris Kearns. *Team of Rivals: The Political Genius of Abraham Lincoln.* Simon & Schuster, New York, 2005

Gossett, Thomas F. *Race: The History of an Idea in America.* New York, Oxford University Press, 1963

Graham, Lawrence Otis. *The Senator and the Socialite: The True Story of America's First Black Dynasty.* HarperCollins, New York, 2006

Grant, Ulysses S. *The Papers of Ulysses S. Grant.* John Y. Simon, editor. Southern Illinois University Press, Carbondale, 2000

Green, Constance M. *The Secret City: A History of Race Relations in the Nation's Capitol.* Princeton University Press, Princeton, 1967

Green, James. *Personal Recollections of Daniel Henry Chamberlain, Once Governor of South Carolina* (booklet). Worcester Society of Antiquity, Worcester, Massachusetts, 1908

Hahn, Steven. *A Nation Under Our Feet: Black Political Struggles in the Rural South from Slavery to the Great Migration.* Harvard University Press, Cambridge, 2003

Hall, Kermit L. *The Oxford Guide to United States Supreme Court Decisions.* Oxford University Press, New York, 1999

Harlan, Malvina S. *Some Memories of a Long Life: 1854–1911.* Modern Library, New York, 2002

Harris, William C. *The Day of the Carpetbagger: Republican Reconstruction in Mississippi.* Louisiana State University Press, Baton Rouge, 1979

Haskins, James. *Pinckney Benton Stewart Pinchback.* Macmillan, New York, 1973

Hendrick, Burton J. *Statesmen of the Lost Cause: Jefferson Davis and His Cabinet.* Literary Guild of America, New York, 1939

Higginson, Thomas Wentworth. *Army Life in a Black Regiment.* Penquin, New York, 1997; originally published 1870

Hirshson, Stanley P. *Farewell to the Bloody Shirt: Northern Republicans and the Southern Negro, 1877–1893.* Indiana University Press, Bloomington, 1962

Hofstadter, Richard. *Great Issues in American History: From Reconstruction to the Present Day, 1864–1969.* New York, Vintage Books, 1969

Holden, Charles J. *In the Great Maelstrom: Conservatives in Post–Civil War South Carolina.* University of South Carolina Press, Columbia, 2002

Hollandsworth, James G., Jr. *An Absolute Massacre: The New Orleans Race Riot of July 30, 1866.* Louisiana State University Press, Baton Rouge, 2001

Holt, Thomas. *Black over White: Negro Political Leadership in South Carolina During Reconstruction.* University of Illinois Press, Urbana, 1977

Horn, Stanley. *Invisible Empire.* Gordon Press, New York, 1972

Howard, Oliver Otis. *Autobiography of General Oliver Otis Howard.* Baker & Taylor, New York, 1907

Humphreys, Benjamin. *Floods and Levees of the Mississippi River.* Mississippi River Levee Association, Memphis, 1914

Jacoby, Susan. *Freethinkers: A History of American Secularism.* Metropolitan, New York, 2004

Jarrell, Hampton M. *Wade Hampton and the Negro: The Road Not Taken.* University of South Carolina Press, Columbia, 1949

Jefferson, Thomas. *Notes on the State of Virginia.* H. C. Carey & I. Lea, Philadelphia, 1825

Keller, Morton. *The Art and Politics of Thomas Nast.* Oxford University Press, New York, 1968

Klement, Frank L. *The Limits of Dissent.* University Press of Kentucky, Lexington, 1970

Kletzing, Henry F. *Progress of a Race.* J. L. Nichols & Co., Atlanta, 1900

Klingman, Peter D. *Josiah Walls: Florida's Black Congressman of Reconstruction.* University Presses of Florida, Gainesville, 1976

Knight, Edgar W. *The Influence of Reconstruction on Education in the South.* Teachers College/Columbia University, New York, 1913

Korngold, Ralph. *Thaddeus Stevens: A Being Darkly Wise and Rudely Great.* Harcourt, Brace, New York, 1955

———. *Two Friends of Man: The Story of William Lloyd Garrison and Wendell Phillips.* Little, Brown, Boston, 1950

Kousser, J. Morgan, and James M. McPherson, editors. *Region, Race, and Reconstruction: Essays in Honor of C. Vann Woodward,* Oxford University Press, New York, 1982

Lamson, Peggy. *The Glorious Failure: Black Congressman Robert Brown Elliott and the Reconstruction in South Carolina.* W. W. Norton & Co., New York, 1973

Lamson, Roswell H. *Lamson of the Gettysburg: The Civil War Letters of Lt. Roswell H. Lamson, U.S. Navy.* James M. and Patricia R. McPherson, editors. Oxford University Press, New York, 1997

Lawson, Elizabeth. *The Gentleman from Mississippi, Our First Negro Congressman, Hiram R. Revels.* New York, 1960

Lemann, Nicholas. *Redemption: The Last Battle of the Civil War.* Farrar, Straus and Giroux, New York, 2006

Les Benedict, Michael. *The Fruits of Victory: Alternatives in Restoring the Union, 1865–1877.* Revised edition. Ohio State University Press/University Press of America, Lanham, Maryland, 1986

Logan, Mrs. John A. *Thirty Years in Washington.* A. D. Worthington, Publisher, Hartford, Connecticut, 1901

Logan, Rayford W. *The Betrayal of the Negro: From Rutherford B. Hayes to Woodrow Wilson.* Da Capo Press, New York, 1997; originally published 1954

Lonn, Ella. *Reconstruction in Louisiana After 1868.* G. P. Putnam's Sons, New York, 1918

Lutz, Alma. *Susan B. Anthony: Rebel, Crusader, Humanitarian.* Beacon Press, Boston, 1959

Lynch, John Roy. *The Facts of Reconstruction.* Arno Press, New York, 1969; originally published 1913

———. *Reminiscences of an Active Life: The Autobiography of John Roy Lynch.* University of Chicago Press, Chicago, 1970

Martin, Samuel J. *Southern Hero: Matthew C. Butler.* Stackpole Books, Mechanicsburg, Pennsylvania, 2001

McCullough, David. *Truman.* Simon & Schuster, New York, 1992

McFeely, William S. *Frederick Douglass.* Touchstone edition, Simon & Schuster, New York, 1992; originally published 1991

——. *Grant: A Biography.* W. W. Norton & Co., New York, 1981

——. *Yankee Stepfather: General O. O. Howard and the Freedmen.* W. W. Norton, New York, 1994; originally published 1968

McGinty, Garnie W. *Louisiana Redeemed: The Overthrow of Carpet-Bag Rule, 1876–1880.* Pelican Publishing Co., New Orleans, 1941

McKay, Nellie Y. *Jean Toomer, Artist.* University of North Carolina Press, Chapel Hill, 1984

McPherson, James M. *The Abolitionist Legacy: From Reconstruction to the NAACP.* Princeton University Press, Princeton, New Jersey, 1975

——. *Abraham Lincoln and the Second American Revolution.* Oxford University Press, New York, 1990

——. *Battle Cry of Freedom: The Civil War Era.* Oxford University Press, New York, 1988

——. *The Negro's Civil War: How American Negroes Felt and Acted During the War for the Union.* Vintage Books, New York, 1965

Miller, Edward A. *Gullah Statesman: Robert Smalls from Slavery to Congress, 1839–1915.* University of South Carolina Press, Columbia, 1995

Miller, Mary J., editor. *The Suffrage: Speeches By Negroes in the Constitutional Convention: the part taken by colored orators in their fight for a fair and impartial ballot.* (self-published), 1895

Montgomery, Frank A. *Reminiscences of a Mississippian in Peace and War.* Robert Clark Co. Press, Cincinnati, 1901

Morgan, Albert T. *Yazoo; or, On the Picket Line of Freedom in the South.* University of South Carolina Press, Columbia, 2000

Morgan, James Morris. *Recollections of a Rebel Reefer.* Houghton Mifflin, Boston, 1917

Morris, Roy, Jr. *Ambrose Bierce: Alone in Bad Company.* Oxford University Press, New York, 1995

——. *Fraud of the Century: Rutherford B. Hayes, Samuel Tilden, and the Stolen Election of 1876.* Simon & Schuster, New York, 2003

Moses, Wilson J. *The Golden Age of Black Nationalism: 1850–1925.* Oxford University Press, New York, 1978

Myers, George A., and James Ford Rhodes. *The Barber and the Historian: The Correspondence of George A. Myers and James Ford Rhodes, 1910–1923.* John A. Garraty, editor. Ohio Historical Society, Columbus, 1956

Nash, Howard P., Jr. *Stormy Petrol: The Life and Times of General Benjamin F. Butler, 1818–1893.* Farleigh Dickinson University Press, Rutherford, New Jersey, 1969

Nelson, Scott R. *Iron Confederacies: Southern Railways, Klan Violence, and Reconstruction.* University of North Carolina Press, Chapel Hill, 1999

Nieman, Donald G., editor. *Black Freedom/White Violence, 1865–1900.* Garland Publishing, New York, 1994

Nordhoff, Charles. *The Cotton States in the Spring and Summer of 1875.* Burt Franklin Publishers, New York, 1971; originally published 1876

Packwood, Cyril O. *Detour—Bermuda, Destination—U.S. House of Represen-*

tatives: The Life of Joseph Hayne Rainey. Baxter's Ltd, Hamilton, Bermuda, 1977

Painter, Nell. *Exodusters: Black Migration to Kansas after Reconstruction.* W. W. Norton, New York, 1992, originally published 1977

———. *Sojourner Truth.* W. W. Norton, New York, 1996

Pearson, Elizabeth Ware, editor. *Letters from Port Royal, 1862–1868.* Arno Press, New York, 1969

Pierce, Edward L. *Memoir and Letters of Charles Sumner.* Roberts Brothers, Boston, 1877

Pike, James S. *The Prostrate State: South Carolina Under Negro Government.* Harper & Row, New York, 1968; originally published 1874

Piston, William G. *Lee's Tarnished Lieutenant James Longstreet and His Place in Southern History.* University of Georgia Press, Athens, 1987

Przybyszewski, Linda. *The Republic According to John Marshall Harlan.* University of North Carolina Press, Chapel Hill, 1999

Rable, George C. *But There Was No Peace: The Role of Violence in the Politics of Reconstruction.* University of Georgia Press, Athens, 1984

Rabinowitz, Howard, editor. *Southern Black Leaders of the Reconstruction Era.* University of Illinois Press, Urbana, 1982

Reuter, Edward B. *The Mulatto in the United States.* Haskell House Publishers, New York, 1969; originally published 1918

Reynolds, John S. *Reconstruction in South Carolina, 1865–1877.* Negro University Press, New York, 1969; originally published 1905

Rollin, Frank A. *Life and Public Services of Martin R. Delany.* Kraus Reprint, New York, 1969; originally published 1868

Rose, Willie Lee. *Rehearsal for Reconstruction: The Port Royal Experiment.* Oxford University Press, New York, 1964

St. Clair, Sadie Daniel. *The National Career of Blanche Kelso Bruce.* Unpublished thesis, University of Michigan, 1947

Salisbury, Robert S. *William Windom: Apostle of Positive Government.* University Press of America, Lanham, Maryland, 1993

Sanger, D. B., and Thomas R. Hay. *James Longstreet.* Louisiana State University Press, Baton Rouge, 1952

Sass, Herbert R. *Outspoken: 150 Years of the News and Courier.* University of South Carolina Press, Columbia, 1953

Simkins, Francis B. *Pitchfork Ben Tillman.* Louisiana State University Press, Baton Rouge, 1944

Simmons, William J. *Men of Mark: Eminent, Progressive, and Rising.* George M. Rewell, Cleveland, 1887

Singletary, Otis A. *Negro Militia and Reconstruction.* McGraw-Hill, New York, 1963

Smith, Samuel D. *The Negro in Congress: 1870–1901.* University of North Carolina Press, Chapel Hill, 1940

Stanton, Elizabeth C., Susan B. Anthony, et al. *History of Women's Suffrage.* Charles Mann, publisher, Rochester, New York, 1887

Sterling, Dorothy, editor. *The Trouble They Seen: The Story of Reconstruction in the*

Words of African Americans. Da Capo Press, New York City, 1994; originally published 1976

Sterling, Dorothy. *We Are Your Sisters: Black Women in the 19th Century.* W. W. Norton, New York, 1984

Sterling, Dorothy. *Captain of the Planter: The Story of Robert Smalls.* Pocket Books edition, New York, 1972; originally published 1958

Stephens, Alexander H. *Alexander H. Stephens, in Public and Private: With Letters and Speeches, Before, During, and Since the War.* Henry Cleveland, editor. Philadelphia, 1886

Stiles, T. J. *Jesse James: Last Rebel of the Civil War.* Alfred A. Knopf, New York, 2001

Storey, Moorfield. *Charles Sumner.* Houghton Mifflin, Boston, 1900

Sumner, Charles. *Works: 1870–83.* Volumes 1–15. Lee and Shepard, Boston, 1873–1883

Swisher, Carl Brent. *Roger B. Taney.* Archon Books, Hamden, Connecticut, 1961; originally published 1935

Taylor, Alrutheus A. *The Negro in South Carolina During the Reconstruction.* Russell & Russell, New York, 1969; originally published 1924

Thomas, Benjamin P., and Harold M. Hyman. *Stanton: The Life and Times of Lincoln's Secretary of War.* Alfred A. Knopf, New York, 1962

Tindall, George. *South Carolina Negroes, 1877–1900.* University of South Carolina Press, Columbia, 1952

Toomer, Jean. *The Wayward and the Seeking: A Collection of Writings by Jean Toomer.* Darwin Turner, editor. Howard University Press, Washington, D.C., 1980

Tourgee, Albion W. *A Fool's Errand.* Harper Torchbooks, New York, 1966; originally published 1879

Towne, Laura M. *The Letters and Diary of Laura M. Towne.* R. S. Holland, editor. Negro Universities Press, New York, 1969; originally published 1912

Trefousse, Hans L. *Thaddeus Stevens: Nineteenth-Century Egalitarian.* Stackpole Books, Mechanicsburg, Pennsylvania, 2001; originally published 1997

Trelease, Allen W. *White Terror: The Ku Klux Klan Conspiracy and Southern Reconstruction.* Louisiana State University Press, Baton Rouge, 1971

Tunnell, Ted. *Crucible of Reconstruction: War, Radicalism, and Race in Louisiana, 1862–1877.* Louisiana State University Press, Baton Rouge, 1984

———. *Edge of the Sword.* Louisiana State University Press, Baton Rouge, 2001

Twitchell, M. H. *Carpetbagger from Vermont: The Autobiography of M. H. Twitchell.* Ted Tunnell, editor. Louisiana State University Press, Baton Rouge, 1989

Ullman, Victor. *Martin R. Delany: The Beginnings of Black Nationalism.* Beacon Press, Boston, 1971

Underwood, James Lowell, and W. Lewis Baker, editors. *At Freedom's Door: African-American Founding Fathers and Lawyers in Reconstruction South Carolina.* University of South Carolina Press, Columbia, 2000

Uya, Okon Edet. *From Slavery to Public Service: Robert Smalls, 1839–1915.* Oxford University Press, New York, 1971

Vandal, Gilles. *The New Orleans Riot of 1866: Anatomy of a Tragedy.* Center for Louisiana Studies, University of Southwest Louisiana, Lafayette, 1983

Vaughn, William P. *Schools for All: The Blacks and Public Education in the South, 1865–1877.* University Press of Kentucky, Lexington, 1974

Vinson, J. Chal. *Thomas Nast: Political Cartoonist.* University of Georgia Press, Athens, 1967

Vorenberg, Michael. *Final Freedom: The Civil War, the Abolition of Slavery, and the Thirteenth Amendment.* Cambridge University Press, New York, 2001

Wallace, David Duncan. *The History of South Carolina.* American Historical Society, New York, 1934

Warmoth, Henry C. *War, Politics, and Reconstruction.* Negro Universities Press, New York, 1970; originally published 1930

Washington, Booker T. *A New Negro for a New Century.* American Publishing House, Chicago, 1900

———. *The Story of the Negro: The Rise of the Race from Slavery.* 2 volumes. Negro University Press, New York, 1969; originally published 1909

Way, Frederick, Jr. *She Takes the Horns: Steamboat Racing on the Western Waters.* Young & Klein, Inc., Cincinnati, 1953

Wharton, Vernon Lane. *The Negro in Mississippi 1865–1890.* Harper & Row, New York, 1965; originally published 1947

Whitman, Walt. *Walt Whitman's Civil War.* Walter Lowenfels, editor. Da Capo Press, New York, 1961

Whyte, James H. *The Uncivil War: Washington During the Reconstruction, 1865–1878.* Twayne Publishers, New York, 1958

Williams, Alfred B. *Hampton and His Red Shirts: South Carolina's Deliverance in 1876.* Books for Libraries Press, Freeport, New York, 1970; originally published 1935

———. *The Liberian Exodus: An Account of the Voyage of the First Emigrants in the Bark "Azor" and Their Reception at Monrovia.* News and Courier Book Presses, Charleston, South Carolina, 1878

Williams, Charles Richard. *The Life of Rutherford B. Hayes.* Houghton Mifflin, Boston, 1914

Williams, George Washington. *History of the Negro Troops in the War of the Rebellion, 1861–1865.* Harper & Bros., New York, 1888

Williams, Lou Falkner. *The Great South Carolina Ku Klux Klan Trials, 1871–72.* University of Georgia Press, Athens, 1996

Williamson, Joel. *After Slavery: The Negro in South Carolina During Reconstruction, 1861–1877.* W. W. Norton, New York, 1975; originally published 1965

Wood, Norman B. *The White Side of a Black Subject.* Negro University Press, 1969; originally published 1896

Woodson, Carter. *Negro Orators and Their Orations.* Associated Publishers, Washington, D.C., 1925

Woodward, C. Vann. *The Burden of Southern History.* New American Library edition, New York, 1969; originally published 1960

———. *Reunion and Reaction: The Compromise of 1877 and the End of Reconstruction.* Little, Brown, Boston, 1951

Yarbrough, Tinsley E. *Judicial Enigma: The First Justice Harlan.* Oxford University Press, New York, 1995

Zuczek, Richard. *Encyclopedia of Reconstruction, Volumes 1 and 2.* Greenwood Press, Westport, Connecticut, 2006

———. *State of Rebellion: Reconstruction in South Carolina.* University of South Carolina Press, Columbia, 1996

Articles, Pamphlets, Speeches

"Anonymous", *Atlantic Monthly,* Feb. 1877: "The Political Condition of South Carolina." *Atlantic Monthly,* Apr. 1877: "South Carolina Morals;" *Atlantic Monthly,* June 1877: "South Carolina Society."

Alilunas, Leo. "A Review of Negro Suffrage Policies Prior to 1915." *Journal of Negro History,* vol. 25, no. 2, Apr. 1940

Anderson, Eric. "James O'Hara of North Carolina: Black Leadership and Local Government," in Rabinowitz, Howard, ed. *Southern Black Leaders of the Reconstruction Era.* University of Illinois Press, Urbana, 1982

Avins, Alfred. "The Civil Rights Act of 1875: Some Reflected Light on the Fourteenth Amendment and Public Accommodations." *Columbia Law Review,* vol. 66, no. 5, May 1966

Blassingame, John W. "The Freedom Fighters." *Negro History Bulletin,* vol. 28, Feb. 1965

Burton, Vernon. "Race and Reconstruction: Edgefield County, South Carolina." *Journal of Social History,* vol. 11, no. 1, fall 1978

Ball, W. W. "An Episode in South Carolina Politics." Reconstruction pamphlet collection, Charleston Historical Society

Bell, Frank C. "The Life and Times of John Roy Lynch: A Case Study 1847–1939." *Journal of Mississippi History,* vol. 38, no. 1, 1976

Belz, Herman. "The New Orthodoxy in Reconstruction Historiography." *Reviews in American History,* vol. 1, no. 1, Mar. 1973

Bigelow, Martha M. "The Significance of Milliken's Bend in the Civil War." *Journal of Negro History,* vol. 45 no. 3, July 1960

Blakely, Allison. "Richard T. Greener and the Talented Tenth's Dilemma." *Journal of Negro History,* vol. 59, no. 4, Oct. 1974

Borome, Joseph H. "The Autobiography of Hiram R. Revels Together with Some Letters by and About Him." *Midwest Journal,* vol. 5, no. 1, winter 1952–53

Bowman, Robert. "Reconstruction in Yazoo County." Mississippi Historical Society Publication, vol. 7, 1903

Brayton, Ellery M. "An Address upon the Election Laws of South Carolina." Columbia, William Sloane, Printer, 1889

Brock, Euline W. "Thomas W. Cardozo: Fallible Black Reconstruction Leader." *Journal of Negro History,* vol. 47, no. 2, May 1981

Brough, Charles Hillman. "The Clinton Riot." Mississippi Historical Society Publication, vol. 6, 1902

Burton, Vernon. "Race and Reconstruction: Edgefield County, South Carolina." *Journal of Social History,* vol. 12, no. 1, fall 1978

Chamberlain, Daniel H. "The Race Problem at the South." *Yale Review,* June 1890
——. "Reconstruction and the Negro." *North American Review,* 1879
——. "Reconstruction in South Carolina." *Atlantic Monthly,* Apr. 1901
Cheek, William F. "A Negro Runs for Congress: John Mercer Langston and the Virginia Campaign of 1888." *Journal of Negro History,* vol. 52, no. 1, Jan. 1967
Christian, Marcus B. "The Theory of the Poisoning of Oscar J. Dunn." *Phylon,* vol. 6, no. 3, third quarter, 1945
Coleman, John A. "The Fight of a Man with a Railroad." *Atlantic Monthly,* Dec. 1872
Coulter, E. Merton. "Negro Legislators in Georgia During the Reconstruction Period." *Georgia History Quarterly,* Athens, 1968
Cox, LaWanda. "The Promise of Land for the Freedmen." *Mississippi Valley Historical Review,* vol. 45, no. 3, Dec. 1958
Cox, LaWanda, and John H. Cox. "Negro Suffrage and Republican Politics: The Problem of Motivation in Reconstruction Historiography." *Journal of Southern History,* vol. 33, no. 3, Aug. 1967
Cresswell, Stephen. "Enforcing the Enforcement Acts: The Department of Justice in Northern Missisippi, 1870–1890." *Journal of Southern History,* vol. 53, no. 3, Aug. 1987
Donaldson, Gary A. "A Window on Slave Culture: Dances at Congo Square in New Orleans, 1800–1862." *Journal of Negro History,* vol. 69, no. 2, spring 1984
Dorris, J. T. "Pardoning the Leaders of the Confederacy." *Mississippi Valley Historical Review,* vol. 15, no. 1, June 1928
Dunbar-Nelson, Alice. "People of Color in Louisiana (Part I)." *Journal of Negro History,* vol. 1, no. 4, Oct. 1916
Durden, Robert F. "The Prostrate State Revisited: James S. Pike and South Carolina Reconstruction." *Journal of Negro History,* vol. 39, no. 2, Apr. 1954
Elliott, Robert Brown. "Oration Delivered by the Hon. R. B. Elliot, April 16, 1872, at the Celebration of the Tenth Anniversary of Emancipation in the District of Columbia." H. Polkinhorn (Publisher), Washington, 1872
Fair, Sophie M. "Distinguished Confederate War Record of Gen. Martin Witherspoon Gary." *Southern Herald and Working Man of New York and Columbia, S.C.,* Feb. 13, 1878
Fischer, Roger A. "A Pioneer Protest: The New Orleans Street Car Controversy of 1867." *Journal of Negro History,* vol. 53, no. 3, July 1968
Fleming, Walter L. "'Pap' Singleton, the Moses of the Colored Exodus." *American Journal of Sociology,* vol. 15, no. 1, July 1909
Foner, Eric. "Thaddeus Stevens, Confiscation, and Reconstruction." Appears in *The Hofstadter Aegis: A Memorial.* Stanley Elkins and Eric McKitrick, eds. Alfred A. Knopf, New York, 1974
Forten, Charlotte. "Life on the Sea Islands." *Atlantic Monthly,* vol. 13, May 1864
Frasure, Carl M. "Charles Sumner and the Rights of the Negro." *Journal of Negro History,* vol. 13, no. 2, Apr. 1928
Fredrickson, George M. "A Man but Not a Brother: Abraham Lincoln and Racial Equality." *Journal of Southern History,* vol. 41, no. 1, Feb. 1975

French, Justus C. "*The Trip of the Steamer Oceanus to Fort Sumter and Charleston . . . (and) the re-raising of the flag over the ruins of Fort Sumter, April 14, 1865.*" Union Steam Printing House, Brooklyn, New York, 1865

Gatewood, Willard B., Jr. "The Remarkable Misses Rollin" — Black Women in Reconstruction South Carolina." *South Carolina Historical Magazine*, vol. 92, 1991

Gelston, Arthur Lewis. Radical Versus Straight-Out in Post-Reconstruction Beaufort County. *South Carolina Historical Magazine*, Oct. 1974

Gilbert, Abby L. "The Comptroller of the Currency and the Freedman's Savings Bank." *Journal of Negro History*, vol. 57, no. 2, Apr. 1972

Gressman, Eugene. "The Unhappy History of Civil Rights Legislation." *Michigan Law Review*, vol. 50, 1952

Grosz, Agnes. "The Political Career of P.B.S. Pinchback." *Louisiana Historical Quarterly*, vol. 27, Apr. 1944

Guignard, John G. "How the Wallace House Met in Carolina Hall." Pamphlet in "Reconstruction" folder, South Carolina Room, Charleston Public Library

Hanchett, William. "Reconstruction and the Rehabilitation of Jefferson Davis: Charles G. Halpine's Prison Life." *Journal of American History*, vol. 56, no. 2, Sept. 1969

Harris, William C. "Blanche K. Bruce of Mississippi: Conservative Assimilationist," in *Southern Black Leaders of the Reconstruction Era*. Howard Rabinowitz, ed. University of Illinois Press, Urbana, 1982

Hennessey, Melinda Meek. "Racial Violence During Reconstruction: The 1876 Riots in Charleston and Cainhoy." *South Carolina Historical Magazine*, vol. 86, no. 2, Apr. 1985

Houston, G. David. "A Negro Senator (Blanche K. Bruce)." *Journal of Negro History*, vol. 7, no. 3, July 1922

Hyman, Sidney. "Washington's Negro Elite." *Look Magazine*, Apr. 6, 1965

Jager, Ronald B. "Charles Sumner, the Constitution, and the Civil Rights Act of 1875." *New England Quarterly*, vol. 42, no. 3, Sept. 1969

Jones, Howard James. "Images of Legislative Reconstruction Participants in Fiction." *Journal of Negro History*, vol. 67, no. 4, winter 1982

Johnson, Manie W. "The Colfax Riot of April 1873." *Louisiana Historical Quarterly*, vol. 13, no. 3, July 1930

Johnston, Frank. "The Conference of October 15th, 1875 Between General George and Governor Ames." Mississippi Historical Society Publication, vol. 6, 1902

Kaczorowski, Robert J. "To Begin the Nation Anew: Congress, Citizenship, and Civil Rights After the Civil War." *American Historical Review*, vol. 92, no. 1, Feb. 1987

Katz, William. "George Henry White: A Militant Negro Congressman in the Age of Booker T. Washington." *Negro History Bulletin*, Mar. 1966

Kindall, George B. "The Question of Race in the South Carolina Constitutional Convention of 1895." *Journal of Negro History*, vol. 37, no. 3, July 1952

Lestage, H. Oscar, Jr. "The White League in Louisiana and Its Participation in Reconstruction Riots." *Louisiana Historical Quarterly*, vol. 28, July 1935

Levy, Leonard W., and Harlan B. Phillips. "The Roberts Case: Source of the 'Separate but Equal' Doctrine." *American Historical Review,* vol. 56, no. 3, Apr. 1951

Libby, Billy W. "Senator Hiram Revels of Mississippi Takes His Seat, January-February, 1870." *Journal of Mississippi History,* vol. 37, no. 4, 1973

Lynch, John Roy. "Civil Rights Speech of Hon. John R Lynch, of Mississippi, in the House of Representatives, Feb. 3, 1875." Government Printing Office, Washington, 1875

———. "Some Historical Errors of James Ford Rhodes." *Journal of Negro History,* vol. 2, no. 4, Oct. 1917

———. "The Tragic Era." *Journal of Negro History,* vol. 15, no. 1, Jan. 1930

Lynd, Staughton. "Rethinking Slavery and Reconstruction." *Journal of Negro History,* vol. 50, no. 3, July 1965

MacDowell, Dorothy A. "Hamburg: A Village of Dreams." *South Carolina Magazine,* June 1969

Mann, Kenneth E. "Richard Harvey Cain: Congressman, Minister, and Champion of Civil Rights." *Negro History Bulletin,* vol. 35, Mar 1972

Marszalek, John F., Jr. "A Black Cadet at West Point." *American Heritage,* Aug. 1971

Matthews, John M. "Jefferson Franklin Long: The Public Career of Georgia's First Black Congressman." *Phylon,* vol. 42, 1981

McFeely, William S. "Amos T. Akerman: The Lawyer and Racial Justice." Appears in *Region, Race, and Reconstruction: Essays in Honor of C. Vann Woodward,* J. Morgan Kousser and James M. McPherson, eds. Oxford University Press, New York, 1982

McKelvey, Blake. "Penal Slavery and Southern Reconstruction." *Journal of Negro History,* vol. 20, no. 2, Apr. 1935

McClure, A. K. "Random Recollections of Half a Century." *Washington Post,* Jan. 5, 1902

McPherson, James M. "Abolitionists and the Civil Rights Act of 1875." *Journal of American History,* vol. 52, no. 3, Dec. 1965

Murphy, L. E. "The Civil Rights Law of 1875." *Journal of Negro History,* vol. 12, no. 2, Apr. 1927

Perkins, A. E. "James Henri Burch and Oscar James Dunn in Louisiana." *Journal of Negro History,* vol. 22, no. 3, July 1937

———. "Oscar James Dunn." *Phylon,* vol. 4, no. 2, 2nd quarter, 1943

Pinkett, Harold T. "Efforts to Annex Santo Domingo to the United States, 1866–1871." *Journal of Negro History,* vol. 26, no. 1, Jan. 1941

Pitre, Merline. "Frederick Douglass and the Annexation of Santo Domingo." *Journal of Negro History,* vol. 62, no. 4, Oct. 1977

Post, Louis. "A 'Carpetbagger' in South Carolina." *Journal of Negro History,* vol. 10, no. 1, Jan. 1925

Quarles, Benjamin. "The Breach Between Douglass and Garrison." *Journal of Negro History,* vol. 23, no. 2, Apr. 1938

———. "Frederick Douglass and the Women's Rights Movement." *Journal of Negro History,* vol. 25, no. 1, Jan. 1940

Reid, George W. "Four in Black: North Carolina's Black Congressmen, 1874–1901." *Journal of Negro History,* vol. 64, no. 3, summer 1979

——. "The Post-Congressional Career of George H. White, 1901–1918." *Journal of Negro History,* vol. 61, no. 4, Oct. 1976

Riddleberger, Patrick W. "The Break in the Radical Ranks: Liberals vs Stalwarts in the Election of 1872." *Journal of Negro History,* vol. 44, no. 2, Apr. 1959

Rockwell, Loula Ayres. "The Red Shirt Election." *Atlantic Monthly,* vol. 194, Nov. 1954

Roper, Laura Wood. "Frederick Law Olmsted and the Port Royal Experiment." *Journal of Southern History,* vol. 31, no. 3, Aug. 1965

Rosbow, M. "The Abduction of the Planter." *Crisis,* Apr. 1949

Ross, Michael A. "Justice Miller's Reconstruction: The Slaughter-House Cases, Health Codes, and Civil Rights in New Orleans, 1861–1873." *Journal of Southern History,* vol. 64, no. 4, Nov. 1998

Ross, Steven Joseph. "Freed Soil, Freed Labor, Freed Men: John Eaton and the Davis Bend Experiment." *Journal of Southern History,* vol. 44, no. 2, May 1978

Runnion, James B. "The Negro Exodus." *Atlantic Monthly,* Aug. 1879

Russ, William A., Jr. "The Negro and White Disenfranchisement During Radical Reconstruction." *Journal of Negro History,* vol. 19, no. 2, Apr. 1934

Ryan, James Gilbert. "The Memphis Riots of 1866: Terror in a Black Community During Reconstruction." *Journal of Negro History,* July 1977

Scroggs, Jack B. "Carpetbagger Constitutional Reform in the South Atlantic States, 1867–1868." *Journal of Southern History,* vol. 27, no. 4, Nov. 1961

Shannon, Fred A. "The Federal Government and the Negro Soldier, 1861–1865." *Journal of Negro History,* vol. 11, no. 4, Oct. 1926

Singer, Donald L. "For Whites Only: The Seating of Hiram Revels in the United States Senate." *Negro History Bulletin,* vol. 35, Mar. 1972

Slap, Andrew. "The Spirit of '76: The Reconstruction of History in the Redemption of South Carolina." *The Historian,* vol. 63, no. 4, summer 2001

Smalls, Robert. "Election Methods in the South." *North American Review,* vol. 151, 1890

——. "An Honest Ballot Is the Safeguard of the Republic — Speech of Hon. Robert Smalls in the House of Representatives, February 24, 1877." *Congressional Record,* 44th Cong, 2nd session, Appendix, pp. 123–36

Stagg, J.C.A. "The Problem of Klan Violence: the South Carolina Up-Country, 1868–1871." *Journal of American Studies,* vol. 8, no. 3, Dec. 1974

Stone, James H. "A Note on Voter Registration Under the Mississippi Understanding Clause." *Journal of Southern History,* vol. 38, no. 2, May 1972

Streifford, David M. "The American Colonization Society: An Application of Republican Ideology to Early Antebellum Reform." *Journal of Southern History,* vol. 45, no. 2, May 1979

Sweat, Edward F. "The Union Leagues and the South Carolina Election of 1870." *Journal of Negro History,* vol. 61, no. 2, Apr. 1976

Swisher, Carl Brent. "Dred Scott One Hundred Years After." *The Journal of Politics,* vol. 19, no. 2, May 1957

Taylor, Alrutheus A. "Negro Congressmen a Generation After." *Journal of Negro History,* vol. 7, no. 2, Apr. 1922

Thomas, Susan H. "Spartanburg's Civil War." *Carologue,* spring 2003

Thompson, Julius. "Hiram Rhodes Revels: 1827–1901, A Reappraisal." *Journal of Negro History,* vol. 79, no. 3, summer 1994

Tindall, George B. "The Liberian Exodus of 1878." *South Carolina Historical Magazine,* vol. 53, no. 3, 1952

——. "The Question of Race in the South Carolina Constitutional Convention of 1895." *Journal of Negro History,* vol. 37, no. 3, July 1952

Tillman, Benjamin. "The Struggles of '76 — An Address Delivered at the Red Shirt Reunion, Anderson, South Carolina, Aug. 25, 1909." Reconstruction pamphlet collection, Charleston Historical Society

Toplin, Robert B. "Between Black and White: Attitudes Toward Southern Mulattoes, 1830–1861." *Journal of Southern History,* vol. 45, no. 2, May 1979

Urofsky, Melvin I. "Blance K. Bruce: United States Senator, 1875–1881." *Journal of Mississippi,* vol. 29, May 1967

Van Deusen, John G. "The Exodus of 1879." *Journal of Negro History,* vol. 21, no. 2, Apr. 1936

Vandal, Gilles. "The Origins of the New Orleans Riot of 1866, Revisited;" in *Black Freedom/White Violence, 1865–1900,* Donald G. Nieman, ed. Garland Publishing, New York, 1994

Vinson, J. Chal. "Thomas Nast and the American Political Scene." *American Quarterly,* vol. 9, no. 3, autumn 1957

Weaver, Valeria W. "The Failure of Civil Right 1875–1883 and Its Repercussions." *Journal of Negro History,* vol. 54, no. 4, Oct. 1969

Weisberger, Bernard A. "The Carpetbagger: A Tale of Reconstruction." *American Heritage,* Dec. 1973

Wells, W. Calvin. "Reconstruction and Its Destruction in Hinds County." Mississippi Historical Publications, vol. 9, 1902

Wesley, Charles H. "Lincoln's Plan for Colonizing the Emancipated Negroes." *Journal of Negro History,* vol. 4 , no. 1, Jan. 1919

Westin, Alan F. "John Marshall Harlan and the Constitutional Rights of Negroes: The Transformation of a Southerner." *Yale Law Journal,* vol. 66, no. 5, Apr. 1957

Westwood, Howard C. "Generals David Hunter and Rufus Saxton and Black Soldiers." *South Carolina Historical Magazine,* vol. 86, 1985

Wharton, Vernon L. "The Race Issue in the Overthrow of Reconstruction in Mississippi." *Phylon,* vol. 2, no. 4, 1941

Wilson, Steve. "A Black Lieutenant in the Ranks." *American Historical Illustrated,* vol. 18, Dec. 1983

Windom, William, and Henry W. Blair. "The Proceedings of a Migration Convention and Congressional Action Respecting the Exodus of 1879." *Journal of Negro History,* vol. 4, no. 1, Jan. 1919

Woodson, Carter G. "Robert Smalls and His Descendants." *Negro History Bulletin,* Nov. 1947

Woody, R. H. "Franklin J. Moses, Jr., Scalawag Governor of South Carolina." *North Carolina Historical Review,* vol. 10, no. 2, Apr. 1933

Wyatt-Brown, Bertram. "The Civil Rights Act of 1875." *Western Political Quarterly,* vol. 18, no. 4, Dec. 1965

Cases

Blyew v. United States, 80 U.S. 581 (1872)
Brown v. Board of Education, 347 U.S. 483 (1954)
Civil Rights Cases, 109 U.S. 3, 3 S Ct 18 (1883)
Munn v. Illinois, 94 U.S. 113 (1877)
Plessy v. Ferguson, 163 U.S. 537, 543 (1896)
Scott v. Sandford, 19 How. 60 U.S., 393 (1857)
Slaughterhouse Cases, 16 Wall (83 U.S.) 36 (1873)
United States v. Cruikshank, 92 U.S. 214 (1876)
Williams v. Mississippi, 170 U.S. 213 (1898)

Collections

American Colonization Society Papers, Library of Congress
Benjamin F. Butler Papers, Library of Congress
Blanche K. Bruce Papers, Library of Congress
Blanche K. Bruce Papers, Moorland-Spingarn Collection, Howard University Library
Carter Woodson Papers, Library of Congress
Charles Sumner Papers, Houghton Library, Harvard University
Christian Fleetwood Papers, Library of Congress
"Committee of 70." "History of the Riot at Colfax, Grant Parish, Louisiana, April 13, 1873" prepared by the "Committee of 70", NO April 13, 1874
The Federal Cases, West Publishing Co., St. Paul, 1894–1897
Frederick Douglass Papers, Library of Congress
Government and Organizational Documents
Hiram Revels Collection, Schomburg Center for Research in Black Culture, New York Public Library
Journal of Proceedings, South Carolina Constitutional Convention, Charles A. Calvo, State Printer, Columbia South Carolina, 1895
Meeting of Colored Men in New Orleans. "Horrible Massacre in Grant Parish, Louisiana: Meeting of Colored Men in New Orleans, Address and Speeches" (Pamphlet printed at the Republican Office, New Orleans 1873)
Mississippi in 1875: Report of the Select Committee to Inquire into the Mississippi Election of 1875, Washington GPO 1876
National Archives, Beltsville, Maryland, Department of Justice Records (RG60)
National Archives, Washington, D.C., Freedmen's Bureau Records (RG105)
P.B.S. Pinchback Papers, Moorland-Spingarn Collection, Howard University Library
Proceedings of the Constitutional Convention of South Carolina, held at Charleston, S.C., beginning January 14th and ending March 17th, 1868. Including the debates and proceedings. Reprint. William L. Katz, ed. Arno Press and the New York Times, 1968
Report on Public Frauds . . . made to the General Assembly of South Carolina, 1877–1878. Columbia, Calvo & Patton, State Printers, 1878

Report from the Select Committee on the Freedman's Savings and Trust Co., Printed April 2, 1880, 46th Cong, 2nd sess, Report No 440

Report of the Select Committee on the New Orleans Riots, Washington GPO 1867

South Carolina in 1878: Senate Report Serial 1840, GPO 1879

Southern Historical Collection, University of North Carolina, Chapel Hill

State of South Carolina, Journal of Proceedings, South Carolina Constitutional Convention, Charles A. Calvo, State Printer, Columbia SC, 1895

U.S. 42nd Congress, 2nd session, House Report 22. Report of the Joint Select Committee to Inquire into the Conditions of Affairs in the Late Insurrectionary States. 13 vols. Washington, D.C., Government Printing Office, 1872

U.S. Senate Executive Documents, 43rd Cong, 2nd session, March 1875, Serial 1629, "Affairs in Louisiana"

Vicksburg Troubles, House Report No 265, 43rd cong, 2nd sess

INDEX

Numbers in italics refer to illustrations.